T0305303

Modern Portfolio Theory

Modern Portfolio Theory

*Foundations, Analysis, and
New Developments*

+ Website

JACK CLARK FRANCIS
DONGCHEOL KIM

WILEY

John Wiley & Sons, Inc.

Library of Congress Cataloging-in-Publication Data:

Francis, Jack Clark.
  Modern portfolio theory : foundations, analysis, and new developments + website / Jack Clark Francis, Dongcheol Kim.
      p. cm. – (Wiley finance series)
  Includes index.
  ISBN 978-1-118-37052-0 (cloth); ISBN 978-1-118-41763-8 (ebk); ISBN 978-1-118-42186-4 (ebk); ISBN 978-1-118-43439-0 (ebk)
  1. Portfolio management. 2. Risk management. 3. Investment analysis. I. Kim, Dongcheol, 1955– II. Title.
  HG4529.5.F727 2013
  332.601–dc23

                                                                                          2012032323

Printed in the United States of America

10 9 8 7 6 5 4 3 2 1

To Harry Markowitz

Contents

PART FIVE

Asset Pricing Models

CHAPTER 12
The Capital Asset Pricing Model   **291**

CHAPTER 13
Extensions of the Standard CAPM   **311**

Preface

Harry Markowitz introduced portfolio theory in a 1952 *Journal of Finance* article. That article has been widely referenced, frequently reprinted, and it was cited when Markowitz was awarded the Nobel prize. A few years later, professors James Tobin (Yale) and William Sharpe (Stanford) made important extensions to Markowitz's original model that both won Nobel prizes. Today, portfolio theory has grown to impact the finance and economics classrooms of universities, portfolio managers, financial service organizations, and many individual investors.

The extraordinary intellectual developments of Markowitz, Tobin, and Sharpe were furthered by increasing college enrollments, an explosive growth of information and computing technology, the global expansion of investment activity, and by decades of contributions by many different insightful authors. This book traces the valuable contributions by many different authors. Contributions involving utility analysis, single and multiple index models, non-normal probability distributions, higher-order statistical moments, investment decision criteria that go beyond the mean and variance framework, value at risk (VaR) models, Monte Carlo simulation models, the zero-beta portfolio, continuous time models, market timing, mutual fund portfolios, several portfolio performance evaluation models, arbitrage pricing theory (APT), and alternative trading systems (ATS) are reviewed and evaluated. The interactions between these diverse schools of thought are pulled together to form *Modern Portfolio Theory*.

Three editions of a book titled *Portfolio Analysis*, coauthored by professor Francis in 1971, 1979, and 1986, laid the foundation for *Modern Portfolio Theory*. The last edition of *Portfolio Analysis* included so many diverse topics we decided to name this latest book *Modern Portfolio Theory* (MPT) to reflect the continually growing number of additions to the book and the differing nature of some of the extensions to Markowitz's original portfolio theory.

MPT reports all important offshoots and recent developments to Markowitz portfolio theory. The book furnishes a concise review of portfolio theory and the derivative literature that can provide busy finance professionals a fast and efficient way to stay current on the theoretical developments in their field. In no particular order, we expect to sell this book to:

- Mutual fund executives working at the approximately 8,000 mutual funds in the United States, plus other mutual funds throughout the rest of the world.
- Security analysts working at the mutual funds in the United States, plus others throughout the rest of the world.
- Financial engineers working at the approximately 8,000 hedge funds in the United States, plus those at other hedge funds throughout the rest of the world.
- Investment researchers working at the few thousand pension funds in the United States.

- Portfolio managers working at mutual funds, pensions, hedge funds, trust funds in the trust departments of commercial banks, and other commingled portfolios.
- Sales-oriented financial analysts working at brokerage houses like Goldman-Sachs, Merrill Lynch, and hundreds of banks throughout the rest of the world.
- Professional organizations that run educational programs in finance; for instance, in the investments arena are the Chartered Financial Analysts (CFA) and Individual Investors programs. In the risk management field are Public Risk Management Association (PRIMA) and Global Association of Risk Professionals (GARP).
- Financial executives at the largest foundations throughout the rest of the world; for example, the Ford Foundation and the Rockefeller Foundation.
- Financial executives managing the investment portfolios at endowment funds at colleges, museums, and libraries in the United States (such as the TIAA-CREF and the CommonFund), plus other endowments throughout the rest of the world.
- Financial executives and analysts at multibillion-dollar sovereign wealth funds (SWFs) around the world.

Business schools can also use the book for a one- or two-semester investments course taught at the undergraduate, MS, MBA, or PhD level; or to supplement another book in an investments course. The book can also be used in a course about the economics of choice or uncertainty, taught in economics departments.

We worked to reduce the level of the math in most of the book's chapters without reducing the level of the content in the entire book. This was accomplished by putting the advanced math in a few designated highly mathematical chapters (like 7, 9, and 15), end-of-chapter mathematical appendixes, and footnotes, instead of scattering it throughout every chapter of the book. We did this to make the book more readily available to those who wish to avoid math. We inserted Chapter 4, titled Graphical Portfolio Analysis, so the book could be used by newcomers to portfolio theory. And, as mentioned above, the advanced mathematics can be avoided by skipping Chapters 7, 9, and 15 and the end-of-chapter appendixes. Skipping these more formal segments will not harm the flow of the book's logic.

The coauthors created several Excel spreadsheets that compute Markowitz efficient frontiers under various assumptions and circumstances. This user-friendly software is available at www.wiley.com/go/francis; it may be freely downloaded to the user's computer, used on the user's computer, and retained by the user. In addition, resources for professors can be found on Wiley's Higher Education website.

CHAPTER 1

Introduction

The number of alternative investments is overwhelming. Thousands of stocks, thousands of bonds, and many other alternatives are worthy of consideration. The purpose of this book is to simplify the investor's choices by treating the countably infinite number of stocks, bonds, and other individual assets as components of portfolios. Portfolios are the objects of choice. The individual assets that go into a portfolio are inputs, but they are not the objects of choice on which an investor should focus. The investor should focus on the best possible portfolio that can be created.

Portfolio theory is not as revolutionary as it might seem. A portfolio is simply a list of assets. But managing a portfolio requires skills.

1.1   THE PORTFOLIO MANAGEMENT PROCESS

The portfolio management process is executed in steps.

Step 1. **Security analysis** focuses on the probability distributions of returns from the various investment candidates (such as individual stocks and bonds).

Step 2. **Portfolio analysis** is the phase of portfolio management that delineates the optimum portfolio possibilities that can be constructed from the available investment opportunities.

Step 3. **Portfolio selection** deals with selecting the single best portfolio from the menu of desirable portfolios.

These three phases are discussed briefly below.

1.2   THE SECURITY ANALYST'S JOB

Part of the security analyst's job is to forecast. The security analyst need not forecast a security's returns for many periods into the future. The forecaster only needs to forecast security returns that are plausible for one period into the future. The length of this one-period forecasting horizon can vary within wide limits. It should not be a short-run period (such as an hour or a day), because portfolio analysis is not designed to analyze speculative trading. The forecasting horizon cannot be very long either, because it is not realistic to assume the security analyst is prescient. Between one month and several years, the portfolio manager can select any planning horizon that fits comfortably within the portfolio owner's holding period (investment horizon).

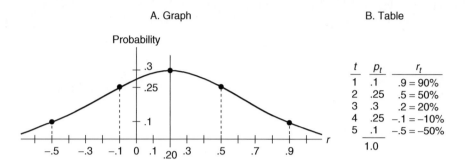

FIGURE 1.1   Tom's Subjective Probability Distribution of Returns

The security analyst's forecast should be in terms of the holding period rate of return, denoted r_1. For instance, for a share of common or preferred stock, r_1 is computed as follows.

$$\begin{pmatrix} \text{One}-\text{period} \\ \text{rate of return} \end{pmatrix} = \frac{\begin{pmatrix} \text{Price change during} \\ \text{the holding period} \end{pmatrix} + \begin{pmatrix} \text{Cash dividends paid during} \\ \text{the holding period, if any} \end{pmatrix}}{\begin{pmatrix} \text{Purchase price at the beginning} \\ \text{of the holding period} \end{pmatrix}}$$

$$\text{or} \quad r_1 = \frac{(P_1 - P_0) + d_1}{P_0} \tag{1.1}$$

where P_0 denotes the price of a share of stock at the beginning of the holding period, P_1 represents the price at the end of the holding period, and d_1 stands for any cash dividend that might have been paid during the holding period (typically one month or one year).[1]

The security analyst should construct a probability distribution of returns for each individual security that is an investment candidate. The needed rates of return may be compiled from historical data if the candidate security already exists (that is, is not an initial public offering). The historically derived probability distribution of returns may then need to be adjusted subjectively to reflect anticipated factors that were not present historically. Figure 1.1 provides an example of a probability distribution of the rates of return for Coca-Cola's common stock that was constructed by a security analyst named Tom. This probability distribution is a finite probability distribution because the outcomes (rates of return) are assumed to be discrete occurrences.

The security analyst must also estimate correlation coefficients (or covariances) between all securities under consideration. Security analysis is discussed more extensively in Chapters 2 and 8. The expected return, variance, and covariance statistics are the input statistics used to create optimal portfolios.

1.3   PORTFOLIO ANALYSIS

Portfolio analysis is a mathematical algorithm created by the Nobel laureate Harry Markowitz during the 1950s.[2] Markowitz portfolio analysis requires the following statistical inputs.

- The expected rate of return, $E(r)$, for each investment candidate (that is, every stock, every bond, etc.).
- The standard deviation of returns, σ, for each investment candidate.
- The correlation coefficients, ρ, between all pairs of investment candidates.

Markowitz portfolio analysis takes the statistical inputs listed above and analyzes them simultaneously to determine a series of plausible investment portfolios. The solutions explain which investment candidates are selected and rejected in creating a list of optimal portfolios that can achieve some expected rate of return. Each Markowitz portfolio analysis solution also gives exact portfolio weightings for the investment candidates in that solution.

1.3.1 Basic Assumptions

Portfolio theory is based on four behavioral assumptions.

1. All investors visualize each investment opportunity (for instance, each stock or bond) as being represented by a probability distribution of returns that is measured over the same planning horizon (holding period).
2. Investors' risk estimates are proportional to the variability of the returns (as measured by the standard deviation, or equivalently, the variance of returns).
3. Investors are willing to base their decisions on only the expected return and risk statistics. That is, investors' utility of returns function, $U(r)$, is solely a function of variability of return (σ) and expected return [$E(r)$]. Symbolically, $U(r) = f[\sigma, E(r)]$. Stated differently, whatever happiness an investor gets from an investment can be completely explained by σ and $E(r)$.
4. For any given level of risk, investors prefer higher returns to lower returns. Symbolically, $\partial U(r)/\partial E(r) > 0$. Conversely, for any given level of rate of return, investors prefer less risk over more risk. Symbolically, $\partial U(r)/\partial \sigma < 0$. In other words, all investors are risk-averse rate of return maximizers.

1.3.2 Reconsidering the Assumptions

The four behavioral assumptions just listed are logical and realistic and are maintained throughout portfolio theory. Considering the four assumptions implies the most desirable investments have:

- The minimum expected risk at any given expected rate of return. Or, conversely,
- The maximum expected rate of return at any given level of expected risk.

Investors described by the preceding assumptions will prefer Markowitz efficient assets. Such assets are almost always portfolios rather than individual assets. The Markowitz efficient assets are called *efficient portfolios*, whether they contain one or many assets.

If all investors behave as described by the four assumptions, portfolio analysis can logically (mathematically) delineate the set of efficient portfolios. The set of efficient portfolios is called the *efficient frontier* and is illustrated in Figure 1.2. The efficient portfolios along the curve between points E and F have the maximum rate of return at each level of risk. The efficient frontier is the menu from which the investor should make his or her selection.

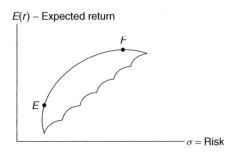

FIGURE 1.2   The Efficient Frontier

Before proceeding to the third step of the portfolio management process, portfolio selection, let us pause to reconsider the four assumptions listed previously. Portfolio theory is admittedly based on some simplifying assumptions that are not entirely realistic. This may raise questions in some people's minds. Therefore, we will examine the validity of the four assumptions underlying portfolio theory.

The first assumption about probability distributions of either terminal wealth or rates of return may be violated in several respects. First, many investors simply do not forecast assets' prices or the rate of return from an investment. Second, investors are frequently heard discussing the "growth potential of a stock," "a glamor stock," or the "quality of management" while ignoring the investment's terminal wealth or rates of return. Third, investors often base their decisions on estimates of the most likely outcome rather than considering a probability distribution that includes both the best and worst outcomes.

These seeming disparities with assumption 1 are not serious. If investors are interested in a security's glamor or growth, it is probably because they (consciously or subconsciously) believe that these factors affect the asset's rate of return and market value. And even if investors cannot define rate of return, they may still try to maximize it merely by trying to maximize their net worth: Maximizing these two objectives can be shown to be mathematically equivalent. Furthermore, forecasting future probability distributions need not be highly explicit. "Most likely" estimates are prepared either explicitly or implicitly from a subjective probability distribution that includes both good and bad outcomes.

The risk definition given in assumption 2 does not conform to the risk measures compiled by some popular financial services. The quality ratings published by Standard & Poor's are standardized symbols like AAA, AA, A, BBB, BB, B, CCC, CC, and C. Studies suggest that these symbols address the probability of default. Firms' probability of default is positively correlated with their variability of return. Therefore, assumption 2 is valid.[3]

As pointed out, investors sometimes discuss concepts such as the growth potential and/or glamor of a security. This may seem to indicate that the third assumption is an oversimplification. However, if these factors affect the expected value and/or variability of a security's rate of return, the third assumption is not violated either.

The fourth assumption may also seem inadequate. Psychologists and other behavioralists have pointed out to economists that business people infrequently maximize profits or minimize costs. The psychologists explain that people usually strive only to do a satisfactory or sufficient job. Rarely do they work to attain the maximum or minimum, whichever may be appropriate. However, if some highly competitive business managers attain near optimization of their objective and other business managers compete with these leaders, then this assumption also turns out to be realistic.

All the assumptions underlying portfolio analysis have been shown to be simplistic, and in some cases overly simplistic. Although it would be nice if none of the assumptions underlying the analysis were ever violated, this is not necessary to establish the value of the theory. If the analysis rationalizes complex behavior (such as diversification), or if the analysis yields worthwhile predictions (such as risk aversion), then it can be valuable in spite of its simplified assumptions. Furthermore, if the assumptions are only slight simplifications, as are the four mentioned previously, they are no cause for alarm. People need only behave *as if* they were described by the assumptions for a theory to be valid.[4]

1.4   PORTFOLIO SELECTION

The final phase of the portfolio management process is to select the one best portfolio from the efficient frontier illustrated in Figure 1.2. The utility of returns function, which aligns with the four basic assumptions previously listed, is very helpful in selecting an optimal portfolio. Utility of return functions can be formulated into indifference curves in $[\sigma, E(r)]$ space. Two different families of indifference curves that were created from similar but different utility of return functions are illustrated in Figure 1.3 to represent the preferences of two different investors. Figure 1.3 shows investor B achieves his maximum attainable happiness from investing in a riskier

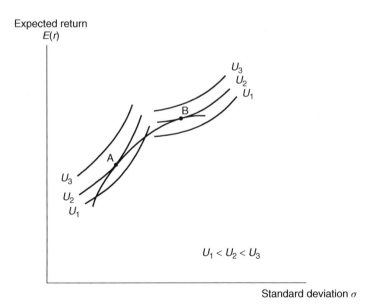

FIGURE 1.3   Different Optimal Portfolios for Different Investors

efficient portfolio than investor A's. In other words, investor A is more risk-averse than investor B.

Portfolio selection is made more difficult because security prices change as more recent information continually becomes available. And as cash dividends are paid, the expected return and risk of a selected portfolio can migrate. When this happens, the portfolio must be revised to maintain its superiority over alternative investments. Thus, portfolio selection leads, in turn, to additional security analysis and portfolio analysis work. Portfolio management is a never-ending process.

1.5   THE MATHEMATICS IS SEGREGATED

What follows can be mathematical. However, the reader who is uninitiated in mathematics can master the material. All that is needed is a remembrance of freshman college algebra, one course in statistics, and persistent interest. Most of the chapters are written at the simplest level that a fair coverage of the model allows. The basic material is presented completely in terms of elementary finite probability theory and algebra supplemented with graphs, explanations, examples, and references to more complete explanations.

Differential calculus and matrix algebra are used in a few chapters (6, 7, 13, 15) and in some of the appendixes. The reader is hereby forewarned and may avoid this material. The book is written so its continuity will not be disturbed by skipping these chapters and appendixes. None of the vocabulary or basic concepts necessary for an acquaintance with the subject is found in the few mathematical chapters and end-of-chapter appendixes. Most of the appendixes contain mathematical solution techniques for large problems, proofs, derivations, and other material of interest only to the so-called rocket scientists.

1.6   TOPICS TO BE DISCUSSED

This book addresses the following aspects of portfolio analysis:

1. *Probability foundations*: This monograph explains probabilistic tools with which risk may be analyzed. See Chapter 2.
2. *Utility analysis*: Chapter 4 focuses on the investor's personal objective, stated in terms of his or her preferences for risk and return.
3. *Mean-variance portfolio analysis*: Portfolio analysis delineates the optimum portfolio possibilities that can be constructed from the available investment opportunities, assuming asset returns are normally distributed. See Chapters 5, 6, and 7.
4. *Non-mean-variance portfolio analysis*: This approach to portfolio analysis delineates the optimum portfolio possibilities when asset returns are not normally distributed. See Chapter 10.
5. *Asset pricing models*: This extension of portfolio analysis investigates models that provide suggestions about the appropriate risk-return trade-off. See Chapters 12 – 16.
6. *Implementation of portfolio theory*: This phase of portfolio analysis is concerned with the construction of the set of optimal portfolios from which an investor can

select the best portfolio based on his or her personal objectives. See Chapters 11 and 19.

7. *Periodic performance evaluations*: The investment performances of invested portfolios should be analyzed to ascertain what is right and what is going wrong. See Chapter 18,

Portfolio analysis deals with only one time period. It assumes that the investor has a given amount of investable wealth and would like to identify, *ex ante* (before the fact), the optimal portfolio to purchase for the next time period. The selected portfolio may not turn out to be optimal *ex post* (after the fact), meaning that it may not turn out to have been the portfolio with the highest realized rate of return. Because the future cannot be forecast perfectly, all portfolio returns can be viewed as random variables. Portfolio theory recognizes this and suggests that the portfolio manager identify the best portfolio by evaluating all portfolios in terms of their risk and expected returns and then choosing the one that best fits his or her preferences.

Although this book uses some mathematical and statistical explanations, the reader who is only slightly initiated in mathematics and statistics can master the basic material. All that is needed is a remembrance of freshman college algebra and calculus, one course in classical statistics, and patience. The material is presented at the simplest level that a fair coverage of the models will allow and is presented in terms of elementary mathematics and statistics supplemented with graphs.

APPENDIX: VARIOUS RATES OF RETURN

The one-period rate of return may be defined in several different, but similar, ways. This appendix considers some alternatives.

A1.1 Calculating the Holding Period Return

If an investor pays a price (P_0) for a stock at the beginning of some period (say, a year) and sells the stock at a price (P_1) at the end of the period after receiving dividends (d_1) during the period, the rate of return for that holding period, r_1, is the discount rate that equates the present value of all cash flows to the cost of investment. Symbolically,

$$P_0 = \frac{(P_1 + d_1)}{1 + r_1} \quad \text{or} \quad r_1 = \frac{[(P_1 - P_0) + d_1]}{P_0} \tag{A1.1}$$

Thus, if \$100 is invested for one year and returns the principal plus capital gains of $(P_1 - P_0) = \$7$, plus \$8 of cash dividends, the rate of return is calculated using equation (A1.1) as follows.

$$r_1 = \frac{[(P_1 - P_0) + d_1]}{P_0}$$

$$r_1 = [(\$107 - \$100) + \$8]/\$100 = 15\% \quad \text{annual rate of return.}$$

The rate of return defined by equation (A1.1) is frequently called the investor's holding period return (HPR).

Equation (A1.1) is defined in terms of the income sources from a common or preferred stock investment, because this analysis is frequently concerned with portfolios of stocks. However, the rates of return from other forms of investment are easily defined, and this analysis is general enough so that all kinds of assets may be considered. For example, the rate of return from a coupon-paying bond is

$$r_1 = \frac{\left[(P_1 - P_0) + c\right]}{P_0} \tag{A1.2}$$

where c denotes the coupon interest paid during the holding period.

The rate of return from a real estate investment can be defined as

$$r_1 = (V_1 - V_0)/V_0 \tag{A1.3}$$

where V_1 is the end-of-period value for a real estate holding and V_0 is the beginning-of-period value. If the investor receives rental income from the real estate, then equation (A1.3a) is appropriate.

$$r_1 = (V_1 - V_0 + \text{Rental Income})/V_0 \tag{A1.3a}$$

A1.2 After-Tax Returns

This analysis can be conducted to fit the needs of an investor in a given tax situation. That is, equation (A1.1) may be adapted to treat tax differentials between the income from cash dividends and capital gains. This would require restating equation (A1.1) in the form

$$r_1 = \frac{\left[(P_1 - P_0)(1 - \tau_G) + d_1(1 - \tau_o)\right]}{P_0} \tag{A1.4}$$

where τ_G is the relevant capital gains tax rate and τ_o is the relevant ordinary income tax rate that is appropriate for the particular investor's income. In addition to the effect of taxes, brokerage commissions and other transactions costs can be included in the computations. Equation (A1.4a) defines a stock's one-period return after commissions and taxes:

$$r_1 = \frac{\left[(P_1 - P_0 - \text{Commissions})(1 - \tau_G) + d_1(1 - \tau_o)\right]}{P_0} \tag{A1.4a}$$

Unless otherwise stated, the existence of taxes and transaction costs such as commissions will be ignored to allow us to proceed more simply and rapidly.

A1.3 Discrete and Continuously Compounded Returns

Equations (A1.1), (A1.2), and (A1.3) define a holding period rate of return that is compounded once per time period. If the rate of return for a one-year holding period is 12 percent, a $1 investment will grow to $1(1 + r) = $1(1 + 0.12) = $1.12

after one year. If the rate is compounded semiannually (two times a year), at what rate of return will the $1 investment become $1.12? In other words, what is the semiannually compounded rate of return? The answer is

$$\$1\,(1+0.12) = \$1\left(1+\frac{r_{semi}}{2}\right)^2$$

$$\Rightarrow \quad r_{semi} = 2 \times \left[(1+0.12)^{1/2} - 1\right] = 0.1166$$

That is, if half of the semiannually compounded return of 11.66 percent is compounded twice a year, it will be the same as the holding period return of 12 percent that is compounded only once per year. The monthly compounded rate of return is

$$\$1\,(1+0.12) = \$1\left(1+\frac{r_{monthly}}{12}\right)^{12}$$

$$\Rightarrow \quad r_{monthly} = 12 \times \left[(1+0.12)^{1/12} - 1\right] = 0.1139$$

If a twelfth of the monthly compounded return of 11.39 percent is compounded for 12 months, it will equal the holding period return of 12 percent. In general, when the holding period return is r_t and the number of compounding is m times per period, the m-compounded rate of return is computed from

$$r_{m-compounded} = m \times \left[(1+r_t)^{1/m} - 1\right] \tag{A1.5}$$

Equation (A1.5) can be rewritten as

$$\left(1+\frac{r_{m-compounded}}{m}\right)^m = 1 + r_t \tag{A1.5a}$$

The continuously compounded return (the frequency of compounding is infinity per period), $\dot{r}_t$, is computed from the following equation:

$$\lim_{m\to\infty}\left(1+\frac{\dot{r}_t}{m}\right)^m \equiv e^{\dot{r}_t} = 1 + r_t \tag{A1.6}$$

Thus, the continuously compounded return is

$$\dot{r}_t = \ln\left(1+r_t\right) \tag{A1.7}$$

where *ln* denotes the natural (or Naperian) logarithm. Hereafter, $\dot{r}_t$ will be referred to as the continuously compounded rate of return or, more concisely, the continuous return, and r_t will be referred to as the holding period return, the noncompounded rate of return or, simply, the return. The continuously compounded rate of return is always less than the holding period return; that is, $\dot{r}_t < r_t$. If r_t is small, these two returns will be close. Thus, if returns are measured over a short period of time, such as daily, the continuously compounded returns and the noncompounded returns would be quite similar.

The continuously compounded rate of return from a stock for a given period, assuming no cash dividend payments, can also be computed as the difference between two natural log prices at the end and beginning of the period. That is,

$$\dot{r}_t = \ln\left(P_t/P_{t-1}\right) = \ln P_t - \ln P_{t-1} \tag{A1.8}$$

NOTES

1. Similar but different definitions for the rate of return may be found in the Appendix to this chapter.
2. For his collected works see Harry M. Markowitz, Editor, *Harry Markowitz Selected Works*, 2010, World Scientific Publishing Company, Hackensack, New Jersey, ISBN-13 978-981-283-363-1.
3. Frank J. Fabozzi, "The Association between Common Stock Systematic Risk and Common Stock Rankings," *Review of Business and Economic Research* 12, no. 3 (Spring 1977): 66–77.
4. Milton Friedman, "The Methodology of Positive Economics," *Essays in Positive Economics* (Chicago: University of Chicago Press, 1953), 3–43.

PART One

Probability Foundations

CHAPTER 2

Assessing Risk

This chapter reviews some fundamental ideas about mathematics and statistics that are useful in analyzing portfolios. The chapter also introduces symbols, definitions, and notations to be used throughout the book.

Essentially, this chapter explains the tools with which risk is analyzed. More specifically, the parts of freshman college algebra and finite probability courses that are relevant to investments analysis are reviewed. The rigor of the explicit definitions used in mathematics turns some people off. Allowing yourself to be turned off and dropping out rather than persevering is short-sighted. If you bite the bullet and master this topic, it will not only teach you how to scientifically analyze investment opportunities, it will also raise your level of consciousness in other academic and nonacademic areas. That is, mathematics applied to real-world problems is powerful stuff that can make your life sweeter. Words such as *expectation* and *risk* will be given fascinating new definitions.

2.1   MATHEMATICAL EXPECTATION

For a fair game paying $1 for heads and $1 for tails on the flip of a coin, the expected value of the outcome from the game is the probability of heads times the $1 loss plus the probability of tails times the $1 gain. Symbolically,

$$\text{Expected value} = p\,(\text{heads})\,(-\$1) + p\,(\text{tails})\,(+\$1)$$

$$= 0.5\,(-\$1) + 0.5\,(+\$1) = 0$$

where p(heads) represents the probability that heads occurs, and p(tails) represents the probability that tails occurs. The symbols above are a very definitive statement of what is meant by the phrase, "we expect that gamblers will break even." Writing this expression for the expected value (or mean) in more general form,

$$E\,(X) = \sum_{s=1}^{S} p_s x_s$$

$$= p_1 x_1 + p_2 x_2 + \cdots + p_S x_S \tag{2.1}$$

where X is a random variable, x_s is the actual (or realized) outcome of X when state s occurs, S is the number of states, and p_s is the probability that state s will occur. It is assumed that the probabilities sum to 1, $\sum_{s=1}^{S} p_s = 1$. In the example of the coin-tossing game above, X might be the random dollar outcome of the game or any other number resulting from an experiment involving chance, $x_1 = -\$1$ and $x_2 = \$1$ are the realized outcomes according to the results of tossing a coin, and $p_1 = p_2 = 1/2$ are the probabilities of heads or tails.

Mathematicians say that the letter E as used in equation (2.1) is an *operator*. They mean that the letter E specifies the operation of multiplying all outcomes times their probabilities and summing those products to get the expected value. Finding the expected values of a set of numbers is roughly analogous to finding the weighted average of the numbers—using probabilities for weights. Do not be confused, however; although the arithmetic is the same, an average is conceptually different from an expectation. An expectation is determined by its probabilities and it represents a hypothesis about an unknown outcome. An average, however, is a summarizing measure. There is some connection between a weighted average and the expectation—the similarity of the calculations. And both the average and the expected value measure what physicists call the center of gravity. Some important proofs that can be done with the expectation operator may be found in an appendix at the end of this book.

The operator E will be used to derive several important formulas. Therefore, consider six properties of expected values, which will be used later.

1. The expected value of a constant number is that constant. Symbolically, if c is any constant number (for example, $c = 2$ or 99 or 1064),

$$E(c) = cp_1 + cp_2 + \cdots + cp_S$$
$$= c(p_1 + p_2 + \cdots + p_S) = c$$

   This simple statement is almost a tautology.

2. The expected value of a constant times a random variable[1] equals the constant times the expected value of the random variable. Thus, if X is a random variable where $X = -1$ represents a loss and $X = +1$ represents a win in a coin flip and c is the constant number of dollars bet on each toss, this situation may be restated as follows:

$$E(cX) = cE(X)$$

   The proof follows:

$$E(cX) = \sum_{s=1}^{S} p_s \cdot cx_s = p_1 \cdot cx_1 + p_2 \cdot cx_2 + \cdots + p_S \cdot cx_S$$
$$= c(p_1 x_1 + p_2 x_2 + \cdots + p_S x_S)$$
$$= c \sum_{s=1}^{S} p_s x_s = cE(X)$$

3. The expected value of the sum of two independent random variables, X and Y, is simply the sum of their expected values. That is,

$$E(X + Y) = E(X) + E(Y)$$

The proof follows:

$$E\left(X+Y\right) = \sum_{s=1}^{S} p_s\left(x_s + y_s\right)$$

$$= p_1\left(x_1 + y_1\right) + p_2\left(x_2 + y_2\right) + \cdots + p_S\left(x_S + y_S\right)$$

$$= p_1 x_1 + p_1 y_1 + p_2 x_2 + p_2 y_2 + \cdots + p_S x_S + p_S y_S$$

$$= \left(p_1 x_1 + p_2 x_2 + \cdots + p_S x_S\right) + \left(p_1 y_1 + p_2 y_2 + \cdots + p_S y_S\right)$$

$$= \sum_{s=1}^{S} p_s x_s + \sum_{s=1}^{S} p_s y_s$$

$$= E\left(X\right) + E\left(Y\right)$$

where p_s is the joint probability of x_s and y_s occurring jointly.

4. The expected value of a constant times a random variable plus a constant equals the constant times the expected value of the random variable plus the constant. Symbolically, if b and c are constants and X is a random variable,

$$E\left(cX + b\right) = cE\left(X\right) + b$$

The proof is a combination of proofs for (1), (2), and (3).

5. The expected value of the sum of n independent random variables, $X_1, X_2, \ldots, X_n$, is simply the sum of their expected values. That is,

$$E\left(X_1 + X_2 + \cdots + X_n\right) = E\left(X_1\right) + E\left(X_2\right) + \cdots + E\left(X_n\right)$$

or

$$E\left(\sum_{i=1}^{n} X_i\right) = \sum_{i=1}^{n} E\left(X_i\right)$$

The proof is an extension of (3).

6. The expected value of the sum of n constants times n independent random variables is simply the sum of n constants times their expected values. That is,

$$E\left(c_1 X_1 + c_2 X_2 + \cdots + c_n X_n\right) = c_1 E\left(X_1\right) + c_2 E\left(X_2\right) + \cdots + c_n E\left(X_n\right)$$

or

$$E\left(\sum_{i=1}^{n} c_i X_i\right) = \sum_{i=1}^{n} c_i E\left(X_i\right)$$

The proof is a combination of (3) and (4).

If you would like to read more about the expected value operator, textbooks on finite probability theory are helpful.

2.2   WHAT IS RISK?

The phrase "dispersion of outcomes around the expected value" could be substituted for the word *risk*. The word *riskier* simply means "more dispersion of outcomes around the expected value." The dispersion-of-outcomes definition of risk squares with the common but less-precise use of the word in everyday conversation. Consider a more formal version of this definition, which lends itself well to analysis.

The mathematics terms *variance* and *standard deviation* measure dispersion of outcomes around the expected value. Symbolically, the variance of a random variable X is

$$\sigma_X^2 = E[X - E(X)]^2$$

$$= \sum_{s=1}^{S} p_s [x_s - E(X)]^2$$

$$= p_1 [x_1 - E(X)]^2 + p_2 [x_2 - E(X)]^2 + \cdots + p_S [x_S - E(X)]^2 \quad (2.2)$$

where $E(X)$ is the expected value of the random variable X. In words, the variance (σ_X^2) is the sum of the products of the squared deviations from the expected value times their probabilities. If all S outcomes are equally likely, $p_s = 1/S$. If a coin-flipping gamble is fair [that is, $E(X) = 0$] and the stakes are \$5, then $S = 2$ (head or tail) and the variance is computed as follows:

$$\text{Var} (\$5 \text{ gamble}) = p_1 [x_1 - E(X)]^2 + p_2 [x_2 - E(X)]^2$$

$$= (1/2)(-5 - 0)^2 + (1/2)(+5 - 0)^2$$

$$= 12.50 + 12.50 = 25.0$$

The variance of the \$5 gamble is 25 "dollars squared." To convert this measure of risk into more intuitively appealing terms, the standard deviation (σ_X) will be used.

$$\sigma_X = \sqrt{E[X - E(X)]^2} = \sqrt{\sum_{s=1}^{S} p_s [x_s - E(X)]^2} = \sqrt{\sigma_X^2} \quad (2.3)$$

Thus, $\sqrt{25 \text{ dollars squared}} = \$5 = $ standard deviation of the \$5 gamble.

Notice in equations (2.2) and (2.3) that the variance and standard deviations are both defined two ways. First, they are defined using the summation sign (Σ) and probabilities. Second, they are defined using the expected value operator (E), which equation (2.1) showed means the same thing as the summation sign and probabilities. The equivalent definitions will be used interchangeably.

2.3 EXPECTED RETURN

If the random variable is a rate of return r from a security, the previously mentioned expected value represents the expected return. The expected return on a security i is calculated using equation (2.1) and substituting the random variable r_i in the equation as follows:

$$E(r_i) = \sum_{s=1}^{S} p_s r_{i,s} \quad (2.1a)$$

EXAMPLE 2.1

Rates of return on two securities, A and B, for a coming year depend on the state of economy as follows:

State of Economy (s)	Probability of State (p_s)	Return on Security A (%)	Return on Security B (%)
Boom	1/4	20	8
Normal	1/2	12	8
Recession	1/4	6	14

The expected returns on Securities A and B are calculated using equation (2.1) as follows:

$$E\left(r_A\right) = \sum_{s=1}^{3} p_s r_{A,s} = (1/4) \times 20 + (1/2) \times 12 + (1/4) \times 6 = 12.5\%$$

$$E\left(r_B\right) = \sum_{s=1}^{3} p_s r_{B,s} = (1/4) \times 8 + (1/2) \times 8 + (1/4) \times 14 = 9.5\%$$

2.4   RISK OF A SECURITY

Risk was defined as dispersion of the outcomes. In discussing securities, it will be assumed that the rate of return is the single most meaningful outcome associated with the securities' performance. Thus, discussion of the risk of a security will focus on dispersion of the security's rate of return around its expected return. That is, one might equate a security i's risk with its variability of return.[2] The standard deviation of rates of return (or variance of rates of return) is a possible measure of the phenomenon defined as risk. Symbolically, this can be written by substituting r_i for X in equation (2.2).

$$\sigma_i^2 = E\left[r_i - E\left(r_i\right)\right]^2 = \sum_{s=1}^{S} p_s \left[r_s - E\left(r_i\right)\right]^2 \tag{2.2a}$$

Equation (2.2a) defines the variance of returns for security i. The value of σ_i^2 is in terms of a rate of return squared. The standard deviation of returns is the square root of the variance.

EXAMPLE 2.2

The variances of the return on Securities A and B in Example 2.1 are computed as follows:

$$\sigma_A^2 = E[r_A - E(r_A)]^2 = \sum_{s=1}^{3} p_s[r_s - E(r_A)]^2$$

$$= (1/4)(20 - 12.5)^2 + (1/2)(12 - 12.5)^2 + (1/4)(6 - 12.5)^2 = 24.74$$

$$\sigma_B^2 = E[r_B - E(r_B)]^2 = \sum_{s=1}^{3} p_s[r_s - E(r_B)]^2$$

$$= (1/4)(8 - 9.5)^2 + (1/2)(8 - 9.5)^2 + (1/4)(14 - 9.5)^2 = 6.75$$

The standard deviations of the return from Securities A and B are $\sigma_A = 4.97\%$ and $\sigma_B = 2.60\%$, respectively.

2.5   COVARIANCE OF RETURNS

Sometimes one random variable is associated with another random variable. A statistical measure of the association between two random variables is the *covariance*. Its sign reflects the direction of the association. The covariance is positive if the variables tend to move in the same direction, while it is negative if they tend to move in opposite directions.

This statistical concept can be applied to analyze the case when a price movement of one security is associated with that of other securities. In this case, the covariance of returns between two securities, i and j, denoted by σ_{ij} or Cov (r_i, r_j) is calculated as

$$\sigma_{ij} = E\{[r_i - E(r_i)][r_j - E(r_j)]\}$$

$$= \sum_{s=1}^{S} p_s\{[r_{is} - E(r_i)][r_{js} - E(r_j)]\} \tag{2.4}$$

where r_{is} is the rate of return on security i when state s occurs. The covariance of some variable with itself equals the variance of that variable. Note that when $i = j$, equation (2.4) becomes equation (2.2a).

$$\sigma_{ii} = E[r_i - E(r_i)]^2 = \sigma_i^2$$

In calculating covariances it makes no difference which variable comes first. Thus, $\sigma_{ij} = \sigma_{ji}$.

EXAMPLE 2.3

The covariance of the returns on Securities A and B in Example 2.1 is computed as follows:

$$\sigma_{AB} = E\{[r_A - E(r_A)][r_B - E(r_B)]\} = \sum_{s=1}^{S} p_s\{[r_{As} - E(r_A)][r_{Bs} - E(r_B)]\}$$

$$= (1/4)(20 - 12.5)(8 - 9.5) + (1/2)(12 - 12.5)(8 - 9.5)$$

$$+ (1/4)(6 - 12.5)(14 - 9.5)$$

$$= -9.75$$

Since the covariance is negative, it is expected that Securities A and B tend to move in the opposite direction.

2.6 CORRELATION OF RETURNS

The *correlation coefficient* is another statistical measure of the association between two random variables and it is derived from the *covariance*. The only difference between these two measures is that the correlation coefficient is standardized by dividing the covariance by the product of the two variables' standard deviations. That is, the correlation coefficient between two random variables X and Y is

$$\rho_{XY} = \frac{\sigma_{XY}}{\sigma_X \sigma_Y} \tag{2.5}$$

The correlation coefficient is always less than or equal to 1 and greater than or equal to −1. That is, $-1 \leq \rho_{XY} \leq +1$.

Within the context of portfolio analysis, *diversification* can be defined as combining securities with less than perfectly positively correlated returns. In order for the portfolio analyst to construct a diversified portfolio, the analyst must know the correlation coefficients between all securities under consideration. If $\rho_{ij} = +1$, the returns on securities i and j are perfectly positively correlated; they move in the same direction at the same time. If $\rho_{ij} = 0$, the returns on securities i and j are uncorrelated; they show no tendency to follow each other. If $\rho_{ij} = -1$, securities i and j vary inversely; they are perfectly negatively correlated.

Using circular definitions, the covariance can be defined in terms of the correlation coefficient and the standard deviations,

$$\sigma_{ij} = \rho_{ij}\sigma_i\sigma_j \tag{2.6}$$

EXAMPLE 2.4

The correlation coefficient of the returns on Securities A and B in Example 2.1 is computed as follows:

$$\rho_{AB} = \frac{\sigma_{AB}}{\sigma_A \, \sigma_B} = \frac{-9.75}{\sqrt{24.75}\sqrt{6.75}} = -0.754.$$

2.7   USING HISTORICAL RETURNS

Calculations of the expected return, variance, and covariance in the previous sections are based on probabilities. In most cases probabilities of future states of nature are uncertain. In this case, the historical observations can be used to estimate the expected return, variance, and covariance. It is convenient to assume that each observation is *equally likely* with probability of $1/T$, where T is the total number of the historical observations. The estimate of the expected return (or the sample mean) from security i is calculated as

$$\bar{r}_i = \frac{1}{T} \sum_{t=1}^{T} r_{it} \tag{2.7}$$

where r_{it} is the rate of return from security i observed at time t. The estimate of the variance of the returns (or the sample variance) for a security i is calculated as

$$\hat{\sigma}_i^2 = \frac{1}{T-1} \sum_{t=1}^{T} \left(r_{it} - \bar{r}_i\right)^2 \tag{2.8}$$

The sample variance measures the dispersion of the security's rate of return around its sample mean. The reason that the divisor is T-1 instead of T is that one degree of freedom is lost by estimating the population mean. If the population mean is known and is used in calculating the variance or covariance instead of the sample mean, the divisor is T. Estimates of the covariance and correlation coefficient between returns from securities i and j are calculated as follows:

$$\hat{\sigma}_{ij} = \frac{1}{T-1} \sum_{t=1}^{T} \left(r_{it} - \bar{r}_i\right) \left(r_{jt} - \bar{r}_j\right) \tag{2.9}$$

and

$$\hat{\rho}_{ij} = \frac{\hat{\sigma}_{ij}}{\hat{\sigma}_i \hat{\sigma}_j} \tag{2.10}$$

EXAMPLE 2.5

The following are monthly return observations on Excelon (X), Jorgenson (J), and Standard & Poor's 500 index (M) over the period from January to December.

t	Excelon (X) (%)	Jorgenson (J) (%)	S&P 500 (M) (%)
1	11.71	−4.26	2.55
2	−4.88	0.77	0.05
3	2.51	2.72	1.11
4	3.65	−1.03	1.22
5	−2.93	3.39	−3.09
6	0.72	−0.05	0.01
7	10.42	4.39	0.51
8	0.37	3.97	2.13
9	−0.84	0.43	2.46
10	6.44	3.79	3.15
11	8.00	−1.65	1.65
12	−0.23	0.17	1.26

By using equation (2.7), the sample mean returns (or the average return) from Excelon (X), Jorgenson (J), and the S&P 500 index (M) are, respectively,

$$\bar{r}_X = \frac{1}{12}(11.71 - 4.88 + \cdots - 0.23) = 2.91\%$$

$$\bar{r}_J = \frac{1}{12}(-4.26 + 0.77 + \cdots + 0.17) = 1.02\%$$

$$\bar{r}_M = \frac{1}{12}(2.55 + 0.05 + \cdots + 1.26) = 1.08\%.$$

Using equation (2.8), the sample variance from Excelon, Jorgenson, and S&P 500 index are, respectively,

$$\hat{\sigma}_X^2 = \frac{1}{12-1}\left[(1.71-2.91)^2 + (-4.88-2.91)^2 + \cdots + (-0.23-2.91)^2\right] = 27.53$$

$$\hat{\sigma}_J^2 = \frac{1}{12-1}\left[(-4.26-1.02)^2 + (0.77-1.02)^2 + \cdots + (0.17-1.02)^2\right] = 7.17$$

$$\hat{\sigma}_M^2 = \frac{1}{12-1}\left[(2.55-1.08)^2 + (0.05-1.08)^2 + \cdots + (1.26-1.08)^2\right] = 2.70$$

(Continued)

EXAMPLE 2.5 (*Continued*)

and the sample standard deviation of Excelon, Jorgenson, and the S&P 500 index are 5.25 percent, 2.68 percent, and 1.64 percent, respectively. By using equation (2.9), the covariance between returns from Excelon and Jorgenson is calculated as

$$\hat{\sigma}_{XJ} = \frac{1}{12-1}[(1.71-2.91)(-4.26-1.02) + \cdots$$
$$+ (-0.23-2.91)(0.17-1.02)] = -3.197$$

and the correlation coefficient between returns from Excelon and Jorgenson is calculated as

$$\hat{\rho}_{XJ} = \frac{-3.197}{\sqrt{27.53} \times \sqrt{7.17}} = -0.228$$

2.8   DATA INPUT REQUIREMENTS

Portfolio analysis requires that the security analyst furnish the following estimates for every security to be considered:

- The expected return ($E(r_i)$)
- The variance of returns (σ_i^2)
- The covariance between all securities (σ_{ij})[3]

The security analyst could obtain these inputs from historical data or they can be estimated subjectively. If the historical data are accurate and conditions in the future are expected to resemble those from the sample period, the historical data may be the best estimate of the future. But if the security analyst is an expert or the market is changing, subjective estimates may be preferable to historical data.

The portfolio analyst must consider many securities at once when constructing an optimum portfolio. That is, the analyst must be concerned with the expected return and risk of the weighted sum of many random variables. In the next few pages the statistical tools for portfolios will be introduced.

2.9   PORTFOLIO WEIGHTS

The portfolio analysis technique that follows does not indicate the dollar amount that should be invested in each security. Rather, it yields the proportions each security in the optimum portfolio should assume. These *proportions, weights,* or *participation levels,* as they are variously called, will be denoted by w_is. Thus, w_i is the fraction of the total value of the portfolio that should be invested in security i. Assuming that all the funds in the portfolio are to be accounted for, the following constraint is placed on all portfolios:

$$\sum_{i=1}^{n} w_i = 1 \qquad\qquad (2.11)$$

In words, the n fractions of the total portfolio invested in n different assets sum to 1. This constraint cannot be violated or the analysis has no rational economic interpretation. Equation (2.11) is simply the well-known balance sheet identity where equity is defined as 100 percent $= 1.0$ and the total assets have a total weight equal to the sum of the n different w_i decision variables. Assuming that the portfolio has no liabilities means that total assets equal equity—as shown in equation (2.11). Portfolios with liabilities will be considered in Chapter 6 and later chapters.

2.10   A PORTFOLIO'S EXPECTED RETURN

Let r_p denote the return from portfolio p which consists of n individual securities. The expected return on portfolio p is defined as

$$E\left(r_p\right) = E\left(\sum_{i=1}^{n} w_i r_i\right) = \sum_{i=1}^{n} w_i E\left(r_i\right) \tag{2.12}$$

where w_i is the investment weight invested in security i. In words, the expected return on a portfolio is the weighted average of the expected returns from the n securities contained in the portfolio. Thus, the expected return of the portfolio with $w_A = 0.4$ and $w_B = 0.6$ in Example 2.1 is

$$E\left(r_p\right) = (0.4)\,(12.5\%) + (0.6)\,(9.5\%) = 10.7\%$$

Note that $\sum_{i=1}^{2} w_i = .4 + .6 = 1$ is the balance sheet identity.

2.11   PORTFOLIO RISK

It is necessary to expand the mathematical definition of risk used for single securities into a form suitable for all securities in the portfolio. Following the "dispersion of outcome" or "variability of return" definitions of risk, the risk of a portfolio is defined as the variability of return, r_p. Denoting the variance of r_p by σ_p^2, it is possible to derive an analytical expression for σ_p^2 in terms of the variances and covariances of all securities in the portfolio. This is the form suitable for portfolio analysis.

A simple two-security portfolio will be used to analyze the portfolio variance. However, the results are perfectly general and follow for an n-security portfolio where n is any positive integer. Substituting the quantity $\left(w_1 r_1 + w_2 r_2\right)$ for the equivalent r_p yields equation (2.13).

$$\sigma_p^2 = E\left[r_p - E\left(r_p\right)\right]^2 = E\{w_1 r_1 + w_2 r_2 - \left[w_1 E\left(r_1\right) + w_2 E\left(r_2\right)\right]\}^2 \tag{2.13}$$

Removing the parentheses, using property (1) of the expectation (because the ws can be treated as constants), collecting terms with like subscripts, and factoring out the w_is gives

$$\sigma_p^2 = E\{w_1 \left[r_1 - E\left(r_1\right)\right] + w_2 \left[r_2 - E\left(r_2\right)\right]\}^2$$

Since $(a + b)^2 = a^2 + b^2 + 2ab,$

$$\sigma_p^2 = E\left\{w_1^2[r_1 - E(r_1)]^2 + w_2^2[r_2 - E(r_2)]^2 + 2w_1w_2[r_1 - E(r_1)][r_2 - E(r_2)]\right\}.$$

Using property (2) of the expectation operation yields

$$\sigma_p^2 = w_1^2\,E[r_1 - E(r_1)]^2 + w_2^2\,E[r_2 - E(r_2)]^2 + 2w_1w_2\,E[r_1 - E(r_1)][r_2 - E(r_2)]$$

and recalling equations (2.2a) and (2.4), which define σ_i^2 and σ_{ij}, we recognize the expression above as

$$\sigma_p^2 = w_1^2\sigma_1^2 + w_2^2\sigma_2^2 + 2w_1w_2\sigma_{12} \tag{2.14}$$

In words, equation (2.14) shows that the variance of a weighted sum is not always simply the sum of the weighted variances. The covariance may increase or decrease the variance of the sum, depending on its sign.

The derivation of equation (2.13) is one of the main points of this chapter. An understanding of equations (2.13) and (2.14) is essential to understanding diversification and portfolio analysis.

EXAMPLE 2.6

A portfolio consisting of 30 percent Excelon and 70 percent Jorgenson from Example 2.5 has a variance of

$$\sigma_p^2 = (0.3)^2(5.25)^2 + (0.7)^2(2.68)^2 + 2(0.3)(0.7)(-3.197) = 4.647$$

Thus, the standard deviation of the portfolio is 2.16 percent. Note that this standard deviation of 2.16 percent is less than either of the two securities' standard deviations. Diversification is a risk-reducer.

The portfolio variance of equation (2.14) can be denoted in different ways:

$$\sigma_p^2 = \begin{matrix} w_1 \\ w_2 \end{matrix}\begin{pmatrix} \sigma_{11} & \sigma_{12} \\ \sigma_{21} & \sigma_{22} \end{pmatrix} = \begin{pmatrix} +w_1w_1\sigma_{11} & +w_1w_2\sigma_{12} \\ +w_2w_1\sigma_{21} & +w_2w_2\sigma_{22} \end{pmatrix} \tag{2.15}$$

$$= w_1w_1\sigma_{11} + w_2w_2\sigma_{22} + w_1w_2\sigma_{12} + w_2w_1\sigma_{21} \tag{2.15a}$$

$$= \sum_{i=1}^{2}\sum_{j=1}^{2} w_iw_j\sigma_{ij}$$

$$= \sum_{i=1}^{2} w_i^2\sigma_i^2 + \sum_{\substack{i=1 \\ \text{for}}}^{2}\sum_{\substack{j=1 \\ i\neq j}}^{2} w_iw_j\sigma_{ij} \tag{2.15b}$$

since $\sigma_{11} = \sigma_1^2$, $\sigma_{22} = \sigma_2^2$, and $\sigma_{12} = \sigma_{21}$. A matrix can be thought of as an array or table of numbers. In the matrix above, the subscript i is the row number and j is the column number. The portfolio variance in equation (2.15b) is exactly the same as equation (2.14). In fact, the portfolio variance equals the sum of all four elements of the (2×2) matrix on the right-hand side in equation (2.15).

The procedure for deriving the variance of a two-security portfolio can be extended to derive the variance of a *three-security* portfolio. Equation (2.13) can be rewritten as

$$\sigma_p^2 = E[r_p - E(r_p)]^2 = E\{w_1 r_1 + w_2 r_2 + w_3 r_3 - [w_1 E(r_1) + w_2 E(r_2) + w_3 E(r_3)]\}^2 \tag{2.16}$$

Removing the parentheses and using property (1) of the expectation and collecting terms with like subscripts and factoring out the w_is gives

$$\sigma_p^2 = E\{w_1 [r_1 - E(r_1)] + w_2 [r_2 - E(r_2)] + w_3 [r_3 - E(r_3)]\}^2$$

Using $(a + b + c)^2 = a^2 + b^2 + c^2 + 2ab + 2bc + 2ca$ and using property (2) of the Expectation operation yields

$$\sigma_p^2 = w_1^2 E[r_1 - E(r_1)]^2 + w_2^2 E[r_2 - E(r_2)]^2 + w_3^2 E[r_3 - E(r_3)]^2$$
$$+ 2w_1 w_2 E[r_1 - E(r_1)][r_2 - E(r_2)] + 2w_2 w_3 E[r_2 - E(r_2)][r_3 - E(r_3)]$$
$$+ 2w_1 w_3 E[r_1 - E(r_1)][r_3 - E(r_3)]$$

We recognize the preceding expression as

$$\sigma_p^2 = w_1^2 \sigma_1^2 + w_2^2 \sigma_2^2 + w_3^2 \sigma_3^2 + 2w_1 w_2 \sigma_{12} + 2w_2 w_3 \sigma_{23} + 2w_1 w_3 \sigma_{13} \tag{2.17}$$

Likewise, the portfolio variance of equation 2.17 can be written differently.

$$\sigma_p^2 = \begin{matrix} & w_1 & w_2 & w_3 \\ w_1 \\ w_2 \\ w_3 \end{matrix} \begin{pmatrix} \sigma_{11} & \sigma_{12} & \sigma_{13} \\ \sigma_{21} & \sigma_{22} & \sigma_{23} \\ \sigma_{31} & \sigma_{32} & \sigma_{33} \end{pmatrix} = \begin{pmatrix} +w_1 w_1 \sigma_{11} & +w_1 w_2 \sigma_{12} & +w_1 w_3 \sigma_{13} \\ +w_2 w_1 \sigma_{21} & +w_2 w_2 \sigma_{22} & +w_2 w_3 \sigma_{23} \\ +w_3 w_1 \sigma_{31} & +w_3 w_2 \sigma_{32} & +w_3 w_3 \sigma_{33} \end{pmatrix} \tag{2.18}$$

Because the portfolio variance equals the sum of all nine elements of the (3×3) matrix on the right-hand side in equation (2.18),

$$\sigma_p^2 = \sum_{i=1}^{3} \sum_{j=1}^{3} w_i w_j \sigma_{ij}$$
$$= \sum_{i=1}^{3} w_i^2 \sigma_i^2 + \sum_{\substack{i=1 \\ \text{for}}}^{3} \sum_{\substack{j=1 \\ i \neq j}}^{3} w_i w_j \sigma_{ij} \tag{2.18a}$$

As a general case, consider a portfolio consisting of n individual securities. Then, the portfolio variance is calculated in a similar way to the case of the preceding two-security and three-security portfolios. That is,

$$
\sigma_p^2 =
\begin{array}{c}
\begin{matrix} w_1 & w_2 & \cdots & w_n \end{matrix} \\
\begin{matrix} w_1 \\ w_2 \\ \vdots \\ w_n \end{matrix}
\begin{pmatrix}
\sigma_{11} & \sigma_{12} & \cdots & \sigma_{1n} \\
\sigma_{21} & \sigma_{22} & \cdots & \sigma_{2n} \\
\vdots & \vdots & \ddots & \vdots \\
\sigma_{n1} & \sigma_{n2} & \cdots & \sigma_{nn}
\end{pmatrix}
\end{array}
$$

$$
=
\begin{pmatrix}
+w_1 w_1 \sigma_{11} & +w_1 w_2 \sigma_{12} & \cdots & +w_1 w_n \sigma_{1n} \\
+w_2 w_1 \sigma_{21} & +w_2 w_2 \sigma_{22} & \cdots & +w_2 w_n \sigma_{2n} \\
\vdots & \vdots & \ddots & \vdots \\
+w_n w_1 \sigma_{n1} & +w_n w_2 \sigma_{n2} & \cdots & +w_n w_n \sigma_{nn}
\end{pmatrix}
\tag{2.19}
$$

Because the portfolio variance equals the sum of all n^2 elements of the $(n \times n)$ matrix on the right-hand side in equation (2.19), it can be reduced to a summation.

$$
\sigma_p^2 = \sum_{i=1}^{n} \sum_{j=1}^{n} w_i w_j \, \sigma_{ij}
$$

$$
= \sum_{i=1}^{n} w_i^2 \sigma_i^2 + \sum_{\substack{i=1 \\ }}^{n} \sum_{\substack{j=1 \\ \text{for } i \neq j}}^{n} w_i w_j \, \sigma_{ij}
\tag{2.19a}
$$

The three components that determine the risk of a portfolio are the weights of the securities, the standard deviation (or variance) of each security, and the correlation coefficient (or covariance) between the securities.

The portfolio variance just given represents the sum of all n variances plus all $(n^2 - n)$ covariances. Thus, a portfolio of 100 securities ($n = 100$) will contain 100 variances and 9,900 ($= 100^2 - 100$) covariances. The security analyst must supply all of these input statistics plus 100 expected returns for the 100 securities being considered. Later, a simplified method will be shown to ease the securities analyst's work.[4]

The preceding matrix is a special type of matrix called the *variance-covariance matrix*:

$$
\Sigma =
\begin{pmatrix}
\sigma_{11} & \sigma_{12} & \cdots & \sigma_{1n} \\
\sigma_{21} & \sigma_{22} & \cdots & \sigma_{2n} \\
\vdots & \vdots & \ddots & \vdots \\
\sigma_{n1} & \sigma_{n2} & \cdots & \sigma_{nn}
\end{pmatrix}
$$

Notice that the spaces in the matrix containing terms with identical subscripts form a diagonal pattern from the upper left-hand corner of the matrix to the lower right-hand corner. These are the n variance terms (for example, σ_{ii}). All the other boxes contain the $(n^2 - n)$ covariance terms (for example, σ_{ij} for $i \neq j$). Because $\sigma_{ij} = \sigma_{ji}$, the variance-covariance matrix is symmetric and each covariance is repeated twice in the matrix. The covariances above the diagonal are the mirror image of the covariances below the diagonal. Thus, only $(n^2 - n)/2$ unique covariances need to be estimated.

2.12   SUMMARY OF NOTATIONS AND FORMULAS

A summary of notation and important equations concludes this chapter. The following notation will be used throughout the analysis:

p_s = probability that state s will occur

w_i = weight of asset i in portfolio, or the participation level of asset i $\left(\sum_{i=1}^{n} w_i = 1 \right)$

r_i = rate of return on asset i = *holding period return* (HPR)

$E(r_i)$ = expected rate of return of asset i

r_{it} = rate of return on asset i at time t (historical return) = HPR_{it}

$\bar{r}_i = (1/T) \sum_{t=1}^{T} r_{it}$ = sample mean return of asset i

σ_i^2 (or σ_{ii}) = variance of the i-th random variable—for example, the variance of returns for asset i

$\sigma_i = \sqrt{\sigma_i^2}$ = standard deviation of the i-th random variable

$\sigma_{ij} = \text{Cov}(r_i, r_j)$ = covariance between returns from asset i and asset j

$\rho_{ij} = \sigma_{ij}/\sigma_i \sigma_j$ = correlation coefficient between returns on asset i and asset j

σ_p^2 = variance of returns from portfolio

The expected rate of return of asset i is

$$E(r_i) = \sum_{s=1}^{S} p_s r_{i,s} = p_1 r_{i,1} + p_2 r_{i,2} + \cdots + p_S r_{i,S} \qquad (2.1a)$$

The variance of returns of asset i is

$$\sigma_i^2 = \sigma_{ii} = E[r_i - E(r_i)]^2 = \sum_{s=1}^{S} p_s [r_s - E(r_i)]^2 \qquad (2.2a)$$

The covariance between returns from asset i and asset j, $\text{Cov}(r_i, r_j)$, is

$$\sigma_{ij} = E\{[r_i - E(r_i)][r_j - E(r_j)]\}$$

$$= \sum_{s=1}^{S} p_s \{[r_{is} - E(r_i)][r_{js} - E(r_j)]\} \qquad (2.4)$$

$$= \rho_{ij} \sigma_i \sigma_j \qquad (2.6)$$

The expected return from the portfolio is

$$E(r_p) = E\left(\sum_{i=1}^{n} w_i r_i \right) = \sum_{i=1}^{n} w_i E(r_i) \qquad (2.12)$$

The variance of returns from a portfolio consisting of two assets is

$$\sigma_p^2 = E[r_p - E(r_p)]^2 = E\{w_1 r_1 + w_2 r_2 - [w_1 E(r_1) + w_2 E(r_2)]\}^2 \qquad (2.13)$$

$$= w_1^2 \sigma_1^2 + w_2^2 \sigma_2^2 + 2 w_1 w_2 \sigma_{12} \qquad (2.14)$$

The variance of returns from a portfolio consisting of three assets is

$$\sigma_p^2 = E[r_p - E(r_p)]^2$$

$$= E\{w_1 r_1 + w_2 r_2 + w_3 r_3 - [w_1 E(r_1) + w_2 E(r_2) + w_3 E(r_3)]\}^2 \qquad (2.16)$$

$$= w_1^2 \sigma_1^2 + w_2^2 \sigma_2^2 + w_3^2 \sigma_3^2 + 2w_1 w_2 \sigma_{12} + 2w_2 w_3 \sigma_{23} + 2w_1 w_3 \sigma_{13} \qquad (2.17)$$

The variance of returns of portfolio consisting of n assets is

$$\sigma_p^2 = \sum_{i=1}^{n} \sum_{j=1}^{n} w_i w_j \, \sigma_{ij} = \sum_{i=1}^{n} w_i^2 \sigma_i^2 + \sum_{\substack{i=1 \\ \text{for}}}^{n} \sum_{\substack{j=1 \\ i \neq j}}^{n} w_i w_j \, \sigma_{ij} \qquad (2.19a)$$

NOTES

1. A random variable is a rule or function that assigns a value to each outcome of an experiment. For example, in the coin toss, the random variable is X and it can assume two values, -1 for x_1 and $+1$ for x_2.
2. Harry M. Markowitz, *Portfolio Selection*, Cowles Foundation Monograph 16 (New York: John Wiley & Sons, 1959), 14.
3. Using Sharpe's simplified model, covariances based on some market index may be used instead of covariances between all possible combinations of securities. These simplified models are examined in Chapter 8.
4. See Chapter 8 about the simplified method.

CHAPTER **3**

Risk and Diversification

Chapter 3 briefly introduces topics such as risk, dominant asset, efficient asset, opportunity set, and capital market line (CML), naive diversification, and Markowitz diversification. These topics are discussed intuitively. Later chapters reexamine the topics in more depth.

3.1   RECONSIDERING RISK

The common dictionary definition of *risk* says it is the chance of injury, damage, or loss. Although this definition is correct, it is not highly suitable for scientific analysis. Analysis cannot proceed very far using verbal definitions, for several reasons. (1) Verbal definitions are not exact; different people interpret them in different ways. (2) Verbal definitions do not yield to analysis; they can only be broken down into more verbose verbal definitions and examples. (3) Verbal definitions do not facilitate ranking or comparison because they are usually not explicit enough to allow measurement. A *quantitative risk surrogate* is needed to replace the verbal definition of risk if risk analysis and portfolio analysis are to proceed very far. Most sciences are moving to refine and quantify their studies. For example, biometrics, econometrics, and psychometrics are focusing on quantification of the studies of biology, economics, and psychology, respectively.

The model used here for analyzing risk focuses on probability distributions of quantifiable outcomes. Because the rate of return from an investment is the most relevant outcome from an investment, risk analysis focuses on probability distributions of returns. A probability distribution of holding period returns is illustrated in Figure 3.1.

The arithmetic mean or expected value of the probability distribution of returns, denoted $E(r)$, represents the mathematical expectation of the possible rates of return. The *expected return* is

$$E(r) = \sum_{i=1}^{N} p_i r_i$$
$$= p_1 r_1 + p_2 r_2 + \cdots + p_N r_N \tag{3.1}$$

where $i = 1, 2, 3, \ldots, N$ are a series of integers that count the possible outcomes, N is the total number of outcomes, and p_i is the probability that rate of return i occurs.

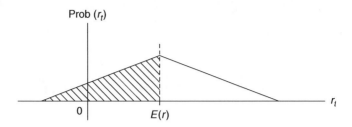

FIGURE 3.1 Probability Distribution of Rates of Return

Continuous probability distributions are used rarely in this book. The estimated returns assume finite values and have finite variances.

Rates of return below $E(r)$ represent disappointing outcomes to someone who has invested his or her funds in the asset's probability distribution of risky returns. The area within the probability distribution that lies to the left of $E(r)$ graphically represents the investor's chance of injury, loss, or damage. These unfortunate outcomes align with the dictionary definition of risk. The *semivariance* (SV) of returns(s), defined in equation (3.2), is a quantitative risk surrogate that measures the area below $E(r)$ in the probability distribution of returns:

$$SV(r) = \sum_{i=1}^{N} p_i \{\min[r_i - E(r), 0]\}^2$$

$$= \sum_{i=1}^{L} p_i [\underline{r_i} - E(r)]^2$$

$$= p_1 [\underline{r_1} - E(r)]^2 + p_2 [\underline{r_2} - E(r)]^2 + \cdots + p_L [\underline{r_L} - E(r)]^2 \qquad (3.2)$$

where $\underline{r_i}$ represents below-average returns. These rates of return are less than $E(r)$ (that is, $\underline{r_i} < E(r)$), N represents the total number of returns, and L represents the number of returns less than $E(r)$. The square root of equation (3.2) is called the *semideviation* of returns and is an equivalent financial risk surrogate that some people may find more intuitively pleasing. The semivariance is described in more detail in Chapter 10.

The semivariance and semideviation of returns are special cases of the variance and standard deviation of returns. The variance of returns, equation (2.2), measures the dispersion or width of the entire probability distribution of returns, rather than merely the portion of the distribution lying below $E(r)$.

$$\sigma^2 = \sum_{i=1}^{N} p_i [r_i - E(r)]^2$$

$$= p_1 [r_1 - E(r)]^2 + p_2 [r_2 - E(r)]^2 + \cdots + p_N [r_N - E(r)]^2 \qquad (2.2)$$

The standard deviation of returns, σ, is the square root of equation (2.2).

3.1.1 Symmetric Probability Distributions

Figures 3.2, 3.3, and 3.4 contrast three different types of skewness in probability distributions of returns. If an asset's probability distribution of rates of return are symmetric, as shown in Figure 3.3, rather than skewed to the left or right, then "an analysis based on expected return and standard deviation would consider these assets as equally desirable" relative to an analysis based on expected return and semideviation. Because most studies published thus far indicate the distributions of returns are approximately symmetric,[1] the semideviation is abandoned in favor of the standard deviation of returns. As Markowitz points out, the standard deviation

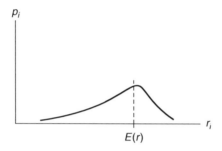

FIGURE 3.2 Probability Distribution Skewed Left

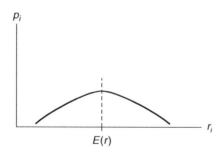

FIGURE 3.3 Symmetric Probability Distribution

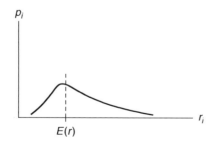

FIGURE 3.4 Probability Distribution Skewed Right

(or variance) "is superior with respect to cost, convenience, and familiarity" and "will produce the same set of efficient portfolios" as the semideviation (or semivariance) if the probability distributions are symmetric.[2]

The variance or standard deviation of returns is the surrogate for total risk that will be employed throughout this book. This is equivalent to defining risk as *variability of return.*

3.1.2 Fundamental Security Analysis

Analyzing only a firm's rate of return may seem oversimplified when compared with fundamental security analysis techniques that use many financial ratios to analyze financial statements, management interviews, industry forecasts, and the economic outlook.[3] However, there is no contradiction in these two approaches. After the fundamental security analyst completes her task, she need only convert the estimates into several possible rates of return and attach probability estimates to each. The security analyst's consideration of such matters as how highly the firm is levered (that is, how much debt is used relative to the equity), its ability to meet fixed obligations, instability within the industry, the possibility of product obsolescence, the aggressiveness of competitors, the productivity of research and development, management depth and ability, and macroeconomic conditions are all dully reflected in the forecasted rates of return and their probabilities. Thus, variability of returns is a measure of risk grounded in fundamental analysis of the firm, its industry, and the economic outlook.[4]

3.2   UTILITY THEORY

Utility is a measure of derived happiness. Economic theory is based on the assumption that the ultimate objective of human behavior is utility maximization. A person's utility (happiness) is determined by many things. But since consumption embraces the variables determining utility over which a person has some control, utility is assumed to be a function of consumption goods (such as food, leisure, health care, and education). Because the consumption goods that a human being can control have a cost, consumption is assumed to be a function of wealth. Thus, utility can be restated as a function of wealth.

Investment activity affects utility through its effects on wealth. Because the rate of return is a measure of the rate at which wealth is accumulated, the utility from investment activity can be restated as a function of the rates of return from a person's wealth. This is all summarized as follows, where U denotes utility and f, h, and g are positive functions.

$$U = f\,(\text{consumption}) \tag{3.3}$$

$$= f\left[h\,(\text{wealth})\right], \text{since consumption} = h\,(\text{wealth}) \tag{3.3a}$$

$$= f\left\{h\left[g\,(\text{rate of return})\right]\right\}, \text{since wealth} = g\,(\text{rate of return}) \tag{3.3b}$$

In a world of certainty where all outcomes are known in advance, a utility maximizer would simply invest his or her wealth in the one asset with the highest expected rate of return. However, in an uncertain world, investors can only maximize what they expect utility to be, not what it will actually turn out to be, because the future is unknown. With the introduction of uncertainty, considerations of risk enter the picture. Equation (3.4) summarizes the relation between an investor's utility and the investor's investments in a world of uncertainty.

$$E(U) = f[E(r), \text{ risk}] \qquad (3.4)$$

Consider the following example of how the "dominance principle" can be used to make rational investment decisions in the context of the two-parameter model.

PRINCIPLES BOX: DEFINITION OF DOMINANCE

A dominant asset has: (1) the lowest risk at its level of return, or (2) the highest expected return in its risk class.

3.2.1 Numerical Example

Assume an investor is trying to select one security from among five securities. These securities and their estimated return and risk statistics are listed in Table 3.1.

The five securities are compared in the two-dimensional Figure 3.5 with expected return on the vertical axis and risk on the horizontal axis. All investors that are averse to accepting risk would agree that GA dominates HT, because they both offer the same expected return but GA is less risky. And all investors that prefer higher returns over lower returns would agree that FT is dominated by AT, because they are both in the same risk class (that is, $\sigma = 4$ percent) but AT offers a higher expected return. Thus, FT and HT can be eliminated from consideration: They would not make good individual investments.

At first glance it appears that the number of desirable choices has been narrowed from five to three. The truth is more complex. Portfolios of the three dominant securities can be combined to create an infinite number of choices that are located approximately along the line r_f Q (or to the right of it—depending on the correlation coefficients between the securities[5]). For example, a portfolio composed of 50 percent AT and 50 percent GA has an expected return of 7.5 percent and a standard deviation

TABLE 3.1 Investment Candidates

Name of Security	Expected return $E(r)$ (%)	Risk σ (%)
American Telephone (AT)	7	4
General Auto (GA)	8	5
Yellow Tractors (YT)	15	15
Fine Tires (FT)	3	4
Hot Tires (HT)	8	12

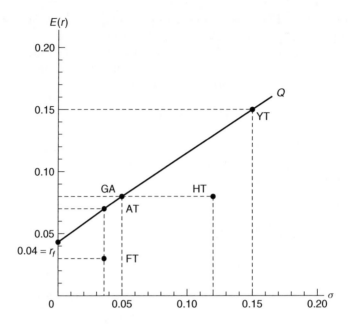

FIGURE 3.5   Investment Opportunities in Risk-return Space

of 4.5 percent, assuming AT and GA are perfectly positively correlated, $\rho_{AT,GA} = +1$. The expected return from this portfolio is calculated as follows:

$$E\left(r_p\right) = \sum_{i=1}^{2} w_i E\left(r_i\right) = w_{AT} E\left(R_{AT}\right) + w_{GA} E\left(R_{GA}\right) \tag{2.11}$$

$$= 1/2\,(7\%) + 1/2\,(8\%) = 7.5 \text{ percent.}$$

The standard deviation of returns from a two-asset portfolio is calculated with equation (2.14).

$$\sigma_p^2 = w_{AT}^2 \sigma_{AT}^2 + w_{GA}^2 \sigma_{GA}^2 + 2w_{AT} w_{GA} \sigma_{AT,GA} \tag{2.14}$$

$$= (1/2)^2 (4\%)^2 + (1/2)^2 (5\%)^5 + 2\,(1/2)\,(1/2)\,(+1)\,(4\%)\,(5\%)$$

$$= 0.002025$$

$$\sigma_p = \sqrt{0.002025} = 0.045 = 4.5 \text{ percent.}$$

Plotting this portfolio in Figure 3.5 produces a point halfway between AT and GA. If point r_f denotes investing in a risk-free asset at 4 percent return (for example, in a short-term FDIC-insured bank deposit), the points between points r_f and AT can be interpreted to be portfolios with varying proportions of bank deposit and AT shares. By borrowing at interest rate r_f (that is, by using leverage) and investing in AT or GA, the investor can create points (investment opportunities) on the line r_f Q that lie to the right and higher than GA.

By eliminating two dominated securities, the choice has been limited to points AT, GA, YT, and the infinite number of diversified portfolios containing various combinations of different securities, which we assume, to keep things simple, lie along the line r_f Q in Figure 3.5. Exactly which point along r_f Q an investor selects depends on the investor's personal preferences in the trade-off between risk and return.

3.2.2 Indifference Curves

Indifference curves can be used to represent investors' preferred trade-off between risk, σ, and return, $E(r)$. Indifference curves are drawn so an investor's satisfaction is the same throughout their length; they are *utility isoquants*. If we assume that investors dislike (get disutility from) risk and like (receive positive utility from) positive expected returns, the indifference curves that result will be positively sloped. The slope depends on the investor's particular preferences for a risk-return trade-off. The indifference map of a timid, risk-averse investor is shown in Figure 3.6. Figure 3.7 depicts a more aggressive risk-averse investor who will accept more risk to get a higher return. Both the timid and aggressive investors dislike risk. However, the timid investor in Figure 3.6 dislikes risk more than the aggressive investor in Figure 3.7.

The higher-numbered utility isoquants represent higher levels of satisfaction (happiness) for the investor. These curves grow more vertical as they rise, reflecting a diminishing willingness to assume risk.

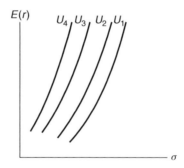

FIGURE 3.6 A Timid
Risk-averter's Indifference Map

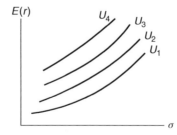

FIGURE 3.7 A Slightly More
Aggressive Risk-averter's
Indifference Map

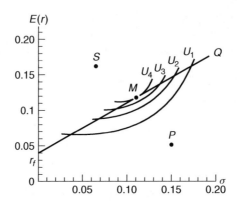

FIGURE 3.8   A Risk-return Preference
Ordering

Combining the line $r_f\,Q$ from Figure 3.5 with the indifference map from either
Figure 3.6 or 3.7 will make this choice analysis determinate, as shown in Figure 3.8.
The investor will seek the highest indifference curve tangent to the dominant
opportunity locus, $r_f\,Q$, and thereby maximize his or her utility at point M.

Asset P in Figure 3.8 is a dominated asset, it will suffer from lack of demand,
and its price will fall.[6] The rate of return is the ratio of the investor's income (from
cash dividends plus capital gains or losses) divided by the purchase price. After
a price fall, the denominator of the ratio will be reduced enough to increase the
value of the rate of return. This means that the equilibrium return on P will move
toward $r_f\,Q$ after the temporary capital losses cease. Points above the line $r_f\,Q$ (like
S) represent undervalued assets whose prices will be bid up. The resulting higher
equilibrium price (that is, higher denominator in rate-of-return ratio) will lower the
expected rate of return on this previously undervalued asset, and it will be relocated
on the line $r_f\,Q$. An equilibrium rate of return is a rate of return on the ray $r_f\,Q$.
Equilibrium returns have no tendency to change.

3.3   RISK-RETURN SPACE

Consider plotting the $E\,(r)$ and σ pairs denoted $[\sigma, E\,(r)]$ that represent the individual
investments in a two-dimensional graph in risk-return space. Next, connect the dots
representing the individual investments with lines representing possible portfolios
made from various combinations of the individual assets. Plotting such a figure
would generate a set of investment opportunities that might take on the escalloped
quarter-moon shape in Figure 3.9A. Within this opportunity set are the individual
securities and the diversified portfolios made up from those securities. Every point
on the edge and within the escalloped quarter-moon shape in Figure 3.9A is a
feasible investment opportunity. The left side of the opportunity set between points
E and F is called the *efficient frontier* of the opportunity set. This efficient frontier is
comprised of an infinite number of efficient portfolios.

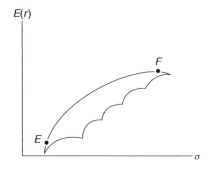

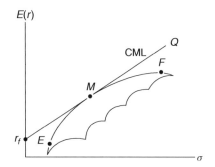

FIGURE 3.9A Investment Opportunities Without Borrowing and Lending

FIGURE 3.9B Investment Opportunities With Borrowing and Lending

---

PRINCIPLES BOX: DEFINITION OF AN EFFICIENT INVESTMENT

An efficient investment has either (1) more return than any other investment in its risk class (that is, any other security with the same variability of return), or (2) less risk than any other security with the same level of return. The efficient frontier of the opportunity set dominates all other investments in the opportunity set. These investments are said to be Markowitz efficient, referring to Harry Markowitz, the Nobel prize winner who created two-parameter portfolio theory.

Hirschleifer expressed the reason for the particular shape of the efficient frontier of the opportunity set as follows:

The curvature shown for the efficient frontier—opposite to that of the [σ, E(r)] indifference curves—follows also from the covariance effect, since moving to higher values of portfolio E (r) progressively reduces the number of securities that can be held in combination so as to lower σ.[7]

Adding the possibility of borrowing or lending at the riskless interest rate, denoted r_f, creates a new opportunity set and the line r_fMQ is created. The line r_fMQ represents the continuum of possible portfolios an investor could construct from various combinations of assets r_f and M by borrowing and lending at the interest rate r_f. r_fMQ is called the capital market line (CML). As shown in Figure 3.9B, the CML is a new and different dominant efficient frontier that is created by borrowing and lending at the riskless rate r_f; this new efficient frontier dominates all other investment opportunities in Figures 3.9A and 3.9B. The CML can be viewed as the locus of the maximum rates of returns in every risk class that exists whenever it is possible to borrow and lend at the riskless rate r_f.

Each point on the CML is determined by a pair of values for $E(r_i)$ and σ_i. The σ_i determines the investment's risk class. $E(r_i)$ is the *expected return, cost of capital, capitalization rate*, or *risk-adjusted discount rate* that is appropriate for that asset's risk class; these phrases are all synonyms.

3.4 DIVERSIFICATION

Markowitz diversification is the particular form of diversification activity implied by portfolio analysis. This type of diversification differs from *naive diversification*, used widely by security salespeople and even in some investment publications. These sources define diversification as "not putting all your eggs in one basket" or "spreading your risks." Naive diversification ignores the covariance between securities and results in superfluous diversification.

Markowitz diversification involves combining assets with less-than-perfect positive correlations in order to reduce risk in the portfolio without sacrificing any of the portfolio's return. In general, the lower the correlation between the assets in a portfolio, the less risky the portfolio will be. This is true regardless of how risky the assets of the portfolio are when analyzed individually. Markowitz explains his approach to diversification as follows:[8]

> *Not only does [portfolio analysis] imply diversification, it implies the "right kind" of diversification for the "right reason." The adequacy of diversification is not thought by investors to depend on the number of different securities held. A portfolio with sixty different railway securities, for example, would not be as well diversified as the same size portfolio with some railroad, some public utility, mining, various sorts of manufacturing, etc. The reason is that it is generally more likely for firms within the same industry to do poorly at the same time than for firms in dissimilar industries. Similarly, in trying to make variance [of returns] small it is not enough to invest in many securities. It is necessary to avoid investing in securities with high covariances [or correlations] among themselves.*

3.4.1 Diversification Illustrated

Consider the characteristics of the two securities in Table 3.2.

Reconsider equation (2.12) from Chapter 2. If Securities A and B are combined in the proportions $w_A = 2/3$ and $w_B = 1/3$, the expected return of the resulting portfolio is 8.3 percent.

$$E(r_p) = w_A E(r_A) + w_A E(r_A) \tag{2.12}$$

$$= (2/3)\,0.05 + (1/3)\,0.15 = 0.083 = 8.3 \text{ percent}$$

TABLE 3.2 Two Investment Assets

Investments:	$E(r)$	σ
A	5%	20%
B	15%	40%

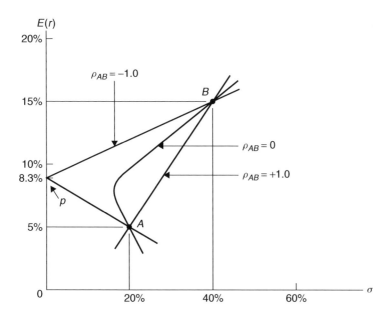

FIGURE 3.10 The Effects of Markowitz Diversification

The risk of the portfolio is given by equation (2.14) from Chapter 2.

$$\sigma_p^2 = w_A^2 \sigma_A^2 + w_B^2 \sigma_B^2 + 2w_A w_B \left[\sigma_{AB} \right] \tag{2.14}$$
$$= (2/3)^2 (0.2)^2 + (1/3)^2 (0.4)^2 + 2\,(2/3)\,(1/3)\,[\rho_{AB}\,(0.2)\,(0.4)]$$
$$= 0.0356 + 0.0356 \times \rho_{AB}$$
$$\sigma_p = \sqrt{0.0356 + 0.0356 \times \rho_{AB}}$$

Although the expected return of this portfolio is fixed at 8.3 percent with these proportions of A and B regardless of the correlation coefficient, ρ_{AB}, the risk of the portfolio varies with ρ_{AB}. Thus, if $\rho_{AB} = +1$, then $\sigma_p = \sqrt{0.0712} = 26.7$ percent. If $\rho_{AB} = 0$, then $\sigma_p = \sqrt{0.0356} = 18.7$ percent. And, if the correlation is -1, then $\sigma_p = 0$. The locus of all possible proportions (w_A and w_B) for investments A and B are plotted in Figure 3.10 for three different values of ρ_{AB}: $+1$, 0, and -1.

3.4.2 Risky A + Risky B = Riskless Portfolio

Consider two risky securities named A and B. Table 3.3 lays out annual rates of return from the two assets over four consecutive years, as well as the returns from portfolio p, which is composed half and half of A and B. The single-period returns from portfolio p for each year are calculated with 50–50 weights on A and B, according to the following formula:

$$r_{pt} = 0.5 r_{At} + 0.5 r_{Bt} \qquad \text{for } t = 1, 2, 3, 4 \text{ years}$$

TABLE 3.3 Riskless Portfolio p is Constructed from Risky Assets A and B

	$t = 1$	$t = 2$	$t = 3$	$t = 4$	Variances
Asset A (r_{At})	10.6%	8.3%	5.1%	14.2%	$\sigma_A^2 > 0$
Asset B (r_{Bt})	6.6%	8.3%	11.5%	2.4%	$\sigma_B^2 > 0$
Portfolio p (r_{pt})	8.3%	8.3%	8.3%	8.3%	$\sigma_p^2 = 0$

where t is a time period counter in Table 3.3. A glance at Table 3.3 reveals that assets A and B experience considerable variability of return from year to year—thus, they are risky assets. In contrast, the diversified portfolio p experiences zero variance of returns, which conforms with our definition of a *riskless asset*. The question is: How can the portfolio p be riskless when it is constructed from the two risky assets? The key to understanding this paradoxical question lies in understanding the correlation between the two assets' returns.

Assets A and B have perfectly negatively correlated returns, $\rho_{AB} = -1$. Their prices always move inversely. Any gains on A are always exactly offset by equal losses from B, and vice versa. As a result, portfolio p experiences zero variability of returns. In short, a riskless portfolio can be constructed from two risky assets whose prices are perfectly inversely correlated. A portfolio like p is illustrated at point p in Figure 3.10.

3.4.3 Graphical Analysis

Figure 3.10 illustrates how Markowitz diversification determines the risk of a 2-asset portfolio.[9] Figure 3.10 shows that the lower the correlation coefficient (ρ_{AB}), the more risk is reduced by combining A and B into a portfolio. The straight line between A and B defines the locus of $E(r)$ and σ pairs for all possible portfolios of A and B when $\rho_{AB} = +1$. Considering the effects of diversification depicted in Figure 3.10, the reader is invited to reexamine Figure 3.9. The curves convex toward the $E(r)$ axis in Figure 3.10 suggest the opportunity set in Figure 3.9 results from risk-reducing diversification.

Figure 3.10 also illustrates graphically that Markowitz diversification reduces the risk (variability of return) only on the owner's equity. The risk and expected return of the individual assets, A and B, are not affected by the formation of a diversified portfolio in which A and B happen to be a part. Throughout this portfolio analysis monograph the focus is ultimately on (1) the expected rate of return on the owner's equity, and (2) the variability of return (the risk) of the owner's equity. The individual assets are mere objects of choice that portfolio analysis endeavors to form into investment portfolios that dominate the individual assets. The risk and return statistics on the individual assets being considered for possible inclusion in the portfolio are *exogenous constants* that are *statistical inputs* for portfolio analysis.

3.5 CONCLUSIONS

Most investors recognize that diversification is a useful way to reduce risk. However, few investors have ever thought about risk scientifically. If an investor's concept of risk is not sufficiently well defined to be measured, that investor must be working with a vague concept of how to diversify. Furthermore, some investors develop erroneous notions about diversification. For instance, some people erroneously believe that low-risk public utility stocks and low-risk government bonds, both of which usually have low average returns, should be added to a portfolio to lower its risk. This chapter has introduced new ideas about using the correlation coefficient to reduce a portfolio's risk.

Markowitz diversification can sometimes be used to reduce risk without decreasing the portfolio's return—such diversification is optimal. Be careful not to misinterpret Figure 3.10 by erroneously thinking the correlation between securities also affects the portfolio's return. The error of this conclusion is seen by noting that the correlation coefficient is not to be found in the formula for the portfolio's return, equation (2.12). Thus, a portfolio's expected return, $E(r_p)$, is independent of the benefits of Markowitz diversification. Of course, naive diversification can reduce risk. However, naive diversification cannot be expected to *minimize* risk, since it ignores the correlation (or covariance) between assets. Naive diversification concentrates on owning many assets—that is, "not putting all your eggs in one basket." In contrast, Markowitz diversification is a scientific approach to diversification.

NOTES

1. M. G. Kendall, "The Analysis of Economic Time Series, I: Prices," *Journal of the Royal Statistical Society*, ser. A (1953): 11–25; M. F. M. Osborne, "Brownian Motion in the Stock Market," *Operations Research* 7 (1959): 173–195; H. V. Roberts, "Stock Market 'Patterns' and Financial Analysis: Methodological Suggestions," *Journal of Finance* 14 (1951): 1–10; E. F. Fama, *Foundations of Finance* (New York: Basic Books, 1976). Chapters 1 and 2 of *Foundations of Finance* discuss empirical statistics measuring the symmetry of the distributions of one-period rates of return. See pages 8–10, 40, and 58.
2. Harry M. Markowitz, "Portfolio Selection," *Journal of Finance* 7, no. 1 (1952): 193–194. See also Harry Markowitz, Editor of *Harry Markowitz Selected Works*, World Scientific Publisher, Singapore, 2010, 693 pages, Volume 1.
3. A classic book about fundamental security analysis is Benjamin Graham, David L. Dodd, and Sidney Cottle, *Security Analysis*, 4th ed. (New York: McGraw-Hill, 1962).
4. Studies showing how financial statement data relate to market-determined risk measures include the following: W.H. Beaver, P. Kettler, and M. Scholes, "The Association between Market-Determined and Accounting-Determined Risk Measures," *The Accounting Review* October 1970, 654–682; J. S. Bildersee, "Market-Determined and Alternative Measures of Risk," *The Accounting Review* January 1975, 81–98; and George Foster, *Financial Statement Analysis* (Englewood Cliffs, NJ: Prentice-Hall, 1978); see especially Chapter 9. Also see Appendix A to Chapter 4 of this monograph about the study by Dr. Thompson.
5. If the correlation coefficients between securities in a portfolio that are considerably below +1 (for example, maybe negative), they might produce points that dominate the line $r_f Q$

and may even represent portfolios containing the two dominated securities HT and FT. These possibilities will be discussed in later chapters.

6. In a more advanced analysis, point P could represent an individual security in equilibrium if that security were held in an efficient portfolio. This will be explained in a later chapter.

7. Jack Hirschleifer, "Efficient Allocation of Capital in an Uncertain World," *American Economic Review*, May 1964, 79.

8. Harry M. Markowitz, "Portfolio Selection," *Journal of Finance* 7, no. 1 (1952): The parenthetical phrases above were added. See also Harry Markowitz, Editor of *Harry Markowitz Selected Works*, World Scientific Publisher, Singapore, 2010, 693 pages, Volume 1.

9. Figure 3.10 was first published in W. F. Sharpe's classic article, "Capital Asset Prices: A Theory of Market Equilibrium under Conditions of Risk," *Journal of Finance*, September 1964. Reprinted by William Sharpe, Editor of *William F. Sharpe: Selected Works*, World Scientific Publishing Company Inc., 2012, ISBN-10: 9814329959, ISBN-13: 978–9814329958, 692 pages.

Utility Foundations

Single-Period Utility Analysis

A person can derive utility from food, an automobile, a diversified portfolio, and from many other things. Utility measures the relative magnitude of satisfaction someone derives from something; it is a subjective index of preference. If a person is faced with a decision, the alternative with the highest utility is the preferred choice. Thus, if the utility from a candy bar is less than the utility from an apple, the apple is preferred to the candy bar. Symbolically, this preference may be written: U(candy bar) < U(apple). In this monograph, utility theory is used to analyze investment decisions.

In a world of certainty, utility theory says a person should assign a numerical value to each alternative and then choose the alternative with the largest numerical value. The investor's utility function is used to determine the numerical values for each alternative investment. The application of utility theory to portfolio selection is complicated by uncertainty. In a world of certainty the rates of return to be earned from alternative portfolios are known and the investor can simply choose the portfolio with the highest return. Under uncertainty the rates of return on alternative portfolios are stochastic variables—that is, random variables. In such a situation, how should the investor proceed? Utility theory states that the investor should act so as to maximize expected utility, where expected utility is a numerical value assigned to a portfolio's probabilistic rates of return. This numerical value is calculated by taking the weighted average of the utilities from the various possible returns.

The weights are the probabilities associated with each possible return.[1] This description of how investors should behave is typically referred to as the expected utility hypothesis and is based on the utility model developed by von Neumann and Morgenstern.[2]

This chapter analyzes single-period investment decisions. The length of time covered by the single period may be as short as a month or as long as a decade. Conceptually, an investor's period of reference is the length of the person's investment *planning horizon*. Risky investments that will be resolved within a few days are not really investments; they are gambles or speculations. In contrast, pension fund managers, endowment fund managers, and others make investments with 30- to 100-year planning horizons. These planning horizons exceed our definition of a single period. Multiperiod (or long-term; for instance, multiple decades) utility analysis is the topic of a later chapter.

4.1 BASIC UTILITY AXIOMS

Rigorous utility analysis begins with the following six assumptions.[3]

1. People have preferences. Thus, given a choice between A and B, a person can tell whether he or she prefers A to B, $U(A) > U(B)$; is indifferent between A and B, $U(A) = U(B)$; or prefers B to A, $U(A) < U(B)$.
2. A person's choices are transitive. Thus, if someone prefers A to B and prefers B to C, it follows that A is preferred to C.
3. Objects with equal utility are equally desirable. Symbolically, if $U(A) = U(D)$ and $U(A) > U(B)$, then $U(D) > U(B)$ follows directly, because A and D are desired equally.
4. Utility can be used with risky decisions. For instance, if $U(A) > U(B)$ and $U(B) > U(C)$, there is some risky lottery involving A and C that is as satisfying as B. Symbolically,

$$[1 - p(C)] \cdot U(A) + p(C) \cdot U(C) = U(B)$$

where $p(C)$ is the probability of C occurring, and $p(A) = 1 - p(C)$.
5. If someone has ranked objects of choice, then adding some irrelevant additional object to each of the already-ranked alternatives does not change their ranking. Symbolically, if $U(A) > U(B)$, then $[U(A) + U(E)] > [U(B) + U(E)]$, where E is something that does not affect A or B.
6. People make risky decisions by maximizing their *expected utility*. The utility of a risky object is equal to the expected utility of the possible outcomes. Symbolically, if a person faces n possible outcomes, that person's expected utility is

$$E(U) = \sum_{i=1}^{n} p_i(O_i) \cdot U(O_i) \tag{4.1}$$

where $U(\cdot)$ is some positive function that assigns utils to the values of the outcomes, O_i is the numerical value assigned to the i-th outcome, and $p_i(O_i)$ is the probability O_i occurs. Utility analysis is based on the six previous assumptions.

Economists use utility analysis to analyze the implications of their decision-making models to see if they are logical and realistic. If you get *positive marginal utility* from ice cream (or dollars, or returns) that simply means that you like ice cream (or dollars, or returns). Positive but *diminishing marginal utility* is one of the characteristics economists expect to find in a realistic economic model. Diminishing positive marginal utility simply means that as you get more and more units of a good, you enjoy each additional unit less. Most people experience diminishing marginal utility when they eat several ice cream cones, as shown below.

$$U(\text{1st cone}) > U(\text{2nd cone}) > U(\text{3rd cone}) > 0$$

Although each cone yields some positive utility, each additional cone yields less utility than the preceding cone.

4.2 THE UTILITY OF WEALTH FUNCTION

Economists rarely analyze the utility from particular commodities (such as ice cream cones, clothes, perfume, etc.) because everyone has different preferences. Instead, economists analyze the utility of purchasing power because the utility of purchasing power allows the dollar cost of clothing to be compared with the dollar cost of perfume. By focusing on the utility of wealth, denoted $U(W)$, economists facilitate utility analysis of different purchasing decisions. Some things that are desirable do not have an explicit dollar cost; for example, leisure time. To use utility of wealth to analyze decisions about leisure time, you must impute a dollar value to leisure time. This might be done, for example, by assuming the dollar value of an hour of leisure time equals the hourly wage foregone while loafing.

A *utility of wealth* function is a formula or a graph that shows how much utility (or how many utils, or how much happiness) a person derives from different levels of wealth. Figure 4.1 illustrates a utility function that has diminishing positive marginal utility.

4.3 UTILITY OF WEALTH AND RETURNS

Utility preference orderings are invariant under a positive linear transformation of the utility function. Speaking mathematically, this means that any utility curve (such as the one in Figure 4.1) can undergo any of the following linear transformations without changing the preference orderings it generates.

- The utility function can be raised or lowered (that is, can have a positive constant added or subtracted).
- The utility function can be scaled down without having its shape changed (that is, can be divided by a positive constant).
- The utility function can be expanded without changing its curvature (that is, it can be multiplied by a positive constant).

The transformations may change the number of utils assigned to any given outcome, but the preference rankings would be invariant under these positive linear transformations.

The one-period rate of return involves a positive linear transformation. An investor's return is simply a linear transformation of wealth. The positive linear

FIGURE 4.1 A Utility of Wealth Function

TABLE 4.1 Beginning- and End-of-Period Prices and One-Period Returns

Security	Purchase price per share	End-of-period sale price	One-period rate of return
A	$ 15	$ 20	$r_A = 33.3\%$
B	$150	$200	$r_B = 33.3\%$

transformation between wealth and the rate of return is

$$W_T = W_0 (1 + r) \tag{4.2}$$

where W_0 denotes the investor's initial wealth (a positive constant), W_T is the end-of-period wealth (a random variable), and r is the one-period rate of return (also a random variable). Equation (4.2) shows that the investor's return is simply a linear transformation of the investor's wealth, and vice versa. This means that the investor's utility of wealth curve shown in Figure 4.1 is simply a positive linear transformation of that investor's rates of return. And that investor's utility of wealth and utility of returns functions will yield identical preference orderings.

In discussing investments, financial economists often prefer to analyze the speed (or rate) at which the investor's wealth changes rather than wealth itself. The one-period rate of return measures the rate at which initial wealth W_0 increases to end-of-period wealth W_T. It is easier to analyze the utility of returns, denoted $U(r)$, than it is to analyze the utility of wealth, because the analysis is not distorted by differences in the dollar amount of the investment (that is, by scaling differences). Thus, as Table 4.1 shows, the $15-per-share security A can yield as much utility as security B, which costs $150 per share, if they both grow at a rate of 33.3 percent.

An investor who was naive might prefer security B because it yielded more dollars of capital gain ($50) than security A (only $5). A more rational investor would realize that 10 shares of security A would provide the identical gain as one share of security B and, therefore, would evaluate the two investments equally in terms of their returns, $U(r_A) = U(r_B) = U(33.3\%)$.

4.4 EXPECTED UTILITY OF RETURNS

In the real world, investments involve risk. Before risky alternatives can be analyzed, the analyst must be supplied with a probability distribution of returns for each alternative investment and a utility function that assigns utils to the returns.

Utility analysis is useful for analyzing the logic in decisions involving risky outcomes. The expected-utility maxim (basic assumption 6) is the heart of the analysis. The expected-utility maxim defines an action that maximizes the decision maker's expected utility to be the most desirable choice.

If the outcomes involve risk, maximizing expected utility is different from maximizing the utility from outcomes that are known in advance. To see the difference, reconsider the definition of expected utility. The expected utility from a decision to undertake a course of action involving risk is the weighted average of the utils from the possible outcomes that are calculated using the probability of each outcome as its weight. For example, if you enter into a coin-tossing gamble, you have decided to undertake a risky course of action. There are two possible outcomes—heads or tails. The utility from the gamble that results if heads turns up is represented by U(head) and the utility of getting a tail is U(tail). Thus, the expected utility of the gamble may be written as

$$E\left[U\left(coin\ toss\right)\right] = p\left(head\right) \cdot U\left(head\right) + p\left(tail\right) \cdot U\left(tail\right) \tag{4.3}$$

where $p\left(head\right)$ indicates the probability a head turns up, and $p\left(tail\right) = 1 - p\left(head\right)$ indicates the probability a tail turns up.

EXAMPLE 4.1

Consider assets named 1, 2, and 3. Table 4.2 defines the probability distribution of returns for the three assets. The assets' expected returns and standard deviations are calculated using equations (2.1) and (2.2) from Chapter 2.

TABLE 4.2 Probability Distributions for Three Assets' Returns

Returns	Probability		
	Asset 1	Asset 2	Asset 3
−3%	0.5	0.0	0.0
0	0.0	0.5	0.0
3%	0.0	0.0	1.0
6%	0.0	0.5	0.0
9%	0.5	0.0	0.0
$E\left(r\right)$	3.0%	3.0%	3.0%
$\sigma\left(r\right)$	6.0%	3.0%	0.0%

Assume that there are three investors, A, B, and C, and these investors have the following three different utility functions.

$$U_A\left(r\right) = 100r - 50r^2 \tag{4.4}$$

$$U_B\left(r\right) = 100r \tag{4.5}$$

$$U_C\left(r\right) = 100r + 50r^2 \tag{4.6}$$

Figures 4.2, 4.3, and 4.4 represent utility functions for (A) a risk-averse, (B) a risk neutral, and (C) a risk-seeking investor, respectively.

Because the three investments all offer the same expected return of three percent, it is clear that investors will rank these three investments purely because of their risk differences.

(Continued)

EXAMPLE 4.1 *(Continued)*

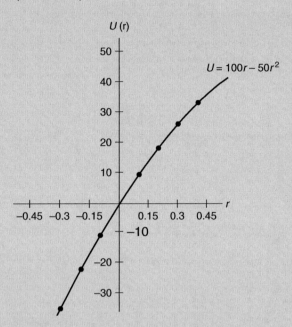

FIGURE 4.2   Risk-averse Investor A's Quadratic
Utility of Returns Function

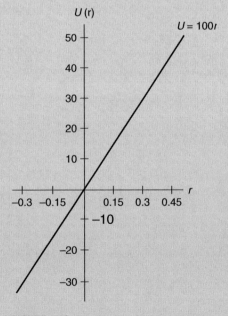

FIGURE 4.3   Risk-neutral Investor B's
Linear Utility of Returns Function

EXAMPLE 4.1 (*Continued*)

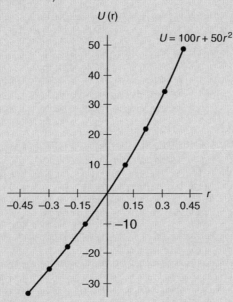

FIGURE 4.4 Risk-seeking Investor C's
Quadratic Utility of Returns Function

Investor A's expected utilities from the three assets are calculated as follows:

$$E\left[U_A\left(r_1\right)\right] = \sum_{i=1}^{2} p_i U(r_i) = 0.5 \times U(-0.03) + 0.5 \times U(0.09)$$

$$= 0.5 \times \left[100\left(-0.03\right) - 50(-0.03)^2\right] + 0.5$$

$$\times \left[100\left(0.09\right) - 50(0.09)^2\right]$$

$$= 0.5 \times (-3.045) + 0.5 \times (8.595) = 2.785 \quad \text{for asset 1,}$$

$$E\left[U_A\left(r_2\right)\right] = 0.5 \times U(0) + 0.5 \times U(0.06) = 0 + 0.5 \times (5.82)$$

$$= 2.91 \quad \text{for asset 2, and,}$$

$$E\left[U_A\left(r_3\right)\right] = 1.0 \times U(0.03) = 1.0 \times (2.955) = 2.955 \quad \text{for asset 3.}$$

Not surprisingly, the risk-averse investor with utility equation (4.4) derives the most satisfaction from asset 1, which has the least variability of return of the three assets.

Investor B's expected utilities from the same three assets are calculated as follows:

$$E\left[U_B\left(r_1\right)\right] = \sum_{i=1}^{2} p_i U(r_i) = 0.5 \times U(-0.03) + 0.5 \times U(0.09)$$

$$= 0.5 \times \left[100\left(-0.03\right)\right] + 0.5 \times \left[100\left(0.09\right)\right]$$

$$= 0.5 \times (-3) + 0.5 \times (9) = 3 \quad \text{for asset 1,}$$

(*Continued*)

EXAMPLE 4.1 (*Continued*)

$E[U_B(r_2)] = 0.5 \times U(0) + 0.5 \times U(0.06) = 0 + 0.5 \times (6) = 3$ for asset 2, and

$E[U_B(r_3)] = 1.0 \times U(0.03) = 1.0 \times (3) = 3$ for asset 3.

The investor with utility equation (4.5) is indifferent among the three assets, because the utilities from all three are the same. Since assets 1, 2, and 3 differ only with respect to their risk, the risk-indifferent investor has an expected utility of three utils from each of the choices.

Investor C's expected utilities from the three assets are as follows:

$$E[U_C(r_1)] = \sum_{i=1}^{2} p_i U(r_i) = 0.5 \times U(-0.03) + 0.5 \times U(0.09)$$

$$= 0.5 \times \left[100(-0.03) + 50(-0.03)^2\right] + 0.5$$

$$\times \left[100(0.09) + 50(0.09)^2\right]$$

$$= 0.5 \times (-2.055) + 0.5 \times (9.405) = 3.225 \quad \text{for asset 1,}$$

$$E[U_C(r_2)] = 0.5 \times U(0) + 0.5 \times U(0.06) = 0 + 0.5 \times (6.18)$$

$$= 3.09 \quad \text{for asset 2, and}$$

$$E[U_C(r_3)] = 1.0 \times U(0.03) = 1.0 \times (3.045) = 3.045 \quad \text{for asset 3.}$$

The risk lover with utility equation (4.6) derives the most satisfaction from asset 1, which has the largest variability of return (the most risk).

Summarizing, when the expected returns of all investments are equal, investor A prefers the investment that has the least risk, as computed with equation (4.4). Risk-indifferent investor B is indifferent among the investments as long as their expected returns are the same. And investor C prefers the investment with the largest risk because investor C's utility function, equation (4.6), represents risk-loving behavior. This example shows how investment decisions are determined by the shape of investors' utility functions.

4.5   RISK ATTITUDES

Some risk averters are more risk-averse than others.

4.5.1   Risk Aversion

The *marginal utility of wealth* is defined as the additional utility a person gets from a tiny change in her wealth. Economics is based on the notion that more wealth is always more desirable than less wealth. In other words, the marginal utility of wealth of every rational person will always be positive. Marginal utility can be measured mathematically by the first derivative of the utility function with respect to wealth. Symbolically, marginal utility of wealth = $U'(W) = \partial U / \partial W > 0$.

To determine whether marginal utility is rising or falling, the slope of the utility function, as measured by the sign of the second derivative of the utility function, is observed. Decreasing marginal utility exists when the utility function rises at a diminishing rate, or, equivalently, when the second derivative of the utility function is negative, $\partial^2 U(W)/\partial W^2 = U''(W) < 0$. Figure 4.1 illustrates an example of decreasing marginal utility. Diminishing marginal utility of wealth leads to risk-avoiding behavior because, from any point on the utility-of-wealth (or utility-of-returns) curve, a risky investment has a lower expected utility than a risk-free investment with the same expected return. Economics assumes it is always rational to be risk averse.[4]

Suppose an investor has a utility function with decreasing marginal utility. Further suppose that this investor is offered a fair game that has a chance of winning \$300 ($= \tilde{z}$) with probability of 1/2 or losing \$300 with probability of 1/2.[5] The investor's initial wealth is \$1,000. Would this investor be willing to enter into this fair game? The answer depends on the investor's attitude toward risk. Figure 4.5 illustrates the amount of utility before and after playing the fair game. If the investor wins this fair game, her wealth increases to \$1,300 $\left(W_+ = W_0 + \tilde{z} \right)$ and the amount of utility is $U\left(W_+ \right)$. If the investor loses the game, her wealth decreases to \$700 $\left(W_- = W_0 - \tilde{z} \right)$ and the amount of utility is $U\left(W_- \right)$. Thus, the expected utility after playing the game will be $E\left[U(W) \right] = \frac{1}{2} U\left(W_+ \right) + \frac{1}{2} U\left(W_- \right)$. Whether or not this investor is willing to play this fair game depends on whether the investor's expected utility is increased or decreased by playing the game. $U\left(W_0 \right)$ indicates the investor's utility of wealth before playing the game. If $E\left[U(W) \right] > U\left(W_0 \right)$, the investor would be willing to play the game, and if $E\left[U(W) \right] < U\left(W_0 \right)$, the investor would not be willing to play. Figure 4.5 shows the game decreases the investor's expected utility by $U\left(W_0 \right) - E\left[U(W) \right]$. Therefore, this investor would decline to participate in this fair game. In other words, this investor exhibits *risk aversion*.

A risk averter's utility function will always be concave (toward the wealth or returns axis), as in Figures 4.1 and 4.5. Risk averters prefer to hold W_0 sure cash

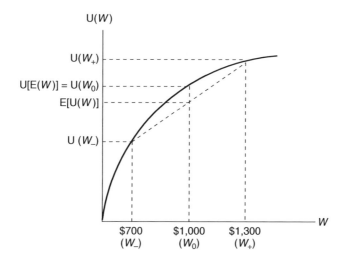

FIGURE 4.5 Risk Averter's Utility Before and After Playing Fair Game

rather than gamble (assume risk) to increase their wealth above W_0. If the probability of winning the risky investment is large enough, or if the reward for winning is large enough, a risk averter can be induced to gamble. Stated differently, risk averters may purchase risky investments if they feel the odds are in their favor.

In the previous example, playing the risky game decreases the risk averter's utility by $U(W_0) - E[U(W)]$. Suppose, the investor's utility after playing the risky game equals the utility of holding a certainty equivalent (CE) amount of cash, symbolically $E[U(W)] = U(CE)$. Figure 4.6 illustrates the *certainty equivalent*; it is a certain amount of cash that leaves the investor indifferent between a risky investment and a certain amount of cash, denoted CE. By playing a risky game, this investor loses utility of $U(W_0) - E[U(W)]$, or equivalently, loses a certainty equivalent amount of cash equal to $E(\tilde{W}) - CE$, where $E(\tilde{W}) = (1/2)(W_0 + \tilde{z}) + (1/2)(W_0 - \tilde{z})$ is the expected wealth from the gamble. In order for this investor to avoid this risky game, she would be willing to pay an amount of cash equal to $E(\tilde{W}) - C$; the amount of this payment is called the *risk premium*.

$$\text{Risk premium} = \text{Expected wealth} - \text{Certainty equivalent}$$

$$\text{or,} \quad \phi(W_0, \tilde{z}) = E(\tilde{W}) - CE \tag{4.7}$$

where $\phi(W_0, \tilde{z})$ is the *risk premium*, which is a function of the initial wealth W_0 and a random payoff $\tilde{z}$. The risk premium is always positive for risk averters.

In summary, the risk-averse investor's utility function is concave and has the following mathematical characteristics:

$$U[E(W)] > E[U(W)] \Longleftrightarrow U'(W) > 0, \quad \text{and} \quad U''(W) < 0 \tag{4.8}$$

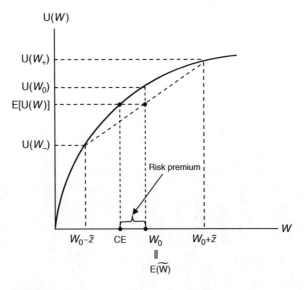

FIGURE 4.6   Risk Averter's Utility Function

EXAMPLE 4.2

An investor whose initial wealth is $1,000 is offered an opportunity to play a fair game with two possible outcomes: winning $200 with probability of 1/2 or losing $200 with probability of 1/2. This investor's utility function equals the natural (or Naperian) logarithm of wealth, $U(W) = \ln(W)$. What are the certainty equivalent (CE) and risk premium of this risky game?

Because the logarithmic utility function has the following first- and second-order derivatives with respect to wealth, it satisfies three conditions.

$$\frac{\partial U(W)}{\partial W} = U'(W) = \frac{1}{W} > 0$$

$$\frac{\partial^2 U(W)}{\partial W^2} = U''(W) = -\frac{1}{W^2} < 0$$

First, the investor prefers to have more wealth rather than less wealth (i.e., the first derivative is positive). Second, the $\ln(W)$ function will always generate risk-averse decisions because the second derivative of $U(W) = \ln(W)$ is negative. Third, the investor will require a positive risk premium. The expected utility is

$$E[U(W)] = 0.5 \times \ln(1,200) + 0.5 \times \ln(800) = 6.8873$$

Because $E[U(W)] = \ln(CE)$, the antilogarithm of $E[U(W)]$ (using base $e = 2.718\ldots$) equals the antilog of $\ln(CE)$. Therefore, the certainty equivalent and the risk premium of this game are

Certainty equivalent (CE) $= e^{6.8873} = \$979.80$

Risk premium = Expected wealth − Certainty equivalent wealth

$= \$1,000 - \$979.80$

$= \$20.20$

EXAMPLE 4.3

Assume the facts used in Example 4.2, except that the payoffs will be more widely dispersed. The probability of winning $500 is 1/2 and the probability of losing $500 is 1/2. Because the payoffs are more volatile than the payoffs in Example 4.2, this game is riskier, and as a result, the investor requires a larger risk premium.

The expected utility is $E[U(W)] = 0.5 \times \ln(1,500) + 0.5 \times \ln(500) = 6.7639$.

Certainty equivalent (CE) $= e^{6.7639} = \$866.03$

Risk premium $= \$1,000 - \$866.03 = \$133.97$

EXAMPLE 4.4

Utilize the facts of Example 4.2 again, except that the investor's initial wealth increases to $2,000. What is the risk premium in this wealthier case?

Depending on the outcome of the game, the investor's wealth will be either [$2,000 + $200 =] $2,200 or [$2,000 − $200 =] $1,800 with equal chance. The expected utility is

$$E\,[U\,(W)] = 0.5 \times \ln\,(2{,}200) + 0.5 \times \ln\,(1{,}800) = 7.5959.$$

$$\text{Certainty equivalent (CE)} = e^{7.5959} = \$1{,}989.97$$

$$\text{Risk premium} = \$2{,}000 - \$1{,}989.97 = \$10.03$$

Note that the risk premium decreases as the wealth increases. This indicates that as the investor gets richer, she becomes less afraid of risk. That is, the investor exhibits decreasing risk aversion.

4.5.2   Risk-Loving Behavior

If an investor has the convex utility function illustrated in Figure 4.7, the investor will make riskier decisions about the same fair game. His expected utility from playing, $E\,[U\,(W)]$, is greater than without playing the game, $U\,(W_0)$. In other words, playing the risky game increases the risk lover's utility by $E\,[U\,(W)] - U\,(W_0)$. This investor expects his utility will be increased by gambling or speculating; this investor is a

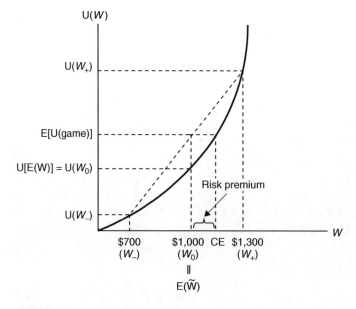

FIGURE 4.7   Risk Lover's Utility Before and After Playing a Fair Game

risk lover. This risk lover's utility after playing the risky game equals the utility of holding a certain amount of cash, denoted CE in Figure 4.7. The certainty equivalent of this fair game is greater than the expected wealth. Thus, the risk premium is negative: $\phi\left(W_0, \tilde{z}\right) = \mathrm{E}(\tilde{W}) - \mathrm{CE} < 0$.

The utility function for the risk lover can be mathematically summarized by

$$\mathrm{U}\left[\mathrm{E}\left(W\right)\right] < E\left[\mathrm{U}\left(W\right)\right] \Longleftrightarrow \mathrm{U}'\left(W\right) > 0 \ \text{ and } \ \mathrm{U}''\left(W\right) > 0 \qquad (4.9)$$

EXAMPLE 4.5

Assume the facts used in Example 4.2 again, except that the investor's utility function is quadratic; $\mathrm{U}\left(W\right) = W^2$. What are the certainty equivalent (CE) and risk premium of this risky game?

Because the quadratic utility function has the following first- and second-order derivatives with respect to wealth, it satisfies three conditions.

$$\frac{\partial U\left(W\right)}{\partial W} = \mathrm{U}'\left(W\right) = 2W > 0$$

$$\frac{\partial^2 U\left(W\right)}{\partial W^2} = \mathrm{U}''\left(W\right) = 2 > 0$$

First, the investor prefers to have more wealth than less wealth (i.e., the first derivative is positive). Second, it will generate risk-loving decisions (i.e., the second derivative is positive). Third, the investor will require a negative risk premium. The expected utility is

$$\mathrm{E}\left[\mathrm{U}\left(W\right)\right] = 0.5 \times 1{,}200^2 + 0.5 \times 800^2 = 1{,}040{,}000$$

Because $\mathrm{E}\left[\mathrm{U}\left(W\right)\right] = \mathrm{U}\left(\mathrm{CE}\right)$, the square root of $\mathrm{E}\left[\mathrm{U}\left(W\right)\right]$ equals the CE. Therefore, the certainty equivalent and risk premium of this game are

$$\text{Certainty equivalent (CE)} = \sqrt{1{,}040{,}000} = \$1{,}019.80$$

$$\text{Risk premium} = \text{Expected wealth} - \text{Certainty equivalent}$$

$$= \$1{,}000 - \$1{,}019.80 = -\$19.80$$

4.5.3 Risk-Neutral Behavior

If an investor has the linear utility function illustrated in Figure 4.8, the investor would be indifferent about playing a fair game. Her expected utility from playing, $\mathrm{E}\left[\mathrm{U}\left(W\right)\right]$, is equal to that from not playing the game, $\mathrm{U}\left(W_0\right)$. It is said that this investor exhibits *risk-neutral* behavior. The certainty equivalent of this fair game equals the expected wealth. As illustrated in Figure 4.8, risk-neutral investors require no risk premium: $\phi\left(W_0, \tilde{z}\right) = \mathrm{E}(\tilde{W}) - \mathrm{CE} = 0$.

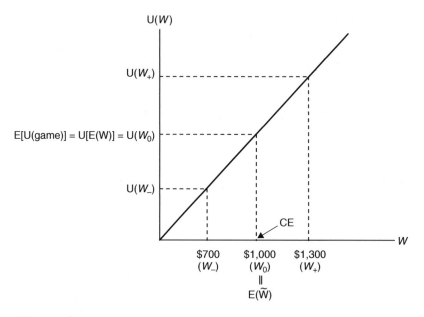

FIGURE 4.8 Risk Neutral Investor's Utility Before and After Playing Fair Game

Mathematically, the utility function for risk-neutral investors is

$$U[E(W)] = E[U(W)] \Longleftrightarrow U'(W) > 0 \quad \text{and} \quad U''(W) = 0 \qquad (4.10)$$

EXAMPLE 4.6

Assume the same facts used in Example 4.2, except that the investor's utility function is a linear function of wealth: $U(W) = W$. What are the certainty equivalent (CE) and risk premium of this risky game?

Because the linear utility function has the following first- and second-order derivatives with respect to wealth, it satisfies three conditions.

$$\frac{\partial U(W)}{\partial W} = U'(W) = 1 > 0$$

$$\frac{\partial^2 U(W)}{\partial W^2} = U''(W) = 0$$

First, the investor prefers to have more wealth than less wealth (i.e., the first derivative is positive). Second, the linear utility function generates risk-neutral decisions (i.e., the second derivative is zero). Third, the investor will require no risk premium. The expected utility is: $E[U(W)] = 0.5 \times \$1,200 + 0.5 \times \$800 = \$1,000$.

> **EXAMPLE 4.6** (*Continued*)
>
> Because $E[U(W)] = U(CE)$, the $E[U(W)]$ itself equals the CE. Therefore, the certainty equivalent and risk premium of this game are
>
> Certainty equivalent (CE) = $1,000
>
> Risk premium = Expected wealth − Certainty equivalent
>
> = $1,000 − $1,000 = 0

4.6 ABSOLUTE RISK AVERSION

It was shown in Figure 4.6 that a risk-averse investor would not be willing to play a fair game, because playing would decrease his or her utility. To avoid this risky game, the investor would be willing to give up an amount of cash, called the risk premium, denoted $\phi(W, \tilde{z})$. After giving up the risk premium, this investor would be indifferent between playing a risky fair game with random payoff $\tilde{z}$ and holding a certain amount of cash equal to the *certainty equivalent*. The utilities of playing the risky game and holding the certain amount of cash (= the total wealth after the game minus the risk premium) are equal. Mathematically,

$$E[U(W + \tilde{z})] = U[W + E(\tilde{z}) - \phi(W, \tilde{z})] \tag{4.11}$$

Because a fair game has $E(\tilde{z}) = 0$, equation (4.11) can be rewritten as

$$E[U(W + \tilde{z})] = U[W - \phi(W, \tilde{z})] \tag{4.12}$$

Solving equation (4.12) yields the risk premium.

$$\phi(W, \tilde{z}) = \frac{1}{2}\sigma_z^2 \left[-\frac{U''(W)}{U'(W)} \right] \tag{4.13}$$

Equation (4.13) is also called the *Pratt-Arrow risk premium*. The derivation is described in Appendix A4.1.

As in Example 4.2, suppose an investor whose initial wealth is $1,000 is offered a chance to play a fair game that has a probability of 1/2 of winning $200 and a probability of 1/2 of losing $200. This investor has a logarithmic utility function, $U(W) = \ln(W)$. Then, the variance of the payoff is $\sigma_z^2 = 0.5 \times (200 - 0)^2 + 0.5 \times (-200 - 0)^2 = 200^2$. Because $\partial U/\partial W = U'(W) = 1/W$ and $\partial^2 U/\partial W^2 = U''(W) = -1/W^2$, the Pratt-Arrow measure of risk premium is

$$\phi(W, \tilde{z}) = \frac{1}{2}\sigma_z^2 \left(\frac{1}{W} \right) = \frac{1}{2}(200^2)\left(\frac{1}{1,000} \right) = \$20$$

This amount is slightly different from the Markowitz measure of risk premium of $20.20 computed in Example 4.2. This difference may be attributed to the Taylor series approximation.

The term in the bracket on the right-hand side in equation (4.13) is individual specific and is referred to as the investor's measure of *absolute risk aversion* (ARA). The absolute risk aversion is defined as

$$A(W) = -\frac{U''(W)}{U'(W)} \qquad (4.14)$$

Note that the absolute risk aversion is a positive value, since $U'(W) > 0$ and $U''(W) < 0$, because rational economic agents prefer more to less and they are risk-averse. The size of the risk premium $\phi(W, \tilde{z})$ is determined by the product of the two terms in equation (4.13); the variance of the payoff $\tilde{z}$ and the absolute risk aversion. A greater risk premium is required as the payoff from the game becomes more volatile (riskier) and as the investor's absolute risk aversion grows, as demonstrated in Examples 4.2, 4.3, and 4.4.

The absolute risk aversion, $A(W)$ in equation (4.14), is a measure of how the investor's preference for risk changes with a change in wealth. If the investor wants to put more wealth (in absolute dollars) in risky investments as his or her wealth increases, it is said that the investor exhibits decreasing absolute risk aversion. This means that as the investor gets richer, he or she becomes less risk averse. Examples 4.2 and 4.4 illustrate examples of decreasing absolute risk aversion. An investor whose initial wealth is $1,000 and whose utility function is logarithmic requires the risk premium of $20.20 for playing a risky game paying $200 or −$200 with equal chance. However, if his or her wealth increases to $2,000, that same investor requires the lesser risk premium of $10.03 to play. Thus, it is said this investor has decreasing absolute risk aversion. Mathematically, decreasing absolute risk aversion is represented by $A'(W) < 0$, where $A'(W)$ is the first derivative of $A(W)$ with respect to wealth. If investment in risky assets is decreased as the investor's wealth increases, it is said that this investor exhibits increasing absolute risk aversion, which is represented by $A'(W) > 0$. If the risky investment is unchanged even though the investor's wealth increases, it is said that this investor exhibits constant absolute risk aversion, which is represented by $A'(W) = 0$.

Most rational investors would increase the (absolute) dollar amount invested in risky assets as their wealth increases. In other words, decreasing absolute risk aversion is the most realistic assumption we can make for most investors.[6]

4.7 RELATIVE RISK AVERSION

The previous discussion of absolute risk aversion focused on the dollar magnitude of the risk premium $\phi(W, \tilde{z})$, for a portfolio whose return remained constant in dollars while the investor's initial wealth increased. It was noted that $\phi(W, \tilde{z})$ is quite reasonably assumed to be a decreasing function of initial wealth. Another method of analysis is to look at the risk premium expressed as a proportion p of the wealth. This is accomplished by redefining $\phi(W, \tilde{z}) = pW$. We also express the random payoff from a game as $\tilde{z} = \tilde{r}W$, where $\tilde{r}$ is the rate of return and $E(\tilde{r}) = 0$ represents a fair game. As a result of these changes, equation (4.12) is rewritten as

$$E[U(W + \tilde{r}W)] = U[W - pW] \qquad (4.15)$$

Based on equation (4.15), the proportional size of the risk premium, p, is

$$p\left(W, \tilde{r}\right) = \frac{1}{2}\sigma_r^2 \left[-W\left(\frac{U''\left(W\right)}{U'\left(W\right)}\right)\right] \tag{4.16}$$

Note that the proportional size of the risk premium is a function of the initial wealth and the variance of the rate of return. This derivation is discussed further in Appendix A4.2.

The term in the bracket on the right-hand side in equation (4.16) is individual specific and is referred to as the investor's measure of *relative risk aversion*. Relative risk aversion (RRA) is defined as

$$R\left(W\right) = W \cdot A\left(W\right) = -W\left(\frac{U''\left(W\right)}{U'\left(W\right)}\right) \tag{4.17}$$

Note that the relative RRA is a positive value for rational investors who want more instead of less and are risk-averse. The proportional size of the risk premium is determined by the product of the two terms in equation (4.16); the variance of returns from the risky game and the measure of relative risk aversion.

Note the effect that greater wealth has on the size of the proportional risk premium p. The relative risk aversion, $R\left(W\right)$ in equation (4.17), is a measure of how the percentage of wealth invested in risky assets changes with a change in wealth. If the investor increases (decreases) the percentage of wealth invested in risky investments as his or her wealth increases, the investor is exhibiting decreasing (increasing) relative risk aversion. This is mathematically denoted $R'\left(W\right) < 0$ [$R'\left(W\right) > 0$]. If the investor maintains the same percentage in risky investments with a change in wealth, the investor is exhibiting constant relative risk aversion, denoted $R'\left(W\right) = 0$.

After examining Internal Revenue Service data on individual investors, Blume and Friend (1975) and Friend and Blume (1975) concluded that a reasonable approximation for describing investors' behavior was constant relative risk aversion. Although there is much less consensus regarding relative risk aversion than absolute risk aversion, it is often assumed that constant relative risk aversion is consistent with most investors' behavior. Note that there is general consensus that most investors exhibit decreasing absolute risk aversion.

As an example, the logarithmic utility function $U\left(W\right) = \ln\left(W\right)$, exhibits constant relative risk aversion. The logarithmic utility function has the absolute risk aversion of $A\left(W\right) = 1$ and the relative risk aversion of $R\left(W\right) = 1$. So, $R'\left(W\right) = 0$. In other words, investors with the logarithmic utility function would maintain the same percentage in risky investments as their wealth changes.

Arrow has interpreted the value of relative risk aversion as follows:

Thus, broadly speaking, the relative risk aversion must hover around 1, being, if anything, somewhat less for low wealths and somewhat higher for high wealths. Two conclusions emerge: (1) it is broadly permissible to assume that relative risk aversion increases with wealth, though theory does not exclude some fluctuations; (2) if, for simplicity, we wish to assume a constant relative risk aversion, then the appropriate value is 1. As can easily be seen, this implies that the utility of wealth equals its logarithm, a relation already suggested by Bernoulli. To be sure, the logarithm is not bounded at either end, but it may still be regarded as an approximation to a bounded utility function, for if the relative risk aversion were ever so slightly greater than 1 at the high end of the wealth scale and ever so slightly less at the lower end, the utility function would be bounded at both ends and yet essentially logarithmic throughout the greater part of the range.[7]

Arrow's discussion of absolute risk aversion and relative risk aversion is not only insightful, it also provides reasons to believe the logarithmic utility function is more logical than alternative utility functions.

4.8 MEASURING RISK AVERSION

The tools just introduced allow the reader to make studied judgments about logic and rationality of alternative utility functions.

4.8.1 Assumptions

The previous sections suggest the following four assumptions are consistent with rational investment behavior.

> Assumption 1: Investors prefer more to less (nonsatiation); $\partial U / \partial W = U'(W) > 0$.
>
> Assumption 2: Investors are risk averse; $\partial^2 U / \partial W^2 = U''(W) < 0$.
>
> Assumption 3: Investors exhibit decreasing absolute risk aversion; $A'(W) < 0$.
>
> Assumption 4: Investors exhibit constant relative risk aversion; $R'(W) = 0$.

Table 4.3 summarizes risk aversion assessments for various utility functions of interest. Subject to the restrictions noted in the table, all these functions meet the first two assumptions about investor behavior; nonsatiation ($U'(W) > 0$) and risk aversion ($U''(W) < 0$). However, the quadratic utility function displays increasing absolute risk aversion, which violates the third assumption. The exponential utility function also violates this assumption, because it has constant absolute risk aversion.[8] Both the logarithmic and power utility functions, on the other hand, are consistent with the assumption of decreasing absolute risk aversion and also have constant relative risk aversion.[9] These latter two functions are of particular interest.[10]

4.8.2 Power, Logarithmic, and Quadratic Utility

Comparisons of the quadratic, logarithmic, and power utility functions, reveal several advantages from using the latter two functions. First, the power function exhibits positive marginal utility over all ranges. In contrast, the quadratic function's marginal utility becomes negative for large wealth levels, an unrealistic and perplexing problem that must be dealt with by appending bounds to the function.[11]

Another advantage of both the logarithmic and power functions relative to the quadratic is that the investor's wealth and returns are separable with the logarithmic and power functions, but not with the quadratic.[12] Separability of wealth and returns means that indifference curves, to be discussed in Section 4.10 in this chapter, and

TABLE 4.3 Assessing Risk Aversion In Various Utility Functions

Utility function	Restrictions	$U'(W)$	$U''(W)$	$A(W)$ Function	$A'(W)$	$R(W)$ Function	$R'(W)$
1. Quadratic: $U = bW - cW^2$	$b > 0; c > 0;$ $W \leq \dfrac{b}{2c}$	$b - 2cW$	$-2c$	$\dfrac{2c}{b - 2cW}$	positive	$\dfrac{2cW}{b - 2cW}$	positive
2. Exponential: $U = -\exp(-cW)$	$c > 0$	$c\exp(-cW)$	$-c^2\exp(-cW)$	c	zero	cW	positive
3. Logarithmic: $U = \ln W$	None	$\dfrac{1}{W}$	$-\dfrac{1}{W^2}$	$\dfrac{1}{W}$	negative	1	zero
4. Power: $U = W^{1-\gamma}$ or	$0 < \gamma < 1$	$(1 - \gamma)\,W^{-\gamma}$	$-\gamma(1 - \gamma)\,W^{-\gamma-1}$	$\dfrac{\gamma}{W}$	negative	γ	zero
$U = -W^{-\gamma}$	$\gamma > 0$	$\gamma\,W^{-\gamma-1}$	$-\gamma(\gamma + 1)\,W^{-\gamma-2}$	$\dfrac{1 + \gamma}{W}$	negative	$1 + \gamma$	zero

hence optimal portfolio allocations, are independent of the level of initial wealth W_0. For example, suppose that an investor has the logarithmic utility of terminal wealth function

$$U\left(W_T\right) = \ln\left(W\right)_T$$

$$= \ln\left[W_0\left(1 + r_p\right)\right] = \ln W_0 + \ln\left(1 + r_p\right) \qquad (4.18)$$

The term $\ln\left(W_0\right)$ on the right-hand side of equation (4.18) is a positive constant that can be ignored because a utility function's preference orderings are invariant under positive linear transformations. Thus, utility analysis can focus on the term involving returns, $\left(1 + r_p\right)$, without being affected by the level of the investor's initial wealth.

Consider next the power utility in terminal wealth. As in the case of the logarithmic function, the investor's initial wealth is separable from the rate of return as shown below:

$$U\left(W_T\right) = W_T^{1-\gamma}$$

$$= \left[W_0\left(1 + r_p\right)\right]^{1-\gamma}$$

$$= W_0^{1-\gamma}\left(1 + r_p\right)^{1-\gamma} \qquad (4.19)$$

The term $W_0^{1-\gamma}$ on the right-hand side of equation (4.19) is a positive constant that can be ignored because a utility function's preference orderings are invariant under positive linear transformations. Thus, utility analysis can focus on the term involving returns, $\left(1 + r_p\right)^{1-\gamma}$, without being affected by the level of the investor's initial wealth. This property of separability has an important consequence for portfolio optimization, which is discussed further in the next section.

The quadratic function does not allow separation of the investor's initial wealth and returns. A quadratic wealth function implies a quadratic returns function, but the coefficients of the returns function are dependent on the level of the investor's initial wealth.

4.8.3 Isoelastic Utility Functions

Isoelastic utility functions enjoy a quality called *constant elasticity of substitution*. The Arrow-Pratt relative risk-aversion measure may be interpreted as a measure of the elasticity of utility with respect to wealth. Those classes of utility functions that have constant relative risk aversion (CRRA) may be called *isoelastic utility* functions. As an example of isoelastic utility functions, consider the following utility function:

$$U\left(W\right) = \frac{1}{1-\gamma} W^{1-\gamma} \qquad (4.20)$$

where $0 < \gamma < 1$ for risk-averse investors. This function can be viewed as a positive linear transformation of the power utility function because the coefficient $1/(1-\gamma)$ can be deleted by such a transformation. This function's name comes from the fact that the elasticity of utility with respect to terminal wealth is constant

$$\left(\frac{\partial U}{U}\right)\bigg/\left(\frac{\partial W}{W}\right) = \left(\frac{\partial U}{\partial W}\right)\left(\frac{W}{U}\right) = 1 - \gamma \qquad (4.21)$$

Isoelastic utility functions allow wealth and returns to be separated so that the investor's expected utility can be maximized by analyzing investment returns without reference to the investor's level of wealth—that is, the optimum portfolio is not dependent on the level of the investor's wealth. This separability property greatly simplifies the analysis of an investor's utility in a multiperiod context where the investor probably begins every period with a different amount of investable wealth. Isoelastic utility functions allow the investor to act as if he or she had a short-term (single-period) horizon even though he or she actually has a long-term (multiperiod) horizon. Investors with isoelastic utility functions can simply maximize the same utility of returns function in every period, regardless of the level of their wealth. Furthermore, this period-by-period utility of returns function is of the same form as the investor's utility of terminal wealth function.

Among those classes of utility functions that possess positive but diminishing marginal utility, Mossin (1968) has shown that three classes of utility functions are isoelastic. These classes are:[13]

1. $U = W^{1-\gamma}$ for $0 < \gamma < 1$, a positive power function.
2. $U = -W^{-\gamma}$ for $\gamma > 0$, a negative power function.
3. $U = \ln(W)$ for $\gamma = 1$, a logarithmic function.

4.8.4 Myopic, but Optimal

An investor who disregards past and future periods in making investment decisions for the current period could be called nearsighted. Instead of calling them nearsighted, financial economists prefer to say they behave myopically. Simply delineating and selecting an optimal single-period efficient portfolio is optimal multiperiod behavior and will maximize multiperiod expected utility under three conditions. These three conditions are:

1. The investor has positive but diminishing utility of terminal wealth, that is, $U'(W) > 0$ and $U''(W) < 0$.
2. The investor has an isoelastic utility function, which makes wealth and returns separable.
3. The single-period rates of return for securities are distributed according to a multivariate normal distribution and are independent of prior period returns.

These conditions simplify the mathematics sufficiently to prove that expected utility in the multiperiod case can be maximized by acting myopically.[14] For example, if the investor has a logarithmic utility function, the utility of the terminal wealth is $U(W_T) = \ln(W_T)$, where $W_T = W_0(1 + r_1)\cdots(1 + r_T)$. In this case, for any single time period t between 0 and T, maximizing $E[U(W_T)]$ is equivalent to maximizing $E[\ln(1 + r_t)]$. In other words, a young investor with a logarithmic utility of retirement-age wealth can behave consistently by maximizing the log of end-of-year wealth year after year until reaching retirement. Stated differently, if you have a log utility function, it is not only easy to be an economically nearsighted (myopic) Markowitz portfolio manager who always focuses on rates of return and ignores wealth levels, it is also optimal wealth-maximizing behavior.

4.9 PORTFOLIO ANALYSIS

Given an investor's utility function $U = f(W)$, it can be demonstrated that the expected utility of a portfolio is a function of the portfolio's mean and variance of returns (and possibly other parameters). That is, the expected utility becomes a functions of the mean and variance of the wealth W,

$$E[U(W)] \cong f[E(W)] + \frac{f''[E(W)]}{2!}\sigma_w^2 \tag{4.22}$$

where $E(W)$ and σ_w^2 are the expected value and variance of wealth, respectively. The derivation of equation (4.22) is reproduced in this chapter's Appendix A4.3.

Because the terminal wealth W_T is a function of the rate of return over the one period, r_p, it can be seen that

$$E(W_T) = W_0[1 + E(r_p)] \tag{4.23}$$

and

$$\sigma_{W_T}^2 = W_0^2\sigma_p^2 \tag{4.24}$$

where $E(r_p)$ and σ_p^2 denote the portfolio's mean return and variance of returns over the period, respectively. Thus, combining equations (4.22), (4.23), and (4.24) yields

$$E[U(W_T)] \cong f[W_0(1 + E(r_p))] + \frac{f''[W_0(1 + E(r_p))]}{2!}W_0^2\sigma_p^2 \tag{4.25}$$

Because the initial wealth W_0 is a given constant, the expected utility of the terminal wealth of equation (4.25) is a function of only the mean and variance of the returns, $E(r_p)$ and σ_p^2. That is,

$$E[U(W_T)] \cong f[E(r_p), \sigma_p^2] \tag{4.26}$$

A question raised by using the preceding approximations, which focuses on only the first two statistical moments, concerns the utility implications of portfolio analysis for the third and fourth statistical moments of the probability distribution of returns. For example, imagine two portfolios that have identical expected returns and variances but that have different third and fourth moments. The distribution most skewed to the left will have the largest probability of a dangerous event—perhaps even enough to bankrupt the portfolio. Or, if one of the distributions is platykurtic, the range of possible returns is wider than a normal distribution. In these situations, questions arise about whether portfolio analysis will find both securities equally desirable. The answer is yes.

Portfolio analysis ignores the third and fourth moments. This is not a flaw in the model for two reasons: (1) Statistical evidence shows that, historically, most distributions of returns are approximately symmetrical.[15] Thus, consideration of skewness is not necessary. (2) Unless investors' utility functions are polynomials of degree four, or higher, the fourth moment does not affect utility. Furthermore, there is some question about what the fourth moment measures.[16]

4.9.1 Quadratic Utility Functions

A quadratic utility function implies certain things about its owner's behavior. Consider the following quadratic utility function of the terminal wealth

$$U\left(W_{T}\right) = \beta W_{T} - \gamma W_{T}^{2} \tag{4.27}$$

where β and γ are positive constants.[17] By substituting $W_{0}\left(1 + r_{p}\right)$ for W_{T} in equation (4.27), the utility can be expressed as a quadratic function in r_{p}:

$$U\left(r_{p}\right) = a + br_{p} - cr_{p}^{2} \tag{4.28}$$

where $a = \beta W_{0} - \gamma W_{0}^{2}$, $b = \beta W_{0} - 2\gamma W_{0}^{2}$, and $c = \gamma W_{0}^{2}$. Thus, utility functions that are quadratic in W_{T} are also quadratic in r_{p}.

When the utility function is quadratic, the expected utility is exactly a function of the mean and variance of the wealth. Taking the expectation of equation (4.27) yields

$$\begin{aligned}
E\left[U\left(W_{T}\right)\right] &= E\left(\beta W_{T} - \gamma W_{T}^{2}\right) \\
&= \beta E\left(W_{T}\right) - \gamma E\left(W_{T}^{2}\right) \\
&= \beta E\left(W_{T}\right) - \gamma \left\{\left[E\left(W_{T}\right)\right]^{2} + \sigma_{W}^{2}\right\}
\end{aligned} \tag{4.29}$$

because $E\left(W_{T}^{2}\right) = \left[E\left(W_{T}\right)\right]^{2} + \sigma_{W}^{2}$.[18] Therefore, portfolio analysis based on the quadratic utility function is identical to the standard mean-variance analysis.[19]

The marginal utility of returns is the change in utility resulting from a tiny change in return. For the quadratic utility function in equation (4.30), the marginal utility of returns is

$$\frac{\partial U\left(r\right)}{\partial r} = b - 2cr > 0 \tag{4.30}$$

The marginal utility from additional returns is positive for $r < b/2c$. At $r = b/2c$, marginal utility is zero and the utility curve in Figure 4.9 peaks. For returns above $b/2c$, the investor receives negative marginal utility—that is, positive returns greater than $r = b/2c$ are distasteful. This violates the first assumption in Section 4.8.1

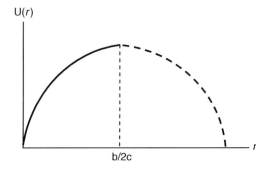

FIGURE 4.9 Quadratic Utility Function of Returns

(nonsatiation). To avoid the unrealistic portion of the utility curve where additional gains yield negative marginal utility (that is, the dashed portion of Figure 4.9), the analysis must be restricted to returns below a limit. This constraint is $r < b/2c$. In other words, we must assume that a quadratic utility of returns function has an upper bound.

4.9.2 Using Quadratic Approximations to Delineate Max[E(Utility)] Portfolios

Most investors are not gratified to hear their investment advisor tell them they should maximize their expected utility. This is because utility theory is abstract. Most investors prefer to discuss dollars or returns or something that is, as a minimum, sufficiently tangible to be measured. Most investors are not interested in utility theory.

Unlike most investors, financial economists like utility theory. They find risk-averse, risk-neutral, and risk-loving behavior interesting. They analyze linear, power, logarithmic, quadratic, and other utility functions and compare and contrast the risk-aversion characteristics of each function, as shown in this chapter's Table 4.3. Utility functions that deliver positive but diminishing marginal utility of wealth are held in esteem because they rationalize complicated human behaviors like wealth maximization, risk aversion, and diversification. An unfortunate disadvantage of utility analysis is that delineating Max[E(U{r})] portfolios provides a slow and cumbersome route to selecting efficient portfolios. Markowitz (1959, 282–289) and Markowitz (1987, 59–68) show that a quadratic function of a portfolio's expected return and standard deviation can provide a fast and easy way to delineate efficient portfolios.

Markowitz (1959) suggests the quadratic utility function

$$U\left(r_p\right) = a + br_p - cr_p^{\,2} \tag{4.28}$$

$$E\left[U\left(r_p\right)\right] = a + bE\left(r_p\right) - c\left\{\left[E\left(r_p\right)\right]^2 + \sigma_r^2\right\} \tag{4.28a}$$

$$= a + bE\left(r_p\right) - c\left[E\left(r_p\right)\right]^2 - c\sigma_r^2 \tag{4.28b}$$

since $E\left(r_p^2\right) = \left[E\left(r_p\right)\right]^2 + \sigma_r^2$. Markowitz proposes this utility function because (1) as shown in equation (4.28b), it is an exact function of the investment's expected return and standard deviation; (2) Markowitz (1959, 282–289), Young and Trent (1969), Levy and Markowitz (1979), Kroll, Levy, and Markowitz (1984), Markowitz (1987, 59–68), and others have shown that a custom-fit quadratic function of a portfolio's expected return and standard deviation can provide a very good shortcut for finding utility-maximizing portfolios for several different types of utility functions;[20] and (3) a quadratic function of an investment's expected return and standard deviation can be combined with mean-standard deviation portfolio analysis to select optimal investment opportunities in risk and return space. This mean-variance approximation technique quickly and efficiently selects portfolios that are almost identical to those selected by the slower and more cumbersome process of computing Max[E(U{r})] portfolios.

As Levy and Markowitz (1979) first noted, if investors with unidentified utility functions choose off the mean-variance efficient frontier, they can approximately maximize their expected utility without ever knowing what their utility function is; in fact, without anyone even mentioning the "expected utility maxim" to them. Finally, in spite of the fact it is possible to find utility-maximizing portfolios without a utility function, this in no way diminishes the insights obtained by analyzing traditional utility functions.

4.9.3 Normally Distributed Returns

Using the expected utility hypothesis causes the investors to maximize their expected utility, even in the presence of uncertainty. If the number of outcomes for a given portfolio p is discrete, its expected utility is

$$E\left[U\left(W_p\right)\right] = \sum_{i=1}^{k} U\left(W_T^i\right) p_i\left(W_T^i\right) \qquad (4.31)$$

where k is the number of possible outcomes, W_T^i is the level of terminal wealth corresponding to outcome i for portfolio p, and $p_i\left(W_T^i\right)$ is the probability it occurs. In the more general case where the outcomes are continuously distributed, expected utility was shown to be calculated as

$$E\left(U_p\right) = \int_{-\infty}^{+\infty} U\left(W_T\right) p\left(W_T\right) dW_T \qquad (4.32)$$

where $p\left(W_T\right)$ is the probability density function for terminal wealth associated with a given portfolio p. Thus, for any utility function, $E\left[U\left(W_p\right)\right]$ depends on $p\left(W_T\right)$.

If the probability density function is normally distributed, it will be of the form

$$p\left(W_T\right) = \frac{1}{\sqrt{2\pi}\,\sigma_{W_T}} \exp\left\{-\frac{\left[W_T - E\left(W_T\right)\right]^2}{2\sigma_{W_T}^2}\right\} \qquad (4.33)$$

In comparing any set of portfolios that have normally distributed returns, meaning that terminal wealth is normally distributed as in equation (4.33), their corresponding levels of $E\left[U\left(W_p\right)\right]$ will differ only to the extent that $p\left(W_T\right)$ differs between alternative portfolios. In this situation, examination of equation (4.33) indicates that $p\left(W_T\right)$ will differ between alternative portfolios if and only if either $E\left(W_T\right)$ or σ_{W_T} differs between the portfolios. Accordingly, if terminal wealth is normally distributed (or, equivalently, if portfolio returns are normally distributed), then portfolios can be evaluated by using the magnitudes of $E\left(W_T\right)$ and σ_{W_T}. Thus, mean-variance analysis is exact not only when utility functions are quadratic, but also when returns are normally distributed.

4.10 INDIFFERENCE CURVES

In the previous sections, we discussed how an investor's expected utility could be expressed as a function of risk, measured by the standard deviation of returns (denoted σ_p) and expected returns (denoted $E\left(r_p\right)$). This section shows how indifference curves can be derived from an investor's utility function and used to represent the investor's preferences in $\left[\sigma_p, E\left(r_p\right)\right]$ space. An indifference curve is drawn in

$[\sigma_p, E(r_p)]$ space such that the investor's satisfaction (that is, expected utility) is equal throughout its length. Indifference curves are utility isoquants. The slope of an indifference curve depends on the investor's particular preference for a lower but safer return versus a larger but riskier return.

Figures 4.10A and 4.10B illustrate positively-sloped indifference curves in $[\sigma_p, E(r_p)]$ space for inverstors A and B. Indiffernce curves for timid, risk-averse investors are positively sloped, because they require higher expected returns as an inducement to assume larger risks. Let us contrast the behavior of the two risk-averse investors illustrated in Figures 4.10A and 4.10B. Investors A's indifference curve has lower slope (is flatter) than investor B's. When an investor increases the level of risks from σ_1 to σ_2, by $\Delta\sigma$, that investor requires more expected return to maintain the same level of utility. He or she would ask for an additional amount of the expected return, denoted $\Delta E(r)$ [from $E(r_1)$ to $E(r_2)$]. Note that portfolios P_1 and P_2 in Figure 4.10A produce the same amount of utility. For the same amount of risk change (from σ_1 to σ_2, by $\Delta\sigma$), investor B would ask for a larger additional amount of expected return, $\Delta E(r)'$, from $E(r_1)'$ to $E(r_2)'$, than investor A to maintain the same level of utility. This difference indicates that investor B is more risk averse than investor A and requires a larger risk premium. In other words, indifference curves with steeper slopes are for the more risk-averse investors. The slope of the indifference curves is discussed further in Section 4.2 of this chapter.

Figure 4.11 illustrates a negatively sloped indifference curve that represents the preferences of a risk seeker. When this *risk lover* increases the level of risk from σ_1 to σ_2, by $\Delta\sigma$, the investor would ask for less expected return to maintain the same level of utility. In other words, when the level of risk is increased, the risk seeker would be willing to give up a certain amount of expected return to maintain the same level of satisfaction. This type of investor enjoys taking risk and would pay money to acquire more risk (that is, would ask for a negative risk premium).

The flat linear indifference curves in Figure 4.12 represent a *risk-neutral* investor. Even though the level of risk is increased, a risk-neutral investor would not ask for additional expected return to maintain the same level of utility. In other words, any change in the level of risk does not affect the utility of a risk-neutral investor. Only the level of expected return determines the utility. No risk premium is required by risk neutral-investors. As long as the expected returns are the same, the utility is

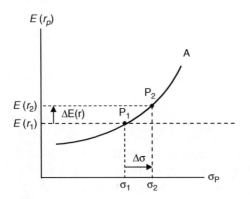
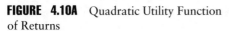

FIGURE 4.10A Quadratic Utility Function of Returns

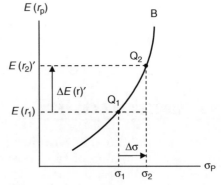

FIGURE 4.10B Indifference Curve for a Moderately Risk-Averse Investor

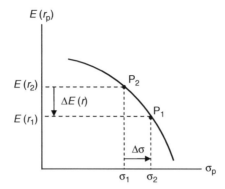

FIGURE 4.11 Indifference Curve for a Risk Seeker

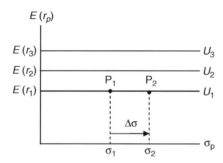

FIGURE 4.12 Indifference Lines for a Risk Neutral Investor

the same. As the expected return increases from $E(r_1)$ to $E(r_3)$, the utility increases from U_1 to U_3, regardless of the level of risk in Figure 4.12.

4.10.1 Selecting Investments

The previous paragraphs showed how an investor's utility function can be used to select a portfolio in terms of risk and expected return statistics; Figure 4.13 illustrates how to do this. The figure is a graph in *risk-return space* illustrating the seven hypothetical portfolios listed in Table 4.4.

Figure 4.13 shows an indifference map in risk-return space representing the preferences of a risk-averse investor whose utility function is a quadratic function of the form $U(r_p) = br_p - cr_p^2$. Because portfolios G, D, and F are all located on indifference curve U_2, the investor obtains equal expected utility from all three, although their expected returns and risks differ considerably.

An infinite number of indifference curves could be drawn for the risk averter depicted in Figure 4.13, but they would all be similar in shape and would all possess the following characteristics:

1. Higher indifference curves represent higher levels of expected utility and thus more investor satisfaction. Symbolically, $U_5 > U_4 > U_3 > U_2 > U_1$. This family

TABLE 4.4 Expected Returns and Standard Deviations of
Seven Hypothetical Portfolios

Portfolio	Expected return (%) $E(r_p)$	Risk (%) σ_p
A	7	3
B	7	4
C	15	15
D	3	3
E	7	12
F	9	13
G	2	0

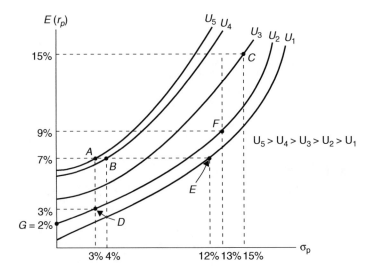

FIGURE 4.13 Opportunities and Preferences in Risk-return Space

of indifference curves indicates the investor likes higher expected return and
dislikes higher risk.

2. All indifference curves slope upward. This is because the investor requires higher
   expected returns as an inducement to assume larger risks. Consider, for example,
   the investor's indifference between D, F, and G. This is due to the fact that F's
   expected return is just enough above the expected return of D to compensate
   the risk-averse investor for assuming the additional risk incurred in going from
   D to F. Riskless portfolio G has just enough reduction in risk below the risk
   of D to compensate the investor for accepting G's lower rate of return. G is
   called the *certainty equivalent* of portfolios D and F because it involves no risk,
   yet is equally desirable. That is, the investor finds the riskless 2 percent return
   (portfolio G) to be equally desirable to 3 percent return with 3 percent risk
   (portfolio D) or 9 percent return with 13 percent risk (portfolio F).

3. The indifference curves grow steeper at higher levels of risk. This reflects the investor's diminishing willingness to assume higher and higher levels of risk.

Given the investment opportunities and the investor preferences shown in Figure 4.13, we see that the investor prefers A over any of the other portfolios because A lies on the highest indifference curve. More generally, if we are given several pairs of risk-return values $[\sigma_p, E(r_p)]$, and each pair represents a different portfolio, an investor could plot these risk-return pairs on a graph that also contains that investor's indifference curves. The portfolio on the highest indifference curve would be optimal (most preferred) because it would provide the investor with the highest level of expected utility.

4.10.2 Risk-Aversion Measures

Figures 4.14, 4.15, and 4.16 illustrate different families of indifference maps for three investors with different risk preferences. Figure 4.14 shows that the slope

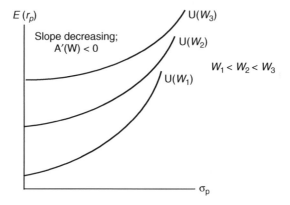

FIGURE 4.14 Indifference Curves Exhibiting Decreasing Absolute Risk Aversion

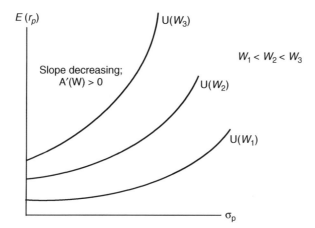

FIGURE 4.15 Indifference Curves Exhibiting Increasing Absolute Risk Aversion

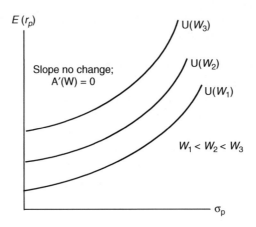

FIGURE 4.16   Indifference Curves Exhibiting
Constant Absolute Risk Aversion

of the indifference curves becomes lower (flatter) as the level of wealth increases
from W_1, W_2 to W_3. Because an indifference curve with lower slope indicates less
risk aversion, this figure represents decreasing absolute risk aversion. In contrast,
Figure 4.15 shows that as the level of wealth increases, the slope of the indifference
curves steepens, indicating more risk aversion and increasing absolute risk aversion.
Figure 4.16 shows that although the level of wealth changes, the slopes of the
indifference curves do not change. The indifference curves in Figure 4.16 remain
parallel with respect to wealth change, representing *constant absolute risk aversion.*[21]

4.11   SUMMARY AND CONCLUSIONS

Roy (1952, 433) is widely quoted for saying that "a man who seeks advice about his
actions will not be grateful for the suggestion that he maximize his expected utility."
Although true, such light remarks do not depreciate the rigor or the usefulness of
utility analysis.

   Rationally seeking to increase one's wealth in a risk-averse fashion was shown
to imply positive but diminishing marginal utility of wealth and decreasing absolute
risk aversion. Utility functions with positive but diminishing marginal utility are
those with positive first derivatives and negative second derivatives. Graphically
speaking, such functions are positively sloped and concave toward the wealth axis.
The expected utility axiom was used to analyze alternative investments and make
risky decisions that maximize the investor's happiness (expected utility).

   The quadratic, exponential, power, and logarithmic utility functions were examined. Subject to certain restrictions on their parameters, all four functions were found
to have positive but diminishing marginal utility. The quadratic was shown to be a
troublesome function to work with because of some unrealistic properties. Unfortunately, the quadratic function can exhibit negative marginal utility and increasing
absolute risk aversion. But by assuming that the rates of return are normally distributed, it is possible to make rational, wealth-maximizing decisions by using more
logical utility functions, such as the power and the logarithmic functions.

An indifference curve was described as the locus of all $[\sigma_p, E(r_p)]$ pairs that provide the investor with the same amount of happiness. Each investor can be represented by a set (family) of indifference curves and each indifference curve represents a given level of expected utility. It was shown that the indifference curves representing rational decisions are positively sloped and convex for risk-averse investors, negatively sloped and concave for risk-seeking investors, and are horizontal lines for risk-neutral investors. Expected utility increases as one moves to higher-level indifference curves, which is in a northwesterly direction for risk-averse investors. For risk-seeking and risk-neutral investors, happiness is increased by moving northeast and north, respectively.

APPENDIX: RISK AVERSION AND INDIFFERENCE CURVES

This appendix describes the derivation of absolute risk aversion (ARA) and relative risk aversion (RRA) by using the Taylor series expansion. It also shows that the expected utility of wealth is a function of a portfolio's mean return and variance, and discusses the slope of indifference curves and the indifference curve for a quadratic utility function.

A4.1   Absolute Risk Aversion (ARA)

Consider a situation in which the utility from playing a risky game and holding a certain amount of cash (the total wealth after the game minus the risk premium) are equal and $E(\tilde{z}) = 0$. The mathematical representation of this situation is

$$E[U(W + \tilde{z})] = U[W - \phi(W, \tilde{z})] \tag{4.12}$$

To evaluate equation (4.12), we first take a Taylor series expansion of $U(W + \tilde{z})$ about the random payoff $\tilde{z}$:

$$U(W + \tilde{z}) = U(W) + \tilde{z}U'(W) + \frac{1}{2!}\tilde{z}^2 U''(W) + O(\tilde{z}^3) \tag{A4.1}$$

where $O(\tilde{z}^3)$ is the remainder that includes the third- or higher-order terms of $\tilde{z}$. Assuming this remainder is near zero, the left-hand side of equation (4.12) is approximated as

$$E[U(W + \tilde{z})] \cong U(W) + \frac{1}{2}U''(W)\sigma_z^2 \tag{A4.2}$$

since $E(\tilde{z}) = 0$ and $E(\tilde{z}^2) = \sigma_z^2$.

The second step in evaluating equation (4.12) is to take a Taylor series expansion of the right-hand side (RHS) about $\phi(\cdot)$:

$$U[W - \phi(W, \tilde{z})] = U(W) - \phi(W, \tilde{z})U'(W) + O[\phi^2(W, \tilde{z})] \tag{A4.3}$$

where $O\left[\phi^2\left(W,\tilde{z}\right)\right]$ is the remainder that contains the second- or higher-order terms of $\phi\left(W,\tilde{z}\right)$. Assuming the remainder in equation (A4.3) is near zero and equating equations (A4.2) and (A4.3) results in

$$U\left(W\right)+\frac{1}{2}U''\left(W\right)\sigma_z^2=U\left(W\right)-\phi\left(W,\tilde{z}\right)U'\left(W\right) \qquad \text{(A4.4)}$$

Thus, the risk premium is derived as

$$\phi\left(W,\tilde{z}\right)=\frac{1}{2}\sigma_z^2\left[-\frac{U''\left(W\right)}{U'\left(W\right)}\right] \qquad \text{(A4.5)}$$

Equation (A4.5) defines the Pratt-Arrow risk premium.

A4.2 Relative Risk Aversion (RRA)

Redefining the risk premium $\phi\left(W,\tilde{z}\right)=pW$ and the random payoff $\tilde{z}=\tilde{r}W$, where p is the proportional size of the risk premium and $\tilde{r}$ is the rate of return, with $E\left(\tilde{r}\right)=0$ permits us to rewrite equation (4.12) as

$$E\left[U\left(W+\tilde{r}W\right)\right]=U\left[W-pW\right] \qquad \text{(A4.15)}$$

Taking a Taylor series expansion of $U\left(W+\tilde{r}W\right)$ about the random payoff $\tilde{r}W$ yields:

$$U\left(W+\tilde{r}W\right)=U\left(W\right)+\left(\tilde{r}W\right)U'\left(W\right)+\frac{1}{2!}(\tilde{r}W)^2U''\left(W\right)+O\left[(\tilde{r}W)^3\right] \qquad \text{(A4.6)}$$

Assuming the remainder term $O(\cdot)$ is near zero, the left-hand side of equation (A4.15) is approximated as

$$E\left[U\left(W+\tilde{r}W\right)\right]\cong U\left(W\right)+\frac{1}{2}U''\left(W\right)W^2\sigma_r^2 \qquad \text{(A4.7)}$$

We also take a Taylor series expansion of the right-hand side of equation (4.15) about pW:

$$U\left[W-pW\right]=U\left(W\right)-\left(pW\right)U'\left(W\right)+O\left[(pW)^2\right] \qquad \text{(A4.8)}$$

Assuming the remainder in equation (A4.8) is near zero and equating equations (A4.7) and (A4.8) results in

$$U\left(W\right)+\frac{1}{2}U''\left(W\right)W^2\sigma_r^2=U\left(W\right)-\left(pW\right)U'\left(W\right) \qquad \text{(A4.9)}$$

The proportional size of risk premium p is expressed as

$$p\left(W,\tilde{r}\right)=\frac{1}{2}\sigma_r^2\left[-W\left(\frac{U''\left(W\right)}{U'\left(W\right)}\right)\right] \qquad \text{(A4.10)}$$

A4.3 Expected Utility of Wealth

Given an investor's utility function $U = f(W)$, it can be demonstrated that the expected utility of a portfolio is a function of the portfolio's mean and variance of returns (and possibly other parameters). A Taylor series expansion is used to approximate the function U about the expected value $E(W)$ associated with any given portfolio:

$$U(W) = f[E(W)] + f'[E(W)][W - E(W)] + \frac{f''[E(W)]}{2!}[W - E(W)]^2$$

$$+ \sum_{n=3}^{\infty} \left\{ \frac{f^{(n)}[E(W)]}{n!}[W - E(W)]^n \right\} \qquad (A4.11)$$

where $f^{(n)}(\cdot)$ is the n-th derivative function. The expected utility is

$$E[U(W)] = f[E(W)] + f'[E(W)]E[W - E(W)] + \frac{f''[E(W)]}{2!}E[W - E(W)]^2$$

$$+ \sum_{n=3}^{\infty} \left\{ \frac{f^{(n)}[E(W)]}{n!}E[W - E(W)]^n \right\} \qquad (A4.12)$$

In evaluating equation (A4.12), note that $f[E(W)]$ is *simply* the value of the utility function evaluated at the expected value of W. The second term on the RHS of equation (A4.12) is zero. The third term on the RHS of equation (A4.12) is the constant $f''[E(W)]/2!$ times $E[W - E(W)]^2$, where $E[W - E(W)]^2$, by definition, is the variance of the random variable W, denoted σ_w^2. Assuming that the remaining terms in equation (A4.12) are approximately (or exactly) zero, the expected utility becomes a function of the mean and variance of the wealth W,

$$E[U(W)] \cong f[E(W)] + \frac{f''[E(W)]}{2!}\sigma_w^2 \qquad (A4.13)$$

Equation (A4.13) proves that the utility (satisfaction, happiness) an investor derives from an investment can be restated to be a function of the investment's mean and variance of the wealth W.

A4.4 Slopes of Indifference Curves

The slope of the indifference curves for risk-averse, risk-seeking, and risk-neutral investors can be shown to be positive, negative, and zero, respectively, by analysis of the Taylor series expansion of an investor's utility function presented in equation (A4.13). Consider the following partial derivatives of equation (A4.13) with respect to $E(W)$, and σ_w^2:

$$\frac{\partial E[U(W)]}{\partial E(W)} = f'[E(W)] + \sigma_w^2 \left[\frac{f'''[E(W)]}{2} \right] \qquad (A4.14)$$

$$\frac{\partial E[U(W)]}{\partial \sigma_w} = \sigma_w [f''[E(W)]] \qquad (A4.15)$$

Due to the nonsatiation assumption, we know that the first derivative, $f'[E(W)]$, is positive for risk-averse, risk-seeking, and risk-neutral investors. Furthermore, for these three types of investors we know that the third derivative $f'''[E(W)] \cong 0$ from our earlier assumption regarding the higher-order terms of the Taylor series expansion in equation (A4.13). This means that $\partial E(U)/\partial E(W) > 0$ in equation (A4.14) for all three types of investors. Accordingly, in Figure A4.1, these investors should all prefer A to C, because it has a higher level of $E(W)$ while still having the same level of σ_w.

In evaluating equation (A4.15), by definition, risk-averse investors have negative second derivatives, $f''[E(W)] < 0$, because they possess decreasing marginal utility. Furthermore, risk-seeking investors have positive second derivatives, $f''[E(W)] > 0$, and, risk-neutral investors have second derivatives that equal zero, $f''[E(W)] = 0$, because they possess increasing and constant marginal utility, respectively. Accordingly, in choosing among B, A, and D in Figure A4.1, risk-averse investors prefer B, because $\partial E[U(W)]/\partial \sigma_w < 0$, while risk-seeking investors prefer D, because $\partial E[U(W)]/\partial \sigma_w > 0$. Risk-neutral investors are indifferent between A, B, and D, because $\partial E[U(W)]/\partial \sigma_w = 0$ for them. More generally, risk-averse investors prefer portfolios lying northwest of A, risk-seeking investors prefer portfolios lying northeast of A, and risk-neutral investors prefer portfolios that are anywhere north of A.[22]

Given these graphically defined preferences, it can now be shown that the risk-averse investor will have positively sloped indifference curves. Consider the level of expected utility associated with investment A in Figure A4.1, denoted $E(U_A)$. Portfolio D has a lower level of expected utility because it has greater variance [that is, $E(U_A) > E(U_D)$ since $\sigma_A < \sigma_D$]. In moving toward C from A we know that expected utility is falling because expected return is falling.

Suppose we seek a portfolio with the same level of expected utility as D in Figure A4.1. The desired portfolio must lie below A, say, at point C. Let us assume C and D have the same expected utility [that is, $E(U_C) = E(U_D)$] and, therefore, will lie on the same indifference curve. The indifference curve containing both A and C must be upward sloped, as in Figure A4.1. Similar arguments can show that the indifference curves for a risk-seeking investor will be negatively sloped, while a risk-neutral investor will have horizontal lines.[23]

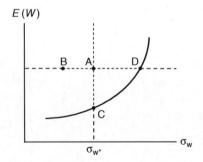

FIGURE A4.1   Indifference Curve Analysis

A4.5 Indifference Curves for Quadratic Utility

Consider the following quadratic utility function:

$$U\left(r_p\right) = br_p - cr_p^2 \tag{A4.16}$$

The expected value of the utility of equation (A4.16) is

$$E\left[U\left(r_p\right)\right] = bE\left(r_p\right) - c\left[E(r_p)^2 + \sigma_p^2\right] \tag{A4.17}$$

since $E\left(r_p^2\right) = E(r_p)^2 + \sigma_p^2$. In equation (A4.17), expected utility varies directly with $E\left(r_p\right)$ and inversely with σ_p, as shown next, for the values to which b, c, and r_p are constrained (namely, b > 0, c > 0, and $r_p < b/2c$):

$$\partial E\left[U\left(r_p\right)\right]/\partial E\left(r_p\right) = b - 2cE\left(r_p\right) > 0 \tag{A4.18}$$

$$\partial E\left[U\left(r_p\right)\right]/\partial \sigma_p = -2c\sigma_p < 0 \tag{A4.19}$$

Thus, risk-averse investors with quadratic utility functions will desire both higher $E\left(r_p\right)$ and less σ_p. Note again that to satisfy equation (A4.18) the upper bound for the expected return is constrained as shown in Figure A4.2, $E\left(r_p\right) < b/2c$.

Solving equation (A4.17) for σ_p^2 yields

$$\sigma_p^2 = -\frac{E\left[U\left(r_p\right)\right]}{c} + \left(\frac{b}{c}\right)E\left(r_p\right) - E(r_p)^2 \tag{A4.20}$$

Equation (A4.20) is quadratic in $\left[\sigma_p, E\left(r_p\right)\right]$ space for a given level of the expected utility $E\left[U\left(r_p\right)\right]$. Modifying the numerical value of $E\left[U\left(r_p\right)\right]$, representing the investor's level of happiness, generates an indifference map in $\left[\sigma_p, E\left(r_p\right)\right]$ space. For an investor with diminishing marginal utility (that is, a risk averter), one indifference curve is shown in Figures 3.6 and 3.7.

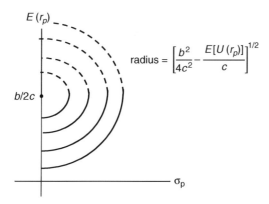

FIGURE A4.2 Indifference Curves for Quadratic Utility Functions

Although none of the graphs show it, (A4.20) defines an ellipse with a center on the $E(r_p)$-axis, where the values of $E[U(r_p)]$ are a series of constants that represent different indifference curves. The center of this indifference map has coordinates of $\sigma_p = 0$ and $E(r_p) = b/2c$. Equation (A4.20) can be rewritten as

$$\sigma_p^2 + \left[E(r_p) - \frac{b}{2c}\right]^2 = \frac{b^2}{4c^2} - \frac{E[U(r_p)]}{c} \qquad (A4.21)$$

Figure A4.2 depicts the ellipses of equation (A4.21) with a center of $[\sigma_p, E(r_p)] = (0, b/2c)$ and a radius of $[(b^2/4c^2) - (E(U)/c)]^{1/2}$. Any pair of risk-return values, σ_p and $E(r_p)$, on the same ellipse produces the same amount of utility. The left half of any such circle is inapplicable because it represents values to the left of the origin that would have $\sigma_p < 0$, which is a statistical impossibility. The upper half of any such circle (dotted part) is also inapplicable, because it represents values of $E(r_p)$ above the upper bound (b/2c) that constrains the investor's utility function. Thus, over the relevant region the indifference curves (solid curves) that correspond to a risk averter's quadratic utility function are convex. Since the radius of the circle is a linear function of the expected utility, $E[U(r_p)]$, the radius indicates the amount of expected utility. Thus, an ellipse with smaller radius provides greater utility.

NOTES

1. In the presence of uncertainty, it is tempting to argue that one should simply choose the alternative with the maximum expected value. However, the St. Petersburg paradox, presented by Daniel Bernoulli over 200 years ago, indicates the fallacy of the expected value criterion. The St. Petersburg paradox involves a game where a fair coin is tossed until a tail occurs, at which time the game ends and the player receives a payoff $\$2^k$, where k denotes the number of the toss where the tail occurred. The expected payoff is therefore

$$\sum_{k=1}^{\infty} \left(\frac{1}{2}\right)^k (\$2)^k = \sum_{k=1}^{\infty} (1)^k = \infty,$$

   where $(1/2)^k$ denotes the probability that the tail will first occur on the k-th toss. Thus, an investor making decisions using an expected value criterion should be willing to pay any finite amount of money to play this game because the expected return is infinite. Because people generally would not be willing to pay, say, \$100 to play this game, it is clear that there is something fundamentally wrong with the expected value criterion.

2. Utility theory actually can be traced back to the work of Daniel Bernoulli in the early part of the eighteenth century. However, von Neumann and Morgenstern in the 1940s were the first to develop and expand on Bernoulli's work, resulting in their seminal book, *The Theory of Games and Economic Behavior*, first published in 1944. Utility theory does not suggest that investors consciously work with a utility function in making decisions. It merely asserts that investors act as if they went through the expected utility optimization process associated with the theory. That is, utility theory is prescriptive, not descriptive. For a review and critique of the expected utility model, see Schoemaker (1982).

3. For the classic discussion of the basic assumptions see John von Neumann and Oskar Morgenstern, *Theory of Games and Economic Behavior*, 3rd ed. (Princeton, N.J.: Princeton University Press, 1953), chap. 3. Much of the other important utility literature is in Harry M. Markowitz, *Portfolio Selection*, Cowles Foundation Monograph 16 (New York: John Wiley & Sons, 1959), chaps. 10–13.

4. We sidestep the impressive work by Daniel Kahneman and Amos Tversky because they did not delineate any utility functions. Instead, they delineated probabilistic curves that resemble utility functions in some respects. See Daniel Kahneman and Amos Tversky, "Prospect Theory: An Analysis of Decisions under Risk," *Econometrica* 47 (March 1979): 263–291.

5. When the expected value of outcomes $(\tilde{z})$ from a risky game equals zero (i.e., $E(\tilde{z}) = 0$), it is an actuarially fair game.

6. Section 4.10.2 of this chapter will also explain the implication of absolute risk aversion using indifference curves.

7. Kenneth Arrow, *Essays in the Theory of Risk-Bearing* (Chicago: Markham Publishing Company, 1971), 98.

8. Henderson and Quandt (1980, 58–59) show that all utility functions having constant absolute risk aversion must be of this form.

9. It can be shown that all utility functions having constant relative risk aversion must be of either the logarithmic or power function form.

10. Friend and Blume (1975), having estimated R(W) to be greater than 1, rejected the logarithmic utility function. A similar conclusion was reached by Landskroner (1977) and is implicit in Grossman and Shiller (1981). Arrow (1971, 98), on the other hand, argues that R(W) should "hover around 1," implying that the utility function is logarithmic. For a description of various utility assessment techniques, see Farquhar (1984).

11. If the utility function is of the form $U = bW - cW^2$, then b and c must be positive constants in order for the function to have positive but diminishing marginal utility. However, this implies a turning point, occurring when $W = b/2c$. Values of W above this level imply negative marginal utility; thus, W must be bounded. Section 4.9.1 in this chapter discusses this point in more detail.

12. Mossin (1968) has shown that separability of wealth and returns occurs only for those utility functions having constant relative risk aversion.

13. Note that the logarithmic utility function is a special case of the power utility function of equation (4.19) in that as the CRRA coefficient γ approaches 1, the power function converges to the logarithmic function; that is, $\lim_{\gamma \to 1} [1/(1 - \gamma)] W^{1-\gamma} = \ln(W)$. These utility functions were shown to have constant relative risk aversion in Table 4.3. Accordingly, they may allow use of the single-period portfolio model in multiperiod applications, thereby resulting in an optimal multiperiod investment strategy, as will be discussed next.

14. A stationary portfolio policy can be defined as one in which the same proportions are invested in each asset at the beginning of every period. In a multiperiod setting, such a policy means that at the beginning of each period the investor simply reweights his or her portfolio to have the original proportions. Mossin (1968) has shown that such a policy is optimal if, in addition to the three conditions listed here, a fourth condition is added. This fourth condition is that the distribution of returns must be stationary.

15. E. F. Fama, *Foundations of Finance* (New York: Basic Books, 1976). Chapters 1 and 2 argue in favor of using the normal distribution. The central limit theorem also contributes to the normality of diversified portfolios.

16. I. Kaplansky, "A Common Error concerning Kurtosis," *Journal of the American Statistical Association*, June 1945.

17. The coefficients β and γ must be positive in order for the utility function to have positive but diminishing marginal utility. The absence of a constant intercept term is unimportant, because it has no bearing on the relative values of expected utility associated with various portfolios. This is because, as mentioned earlier, any positive linear transformation of a utility function does not affect portfolio rankings; hence, a constant intercept can be deleted from the analysis.

18. The variance of a random variable W_T is defined as $\sigma_W^2 = E[W_T - E(W_T)]^2$. Expanding the expectation yields

$$\sigma_W^2 = E\left\{W_T^2 - 2W_T E(W_T) + [E(W_T)]^2\right\}$$

$$= E\left(W_T^2\right) - 2E(W_T)E(W_T) + [E(W_T)]^2 = E\left(W_T^2\right) - [E(W_T)]^2.$$

Thus, $E\left(W_T^2\right) = [E(W_T)]^2 + \sigma_W^2$.

19. Because the second derivative of the utility function in equation (4.27) is $U'' = -2\gamma$, the expected utility in equation (4.27) can be approximated by using equation (4.22), resulting in

$$E[U(W_T)] \cong \left\{\beta E(W_T) - \gamma[E(W_T)]^2\right\} + \sigma_W^2(-2\gamma/2)$$

$$\cong \beta E(W_T) - \gamma\left\{[E(W_T)]^2 + \sigma_W^2\right\}.$$

The above equation is exactly the same as equation (4.29), indicating that for quadratic utility functions the Taylor's series expansion is exact. In this situation, mean-variance analysis of portfolios is exact.

20. To avoid the dashed segment of the quadratic utility function shown in Figure 4.9, only returns less than $b - 2c$ should be analyzed. And, to obtain the best possible custom-made fit, Markowitz (1959, 282–289) suggests using returns from within the range $-30\% \leq r \leq +40\% < b - 2c$. Monthly stock and bond returns will typically fall within this range.

21. This utility function is called homothetic.

22. Because the end-period wealth is a linear function of the one-period return [i.e., $W_T = W_0(1 + r_p)$], the partial derivatives $\partial E[U(W_T)]/\partial E(r_p)$ and $\partial E[U(W_T)]/\partial \sigma_p$ have the same sign as the partial derivatives of $\partial E[U(W_T)]/\partial E(W)$ and $\partial E[U(W_T)]/\partial \sigma_w$ presented here.

23. It can be shown that the indifference curves for a risk-averse investor are convex, while those for a risk-seeking investor are concave; see Copeland and Weston (1983, 95–99) for a proof of this property along with a more rigorous proof of the sign of the slope of the indifference curves.

Three

Mean-Variance Portfolio Analysis

CHAPTER **5**

Graphical Portfolio Analysis

Markowitz portfolio analysis is a mathematical procedure to determine the optimum portfolios in which to invest. The procedure was first made public in 1952 by HarryMarkowitz.[1] The theory caused a profound scientific revolution in finance. Before Markowitz's scientific procedure, investment counselors passed off commonsense guidelines to their clients and pretended it was valuable expert advice—and, unfortunately, many still do.

The objective of portfolio analysis is to find the set of *efficient portfolios*. *Efficient portfolios*:

- Have the greatest expected return for a given level of risk, or, conversely,
- Offer the lowest risk for a given level of expected return.

The collection of all the efficient portfolios comprises a curve in risk-return space called the *efficient frontier*. In terms of Figure 5.1, the objective is to find the heavy dark curve from E to F—the *efficient frontier*—from some opportunity set of potential investments (individual stocks, bonds, and other assets).

5.1 DELINEATING EFFICIENT PORTFOLIOS

There are three methods of solving for the efficient set:

1. Graphically
2. With calculus
3. By quadratic programming (QP)[2]

For any given set of candidate assets, all three algorithms will yield the same efficient set of portfolios. Stated differently, the same stocks and bonds will be selected, and in the same proportions, whether you use graphs, calculus, or a quadratic program (QP). Graphical portfolio analysis is the subject of this chapter. The primary advantage of this technique is that it is simpler. Most people internalize the analysis more effectively if they have something graphical to which they may refer. Furthermore, leveraged portfolios may be represented graphically. The disadvantage of the graphical analysis is that it cannot handle portfolios containing more than a few securities.

Two solution methods that employ calculus will be presented in Chapter 6. The primary advantage of the calculus method lies in its ability to handle portfolios

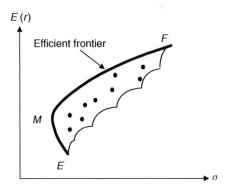

FIGURE 5.1 The Opportunity Set in (σ, μ) Space

containing a large number of securities. Any number of securities may be analyzed. As a result of these and other advantages, the calculus solution is useful to researchers. The disadvantage of calculus solutions is that they cannot handle inequality constraints.

Quadratic programming techniques are most useful in handling large-portfolio problems that are solved frequently. Like linear programming, quadratic programming (QP) can accommodate inequality constraints such as short sales constraints and budget constraints. Thus, the portfolio may be optimized with a large number of different kinds of constraints that the portfolio manager might want to impose. For practical management of mutual funds or other large portfolios, the QP solution method is the most desirable. QP will be discussed further in Chapter 6.

5.2 PORTFOLIO ANALYSIS INPUTS

Whether you use a graph, calculus, or QP, portfolio analysis requires certain statistical data as inputs. The inputs to the portfolio analysis of a set of n candidate assets are:

- n expected returns: $\{E(r_i)\}$, $i = 1, 2, \ldots, n$
- n variances of returns: $\{\sigma_i^2\}$, $i = 1, 2, \ldots, n$
- $(n^2 - n)/2$ covariances: $\{\sigma_{ij}\}$, $i = 1, 2, \ldots, n$; $\quad j = 1, 2, \ldots, n$; $\quad i \neq j$

This chapter shows how to solve two-security portfolios and three-security portfolios graphically. The analysis is conducted on the graphical plane representing two weights, as shown in Figure 5.2. Point A represents a portfolio that has 50 percent (or one-half, or 0.5) of the portfolio's net worth invested in each of Securities 1 and 2. Point L represents a leveraged portfolio with 150 percent of the original capital invested in security 1 and −50 percent of the capital invested in security 2. In other words, a security like security number 2 [for example, a bond with the same $E(r)$ and σ] is printed and sold in an amount equal to 50 percent of the equity value of the portfolio. The short sale of security 2, or leverage, is achieved

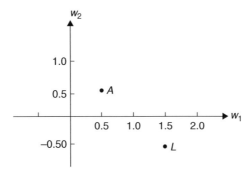

FIGURE 5.2 Graph of Two-weight Variables: w_1 and w_2

by issuing a security like number 2 that is represented by a negative value for w_2. For example, suppose that the portfolio represented by point L in Figure 5.2 had $1,000 of original equity invested. Then, the portfolio manager purchased $1,500 of security 1, so $w_1 = 1.5$. To cover the $500 shortage, the portfolio manager issues $500 worth of a security like number 2, so $w_2 = -0.5$ The total of the two weights is 1. In other words, $w_1 + w_2 = 1.5 - 0.5 = 1.0$: This equality signifies that the total net worth of the portfolio has been accounted for.

The variables w_1 and w_2 are weights or percentages of the portfolio owner's equity capital that is invested in each security. The sum of the weights must be 1 or the analysis has no meaningful interpretation. Thus, throughout portfolio analysis, either implicitly or explicitly, the following mathematical condition can never be violated:

$$\sum_{i=1}^{n} w_i = 1.0 = 100\% \tag{5.1}$$

where n represents the number of candidate investments being analyzed. This equality is called either the *budget constraint* or the *balance sheet identity*. The budget constraint does not mean that all the wealth must be invested. Cash can be one of the n assets.

5.3 TWO-ASSET ISOMEAN LINES

For a two-security portfolio, the analysis requires the five statistics in Table 5.1.

The portfolio's expected return is

$$E(r_p) = w_1 E(r_1) + w_2 E(r_2) \tag{5.2}$$

First let us rewrite equation (5.2) as follows:

$$w_2 = \frac{E(r_p)}{E(r_2)} - \frac{E(r_1)}{E(r_2)} w_1 \tag{5.2a}$$

This is a linear equation with $E(r_p)/E(r_2)$ as the vertical intercept and with a negative slope of $E(r_1)/E(r_2)$. $E(r_1)$ and $E(r_2)$ are exogenous constants that are

TABLE 5.1   Return and Variance of Two Assets and Their Covariance

Expected return $E(r_i)$	Variance (σ_i^2)	Covariance (σ_{ij})
$E(r_1)$	σ_1^2	
		σ_{12}
$E(r_2)$	σ_2^2	

estimated by a statistically oriented securities analyst. We have three unknown variables: w_1, w_2, and the portfolio's expected return $E(r_p)$. Thus, the slope of the linear equation (5.2a) is fixed at $E(r_1)/E(r_2)$. The value of the intercept term depends on the value assigned to $E(r_p)$. If an expected return of eight percent, for instance, is the portfolio manager's target, there are many pairs of w_1 and w_2 that can produce portfolios with an expected return of eight percent. In fact, a countably infinite number of lines exist that each consist of combinations of w_1 and w_2 that will yield a given expected return. We call these lines *isomean lines* or simply *isomeans*. Since the word "iso" means equal, it follows that isomean lines must be lines that have equal mean returns—that is, equal $E(r_p)$ values—throughout their length. Figure 5.3 shows a family of three isomean lines. The larger the expected return, the higher the isomean line. From the figure, it is clear that the isomean line E_3 has the highest expected return, the isomean line E_2 has the next highest, and the isomean line E_1 has the lowest, because E_3 shows the highest vertical intercept and E_1 has the lowest vertical intercept. These lines are parallel because their slopes all equal the fixed value of $-E(r_1)/E(r_2)$.

Investors all desire to reach the highest possible isomean line. However, they cannot invest infinite amounts because of the budget constraint, equation (5.1). The

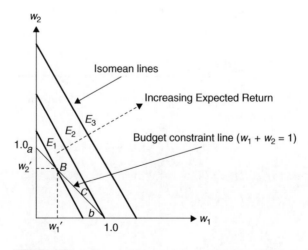

FIGURE 5.3   Isomean Lines and the Budget Constraint Line

budget constraint requires that the sum of all investment proportions is one; that is, $w_1 + w_2 = 1$, which can be rewritten as $w_2 = 1 - w_1$. This budget constraint line is denoted $\overline{ab}$ in Figure 5.3. This is a linear equation with a 45° slope. The attainable expected return lies only on this budget constraint line. Because the isomean line E_1 intersects with the budget constraint line at B, the amount of the expected return implied in the isomean line E_1 is attainable by investing w_1' in security 1 and w_2' in security 2. However, this amount of the expected return is not the maximum attainable. The maximum amount of expected return that can be earned is at point b on the highest attainable isomean line that passes through point b. Point b in Figure 5.3 represents investing 100 percent in security 1 and nothing in security 2. In contrast, point a represents investing nothing in security 1 and 100 percent in security 2. The expected return implied by this latter isomean line is not attainable without violating the budget constraint. Stated differently, every point on isomean E_3 represents the unattainable inequality: $w_1 + w_2 > 1$.

EXAMPLE 5.1

Table 5.2 summarizes rate of return statistics from two hypothetical stocks named Excelon and Jorgenson.

TABLE 5.2   An Example of Two Assets

Company	i	Investment weight (w_i)	Expected return $E(r_i)$	Variance σ_i^2	Covariance σ_{ij}
Excelon	1	w_1	2.07%	48.20	$\sigma_{12} = -2.65$
Jorgenson	2	w_2	1.01%	34.25	

Substituting the two stocks' numerical values for $E(r_i)$ into equation (5.2) yields

$$E(r_p) = 2.07w_1 + 1.01w_2 \qquad (5.3)$$

Because $w_1 = 1 - w_2$, the isomean line above can be rewritten as

$$w_2 = \frac{E(r_p)}{1.01} - \frac{2.07}{1.01}w_1 = 0.99E(r_p) - 2.05w_1$$

Since the slope is fixed as 2.05, the isomean lines are parallel, but the intercept, $0.99E(r_p)$, depends on the amount of $E(r_p)$ the portfolio manager is seeking. The greater the expected return, the higher the intercept. The maximum expected return attainable in this example occurs where $w_1 = 1.0$ and $w_2 = 0$. This point equals 2.07 percent, which is security 1's expected return.

5.4   TWO-ASSET ISOVARIANCE ELLIPSES

The variance of returns from a two-security portfolio is

$$\sigma_p^2 = w_1^2\sigma_1^2 + w_2^2\sigma_2^2 + 2w_1w_2\sigma_{12} \tag{2.14}$$

This quadratic equation defines an *ellipse*. Figure 5.4 shows a family of ellipses. Each ellipse represents a constant level of variance. There are many combinations of the weights w_1 and w_2 that produce the same level of portfolio variance. This means that every ellipse consists of the numerous different combinations of w_1 and w_2 that yield the same variance. We call these ellipses *isovariances*. An isovariance ellipse is a locus of points that represents portfolios that all have the same variance. Isovariances are risk isoquants. Recalling that *iso* means equal, isovariances are ellipses with the same variance everyplace. The larger ellipses represent greater variance than the inner ellipses; that is, $\sigma_Q^2 < \sigma_R^2 < \sigma_S^2$. Like the isomean lines, the isovariance ellipses never intersect because a single point on an isovariance ellipse cannot represent two different levels of portfolio variance.

As with the isomean lines, different levels of variance do not exist on any given isovariance. The attainable variances are all located along the budget constraint line $\overline{ab}$ in Figure 5.4. Any point of intersection or tangency between an isovariance and the budget constraint line represents an attainable portfolio variance. In Figure 5.4, the variances at intersection points A, B, and C are attainable within the budget constraint. Among these, the point B, which is a tangency point between one ellipse and the budget constraint line, represents the minimum attainable portfolio variance. All portfolios on the budget constraint line $\overline{ab}$ can be identified with the weights, w_1 and w_2. By using a trial and error search for the weights that give the least amount of variance, the minimum variance portfolio (MVP) located at the point B can be identified.

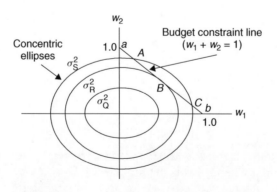

FIGURE 5.4   A Family of Isovariance Ellipses

EXAMPLE 5.2

Using the two securities considered in Table 5.2, we identify the minimum variance portfolio (MVP). Table 5.3 lists the variances for various pairs of the weights for Securities 1 and 2. By changing w_1 incrementally by 0.01 (that is, moving from point *b* toward point *a* in Figure 5.4), we can compute a series of portfolio variances by using equation (2.14). At the point with $w_1 = 0.42$ and $w_2 = 0.58$ we find the MPV of $\sigma_p^2 = 18.73$.

TABLE 5.3 Two-Security Portfolio Variances for Various Sets of Weights

w_1	w_2 $(= 1 - w_1)$	σ_p^2
1.00	0.00	48.20
0.99	0.01	47.19
0.98	0.02	46.20
⋮	⋮	⋮
0.45	0.55	18.81
0.44	0.56	18.77
0.43	0.57	18.74
0.42	0.58	18.73 ← MVP
0.41	0.59	18.74
0.40	0.60	18.77
0.39	0.61	18.81
⋮	⋮	⋮
0.02	0.98	32.81
0.01	0.99	33.52
0.00	1.00	34.25

The attainable portfolios on the budget constraint line in Figure 5.4 can be mapped into the mean-standard deviation plane. Every point on the budget constraint line in Figure 5.4 represents a given pair of weights (w_1, w_2) for the two securities, and this point can be mapped to a point in $[\sigma, E(r)]$ space by computing the expected return and standard deviation with the associated pair of weights. This is how all points on the budget constraint line can be mapped into $[\sigma, E(r)]$ space. Figure 5.5 shows all points from (w_1, w_2) space that have been mapped into $[\sigma, E(r)]$ space. The curve in Figure 5.5 traces out the edge of the investment opportunity set. The lower section of the budget constraint line in Figure 5.4, $\overline{BCb}$, is mapped into the upper part of the investment opportunity set in Figure 5.5. And

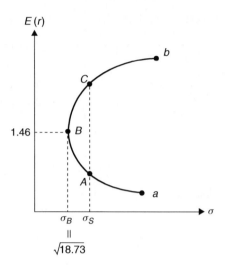

FIGURE 5.5 Investment Opportunity
Set in $[\sigma, E(r)]$ Space

the upper section of the budget constraint line in Figure 5.4, located along the curve $\overline{BAa}$, is mapped into the lower part of the investment opportunity set in Figure 5.5. The inefficient portfolios, denoted $\overline{BAa}$ in the lower half of the curve in Figure 5.5, are the minimum risk portfolios that exist at each of the minimum return portfolios.

Because the intersection points A and C in Figure 5.4 are on the same ellipse, they have the same variance, σ_S^2. These two points may both be found in Figure 5.5 on the investment opportunity set where their standard deviations both equal σ_S. *Dominant assets* have the maximum return in their risk class, or the minimum risk at their level of returns. Point C dominates point A, for example, because point C is on a higher isomean line than point A in Figure 5.5, but they are both on the same isovariance ellipse.

5.5 THREE-ASSET PORTFOLIO ANALYSIS

Portfolio analysis requires the input statistics listed in Table 5.4 to analyze a three-security portfolio.

TABLE 5.4 Inputs Necessary for
Three-Security Portfolio Analysis

$E(r_i)$	σ_i^2	σ_{ij}
$E(r_1)$	σ_1^2	σ_{12}
$E(r_2)$	σ_2^2	σ_{23}
$E(r_3)$	σ_3^2	σ_{31}

TABLE 5.5 Return and Variance of Three Assets and Their Covariances

Company	i	Investment weight (w_i)	Expected return $E(r_i)$	Variance σ_i^2	Covariance σ_{ij}
Excelon	1	w_1	2.07%	48.20	$\sigma_{12} = 7.82$
IH	2	w_2	0.21%	16.34	$\sigma_{23} = 0.99$
Citi-Guys	3	w_3	1.01%	34.25	$\sigma_{13} = -2.65$

The input data in Table 5.5 are obtained with monthly rates of return from Excelon, International Holdings (IH), and Citi-Guys during a representative sample period.

It is possible for an extremely careful draftsman (with a very sharp pencil) to find the set of efficient portfolios made from three securities with a three-dimensional drawing. However, it is difficult to create a three-dimensional drawing with as much precise detail as we enjoyed when we analyzed two assets in two dimensions in the preceding section.

To solve a three-asset portfolio problem in two-dimensional space, the following seven steps will be performed:

1. Convert the formulas for the portfolio's expected return (the isomeans) and the portfolio's risk (the isovariances) from three to two variable equations.
2. Find the MVP.
3. Graph the isomean lines.
4. Graph the isovariance ellipses.
5. Delineate the efficient set (that is, draw the critical line).
6. Calculate the expected return, $E(r_p)$, and risk, σ_p^2, for the efficient portfolios.
7. Graph the efficient frontier in $[\sigma, E(r)]$ space.

5.5.1 Solving for One Variable Implicitly

In order to analyze the efficient frontier graphically, it is necessary to convert the three dimensional problem associated with a three-security portfolio to a two-dimensional problem that is easier to graph. This conversion is accomplished by transforming the weight of the third security into an implicit solution from the other two securities. That is,

$$w_3 = 1 - w_1 - w_2 \qquad (5.4)$$

First, the conversion of $E(r_p)$ will be considered. This conversion is done by substituting equation (5.4) into equation (2.12) to obtain equation (5.5):

$$E(r_p) = \sum_{i=1}^{3} w_i E\left(r_i\right) = w_1 E(r_1) + w_2 E(r_2) + w_3 E(r_3) \qquad (2.12)$$

$$= w_1 E(r_1) + w_2 E(r_2) + \left(1 - w_1 - w_2\right) E(r_3) \quad \text{by substituting for } w_3$$

$$= \left[E(r_1) - E(r_3)\right] w_1 + \left[E(r_2) - E(r_3)\right] w_2 + E(r_3) \qquad (5.5)$$

Equation (5.5) is a linear equation in two variables (w_1 and w_2). Substituting the three stocks' numerical values in Table 5.5 for $E(r_i)$ in equation (5.5) yields equation (5.6).

$$E(r_p) = (2.07 - 1.01) w_1 + (0.21 - 1.01) w_2 + 1.01$$
$$= 1.06w_1 - 0.80w_2 + 1.01 \tag{5.6}$$

Equation (5.6) gives the expected return of the three-security portfolio in terms of w_1 and w_2 explicitly and w_3 implicitly. It is a linear function in two variables, w_1 and w_2, and can be readily graphed in two dimensions.

The three-security portfolio variance formula is similarly converted to two variables by substituting equation (5.4) into equation (2.18a) to obtain equation (5.7).

$$\sigma_p^2 = \sum_{i=1}^{3} \sum_{j=1}^{3} w_i w_j \sigma_{ij}$$

$$= w_1^2 \sigma_{11} + w_2^2 \sigma_{22} + w_3^2 \sigma_{33} + 2w_1 w_2 \sigma_{12} + 2w_1 w_3 \sigma_{13} + 2w_2 w_3 \sigma_{23}$$

$$= w_1^2 \sigma_{11} + w_2^2 \sigma_{22} + \left(1 - w_1 - w_2\right)^2 \sigma_{33} + 2w_1 w_2 \sigma_{12} + 2w_1 \left(1 - w_1 - w_2\right) \sigma_{13}$$
$$\quad + 2w_2 \left(1 - w_1 - w_2\right) \sigma_{23}$$

$$= w_1^2 \sigma_{11} + w_2^2 \sigma_{22} + \left(1 + w_1^2 + w_2^2 - 2w_1 - 2w_2 + 2w_1 w_2\right) \sigma_{33} + 2w_1 w_2 \sigma_{12}$$
$$\quad + \left(2w_1 - 2w_1^2 - 2w_1 w_2\right) \sigma_{13} + \left(2w_2 - 2w_1 w_2 - 2w_2^2\right) \sigma_{23}$$

$$= w_1^2 \sigma_{11} + w_2^2 \sigma_{22} + \sigma_{33} + w_1^2 \sigma_{33} + w_2^2 \sigma_{33} - 2w_1 \sigma_{33} - 2w_2 \sigma_{33} + 2w_1 w_2 \sigma_{33}$$
$$\quad + 2w_1 w_2 \sigma_{12} + 2w_1 \sigma_{13} - 2w_1^2 \sigma_{13} - 2w_1 w_2 \sigma_{13}$$
$$\quad + 2w_2 \sigma_{23} - 2w_1 w_2 \sigma_{23} - 2w_2^2 \sigma_{23}$$

$$= \left(\sigma_{11} + \sigma_{33} - 2\sigma_{13}\right) w_1^2 + \left(2\sigma_{33} + 2\sigma_{12} - 2\sigma_{13} - 2\sigma_{23}\right) w_1 w_2$$
$$\quad + \left(\sigma_{22} + \sigma_{33} - 2\sigma_{23}\right) w_2^2 + \left(-2\sigma_{33} + 2\sigma_{13}\right) w_1$$
$$\quad + \left(-2\sigma_{33} + 2\sigma_{23}\right) w_2 + \sigma_{33} \tag{5.7}$$

Equation (5.7) is a second-degree equation in two variables, w_1 and w_2. Recall that such equations have the following general quadratic form.[3]

$$Ax^2 + Bxy + Cy^2 + Dx + Ey + F = 0 \tag{5.8}$$

Inserting the variances and covariances from Table 5.5 into equation (5.8) yields equation (5.9).

$$\sigma_p^2 = [48.20 + 34.25 - 2\,(-2.65)]\,w_1^2$$
$$\quad + [2\,(34.25) + 2\,(7.82) - 2\,(-2.65) - 2\,(0.99)]\,w_1 w_2$$
$$\quad + [16.34 + 34.25 - 2\,(0.99)]\,w_2^2 + [-2\,(34.25) + 2\,(-2.65)]\,w_1$$
$$\quad + [-2\,(34.25) + 2\,(0.99)]\,w_2 + 34.25$$
$$= 87.75w_1^2 + 87.46w_1 w_2 + 48.61w_2^2 - 73.80w_1 - 66.52w_2 + 34.25 \tag{5.9}$$

To find the weights for three securities that minimize the portfolio variance in equation (5.7), we try all possible combinations of w_1 and w_2. Table 5.6 provides variances for various sets of the weights. By changing w_1 and w_2 with an increment of 0.1, we compute the portfolio variance with equation (5.9) that equals equation (5.7) with substituted values for the relevant variances and covariances. With $w_1 = 0.1$, $w_2 = 0.60$, and $w_3 = 0.3$, we can find the MVP is $\sigma_p^2 = 10.58$.

TABLE 5.6 Three-Security Portfolio Variances for Various Sets of Weights

w_1	w_2	w_3 $(= 1 - w_1 - w_2)$	σ_p^2
0.0	1.0	0.0	16.34
0.0	0.9	0.1	13.76
0.0	0.8	0.2	12.14
0.0	0.7	0.3	11.50
0.0	0.6	0.4	11.84
0.0	0.5	0.5	13.14
0.0	0.4	0.6	15.42
0.0	0.3	0.7	18.67
0.0	0.2	0.8	22.89
0.0	0.1	0.9	28.08
0.0	0.0	1.0	34.25
⋮	⋮	⋮	⋮
0.1	1.0	−0.1	18.58
0.1	0.9	0.0	15.13
0.1	0.8	0.1	12.64
0.1	0.7	0.2	11.12
0.1	**0.6**	**0.3**	**10.58** ← MVP
0.1	0.5	0.4	11.01
0.1	0.4	0.5	12.42
0.1	0.3	0.6	14.79
0.1	0.2	0.7	18.14
0.1	0.1	0.8	22.46
0.1	0.0	0.9	27.75
⋮	⋮	⋮	⋮
⋮	⋮	⋮	⋮
1.0	1.0	−1.0	117.75
1.0	0.9	−0.9	106.42
1.0	0.8	−0.8	96.06
1.0	0.7	−0.7	86.68
1.0	0.6	−0.6	78.26
1.0	0.5	−0.5	70.82
1.0	0.4	−0.4	64.35
1.0	0.3	−0.3	58.86
1.0	0.2	−0.2	54.33
1.0	0.1	−0.1	50.78
1.0	0.0	0.0	48.20

Of course, these answers are not accurate, because we consider only an increment of 0.1. If we consider a finer increment, such as 0.001, more accurate answers can be obtained. In this case, however, many more combinations of the weights will be considered.[4] In fact, the accurate answers for the weights are $w_1 = 0.1442$, $w_2 = 0.5545$, and $w_3 = 0.3013$, and the minimum variance is $\sigma^2_{mvp} = 10.49$.

5.5.2 Isomean Lines

The portfolio analysis graphing may begin after the formulas for the variance and expected return for the portfolio are reduced to two variables and the MVP weights are discovered. The isomean lines are graphed first in this example; but, just as easily, we could have begun with the isovariance ellipses.

After arbitrarily selecting a few values of $E(r_p)$ in the neighborhood of the $E(r_i)$'s of the securities in the portfolio, the isomean lines may be determined. By selecting four arbitrary values (0.4, 0.8, 1.2, and 1.6 percent per month) of $E(r_p)$ and using equation (5.6), the formulas for four isomean lines are derived:

$$E(r_p) = 0.4\% = 1.06w_1 - 0.80w_2 + 1.01$$

$$E(r_p) = 0.8\% = 1.06w_1 - 0.80w_2 + 1.01$$

$$E(r_p) = 1.2\% = 1.06w_1 - 0.80w_2 + 1.01$$

$$E(r_p) = 1.6\% = 1.06w_1 - 0.80w_2 + 1.01$$

The easiest way to graph these four linear equations in a Cartesian plane, as shown in Figures 5.3 and 5.4, is to set one weight equal to zero and then solve the equation for the other weight. Because the isomean lines intersect the w_1 axis when w_2 is zero, and vice versa, this process will yield points on the two axes. Connecting these points with a line yields the isomean lines. For example, the 0.5 percent isomean line must have $w_1 = -0.5755$ when w_2 is set equal to zero:

$$0.4 = 1.06w_1 - 0.80\,(0.0) + 1.01 \Rightarrow w_1 = -0.5755$$

When the 0.5 percent isomean has $w_1 = 0.0$ and $w_2 = 0.7625$

$$0.4 = 1.06\,(0.0) - 0.80w_2 + 1.01 \Rightarrow w_2 = 0.7625$$

The points in Table 5.7 are derived similarly.

TABLE 5.7 Isomeans

Isomean	w_1-axis intercept given $w_2 = 0$	w_2-axis intercept given $w_1 = 0$
0.4	−0.5755	0.7625
0.8	−0.1981	0.2625
1.2	0.1792	−0.2375
1.6	0.5566	−0.7375

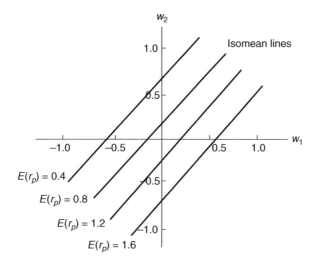

FIGURE 5.6 Four Isomean Lines for a Three-security Portfolio

Plotting the four isomeans from Table 5.7 yields the four parallel straight lines in Figure 5.6.

There are an infinite number of isomean lines, but only a few have been graphed. The primary characteristic of the isomean lines is that they are all parallel to each other. Knowledge of this characteristic provides a good check when graphing the isomean lines. Because the budget constraint $(w_1 + w_2 + w_3 = 1)$ is already contained in the isomean lines in Figure 5.6, the expected return implied in any isomean line is attainable without violating the budget constraint.

5.5.3 Isovariance Ellipses

The next step of the graphical analysis is graphing the isovariances. Isovariances are ellipses with a common center, orientation, and egg shape.

Graphing the isovariances should ideally be preceded by finding the MVP. The MVP is the center point for all the isovariance ellipses, it represents the portfolio with the least (but not necessarily zero) variance. It is impossible to graph isovariance ellipses for variances less than the variance of the MVP.

To graph isovariances, it is necessary to solve equation (5.7) or (5.9) in terms of one of the variables (that is, weights), while treating the remaining variables as constants. Arbitrarily selecting w_1 as the variable to be solved for, and treating w_2 as a constant, reduces equation (5.7) to a quadratic equation in one variable. The general form of a quadratic equation is $ax^2 + bx + c = 0$, where the x is a variable and the other symbols are any constant values. Solution of such second-order equations in one variable may be obtained with the well-known quadratic formula:

$$x = \frac{-b \pm \sqrt{b^2 - 4ac}}{2a}$$

Let $x = w_1$ in equations (5.7) and (5.9) and treat w_2 as a constant. Then, let

$a =$ all coefficients of x^2—that is, all coefficients of w_1^2 in equations (5.7) and (5.9),

$b =$ all coefficients of x—that is, all coefficients of w_1 in equations (5.7) and (5.9),

$c =$ all values that are not coefficients of x_1^2 or w_1—that is, all constants, which includes the w_2s and the σ_p^2 in equations (5.7) and (5.9).

For equation (5.7), set the entire expression equal to zero as follows:

$$0 = \left(\sigma_{11} + \sigma_{33} - 2\sigma_{13}\right)w_1^2 + \left(2\sigma_{33} + 2\sigma_{12} - 2\sigma_{13} - 2\sigma_{23}\right)w_1 w_2$$
$$+ \left(\sigma_{22} + \sigma_{33} - 2\sigma_{23}\right)w_2^2 + \left(-2\sigma_{33} + 2\sigma_{13}\right)w_1$$
$$+ \left(-2\sigma_{33} + 2\sigma_{23}\right)w_2 + \sigma_{33} - \sigma_p^2$$

Then the values of a, b, and c are

$$a = \left(\sigma_{11} + \sigma_{33} - 2\sigma_{13}\right)$$
$$b = \left(2\sigma_{33} + 2\sigma_{12} - 2\sigma_{13} - 2\sigma_{23}\right)w_2 + \left(-2\sigma_{33} + 2\sigma_{13}\right)$$
$$c = \left(\sigma_{22} + \sigma_{33} - 2\sigma_{23}\right)w_2^2 + \left(-2\sigma_{33} + 2\sigma_{23}\right)w_2 + \sigma_{33} - \sigma_p^2$$

The value of w_1 can be found by substituting these values of a, b, and c into the quadratic formula.

Following the procedure outlined above, equation (5.9) yields the following results:

$$\sigma_p^2 = 87.75w_1^2 + 87.46w_1 w_2 + 48.61w_2^2 - 73.80w_1 - 66.52w_2 + 34.25$$
$$0 = 87.75w_1^2 + 87.46w_1 w_2 + 48.61w_2^2 - 73.80w_1 - 66.52w_2 + 34.25 - \sigma_p^2$$

Thus,
$$a = 87.75$$
$$b = 87.46w_2 - 73.80$$
$$c = 48.61w_2^2 - 66.52w_2 + 34.25 - \sigma_p^2$$

Inserting these values of a, b, and c into the quadratic formula yields

$$w_1 = \frac{-b \pm \sqrt{b^2 - 4ac}}{2a}$$

$$= \frac{-\left(87.46w_2 - 73.80\right) \pm \sqrt{\begin{array}{l}\left(87.46w_2 - 73.80\right)^2 - 4\,(87.75)\\ \left(48.61w_2^2 - 73.80w_2 + 34.25 - \sigma_p^2\right)\end{array}}}{2\,(87.75)} \tag{5.10}$$

Equation (5.10) is the solution to equation (5.9) for w_1 while treating w_2 as a constant. It is necessary to solve the formula to graph the isovariances. To obtain points on the isovariance ellipse, some arbitrary values for σ_p^2 and w_2 are selected and equation (5.10) is then solved for two values of w_1. It is easiest to select a value for σ_p^2 that is slightly larger than the variance of the MVP and select a value of w_2 at or near the MVP to get the first two values for w_1. For example, for $\sigma_p^2 = 13.43$ and $w_2 = 0.3$, equation (5.10) yields the following two values for w_1:

$$w_1 = \frac{-[87.46\,(0.3) - 73.80] \pm \sqrt{\frac{[87.46\,(0.3) - 73.80]^2 - 4\,(87.75)}{[48.61(0.3)^2 - 73.80\,(0.3) + 34.25 - 15.29]}}}{2\,(87.75)}$$

$$= 0.388 \text{ and } 0.154$$

The variance chosen in this example ($\sigma_p^2 = 13.43$) is the variance of the portfolio when $E(r_p) = 1.20$ percent. Of course, any value for σ_p^2 could have been chosen as long as it exceeded the variance of the MVP (that is, 10.49). In this way, we can find the value of w_1 for a given value of w_2 and the portfolio variance. Table 5.8 shows those values of w_1 and w_2. It is left as an exercise for the reader to verify the points on the isovariance ellipses listed in Table 5.8.

Beyond the given values of w_2, the solutions for w_1 in equation (5.10) are not available, because the value of the equation inside the square root is negative.

The values of w_1 and w_2 and the portfolio variances in Table 5.8 are graphed in $(w_1,\ w_2)$ space to obtain the isovariance ellipses in Figure 5.7.

In Figure 5.7, V_1 is the isovariance ellipse with a variance of $\sigma_p^2 = 10.57$. In a similar manner, V_2, V_3, and V_4 indicate the isovariance ellipses having the variances $\sigma_p^2 = 11.78$, 13.43, and 20.36, respectively. The more outer ellipse indicates the greater variance (i.e., $V_1 < V_2 < V_3 < V_4$).

5.5.4 The Critical Line

The isomeans in Figure 5.6 and isovariances in Figure 5.7 are all graphed in the same $(w_1,\ w_2)$ space in Figure 5.8. After the isomeans and isovariances are graphed, it is simple to determine the efficient set of portfolios. An efficient portfolio is defined as the portfolio with the maximum return for any given risk class. Because each isovariance traces out a risk class, the point where the highest-value isomean is just tangent to an isovariance is an efficient portfolio. On V_3 isovariance ellipse, for example, point O is an efficient portfolio. At this given level of the variance of $V_3 = 13.43$, the portfolio at point O earns the highest expected return of 1.2 percent. Note that point O is the tangency point between V_3 and the isomean line of $E(r_p) = 1.2$ percent. Point J is also on the same isovariance ellipse V_3. However, the portfolio at point J is dominated because it has a lower expected return than the portfolio at point O. The portfolio at point O' is also dominated (inefficient), because it has the same expected return as the portfolio at point O, but has greater amount of variance of $V_3 = 13.43$.

In the same vein, portfolios at points M, N, and P are efficient portfolios at the variance levels of 10.57, 11.78, and 20.36, respectively. The straight line starting from the MVP and connecting these points is the critical line. This *critical line* is the locus of points in $(w_1,\ w_2)$ space representing the efficient set. In Figure 5.8, the set of efficient portfolios starts at the MVP and runs downward to the right through

TABLE 5.8   Isovariance Points in (w_1, w_2) Space

w_2	Two values of w_1		Variance (σ_p^2)
less	n.a.	n.a.	n.a.
0.5	0.178	0.165	10.57
0.6	0.139	0.104	10.57
greater	n.a.	n.a.	n.a.
less	n.a.	n.a.	n.a.
0.4	0.307	0.135	11.78
0.5	0.289	0.054	11.78
0.6	0.240	0.003	11.78
0.7	0.163	−0.019	11.78
greater	n.a.	n.a.	n.a.
less	n.a.	n.a.	n.a.
0.3	0.388	0.154	13.43
0.4	0.383	0.059	13.43
0.5	0.352	−0.009	13.43
0.6	0.303	−0.066	13.43
0.7	0.236	−0.093	13.43
0.8	0.145	−0.101	13.43
greater	n.a.	n.a.	n.a.
less	n.a.	n.a.	n.a.
0.0	0.557	0.284	20.36
0.1	0.593	0.148	20.36
0.2	0.593	0.049	20.36
0.3	0.576	−0.033	20.36
0.4	0.546	−0.103	20.36
0.5	0.505	−0.163	20.36
0.6	0.456	−0.213	20.36
0.7	0.397	−0.254	20.36
0.8	0.329	−0.285	20.36
0.9	0.248	−0.304	20.36
1.0	0.150	−0.306	20.36
1.1	0.019	−0.275	20.36
greater	n.a.	n.a.	n.a.

Note: n.a. indicates not available.

points M, N, O, and P. On the other hand, the dotted critical line starting at the MVP and running upward by connecting points L, K, J, and I indicates inefficient (dominated, the least desirable) portfolios.

Once the critical line is graphed, the efficient frontier may be graphed with ease. Reading weights (w_1, w_2) off the critical line at a few points (such as points M, N, O, and P in Figure 5.8), it is possible to calculate the $E(r)$ and σ of portfolios that have the highest rate of return for their risk class. Table 5.9 shows these values. The efficient frontier is found by plotting $E(r_p)$ and σ_p as done in Figure 5.9. The graphical method is only approximate because of problems in pencil drafting. This completes the graphical portfolio analysis.

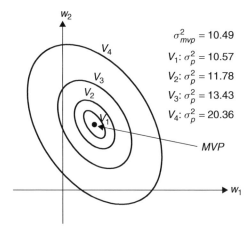

FIGURE 5.7   Isovariance Ellipses

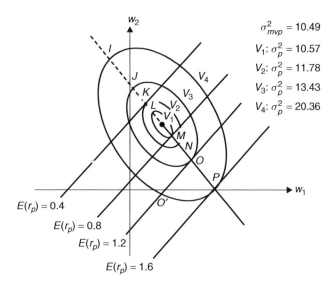

FIGURE 5.8   Three-asset Graphical Solution

5.5.5   Inefficient Portfolios

Inexperienced portfolio analysts must take care not to draw the critical line in the wrong direction away from the MVP. Such a line would be the locus of points representing the set of most inefficient portfolios. The dotted line in Figure 5.8 is such a line; it is the locus of points representing the minimum return in each risk class; these portfolios are highly undesirable investments.

Earlier in this chapter the objective of portfolio analysis was said to be the determination of the efficient set of portfolios. The efficient set is represented by the infinite number of portfolios whose weights lie along the critical line. The reader who understands this and the preceding chapters will recognize that portfolio analysis utilizes

TABLE 5.9 The Weights for the Portfolios on the Critical Line

Points	w_1	w_2	w_3	$E(r_p)$	σ_p^2	σ_p
K	−0.0051	0.7557	0.2494	0.40	11.78	3.43
M	0.1820	0.5036	0.3144	0.80	10.57	3.25
MVP	0.1445	0.5540	0.3015	0.72	10.49	3.24
O	0.3691	0.2515	0.3794	1.20	13.43	3.66
P	0.5562	−0.0006	0.4444	1.60	20.36	4.51

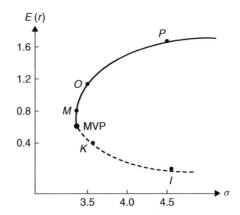

FIGURE 5.9 Three-asset Efficient Frontier

Markowitz diversification. In fact, it could be said that the objective of portfolio analysis is to maximize the benefits from Markowitz's optimal diversification at each possible rate of return.

5.6 LEGITIMATE PORTFOLIOS

Markowitz tells us an efficient portfolio must meet three conditions:

1. It must have the maximum return in its risk class.
2. It must have the minimum risk in its return class.
3. It must not involve any negative weights.

The third condition for efficiency has not been imposed so far in this book. Graphically, the third condition means that the critical line may not leave the upper-right quarter of the (w_1, w_2) space in Figure 5.8. Consequently, the efficient portfolios comprise only part of the unconstrained critical line. Financially speaking, denying negative weights means no leverage or short sales are permitted.

More realistically, negative weights are possible and have a rational economic interpretation. In this book the non-negativity constraint will not be observed. Only public investment funds that are constrained by regulations need adhere to the third condition.

5.7   "UNUSUAL" GRAPHICAL SOLUTIONS DON'T EXIST

After performing graphical portfolio analysis, some analysts are surprised to find that their MVP has negative weights in it, or their isomeans are not tangent to their isovariances, or their entire set of efficient portfolios has negative weights, or their isomeans slope at an angle different from the previous examples they have seen. These and other occurrences are not unusual or abnormal. Figure 5.10 is an example containing characteristics that might erroneously surprise a beginning portfolio analyst. For examples of other graphical solutions, including a four-security portfolio, see Chapter 7 of Markowitz's (1959) book.

5.8   REPRESENTING CONSTRAINTS GRAPHICALLY

Sometimes laws or corporate policies constrain portfolios. For example, laws require that some mutual funds may not borrow money to finance purchases—that is, leveraged portfolios are illegal. This hypothetical borrowing constraint allows legal formation of portfolios only within the triangle bounded by J, P, and R in Figure 5.11. While the legislators who wrote such laws had good intentions, this analysis shows that such laws can make investments along the critical line from the MVP to T in Figure 5.11 illegal.

5.9   THE INTERIOR DECORATOR FALLACY

Brealey (1969) explains the "interior decorator" concept of portfolio management as the commonly held view that the mix of common stocks maintained by an investor should depend on his willingness to bear risk. According to this view, a broker or investment counselor is a kind of financial interior decorator, skillfully designing portfolios to reflect his client's personality.

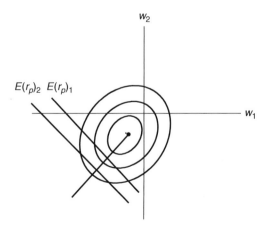

FIGURE 5.10   A Hypothetical "Unusual" Solution

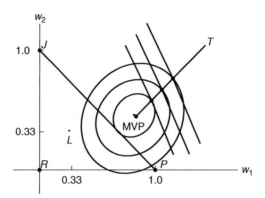

FIGURE 5.11   Graphical Representation of
Legal Constraint

According to the interior decorator school, a highly risk-averse investor should hold government bonds and high-quality utility stocks, for example, while a more aggressive investor would shun these assets.

The Markowitz portfolio analysis technique explained in this chapter is at odds with the financial interior decorator concept of portfolio management. For example, portfolio analysis may indicate that a person desiring to minimize risk should own a portfolio of only two stocks that are very risky individually. But if the two risky stocks covary inversely, the portfolio will most likely have less risk (that is, variability of return) than any portfolio prepared by less analytical techniques.

5.10   SUMMARY

Markowitz portfolio analysis is a new scientific approach to an old problem. Portfolios were never analyzed scientifically until Markowitz's theory was published in 1952.[5] In fact, highly intelligent Wall Street investment advisors who have years of experience are sometimes awed when they are introduced to the Markowitz model. Of course, the algebra intimidates anyone who is unaccustomed to it. More important, the precision of the solutions are viewed dubiously. After years of following "hot tips," reading subjective economic forecasts that are often misleading, studying charts of stocks' prices, and reading vaguely suggestive industry reports, experienced investment advisors are often shocked to see investment decisions with decimal-point precision. In fact, experience with actual Markowitz portfolios is necessary to understand the strengths and weaknesses of the analysis. This chapter concludes with a discussion of two caveats about portfolio analysis that the successful analyst should bear in mind. Efficient portfolios are derived from input statistics (namely, the expected returns, variances, and covariances) that are supplied to the portfolio analyst by security analysts. Of course, the value of the portfolio analysis is dependent on the validity of these input statistics. Therefore, considerable attention should be given to the input statistics. Ample resources should be expended on analyzing the individual assets before proceeding to the portfolio analysis and portfolio selection. The investment decisions delineated by portfolio analysis can be no better than the input statistics from which the efficient frontier is derived.

After an optimal-efficient portfolio has been selected and the assets purchased, more work remains. Portfolio analysis does not yield permanent solutions—only temporary solutions. As new information arrives continuously, the security analysts must reassess the statistical inputs that were provided to the portfolio analyst. The input statistics change every time the prospects for an actual or a potential investment change. Furthermore, a change in one security that lowers its covariance with the other securities, reduces its variance, and/or increases its expected return can shift the entire efficient frontier. Thus, security analysts and portfolio analysts never finish their work. Valuable investment decisions require continual updating of the input statistics and the efficient frontier.

APPENDIX: QUADRATIC EQUATIONS

The venerable quadratic equation plays an important role in modern portfolio theory.

A5.1   Quadratic Equations

Two major types of quadratic equations must be considered in portfolio analysis. The first type of quadratic equation is the equation in one unknown. Its general form is

$$ax^2 + bx + c = 0, \qquad (A5.1)$$

where x is the unknown, a and b are coefficients, and c is a constant. Three quadratic equations in one unknown (x) are graphed in Figure A5.1.

In the top equation in Figure A5.1, $a = 1$, $b = -6$, and $c = 14 - y$. Only part of the three parabolas is graphed—actually the figures could be traced out indefinitely

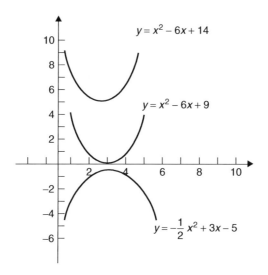

FIGURE A5.1   Parabolas

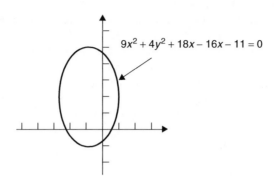

FIGURE A5.2 Ellipse

far if desired. Not all quadratic equations in one unknown are parabolas that point up or down—some point to the left or right.

The second type of quadratic equations is the equation in two unknowns. Its general form is

$$Ax^2 + Bxy + Cy^2 + Dx + Ey + F = 0. \tag{A5.2}$$

Here, the two unknown variables are x and y, and the coefficients A, B, C, D, and E, and F are constants. This equation is essentially the same as the formula for an isovariance ellipse. However, the variables x and y will be used here instead of w_1 and w_2. Figure A5.2 is a graph of a quadratic equation in two unknowns. The particular equation graphed has $A = 9$, $B = 0$, $C = 4$, $D = 18$, $E = -16$, and $F = -11$.

Other types of quadratic equations exist, those with three unknowns, four unknowns, and so on. However, all quadratics have one thing in common. The highest exponent of any variable in a quadratic equation is two.

A5.2 Analysis of Quadratics in Two Unknowns

Depending on the signs and values of the different terms, the graph of a quadratic in two unknowns can take any one of the several forms. The form depends mainly on the value of the coefficients A, B, and C and may be determined by the relationship $B^2 - 4AC$. The rules are:

- If $B^2 < 4AC$ the graph will usually be that of an ellipse. However, if $B = 0$ and $A = C$, the graph may be that of a circle, or a point, or may not exist.
- If $B^2 = 4AC$, the graph will be that of a parabola, or two parallel lines, or may not exist.
- If $B^2 > 4AC$, the graph will be that of a hyperbola or of two intersecting lines.

In considering ellipses, we will be mainly concerned with the first bullet.

The most common method of solving a quadratic equation in two unknowns is to set one of the unknowns to a constant and derive the value or values of the others. In other words, to solve a quadratic in two unknowns, we change the equation being solved to a quadratic in one unknown and solve enough points to enable graphing it.

Changing quadratics in two unknowns to quadratics in one unknown can be shown as follows for the general case. If we set one of the variables in equation (A5.2) to a constant, (that is, if we set y equal to zero), equation (A5.2) becomes

$$Ax^2 + Dx + F = 0. \tag{A5.3a}$$

Or, if we set y equal to 1, equation (A5.2) becomes

$$Ax^2 + Bx\,(1) + C(1)^2 + Dx + E\,(1) + F = 0,$$

and, by rearranging terms,

$$Ax^2 + (B + D)\,x + (C + E + F) = 0. \tag{A5.3b}$$

Equation (A5.3b) is in essentially the same form as Equation (A5.3a). The same general form will result, in fact, regardless of the value we assign to y. The form is

$$ax^2 + bx + c = 0, \tag{A5.1}$$

where $a = A$, $b = (By + D)$, and $c = \left(Cy^2 + Ey + F\right)$.

Quadratic equations in two unknowns that are converted to quadratic equations in one unknown (by setting one unknown equal to some real value, as shown above) may be solved with the *quadratic formula* below,

$$x = \frac{-b \pm \sqrt{b^2 - 4ac}}{2a}. \tag{A5.4}$$

A5.3   Analysis of Quadratics in One Unknown

Solving for x in terms of a, b, and c is done by "completing the square" as follows,

$ax^2 + bx + c = 0$	to be solved for x,
$4a^2x^2 + 4abx + 4ac = 0$	multiply through by $4a$,
$4a^2x^2 + 4abx = -4ac$	rearrange terms,
$4a^2x^2 + 4abx + b^2 = b^2 - 4ac$	add b^2 to both sides of equation,
$\left(2ax + b\right)^2 = b^2 - 4ac$	rearrange terms,
$2ax + b = \pm\sqrt{b^2 - 4ac}$	take the square root of both sides,
$x = \dfrac{-b}{2a} \pm \dfrac{\sqrt{b^2 - 4ac}}{2a}$	rearrange terms. (A5.4a)

Equation (A5.4) is called the *quadratic formula*. It can be seen in equation (A5.4a) that the unknown, x, is equal to a constant $(b/2a)$ plus or minus a constant $\frac{\sqrt{b^2-4ac}}{2a}$. Thus, there are usually two roots to consider. However, if the quantity under the radical equals zero (that is, b^2 equals $4ac$), then there is only one possibility (that is, $-b/2a$). The quantity under the radical may also be less than zero. If this is the case, since we have no way to take the square root of a negative number, the roots will be imaginary numbers.

Because of the possibility of deriving imaginary points, the quantity under the radical ($b^2 - 4ac$) must be evaluated. This term is known as the *discriminant* of a quadratic equation. Regardless of the sign of b, it is obvious that b^2 must be positive. If a and c have opposite signs, the term ($-4ac$) must also be positive. If this is the case, the square roots of the quantity ($b^2 - 4ac$) will always be real, since the quantity will always be positive. Conversely, it is only when both a and c have the same sign that the term ($-4ac$) may be negative. If this term is negative and greater in value than b^2, no real roots are possible.

A5.4   Solving an Ellipse

To illustrate the solution of a simple ellipse in twoknowns, consider

$$4x^2 + 9y^2 - 36 = 0 \qquad\qquad\qquad (A5.5)$$

Here, the coefficients are as follows for the quadratic in two unknowns:

$A = 4,$
$B = 0,$ (that is, the Bxy term does not exist)
$C = 9,$
$D = 0,$ (that is, the Dx term does not exist)
$E = 0,$ (that is, the Ey term does not exist)
$F = -36$

Since the coefficients of the quadratic in one unknown are a combination of the preceding coefficients,

$$a = A = 4,$$

$$b = (By + D) = (0)\,y + 0 = 0,$$

$$c = \left(Cy^2 + Ey + F\right) = 9y^2 + (0)\,y + (-36) = 9y^2 - 36$$

Plugging these values into equation (A5.4) gives

$$x = \frac{(0)}{2\,(4)} \pm \frac{\sqrt{(0)^2 - 4\,(4)\,(9y^2 - 36)}}{2\,(4)} = \pm\frac{\sqrt{(16)\,(36 - 9y^2)}}{8}$$

and

$$x = \pm\frac{\sqrt{36 - 9y^2}}{2}$$

To solve a few points now for this ellipse set y equal to zero.

$$x = \pm\frac{\sqrt{36}}{2} = +3 \text{ and} - 3$$

Setting y equal to one,

$$x = \pm \frac{\sqrt{36 - 9(1)^2}}{2} = +2.6 \text{ or} - 2.6$$

Setting y equal to three,

$$x = \pm \frac{\sqrt{36 - 9(3)^2}}{2} = \pm \frac{\sqrt{-45}}{2}$$

This last root is an imaginary number because the square root of a negative number is imaginary. Figure A5.3 shows the graphing of the ellipse $4x^2 + 9y^2 - 36 = 0$. The point where the quantity under the radical becomes less than zero is, therefore, the effective limit of the ellipse. Determination of the values of y to set in order to find the limits of the ellipse with regard to x is possible, but not analytical (that is, it is clumsy). Therefore, it is sufficient to solve for x values at increasing intervals of y above and below the center until an infeasible solution is found.

In physics the centroid of an ellipse is the center of gravity. In Markowitz portfolio analysis the centroid is the MVP. The *centroid* of an ellipse is found from the general equation in two unknowns:

$$Ax^2 + Bxy + Cy^2 + Dx + Ey + F = 0, \tag{A5.2}$$

By taking partial derivatives with respect to x and y as follows:

$$\frac{\partial}{\partial x} = 2Ax + By + D = 0 \tag{A5.6}$$

$$\frac{\partial}{\partial y} = Bx + 2Cy + E = 0 \tag{A5.7}$$

Solving these two resultant linear equations simultaneously follows:

$2ABx_0 + B^2 y_0 + BD = 0$ (multiply the first partial by B),

$2ABx_0 + 4ACy_0 + 2AE = 0$ (multiply the lower partial by $2A$),

$(B^2 - 4AC)y_0 = 2AE - BD$ (by subtraction).

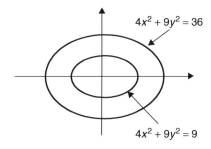

$4x^2 + 9y^2 = 36$

$4x^2 + 9y^2 = 9$

FIGURE A5.3 Ellipse

Thus,

$$y_0 = \frac{2AE - BD}{B^2 - 4AC} \tag{A5.8}$$

Substituting y_0 of equation (A5.8) into equation (A5.6) yields

$$x_0 = \frac{2CD - BE}{B^2 - 4AC} \tag{A5.9}$$

A5.5   Solving for Lines Tangent to a Set of Ellipses

The common method of finding the points where two equations meet is to rearrange one equation to solve for one unknown in terms of the other unknown. Then, we substitute that equation into the other equation in place of the solved variable. This may be illustrated for the ellipse and straight line as follows:

$$Ax^2 + Bxy + Cy^2 + Dx + Ey + F = 0 \qquad \text{(ellipse)} \tag{A5.2}$$

$$y = Mx + K \qquad \text{(straight line)} \tag{A5.10}$$

Substituting equation (A5.10) into equation (A5.2) yields

$$Ax^2 + Bx\,(Mx + K) + C(Mx + K)^2 + Dx + E\,(Mx + K) + F = 0$$

Simplifying,

$$\left(A + BM + CM^2\right)x^2 + (BK + 2CMK + EM + D)\,x + CK^2 + EK + F = 0$$

In order to find the *one* point of coincidence of the two equations, take the derivative with respect to x, as follows:

$$\frac{\partial}{\partial x} = 2\left(A + BM + CM^2\right)x + (BK + 2CMK + EM + D) = 0$$

and therefore,

$$x = \frac{BK + 2CMK + EM + D}{2\left(A + BM + CM^2\right)} \tag{A5.11}$$

The value of y may then be found by substituting x into either equation (A5.8) or (A5.2) and solving. The benefits of this solution are two points that lie on the critical line—that is, the centroid or MVP and a point of tangency of one isomean line with one isovariance ellipse. Which tangency does not matter, because taking the derivative ensures that *one* ellipse is coincident *at one point* with a specific straight line. This is the result of dropping the constant term for the ellipse when its equation is differentiated. The ellipse thus will assume the size necessary to coincide with the straight line at one point.

It is now possible to derive an equation for the critical line connecting the minimum variance centroid point and the tangency point. Where the point of tangency is (x_1, y_1), and the centroid point is (x_0, y_0), solving the following equation will result in the appropriate linear equation for the critical line.

$$(y - y_0) = \frac{y_1 - y_0}{x_1 - x_0}(x - x_0) \tag{A5.12}$$

In this equation, the unsubscripted variables x and y are the general case. To illustrate, suppose $(x_1, y_1) = (1, 3)$ and $(x_0, y_0) = (5, -2)$. Equation (A5.12) becomes

$$(y + 2) = \frac{3 + 2}{1 - 5}(x - 5)$$

$$y = -\frac{5}{4}x + \frac{17}{4}$$

$$5x + 4y = 17 \quad \text{(equation for critical line)}$$

This method of solution yields a specific equation for the critical line on which all minimum variances for each return class must lie. Also, a general equation for each return class follows.

Critical line equation:

$$I_2x + J_2y + K_2 = 0$$

Isomean equation:

$$I_1x + J_1y + K_1 = r_p \quad \text{or} \quad I_1x + J_1y + (K_1 - r_p) = 0$$

where I and J are coefficients of the x and y terms in equation (A5.12) and the isomean, and where K is a constant. To find the points where these two equations are common (intersect), simply solve them simultaneously for each assigned value of portfolio return (r_p).

$$I_1I_2x + I_1J_2y + I_1K_2 = 0$$

$$-I_1I_2x - I_2J_1y - I_2K_1 + I_2r_p = 0$$

and therefore,

$$(I_1J_2 - I_2J_1)y + I_1K_2 - I_2K_1 + I_2r_p = 0$$

Rearranging terms,

$$y = \frac{I_2K_1 - I_1K_2 - I_2r_p}{I_1J_2 - I_2J_1}$$

Substituting the derived y into either the critical line equation or the isomean equation will yield a value for x on the critical line where the particular isomean crosses it.

Once the points (x, y) are found for a given value of portfolio return (r_p), the portfolio variance of this point may then be found by substituting the x and y points derived into the general equation (A5.1):

$$Ax^2 + Bxy + Cy^2 + Dx + Ey + F = \text{Var}(r_p)$$

and solving for $\text{Var}(r_p)$.

NOTES

1. The analysis was originally presented in the article "Portfolio Selection," *Journal of Finance*, March 1952, 77–91. Later Markowitz expanded his presentation in a book, *Portfolio Selection*, Cowles Foundation Monograph 16 (New York: John Wiley & Sons, 1959). Many of Markowitz's most important articles are reprinted in Harry M. Markowitz, Editor, *Harry Markowitz Selected Works*, World Scientific Publisher, Singapore, 2010, 693 pages, Volume 1.

2. Also, Sharpe has written a linear programming algorithm that provides approximate solutions: W. F. Sharpe, "A Linear Programming Algorithm for Mutual Fund Portfolio Selection," *Management Science*, March 1967, 499–510. Furthermore, Sharpe and others have developed simplified solution methods—see Chapter 17. Many of Sharpe's most important articles are reprinted in William F. Sharpe, Editor, *William F. Sharpe: Selected Works*, World Scientific Publishing Company Inc., 2012, ISBN-10: 9814329959, ISBN-13: 978–9814329958, 692 pages.

3. The curve represented by equation (5.9) is a parabola if $B^2 - 4AC = 0$, an ellipse if $B^2 - 4AC < 0$, and a hyperbola if $B^2 - 4AC > 0$. See details in Thomas and Finney, *Calculus and Analytic Geometry*, 9th ed.(Reading, MA: Addison-Wesley, 1996). See also the appendix of this chapter.

4. The accurate answers can be obtained from standard calculus techniques, which are explained in Chapter 6.

5. Harry Markowitz, "Portfolio Selection," *Journal of Finance*, March 1952, 77–91.

Efficient Portfolios

The graphical approach to Markowitz portfolio analysis presented in Chapter 5 provides an excellent visual introduction. However, for those who wish to be able to solve portfolio problems involving many assets, this chapter is more appropriate. This chapter's mathematical techniques yield the same answers as the graphical technique. However, the mathematical techniques in this chapter are more general, more precise, and offer the tools for solving larger problems.

6.1   RISK AND RETURN FOR TWO-ASSET PORTFOLIOS

A portfolio manager must consider many different securities at once when attempting to delineate an optimal portfolio. In this section, the statistical tools the portfolio manager uses for evaluating securities (and thus portfolios) within the modern portfolio theory framework are developed.

If r_p denotes the return from a portfolio consisting of n securities, that portfolio's expected return, $E\left(r_p\right)$, can be expressed as

$$E\left(r_p\right) = \sum_{i=1}^{n} w_i\, E\left(r_i\right) \tag{2.12}$$

and its variance, σ_p^2, can be expressed as

$$\sigma_p^2 = \sum_{i=1}^{n} \sum_{j=1}^{n} w_i w_j \sigma_{ij}$$
$$= \sum_{i=1}^{n} w_i^2 \sigma_i^2 + \sum_{\substack{i=1 \\ for}}^{n} \sum_{\substack{j=1 \\ i \neq j}}^{n} w_i w_j \sigma_{ij} \tag{2.19a}$$

Equation series (2.19a) decomposes the first equation into two parts. The first part of the second equation indicates the sum of n variances, and the second part represents the sum of $\left(n^2 - n\right)$ covariance terms. Overall, the portfolio variance, σ_p^2, equals the sum of the terms in the cells of the following matrix:

$$\begin{pmatrix} +w_1 w_1 \sigma_{11} & +w_1 w_2 \sigma_{12} & \cdots & +w_1 w_n \sigma_{1n} \\ +w_2 w_1 \sigma_{21} & +w_2 w_2 \sigma_{22} & \cdots & +w_2 w_n \sigma_{2n} \\ \vdots & \vdots & \ddots & \vdots \\ +w_n w_1 \sigma_{n1} & +w_n w_2 \sigma_{n2} & \cdots & +w_n w_n \sigma_{nn} \end{pmatrix}$$

For example, in a portfolio of 100 securities ($n = 100$) there will be 100 variances and $(100^2 - 100 =)$ 9,900 covariances. To use Markowitz portfolio theory, the security analyst must estimate all of these parameters (plus 100 expected returns) exogenously. Chapter 8 shows a simplified method that will ease the security analyst's work.

Notice that the terms in the matrix containing identical subscripts (for example, $w_i w_i \sigma_{ii}$) form a diagonal pattern from the upper left-hand corner to the lower right-hand corner. These are the n weighted variances. All the other cells (the off-diagonal cells) contain the $(n^2 - n)$ weighted covariance terms (denoted $w_i w_j \sigma_{ij}$ for $i \neq j$). Because $w_i w_j \sigma_{ij} = w_j w_i \sigma_{ji}$, the matrix is symmetric, and each covariance is repeated twice in the matrix. The covariances above the diagonal are the mirror image of the covariances below the diagonal. As a result, the security analyst must actually estimate only $\frac{1}{2}(n^2 - n)$ unique covariance terms instead of $(n^2 - n)$. In the example with $n = 100$, this means there will be 9,900 total covariances but only 4,950 unique covariances.

6.2 THE OPPORTUNITY SET

The *opportunity set*, also known as the *feasible set*, represents all portfolios that could be formed from a group of n securities, plus the n securities. The set of all possible portfolios formed from a group of n securities lies either on or within the boundary of the opportunity set. This opportunity set can be plotted in $[\sigma, E(r)]$ space. A simple two-security portfolio will be used initially to show how to construct the opportunity set. Later in this chapter, an n-security portfolio is analyzed.

6.2.1 The Two-Security Case

Suppose two securities are used to construct an opportunity set. Table 6.1 gives their information.

The correlation coefficient between these two securities is assumed to be $\rho_{12} = 0$. The expected return and variance on all possible portfolios are determined according to the investment weights w_1 and w_2, as follows:

$$E(r_p) = w_1 E(r_1) + w_2 E(r_2)$$

$$\sigma_p = \sqrt{w_1^2 \sigma_1^2 + w_2^2 \sigma_2^2 + 2 w_1 w_2 \rho_{12} \sigma_1 \sigma_2}$$

The covariance under the radical sign above is restated using the following equation (2.6).

$$\sigma_{12} = \rho_{12} \sigma_1 \sigma_2 \tag{2.6}$$

TABLE 6.1 Input Data for a Two-Asset Portfolio

	Security 1	Security 2
$E(r)$	5%	15%
σ	20%	40%

TABLE 6.2 Expected Return and Standard Deviation of Selected Portfolios

Portfolio	w_1	w_2	$\mu_p(\%)$	$\sigma_p(\%)$
A	1.2	−0.2	3.0	25.3
B	1.0	0.0	5.0	20.0
C	5/6	1/6	6.7	17.9
D (MVP)	4/5	1/5	7.0	17.89
E	2/3	1/3	8.3	18.8
F	1/2	1/2	10.0	22.4
G	1/3	2/3	11.7	27.6
H	1/6	5/6	13.3	33.4
I	0.0	1.0	15.0	40.0
J	−0.2	1.2	17.0	48.2

Among the infinite number of possible Markowitz efficient portfolios, a few are listed in Table 6.2.

For example, when $w_1 = 5/6$ and $w_2 = 1/6$ (portfolio C in Table 6.2), the expected return and standard deviation of the portfolio are

$$E\left(r_p\right) = (5/6)\,(0.05) + (1/6)\,(0.15) = 0.067 = 6.7\%$$

$$\sigma_p = \sqrt{(5/6)^2(0.20)^2 + (1/6)^2(0.40)^2 + 2\,(5/6)\,(1/6)\,(0.0)\,(0.20)\,(0.40)}$$
$$= 0.179 = 17.9\%$$

The expected return and standard deviation for various combinations of w_1 and w_2 are plotted in Figure 6.1. All the portfolios that can be formed from the two risky securities should lie on the elliptical curve $\overline{AJ}$.

Table 6.2 shows that portfolio *B* includes only security 2, and portfolio *I* includes only security 1. All the portfolios from *B* through *I* have nonnegative weights: They

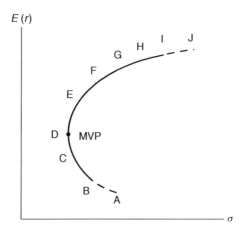

FIGURE 6.1 Opportunity Set with Two Securities

all lie on the solid curve in Figure 6.1. In contrast, portfolio J has weights of $w_1 = 120$ percent and $w_2 = -20$ percent, indicating that a security with the same risk and return as security 2 was printed and sold (issued) to raise borrowed money (leverage the portfolio). Alternatively, we can assume security 2 was sold short in an amount equal to 20 percent of the initial investment and the cash inflow from the short sale was invested in security 1. The borrowed cash, or the cash from the short sale, was used to buy (take a long position in) security 1. The expected return and the risk of this portfolio increase as more funds are borrowed and invested. Thus, portfolios comprised of short-selling security 2 (to raise funds at the low rate) and purchasing security 1 (to earn the high return) lie on the dotted line at the top of the opportunity set in Figure 6.1. Selling short security 1 (the high-return security) and buying long security 2 (the low-return security) is another strategy plotted on the dotted line at the bottom of the opportunity set. This latter strategy is economically irrational (financially counterproductive); it was constructed only to show another example of how a negative weight can arise.

The portion of the opportunity curve that lies above the minimum variance portfolio (MVP is portfolio D) is concave toward the E(r)-axis, while the portion that lies below the minimum variance portfolio (MVP) is convex. This is not due to the peculiarities of the example above; it is a general characteristic of all Markowitz efficient frontiers.

6.2.2   Minimizing Risk in the Two-Security Case

The weights that minimize a portfolio's variance can be found by standard calculus optimization techniques. We take the first derivative of the portfolio's variance with respect to the weight of asset 1, w_1, set that derivative equal to zero, and solve for w_1. The derivative is

$$\frac{\partial \sigma_p^2}{\partial w_1} = \frac{\partial}{\partial w_1}\left[w_1^2 \sigma_1^2 + \left(1 - w_1\right)^2 \sigma_2^2 + 2w_1\left(1 - w_1\right)\sigma_{12}\right]$$

$$= 2w_1\sigma_1^2 - 2\left(1 - w_1\right)\sigma_2^2 + 2\left(1 - 2w_1\right)\sigma_{12} \tag{6.1}$$

Setting the derivative equal to zero and solving for w_1 yields

$$w_1 = \frac{\sigma_2^2 - \sigma_{12}}{\sigma_1^2 + \sigma_2^2 - 2\sigma_{12}} \tag{6.2}$$

The weight for the second security is

$$w_2 = 1 - w_1 = \frac{\sigma_1^2 - \sigma_{12}}{\sigma_1^2 + \sigma_2^2 - 2\sigma_{12}} \tag{6.3}$$

In the above example, the weights for securities 1 and 2 that minimize the portfolio variance are obtained using equations (6.2) and (6.3) as follows

$$w_1 = \frac{(40)^2 - (0.0)(20)(40)}{(20)^2 + (40)^2 - 2(0.0)(20)(40)} = \frac{4}{5}$$

$$w_2 = 1 - w_1 = \frac{1}{5}$$

Thus, the variance of the MVP is

$$\sigma^2_{MVP} = \left(\frac{4}{5}\right)^2 (20)^2 + \left(\frac{1}{5}\right)^2 (40)^2 + 2\left(\frac{4}{5}\right)\left(\frac{1}{5}\right)(0) = 320$$

EXAMPLE 6.1

In Chapter 5's Example 5.2, a trial-and-error method is used to find the weights minimizing the portfolio's variance by searching through numerous possible values of the weights for the two securities. The possible values considered for the weights are listed in Chapter 5's Table 5.3. Unfortunately, this method provides an approximate answer. Mathematical analysis can provide the more precise answers that follow.

$$w_1 = \frac{(34.25) - (-2.65)}{(48.20) + (34.25) - 2(-2.65)} = 0.4205$$

$$w_2 = 1 - 0.4205 = 0.5795$$

Note that the trial-and-error method in Chapter 5 provides the values of $w_1 = 0.42$ and $w_2 = 0.58$, which might not be accurate to as many decimal places as desired.

6.2.3   The Three-Security Case

Extending the case of two risky securities to include a third risky security results in Figure 6.2, when short sales (negative weights) are not considered. All possible portfolios that can be formed from three risky securities should lie either on or within the boundary of the opportunity set as in Figure 6.2. Note that when short

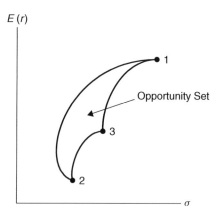

FIGURE 6.2   Opportunity Set Formed by Three Securities with Short Sales Not Allowed

sales are allowed, the opportunity set has open ends on the right-hand side (like Figure 6.3B later).

The expected return and the variance pairs from all possible portfolios formed from three securities are computed with equations (5.5) and (5.7).

$$E\left(r_p\right) = \sum_{i=1}^{3} w_i E\left(r_i\right) = w_1 E\left(r_1\right) + w_2 E\left(r_2\right) + w_3 E\left(r_3\right) \tag{5.5}$$

$$\begin{aligned}
\sigma_p^2 &= w_1^2 \sigma_{11} + w_2^2 \sigma_{22} + w_3^2 \sigma_{33} + 2w_1 w_2 \sigma_{12} + 2w_1 w_3 \sigma_{13} + 2w_2 w_3 \sigma_{23} \\
&= \left(\sigma_{11} + \sigma_{33} - 2\sigma_{13}\right) w_1^2 + \left(2\sigma_{33} + 2\sigma_{12} - 2\sigma_{13} - 2\sigma_{23}\right) w_1 w_2 \\
&\quad + \left(\sigma_{22} + \sigma_{33} - 2\sigma_{23}\right) w_2^2 + \left(-2\sigma_{33} + 2\sigma_{13}\right) w_1 \\
&\quad + \left(-2\sigma_{33} + 2\sigma_{23}\right) w_2 + \sigma_{33}
\end{aligned} \tag{5.7}$$

The weights that minimize the portfolio variance can be found by standard calculus optimization techniques, as in the case of the portfolio with two securities. Taking the partial derivatives of equation (5.7) with respect to both w_1 and w_2 and setting the resulting equations equal to zero yields two linear equations, (6.4) and (6.5):

$$\frac{\partial \sigma_p^2}{\partial w_1} = 2\left(\sigma_{11} + \sigma_{33} - 2\sigma_{13}\right) w_1 + \left(2\sigma_{33} + 2\sigma_{12} - 2\sigma_{13} - 2\sigma_{23}\right) w_2 + \left(-2\sigma_{33} + 2\sigma_{13}\right) = 0 \tag{6.4}$$

$$\frac{\partial \sigma_p^2}{\partial w_2} = \left(2\sigma_{33} + 2\sigma_{12} - 2\sigma_{13} - 2\sigma_{23}\right) w_1 + 2\left(\sigma_{22} + \sigma_{33} - 2\sigma_{23}\right) w_2 + \left(-2\sigma_{33} + 2\sigma_{23}\right) = 0 \tag{6.5}$$

Inserting the numerical values for the variances and covariances from Table 5.5 into equations (6.4) and (6.5) yields equations (6.6) and (6.7):

$$\frac{\partial \sigma_p^2}{\partial w_1} = 175.50\, w_1 + 87.46\, w_2 - 73.80 = 0 \tag{6.6}$$

$$\frac{\partial \sigma_p^2}{\partial w_2} = 87.46\, w_1 + 97.22\, w_2 - 66.52 = 0 \tag{6.7}$$

Equations (6.6) and (6.7) must be solved simultaneously to find the MVP.[1] Solving equations (6.6) and (6.7) yields

$$w_1 = 0.1442, \quad w_2 = 0.5545, \quad w_3 = 1 - w_1 - w_2 = 0.3013.$$

The variance of the MVP is

$$\begin{aligned}
\sigma_{MVP}^2 &= (0.1442)^2 (48.20) + (0.5545)^2 (16.34) + (0.3013)^2 (34.25) \\
&\quad + 2 (0.1442)(0.5545)(7.82) + 2 (0.5545)(0.3013)(0.99) \\
&\quad + 2 (0.1442)(0.3013)(-2.65) \\
&= 10.49
\end{aligned}$$

and its expected return is

$$E\left(r_{MVP}\right) = (0.1442)\,(2.07) + (0.5545)\,(0.21) + (0.3013)\,(1.01) = 0.72\%$$

Note that these answers for the weights can be carried to as many decimal points as desired without invoking any approximations.

6.2.4   The *n*-Security Case

The opportunity set formed from *n* risky securities is depicted in Figures 6.3A and 6.3B. All possible portfolios that could be formed from the *n* securities lie either on or within the boundary of the opportunity set shown in Figure 6.3A. When short sales and borrowing are not allowed, the opportunity set will have the scalloped quarter-moon shape shown in Figure 6.3A. When short sales and/or borrowing are allowed, all possible portfolios lie on or behind the boundary of the opportunity set in Figure 6.3B. Within the opportunity set are all individual securities and portfolios.

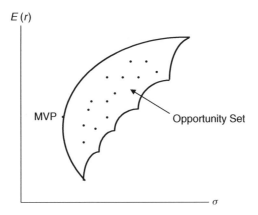

FIGURE 6.3A   Opportunity Set Formed by Many Securities with Short Sales Not Allowed

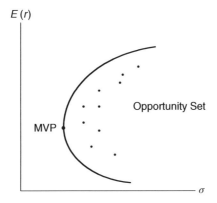

FIGURE 6.3B   Opportunity Set Formed by Many Securities with Short Sales Allowed

Thus, all points within this space are *feasible investments*. Note that Figures 6.2 and 6.3A depict an opportunity set that is a solid mass of investment opportunities within the scalloped quarter-moon-shaped set. This solid mass of investment opportunities is achieved by not using any negative portfolio weights.

6.3 MARKOWITZ DIVERSIFICATION

The phrase *Markowitz diversification* refers to its creator, Harry M. Markowitz (1952, 1959, 2010). Markowitz diversification differs from *simple (or random) diversification*, used widely by security salesmen and some investment books. These sources define diversification as "not putting all your eggs in one basket" or "spreading your risks." The possible benefits of naive diversification will be discussed later. Naive diversification ignores the covariance between securities and results in superfluous diversification.

PRINCIPLE BOX: DEFINITION OF MARKOWITZ DIVERSIFICATION

Markowitz diversification involves combining securities with less-than-perfect positive correlation in order to reduce risk in the portfolio without sacrificing any of the portfolio's expected return. In general, the lower the correlations (or, equivalently, covariances) of the assets in a portfolio, the less risky the resulting portfolio will be. This is true regardless of how risky the portfolio's assets are when analyzed in isolation.

Markowitz (1952, 89) put it this way:

Not only does [portfolio analysis] imply diversification, it implies the "right kind" of diversification for the "right reason." The adequacy of diversification is not thought by investors to depend on the number of different securities held. A portfolio with sixty different railway securities, for example, would not be as well diversified as the same size portfolio with some railroad, some public utility, mining, various sorts of manufacturing, etc. The reason is that it is generally more likely for firms within the same industry to do poorly at the same time than for firms in dissimilar industries. Similarly, in trying to make variance [of returns] small it is not enough to invest in many securities. It is necessary to avoid investing in securities with high covariances among themselves.

We introduce Markowitz diversification by using the statistics in Table 6.1. Note that the opportunity set in Table 6.2 and Figure 6.1 was formed with these two securities after we assumed the correlation coefficient between these two securities is $\rho_{12} = 0$. Combining securities 1 and 2 with the weights $w_1 = 2/3$ and $w_2 = 1/3$ produces a portfolio with expected return of 8.3 percent.

$$E\left(r_p\right) = (2/3)\,(0.05) + (1/3)\,(0.15) = 0.083 \quad \text{or } 8.3\%$$

$$\sigma_p = \sqrt{(2/3)^2(0.20)^2 + (1/3)^2(0.40)^2 + 2\,(2/3)\,(1/3)\left(\rho_{12}\right)(0.20)\,(0.40)}$$

$$= \sqrt{0.0356 + 0.0356\left(\rho_{12}\right)}$$

Although the expected return of this portfolio is fixed at 8.3 percent for the investment weights assumed for securities 1 and 2, the risk of the portfolio varies with the correlation coefficient, ρ_{12}. Thus, if $\rho_{12} = +1$, then $\sigma_p = 26.7$ percent. If $\rho_{12} = 0$, then $\sigma_p = 18.9$ percent. And if $\rho_{12} = -1$, then $\sigma_p = 0$ percent. That is, if the correlation coefficient decreases from $\rho_{12} = +1$ to $\rho_{12} = 0$, the risk decreases from 26.7 percent to 18.9 percent, although the assets' expected returns remain unchanged. The locus of portfolios corresponding to all possible proportions for securities 1 and 2 (w_1 and w_2) is plotted in Figures 6.4A and 6.4B for three correlation values, $\rho_{12} = +1$, 0, and -1, and with short sales not allowed and allowed, respectively. The equations for a relationship between $E\left(r_p\right)$ and σ_p when the correlation coefficients are $+1$ and -1, respectively, are given in an appendix at the end of this chapter.

Figure 6.4A graphically depicts how Markowitz diversification affects the risk of the portfolio when borrowing and/or short sales are not allowed.[2] It shows that lowering ρ_{12} reduces risk when combining securities 1 and 2 into a portfolio. The straight line between securities 1 and 2 defines the locus of $E\left(r_p\right)$ and σ_p from all possible portfolios of securities 1 and 2 when $\rho_{12} = +1$. This straight line is the upper bound for the portfolio's risk (standard deviation). The lower the value

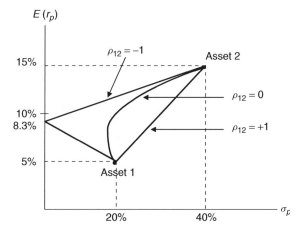

FIGURE 6.4A Markowitz Diversification without Short Sales

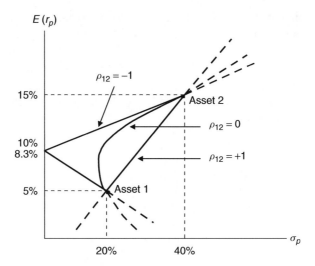

FIGURE 6.4B   Markowitz Diversification with
Borrowing or Short Sales

of ρ_{12}, the more the curve connecting securities 1 and 2 curves or bows to the left. When the lowest possible correlation is encountered, $\rho_{12} = -1$, the portfolio's risk is minimized. Typically, $-1 < \rho_{12} < +1$, and, as a result, the line is usually curved to the left, meaning the line is typically concave. This bowing or curvature property of portfolio variance is called the covariance effect or the correlation effect. The dotted line segments in Figure 6.4B indicate a negative weight for one security (that is, short sales or leverage).

The previous illustration of the diversification effect shows that the expected return of the portfolio equals the weighted average of two securities' expected returns. But the standard deviation of the portfolio is less than or equal to the weighted average of two securities' standard deviations. That is, while $\sigma_p^2 = w_1^2\sigma_1^2 + w_2^2\sigma_2^2 + 2w_1w_2\rho_{12}\sigma_1\sigma_2$ is true, the inequality (6.8) is also true.

$$\sigma_p \leq w_1\sigma_1 + w_2\sigma_2 \qquad (6.8)$$

The equality holds only when the correlation coefficient between the assets equals positive one, $\rho_{12} = +1$.

Figure 6.4A illustrates how Markowitz diversification can reduce the risk (variability of return) on the owner's equity. The risk and expected return of the individual assets is not affected by their inclusion in a diversified portfolio. In modern portfolio theory the focus is ultimately on (1) the expected rate of return on the owner's equity, and (2) the variability of return (risk) on the owner's equity. The individual securities are merely the objects of choice that a portfolio manager uses to form into dominant portfolios. The risk and return statistics on the individual securities being considered for possible inclusion in the portfolio are exogenous constants that are estimated by a statistically oriented security analyst. In contrast, the security weights are the *decision variables* that are determined endogenously by the portfolio manager (or the portfolio manager's computer program).

Most investors realize that diversification reduces risk. However, few people have ever thought about risk analytically. If an investor's concept of risk is not sufficiently well defined to be measured empirically, it follows logically that the investor must be working with only a vague concept of how to diversify. Furthermore, some investors erroneously develop perverted notions about diversification. For instance, some people erroneously believe that low-risk (for example, public utility) stocks and (say, government) bonds, both of which may have low returns, are the best ways to reduce a portfolio's risk.

Risk can be reduced by means of Markowitz diversification without decreasing return at all—in fact, such diversification can be optimal. Simple (random) diversification can usually reduce risk. However, simple diversification cannot be expected to minimize risk because it ignores the correlation (or covariance) between assets. Simple diversification concentrates on owning different assets; that is, not putting all your eggs in one basket. In contrast, Markowitz diversification provides an analytical approach to diversification.

6.4   EFFICIENT FRONTIER WITHOUT THE RISK-FREE ASSET

Figure 6.5 contains an opportunity set derived from many individual securities. The upper left quadrant between points *E* and *F* in Figure 6.5 is the *efficient frontier* of the opportunity set. It is comprised of efficient portfolios.

PRINCIPLES BOX: DEFINITION OF EFFICIENT PORTFOLIOS

An *efficient portfolio* is the portfolio that has either (1) more return than any other portfolio in its risk class (that is, any other asset with the same variability of returns), or (2) less risk than any other security with the same return.

The portfolios on the efficient frontier *EF* in Figure 6.5 are all efficient. The efficient frontier of the opportunity set dominates all other portfolios in the opportunity set. These portfolios are sometimes said to be Markowitz efficient.

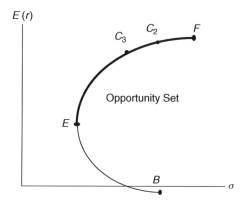

FIGURE 6.5   Efficient Frontier

Mathematical solutions for delineating the efficient portfolios are presented in Section 7.1 of Chapter 7.

Hirschleifer (1964, 79) expressed the reason for the particular shape of the efficient frontier as follows:

> *The curvature shown for the efficient frontier—opposite to that of the* $[\sigma, E(r)]$ *indifference curves—follows also from the covariance effect, since moving to higher values of portfolio $E(r)$ progressively reduces the number of securities that can be held in combination so as to lower σ.*

Chapter 4 showed that the indifference curves for a risk-averse investor were convex away from the $E(r)$ axis. The efficient frontier is concave toward the $E(r)$ axis due to the covariance effect. Consider a situation where the efficient frontier is not concave.[3] The efficient frontier in Figure 6.6 is convex between points D and T. Can such convexity actually exist? The answer is no.

Points D and T, which represent two different portfolios of securities, may themselves be combined into a third portfolio. This third portfolio will have an expected return and variance based on the expected returns and variances of D and T. Furthermore, the covariance between D and T plays a role in determining the variance of the third portfolio. It is the covariance effect that will prevent such convexity from occurring. If the correlation coefficient was as large as possible, $\rho_{DT} = +1$, the third portfolio will lie on a straight line that connects D and T and is outside the convex region. This shows that the original convex section of the efficient frontier was actually not on the minimum variance boundary and thus was not efficient. If the correlation coefficient was less than $+1$, then the third portfolio will lie on a curve that is bowed to the left of a straight line between D and T, proving again that the original convex section of the efficient frontier was not actually efficient. Arguing by induction, the efficient frontier can be shown to be a smooth continuous concave surface similar to that shown in Figure 6.5 and to have a positive slope everywhere (increase monotonically).

The efficient frontier in Figure 6.5 is bounded at one end by point E, and at the other end by point F. Point E is typically referred to as the *global minimum variance*

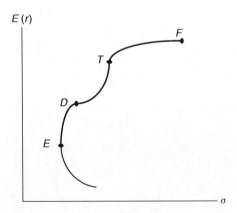

FIGURE 6.6   Concavity of the Efficient
Frontier for the Markowitz Model

portfolio (MVP) because no other portfolio exists that has lower variance. Point *F* is typically referred to as the *maximum return portfolio* because no other portfolio exists that has a higher level of expected return. The latter portfolio will generally consist of the one security that has the highest expected return. (*F* could consist of more than one security if two or more securities tied for having the highest expected return.) The locus of the MVPs at each level of return in Figure 6.5 is the curve bounded at the upper end by *F* and at the lower end by *B*.

When the weights w_i are constrained to being nonnegative, the efficient frontier is generated by a sequence of "corner portfolios." As we go down the efficient frontier from point *F* (or up from point *E*), new corner portfolios are encountered periodically. Adjacent corner portfolios differ in that as we move from one to the next, a new security is added and/or an old security is dropped from the solution. For example, suppose the maximum return portfolio, denoted F in Figure 6.5, is a corner portfolio consisting of one security (thus all the other securities have zero weights). The next corner portfolio, C_2, might consist of both the security in *F* and a second security, with all the other securities having zero weights. All efficient portfolios between C_2 and *F* would simply be linear combinations of these two portfolios. Moving down from C_2 in Figure 6.5, we would encounter C_3 next, which might consist of the two securities in C_2 plus a third security with nonzero weight. Combinations of C_3 and C_2 would result in efficient portfolios plotting between C_3 and C_2. Knowledge of all the corner portfolios enables construction of the efficient frontier. Establishing the convexity of a risk-averse investor's indifference curves and the concavity of the efficient frontier allows us to state the efficient frontier theorem (also known as the efficient set theorem):

PRINCIPLES BOX: DEFINITION OF THE EFFICIENT FRONTIER THEOREM

The optimal portfolio for a risk-averse investor will be located on the efficient frontier.

This theorem can be proven intuitively by noting that the risk-averse investor's convex indifference curves represent increasing expected utility as one moves from one curve (utility isoquant) to another in a northwesterly direction. Because (1) the investor seeks a portfolio on the most northwestern indifference curve possible, (2) the opportunity set is concave on its northwest boundary, and (3) the northwest boundary of the opportunity set is by definition the efficient frontier, the investor's optimal portfolio will be an efficient portfolio.[4]

Figure 6.7 depicts the identification of a risk-averse investor's optimal portfolio O^*. Indifference curve I_3 is preferred to I_2 because it has a higher level of expected utility. Similarly, I_2 is preferred to I_1. There are many feasible portfolios the investor could choose that provide the same amount of expected utility along the curve I_1. These portfolios lie on I_1 and are bounded by efficient portfolios O_1 and O_2. However, O^* is also feasible and provides a greater amount of expected utility because it lies on I_2; accordingly, O^* is preferred to O_1, O_2, or any other portfolio on I_1. Finally, note that while I_3 is preferred to I_2, no portfolios exist that touch I_3.

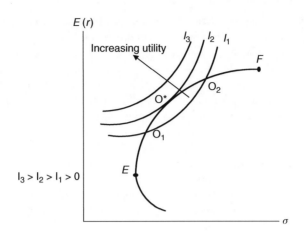

FIGURE 6.7   Identifying the Optimal Portfolio for the Markowitz Model

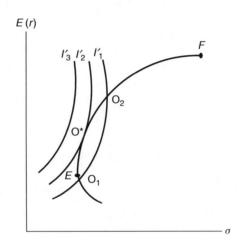

FIGURE 6.8   Identifying the Optimal Portfolio for a Highly Risk-averse Investor

Therefore, the optimal portfolio is the efficient portfolio O^*, which is a tangency point between the efficient frontier and the highest feasible indifference curve.

The choice of the optimal portfolio depends on an investor's degree of risk aversion. If the investor is highly risk averse, the slope of the indifference curve is steeper. In this case, the investor's optimal portfolio will be located on the lower part of the efficient frontier as illustrated in Figure 6.8. Highly risk-averse investors generally prefer portfolios with low risk and low return.

6.5   INTRODUCING A RISK-FREE ASSET

Up to this point we have been dealing with portfolios that contain only risky assets. Every candidate asset has positive variance, $\sigma^2 > 0$. If we assume the existence of the risk-free asset, $\sigma^2 = 0$, that one small additional assumption introduces the possibilities of borrowing and lending at a risk-free interest rate. For example, borrowing at a risk-free interest rate might involve going to an FDIC-insured bank and taking out a short-term loan at a low interest rate. Borrowing can also be accomplished by selling a risk-free asset short and collecting the cash proceeds from the short sale, while delivering a *borrowed* risk-free asset to the buyer. Short sales are more complex beause they involve selling something not owned. Lending at some risk-free interest rate can be as simple as going to an FDIC-insured bank and making a deposit at some low fixed rate of interest. Making the bank deposit is economically equivalent to investing in a riskless asset and holding it in a long position.

Consider what happens when a risk-free security is held in a long position in conjunction with a long position in a risky asset. Denote the proportions held in the risky asset and the risk-free asset as w_1 and $1 - w_1$, respectively. The expected return of this portfolio is defined by the unambiguously linear equation (6.9).

$$E\left(r_p\right) = \left(1 - w_1\right) r_f + w_1 E\left(r_1\right) \tag{6.9}$$

where r_f denotes the risk-free rate of return and $E\left(r_1\right)$ denotes the expected return on the risky asset 1. The variance of this two-asset portfolio is defined by equation (6.10).

$$\sigma_p^2 = w_1^2 \sigma_1^2 + \left(1 - w_1^2\right) \sigma_f^2 + 2w_1 \left(1 - w_1\right) \sigma_{1f} \tag{6.10}$$

where σ_f^2 is the variance of the risk-free asset's rate of return, and σ_{1f} is the covariance between returns of the risky asset and the risk-free asset. By definition, $\sigma_f^2 = 0$. The covariance also equals zero, $\sigma_{1f} = 0$, because there is no association (correlation) between a series of constant (riskless) returns and a series of fluctuating (risky) returns. The preceding sentence also follows from the fact (shown in Theorem A6 of the appendix at the end of this book) that the correlation (or covariance) of a constant (zero variance asset) with a random variable (positive variance) is zero. Reconsidering equation (6.10) in view of these facts allows us to equivalently rewrite equation (6.10) to become (6.10a) below.

$$\sigma_p^2 = w_1^2 \sigma_1^2 + \left(1 - w_1\right)^2 \sigma_f^2 + 2w_1 \left(1 - w_1\right) \sigma_{1f} \tag{6.10}$$

$$= w_1^2 \sigma_1^2 + \left(1 - w_1\right)^2 (0) + 2w_1 \left(1 - w_1\right) (0)$$

$$\sigma_p^2 = w_1^2 \sigma_1^2 \tag{6.10a}$$

Taking the square root of equation (6.10a) reduces it to the simple linear equation (6.11).

$$\sigma_p = w_1 \sigma_1 \tag{6.11}$$

Solving equation (6.11) for w_1 yields $w_1 = \sigma_p / \sigma_1$. Substituting this expression above for w_1 into equation (6.9) and simplifying results in

$$E\left(r_p\right) = r_f + \left(\frac{E\left(r_1\right) - r_f}{\sigma_1}\right) \sigma_p \tag{6.12}$$

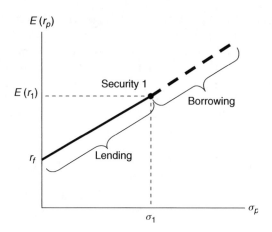

FIGURE 6.9 Opportunity Line from Combining
a Risky Asset with the Risk-free Asset

Equation (6.12) shows that $E(r_p)$ is linearly related to σ_p. This linear relationship is depicted in Figure 6.9. These examples generalize to mean that any
portfolio formed from the risk-free asset and any risky asset (like security 1) will
lie on a straight line connecting those two points, the exact location depending
on the weights in the two securities. If $w_1 = 0$, then from equations (6.9) and
(6.11) it can be seen that $\sigma_p = 0$ and $E(r_1) = r_f$. The resulting portfolio is the
risk-free asset itself. Similarly, if $w_1 = 0$, then $\sigma_p = \sigma_1$ and $E(r_p) = E(r_1)$, which
is risky asset 1. Assuming that $r_f < E(r_1)$, if $0 < w_1 < 1$, then $0 < \sigma_p < \sigma_1$ and
$r_f < E(r_p) < E(r_1)$.

Depositing some money in an FDIC-insured bank and some more money in
risky security 1 results in a two-asset portfolio located somewhere on the solid
line segment between r_f and asset 1 in Figure 6.9. This line segment is labeled
lending, because $w_f > 0$, where $w_f = 1 - w_1$. Next, assume $r_f < E(r_1)$, if $w_1 > 1$,
then $\sigma_p > \sigma_1$ and $E(r_p) > E(r_1)$. This corresponds to a point located somewhere on
the dotted line segment above asset 1 in Figure 6.9, which is labeled borrowing,
because $w_f < 0$. The more borrowing that is done, the farther out on this dashed
line segment the investor's portfolio will lie.

Because asset 1 can be viewed as a portfolio just as easily as a single asset, this
analysis can be extended to a general case of combining any risky portfolio in the
opportunity set with the risk-free asset. In other words, combining the risk-free asset
with any risky portfolio will result in a new portfolio somewhere on the straight
line connecting the two. Next, consider how the efficient frontier is changed when
the risk-free asset is introduced into an opportunity set comprised of risky assets.
Figure 6.10 shows the combination of the risk-free asset with various risky assets in
the opportunity set. Combinations of portfolio B with the risk-free asset along the
line $\overline{r_f B}$ are more desirable than (dominant) combinations of portfolio A with the
risk-free asset along the line $\overline{r_f A}$, because portfolios along the line $\overline{r_f B}$ have the higher
expected returns in the same risk class than portfolios along the line $\overline{r_f A}$. However,
combinations of portfolio B with the risk-free asset along the line $\overline{r_f B}$ are dominated

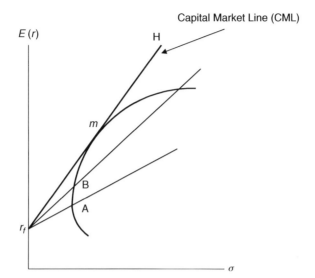

FIGURE 6.10 Combining the Risk-free Asset with
Various Risky Portfolios

by combinations of portfolio m with the risk-free asset along the line $\overline{r_f mH}$. In fact, in Figure 6.10 the portfolios along the line $\overline{r_f mH}$ have the highest returns at every level of risk.

Within Figure 6.10, any ray out of the riskless rate, r_f, that has a smaller slope than the tangency ray (line $\overline{r_f mH}$) will be dominated by the tangency ray because it represents a less favorable risk-return trade-off than the ray $\overline{r_f mH}$. Any ray with a slope greater than the tangency ray is infeasible, because such a line would lie entirely outside the opportunity set of assets that exist. Thus, over all the levels of risk illustrated in Figure 6.10, the tangency ray (line $\overline{r_f mH}$) represents dominant portfolios.

The result is that the new efficient frontier is a straight line where all efficient portfolios are simply linear combinations of the risk-free asset and the tangency portfolio m.[5] Because this efficient frontier is a straight line, it can be described by the linear equation (6.13) where m is the tangency portfolio [the role previously assumed by security 1 in both equation (6.12) and in Figure 6.9].

$$E\left(r_p\right) = r_f + \left(\frac{\mu_m - r_f}{\sigma_m}\right)\sigma_p \tag{6.13}$$

In this case, and in general, efficient portfolios between r_f and m involve lending at the risk-free interest rate, and efficient portfolios above m involve borrowing at the risk-free interest rate. This new linear efficient frontier is called the *capital market line* (CML).

Given a linear efficient frontier and convex indifference curves for a risk-averse investor, the efficient frontier theorem still holds and the investor optimally will choose a portfolio on this new linear efficient frontier. Figure 6.11 displays the portfolio chosen by a risk-averse investor. This investor chooses portfolio

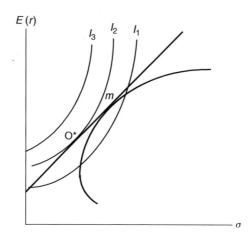

FIGURE 6.11 Identifying the Optimal Portfolio on the Straight Line Efficient Frontier

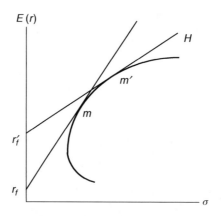

FIGURE 6.12 Tangency Portfolios with Two Different Risk-free Interest Rates

O^* because it will give the maximum utility, I_2. This optimal portfolio O^* in Figure 6.11 involves positive investments in both the risk-free asset and the tangency portfolio m.

The tangency portfolios, m in Figures (6.10) and (6.11), change their location as the level of the risk-free interest rate changes. As seen in Figure 6.12, as the risk-free rate of return increases from r_f to r_f', the tangency portfolio moves from m to m'. Figure 6.12 also represents the shape of the efficient frontier when investors borrowing at the risk-free interest rate r_f' pay an interest rate that exceeds the risk-free lending rate r_f. If investors can lend at r_f but not borrow at this low interest rate, the efficient frontier becomes the discontinuous line $\overline{r_f mm'}$ (first linear and then curved). If the investor can lend at the lower rate r_f but must borrow at the higher rate r_f', the efficient frontier becomes $\overline{r_f mm' H}$ (linear, curved, and linear with less slope).

6.6   SUMMARY AND CONCLUSIONS

This chapter discusses some financial engineering that shows how to calculate the expected return and variance for a portfolio. Markowitz diversification was shown to be attributable to the existence of less-than-perfect positive correlations within any set of risky securities. Investment opportunity sets and efficient frontiers were first developed without the risk-free asset by using two risky assets, three risky assets, and many risky assets. Investment opportunity sets and efficient frontiers were then developed by introducing the risk-free asset under differing sets of assumptions. These assumptions differed in how they treated short selling, borrowing, and lending at the risk-free interest rate. Regardless of the set of assumptions used, it was shown that the efficient frontier theorem still held. However, the shape and location of the efficient frontier were shown to vary to reflect the particular set of assumptions.

APPENDIX: EQUATIONS FOR A RELATIONSHIP BETWEEN $E(r_p)$ AND σ_p

This appendix presents the equations for the opportunity line when the correlation coefficients between the two assets' returns are perfectly positive and perfectly negative (i.e., $\rho_{12} = +1$ and -1).

Suppose a portfolio is formed from two securities whose expected returns are not equal and variances are not equal either (i.e., $E(r_1) \neq E(r_2)$ and $\sigma_1^2 \neq \sigma_2^2$).

(1) When portfolios are formed from two securities and the correlation coefficient between these two securities is $\rho_{12} = +1$, the expected return and standard deviation of the portfolio are

$$E(r_p) = w_1 E(r_1) + w_2 E(r_2) \tag{A6.1}$$

$$\sigma_p = \sqrt{w_1^2 \sigma_1^2 + w_2^2 \sigma_2^2 + 2w_1 w_2 \sigma_1 \sigma_2} = \sqrt{(w_1 \sigma_1 + w_2 \sigma_2)^2}$$

$$= w_1 \sigma_1 + w_2 \sigma_2 \tag{A6.2}$$

From equation (A6.1),

$$w_1 = \frac{E(r_p) - E(r_2)}{E(r_1) - E(r_2)} \tag{A6.3}$$

Substituting w_1 of equation (A6.2) with equation (A6.3) and rearranging yields

$$E(r_p) = \left[\frac{E(r_1) - E(r_2)}{\sigma_1 - \sigma_2} \right] \sigma_p + \left[\frac{\sigma_1 E(r_2) - \sigma_2 E(r_1)}{\sigma_1 - \sigma_2} \right] \tag{A6.4}$$

Equation (A6.4) represents the straight line connecting asset 1 and asset 2 for $\rho_{12} = +1$ in Figure 6.4A.

(2) When the correlation coefficient between two securities is $\rho_{12} = -1$, the expected return and standard deviation of the portfolio are

$$E(r_p) = w_1 E(r_1) + w_2 E(r_2) \tag{A6.1}$$

$$\sigma_p = \sqrt{w_1^2\sigma_1^2 + w_2^2\sigma_2^2 - 2w_1 w_2\sigma_1\sigma_2} = \sqrt{(w_1\sigma_1 - w_2\sigma_2)^2}$$
$$= |w_1\sigma_1 - w_2\sigma_2| \tag{A6.5}$$

Substituting w_1 of equation (A6.2) with equation (A6.5) and rearranging yields

$$\sigma_p = \left| \frac{E(r_p)[\sigma_1 + \sigma_2] - [\sigma_1 E(r_2) + \sigma_2 E(r_1)]}{E(r_1) - E(r_2)} \right| \tag{A6.5a}$$

If $w_1\sigma_1 - w_2\sigma_2 > 0$, or equivalently, if $E(r_p) > [\sigma_1 E(r_2) + \sigma_2 E(r_1)]/[\sigma_1 + \sigma_2]$, then

$$E(r_p) = \left[\frac{E(r_1) - E(r_2)}{\sigma_1 + \sigma_2}\right]\sigma_p + \left[\frac{\sigma_1 E(r_2) + \sigma_2 E(r_1)}{\sigma_1 + \sigma_2}\right] \tag{A6.6}$$

Equation (A6.6) represents the upper part in the piecewise straight line for $\rho_{12} = -1$ in Figure 6.4A.

If $w_1\sigma_1 - w_2\sigma_2 < 0$, or equivalently, if $E(r_p) < [\sigma_1 E(r_2) + \sigma_2 E(r_1)]/[\sigma_1 + \sigma_2]$, then

$$E(r_p) = -\left[\frac{E(r_1) - E(r_2)}{\sigma_1 + \sigma_2}\right]\sigma_p + \left[\frac{\sigma_1 E(r_2) + \sigma_2 E(r_1)}{\sigma_1 + \sigma_2}\right] \tag{A6.7}$$

Equation (A6.7) represents the lower part in the piecewise straight line for $\rho_{12} = -1$ in Figure 6.4A.

NOTES

1. When we have the following (2×2) simultaneous equations for the two unknown variables x_1 and x_2

$$a_1 x_1 + b_1 x_2 = c_1$$
$$a_2 x_1 + b_2 x_2 = c_2$$

the solutions are

$$x_1 = \frac{b_2 c_1 - b_1 c_2}{a_1 b_2 - a_2 b_1} \quad \text{and} \quad x_2 = \frac{a_1 c_2 - a_2 c_1}{a_1 b_2 - a_2 b_1}$$

Thus, the solutions for equations (6.6) and (6.7) are

$$w_1 = \frac{(97.22)(73.80) - (87.46)(66.52)}{(175.50)(97.22) - (87.46)(87.46)} = 0.1442$$

and

$$w_2 = \frac{(175.50)(66.52) - (87.46)(73.80)}{(175.50)(97.22) - (87.46)(87.46)} = 0.5545$$

Other methods of solving simultaneous equations are described in an appendix at the end of this book.

2. Figure 6.4A was first published in W. F. Sharpe (1964). Reprinted in William F. Sharpe, Editor, *William F. Sharpe: Selected Works*, World Scientific Publishing Company Inc., 2012, ISBN-10: 9814329959, ISBN-13: 978–9814329958, 692 pages.
3. Dybvig and Ross (1982) point out that under certain circumstances (which include non-normality of return distributions) the efficient frontier may not be convex.
4. Bawa (1976) has shown that the optimal portfolio for a risk seeker will not necessarily be efficient.
5. Of course, if r_f is greater than the expected returns of all the risky assets, then the efficient frontier will degenerate to one point, r_f.

CHAPTER 7

Advanced Mathematical Portfolio Analysis

This chapter presents a more advanced mathematical solution for the same portfolio problem that was discussed in Chapter 6. A specific solution for the optimal weights for efficient portfolios is presented with and without a risk-free asset. Several numerical examples are provided. An equation specifying the relationship between the expected returns and variances of efficient portfolios is presented: this equation represents the efficient frontier. Although this chapter employs more concise vector and matrix notations to represent the same problem used in Chapter 6, no new financial insights will be presented and this book's reading continuity will not be lost if this chapter is passed over.

7.1   EFFICIENT PORTFOLIOS WITHOUT A RISK-FREE ASSET

As shown in Chapters 5 and 6, if a risk-free asset is included in the list of risky investment candidates, a linear efficient frontier results. This section omits the risk-free asset from the list of risky investment candidates. As a result of this omission, this section derives a convex efficient frontier.

7.1.1   A General Formulation

Consider how a portfolio on the efficient frontier can be identified. What is desired are weights for the portfolio that minimize the portfolio variance, σ_p^2, at a given level of the expected return, $E(r_p)$. As mentioned in the previous paragraph, this section's optimization problem omits the risk-free asset.

The problem involves finding the weights that minimize the portfolio variance.

$$\text{Minimize}\quad \sigma_p^2 = \sum_{i=1}^{n}\sum_{j=1}^{n} w_i w_j \sigma_{ij} \tag{7.1}$$

subject to two mathematical constraints that are explained in the next paragraphs. As is common, we multiply the constant fraction $1/2$ times the objective function in equation (7.1) to simplify the solution that follows. This is a cosmetic change. This multiplication does not change any of the conclusions that follow.

The first constraint on minimizing equation (7.1) requires that some desired (or target) level of expected return, $E(r_p)$, from the portfolio be achieved. This constraint is equivalent to requiring that equation (7.2) not be violated.

$$\sum_{i=1}^{n} w_i E(r_i) = E(r_p) \tag{7.2}$$

The second constraint on minimizing equation (7.1) is the familiar requirement that the weights sum to 1.

$$\sum_{i=1}^{n} w_i = 1 \tag{2.11}$$

Note that short sales (negative weights) are allowed.

Equations (2.11) and (7.2) are called *Lagrangian constraints*. Combining the three equations, (7.1), (7.2), and (2.11), allows us to form a *Lagrangian objective function* for the risk-minimization problem with two constraints.

$$\text{Minimize } L = \frac{1}{2} \sum_{i=1}^{n} \sum_{j=1}^{n} w_i w_j \sigma_{ij} + \lambda \left[E(r_p) - \sum_{i=1}^{n} w_i E(r_i) \right] + \gamma \left(1 - \sum_{i=1}^{n} w_i \right) \tag{7.3}$$

The lower-case Greek letters lambda and gamma, denoted λ and γ in equation (7.3), are called *Lagrangian multipliers* because they are multiplied by the two Lagrangian constraints defined in equations (2.11) and (7.2).

The minimum-risk portfolio is found by setting the partial derivatives, denoted $\partial L / \partial w_i$, equal to zero, for all integer values of the subscript i ranging from one to n. In other words, set $\partial L / \partial w_i = 0$ for $i = 1, \ldots, n$. The partial derivatives of the two Lagrangian constraints are also set equal to zero, thus, $\partial L / \partial \lambda = 0$ and $\partial L / \partial \gamma = 0$. These $n + 2$ partial derivatives result in the following system of $n + 2$ equations.

$$\left. \begin{aligned} \frac{\partial L}{\partial w_1} &= w_1 \sigma_{11} + w_2 \sigma_{12} + \cdots + w_n \sigma_{1n} - \lambda E(r_1) - \gamma = 0 \\ \frac{\partial L}{\partial w_2} &= w_1 \sigma_{21} + w_2 \sigma_{22} + \cdots + w_n \sigma_{2n} - \lambda E(r_2) - \gamma = 0 \\ &\quad\vdots \\ \frac{\partial L}{\partial w_n} &= w_1 \sigma_{n1} + w_2 \sigma_{n2} + \cdots + w_n \sigma_{nn} - \lambda E(r_n) - \gamma = 0 \end{aligned} \right\} \tag{7.4}$$

$$\frac{\partial L}{\partial \lambda} = w_1 E(r_1) + w_2 E(r_2) + \cdots + w_n E(r_n) - E(r_p) = 0 \tag{7.5}$$

$$\frac{\partial L}{\partial \gamma} = w_1 + w_2 + \cdots + w_n - 1 = 0 \tag{7.6}$$

The last two partial derivatives above are equations (7.2) and (2.11). They were obtained by taking the partial derivatives of the Lagrangian objective function (7.3) with respect to the two Lagrangian multipliers, λ and γ, which are included to provide the two constraints that are necessary for a rational solution.

The $n + 2$ equations in equation system (7.4), (7.5), and (7.6) all happen to be linear equations. Stated differently, every weight variable in the equations has a superscript equal to one. To simplify writing out these $n + 2$ equations, the superscripts of one are not written explicitly; they are implicit.

The first n terms in the first n partial derivatives in equation system (7.4) were obtained by taking partial derivatives of the variance formula shown next with respect to each of the n weight variables.

$$\sigma_p^2 = \sum_{i=1}^{n} \sum_{j=1}^{n} w_i w_j \sigma_{ij} = \begin{pmatrix} +w_1 w_1 \sigma_{11} & +w_1 w_2 \sigma_{12} & \cdots & +w_1 w_n \sigma_{1n} \\ +w_2 w_1 \sigma_{21} & +w_2 w_2 \sigma_{22} & \cdots & +w_2 w_n \sigma_{2n} \\ \vdots & \vdots & \ddots & \vdots \\ +w_n w_1 \sigma_{n1} & +w_n w_2 \sigma_{n2} & \cdots & +w_n w_n \sigma_{nn} \end{pmatrix} \quad (2.19)$$

The preceding variance is the first term in the Lagrangian equation (7.3). The partial derivative of the variance with respect to the i-th weight variable is shown below in an expanded form.

$$\frac{\partial \sigma_p^2}{\partial w_i} = \begin{bmatrix} +w_1 \sigma_{1i} \\ +w_2 \sigma_{2i} \\ \vdots \\ +w_i \sigma_{i1} + w_i \sigma_{i2} + \cdots + 2w_i \sigma_{ii} + \cdots + w_i \sigma_{iN} \\ \vdots \\ +w_N \sigma_{Ni} \end{bmatrix} \quad (7.7)$$

The preceding expanded first partial derivative may be equivalently rewritten in more compact notation, after making an inconsequential (purely cosmetic) multiplication by one-half, as mentioned earlier.

$$\frac{\partial \sigma_p^2}{\partial w_i} = w_i \sigma_{i1} + w_i \sigma_{i2} + \cdots + w_i \sigma_{in} = 0 \quad (7.8)$$

The preceding equation differs from the n partial derivatives in equation system (7.4) because it fails to include the last two terms with the n differential equations. These last two terms (omitted here) were obtained by taking the partial derivatives of equations (7.2) and (2.11) with respect to the i-th weight variable, w_i, as the two Lagrangian constraints were encountered in differentiating the Lagrangian objective function (7.3).

Because the $(n + 2)$ differential equations in equation system (7.4), (7.5), and (7.6) are all linear equations, they can be reformulated into a matrix algebra format that is more concise. The $(n + 2)$ first-order partial derivatives are restated as *Jacobian matrix* equation (7.9).

$$\begin{bmatrix} \sigma_{11} & \sigma_{12} & \cdots & \sigma_{1n} & E(r_1) & 1 \\ \sigma_{21} & \sigma_{22} & \cdots & \sigma_{2n} & E(r_2) & 1 \\ \vdots & \vdots & \ddots & \vdots & \vdots & \vdots \\ \sigma_{n1} & \sigma_{n2} & \cdots & \sigma_{nn} & E(r_n) & 1 \\ E(r_1) & E(r_2) & \cdots & E(r_n) & 0 & 0 \\ 1 & 1 & \cdots & 1 & 0 & 0 \end{bmatrix} \begin{bmatrix} w_1 \\ w_2 \\ \vdots \\ w_n \\ -\lambda \\ -\gamma \end{bmatrix} = \begin{bmatrix} 0 \\ 0 \\ \vdots \\ 0 \\ E(r_p) \\ 1 \end{bmatrix} \quad (7.9)$$

Using matrix notation, we can equivalently rewrite equation (7.9) as follows.

$$Cx = b \tag{7.10}$$

where the coefficient matrix C is an $(n + 2)$ by $(n + 2)$ matrix, the weight vector x is an $(n + 2)$ by 1 matrix, and b is an $(n + 2)$ by 1 matrix (vector) of constants. This system may be solved in several different ways. Using matrix notation, the inverse of the coefficients matrix (C^{-1}) may be used to find the solution (weight) vector (x) as follows:

$$Cx = b$$

$$C^{-1}Cx = C^{-1}b$$

$$Ix = C^{-1}b$$

$$\Rightarrow \quad x = C^{-1}b \tag{7.11}$$

where I is an identity matrix that has dimensions of $(n + 2)$ by $(n + 2)$.[1] The solution of equation (7.11) will give the n values for the weights, $w_1, w_2, \ldots, w_n$, which minimize the variance of the portfolio with a desired expected return (constrained solution), $E(r_p)$, and two values for the Lagrangian multipliers λ and γ. The weights of the individual assets in the solution equation (7.11) will be expressed in terms of the independent variable, $E(r_p)$, because the solution for the weights in equation (7.11) is expressed as a function of $E(r_p)$. Exact mathematical expressions for the weights in terms of $E(r_p)$ will be provided later in this chapter.

EXAMPLE 7.1

Consider three securities whose expected returns and variance-covariances are given as follows:

$$\begin{bmatrix} E(r_1) \\ E(r_2) \\ E(r_3) \end{bmatrix} = \begin{pmatrix} 2.07 \\ 0.21 \\ 1.01 \end{pmatrix} \qquad \text{and}$$

$$\begin{pmatrix} \sigma_{11} & \sigma_{12} & \sigma_{13} \\ \sigma_{21} & \sigma_{22} & \sigma_{23} \\ \sigma_{31} & \sigma_{32} & \sigma_{33} \end{pmatrix} = \begin{pmatrix} 48.20 & 7.82 & -2.65 \\ 7.82 & 16.34 & 0.99 \\ -2.65 & 0.99 & 34.25 \end{pmatrix}$$

The information above is also available in Chapter 5's Table 5.5. In order to find the weights minimizing the variance of an efficient portfolio that earns $E(r_p) = 1.5$ percent, we create the following matrix equation by substituting the preceding numerical values into equation (7.9):

$$\begin{bmatrix} 48.20 & 7.82 & -2.65 & 2.07 & 1 \\ 7.82 & 16.34 & 0.99 & 0.21 & 1 \\ -2.65 & 0.99 & 34.25 & 1.01 & 1 \\ 2.07 & 0.21 & 1.01 & 0 & 0 \\ 1 & 1 & 1 & 0 & 0 \end{bmatrix} \begin{bmatrix} w_1 \\ w_2 \\ w_3 \\ -\lambda \\ -\gamma \end{bmatrix} = \begin{bmatrix} 0 \\ 0 \\ 0 \\ 1.5 \\ 1 \end{bmatrix} \tag{7.12}$$

EXAMPLE 7.1 (*Continued*)

Equation (7.12) is identical to equation (7.9); it is merely the specific case of equation (7.9) that exists when $n = 3$. Equation (7.12) is solved by evaluating the following matrix equation:

$$x = \begin{bmatrix} w_1 \\ w_2 \\ w_3 \\ -\lambda \\ -\gamma \end{bmatrix} = \begin{bmatrix} 48.20 & 7.82 & -2.65 & 2.07 & 1 \\ 7.82 & 16.34 & 0.99 & 0.21 & 1 \\ -2.65 & 0.99 & 34.25 & 1.01 & 1 \\ 2.07 & 0.21 & 1.01 & 0 & 0 \\ 1 & 1 & 1 & 0 & 0 \end{bmatrix}^{-1} \begin{bmatrix} 0 \\ 0 \\ 0 \\ 1.5 \\ 1 \end{bmatrix} \qquad (7.13)$$

$$= \begin{bmatrix} 0.5094 \\ 0.0625 \\ 0.4281 \\ -9.9350 \\ -3.3416 \end{bmatrix}$$

The weights that minimize the variance of the portfolio whose expected return is constrained to be 1.5 percent are $w_1 = 0.5094$, $w_2 = 0.0625$, and $w_3 = 0.4281$, as shown in the top portion of the vector above. Not surprisingly, the portfolio's constrained expected return of 1.5 percent is what the portfolio is attained in equation (7.2a):

$$E(r_p) = w_1 E(r_1) + w_2 E(r_2) + w_3 E(r_3)$$

$$= (0.5094)(2.07\%) + (0.0625)(0.21\%) + (0.4281)(1.01\%)$$

$$= 1.5\% \qquad (7.2a)$$

The standard deviation of this efficient portfolio is $\sigma_p = \sqrt{18.244} = 4.27\%$, as shown below.

$$\sigma_p^2 = w_1^2 \sigma_1^2 + w_2^2 \sigma_2^2 + w_3^2 \sigma_3^2 + 2w_1 w_2 \sigma_{12} + 2w_1 w_3 \sigma_{13} + 2w_2 w_3 \sigma_{23}$$

$$= (0.5094)^2 (48.20) + (0.0625)^2 (16.34) + (0.4281)^2 (34.25)$$

$$+ 2(0.5094)(0.0625)(7.82) + 2(0.5094)(0.4281)(-2.65)$$

$$+ 2(0.0625)(0.4281)(0.99)$$

$$= 18.244$$

Thus, $\sigma_p = \sqrt{18.244} = 4.27\%$.

For any desired value of the expected return $E(r_p)$ (1.5% in this example), equation (7.13) gives the weights of the minimum-variance portfolio (MVP). The weights of the portfolios in the efficient set are generated by varying the target expected return $E(r_p)$ and evaluating the values of the weights w_i's that result.

7.1.2   Formulating with Concise Matrix Notation

This section solves the same portfolio problem that was solved in Section 7.1.1, except that a more specific mathematical expression for the optimal weights is derived in this section by using some vector and matrix differentiation.

To begin, we restate the objective function and the two constraints of equations (7.1), (7.2), and (2.10) in vector and matrix notation. A boldface letter or number indicates a vector or matrix. The two constraints of equations (7.2) and (2.10) can be rewritten as follows;

$$\sum_{i=1}^{n} w_i E\left(r_i\right) = E(r_p) \qquad \Rightarrow \qquad \boldsymbol{w}'\boldsymbol{E} = E(r_p) \tag{7.2a}$$

$$\sum_{i=1}^{n} w_i = 1 \qquad \Rightarrow \qquad \boldsymbol{w}'\boldsymbol{1} = 1 \tag{2.11a}$$

where $\boldsymbol{w}' = \left(w_1, w_2, \dots, w_n\right)$ is the weight vector of n assets, $\boldsymbol{E}' = \left[E\left(r_1\right), E\left(r_2\right), \dots, E\left(r_n\right)\right]$ is the expected return vector, and $\boldsymbol{1}' = (1, 1, \dots, 1)$ is the n-vector of ones. The objective function can be transformed as follows:

$$\text{Minimize } \sigma_p^2 = \sum_{i=1}^{n} \sum_{j=1}^{n} w_i w_j \sigma_{ij} \qquad \Rightarrow \qquad \text{Minimize } \sigma_p^2 = \boldsymbol{w}'\boldsymbol{\Sigma}\boldsymbol{w} \tag{7.1a}$$

where $\boldsymbol{\Sigma}$ is the $(n \times n)$ variance-covariance matrix.

The problem formulation, using matrix notation, is therefore

$$\text{Minimize } L = \frac{1}{2}\boldsymbol{w}'\boldsymbol{\Sigma}\boldsymbol{w} \tag{7.1a}$$

$$\text{subject to } \boldsymbol{w}'\boldsymbol{E} = E(r_p). \tag{7.2a}$$

$$\boldsymbol{w}'\boldsymbol{1} = 1 \tag{2.11a}$$

As mentioned previously, the constant 1/2 is multiplied in equation (7.1a) only for computational and writing simplicity.

Because the constraints are equalities, we use the Lagrangian multipliers and form the following optimization;

$$\text{Minimize } L = \frac{1}{2}\boldsymbol{w}'\boldsymbol{\Sigma}\boldsymbol{w} + \lambda\left[E(r_p) - \boldsymbol{w}'\boldsymbol{E}\right] + \gamma\left(1 - \boldsymbol{w}'\boldsymbol{1}\right) \tag{7.3a}$$

where λ and γ are Lagrangian multipliers. Equation (7.3a) is a matrix notation restatement of equation (7.3). First-order conditions for the solution to this problem require that the partial derivatives of L with respect to the three unknown variables, $\boldsymbol{w}$, λ, and γ, be set equal to zero.[2] That is,

$$\frac{\partial L}{\partial \boldsymbol{w}} = \boldsymbol{\Sigma}\boldsymbol{w} - \lambda\boldsymbol{E} - \gamma\boldsymbol{1} = 0 \tag{7.4a}$$

$$\frac{\partial L}{\partial \lambda} = E(r_p) - \boldsymbol{w}'\boldsymbol{E} = 0 \tag{7.5a}$$

$$\frac{\partial L}{\partial \gamma} = 1 - \boldsymbol{w}'\boldsymbol{1} = 0 \tag{7.6a}$$

where $\mathbf{0}$ is the *n*-vector of zeros. If the covariance matrix, $\boldsymbol{\Sigma}$, conforms to certain plausible assumptions (that are mathematically referred to as a positive definite covariance matrix), the first-order conditions are necessary and sufficient for a global optimum.[3] Explanations for vector and matrix differentiation may be found in a mathematical appendix at the end of this book.

Using equation (7.4a), we have

$$w = \lambda \boldsymbol{\Sigma}^{-1} E + \gamma \boldsymbol{\Sigma}^{-1} \mathbf{1} \qquad (7.4b)$$

Combining equations (7.5a) and (7.4b) yields

$$E(r_p) = \mathbf{w}' E = E' \mathbf{w} = \lambda \left(E' \boldsymbol{\Sigma}^{-1} E \right) + \gamma \left(E' \boldsymbol{\Sigma}^{-1} \mathbf{1} \right) \qquad (7.5b)$$

and combining equations (7.6a) and (7.4b) yields

$$1 = \mathbf{w}' \mathbf{1} = \mathbf{1}' \mathbf{w} = \lambda \left(\mathbf{1}' \boldsymbol{\Sigma}^{-1} E \right) + \gamma \left(\mathbf{1}' \boldsymbol{\Sigma}^{-1} \mathbf{1} \right) \qquad (7.6b)$$

Solving the last two equations (7.5b) and (7.6b) with respect to λ and γ yields

$$\lambda = \frac{C\, E(r_p) - A}{D} \qquad (7.14)$$

$$\gamma = \frac{B - A\, E(r_p)}{D} \qquad (7.15)$$

where

$$A = \mathbf{1}' \boldsymbol{\Sigma}^{-1} E \qquad\qquad B = E' \boldsymbol{\Sigma}^{-1} E$$

$$C = \mathbf{1}' \boldsymbol{\Sigma}^{-1} \mathbf{1} \qquad\qquad D = BC - A^2 \qquad (7.16)$$

The inverse of a positive definite matrix is also a positive definite matrix, therefore $B > 0$ and $C > 0$.[4] By the Cauchy-Schwarz inequality (or the correlation inequality)[5], $BC > A^2$. Thus, $D > 0$. Plugging equations (7.14) and (7.15) into equation (7.4b) gives us the optimal weights for the mean-variance efficient portfolios, or efficient frontier portfolios, as

$$w_p = \left[\frac{C\, E(r_p) - A}{D} \right] \boldsymbol{\Sigma}^{-1} E + \left[\frac{B - A\, E(r_p)}{D} \right] \boldsymbol{\Sigma}^{-1} \mathbf{1}$$

$$= \mathbf{g} + \mathbf{h}\, E(r_p) \qquad (7.17)$$

where

$$\mathbf{g} = \frac{1}{D} \left(B \boldsymbol{\Sigma}^{-1} \mathbf{1} - A \boldsymbol{\Sigma}^{-1} E \right) \qquad (7.18)$$

$$\mathbf{h} = \frac{1}{D} \left(C \boldsymbol{\Sigma}^{-1} E - A \boldsymbol{\Sigma}^{-1} \mathbf{1} \right) \qquad (7.19)$$

Thus, the optimal weights of the mean-variance efficient portfolios are represented as a linear function of the given level of the expected return of the portfolio,

$E(r_p)$, because g and h are fixed constants. Note that the efficient portfolio represented by equation (7.17) has the expected return equal to $E(r_p)$; that is, $w_p'E = E(r_p)$. Any efficient portfolio can be represented by equation (7.17), and any portfolio that can be represented by equation (7.17) is an efficient portfolio. The variance of the efficient portfolio p is computed as $\sigma_p^2 = w_p' \Sigma \, w_p$.

EXAMPLE 7.2

Consider three securities: 1, 2, and 3. Their expected returns and covariance matrix are:

$$E = \begin{bmatrix} E(r_1) \\ E(r_2) \\ E(r_3) \end{bmatrix} = \begin{pmatrix} 2.07 \\ 0.21 \\ 1.10 \end{pmatrix} \text{ and } \Sigma = \begin{pmatrix} \sigma_{11} & \sigma_{12} & \sigma_{13} \\ \sigma_{21} & \sigma_{22} & \sigma_{23} \\ \sigma_{31} & \sigma_{32} & \sigma_{33} \end{pmatrix} = \begin{pmatrix} 48.20 & 7.82 & -2.65 \\ 7.82 & 16.34 & 0.99 \\ -2.65 & 0.99 & 34.25 \end{pmatrix}$$

We will find an efficient portfolio whose expected return is 1.5 percent for these three securities. In Figure 7.1, portfolio p has the smallest variance among portfolios earning 1.5 percent return.

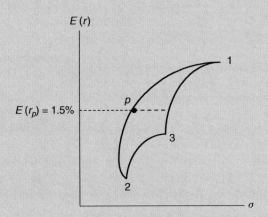

FIGURE 7.1 Identifying an Efficient Portfolio with $E(r_p) = 1.5\%$

To find the optimal values of the three weights for the efficient portfolio p in equation (7.17), we first compute the values of A, B, C, and D in equation (7.16).

$$A = 1'\Sigma^{-1}E = \begin{pmatrix} 1 & 1 & 1 \end{pmatrix} \begin{pmatrix} 48.20 & 7.82 & -2.65 \\ 7.82 & 16.34 & 0.99 \\ -2.65 & 0.99 & 34.25 \end{pmatrix}^{-1} \begin{pmatrix} 2.07 \\ 0.21 \\ 1.10 \end{pmatrix} = 0.0686$$

$$B = E'\Sigma^{-1}E = \begin{pmatrix} 2.07 & 0.21 & 1.01 \end{pmatrix} \begin{pmatrix} 48.20 & 7.82 & -2.65 \\ 7.82 & 16.34 & 0.99 \\ -2.65 & 0.99 & 34.25 \end{pmatrix}^{-1} \begin{pmatrix} 2.07 \\ 0.21 \\ 1.10 \end{pmatrix} = 0.1279$$

EXAMPLE 7.2 (*Continued*)

$$C = \mathbf{1}' \boldsymbol{\Sigma}^{-1} \mathbf{1} = \begin{pmatrix} 1 & 1 & 1 \end{pmatrix} \begin{pmatrix} 48.20 & 7.82 & -2.65 \\ 7.82 & 16.34 & 0.99 \\ -2.65 & 0.99 & 34.25 \end{pmatrix}^{-1} \begin{pmatrix} 1 \\ 1 \\ 1 \end{pmatrix}$$

$$= 0.0954$$

$$D = BC - A^2 = (0.1279)(0.0954) - (0.0686)^2$$

$$= 0.0075$$

Then, we compute the values of g and h in equations (7.18) and (7.19).

$$g = \frac{1}{D}\left(B\boldsymbol{\Sigma}^{-1}\mathbf{1} - A\boldsymbol{\Sigma}^{-1}E\right) = \begin{pmatrix} -0.1922 \\ 1.0078 \\ 0.1845 \end{pmatrix} \qquad (7.18a)$$

$$h = \frac{1}{D}\left(C\boldsymbol{\Sigma}^{-1}E - A\boldsymbol{\Sigma}^{-1}\mathbf{1}\right) = \begin{pmatrix} 0.4678 \\ -0.6302 \\ 0.1624 \end{pmatrix} \qquad (7.19a)$$

Finally, we compute the optimal weights of the three securities for the efficient portfolio earning 1.5 percent return by using equation (7.17), as shown in equation (7.20).

$$w_p = g + h\,E(r_p) = \begin{pmatrix} -0.1922 \\ 1.0078 \\ 0.1845 \end{pmatrix} + \begin{pmatrix} 0.4678 \\ -0.6302 \\ 0.1624 \end{pmatrix} \times (1.5)$$

$$= \begin{pmatrix} 0.5094 \\ 0.0625 \\ 0.4281 \end{pmatrix} \qquad (7.20)$$

These optimal weights of the three assets in equation (7.20) are the same as in Example 7.1. The minimum variance at the given level of the expected return equal to 1.5 percent is computed with these optimal weights as

$$\sigma_p^2 = w_p' \,\boldsymbol{\Sigma}\, w_p$$

$$= \begin{pmatrix} 0.5094 & 0.0625 & 0.4281 \end{pmatrix} \begin{pmatrix} 48.20 & 7.82 & -2.65 \\ 7.82 & 16.34 & 0.99 \\ -2.65 & 0.99 & 34.25 \end{pmatrix} \begin{pmatrix} 0.5094 \\ 0.0625 \\ 0.4281 \end{pmatrix}$$

$$= 18.244$$

Thus, the standard deviation of the efficient portfolio is

$$\sigma_p = \sqrt{18.244} = 4.27\%$$

MEAN-VARIANCE PORTFOLIO ANALYSIS

EXAMPLE 7.3

If the target expected return changes from 1.5 percent to 2.0 percent using the same securities in Examples 7.1 and 7.2, we can easily obtain the optimal weights for another efficient portfolio q by using equation (7.20) again. Note that g and h are fixed and independent of the given target expected return. Thus, we simply replace the target expected return 1.5 percent in equation (7.20) with 2.0 percent:

$$w_q = g + h\, E\left(r_q\right) = \begin{pmatrix} -0.1922 \\ 1.0078 \\ 0.1845 \end{pmatrix} + \begin{pmatrix} 0.4678 \\ -0.6302 \\ 0.1624 \end{pmatrix} \times (2.0) = \begin{pmatrix} 0.7433 \\ -0.2526 \\ 0.5093 \end{pmatrix}$$

And the minimum variance at a given level of the expected return equal to 2.0 percent is computed as

$$
\begin{aligned}
\sigma_q^2 &= w_q'\, \Sigma\, w_q \\
&= (0.7433 \;\; -0.2526 \;\; 0.5093) \begin{pmatrix} 48.20 & 7.82 & -2.65 \\ 7.82 & 16.34 & 0.99 \\ -2.65 & 0.99 & 34.25 \end{pmatrix} \begin{pmatrix} 0.7433 \\ -0.2526 \\ 0.5093 \end{pmatrix} \\
&= 31.360
\end{aligned}
$$

Thus, the standard deviation of the efficient portfolio is

$$\sigma_q = \sqrt{31.360} = 5.60\%$$

This solution technique can be repeated iteratively using different values for the desired expected return constraint and the risk-return statistics for all the efficient portfolios can be computed. Figure 7.2 illustrates the two efficient portfolios p and q identified in Examples 7.2 and 7.3.

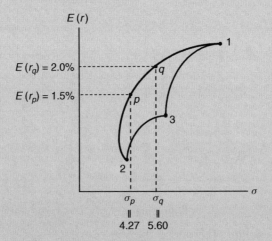

FIGURE 7.2 Two Efficient Portfolios with No Risk-free Asset

As seen in Examples 7.2 and 7.3, when the expected return of an efficient portfolio changes, its variance also changes in a functional way. In other words, a functional relationship between the expected return, $E(r_p)$, and variance, σ_p^2, of an efficient portfolio can be obtained. The equation representing the functional relationship between $E(r_p)$ and σ_p for efficient portfolios is derived in this chapter's Appendix A7.1. This equation represents the efficient frontier depicted in Figure 6.5 of Chapter 6 with no risk-free asset. A function to explain the covariance between an efficient portfolio and any other portfolio is also derived in Appendix A7.2.

7.1.3 The Two-Fund Separation Theorem

All portfolios on the mean-variance efficient frontier can be formed as a linear combination of any two portfolios (or funds) on the efficient frontier. Let portfolios p_1 and p_2 be on the efficient frontier $\overline{EF}$ in Figure 6.5 of Chapter 6 (or $\overline{BD}$ in Figure A7.1 of the appendix to this chapter), assuming the expected returns on these two portfolios are not equal, $E\left(r_{p_1}\right) \neq E\left(r_{p_1}\right)$. Let a portfolio formed by these two efficient portfolios be denoted q. Then, there exists a constant, α, such that

$$E\left(r_q\right) = \alpha\, E\left(r_{p_1}\right) + (1 - \alpha)\, E\left(r_{p_2}\right) \tag{7.21}$$

The investment weight for portfolio q is determined as

$$w_q = \alpha\, w_{p_1} + (1 - \alpha)\, w_{p_2} \tag{7.22}$$

Because the optimal weight vector for an efficient portfolio is expressed as equation (7.17),

$$w_q = \alpha\, \left[g + h\, E\left(r_{p_1}\right)\right] + (1 - \alpha) \left[g + h\, E\left(r_{p_2}\right)\right] \tag{7.23}$$

Rearranging equation (7.23) yields

$$w_q = g + h\, \left[\alpha\, E\left(r_{p_1}\right) + (1 - \alpha)\, E\left(r_{p_2}\right)\right]$$
$$= g + h\, E\left(r_q\right) \tag{7.24}$$

As seen in equation (7.24), portfolio q is also represented in the form of equation (7.17). Thus, portfolio q is an efficient portfolio.

We have shown that a portfolio formed by a linear combination of two efficient portfolios is also an efficient portfolio. In other words, if any two portfolios on the efficient frontier (i.e., any two points on the efficient frontier $\overline{EF}$ in Figure 6.5 of Chapter 6) are given, the entire efficient frontier can be generated by a linear combination of these two portfolios. If an investor prefers an efficient portfolio, the investor can simply hold a linear combination of two efficient portfolios or mutual funds. In that case, there exists a portfolio (or a linear combination of two efficient portfolios) the investor desires at least as much as the original portfolio. This phenomenon is called the *two-fund separation*.

Some important implications arise from the property of the weights for an efficient portfolio represented in equation (7.22). First, the proportion invested in any particular asset changes monotonically as one moves up the efficient frontier from the vertex. This can be seen by noting that α changes monotonically as one moves up the efficient frontier and that equation (7.22) can be rewritten as $w_{p_2} + \alpha(w_{p_1} - w_{p_2})$. Thus, the weights will change monotonically with changes in α. Second, if security i has a nonzero weight in two efficient portfolios, then it will have a nonzero weight in all efficient portfolios except, at most, one efficient portfolio. Letting w_{i1} and w_{i2} denote the weight of security i in portfolios 1 and 2, respectively, this can be seen by noting that if $w_{i2} + \alpha\left(w_{i1} - w_{i2}\right)$ is nonzero for at least one value of α, then it is nonzero for all values except, at most, for one efficient portfolio when $\alpha = -w_{i2}/\left(w_{i1} - w_{i2}\right)$ and $w_1 \neq w_{i2k}$. Third, if $w_{i1} = w_{i2}$, then the proportion for security i is the same everywhere on the efficient frontier because $w_{i2} + \alpha(w_{i1} - w_{i2})$ = nonzero constant.[6] Fourth, it follows that it is possible for no efficient portfolios to exist that have $w > 0$ (that is, all positive weights).

7.1.4   Caveat about Negative Weights

The weights of the efficient portfolio can be negative. Such solutions are not always realistic. Some large public portfolios and some mutual funds are legally forbidden to use leverage. Also, securities having the same risk and return as the security with the negative weight may not be easy to create and issue. Furthermore, because of U.S. securities regulations, a mutual fund manager is required to hold no more than five percent of the portfolio in any given security.

When negative weights are not permitted, quadratic programming (QP) should be used to optimize equations (7.1a), (7.2a), and (2.11a) by adding nonnegative constraints and upper bounds of five percent on any security entering the optimization system. Another way to optimize without using QP is to continue the optimization just described to the point where it begins to produce negative weights. At the point where the weight for an asset reaches zero (before becoming negative), stop the analysis. Remove the asset in the optimization system of equations (7.1a), (7.2a), and (2.11a) that corresponds to the security with the zero weight. The solution now has one less asset from which to select. Then, solve the new optimization system of equations for a new set of optimal weights. This set of efficient portfolios will intersect the original efficient set where the eliminated asset's weight went to zero. Thus, the analysis proceeds. Each time another asset's weight reaches zero, that asset is eliminated, and the new smaller optimization system is solved. Of course, this recommended process provides an approximate solution, not an exact solution.

7.2   EFFICIENT PORTFOLIOS WITH A RISK-FREE ASSET

We now introduce the risk-free asset to the opportunity set formed with n risky assets. Thus, there are $n + 1$ candidate assets available to form efficient portfolios. Let w equal an n-vector of investment weights only for the n risky assets. In order to find optimal weights for the efficient portfolios when the riskless asset exists, we formulate the following objective statement.

$$\text{Minimize} \quad L = \frac{1}{2}w'\Sigma w \tag{7.25}$$

$$\text{subject to} \quad w'E + w_f r_f = E(r_p) \tag{7.26}$$

where L represents a Lagrangian objective function, and $w_f = 1 - w'\mathbf{1}$ is the weight for the risk-free asset. Note that the variance of the portfolio formed from $n + 1$ assets (n risky assets plus the risk-free asset) is equal to the variance of the portfolio formed from n risky assets only, because

$$\sigma_p^2 = w'\, \Sigma\, w + w_f \sigma_f^2 + 2 w_f w' \sigma_{1f} = w'\, \Sigma\, w \qquad (7.27)$$

where σ_f^2 is the variance of the risk-free rate of return which equals zero, and σ_{1f} is the n-covariance vector between n risky assets and the risk-free asset which also equals zero. That is, although the risk-free asset is added to a set of risky assets, there is no change in the portfolio's variance. As mentioned previously, the only reasons that a constant 1/2 is multiplied in equation (7.25) is for computation convenience and cosmetic reasons.

Because the constraint is an equality, we use the Lagrangian multiplier and form the following optimization objective statement.

$$\text{Minimize} \quad L = \frac{1}{2} w'\, \Sigma\, w + \lambda \left[E(r_p) - w'E - \left(1 - w'\mathbf{1}\right) r_f \right] \qquad (7.28)$$

where λ is a Lagrangian multiplier. First-order conditions for the solution to this problem require that the partial derivatives of L with respect to the two unknowns w and λ be set equal to zero. That is,

$$\frac{\partial L}{\partial w} = \Sigma\, w - \lambda \left(E - r_f\, \mathbf{1} \right) = 0 \qquad (7.29)$$

$$\frac{\partial L}{\partial \lambda} = E(r_p) - w'E - \left(1 - w'\mathbf{1}\right) r_f = 0 \qquad (7.30)$$

Because Σ is a positive definite covariance matrix, the first-order conditions are necessary and sufficient for a global optimum. From equations (7.29) and (7.30), we have

$$w = \lambda\, \Sigma^{-1} \left(E - r_f \mathbf{1} \right) \qquad (7.29a)$$

$$E(r_p) = r_f + w' \left(E - r_f \mathbf{1} \right) \qquad (7.30a)$$

Substituting equation (7.29a) into equation (7.30a) yields

$$E(r_p) = r_f + \lambda \left(E - r_f \mathbf{1} \right)' \Sigma^{-1} \left(E - r_f \mathbf{1} \right) \qquad (7.31)$$

From equation (7.31), the Lagrangian multiplier is

$$\lambda = \frac{\left[E(r_p) - r_f \right]}{H} \qquad (7.32)$$

where

$$H = \left(E - r_f \mathbf{1} \right)' \Sigma^{-1} \left(E - r_f \mathbf{1} \right)$$
$$= B - 2 r_f A + r_f^2 C \qquad (7.33)$$

Note that because Σ^{-1} is positive definite, $H > 0$. Therefore, by plugging equation (7.32) into equation (7.29a), we obtain the following optimal weight n-vector of the risky assets for the efficient portfolio

$$w_p = \Sigma^{-1}(E - r_f 1)\left[\frac{E(r_p) - r_f}{H}\right] \qquad (7.34)$$

Thus, the weight of the riskless asset for the efficient portfolio is

$$w_f = 1 - w_p' 1 \qquad (7.35)$$

Like the previous case using the risky assets only, the optimal weights for the mean-variance efficient portfolios in equation (7.34) can also be represented as a linear function of the given level of the expected return of the portfolio, $E(r_p)$. That is,

$$w_p = u + v\,E(r_p) \qquad (7.36)$$

where

$$u = -\Sigma^{-1}(E - r_f 1)\left(\frac{r_f}{H}\right) \qquad (7.37)$$

and

$$v = \Sigma^{-1}(E - r_f 1)\left(\frac{1}{H}\right) \qquad (7.38)$$

Note that u and v are fixed. Thus, the two-fund separation theorem mentioned in Section 7.1.3 of this chapter also holds in the case that the risk-free asset is introduced.

EXAMPLE 7.4

As in Example 7.2 of this chapter, an investor looks for an efficient portfolio with a target expected return of 1.5 percent. This investor wants to form a portfolio by using the three securities used in Example 7.2 plus the risk-free asset with $r_f = 0.18\%$. What are the optimal weights of the three risky assets and the risk-free asset for the efficient portfolio p?

The optimal weights for the risky assets are given in equation (7.34). In order to use this equation, we have to first compute the value of H.

$$H = B - 2r_f A + r_f^2 C = 0.1279 - 2(0.18)(0.0686) + (0.18)^2(0.0954)$$

$$= 0.1063$$

The optimal weights for the efficient portfolio are

$$w_p = \begin{pmatrix} w_1 \\ w_2 \\ w_3 \end{pmatrix} = \begin{pmatrix} 48.20 & 7.82 & -2.65 \\ 7.82 & 16.34 & 0.99 \\ -2.65 & 0.99 & 34.25 \end{pmatrix}^{-1} \begin{pmatrix} 2.07 - 0.18 \\ 0.21 - 0.18 \\ 1.01 - 0.18 \end{pmatrix} \left(\frac{1.5 - 0.18}{0.1063}\right)$$

EXAMPLE 7.4 (*Continued*)

$$= \begin{pmatrix} 0.5486 \\ -0.2610 \\ 0.3509 \end{pmatrix}$$

and the weight for the risk-free asset is $w_f = 1 - \sum_{i=1}^{3} w_i = 1 - (0.5486 - 0.2610 + 0.3509) = 0.3616$. In order to construct the efficient portfolio, the investor buys two long positions equal to portfolio weights of 54.86 percent in security 1 and 35.09 percent in security 3, and also sells short an amount equal to a portfolio weight of 26.10 percent in security 2. Furthermore, this investor should buy one more long position with a portfolio weight of 36.16 percent in the risk-free asset (that is, lend 36.16% of the net investment at the risk-free rate). The variance of this efficient portfolio is

$$\sigma_p^2 = w_p' \Sigma w_p$$
$$= (0.5486 \quad -0.2610 \quad 0.3509) \begin{pmatrix} 48.20 & 7.82 & -2.65 \\ 7.82 & 16.34 & 0.99 \\ -2.65 & 0.99 & 34.25 \end{pmatrix} \begin{pmatrix} 0.5486 \\ -0.2610 \\ 0.3509 \end{pmatrix}$$
$$= 16.389, \quad \text{or}$$
$$\sigma_p = 4.05$$

Note again that the addition of the risk-free asset to the portfolio consisting of risky assets does not change portfolio variance.

Figure 7.3 illustrates the efficient portfolio p with standard deviation of 4.05 percent which locates on the efficient frontier (straight line $\overline{r_f S}$). This efficient portfolio (with the risk-free asset) is compared with portfolio p' which is the efficient portfolio obtained with no risk-free asset in Example 7.2. By introducing the risk-free asset, the investor earns the same expected return of 1.5 percent but reduces the standard deviation (risk) from $\sigma_p = 4.27\%$ to $\sigma_p = 4.05\%$.

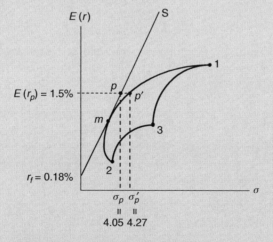

FIGURE 7.3 An Efficient Portfolio with the Risk-free Asset

7.3   IDENTIFYING THE TANGENCY PORTFOLIO

The tangency portfolio is the portfolio of risky assets on the efficient frontier at the point where the capital market line (CML) is tangent to the efficiency frontier. Linear combinations of the tangency portfolio and the risk-free asset compose the CML. The tangency portfolio, m, is illustrated in Figure (6.10) of Chapter 6. The location of the tangency portfolio is changed as the level of the risk-free interest rate changes. In this section, we describe a simple method of identifying the weights for the tangency portfolio. A detailed method is also described in Appendix A7.2.

The weights for the tangency portfolio can be obtained simply by using equation (7.29). Dividing all terms of equation (7.29) by the constant λ yields

$$\Sigma\left(\frac{w}{\lambda}\right) - \left(E - r_f\,\mathbf{1}\right) = 0 \tag{7.39}$$

If we let $z = w/\lambda$, we can rewrite equation (7.39) as

$$\Sigma\,z = \left(E - r_f\,\mathbf{1}\right) \tag{7.40}$$

More specifically, when there are three risky assets ($n = 3$), we have the following (3×3) simultaneous equations with three unknown variables, z_1, z_2, and z_3.

$$\sigma_{11}z_1 + \sigma_{12}z_2 + \sigma_{13}z_3 = E(r_1) - r_f$$

$$\sigma_{21}z_1 + \sigma_{22}z_2 + \sigma_{23}z_3 = E(r_2) - r_f$$

$$\sigma_{31}z_1 + \sigma_{32}z_2 + \sigma_{33}z_3 = E(r_3) - r_f$$

The solution of the above simultaneous equations is obtained from

$$z = \Sigma^{-1}\left(E - r_f\mathbf{1}\right) \tag{7.41}$$

The actual weights w for the tangency portfolio can be obtained by normalizing the transformed weights z. In general,

$$w_i = \frac{z_i}{\sum_{j=1}^{n} z_j} \tag{7.42}$$

Note that the tangency portfolio is composed of risky assets only. The next example shows how to obtain the optimal weights for the efficient portfolio described in Example 7.4.

EXAMPLE 7.5

As in Example 7.2, suppose that we have three risky securities: 1, 2, and 3. Their expected return and covariance matrix are:

$$E = \begin{bmatrix} E(r_1) \\ E(r_2) \\ E(r_3) \end{bmatrix} = \begin{pmatrix} 2.07 \\ 0.21 \\ 1.10 \end{pmatrix} \text{ and } \Sigma = \begin{pmatrix} \sigma_{11} & \sigma_{12} & \sigma_{13} \\ \sigma_{21} & \sigma_{22} & \sigma_{23} \\ \sigma_{31} & \sigma_{32} & \sigma_{33} \end{pmatrix} = \begin{pmatrix} 48.20 & 7.82 & -2.65 \\ 7.82 & 16.34 & 0.99 \\ -2.65 & 0.99 & 34.25 \end{pmatrix}$$

EXAMPLE 7.5 (*Continued*)

And suppose that the risk-free rate of return is $r_f = 0.18\%$. In this case, the simultaneous equations for the weights of the tangency portfolio m are

$$48.20\, z_1 + 7.82\, z_2 - 2.65 z_3 = 2.07 - 0.18$$

$$7.82\, z_1 + 16.34\, z_2 + 0.99\, z_3 = 0.21 - 0.18$$

$$-2.65\, z_1 + 0.99\, z_2 + 34.25\, z_3 = 1.10 - 0.18$$

The solution of the preceding equations is

$$z = \begin{pmatrix} z_1 \\ z_2 \\ z_3 \end{pmatrix} = \begin{pmatrix} 48.20 & 7.82 & -2.65 \\ 7.82 & 16.34 & 0.99 \\ -2.65 & 0.99 & 34.25 \end{pmatrix}^{-1} \begin{pmatrix} 2.07 - 0.18 \\ 0.21 - 0.18 \\ 1.10 - 0.18 \end{pmatrix} = \begin{pmatrix} 0.0442 \\ -0.0210 \\ 0.0283 \end{pmatrix}$$

Thus, the actual weights of the three assets for the tangency portfolio m are

$$w_1 = \frac{z_1}{z_1 + z_2 + z_3} = \frac{0.0442}{0.0442 - 0.0210 + 0.0283} = 0.859$$

$$w_2 = \frac{z_2}{z_1 + z_2 + z_3} = \frac{-0.0210}{0.0442 - 0.0210 + 0.0283} = -0.409$$

$$w_3 = \frac{z_3}{z_1 + z_2 + z_3} = \frac{0.0283}{0.0442 - 0.0210 + 0.0283} = 0.550$$

Based on these actual weights, we compute the expected return and variance of the tangency portfolio. They are $E(r_m) = 2.248\%$ and $\sigma_m^2 = 40.215$.

EXAMPLE 7.6

Continuing from Example 7.5, if an investor looks for an efficient portfolio with a target expected return of 1.5 percent, what are the optimal weights of the three risky assets and the risk-free asset for the efficient portfolio p?

Because the efficient portfolio p is located on the tangency ray passing through the tangency portfolio m and the risk-free asset, it is made by a linear combination of the tangency portfolio m and the risk-free asset. We let w_m be the weight for the tangency portfolio. Then, we have

$$E(r_p) = w_m E(r_m) + (1 - w_m) r_f \tag{7.43}$$

$$\Rightarrow \quad 1.5\% = w_m (2.248\%) + (1 - w_m)(0.18\%)$$

$$\Rightarrow \quad w_m = 0.6383$$

(*Continued*)

EXAMPLE 7.6 (*Continued*)

and the weight for the risk-free asset is $w_f = 1 - 0.6383 = 0.3617$. Therefore, the optimal weights of the three risky assets for the efficient portfolio p can be obtained by allocating w_m into the three assets according to the weights for the tangency portfolio that are obtained in Example 7.5. That is,

$$w_1 = 0.6383 \, (0.859) = 0.5483$$

$$w_2 = 0.6383 \, (-0.409) = -0.2611$$

$$w_3 = 0.6383 \, (0.550) = 0.3511$$

These answers are exactly the same as those directly obtained from equation (7.34) in Example 7.4. Note that a small amount of difference between these answers and those in Example 7.4 is due to rounding. For a different target expected return, the optimal weights for the efficient portfolio can be similarly obtained through equation (7.43).

7.4 SUMMARY AND CONCLUSIONS

This chapter provided a mathematical solution for efficient portfolios for the cases where a risk-free asset is considered and not considered. Whereas Chapter 6 focuses on the conceptual explanations for diversification and efficient portfolios, this chapter focuses on providing the mathematical solution for efficient portfolios. The appendix to this chapter provides the mathematical equation for the efficient frontier and the weights for some key portfolios in the mean-variance portfolio analysis such as the optimal risky portfolio and the global minimum variance portfolio.

APPENDIX: MATHEMATICAL DERIVATION OF THE EFFICIENT FRONTIER

This appendix derives an equation for the efficient frontier.

A7.1 No Risk-Free Asset

The equation for the efficient frontier can be derived with and without the risk-free asset. The case that has no risk-free asset is derived first.

A. Deriving the Equation for the Efficient Frontier   The efficient frontier is depicted in Figure 6.5 of Chapter 6 when there is no risk-free asset. The mathematical equation for the efficient frontier $\overline{EF}$ in Figure 6.5 can be derived by constructing a mathematical relationship between $E(r_p)$ and σ_p.

Let w_p denote the optimal weight vector for a portfolio p located on the efficient frontier $\overline{EF}$. By using equation (7. 17), the variance of the portfolio can be expressed as

$$\sigma_p^2 = w_p' \, \Sigma \, w_p$$

$$= \left[g + h \, E(r_p) \right]' \Sigma \left[g + h \, E(r_p) \right] \tag{A7.1}$$

Rearranging equation (A7.1) by using the definition of the vectors **g** and **h** from equations (7.18) and (7.19) yields

$$\sigma_p^2 = \frac{C}{D}\left[E(r_p) - \frac{A}{C}\right]^2 + \frac{1}{C} \tag{A7.2}$$

Equation (A7.2) is the equation of a parabola in the mean-variance space or a hyperbola in the mean-standard deviation with vertex $\left[\sigma_p, E(r_p)\right] = \left(\frac{1}{\sqrt{C}}, \frac{A}{C}\right)$. The variance of the portfolio in equation (A7.2) will be minimized when $E(r_p) = A/C$. Thus, the variance of the global minimum variance portfolio (global MVP) is $1/C$, and its expected return is A/C. The efficient frontier represented by equation (A7.2) is depicted on $\left[\sigma_p, E(r_p)\right]$ space in Figure A7.1. Note that this minimum variance boundary, denoted $\overline{BD}$, is unbounded from both above and below; that is, for any level of expected return, a portfolio located on $\overline{BD}$ can be found. The parabola represented in equation (A7.2) is parallel to the horizontal axis because it has a term of the squared y-variable, $\left[E(r_p)\right]^2$, and is without a term of the squared x-variable, $\left(\sigma_p^2\right)^2$. Furthermore, it opens to the right because the coefficient term is positive, $C/D > 0$. The location of the vertex is important because the efficient frontier is simply the upper half of the parabola where the dividing point is the vertex.

In general, hyperbolas have two asymptotes (the dotted lines in Figure A7.1), both of which pass through a point called the center of the hyperbola. Given the hyperbola represented in equation (A7.2), it can be shown that its center lies on the vertical axis at the point A/C, meaning that its coordinates are $(0, A/C)$, and they correspond to those of the vertex for the parabola in mean-variance space. Not surprisingly, A/C corresponds to the rate of return on the global MVP. Given this center, the two asymptotes can be viewed as rays emanating from it with slopes equal to $\sqrt{D/C}$ and $-\sqrt{D/C}$, respectively. Thus, the equations of the asymptotes are

$$E(r_p) = \frac{A}{C} + \sqrt{\frac{D}{C}}\,\sigma_p \tag{A7.3}$$

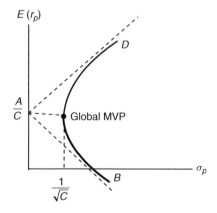

FIGURE A7.1 Efficient Frontier with Vertex $(1/\sqrt{C}, A/C)$

and
$$E(r_p) = \frac{A}{C} - \sqrt{\frac{D}{C}}\, \sigma_p \qquad\qquad (A7.4)$$

Much of the previous analysis was conducted using mean-variance dimensions, whereas portfolio theory typically is presented graphically in mean-standard deviation dimensions. However, it should be apparent, aside from the shape of the minimum variance boundary changing from a parabola to a hyperbola, that the previous observations hold regardless of whether the variance or standard deviation is used as the risk measure.

B. Covariance between an Efficient Portfolio and Any Portfolio   Because the optimal weights for an efficient portfolio have the form of equation (7.4b), the covariance of an efficient portfolio p and any risky portfolio q is expressed as

$$\sigma_{pq} = w_q' \, \Sigma \, w_p$$
$$= w_q' \, \Sigma \left(\lambda \Sigma^{-1}\mu + \gamma \Sigma^{-1}l\right) = \lambda\, E(r_q) + \gamma$$

Using the expression of λ and γ from equations (7.14) and (7.15) and rearranging yields

$$\sigma_{pq} = \left[\frac{CE(r_p) - A}{D}\right] E(r_q) + \left[\frac{B - AE(r_p)}{D}\right]$$
$$= \frac{C}{D}\left[E(r_p) - \frac{A}{C}\right]\left[E(r_q) - \frac{A}{C}\right] + \frac{1}{C} \qquad (A7.5)$$

C. Identifying the Global MVP   The global MVP is on the vertex in Figure A7.1; that is, its mean return is $E(r_{MVP}) = A/C$, and its variance is $\sigma^2_{MVP} = 1/C$. Because the global minimum variance portfolio is on the efficient frontier, its weights are determined as in equation (7.4b). That is,

$$w_{MVP} = \lambda \Sigma^{-1}E + \gamma \Sigma^{-1}\mathbf{1} \qquad\qquad (A7.6)$$

For the global MVP, the Lagrangian multipliers become

$$\lambda = \frac{C\,E(r_p) - A}{D} = 0 \quad\text{and}\quad \gamma = \frac{B - A\,E(r_p)}{D} = \frac{1}{C} \qquad (A7.7)$$

since $E(r_p) = A/C$ for the global MVP and $D = BC - A^2$. Thus, the weights for the global MVP are determined as follows.

$$w_{MVP} = \frac{1}{C}\, \Sigma^{-1}\mathbf{1} = \frac{\Sigma^{-1}\mathbf{1}}{\mathbf{1}'\Sigma^{-1}\mathbf{1}} \qquad\qquad (A7.8)$$

For example, when $n = 2$, the weight for the MVP is

$$w_{MVP} = \frac{1}{C}\begin{pmatrix}\sigma_1^2 & \sigma_{12} \\ \sigma_{21} & \sigma_2^2\end{pmatrix}^{-1}\begin{pmatrix}1 \\ 1\end{pmatrix}$$
$$= \frac{1}{\left(\sigma_1^2 + \sigma_2^2 - 2\sigma_{12}\right)}\begin{pmatrix}\sigma_2^2 - \sigma_{12} \\ \sigma_1^2 - \sigma_{12}\end{pmatrix} \qquad (A7.9)$$

Note that

$$\boldsymbol{\Sigma}^{-1} = \begin{pmatrix} \sigma_1^2 & \sigma_{12} \\ \sigma_{21} & \sigma_2^2 \end{pmatrix}^{-1} = \frac{1}{(\sigma_1^2 \sigma_2^2 - \sigma_{12}^2)} \begin{pmatrix} \sigma_2^2 & -\sigma_{21} \\ -\sigma_{12} & \sigma_1^2 \end{pmatrix}$$

and $\quad C = \mathbf{1}' \boldsymbol{\Sigma}^{-1} \mathbf{1} = \dfrac{\sigma_1^2 + \sigma_2^2 - 2\sigma_{12}}{\sigma_1^2 \sigma_2^2 - \sigma_{12}^2}$

The weights for securities in equation (A7.9) are exactly the same as in equations (6.2) and (6.3) of Chapter 6.

EXAMPLE A7.1

Suppose the three securities described in Example 7.2 comprise the opportunity set. What are the weights of the three assets for the global MVP? The expected returns and variance-covariances of the three assets are given as

$$E = \begin{bmatrix} E(r_1) \\ E(r_2) \\ E(r_3) \end{bmatrix} = \begin{pmatrix} 2.07 \\ 0.21 \\ 1.10 \end{pmatrix} \text{ and } \boldsymbol{\Sigma} = \begin{pmatrix} \sigma_{11} & \sigma_{12} & \sigma_{13} \\ \sigma_{21} & \sigma_{22} & \sigma_{23} \\ \sigma_{31} & \sigma_{32} & \sigma_{33} \end{pmatrix} = \begin{pmatrix} 48.20 & 7.82 & -2.65 \\ 7.82 & 16.34 & 0.99 \\ -2.65 & 0.99 & 34.25 \end{pmatrix}$$

First, we compute the value of C in equation (A7.8). That is,

$$C = \mathbf{1}' \boldsymbol{\Sigma}^{-1} \mathbf{1} = (1 \ \ 1 \ \ 1) \begin{pmatrix} 48.20 & 7.82 & -2.65 \\ 7.82 & 16.34 & 0.99 \\ -2.65 & 0.99 & 34.25 \end{pmatrix}^{-1} \begin{pmatrix} 1 \\ 1 \\ 1 \end{pmatrix} = 0.0954$$

Thus, the weights for the minimum variance portfolio are obtained as

$$w_{\text{MVP}} = \frac{1}{C} \boldsymbol{\Sigma}^{-1} \mathbf{1}$$

$$= \left(\frac{1}{0.0954} \right) \begin{pmatrix} 48.20 & 7.82 & -2.65 \\ 7.82 & 16.34 & 0.99 \\ -2.65 & 0.99 & 34.25 \end{pmatrix}^{-1} \begin{pmatrix} 1 \\ 1 \\ 1 \end{pmatrix} = \left(\frac{1}{0.0954} \right) \begin{pmatrix} 0.0138 \\ 0.0529 \\ 0.0287 \end{pmatrix}$$

$$= \begin{pmatrix} 0.1437 \\ 0.5545 \\ 0.3008 \end{pmatrix}$$

The expected return and variance of the MVP are

$$E(r_{\text{MVP}}) = \frac{A}{C} = \frac{0.0686}{0.0954} = 0.719\%, \text{ and}$$

$$\sigma_{\text{MVP}}^2 = \frac{1}{C} = \frac{1}{0.0954} = 10.482$$

(Continued)

EXAMPLE A7.1 (*Continued*)

Of course, the expected return and variance in the above can be obtained by using the regular formula. That is,

$$E\left(r_{\text{MVP}}\right) = w'_{\text{MVP}}\, E = (0.1437 \quad 0.5545 \quad 0.3008) \begin{pmatrix} 2.07 \\ 0.21 \\ 1.10 \end{pmatrix} = 0.719\%, \quad \text{and}$$

$$\sigma^2_{\text{MVP}} = w'_{\text{MVP}}\, \Sigma\, w_{\text{MVP}}$$

$$= (0.1437 \quad 0.5545 \quad 0.3008) \begin{pmatrix} 48.20 & 7.82 & -2.65 \\ 7.82 & 16.34 & 0.99 \\ -2.65 & 0.99 & 34.25 \end{pmatrix} \begin{pmatrix} 0.1437 \\ 0.5545 \\ 0.3008 \end{pmatrix}$$

$$= 10.482$$

A7.2   With a Risk-Free Asset

This section extends Section A7.1 by bringing the risk-free asset into the solution.

A. Deriving the Equation for the Efficient Frontier   The mathematical equation for the efficient frontier $\overline{r_f mH}$ in Figure 6.10 of Chapter 6 can be derived by constructing a mathematical relationship between the expected return, $E(r_p)$, and variance, σ_p^2, of a portfolio p on the efficient frontier. Let w_p denote the optimal weight vector for the portfolio p on the efficient frontier. Then, using equation (7.34), the variance of the portfolio is expressed as

$$\sigma_p^2 = w'_p\, \Sigma\, w_p = (E - r_f \mathbf{1})'\, \Sigma^{-1}\, (E - r_f \mathbf{1}) \left[\frac{E(r_p) - r_f}{H} \right]^2$$

$$= \frac{\left[E(r_p) - r_f \right]^2}{H} \tag{A7.10}$$

Thus,

$$\sigma_p = \begin{cases} \left[E(r_p) - r_f \right]/\sqrt{H} & \text{if } E(r_p) \geq r_f \\ -\left[E(r_p) - r_f \right]/\sqrt{H} & \text{if } E(r_p) < r_f \end{cases} \tag{A7.11}$$

That is, the efficient frontier of all assets is composed of two half-lines emanating from the intercept r_f in the $[\sigma_p, E(r_p)]$ space with slopes $\sqrt{H}$ and $-\sqrt{H}$, respectively.

The mathematical relationship between $E(r_p)$ and σ_p in equation (A7.10) is depicted in Figure A7.2. The upper solid line indicates the efficient frontier. The portfolio at the tangency point m is termed "tangency portfolio," "optimal risky portfolio," or the "market portfolio." As mentioned previously, the dotted lines are two asymptotes for the parabola (or hyperbola).

It can be shown that if $r_f > A/C$, then a tangency portfolio on the efficient frontier does not exist (but one does exist on the negatively sloped or bottom half

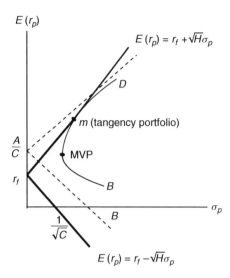

FIGURE A7.2 Efficient Frontier with the
Risk-free Asset

of the minimum variance boundary). Only when $r_f < A/C$ will a tangency portfolio
on the efficient frontier exist (but in this case, no tangency portfolio exists on the
bottom half of the minimum variance boundary). Intuitively, this can be shown by
considering the properties of a hyperbola.

Consider three cases: Case (1) occurs when $r_f > A/C$. In Case (1) any ray
emanating from the risk-free rate must have a slope less than the asymptote's slope
if it is to be a candidate for a tangency portfolio, because a slope greater than or
equal to that of the asymptote would cause the ray emanating from r_f to miss the
opportunity set entirely. But in order to be a tangency portfolio, the ray must have
the same slope as the efficient frontier at the tangency point.

Case (2) occurs when $r_f < A/C$. In Case (2) any ray emanating from the risk-free
rate must have a slope greater than the asymptote's slope if it is to be a candidate
for a tangency portfolio, because a smaller slope would cause the ray to intersect
the boundary. The slope of the efficient frontier decreases monotonically from a
value of $+\infty$ when $E(r_p) = A/C$ to a value of $\sqrt{D/C}$ when $E(r_p) = \infty$. The latter
value corresponds to that of the asymptote. Accordingly, there will exist an efficient
portfolio with a finite value of $E(r_p)$ such that the slope of the efficient frontier at that
point is equal to that of the ray emanating from r_f. Therefore, a tangency portfolio
on the efficient frontier exists, and the equation for the efficient frontier will be
of the same form as equation (7.34). Furthermore, because the efficient frontier is
linear, the efficient frontier theorem again holds. As shown in Figure 6.11, investors
will choose their optimal portfolios in a manner analogous to that discussed in the
previous section.

Case (3) occurs when $r_f = A/C$. In this case, the slope of the line in Figure A7.2
becomes $\sqrt{H} = \left(B - 2r_f A + r_f^2 C\right)^{1/2} = \left[B - 2\,(A/C)\,A + (A/C)^2\right]^{1/2} = \sqrt{D/C}.$

This is the same as the slope of the asymptotes of the efficient frontier composed
of only risky assets. In this case, there is no tangency portfolio. Thus, the portfolio

frontier is not generated by the risk-free asset and the tangency portfolio. In this case, the sum of the weights for the risky assets in the frontier portfolio is

$$w'_p 1 = (E - r_f 1)' \Sigma^{-1} 1 \left[\frac{E(r_p) - r_f}{H} \right]$$

$$= (A - r_f C) \left[\frac{E(r_p) - r_f}{H} \right] = 0 \qquad (A7.12)$$

This indicates that any portfolio on the frontier consists of investing 100 percent in the riskless asset and 0 percent in the risky assets. Here, the portfolio consisting of only the risky assets is a zero-investment arbitrage portfolio. Note that in the previous two cases when $r_f > A/C$ or $r_f < A/C$, there does exist a tangency portfolio on the bottom or top half of the portfolio frontier $\overline{BD}$. Therefore, portfolios on the half-line $E(r_p) = r_f + \sqrt{H}\sigma_p$ or the half-line $E(r_p) = r_f - \sqrt{H}\sigma_p$ are generated by the risk-free asset and the tangency portfolio. That is, the two-fund separation theorem holds in those cases.

B. Identifying the Tangency Portfolio The tangency portfolio (or the optimal risky portfolio) m in Figure A7.2 does not contain the risk-free asset; it contains only the n risky assets. At tangency portfolio m, $w_f = 0$. Let w_m be the $(n \times 1)$ weight vector of risky assets that comprise the tangency portfolio m. From equation (7.35), the weight of the risk-free asset for any efficient portfolio is one minus the sum of the weights of all risky assets in the portfolio. In other words, for the tangency portfolio m that is an efficient portfolio,

$$w_f = 1 - w'_m 1 = 0 \qquad (A7.13)$$

Thus, using equations (7.34), (A7.13), and (7.16) yields

$$w'_m 1 = (E - r_f 1)' \Sigma^{-1} 1 \left[\frac{E(r_m) - r_f}{H} \right]$$

$$= (A - r_f C) \left[\frac{E(r_m) - r_f}{H} \right] \equiv 1 \qquad (A7.14)$$

From equation (A7.14), $[E(r_m) - r_f]/H = 1/(A - r_f A)$. Thus, the weight vector for the tangency portfolio m is

$$w_m = \frac{\Sigma^{-1}(E - r_f 1)}{(A - r_f C)} \qquad (A7.15)$$

The expected return and variance of the tangency portfolio m are computed as

$$E(r_m) = E' w_m = \frac{E'\Sigma^{-1}(E - r_f 1)}{A - r_f C} = \frac{B - r_f A}{A - r_f C} \qquad (A7.16)$$

and $\qquad \sigma_m^2 = w'_m \Sigma w_m = \frac{(\mu' - 1' r_f)\Sigma^{-1}\Sigma\Sigma^{-1}(\mu - 1 r_f)}{(A - r_f C)^2} = \frac{H}{(A - r_f C)^2}$
$$\qquad (A7.17)$$

The weights for the tangency portfolio in equation (A7.15) can also be obtained in a different way. As seen in Figure 6.10 of Chapter 6, all efficient portfolios are on the CML. From the two funds separation theorem, an efficient portfolio can be obtained from a linear combination of the tangency portfolio m (the optimal risky portfolio) and the risk-free asset. In other words, the sum of all the weights of the risky assets in portfolio p is the amount invested in the tangency portfolio, and the remaining weight is the amount invested in the risk-free asset.

Let w_p be the weight vector of n risky assets for the efficient portfolio p. Then, the weights for the tangency portfolio can be obtained by normalizing w_p. That is,

$$w_m = \frac{w_p}{w_p'1} \tag{A7.18}$$

Plugging equation (7.34) for w_p into equation (A7.18) yields

$$
\begin{aligned}
w_m &= \frac{\Sigma^{-1}\left(E - r_f 1\right)\left\{\left[E(r_p) - r_f\right]/H\right\}}{\left(E - r_f 1\right)'\Sigma^{-1}1\left\{\left[E(r_p) - r_f\right]/H\right\}} \\
&= \frac{\Sigma^{-1}\left(E - r_f 1\right)}{\left(E - r_f 1\right)'\Sigma^{-1}1} = \frac{\Sigma^{-1}\left(E - r_f 1\right)}{A - r_f C}
\end{aligned}
\tag{A7.19}
$$

EXAMPLE A7.2

Consider two risky securities. Their expected returns and variances are given in the following table, and their correlation coefficient is zero.

	Security 1	Security 2
$E(r)$	10%	6%
σ	25%	12%

The risk-free asset's rate of return is 5 percent. What are the weights of securities 1 and 2 for the optimal risky portfolio m in Figure A7.3?

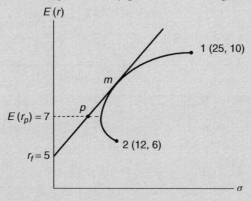

FIGURE A7.3 Tangency Portfolio with Two Risky Assets and the Risk-free Asset

(Continued)

EXAMPLE A7.2 (*Continued*)

To compute the weights of securities 1 and 2 for the tangency portfolio m in equation (A7.15), we first have to compute the values of A and C contained in equation (A7.15). With $n = 2$,

$$A = 1'\Sigma^{-1}E = \frac{(\sigma_2^2 - \sigma_{12})\,E(r_1) + (\sigma_1^2 - \sigma_{12})\,E(r_2)}{\sigma_1^2\,\sigma_2^2 - \sigma_{12}^2} \tag{A7.20}$$

$$C = 1'\Sigma^{-1}1 = \frac{\sigma_1^2 + \sigma_2^2 - 2\sigma_{12}}{\sigma_1^2\,\sigma_2^2 - \sigma_{12}^2} \tag{A7.21}$$

Note that $\Sigma^{-1} = \frac{1}{(\sigma_1^2\sigma_2^2 - \sigma_{12}^2)}\begin{pmatrix} \sigma_2^2 & -\sigma_{21} \\ -\sigma_{12} & \sigma_1^2 \end{pmatrix}$. Using equations (A7.20) and (A7.21), the denominator in equation (A7.15) is expressed as

$$A - r_fC = \frac{[E(r_1) - r_f]\sigma_2^2 + [E(r_2) - r_f]\sigma_1^2 - [E(r_1) + E(r_1) - 2r_f]\sigma_{12}}{\sigma_1^2\,\sigma_2^2 - \sigma_{12}^2} \tag{A7.22}$$

and the numerator is expressed as

$$\Sigma^{-1}(E - r_f1) = \frac{1}{(\sigma_1^2\sigma_2^2 - \sigma_{12}^2)}\begin{pmatrix} \sigma_2^2 & -\sigma_{21} \\ -\sigma_{12} & \sigma_1^2 \end{pmatrix}\begin{bmatrix} E(r_1) - r_f \\ E(r_2) - r_f \end{bmatrix}$$

$$= \frac{1}{(\sigma_1^2\sigma_2^2 - \sigma_{12}^2)}\begin{bmatrix} \sigma_2^2(E(r_1) - r_f) - \sigma_{12}(E(r_2) - r_f) \\ \sigma_1^2(E(r_2) - r_f) - \sigma_{12}(E(r_1) - r_f) \end{bmatrix} \tag{A7.23}$$

Let w_{m1} and w_{m2} be the weights of securities 1 and 2 for the tangency portfolio. Then, $w_m = (w_{m1}, w_{m2})' = \Sigma^{-1}(E - r_f1)/(A - r_fC)$. From equations (A7.22) and (A7.23), the weights of securities 1 and 2 are, respectively,

$$w_{m1} = \frac{\sigma_2^2[E(r_1) - r_f] - \sigma_{12}[E(r_2) - r_f]}{[E(r_1) - r_f]\sigma_2^2 + [E(r_2) - r_f]\sigma_1^2 - [E(r_1) + E(r_1) - 2r_f]\sigma_{12}}$$

$$= \frac{(12)^2(10 - 5) - (0)(6 - 5)}{(10 - 5)(12)^2 + (6 - 5)(25)^2 - (10 + 6 - 2 \times 5)(0)}$$

$$= 0.5353$$

$$w_{m2} = \frac{\sigma_1^2[E(r_2) - r_f] - \sigma_{12}[E(r_1) - r_f]}{[E(r_1) - r_f]\sigma_2^2 + [E(r_2) - r_f]\sigma_1^2 - [E(r_1) + E(r_1) - 2r_f]\sigma_{12}}$$

$$= \frac{(25)^2(6 - 5) - (0)(10 - 5)}{(10 - 5)(12)^2 + (6 - 5)(25)^2 - (10 + 6 - 2 \times 5)(0)}$$

$$= 0.4647$$

EXAMPLE A7.2 (*Continued*)

The expected return and variance of the tangency portfolio m are

$$E(r_m) = (0.5353)(10\%) + (0.4647)(6\%) = 8.1412\%$$

$$\sigma_m = \sqrt{(0.5353)^2(25)^2 + (0.4647)^2(12)^2 + 0} = 14.50\%$$

EXAMPLE A7.3

Continuing from Example A7.2, what are the weights of the securities for efficient portfolio p in Figure A7.3 whose expected return is $E(r_p) = 7\%$?

There are two ways to identify the optimal weights for efficient portfolio p. One way is to apply equation (7.34) directly. Another way is to apply the two-fund separation theorem by using the information about the tangency portfolio m.

First, we find the optimal weights by directly applying equation (7.34).

$$w_p = \begin{pmatrix} w_1 \\ w_2 \end{pmatrix} = \Sigma^{-1}(E - r_f 1)\left[\frac{E(r_p) - r_f}{H}\right]$$

$$= \frac{1}{(\sigma_1^2\sigma_2^2 - \sigma_{12}^2)}\begin{bmatrix} \sigma_2^2(E(r_1) - r_f) - \sigma_{12}(E(r_2) - r_f) \\ \sigma_1^2(E(r_2) - r_f) - \sigma_{12}(E(r_1) - r_f) \end{bmatrix}\left[\frac{E(r_p) - r_f}{H}\right]$$

$$= \frac{1}{[(25)^2(12)^2 - 2]}\begin{bmatrix} (12)^2(10 - 5) - (0)(6 - 5) \\ (25)^2(6 - 5) - (0)(10 - 5) \end{bmatrix}\left(\frac{7 - 5}{0.0469}\right)$$

$$= \begin{pmatrix} 0.3408 \\ 0.2959 \end{pmatrix} \tag{A7.24}$$

since $H = B - 2r_f A + r_f^2 C = 0.41 - 2(5)(0.05767) + (5)^2(0.008544) = 0.0469$. We leave the computations for A, B, and C in the equation of H to the readers. The weight of the risk-free asset is $w_f = 1 - (0.3408 + 0.2959) = 0.3633$. Because the weights in equation (A7.24), w_p, are only for the risky assets in the efficient portfolio, we can obtain the weights for the tangency portfolio m by normalizing these weights as in equation (A7.18). That is,

$$w_{m1} = \frac{w_1}{w_1 + w_2} = \frac{0.3408}{0.3408 + 0.2959} = 0.5353$$

and $$w_{m2} = \frac{w_2}{w_1 + w_2} = \frac{0.2959}{0.3408 + 0.2959} = 0.4647$$

(*Continued*)

EXAMPLE A7.3 *(Continued)*

These weights for the tangency portfolio m are the same as the answers in the previous Example A7.2.

Secondly, we find the optimal weights by applying the two-fund theorem, which means that all efficient portfolios are generated from a linear combination of the tangency portfolio and the risk-free asset. Thus, the efficient portfolio p can also be constructed by investing x_m in the tangency portfolio and $w_f (= 1 - x_m)$ in the risk-free asset. Note that the composition of the securities in the tangency portfolio is fixed as $w_{m1} = 0.5353$ and $w_{m2} = 0.4647$ (from Example A7.2) for any efficient portfolio. The expected return on the portfolio p is represented by

$$E(r_p) = x_m E(r_m) + (1 - x_m) r_f \qquad (A7.25)$$

However, we already know from Example A7.2 that the expected return on the tangency portfolio m is 8.1412 percent. Thus,

$$7\% = x_m (8.1412\%) + (1 - x_m)(5\%) \qquad (A7.26)$$

From the preceding equation, we obtain the weights for the tangency portfolio and the risk-free asset.

$$x_m = 0.6367 \quad \text{and} \quad w_f = 1 - 0.6367 = 0.3633$$

Because this is the total weight invested in the risky assets contained in the tangency portfolio, this weight is allocated into the two risky assets according to the proportions of $w_{m1} = 0.5353$ and $w_{m2} = 0.4647$. Thus, the optimal weights of the two securities for the efficient portfolio p are

$$w_1 = x_m w_{m1} = (0.6367)(0.5353) = 0.3408$$

$$\text{and} \qquad w_2 = x_m w_{m2} = (0.6367)(0.4647) = 0.2959$$

These answers are the same as the answers obtained before in equation (A7.24).

EXAMPLE A7.4

Let us use the same values in Example A7.3, except that the expected return for a new efficient portfolio will be $E(r_p) = 9\%$. What are the optimal weights for this efficient portfolio?

Because equation (A7.25) holds for any efficient portfolio and the tangency portfolio is the same as before, we replace 7 percent in equation (A7.26) with 9 percent:

$$9\% = x_m (8.1412\%) + (1 - x_m)(5\%) \qquad (A7.27)$$

> **EXAMPLE A7.4** (*Continued*)
>
> From equation (7.31), we have $x_m = 1.2734$ and $w_f = -0.2734$. Because $x_m = 1.2734$ is the total investment in the risky assets contained in the tangency portfolio, this weight is also allocated into the two risky assets according to the proportions of $w_{m1} = 0.5353$ and $w_{m2} = 0.4647$. Thus, the optimal weights of the two securities for the efficient portfolio p are
>
> $$w_1 = x_m w_{m1} = (1.2734)(0.5353) = 0.6817$$
>
> and $\quad w_2 = x_m w_{m2} = (1.2734)(0.4647) = 0.5917$
>
> Therefore, if the expected return on an efficient portfolio (or the target return) is given and the information on the tangency portfolio is also given, we can easily find the optimal weights for any efficient portfolio.

NOTES

1. Matrix inversion is discussed at the end of this book in a mathematical appendix that discusses solving linear equations simultaneously.
2. Formulation (7.3a) requires no constraints for investment weights, w. If some constraints on investment weights are imposed, the computation of efficient portfolios becomes more difficult. If short selling of assets is prohibited, investment weights must be nonnegative and the constraint has the form of $w \geq 0$. However, a more general constraint with upper and lowerbounds is required sometimes. For this case, the optimal solution for investment weights will lie within their respective bounds. Recently, Niedermayer and Niedermayer (2010) provide a MATLAB quadratic optimization tool based on Markowitz's critical line algorithm that significantly outperforms standard software packages and a recently developed operations research algorithm. For example, for a universe of 2,000 assets, the Niedermayer method needs less than a second to compute the whole frontier, whereas the quickest competitor needs several hours.
3. A symmetric matrix A is positive definite if and only if $x'Ax > 0$ for all $x \neq 0$. A symmetric matrix A is nonnegative definite (positive semidefinite) if and only if $x'Ax \geq 0$ for all $x \neq 0$. For further information, see Judge, Hill, Griffiths, Lütkepohk, and Lee, *Introduction to the Theory and Practice of Econometrics*, 2nd ed. (New York: John Wiley & Sons, 1988), 960.
4. Σ^{-1} exists because it has been assumed that $\sigma_i^2 > 0$ for all i and $\rho_{ij} > -1$ for all i and j.
5. For more detailed information of the Cauchy-Schwarz inequality, see Mood, Graybill, and Boes, *Introduction to the Theory of Statistics*, 3rd ed., (New York: McGraw Hill, 1974), 162.
6. Assuming, of course, that w_{i1} and w_{i2} are nonzero. Note that if both w_{i1} and w_{i2} are zero, then the security does not appear anywhere on the efficient frontier.

CHAPTER 8

Index Models and Return-Generating Process

Index models are more than regressions that explain an investment's holding period returns, they are also important statements about the economic process that generates the returns. This chapter considers single-index models, two-index models, and multi-index models.

8.1 SINGLE-INDEX MODELS

Single-index models are the simplest and most popular type of generating process used to explain what economic forces create investors' returns. They are also used to estimate a firm's undiversifiable systematic risk.

8.1.1 Return-Generating Functions

Preceding chapters suggested the single-period rate of return is the *basic random variable* of portfolio theory. As explained previously, for a share of common or preferred stock, a bond, a real estate investment, or other investments, this *holding period return* (HPR) is computed as follows.

$$\left(\begin{array}{c}\text{Holding period}\\ \text{return, } r_t\end{array}\right) = \frac{\left(\begin{array}{c}\text{Price change during}\\ \text{the holding period}\end{array}\right) + \left(\begin{array}{c}\text{Cash income received during}\\ \text{the holding period, if any}\end{array}\right)}{\left(\begin{array}{c}\text{Purchase price at the beginning of}\\ \text{the holding period}\end{array}\right)}$$

or equivalently,

$$r_t = \frac{\left(P_t - P_{t-1}\right) + d_t}{P_{t-1}} \tag{1.1}$$

where r_t, is the rate of return, or holding period return (HPR); P_t represents the market price at time t; and d_t stands for cash dividend income, or other source of income received during the holding period.

This chapter reviews the historical development of two similar, yet significantly different, return-generating functions that underlie equation (1.1). These two return-generating functions are fundamental components of portfolio theory.

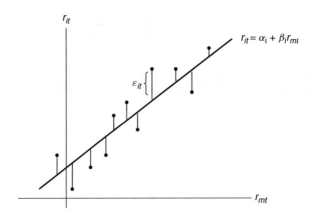

FIGURE 8.1   One Possible Form for Equation (8.1)

In 1959 Harry Markowitz published graphs illustrating the *return-generating function* defined in equation (8.1). This equation is referred to as the single-index model,[1]

$$r_{it} = \alpha_i + \beta_i r_{mt} + \varepsilon_{it} \tag{8.1}$$

where α_i and β_i are the intercept and slope coefficients that result from regressing the rate of return from asset i in period t, denoted r_{it}, onto the simultaneous rate of return on some market index in period t, denoted r_{mt}; and ε_{it} is the unexplained residual error term for asset i in period t. This model is based on the assumption that the joint probability distribution between r_{it} and r_{mt} is stationary and bivariate normal.[2] Figure 8.1 illustrates equation (8.1). Markowitz's 1959 monograph provides the earliest presentation of this well-known model of which we are aware.

In the early 1960s William F. Sharpe finished his PhD in economics at UCLA while working at the RAND Corporation in Los Angeles. Sharpe collaborated with Harry Markowitz, who was also a RAND employee at that time. As a result of this collaboration, in 1963 Sharpe published a classic analysis of equation (8.1), referring to the equation as the diagonal model in that paper.[3] In later papers Sharpe variously referred to equation (8.1) as the single-index model, the one-factor model, and the single-factor market model.

Working independently, in 1965 Jack L. Treynor published a paper about equation (8.1), which he called the characteristic line.[4] Other people like to call equation (8.1) the market model. The return-generating function in equation (8.1) obviously has several different names. Treynor's classic paper delved into the portfolio management and risk management implications the classic Markowitz-Sharpe-Treynor characteristic line has for mutual fund managers.

Assuming that the error terms average out to zero, $E\left(\varepsilon_{it}\right) = 0$, the *conditional expectation* of equation (8.1) is shown as equation (8.2).

$$E\left(r_{it} | r_{mt}\right) = \alpha_i + \beta_i \left(r_{mt}\right) \tag{8.2}$$

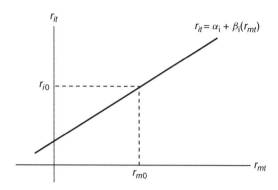

FIGURE 8.2 Another Possible Form for Equation (8.1)

Using this conditional expectation facilitates prediction. For example, if a financial economist predicts that the rate of return on the market index (r_{mt}) at time period $t = 0$ assumes the value r_{m0}, then equation (8.2) implies that r_{i0} is the expected value of the i-th asset's rate of return, where $r_{i0} = \alpha_i + \beta_i (r_{m0})$. Figure 8.2 graphically depicts this process. Note, however, that this form of forecasting is dependent on the constancy over time of the underlying regression model of equation (8.1).

The regression model such as equation (8.1) makes five assumptions about the random error term.

1. The expected value of the random error term is zero—that is, $E\left(\varepsilon_{it}\right) = 0$.
2. The variance of ε_{it}, denoted $\sigma_{\varepsilon i}^2$, is constant—that is, the error terms are homoscedastic.
3. The random error terms are uncorrelated with r_{mt}—that is, $\text{Cov}\left(\varepsilon_{it}, r_{mt}\right) = 0$.
4. The random error terms are serially uncorrelated—that is, $\text{Cov}\left(\varepsilon_{it}, \varepsilon_{is}\right) = 0$ for $t \neq s$.
5. The random error terms of an asset are uncorrelated with those of any other asset—that is, $\text{Cov}\left(\varepsilon_{it}, \varepsilon_{jt}\right) = 0$ for $i \neq j$.

If the sample data conforms to the assumptions above, the least square estimates of α_i and β_i will be unbiased, minimum-variance, linear estimates of the true regression parameters.

The return-generating equation (8.1) can be partitioned into two mutually exclusive components: a systematic part and an unsystematic part:

$$\underbrace{r_{it}}_{\text{Total return}} = \underbrace{\alpha_i + \beta_i r_{mt}}_{\text{Systematic part}} + \underbrace{\varepsilon_{it}}_{\text{Unsystematic part}} \qquad (8.1a)$$

The systematic part of the total return is systematically explained by the explanatory variable, the return on the market index (r_{mt}). The unsystematic part is the remaining portion of the total return that is left unexplained by the explanatory variable. Economic insights can be gained from equation (8.1a)'s return-generating function by partitioning its total variance into two economically meaningful components.

Taking the variance of both the left- and right-hand sides of equation (8.1a) produces equation (8.3)

$$
\begin{aligned}
\text{Var}\left(r_{it}\right) &= \text{Var}\left(\alpha_i + \beta_i r_{mt} + \varepsilon_{it}\right) \\
&= \text{E}\left[\left(\alpha_i + \beta_i r_{mt} + \varepsilon_{it}\right) - \text{E}\left(\alpha_i + \beta_i r_{mt} + \varepsilon_{it}\right)\right]^2 \\
&= \text{E}\left[\beta_i^2\left(r_{mt} - \mu_m\right)^2 + \varepsilon_{it}^2 + 2\beta_i\left(r_{mt} - \mu_m\right)\varepsilon_{it}\right] \\
&= \beta_i^2 \sigma_m^2 + \sigma_{\varepsilon i}^2
\end{aligned}
\tag{8.3}
$$

The total variance of equation (8.3) measures the total variability of return, or total risk, of the basic random variable r_{it}. The first term of the equation (8.3), $\beta_i^2 \sigma_m^2$, measures systematic (or undiversifiable) risk, and the second term, $\sigma_{\varepsilon i}^2$, measures the unsystematic (or diversifiable) risk of asset i. Since all assets experience the same market variance, σ_m^2, the beta emerges as an index of systematic (or diversifiable) risk. This relation may clarify partitioning the total variance:

$$
\underbrace{\sigma_i^2}_{\text{Total risk}} = \underbrace{\beta_i^2 \sigma_m^2}_{\text{Systematic risk}} + \underbrace{\sigma_{\varepsilon i}^2}_{\text{Unsystematic risk}}
$$

The insights just introduced are the topics of several of the following chapters.

Because the return from stock j in period t is also described by the following single-index model,

$$
r_{jt} = \alpha_j + \beta_j r_{mt} + \varepsilon_{jt}
\tag{8.1b}
$$

the covariance between two different securities i and j can be expressed as

$$
\begin{aligned}
\text{Cov}\left(r_{it}, r_{jt}\right) &= \text{E}\left[r_{it} - E\left(r_{it}\right)\right]\left[r_{jt} - E\left(r_{jt}\right)\right] \\
&= \text{E}\left[\left(\alpha_i + \beta_i r_{mt} + \varepsilon_{it}\right) - \text{E}\left(\alpha_i + \beta_i r_{mt} + \varepsilon_{it}\right)\right] \\
&\quad \times \left[\left(\alpha_i + \beta_i r_{mt} + \varepsilon_{it}\right) - \text{E}\left(\alpha_i + \beta_i r_{mt} + \varepsilon_{it}\right)\right] \\
&= \text{E}\left[\beta_i\left(r_{mt} - E\left(r_{mt}\right)\right) + \varepsilon_{it}\right]\left[\beta_j\left(r_{mt} - E\left(r_{mt}\right)\right) + \varepsilon_{jt}\right] \\
&= \beta_i \beta_j E\left[r_{mt} - E\left(r_{mt}\right)\right]^2
\end{aligned}
$$

Thus, $\sigma_{ij} = \beta_i \beta_j \sigma_m^2$.

8.1.2   Estimating the Parameters

Assuming that the historical data have been generated by a stationary distribution, the statistical technique of simple regression [that is, ordinary least squares (OLS)] can be used to estimate the security-specific regression parameters α_i, β_i, and $\sigma_{\varepsilon i}^2$. This statistical technique takes the set of paired sample values of $\left(r_{mt}, r_{it}\right)$ and attempts to find the values of α_i and β_i that create a line of best fit. Here "best fit" means that the sum of the squared *vertical distances* of the actual values of r_{it} from the regression line is minimized. Figure 8.1 indicates that it is the squared vertical distances, not the squared perpendicular distances, and not the squared horizontal distances, that is minimized in an OLS regression. The OLS α_i, β_i, and $\sigma_{\varepsilon i}^2$ can be estimated from T sample observations using the following formulas:

$$\hat{\beta}_i = \frac{\sum_{t=1}^{T} \left(r_{it} - \bar{r}_i\right)\left(r_{mt} - \bar{r}_m\right)}{\sum_{t=1}^{T}\left(r_{it} - \bar{r}_i\right)^2}$$

$$\hat{\alpha}_i = \bar{r}_i - \hat{\beta}_i \bar{r}_m$$

$$\hat{\sigma}_{\varepsilon i}^2 = \left(\frac{1}{T-2}\right)\sum_{t=1}^{T}\left[r_{it} - \left(\hat{\alpha}_i + \hat{\beta}_i r_{mt}\right)\right]^2$$

Here $\bar{r}_i$ and $\bar{r}_m$ are the estimated sample mean values of r_{it} and r_{mt}; these means are computed during the estimation period using equation (2.7).

EXAMPLE 8.1

Table 8.1 lists the monthly rates of return from stock i and the market portfolio m over the period from January through December of a recent year.

TABLE 8.1　Hypothetical Monthly Holding Period Returns[5]

Month	t	Return on stock i r_{it}	Return on the market r_{mt}	Fitted return on stock i $\hat{\alpha}_i + \hat{\beta}_i r_{mt}$	$(r_{it} - \bar{r}_i) \times$ $(r_{mt} - \bar{r}_m)$	Residuals $\hat{\varepsilon}_{it}$
		(1)	(2)	(3)	(4)	(1)–(3)
January	1	0.0206	0.0194	0.0242	0.0001	−0.0036
February	2	−0.0596	−0.0140	−0.0087	0.0014	−0.0510
March	3	0.0142	0.0129	0.0178	0.0000	−0.0036
April	4	0.0843	0.0399	0.0443	0.0025	0.0400
May	5	0.0469	0.0389	0.0434	0.0012	0.0035
June	6	−0.0127	−0.0148	−0.0094	0.0005	−0.0033
July	7	0.0513	−0.0317	−0.0261	−0.0015	0.0774
August	8	0.0582	0.0116	0.0165	0.0003	0.0417
September	9	0.0095	0.0409	0.0453	−0.0001	−0.0358
October	10	−0.0143	0.0259	0.0305	−0.0005	−0.0448
November	11	−0.0908	−0.0493	−0.0434	0.0057	−0.0474
December	12	0.0278	−0.0043	0.0009	−0.0002	0.0269
Total		0.1355	0.0754	0.1355	0.00936	0.0000
Average ($\bar{r}$)		0.0113	0.0063	0.0113	—	0.0000
Sum of squares*		0.02744	0.00952	0.00921	—	0.01824
Stddev ($\hat{\sigma}_r$)		0.0499	0.0294	0.0289	—	0.0407

*Sum of squares $= \sum_{t=1}^{T}\left(r_t - \bar{r}\right)^2$

(*Continued*)

EXAMPLE 8.1 (*Continued*)

The scatter plot for the returns from stock i and the market portfolio is drawn in Figure 8.3.

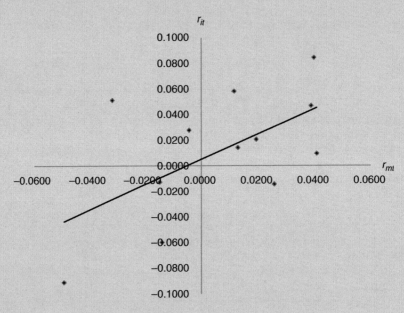

FIGURE 8.3 Plot of the Returns from a Stock and the Market Portfolio

The estimates of the regression parameters are calculated as

$$\hat{\beta}_i = \frac{\sum_{t=1}^{12} (r_{it} - r_i)(r_{mt} - \bar{r}_m)}{\sum_{t=1}^{T} (r_{it} - \bar{r}_i)^2}$$

$$= \frac{0.00936}{0.00952} = 0.983$$

$$\hat{\alpha}_i = \bar{r}_i - \hat{\beta}_i \bar{r}_m$$

$$= 0.0113 - (0.983)(0.0063) = 0.00511$$

$$\hat{\sigma}_{\varepsilon i}^2 = \left(\frac{1}{T-2}\right) \sum_{t=1}^{12} \hat{\varepsilon}_{it}^2$$

$$= \left(\frac{1}{T-2}\right) \sum_{t=1}^{12} \left[r_{it} - \left(\hat{\alpha}_i + \hat{\beta}_i r_{mt}\right)\right]^2$$

$$= \left(\frac{1}{12-2}\right) \left[(-0.0036)^2 + (-0.0510)^2 + \cdots + 0.0269^2\right]$$

$$= \left(\frac{1}{12-2}\right)(0.01824) = 0.001824$$

8.1.3 The Single-Index Model Using Excess Returns

During the late 1960s Michael C. Jensen, a PhD student at the University of Chicago, suggested advantages to using the excess return (risk premium) defined in equation (8.4) as the basic random variable.[6]

$$\underbrace{R_{it}}_{\text{Excess return}} = \underbrace{r_{it}}_{\text{HPR}} - \underbrace{r_f}_{\text{Riskless return}} \tag{8.4}$$

It can be argued that the excess return defined in equation (8.4) differs from the holding period return (HPR) defined in equation (1.1) by a positive constant and, therefore, the two return measures are not substantially different. Section 18.4.3 of Chapter 18 explains how Jensen uses the excess return defined in equation (8.4) to make a valuable contribution to investment performance evaluation. The riskless rate of return, r_f, may be a meaningful random variable in its own right. When the riskless rate of return fluctuates over time, it is given a time subscript, denoted r_{ft}.

Jensen showed that excess returns may also come from a return-generating function that is similar to, but different from, the Markowitz-Sharpe-Treynor return-generating function of equation (8.1). Jensen reformulated the single-index market model in HPRs of equation (8.1) to become the single-index market model stated in terms of excess returns shown in equations (8.5) and (8.5a).

$$r_{it} - r_f = \alpha_i' + \beta_i \left(r_{mt} - r_f \right) + \varepsilon_{it} \tag{8.5}$$

or

$$R_{it} = \alpha_i' + \beta_i R_{mt} + \varepsilon_{it} \tag{8.5a}$$

where $R_{it} = r_{it} - r_f$ and $R_{mt} = r_{mt} - r_f$ are the excess return of asset i and the market index, respectively, for time period t. The original version of the single-index model of equation (8.1) and its excess return version, equation (8.5), are very similar. The beta slope coefficient, β_i, and the error term, ε_{it}, of the two versions are the same, because the dependent and independent variables are reduced by the same constant, r_f. Only the intercept terms differ. The relationship between the two intercepts is

$$\alpha_i' = \alpha_i - r_f \left(1 - \beta_i \right) \tag{8.6}$$

The intercept of Jensen's excess return version of the single-index model is called Jensen's alpha. A variance decomposition resembling earlier equation (8.3) also holds for the excess return version of the single-index model.

$$\begin{aligned}
\text{Var}\left(R_{it}\right) &= \text{Var}\left(\alpha_i + \beta_i R_{mt} + \varepsilon_{it}\right) \\
&= \text{E}\big[\left(\alpha_i + \beta_i R_{mt} + \varepsilon_{it}\right) - \text{E}\left(\alpha_i + \beta_i R_{mt} + \varepsilon_{it}\right)\big]^2 \\
&= E\left[\beta_i^2 \left(R_{mt} - \mu_m\right)^2 + \varepsilon_{it}^2 + 2\beta_i \left(R_{mt} - \mu_m\right)\varepsilon_{it}\right] \\
&= \beta_i^2 \sigma_m^2 + \sigma_{\varepsilon i}^2
\end{aligned}$$

EXAMPLE 8.2

Assume an invariant riskless interest rate of three percent per year exists. This annual rate of interest is converted into monthly returns by dividing $r_f = 3.0$ percent by the number of months in one year to obtain an equivalent riskless interest rate of $(3\% / 12 \text{ months} =) 0.25\% = 0.0025$ per month. Table 8.2 reproduces the holding period excess returns from Table 8.1 by subtracting the monthly riskless rate of return $r_f = 0.0025$ from the monthly HPRs from the stock and from the monthly returns on the market.

TABLE 8.2 Hypothetical Monthly Holding Period Excess Returns from a Stock and the Market

Month	t	Excess return on stock i R_{it} $(= r_{it} - r_f)$ (1)	Excess return on the market R_{mt} $(= r_{mt} - r_f)$ (2)	Fitted excess return on stock i $\hat{\alpha}_i + \hat{\beta}_i R_{mt}$ (3)	Product $(R_{it} - \overline{R}_i) \times$ $(R_{mt} - \overline{R}_m)$ (4)	Unexplained residuals $\hat{\varepsilon}_{it}$ (1)–(3)
January	1	0.0181	0.0169	0.0217	0.0001	−0.0036
February	2	−0.0621	−0.0165	−0.0112	0.0014	−0.0510
March	3	0.0117	0.0104	0.0153	0.0000	−0.0036
April	4	0.0818	0.0374	0.0418	0.0025	0.0400
May	5	0.0444	0.0364	0.0409	0.0012	0.0035
June	6	−0.0152	−0.0173	−0.0119	0.0005	−0.0033
July	7	0.0488	−0.0342	−0.0286	−0.0015	0.0774
August	8	0.0557	0.0091	0.0140	0.0003	0.0417
September	9	0.0070	0.0384	0.0428	−0.0001	−0.0358
October	10	−0.0168	0.0234	0.0280	−0.0005	−0.0448
November	11	−0.0933	−0.0518	−0.0459	0.0057	−0.0474
December	12	0.0253	−0.0068	−0.0016	−0.0002	−0.0269
Total		0.1055	0.0454	0.1055	0.00936	0.0000
Average ($\overline{R}$)		0.0088	0.0038	0.0088	—	0.0000
Sum of squares*		0.02744	0.00952	0.00921	—	0.01824
Stddev ($\hat{\sigma}_R$)		0.0499	0.0294	0.0289	—	0.0407

*Sum of squares $= \sum_{t=1}^{T}(r_t - \overline{r})^2$

As in Example 8.1, statistical estimates of the regression's population parameters are calculated next.

$$\hat{\beta}_i = \frac{\sum_{t=1}^{12}\left(R_{it} - \overline{R}_i\right)\left(R_{mt} - \overline{R}_m\right)}{\sum_{t=1}^{T}\left(R_{it} - \overline{R}_i\right)^2}$$

$$= \frac{\sum_{t=1}^{12}\left(r_{it} - r_i\right)\left(r_{mt} - \overline{r}_m\right)}{\sum_{t=1}^{T}\left(r_{it} - \overline{r}_i\right)^2} = \frac{0.00936}{0.00952} = 0.983$$

EXAMPLE 8.2 *(Continued)*

$$\hat{\alpha}_i' = \overline{R}_i - \hat{\beta}_i \overline{R}_m$$

$$= 0.0088 - (0.983)(0.0038) = 0.00506$$

$$\hat{\sigma}_{\varepsilon i}^2 = \left(\frac{1}{T-2}\right) \sum_{t=1}^{12} \hat{\varepsilon}_{it}^2 = \left(\frac{1}{T-2}\right) \sum_{t=1}^{12} \left[R_{it} - \left(\hat{\alpha}_i + \hat{\beta}_i R_{mt}\right) \right]^2$$

$$= \left(\frac{1}{12-2}\right)(0.01824) = 0.001824$$

The estimates of the slope coefficient (β_i) and the error variance $(\sigma_{\varepsilon i}^2)$ in this example are exactly the same as those in Example 8.1. Only the intercept estimate is different. In fact, as mentioned previously, the intercept estimate in this example $(\hat{\alpha}_i')$ can be obtained through equation (8.6).

If Jensen's single-index market model stated in terms of excess returns in Table 8.2 were graphed, that graph would differ slightly from Figure 8.3. All the little differences that occur can be attributed to the two alpha intercept terms that differ slightly. The difference in the two illustrations would be so small it would be difficult to see in this particular numerical example. If the underlying sample of market data were different, sometimes it would be possible to find a graph of Jensen's single-index market model stated in terms of excess returns that would differ noticeably from a graph of the Markowitz-Sharpe-Treynor single-index market model computed with holding period returns.

8.1.4 The Riskless Rate Can Fluctuate

Portfolio theory equates risk with variability of return. Thus, it would seem that the riskless interest rate should be invariant. However, over a century ago a well-known economics professor named Irving Fisher taught us that the level of market interest rates rise and fall with the rate of inflation.[7] Figure 8.4 illustrates the way the one-year U.S. Treasury bill interest rate (solid line) and the annualized inflation rate in the consumer price index (CPI) (dashed line) covary through time; their correlation is 0.70.

When financial analysts perform empirical work, they often use U.S. Treasury bill interest rates as surrogates for the riskless interest rate. Although U.S. Treasury bills are U.S. government bonds that are default free, their prices and yields nevertheless fluctuate because of changing inflationary expectations and other factors. In other words, empirical researchers sometimes use a riskless interest rate that involves risky variations, $\text{Var}\left(r_{ft}\right) > 0$. All U.S. Treasury bills mature within one year. The prices of these short-term bonds fluctuate less than the prices of the longer-term U.S. Treasury bonds. And, default-free U.S. Treasury bonds fluctuate less than corporate bonds with equal maturities, because the corporate bonds also involve default risk. But, as illustrated in Figure 8.4, the one-year T-bill rate fluctuates significantly over time.

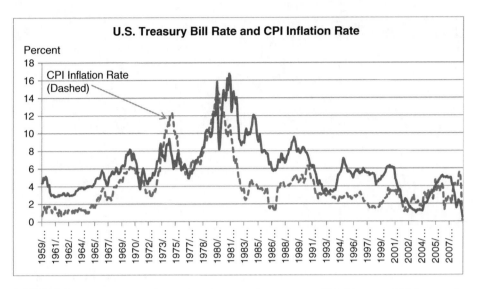

FIGURE 8.4   Time-series Relationship Between the One-year U.S. Treasury Bill Interest Rate and the Annualized Inflation Rate
Source: Federal Reserve Economic Database.

When the riskless interest rate fluctuates over time, Jensen's single-index model of equation (8.5) can be formulated by simply replacing the constant riskless rate of return, r_f, with a time-varying riskless rate of return, r_{ft}. That is,

$$r_{it} - r_{ft} = \alpha_i' + \beta_i \left(r_{mt} - r_{ft} \right) + \varepsilon_{it} \tag{8.5}$$

or

$$R_{it} = \alpha_i' + \beta_i R_{mt} + \varepsilon_{it} \tag{8.5a}$$

where $R_{it} = r_{it} - r_{ft}$ and $R_{mt} = r_{mt} - r_{ft}$. When the riskless interest rate fluctuates over time, the covariance between the excess return from asset i and the excess return from the market is affected. And, in turn, the beta slope coefficient and the alpha intercept term are also affected by variation in the riskless rate. Because the variation of the riskless rate of return r_{ft} is usually much smaller than the variations in holding period returns from the stock and the market, the impact on the beta slope coefficient estimate is small. Consequently, the difference between the two beta slope estimates in equations (8.1) and (8.5a) is small.

EXAMPLE 8.3

Consider the parameters of the single-index model when the riskless rate of return fluctuates over time. Table 8.3 repeats the holding period returns from Tables 8.1 and 8.2, but inserts a fluctuating riskless interest rate.

EXAMPLE 8.3 (*Continued*)

TABLE 8.3 Hypothetical Monthly Holding Period Returns with Fluctuating Riskless Rates of Return

Month	t	Excess return on stock i R_{it} $(= r_{it} - r_{ft})$ (1)	Excess return on the market R_{mt} $(= r_{mt} - r_{ft})$ (2)	Riskless rate of return r_{ft} (3)	Fitted excess return on stock i $\hat{\alpha}_i + \hat{\beta}_i R_{mt}$ (4)	Product $(R_{it} - \overline{R}_i) \times$ $(R_{mt} - \overline{R}_m)$ (5)	Unexplained residuals $\hat{\varepsilon}_{it}$ (1)–(4)
January	1	0.0201	0.0189	0.0005	0.0236	0.0001	−0.0035
February	2	−0.0599	−0.0143	0.0003	−0.0088	0.0014	−0.0512
March	3	0.0135	0.0122	0.0008	0.0170	0.0000	−0.0036
April	4	0.0830	0.0386	0.0013	0.0426	0.0024	0.0404
May	5	0.0451	0.0371	0.0018	0.0412	0.0011	0.0039
June	6	−0.0132	−0.0153	0.0005	−0.0097	0.0005	−0.0035
July	7	0.0504	−0.0327	0.0009	−0.0266	−0.0015	0.0770
August	8	0.0570	0.0104	0.0013	0.0152	0.0002	0.0417
September	9	0.0093	0.0407	0.0002	0.0447	0.0000	−0.0354
October	10	−0.0148	0.0253	0.0006	0.0297	−0.0005	−0.0446
November	11	−0.0912	−0.0497	0.0004	−0.0431	0.0056	−0.0481
December	12	0.0277	−0.0044	0.0001	0.0009	−0.0002	0.0268
Total		0.1269	0.0669	0.0086	0.1269	0.00914	0.0000
Average ($\overline{R}$)		0.0106	0.0056	0.0007	0.0106	—	0.0000
Sum of squares[*]		0.02711	0.00940	0.00000	0.00887	—	0.01823
Stddev ($\hat{\sigma}_R$)		0.0496	0.0292	0.0005	0.0284	—	0.0407

[*] Sum of squares $= \sum_{t=1}^{T} (r_t - \overline{r})^2$

As in Example 8.2, the estimates of the regression parameters are calculated below.

$$\hat{\beta}_i = \frac{\sum_{t=1}^{12} \left(R_{it} - \overline{R}_i\right)\left(R_{mt} - \overline{R}_m\right)}{\sum_{t=1}^{T} \left(R_{it} - \overline{R}_i\right)^2}$$

$$= \frac{0.00914}{0.00940} = 0.972$$

$$\hat{\alpha}'_i = \overline{R}_i - \hat{\beta}_i \overline{R}_m$$

$$= 0.0106 - (0.972)(0.0056) = 0.00516$$

$$\hat{\sigma}_{\varepsilon i}^2 = \left(\frac{1}{T-2}\right)\sum_{t=1}^{12} \hat{\varepsilon}_{it}^2 = \left(\frac{1}{T-2}\right)\sum_{t=1}^{12} \left[R_{it} - \left(\hat{\alpha}_i + \hat{\beta}_i R_{mt}\right)\right]^2$$

$$= \left(\frac{1}{12-2}\right)(0.01823) = 0.001823$$

The beta slope coefficient computed with Jensen's excess returns is smaller than the beta slope coefficient computed with holding period returns: $0.983 > 0.972$. Generally speaking, the beta may be smaller, equal, or larger when it is computed with Jensen's excess returns during a sample period in which the riskless interest rate fluctuates. However, the values of the betas from the two models do not usually differ significantly.

Figure 8.3 illustrated the Markowitz-Sharpe-Treynor single-index market model in terms of the holding period returns from Example 8.1. If Jensen's single-index market model stated in terms of excess returns in Table 8.3 were graphed, that graph would differ from Figure 8.3 because the alpha and beta statistics differ. The size of this difference will vary with the sample data. If the underlying sample of market data is substantially different, a graph of Jensen's single-index market model will differ from a graph of the Markowitz-Sharpe-Treynor single-index market model enough to be noticed. Most differences in the alphas, betas, and residual variances can be attributed to the fluctuations in the riskless interest rate. Nonetheless, when a firm's systematic risk (or market beta) is estimated, it is satisfactory to use the single-index market models of either equation (8.1) or (8.5a).

8.1.5   Diversification

When securities' returns follow the single-index model, the return of a portfolio of those securities also follows the single-index model. That is, the portfolio's return can be described as

$$r_{pt} = \sum_{i=1}^{n} w_i \left(\alpha_i + \beta_i r_{mt} + \varepsilon_{it} \right)$$

$$= \sum_{i=1}^{n} w_i \alpha_i + \left(\sum_{i=1}^{n} w_i \beta_i \right) r_{mt} + \sum_{i=1}^{n} w_i \varepsilon_{it}$$

$$= \alpha_p + \beta_p r_{mt} + \varepsilon_{pt} \tag{8.7}$$

where $\alpha_p = \sum_{i=1}^{n} w_i \alpha_i$, $\beta_p = \left(\sum_{i=1}^{n} w_i \beta_i \right)$, and $\varepsilon_{pt} = \sum_{i=1}^{n} w_i \varepsilon_{it}$. Thus, when the single-index model holds for individual securities, it also holds for portfolios. Like individual stocks, the variance of the return of a portfolio can be decomposed into two components:

$$\mathrm{Var}\left(r_{pt} \right) \equiv \sigma_p^2 = E\big[\left(\alpha_p + \beta_p r_{mt} + \varepsilon_{pt} \right) - E\left(\alpha_p + \beta_p r_{mt} + \varepsilon_{pt} \right) \big]^2$$

$$= \beta_p^2 E\left(r_{mt} - \mu_m \right)^2 + E\left(\varepsilon_{pt}^{\ 2} \right) + 2\beta_p E\big[\left(r_{mt} - \mu_m \right) \varepsilon_{pt} \big]$$

$$= \beta_p^2 \sigma_m^2 + \sigma_{\varepsilon p}^2 \tag{8.8}$$

The term on the left-hand side (LHS), σ_p^2, is known as the total risk of the portfolio. The first term on the RHS of equation (8.8), $\beta_p^2 \sigma_m^2$, is known as the portfolio's undiversifiable or systematic risk, and the second term, $\sigma_{\varepsilon p}^2$, is known as the diversifiable or unsystematic risk of the portfolio:

$$\text{Total risk} = \frac{\text{Systematic or}}{\text{nondiversifiable risk}} + \frac{\text{Unsystematic or}}{\text{diversifiable risk}}$$

The reason for this portfolio nomenclature can be found in considering a well-diversified portfolio that has the investor's funds spread evenly over n different securities. For the n securities held in the portfolio, $w_i = 1/n$. Reconsider the second term on the right-hand side (RHS) of equation (8.8), $\sigma^2_{\varepsilon_p}$.

$$\sigma^2_{\varepsilon_p} = \text{Var}\left(\sum_{i=1}^{n} w_i \varepsilon_{it}\right) = \sum_{i=1}^{n} w_i^2 \sigma^2_{\varepsilon i}$$

$$= \left(\frac{1}{n}\right)\left(\frac{1}{n}\sum_{i=1}^{n} \sigma^2_{\varepsilon i}\right)$$

$$= \left(\frac{1}{n}\right)\overline{\sigma}^2_{\varepsilon} \tag{8.9}$$

where $\overline{\sigma}^2_{\varepsilon}$ is the average value of the residual variances. As n increases, due to the law of large numbers, $\overline{\sigma}^2_{\varepsilon}$ will approach its true value, a positive constant. However, $1/n$ will approach zero as n increases. Thus, the product $(1/n)\,\overline{\sigma}^2_{\varepsilon}$ will approach to zero as n increases.

As n increases, there is no a priori reason to expect $\overline{\beta}_p$ (the average beta of the securities in the portfolio) to move in a particular direction (assuming that the securities added are drawn randomly from a population with mean $\overline{\beta}_p$). Thus, because σ^2_m can be viewed as a constant, the value of the product $\beta^2_p \sigma^2_m$ will not move in a systematic direction as n is increased. Combining equations (8.8) and (8.9), we can see that, with the market model, the portfolio variance can be expressed as

$$\sigma^2_p = \beta^2_p \sigma^2_m + \sigma^2_{\varepsilon p}$$

$$= \beta^2_p \sigma^2_m + \left(\frac{1}{n}\right)\overline{\sigma}^2_{\varepsilon}$$

$$\rightarrow \beta^2_p \sigma^2_m \quad \text{as } n \text{ increases large,}$$

so that for arbitrarily large values of n, $\sigma^2_p \cong \beta^2_p \sigma^2_m$. Thus, for a relatively large number of securities in a portfolio, the unsystematic risk of the portfolio can be diversified away, and only the systematic risk remains. William Sharpe said: ".... a little diversification can go a long way toward reducing risk. A portfolio containing 15 or 20 securities may be considered well-diversified in this respect."[8]

Note that even if the weights for the securities are not equal to $1/n$, it still can be shown that $\sigma^2_p \cong \beta^2_p \sigma^2_m$, where β_p equals the weighted average beta of the securities in the portfolio. U.S. securities law limits the maximum proportion that a mutual fund is allowed to invest in any one security to the arbitrarily small amount of 5 percent (a constraint that is set forth by the U.S. Investment Company Act of 1940). This legal stipulation ensures that U.S. mutual fund betas will resemble betas from individual securities.

8.1.6 About the Single-Index Model

The Markowitz-Sharpe-Treynor single-index market model first appeared in print in 1959. In 1968 Jensen published his doctoral dissertation, which introduced his single-index market model (or characteristic line) formulated with excess returns. These two return-generating functions may seem to be similar, and, in some important respects, they are alike. First, the beta coefficients in both return-generating functions provide satisfactory indexes of systematic (undiversifiable) risk. And these two beta coefficients from different return-generating models will be identical, if the riskless interest rate is invariant. Second, partitioning the risk from these two different return-generating functions separates systematic risk and unsystematic risk into insightful components that have similar interpretations. However, even if the riskless interest rate is invariant, the two return-generating functions differ in other ways. Important implications of both models, which are not explored until later chapters, differentiate the two models. Although the alpha intercept terms from both models measure important idiosyncratic characteristics of the underlying asset, these two alphas have different values, different meanings, and different applications.

When excess returns are calculated with a fluctuating riskless interest rate, the Markowitz-Sharpe-Treynor single-index market model and the Jensen model produce numerically different beta coefficients. But, whether a fluctuating or a constant riskless interest rate is used to compute the excess returns, the Markowitz-Sharpe-Treynor single-index market model and the Jensen model will always have conceptually different alphas. Chapter 18 shows that Jensen's alpha has investment performance implications that are insightful, useful, and unrelated to the alphas from the Markowitz-Sharpe-Treynor single-index market model.

8.2   EFFICIENT FRONTIER AND THE SINGLE-INDEX MODEL

If a portfolio analyst is going to derive the efficient frontier from a group of n assets (where n is any positive integer), the following three statistics (also referred to as parameter estimates) are required as inputs to portfolio analysis:

1. Expected return estimates for all n assets under consideration.
2. Standard deviations (or variances) of the rates of return for all n assets.
3. All the covariances (or, equivalently, correlation coefficients) between these assets' rates of return.[9] It can be shown that $(n^2 - n)/2$ covariances (or correlations) are required to analyze n assets.

These statistics are the *input data* used to fill the cells in the expected return vector and variance-covariance matrix that are explored in this chapter. The sample statistics must be estimated because their "true" population parameters are unobservable. The formulas for the expected return, $E(r)$; standard deviation, σ; and the covariance, $\text{Cov}(r_i, r_j)$ or σ_{ij}, were introduced in Chapter 2.

The efficient portfolios generated by portfolio analysis are no better than the statistical input data on which they are based. Therefore, it is imperative that attention be devoted to this phase of portfolio management. Three different approaches are suggested for generating the statistical inputs: (1) The parameters may be directly estimated on an asset-by-asset basis without assuming any return-generating process; (2) a one-factor return-generating process can be used to estimate the parameters; or (3) a multiple-factor return-generating process can be assumed to exist, from which the parameters may be estimated.[10] Regardless of the approach used, the security analyst may base his or her estimates on either ex post (historical) returns or, alternatively, subjective judgment. Information used for subjective estimates could include, but not be limited to, ex post returns. The probability distributions of returns often demonstrate sufficient intertemporal statistical stability to make historical data useful in preparing estimates of future-oriented input statistics.

Approach (1) to generating the statistical inputs involves estimating each candidate security's expected return, variance, and covariances with all the other candidate securities. Accordingly, the security analyst must estimate $(n^2 + 3n)/2$ parameters [that is, n expected returns, n variances, plus $(n^2 - n)/2$ covariances] for n securities. For example, if an analyst follows 500 stocks, he/she must estimate 125,750 parameters [that is, 500 average returns, 500 variances, and 124,750 covariance terms]. This is the input requirement for Markowitz's full-covariance model. The estimation method of each parameter was described in Chapter 2.

It seems unlikely that the security analyst will be able to directly estimate huge numbers of parameters (especially covariances or correlation coefficients) with ease, because it would be inconvenient to keep the data on a huge number of the estimated values. Because the number of parameters to be estimated rises exponentially relative to the number of securities, Markowitz made certain suggestions to expedite the use of his portfolio analysis model. Following his suggestion, Sharpe (1963) developed a simplified model of portfolio analysis called the *single-index model*. This simplified model requires fewer input data, thus simplifying both the parameter estimation process and the derivation of the efficient frontier. As a result, the computer running time for solving this simplified portfolio analysis problem is a small fraction of the time required to solve the same problem using the full-covariance model. But, as might be expected, the efficient frontiers obtained using these simplifications may differ somewhat from the efficient frontiers obtained with the full-covariance model.

In addition to the benefit of having to input fewer estimated parameters, a second benefit can be obtained by using the single-index model. The portfolio analysis problem itself may be reformulated in terms of the market index variables $E(r_m)$ and σ_m^2, thereby offering computational shortcuts in deriving the efficient frontier. This formulation is analogous to the regular Markowitz formulation. The return of a portfolio is defined as before:

$$r_{pt} = \sum_{i=1}^{n} w_i r_{it}$$

However, using equation (8.1) permits us to redefine the portfolio's return as follows.

$$r_{pt} = \sum_{i=1}^{n} w_i \left(\alpha_i + \beta_i r_{mt} + \varepsilon_{it} \right)$$

Sharpe suggests that the portion of the portfolio invested in security i can be viewed as having two components:

1. An investment in the basic characteristics of the security—that is, $w_i \left(\alpha_i + \varepsilon_{it} \right)$.
2. An investment in the index—that is, $w_i \left(\beta_i r_{mt} \right)$.

Thus, the portfolio return is a combination of n basic securities and an investment in the index, as represented by equation (8.10):

$$r_{pt} = \sum_{i=1}^{n} w_i \left(\alpha_i + \varepsilon_{it} \right) + \left(\sum_{i=1}^{n} w_i \beta_i \right) r_{mt} \qquad (8.10)$$

Sharpe decomposes the rates of change in the market index into two parts in formulating the simplified diagonal portfolio analysis model:

$$r_{mt} = E(r_m) + \varepsilon_{mt}$$

$$= \alpha_{n+1} + \varepsilon_{n+1,t} \tag{8.11}$$

where $E(r_m) = \alpha_{n+1}$ is a constant that estimates the expected rate of return on the market index and $\varepsilon_{mt} = \varepsilon_{n+1,t}$ is a random-error term with a mean of zero that measures the period-by-period fluctuations of r_{mt} around α_{n+1}. Accordingly, the variance of the market index, σ_m^2, is equal to the variance of $\varepsilon_{n+1,t}$, denoted $\sigma_{\varepsilon_{n+1}}^2$. To gain a significant notational convenience that will become apparent as the single-index model of portfolio analysis is introduced, the market index is subsequently treated as security $(n + 1)$ in a portfolio consisting of n individual securities.

Sharpe defines the weight of this artificial security (which is, as just mentioned, the market index), denoted w_{n+1}, as

$$w_{n+1} = \sum_{i=1}^{n} w_i \beta_i \tag{8.12}$$

The term w_{n+1} simply equals the weighted average of the beta coefficients—which should equal a number near unity, because all betas in the market average out to unity. The purpose of defining variables α_{n+1}, $\varepsilon_{n+1,t}$, and w_{n+1} is to simplify equation (8.10) into a form suitable for portfolio analysis. Substituting equations (8.11) and (8.12) into the RHS of equation (8.10) yields equation (8.13).

$$r_{pt} = \sum_{i=1}^{n} w_i (\alpha_i + \varepsilon_{it}) + w_{n+1} (\alpha_{n+1} + \varepsilon_{n+1,t})$$

$$= \sum_{i=1}^{n+1} w_i (\alpha_i + \varepsilon_{it}) \tag{8.13}$$

Because the expected value of all $(n + 1)$ error terms is zero, the expectation of equation (8.13) is

$$E(r_{pt}) = E\left[\sum_{i=1}^{n+1} w_i (\alpha_i + \varepsilon_{it})\right]$$

$$= \sum_{i=1}^{n+1} w_i \alpha_i \tag{8.14}$$

Examination of the algebraic simplifications leading to equation (8.14) reveals why the notation using w_{n+1} and α_{n+1} was used—it facilitates compact notation for deriving the portfolio expected return formulation.

Sharpe also simplified the expression for portfolio risk. Portfolio risk may be measured by taking the weighted sum of the variances and covariances for all the assets in the portfolio. Or, equivalently, portfolio risk may be measured directly from the portfolio's returns as

$$\text{Var}(r_{pt}) \equiv \sigma_p^2 = E[r_{pt} - E(r_{pt})]^2$$

Substituting equations (8.13) and (8.14) into the equation above yields

$$\sigma_p^2 = E\left\{\left[\sum_{i=1}^{n+1} w_i\left(\alpha_i + \varepsilon_{it}\right) - \sum_{i=1}^{n+1} w_i\alpha_i\right]^2\right\}$$

$$= E\left\{\left[\sum_{i=1}^{n+1} w_i\varepsilon_{it}\right]^2\right\}$$

$$= \text{Var}\left(\sum_{i=1}^{n+1} w_i\varepsilon_{it}\right) \tag{8.15}$$

since $E\left(\sum_{i=1}^{n+1} w_i\varepsilon_{it}\right) = 0$. Using the portfolio risk formula from equation (2.18a) reveals that equation (8.15) is equal to

$$\sigma_p^2 = \sum_{i=1}^{n+1} w_i^2\sigma_{\varepsilon_i}^2 + \sum_{i=1}^{n+1}\sum_{\substack{j=1 \\ \text{for } j \neq i}}^{n+1} w_i w_j \text{Cov}\left(\varepsilon_{it}, \varepsilon_{jt}\right) \tag{8.16}$$

because $\text{Cov}\left(\varepsilon_{it}, \varepsilon_{jt}\right) = 0$ for $i \neq j$, equation (8.16) can be simplified, leaving the following:

$$\sigma_p^2 = \sum_{i=1}^{n+1} w_i^2\sigma_{\varepsilon_i}^2 \tag{8.17}$$

The significance of the name "diagonal model" can be seen in matrix equation (8.18). The variance-covariance matrix displayed on the RHS of equation (8.17) has zeros in all positions other than the diagonal, as shown in equation (8.18).

$$\sigma_p^2 = \begin{bmatrix} w_1 & w_2 & \cdots & w_n & w_{n+1} \end{bmatrix}\begin{pmatrix} \sigma_{\varepsilon_1}^2 & 0 & \cdots & 0 & 0 \\ 0 & \sigma_{\varepsilon_2}^2 & \cdots & 0 & 0 \\ \vdots & \vdots & \ddots & 0 & \vdots \\ 0 & 0 & 0 & \sigma_{\varepsilon_n}^2 & 0 \\ 0 & 0 & \cdots & 0 & \sigma_m^2 \end{pmatrix}\begin{pmatrix} w_1 \\ w_2 \\ \vdots \\ w_n \\ w_{n+1} \end{pmatrix} \tag{8.18}$$

The diagonal matrix of equation (8.18) can be inverted with less computation than a full variance-covariance matrix, because all that is necessary is to calculate the reciprocal of each diagonal entry. The resulting inverted matrix is also a diagonal matrix with these reciprocals appearing on its diagonal. This computational ease leads to considerable computational savings in large portfolio problems.

With the single-index model, the problem of identifying a portfolio on the efficient frontier involves finding the weights that minimize the portfolio variance,

$$\text{Minimize} \quad \sigma_p^2 = \sum_{i=1}^{n+1} w_i^2\sigma_{\varepsilon_i}^2 \tag{8.19}$$

subject to three mathematical constraints. Note that multiplying a constant fraction $(1/2)$ times the objective function in equation (8.19), as we do below, does not change any of the conclusions that follow. We multiply the fraction times a Lagrangian objective function merely to simplify the equations that follow. The first constraint on minimizing equation (8.19) requires that some desired (or target) level of expected return, $E(r_p)$, from the portfolio be achieved.

$$\sum_{i=1}^{n+1} w_i \alpha_i = E(r_p) \tag{8.20}$$

This constraint is based on equation (8.14). The second constraint on minimizing equation (8.19) is that the weights sum to 1.

$$\sum_{i=1}^{n} w_i = 1 \tag{2.10}$$

Equation (8.12) is the third constraint.

$$\sum_{i=1}^{n} w_i \beta_i = w_{n+1} \tag{8.12}$$

Equations (8.20), (2.11), and (8.12) are called the *Lagrangian constraints*.

Combining the equations (8.19), (8.20), (2.11), and (8.12), we form a Lagrangian objective function for the risk-minimization problem.

$$\text{Minimize } L = \frac{1}{2} \sum_{i=1}^{n+1} w_i^2 \sigma_{\varepsilon_i}^2 + \lambda_1 \left[E(r_p) - \sum_{i=1}^{n+1} w_i \alpha_i \right] + \lambda_2 \left(1 - \sum_{i=1}^{n} w_i \right)$$
$$+ \lambda_3 \left(w_{n+1} - \sum_{i=1}^{n} w_i \beta_i \right) \tag{8.21}$$

where λ_1, λ_2, and λ_3 are *Lagrangian multipliers*. Note that α_i, β_i, and $\sigma_{\varepsilon_i}^2$ are exogenous values which are obtained by estimating the single-index model of equation (8.1).

The minimum-risk portfolio is found by setting the partial derivatives of the Lagrangian objective function L with respect to w_i, denoted $\partial L/\partial w_i$, equal to zero, for $i = 1, 2, \ldots, n, n+1$ differential equations. The partial derivatives of the objective function with respect to the three Lagrangian multipliers are also set equal to zero, thus, $\partial L/\partial \lambda_j = 0$ for $j = 1, 2, 3$. These $(n+4)$ partial derivatives result in a system of $(n+4)$ simultaneous equations with $(n+4)$ unknowns $(w_1, \ldots, w_n, w_{n+1}, \lambda_1, \lambda_2, \lambda_3)$, as shown below.

$$\frac{\partial L}{\partial w_i} = w_i \sigma_{\varepsilon_i}^2 - \lambda_1 \alpha_i - \lambda_2 - \lambda_3 \beta_i = 0 \quad \text{for } i = 1, 2, \ldots, n \text{ equations} \tag{8.22}$$

$$\frac{\partial L}{\partial w_{n+1}} = w_{n+1} \sigma_{\varepsilon_{n+1}}^2 - \lambda_1 \alpha_{n+1} + \lambda_3 = 0 \tag{8.23}$$

$$\frac{\partial L}{\partial \lambda_1} = \sum_{i=1}^{n+1} w_i \alpha_i - E(r_p) = 0 \tag{8.24}$$

$$\frac{\partial L}{\partial \lambda_2} = \sum_{i=1}^{n} w_i - 1 = 0 \qquad (8.25)$$

$$\frac{\partial L}{\partial \lambda_3} = \sum_{i=1}^{n} w_i \beta_i - w_{n+1} = 0 \qquad (8.26)$$

It is well known from linear algebra that when the number of linear equations equals the number of unknown variables contained in those equations, it is possible to solve those linear equations simultaneously.[11] Thus, solving the above $(n+4)$ simultaneous linear equations can be done to obtain solutions for the $(n+4)$ unknowns.

Specifically, from equations (8.22) and (8.23), we obtain equations (8.22a) and (8.23a), respectively.

$$w_i = \frac{1}{\sigma_{\varepsilon_i}^2} \left(\lambda_1 \alpha_i + \lambda_2 + \lambda_3 \beta_i \right) \text{ for } i = 1, 2, \ldots, n \qquad (8.22a)$$

$$w_{n+1} = \frac{1}{\sigma_{\varepsilon_{n+1}}^2} \left(\lambda_1 \alpha_{n+1} - \lambda_3 \right) \qquad (8.23a)$$

Plugging equations (8.22a) and (8.23a) into equations (8.24), (8.25), and (8.26) results in the following three simultaneous equations in the three unknowns $\lambda_1, \lambda_2, \lambda_3$.

$$\lambda_1 \left(\sum_{i=1}^{n} \frac{\alpha_i^2}{\sigma_{\varepsilon_i}^2} + \frac{\alpha_{n+1}^2}{\sigma_{\varepsilon_{n+1}}^2} \right) + \lambda_2 \left(\sum_{i=1}^{n} \frac{\alpha_i}{\sigma_{\varepsilon_i}^2} \right) + \lambda_3 \left(\sum_{i=1}^{n} \frac{\alpha_i \beta_i}{\sigma_{\varepsilon_i}^2} - \frac{\alpha_{n+1}}{\sigma_{\varepsilon_{n+1}}^2} \right) = E\left(r_p\right) \qquad (8.24a)$$

$$\lambda_1 \left(\sum_{i=1}^{n} \frac{\alpha_i}{\sigma_{\varepsilon_i}^2} \right) + \lambda_2 \left(\sum_{i=1}^{n} \frac{1}{\sigma_{\varepsilon_i}^2} \right) + \lambda_3 \left(\sum_{i=1}^{n} \frac{\beta_i}{\sigma_{\varepsilon_i}^2} \right) = 1 \qquad (8.25a)$$

$$\lambda_1 \left(\sum_{i=1}^{n} \frac{\alpha_i \beta_i}{\sigma_{\varepsilon_i}^2} - \frac{\alpha_{n+1}}{\sigma_{\varepsilon_{n+1}}^2} \right) + \lambda_2 \left(\sum_{i=1}^{n} \frac{\beta_i}{\sigma_{\varepsilon_i}^2} \right) + \lambda_3 \left(\sum_{i=1}^{n} \frac{\beta_i^2}{\sigma_{\varepsilon_i}^2} + \frac{1}{\sigma_{\varepsilon_{n+1}}^2} \right) = 0 \qquad (8.26a)$$

By solving the above three simultaneous equations, the values of λ_1, λ_2, and λ_3 are obtained. Then, we put the values of λ_1, λ_2, and λ_3 in equation (8.22a) to find the optimal weights, $w_1, w_2, \ldots$, and w_n. The value of w_{n+1} is obtained from equation (8.23a). Note that $\alpha_{n+1} = E\left(r_m\right)$ and $\sigma_{\varepsilon_{n+1}}^2 = \sigma_m^2$. For a solution with matrix notation, refer to the end-of-chapter appendix. This appendix also provides an equation for a relationship between the expected return and variance pairs for the portfolios along the efficient frontier; this equation represents the efficient frontier in the mean-variance space.

EXAMPLE 8.4

Assume we would like to earn a 1.20 percent target return from three stocks. The expected returns and variance-covariances of the three stocks are given as follows.

(Continued)

EXAMPLE 8.4 (*Continued*)

$$E = \begin{bmatrix} E(r_1) \\ E(r_2) \\ E(r_3) \end{bmatrix} = \begin{pmatrix} 2.40 \\ 1.37 \\ 0.76 \end{pmatrix}$$

and

$$\Sigma = \begin{pmatrix} \sigma_1^2 & \sigma_{12} & \sigma_{13} \\ \sigma_{21} & \sigma_2^2 & \sigma_{22} \\ \sigma_{31} & \sigma_{32} & \sigma_3^2 \end{pmatrix} = \begin{pmatrix} 20.35 & 6.63 & 4.23 \\ 6.63 & 21.60 & 5.53 \\ 4.23 & 5.53 & 23.65 \end{pmatrix}$$

The parameter estimates of the single-index model of equation (8.1) for these three stocks are also given:

$$\begin{pmatrix} \alpha_1 \\ \alpha_2 \\ \alpha_3 \end{pmatrix} = \begin{pmatrix} 1.488 \\ 0.035 \\ -0.025 \end{pmatrix}, \quad \begin{pmatrix} \beta_1 \\ \beta_2 \\ \beta_3 \end{pmatrix} = \begin{pmatrix} 0.959 \\ 1.055 \\ 1.065 \end{pmatrix}, \quad \text{and} \quad \begin{pmatrix} \sigma_{\varepsilon1}^2 \\ \sigma_{\varepsilon2}^2 \\ \sigma_{\varepsilon3}^2 \end{pmatrix} = \begin{pmatrix} 15.42 \\ 15.50 \\ 17.51 \end{pmatrix}$$

In addition, the average return and variance of the market portfolio are $E(r_m) = 0.954$ and $\sigma_m^2 = 6.08$, respectively. What are the optimal weights of these three stocks that give the lowest risk at the level of the given return of $E(r_p) = 1.20$ percent? For this example, the solutions by the full-covariance model and by the single-index model are provided for comparison.

First, we obtain the optimal weights for the mean-variance efficient portfolio under the full-covariance model. The detailed procedure of obtaining the optimal weights is described in Section 7.1.2 of Chapter 7. Therefore, only the final solution is provided here. The optimal weights for the full-covariance model from equation (7.17) are

$$w_p = \begin{pmatrix} w_1 \\ w_2 \\ w_3 \end{pmatrix} = \begin{pmatrix} 0.129 \\ 0.376 \\ 0.495 \end{pmatrix} \tag{8.27}$$

The return and variance of this portfolio are

$$E(r_p) = (0.129)(2.40) + (0.376)(1.37) + (0.497)(0.76) = 1.20$$

$$\sigma_p^2 = w_p' \Sigma w_p$$

$$= (0.129 \ 0.376 \ 0.497) \begin{pmatrix} 20.35 & 6.63 & 4.23 \\ 6.63 & 21.60 & 5.53 \\ 4.23 & 5.53 & 23.65 \end{pmatrix} \begin{pmatrix} 0.129 \\ 0.376 \\ 0.495 \end{pmatrix}$$

$$= 12.431 \tag{8.28}$$

Second, we can also obtain the optimal weights for the mean-variance efficient portfolio under the single-index model by using equations (8.22a) through (8.26a). Based on the given information of the single-index model parameters for the three stocks and the market portfolio, equations (8.24a), (8.25a), and (8.26a) become

EXAMPLE 8.4 *(Continued)*

$$\lambda_1 (0.305) + \lambda_2 (0.105) + \lambda_3 (-0.055) = 1.20$$

$$\lambda_1 (0.105) + \lambda_2 (0.186) + \lambda_3 (0.191) = 1$$

$$\lambda_1 (-0.055) + \lambda_2 (0.191) + \lambda_3 (0.361) = 0$$

Rewriting the above three simultaneous equations in a matrix form yields

$$\begin{pmatrix} 0.305 & 0.105 & -0.055 \\ 0.105 & 0.186 & 0.191 \\ -0.055 & 0.191 & 0.361 \end{pmatrix} \begin{pmatrix} \lambda_1 \\ \lambda_2 \\ \lambda_3 \end{pmatrix} = \begin{pmatrix} 1.20 \\ 1 \\ 0 \end{pmatrix} \qquad (8.29)$$

From equation (8.29), the values of the Lagrangian multipliers are

$$\begin{pmatrix} \lambda_1 \\ \lambda_2 \\ \lambda_3 \end{pmatrix} = \begin{pmatrix} 0.305 & 0.105 & -0.055 \\ 0.105 & 0.186 & 0.191 \\ -0.055 & 0.191 & 0.361 \end{pmatrix}^{-1} \begin{pmatrix} 1.20 \\ 1 \\ 0 \end{pmatrix} = \begin{pmatrix} -4.47 \\ 18.78 \\ -10.64 \end{pmatrix}$$

To find the optimal weights, we plug the values of the Lagrangian multipliers into equation (8.22a).

$$w_1 = \frac{1}{\sigma_{\varepsilon_1}^2} \left(\lambda_1 \alpha_1 + \lambda_2 + \lambda_3 \beta_1 \right)$$

$$= \frac{1}{15.42} \left[(-4.47)(1.488) + 18.78 + (-10.64)(0.959) \right]$$

$$= 0.125$$

$$w_2 = \frac{1}{\sigma_{\varepsilon_2}^2} \left(\lambda_1 \alpha_2 + \lambda_2 + \lambda_3 \beta_2 \right)$$

$$= \frac{1}{15.50} \left[(-4.47)(0.359) + 18.78 + (-10.64)(1.055) \right]$$

$$= 0.384$$

$$w_3 = \frac{1}{\sigma_{\varepsilon_3}^2} \left(\lambda_1 \alpha_3 + \lambda_2 + \lambda_3 \beta_3 \right)$$

$$= \frac{1}{17.51} \left[(-4.47)(-0.253) + 18.78 + (-10.64)(1.065) \right]$$

$$= 0.490$$

and

$$w_4 = \frac{1}{\sigma_{\varepsilon_4}^2} \left(\lambda_1 \alpha_4 - \lambda_3 \right) = \frac{1}{\sigma_m^2} \left[\lambda_1 E \left(r_m \right) - \lambda_3 \right]$$

$$= \frac{1}{6.08} \left[(-4.47)(0.954) - (10.64) \right] = 1.048$$

(Continued)

EXAMPLE 8.4 (*Continued*)

Therefore, the optimal weights of the three assets under the single-index model are

$$w_p = \begin{pmatrix} w_1 \\ w_2 \\ w_3 \end{pmatrix} = \begin{pmatrix} 0.125 \\ 0.384 \\ 0.490 \end{pmatrix} \tag{8.30}$$

Based on these weights, the return and variance of this portfolio are calculated as

$$E(r_p) = (0.125)\,(2.40) + (0.384)\,(1.37) + (0.490)\,(0.76) = 1.20$$

$$\sigma_p^2 = w_p' \Sigma w_p = (0.125 \ \ 0.384 \ \ 0.490) \begin{pmatrix} 20.35 & 6.63 & 4.23 \\ 6.63 & 21.60 & 5.53 \\ 4.23 & 5.53 & 23.65 \end{pmatrix} \begin{pmatrix} 0.125 \\ 0.384 \\ 0.490 \end{pmatrix}$$

$$= 12.433$$

The variance can also be calculated by using the error variance matrix, Σ_ε, as

$$\sigma_p^2 = w' \Sigma_\varepsilon w = (w_1 \ \ w_2 \ \cdots \ w_n \ \ w_{n+1}) \begin{pmatrix} \sigma_{\varepsilon 1}^2 & 0 & 0 & 0 \\ 0 & \sigma_{\varepsilon 2}^2 & 0 & 0 \\ 0 & 0 & \sigma_{\varepsilon 3}^2 & 0 \\ 0 & 0 & 0 & \sigma_m^2 \end{pmatrix}^{-1} \begin{pmatrix} w_1 \\ w_2 \\ \vdots \\ w_n \\ w_{n+1} \end{pmatrix}$$

$$= (0.125 \ \ 0.384 \ \ 0.490 \ \ 1.048) \begin{pmatrix} 15.42 & 0 & 0 & 0 \\ 0 & 15.50 & 0 & 0 \\ 0 & 0 & 17.51 & 0 \\ 0 & 0 & 0 & 6.08 \end{pmatrix} \begin{pmatrix} 0.125 \\ 0.384 \\ 0.490 \\ 1.048 \end{pmatrix}$$

$$= 12.433.$$

The optimal weights calculated with the full-covariance model and the single-index model in equations (8.27) and (8.30) are very similar. Based on these weights, the average returns on the portfolio are approximately the same, and the variances are only slightly different. Because the optimal weights obtained under the full-covariance matrix are the exact solution, the portfolio variance with these weights should be smaller than that of the variance obtained under the simplified single-index model. The difference in this example is small (12.433 versus 12.431). In other words, the solution for the optimal weights under the single-index model is close to the exact solution, and is quite acceptable.

8.3 TWO-INDEX MODELS

Single-index models contain only a single explanatory factor (or market index) to capture a systematic part of the stochastic movement of stock returns. If the single explanatory factor is not sufficient to capture its systematic part, additional explanatory factors can be added. If one more factor is added in the single-index model, the single-index model becomes a *two-index model*. If two-index models (or multi-index models) are constructed correctly, two-index models yield more precise solutions than single-index models.

8.3.1   Generating Inputs

Our discussion of multi-index models begins with two-index models. The two-index model provides a concrete example of how single-index models can be extended to multi-index models. One of the key assumptions of the single-index market model is that the covariance between the error terms of any two securities is zero [that is, $\text{Cov}\left(\varepsilon_{it}, \varepsilon_{jt}\right) = 0$ for $i \neq j$]. This assumption leads to the insight that the covariance of returns between any two securities arises primarily through their relationship with a common market factor. This important insight is represented symbolically as $\sigma_{ij} = \beta_i \beta_j \sigma_m^2$. However, if one or more additional underlying (statistically significant explanatory) factors are omitted from the model, the first key assumption will no longer be valid; symbolically, $\text{Cov}\left(\varepsilon_{it}, \varepsilon_{jt}\right) \neq 0$ for $i \neq j$. Violating the first assumption leads to the second insight. The second insight is that the covariance of returns between any two securities arises through their common relationships with more than a single common factor.[12] An example of a second common factor could be the growth rate in the index of the nation's industrial production. That is, security returns could be assumed to be related to both a market factor and an industrial growth factor.[13] The return on such a stock in period t is described by the following two-factor return-generating process:

$$r_{it} = \alpha_i + \beta_{i1} r_{mt} + \beta_{i2} g_t + \varepsilon_{it} \qquad (8.31)$$

where β_{i1} and β_{i2} are the first and second slope coefficients, respectively, which measure the sensitivity of stock i's returns to the two corresponding risk factors. The symbol g_t denotes the growth rate of industrial production, the second explanatory (risk) factor.[14]

The two-index model of equation (8.31) can be constructed so that the two independent variables, r_{mt} and g_t, are orthogonal, meaning that $\text{Cov}\left(r_{mt}, g_t\right) = 0$, by removing the market effect from the growth rate in the index of industrial production. We assume that the market effect has been already removed in equation (8.31) and the two independent variables are orthogonal. These two independent variables are also assumed to be uncorrelated with the error term. That is, $\text{Cov}\left(r_{mt}, \varepsilon_{it}\right) = 0$, and $\text{Cov}\left(g_t, \varepsilon_{it}\right) = 0$. The orthogonalization procedure for removing each factor's effect on the other factor under multi-index models is described in an appendix at the end of this chapter.

Using the above properties, along with the properties of bivariate normality, the variance of a security i can be expressed as

$$\sigma_i^2 = \beta_{i1}^2 \sigma_m^2 + \beta_{i2}^2 \sigma_g^2 + \sigma_{\varepsilon i}^2 \qquad (8.32)$$

where $\sigma_m^2 = \text{Var}\left(r_{mt}\right)$ and $\sigma_g^2 = \text{Var}\left(g_t\right)$. The proof for the derivation of equation (8.32) is provided in the end-of-chapter appendix A8.2. The sum of the first two terms on the RHS of equation (8.32), $\beta_{i1}^2 \sigma_m^2 + \beta_{i2}^2 \sigma_g^2$, measures systematic risk, and the third term, $\sigma_{\varepsilon i}^2$, measures unsystematic risk. As with the single-index model, this relation expedites the partitioning of the total variance as shown below.

$$\underbrace{\sigma_i^2}_{\substack{\text{Total} \\ \text{risk}}} = \underbrace{\beta_{i1}^2 \sigma_m^2 + \beta_{i2}^2 \sigma_g^2}_{\substack{\text{Systematic} \\ \text{risk}}} + \underbrace{\sigma_{\varepsilon i}^2}_{\substack{\text{Unsystematic} \\ \text{risk}}} \qquad (8.32\text{a})$$

Because the return from stock j in period t is also described by the following return-generating process,

$$r_{jt} = \alpha_j + \beta_{j1} r_{mt} + \beta_{j2} g_t + \varepsilon_{jt} \qquad (8.33)$$

the covariance between two different securities i and j can be expressed as

$$\sigma_{ij} = \beta_{i1} \beta_{j1} \sigma_m^2 + \beta_{i2} \beta_{j2} \sigma_g^2. \qquad (8.34)$$

Like the single-index model, the expected value of security i's return can be represented as a (conditional) expectation for a given value of r_{mt} and g_t:

$$E\left(r_{it} | r_{mt}, g_t\right) = \alpha_i + \beta_{i1} E\left(r_{mt}\right) + \beta_{i2} E\left(g_t\right) \qquad (8.35)$$

In estimating the expected returns, variances, and covariances for n securities, the security analyst using a two-index model must estimate each security's $\alpha_i, \beta_{i1}, \beta_{i2},$ and $\sigma_{\varepsilon i}^2$ statistics for total of $4n$ security-specific inputs. In addition, the estimates for four parameters of the factors, $E(r_{mt}), \sigma_m^2, E(g_t),$ and σ_g^2, must be provided. The result is that by using a two-index model, the security analysts need to estimate $(4n + 4)$ parameters. This is a substantial reduction from $(n^2 + 3n)/2$ inputs needed for the full-covariance model, especially when n is large. Although $(4n + 4)$ is a larger number than needed with the single-index market model, it is potentially beneficial because it is hypothetically a more accurate model of security returns. Furthermore, it is preferred to the full-covariance model because for large n it will involve the estimation of far fewer parameters than $(n^2 + 3n)/2$. Estimation of the parameters is discussed next.

8.3.2 Diversification

When securities' returns follow the two-index model of equation (8.31), the return from a portfolio of n securities follows the two-index model described as

$$
\begin{aligned}
r_{pt} &= \sum_{i=1}^{n} w_i \left(\alpha_i + \beta_{i1} r_{mt} + \beta_{i2} g_t + \varepsilon_{it} \right) \\
&= \sum_{i=1}^{n} w_i \alpha_i + \left(\sum_{i=1}^{n} w_i \beta_{i1} \right) r_{mt} + \left(\sum_{i=1}^{n} w_i \beta_{i2} \right) g_t + \sum_{i=1}^{n} w_i \varepsilon_{it} \\
&= \alpha_p + \beta_{p1} r_{mt} + \beta_{p2} g_t + \varepsilon_{pt} \qquad (8.36)
\end{aligned}
$$

where $\alpha_p = \sum_{i=1}^{n} w_i \alpha_i$, $\beta_{p1} = \left(\sum_{i=1}^{n} w_i \beta_{i1} \right)$, $\beta_{p2} = \left(\sum_{i=1}^{n} w_i \beta_{i2} \right)$, and $\varepsilon_{pt} = \sum_{i=1}^{n} w_i \varepsilon_{it}$. As with individual securities, the variance of returns from a portfolio can be decomposed into two components:

$$Var\left(r_{pt}\right) \equiv \sigma_p^2 = \beta_{p1}^2 \sigma_m^2 + \beta_{p2}^2 \sigma_g^2 + \sigma_{\varepsilon_p}^2 \tag{8.37}$$

As shown in the case of individual securities of equation (8.9), the unsystematic risk, $\sigma_{\varepsilon_p}^2$, will approach zero as the number of individual securities in the portfolio, n, increases. For a relatively large number of securities in a portfolio, the unsystematic risk of the portfolio can be diversified away ($\sigma_{\varepsilon_p}^2 \to 0$), and only systematic risk remains. Thus, the total risk of a well-diversified portfolio converges to its systematic risk for large n. That is, $\sigma_p^2 \cong \beta_{p1}^2 \sigma_m^2 + \beta_{p1}^2 \sigma_g^2$.

8.4   MULTI-INDEX MODELS

The single-index model assumes that only one independent variable, typically, the market portfolio's return, can explain an asset's expected return and the comovements among securities. However, many researchers and practitioners believe there are more variables necessary to explain stock price movements. In order to use additional variables for the explanation of asset returns and their comovements, multi-index models have been proposed. Multi-index models simplify the parameter estimation process relative to the full-covariance model. Although these simplifications are not as great as the simplifications provided by the single-index market model, they are arguably more accurate and realistic. When there are influential factors in addition to the single-index model, the return-generating process for stock i can be described as follows:

$$r_{it} = \alpha_i + \beta_{i1} I_{1t} + \beta_{i2} I_{2t} + \cdots + \beta_{iK} I_{Kt} + \varepsilon_{it} \tag{8.38}$$

where
$\quad I_{kt} =$ the level of index k ($k = 1, 2, \ldots K$), and
$\quad \beta_{ik} =$ a measure of the sensitivity (or responsiveness, or the beta slope coefficient) of stock i's returns to changes in the k-th index.

As with the single-index model, $\sum_{k=1}^{K} \beta_{ik} I_{kt}$ indicates the portion of the security return related to the indexes, the term α_i represents the unique portion of the security return unrelated the indexes, and the term ε_{it} corresponds to the unexplained component of the security return, with a mean of zero and variance of $\sigma_{\varepsilon_i}^2$. The comovements among securities are captured by the K indexes.

To obtain computational advantages in computing risk and in selecting optimal portfolios using multi-index models, we construct multi-index models so that all the indexes are orthogonal (uncorrelated). Thus, we assume that all the indexes in equation (8.38) are uncorrelated, that is, $\text{Cov}\left(I_{kt}, I_{lt}\right) = 0$ for all k and all l. Of course, the real raw indexes are frequently correlated to one another. After orthogonalizing these raw indexes by removing each factor's effect on the other factors, we use the orthogonalized indexes in the multi-index models. As mentioned previously, this procedure does not create any problems. The orthogonalization procedure is described in an end-of-chapter appendix.

Six basic assumptions underlying equation (8.38) for the multi-index models are:

1. The expected value of the random error term ε_{it} is zero—that is, $E\left(\varepsilon_{it}\right) = 0$.
2. The variance of ε_{it}, denoted $\sigma_{\varepsilon_i}^2$, is constant—that is, homoscedastic.
3. The covariance between indexes k and l equals zero, $\sigma_{kl} = \text{Cov}\left(I_{kt}, I_{lt}\right) = 0$, for all k and all l.
4. The random error terms are uncorrelated with the indexes—that is, $\text{Cov}\left(\varepsilon_{it}, I_{kt}\right) = 0$ for $k = 1, 2, \ldots, K$.
5. The random error terms are serially uncorrelated—that is, $\text{Cov}\left(\varepsilon_{it}, \varepsilon_{is}\right) = 0$ for $t \neq s$.
6. The random error terms of an asset are uncorrelated with those of any other asset—that is, $\text{Cov}\left(\varepsilon_{it}, \varepsilon_{jt}\right) = 0$ for $i \neq j$.

If there are no missing indexes (or risk factors) that account for comovements among securities, as in the two-index model, the expected return, variance, and covariance can be defined. The expected return of security i is

$$E\left(r_{it} | \text{all } I_{kt}\right) = \alpha_i + \beta_{i1} E\left(I_{1t}\right) + \beta_{i2} E\left(I_{2t}\right) + \cdots + \beta_{iK} E\left(I_{Kt}\right) \tag{8.39}$$

the variance of security i's returns is

$$\text{Var}\left(r_{it} | \text{all } I_{kt}\right) \equiv \sigma_i^2 = \beta_{i1}^2 \sigma_{I_1}^2 + \beta_{i2}^2 \sigma_{I_2}^2 + \cdots + \beta_{iK}^2 \sigma_{I_K}^2 + \sigma_{\varepsilon_i}^2 \tag{8.40}$$

and the covariance between returns of securities i and j is

$$\text{Cov}\left(r_{it}, r_{jt} | \text{all } I_{kt}\right) \equiv \sigma_{ij} = \beta_{i1} \beta_{j1} \sigma_{I_1}^2 + \beta_{i2} \beta_{j2} \sigma_{I_2}^2 + \cdots + \beta_{iK} \beta_{jK} \sigma_{I_K}^2 \tag{8.41}$$

This expected return, variance, and covariance are conditional on the given indexes.

To estimate the expected returns, variances, and covariances for n securities, the security analyst can use a multi-index model with K indexes to estimate each security's $\alpha_i, \beta_{i1}, \beta_{i2}, \ldots, \beta_{iK}$ and $\sigma_{\varepsilon_i}^2$, for total of $(K + 2) \times n$ security-specific inputs. In addition, the estimates for $2K$ parameters of the factors, $\mu_{I_1}, \mu_{I_2}, \ldots, \mu_{I_K}$ and $\sigma_{I_1}^2, \sigma_{I_2}^2, \ldots, \sigma_{I_K}^2$, must be provided. The result is that by using a multi-index model, the security analysts need to estimate $(K + 2) \times n + 2K$ parameters, which is a substantial reduction from the number of parameters to be estimated in the full-covariance model, $\left(n^2 + 3n\right)/2$. For example, when the number of securities under consideration is $n = 500$, the number of parameters to be estimated in the full-covariance model is 125,750, whereas it is only 3,510 in a five-index model.

8.5   CONCLUSIONS

To determine the efficient frontier, the expected return vector and variance-covariance matrix must be estimated. If one or more security analysts estimated the requisite parameters on an asset-by-asset basis, although possible, the work could become exceedingly time consuming as the number of securities grows. This chapter presented alternative estimation methods that are based on the assumption that security returns can be described by either a one-factor or a multifactor return-generating process. These return-generating processes also provide interesting insights into portfolio diversification and simplify the quadratic programming problem that must be solved to determine the efficient frontier. Furthermore, the multi-index return-generating processes discussed in this chapter can be viewed as predecessors of the return-generating process underlying arbitrage pricing theory, which is discussed in Chapter 16.

APPENDIX: INDEX MODELS

This appendix presents a derivation of the optimal solution (using matrix notation) for efficient portfolios under the single-index model. It also derives the variance decomposition in the two-index model, and it presents a procedure of orthogonalizing multiple indexes.

A8.1 Solving for Efficient Portfolios with the Single-Index Model

This section explains the portfolio risk minimization problem described in Section 8.2 from equations (8.19) through (8.23a) in matrix notation.

With the single-index model, the minimization problem in equation (8.19) can be rewritten in a matrix notation as equation (A8.1). Likewise, the constraints of equations (8.20), (2.11), and (8.12) can also be rewritten as equations (A8.2), (A8.3), and (A8.4), respectively. Thus, the minimization problem is reformulated as follows:

$$\text{Minimize} \quad L = \frac{1}{2} w' \Sigma_\varepsilon w \tag{A8.1}$$

$$\text{subject to} \quad w' \alpha = E(r_p) \tag{A8.2}$$

$$w' l = 1 \tag{A8.3}$$

$$w' \beta = 0 \tag{A8.4}$$

where

$$w = \begin{pmatrix} w_1 \\ w_2 \\ \vdots \\ w_n \\ w_{n+1} \end{pmatrix}, \quad \alpha = \begin{pmatrix} \alpha_1 \\ \alpha_2 \\ \vdots \\ \alpha_n \\ \alpha_{n+1} \end{pmatrix}, \quad \beta = \begin{pmatrix} \beta_1 \\ \beta_2 \\ \vdots \\ \beta_n \\ -1 \end{pmatrix}, \quad l = \begin{pmatrix} 1 \\ 1 \\ \vdots \\ 1 \\ 0 \end{pmatrix},$$

$$\Sigma_\varepsilon = \begin{pmatrix} \sigma_{\varepsilon_1}^2 & 0 & \cdots & 0 & 0 \\ 0 & \sigma_{\varepsilon_2}^2 & \cdots & 0 & 0 \\ \vdots & \vdots & \ddots & 0 & \vdots \\ 0 & 0 & 0 & \sigma_{\varepsilon_n}^2 & 0 \\ 0 & 0 & \cdots & 0 & \sigma_m^2 \end{pmatrix}$$

and $E(r_p)$ is a scalar indicating the given target expected return. Notice that $\boldsymbol{\alpha}$ is an $(n+1) \times 1$ column vector of alphas (the intercept terms of the single-index model) where the last cell has a value of $\alpha_{n+1} = E(r_m)$, $\boldsymbol{\beta}$ is an $(n+1) \times 1$ column vector of beta coefficients for the securities where the last cell has a value of -1, and l is an $(n+1) \times 1$ column vector of ones except that it has a zero as the entry in its last cell. Σ_ε is an $(n+1) \times (n+1)$ diagonal variance-covariance matrix in which the first n diagonal terms are the error variances and the last diagonal term is the variance of the market. Again, the constant $1/2$ is multiplied in equation (A8.1) only for computational and writing simplicity.

Because the constraints to this problem are equalities, the following Lagrangian objective function can be formed:

$$\text{Minimize} \ \ L = \frac{1}{2} w' \Sigma_\varepsilon w + \lambda_1 \left[E(r_p) - w' \boldsymbol{\alpha} \right] + \lambda_2 \left(1 - w' l \right) + \lambda_3 \left(w' \boldsymbol{\beta} \right) \qquad \text{(A8.5)}$$

where λ_1, λ_2, and λ_3 are scalars indicating Lagrangian multipliers. The above objective function is exactly the same as equation (8.21). First-order conditions for the solution require the following equations to hold:[15]

$$\frac{\partial L}{\partial w} = \Sigma_\varepsilon w - \lambda_1 \boldsymbol{\alpha} - \lambda_2 l - \lambda_3 \boldsymbol{\beta} = 0 \qquad \text{(A8.6)}$$

$$\frac{\partial L}{\partial \lambda_1} = E(r_p) - w' \boldsymbol{\alpha} = 0 \qquad \text{(A8.7)}$$

$$\frac{\partial L}{\partial \lambda_2} = 1 - w' l = 0 \qquad \text{(A8.8)}$$

$$\frac{\partial L}{\partial \lambda_3} = w' \boldsymbol{\beta} = 0 \qquad \text{(A8.9)}$$

From equation (A8.6), we have

$$\Sigma_\varepsilon w = \lambda_1 \boldsymbol{\alpha} + \lambda_2 l + \lambda_3 \boldsymbol{\beta}$$

$$\text{or} \qquad w = \lambda_1 \Sigma_\varepsilon^{-1} \boldsymbol{\alpha} + \lambda_2 \Sigma_\varepsilon^{-1} l + \lambda_3 \Sigma_\varepsilon^{-1} \boldsymbol{\beta}$$

$$= \Sigma_\varepsilon^{-1} \left[\boldsymbol{\alpha} \ \ l \ \ \boldsymbol{\beta} \right] \left(\lambda_1 \ \ \lambda_2 \ \ \lambda_3 \right)' \qquad \text{(A8.10)}$$

where $\left[\boldsymbol{\alpha} \ \ l \ \ \boldsymbol{\beta} \right]$ is an $(n+1) \times 3$ matrix that stacks the three vectors $\boldsymbol{\alpha}$, l, and $\boldsymbol{\beta}$ in a column as

$$\left[\boldsymbol{\alpha} \ \ l \ \ \boldsymbol{\beta} \right] = \begin{bmatrix} \alpha_1 & 1 & \beta_1 \\ \alpha_2 & 1 & \beta_2 \\ \vdots & \vdots & \vdots \\ \alpha_n & 1 & \beta_n \\ \alpha_{n+1} & 0 & -1 \end{bmatrix}$$

and $\left(\lambda_1 \ \ \lambda_2 \ \ \lambda_3 \right)'$ is a (3×1) column vector of the Lagrangian multipliers. Premultiplying equation (A8.10) by $\left[\boldsymbol{\alpha} \ \ l \ \ \boldsymbol{\beta} \right]'$ yields

$$\left[\boldsymbol{\alpha} \ \ l \ \ \boldsymbol{\beta} \right]' w = \left[\boldsymbol{\alpha} \ \ l \ \ \boldsymbol{\beta} \right]' \Sigma_\varepsilon^{-1} \left[\boldsymbol{\alpha} \ \ l \ \ \boldsymbol{\beta} \right] \left(\lambda_1 \ \ \lambda_2 \ \ \lambda_3 \right)' \qquad \text{(A8.11)}$$

Notice that $[\alpha \; I \; \beta]'$ is a transpose of $[\alpha \; I \; \beta]$.[16] From equation (A8.11), the Lagrangian multipliers are calculated as

$$(\lambda_1 \;\; \lambda_2 \;\; \lambda_3)' = G^{-1}[\alpha \; I \; \beta]'w \tag{A8.12}$$

where

$$G = [\alpha \; I \; \beta]'\Sigma_\varepsilon^{-1}[\alpha \; I \; \beta] \tag{A8.13}$$

Notice that G is a (3×3) matrix. From equations (A8.7), (A8.8), and (A8.9), we have

$$[\alpha \; I \; \beta]'w = [E(r_p) \;\; 1 \;\; 0]' \tag{A8.14}$$

By using equations (A8.14) and (A8.12), the Lagrangian multipliers are calculated as

$$(\lambda_1 \;\; \lambda_2 \;\; \lambda_3)' = G^{-1}[E(r_p) \;\; 1 \;\; 0]' \tag{A8.15}$$

Plugging equation (A8.15) into equation (A8.10) yields the optimal weights for mean-variance efficient portfolios.

$$w = \Sigma_\varepsilon^{-1}[\alpha \; I \; \beta]G^{-1}[E(r_p) \;\; 1 \;\; 0]' \tag{A8.16}$$

The optimal weights of the mean-variance efficient portfolios in equation (A8.16) also are represented as a linear function of the given level of the portfolio's expected return, $E(r_p)$, as in equation (7.17). Note that α, β, Σ_ε, and G are fixed constants.

By using equation (A8.16), the variance of an efficient portfolio is expressed as

$$
\begin{aligned}
\sigma_p^2 &= w'\Sigma_\varepsilon w \\
&= [E(r_p) \;\; 1 \;\; 0]G^{-1}[\alpha \; I \; \beta]'\Sigma_\varepsilon^{-1}\Sigma_\varepsilon\Sigma_\varepsilon^{-1}[\alpha \; I \; \beta]G^{-1}[E(r_p) \;\; 1 \;\; 0]' \\
&= [E(r_p) \;\; 1 \;\; 0]G^{-1}[E(r_p) \;\; 1 \;\; 0]' \\
&= g_{11}[E(r_p)]^2 + 2g_{12}E(r_p) + g_{22} \tag{A8.17}
\end{aligned}
$$

where g_{ij} is the (i,j)-th element of G^{-1}. Equation (A8.17) is the equation of a parabola in the mean-variance space or a hyperbola in the mean-standard deviation under the single-index model. This equation is analogous to equation (A7.2) under the full-covariance model.

Compared with the optimal weights for mean-variance efficient portfolios for the full-covariance model, equation (7.17) of Chapter 7, the optimal weights under the single-index model in equation (A8.16) have some computational benefits. The inverse of the diagonal matrix Σ_ε in equation (A8.16) is obtained simply by taking a reciprocal of its diagonal elements. The covariances among assets are not needed. On the other hand, there is a computational burden in computing the inverse of the full covariance matrix Σ in equation (7.17), especially when the number of assets is large. In particular, when the number of assets, n, is larger than the number of time-series return observations, T, the inverse of the covariance matrix, Σ^{-1}, does not exist.

EXAMPLE A8.1

Example 8.4 is used to show a procedure to obtain the optimal weights using equation (A8.16). Here we repeat the information about the parameters of the single-index model for the three stocks as follows:

$$\begin{pmatrix} \alpha_1 \\ \alpha_2 \\ \alpha_3 \end{pmatrix} = \begin{pmatrix} 1.488 \\ 0.035 \\ -0.025 \end{pmatrix}, \quad \begin{pmatrix} \beta_1 \\ \beta_2 \\ \beta_3 \end{pmatrix} = \begin{pmatrix} 0.959 \\ 1.055 \\ 1.065 \end{pmatrix}, \text{ and } \begin{pmatrix} \sigma_{\varepsilon1}^2 \\ \sigma_{\varepsilon2}^2 \\ \sigma_{\varepsilon3}^2 \end{pmatrix} = \begin{pmatrix} 15.42 \\ 15.50 \\ 17.51 \end{pmatrix}$$

The average return and variance of the market portfolio are $E(r_m) = 0.954$ and $\sigma_m^2 = 6.08$, respectively. We assume the portfolio manager sets the desired target return as $E(r_p) = 1.20$ percent.

The necessary information to compute the optimal weights in equation (A8.16) is

$$\alpha = \begin{pmatrix} \alpha_1 \\ \alpha_2 \\ \alpha_3 \\ \alpha_4 \end{pmatrix} = \begin{pmatrix} \alpha_1 \\ \alpha_2 \\ \alpha_3 \\ \bar{r}_m \end{pmatrix} = \begin{pmatrix} 1.488 \\ 0.359 \\ -0.253 \\ 0.954 \end{pmatrix}, \quad \beta = \begin{pmatrix} \beta_1 \\ \beta_2 \\ \beta_3 \\ \beta_4 \end{pmatrix} = \begin{pmatrix} \beta_1 \\ \beta_2 \\ \beta_3 \\ -1 \end{pmatrix} = \begin{pmatrix} 0.959 \\ 1.055 \\ 1.065 \\ -1 \end{pmatrix},$$

$$l = \begin{pmatrix} 1 \\ 1 \\ 1 \\ 0 \end{pmatrix}, \quad \Sigma_\varepsilon = \begin{pmatrix} \sigma_{\varepsilon1}^2 & 0 & 0 & 0 \\ 0 & \sigma_{\varepsilon2}^2 & 0 & 0 \\ 0 & 0 & \sigma_{\varepsilon3}^2 & 0 \\ 0 & 0 & 0 & \sigma_m^2 \end{pmatrix} = \begin{pmatrix} 15.42 & 0 & 0 & 0 \\ 0 & 15.50 & 0 & 0 \\ 0 & 0 & 17.51 & 0 \\ 0 & 0 & 0 & 6.08 \end{pmatrix}$$

Thus,

$$G = \begin{bmatrix} \alpha & l & \beta \end{bmatrix}' \Sigma_\varepsilon^{-1} \begin{bmatrix} \alpha & l & \beta \end{bmatrix}$$

$$= \begin{bmatrix} \alpha_1 & 1 & \beta_1 \\ \alpha_2 & 1 & \beta_2 \\ \alpha_3 & 1 & \beta_3 \\ \bar{r}_m & 0 & -1 \end{bmatrix}' \begin{pmatrix} \sigma_{\varepsilon1}^2 & 0 & 0 & 0 \\ 0 & \sigma_{\varepsilon2}^2 & 0 & 0 \\ 0 & 0 & \sigma_{\varepsilon3}^2 & 0 \\ 0 & 0 & 0 & \sigma_m^2 \end{pmatrix}^{-1} \begin{bmatrix} \alpha_1 & 1 & \beta_1 \\ \alpha_2 & 1 & \beta_2 \\ \alpha_3 & 1 & \beta_3 \\ \bar{r}_m & 0 & -1 \end{bmatrix}$$

$$= \begin{bmatrix} 1.488 & 1 & 0.959 \\ 0.359 & 1 & 1.055 \\ -0.253 & 1 & 1.065 \\ 0.954 & 0 & -1 \end{bmatrix}' \begin{pmatrix} 15.42 & 0 & 0 & 0 \\ 0 & 15.50 & 0 & 0 \\ 0 & 0 & 17.51 & 0 \\ 0 & 0 & 0 & 6.08 \end{pmatrix}^{-1} \begin{bmatrix} 1.488 & 1 & 0.959 \\ 0.359 & 1 & 1.055 \\ -0.253 & 1 & 1.065 \\ 0.954 & 0 & -1 \end{bmatrix}$$

$$= \begin{pmatrix} 0.305 & 0.105 & -0.055 \\ 0.105 & 0.186 & 0.191 \\ -0.055 & 0.191 & 0.361 \end{pmatrix}.$$

EXAMPLE A8.1 (*Continued*)

In fact, the matrix G is the same as the coefficient matrix in equation (8.29). From equation (A8.15), the Lagrangian multipliers are calculated as

$$
\begin{pmatrix} \lambda_1 \\ \lambda_2 \\ \lambda_3 \end{pmatrix} = G^{-1} \begin{pmatrix} E(r_p) \\ 1 \\ 0 \end{pmatrix} = \begin{pmatrix} 0.305 & 0.105 & -0.055 \\ 0.105 & 0.186 & 0.191 \\ -0.055 & 0.191 & 0.361 \end{pmatrix}^{-1} \begin{pmatrix} 1.20 \\ 1 \\ 0 \end{pmatrix}
$$

$$
= \begin{pmatrix} -4.47 \\ 18.78 \\ -10.64 \end{pmatrix}
$$

Therefore, the optimal weights for the mean-variance efficient portfolio from equation (A8.16) is calculated as

$$
w = \begin{pmatrix} w_1 \\ w_2 \\ \vdots \\ w_n \\ w_{n+1} \end{pmatrix} = \begin{pmatrix} w_1 \\ w_2 \\ \vdots \\ w_n \\ \sum_{i=1}^{n} w_i \beta_i \end{pmatrix} = \Sigma_\varepsilon^{-1} \begin{bmatrix} \alpha & l & \beta \end{bmatrix} G^{-1} \begin{bmatrix} E(r_p) & 1 & 0 \end{bmatrix}'
$$

$$
= \begin{pmatrix} 15.42 & 0 & 0 & 0 \\ 0 & 15.50 & 0 & 0 \\ 0 & 0 & 17.51 & 0 \\ 0 & 0 & 0 & 6.08 \end{pmatrix}^{-1} \begin{bmatrix} 1.488 & 1 & 0.959 \\ 0.359 & 1 & 1.055 \\ -0.253 & 1 & 1.065 \\ 0.954 & 0 & -1 \end{bmatrix}
$$

$$
\times \begin{pmatrix} 0.305 & 0.105 & -0.055 \\ 0.105 & 0.186 & 0.191 \\ -0.055 & 0.191 & 0.361 \end{pmatrix}^{-1} \begin{pmatrix} 1.20 \\ 1 \\ 0 \end{pmatrix}
$$

$$
= \begin{pmatrix} 0.125 \\ 0.384 \\ 0.490 \\ 1.048 \end{pmatrix} \tag{A8.18}
$$

Therefore, the optimal weights of the three assets using the single-index model are

$$
w_p = \begin{pmatrix} w_1 \\ w_2 \\ w_3 \end{pmatrix} = \begin{pmatrix} 0.125 \\ 0.384 \\ 0.490 \end{pmatrix}
$$

When a different target return is given, the optimal weights can be easily obtained by replacing the given target return of $E(r_p) = 1.20$ in equation (A8.18) with the new value of the target return.

A8.2   Variance Decomposition

The variance decomposition in the two-index model proceeds as follows:

$$
\begin{aligned}
Var\left(r_{pt}\right) \equiv \sigma_p^2 &= E\big[\left(\alpha_p + \beta_{p1}r_{mt} + \beta_{p2}g_t + \varepsilon_{pt}\right) - E\left(\alpha_p + \beta_{p1}r_{mt} + \beta_{p2}g_t + \varepsilon_{pt}\right)\big]^2 \\
&= E\{\beta_{p1}\left[r_{mt} - E\left(r_{mt}\right)\right] + \beta_{p2}\left[g_t - E\left(g_t\right)\right] + \varepsilon_{pt}\}^2 \\
&= \beta_{p1}^2 E\left[r_{mt} - E\left(r_{mt}\right)\right]^2 + \beta_{p2}^2 E\left[g_t - E\left(g_t\right)\right]^2 + E\left(\varepsilon_{pt}^2\right) \\
&\quad + 2\beta_{p1}\beta_{p2}\mathrm{Cov}\left[r_{mt} - E\left(r_{mt}\right), g_t - E\left(g_t\right)\right] \\
&\quad + 2\beta_{p1}\mathrm{Cov}\left[r_{mt} - E\left(r_{mt}\right), \varepsilon_{pt}\right] + 2\beta_{p2}\mathrm{Cov}\left[g_t - E\left(g_t\right), \varepsilon_{pt}\right] \\
&= \beta_{p1}^2\sigma_m^2 + \beta_{p1}^2\sigma_g^2 + \sigma_{\varepsilon p}^2
\end{aligned}
$$

where $\sigma_m^2 = \mathrm{Var}\left(R_{mt}\right)$ and $\sigma_g^2 = \mathrm{Var}\left(g_t\right)$. Notice that the first and second indexes, r_{mt} and g_t, are assumed independent. That is, $\mathrm{Cov}\left[r_{mt} - E\left(r_{mt}\right), g_t - E\left(g_t\right)\right] = 0$. Because the indexes are independent of the error term $\left(\varepsilon_{pt}\right)$, $\mathrm{Cov}\left[r_{mt} - E\left(r_{mt}\right), \varepsilon_{pt}\right] = 0$ and $\mathrm{Cov}\left[g_t - E\left(g_t\right), \varepsilon_{pt}\right] = 0$.

A8.3   Orthogonalizing Multiple Indexes

We begin with a two-index model with two explanatory variables, x_{1t} and x_{2t}. Suppose they are correlated with each other; that is, $\mathrm{Cov}\left(x_{1t}, x_{2t}\right) \neq 0$. Then, the two-index model is described as

$$ r_{it} = b_{i0} + b_{i1}x_{1t} + b_{i2}x_{2t} + \varepsilon_{it} \tag{A8.19}$$

We let x_{1t} equal I_{1t}. In order to remove the effect of x_{1t} from x_{2t}, we can regress x_{2t} on x_{1t}. That is, we estimate the following regression model:

$$ x_{2t} = \delta_0 + \delta_1 x_{1t} + \xi_t, $$

where δ_0 and δ_1 are the regression coefficients and ξ_t is the random error term. In the standard regression analysis, ξ_t is uncorrelated with x_{1t}; that is, $\mathrm{Cov}\left(x_{1t}, \xi_t\right) = 0$. The random error term

$$ \xi_t = x_{2t} - \left(\delta_0 + \delta_1 x_{1t}\right), $$

represents the second explanatory variable, x_{2t}, after the effect of x_{1t} is removed. If we define

$$ I_{2t} \equiv \xi_t $$

and rearrange terms, the two-index model of equation (A8.19) becomes

$$
\begin{aligned}
r_{it} &= b_{i0} + b_{i1}x_{1t} + b_{i2}(\delta_0 + \delta_1 x_{1t} + \xi_t) + \varepsilon_{it} \\
&= b_{i0} + b_{i2}\delta_0 + (b_{i1} + b_{i2}\delta_1)x_{1t} + b_{i2}\xi_t + \varepsilon_{it} \\
&= \alpha_i + \beta_{i1}I_{1t} + \beta_{i2}I_{2t} + \varepsilon_{it},
\end{aligned}
\tag{A8.20}
$$

where $\alpha_i = b_{i0} + b_{i2}\delta_0$, $\beta_{i1} = b_{i1} + b_{i2}\delta_1$, and $\beta_{i2} = b_{i2}$. Thus, the two indexes in the model of equation (A8.20), I_{1t} and I_{2t}, are constructed to be orthogonal.

If a third variable, x_{3t}, is added into the two-index model, then the three-index model is

$$r_{it} = b_{i0} + b_{i1}x_{1t} + b_{i2}x_{2t} + b_{i3}x_{3t} + \varepsilon_{it}. \tag{A8.21}$$

By removing the effect of x_{1t} and x_{2t} from x_{3t}, we can construct a third index that is orthogonal to the other two indexes. That is, we regress x_{3t} on x_{1t} and x_{2t} by estimating the following regression model:

$$x_{3t} = \phi_0 + \phi_1 x_{1t} + \phi_2 x_{2t} + \varphi_t.$$

Then, the random error term φ_t will be orthogonal to x_{1t} and x_{2t}. We define φ_t as the third index I_{3t}. That is,

$$I_{3t} \equiv \varphi_t = x_{3t} - \left(\phi_0 + \phi_1 x_{1t} + \phi_2 x_{2t} \right).$$

Because I_{2t} is orthogonal to x_{1t} and I_{3t} is also orthogonal to x_{1t}, I_{2t} is uncorrelated with I_{3t}. Thus, the initial three-index model, equation (A8.3), whose variables are correlated each other can be rewritten as

$$r_{it} = \alpha_i + \beta_{i1}I_{1t} + \beta_{i2}I_{2t} + \beta_{i3}I_{3t} + \varepsilon_{it} \tag{A8.22}$$

because the indexes in the model of equation (A8.22) are constructed to be orthogonal.

In a similar fashion, a *K*-index model whose original variables, $x_{1t}, \ldots, x_{Kt}$, are correlated each other can be transformed to be another *K*-index model whose indexes are constructed to be orthogonal. That is, the first variable x_{1t} is defined as the first index I_{1t}. The second index I_{2t} is defined as the random error term generated from regressing x_{2t} on x_{1t}. The third index I_{3t} is defined as the random error term generated from regressing x_{3t} on x_{1t} and x_{2t}. In this way, the last *K*-th index I_{Kt} is defined as the random error term generated from regressing x_{Kt} on $x_{1t}, x_{2t}, \ldots, x_{K-1t}$. These newly constructed indexes, $I_{1t}, I_{2t}, \ldots, I_{Kt}$, are orthogonal.

NOTES

1. Harry Markowitz, *Portfolio Selection* (New York: John Wiley and Sons, 1959), 97–100. In particular, note Figures 10a and 10b on page 98 and footnote 1 on page 100. For related work see Markowitz, Harry M., Editor, *Harry Markowitz Selected Works*, World Scientific Publisher, Singapore, 2010, 693 pages, Volume 1.
2. More generally, assume that the joint probability distribution of security returns is multivariate normal and the underlying factor r_{mt} is some type of stock market index. In particular, let it be a linear combination of the returns on the individual securities. If so, then the joint probability distribution of r_{it} and r_{mt} is bivariate normal distribution. However, with this type of index, equation (8.1) can hold for only n−1 securities. The reason for this is that once the parameters in equation (8.1) have been estimated for n−1 securities (and the composition of r_{mt} is known and fixed), then the parameters for the n-th security are deterministic and the error term is no longer stochastic (see Bawa,

Brown, and Klein, eds., "Estimation risk and optimal portfolio choice: The Sharpe index model," *Estimation Risk and Optimal Portfolio Choice* (Amsterdam: North Holland, 1979), 42, 148; and Eugene F. Fama, *Foundations of Finance* (New York: Basic Books, 1976), chap. 3).

3. William F. Sharpe, "A Simplified Model for Portfolio Analysis," *Management Science*, January 1963, 277–293. Reprinted in William F. Sharpe, Editor, *William F. Sharpe: Selected Works*, World Scientific Publishing Company Inc., 2012, ISBN-10: 9814329959, ISBN-13: 978–9814329958, 692 pages.

4. Jack L. Treynor,"How to Rate Management of Investment Funds," *Harvard Business Review*, 1965.

5. This hypothetical numerical example employs a sample that is computationally simple, but it is too small to provide a representative sample. A representative sample should cover one complete business cycle from peak to peak, or, from trough to trough. Complete business cycles last from five to ten years.

6. Two articles followed from Jensen's PhD dissertation: M. C. Jensen, "The Performance of Mutual Funds in the Period 1945–1964," *Journal of Finance* 23 (1968): 389–416; also M. C. Jensen, "Risk, the Pricing of Capital Assets, and the Evaluation of Investment Portfolios," *Journal of Business* 42 (1969).

7. See Irving Fisher, *Appreciation and Interest* (New York: Macmillan, 1896), 75–76. Also, see Irving Fisher, *The Theory of Interest* (New York: Macmillan, 1930).

8. William F. Sharpe, *Portfolio Theory and Capital Markets* (New York: McGraw-Hill, 1970),130.

9. As explained earlier in this chapter, some single-index market models require one or more risk-free interest rates to be estimated. Typically, U.S. Treasury securities with appropriate maturities are used as surrogates for the risk-free interest rate.

10. The reader is cautioned not to confuse the estimation models discussed in this chapter with the various models of the efficient frontiers presented in Chapter 6.

11. A mathematical appendix at the end of this book shows how to solve simultaneous linear equations.

12. Chapter 16 presents the arbitrage pricing theory, which is based on a return-generating process with an arbitrary number of factors. Similar multifactor return-generating processes are discussed by Sharpe (1977) and Rosenberg (1974).

13. For explanation on the industrial production growth factor, see Chen, Roll, and Ross (1985). We can also consider the industry effect as another common factor. For evidence on the existence of an industry factor, see King (1966), Meyers (1973), Farrell (1974, 1975), and Fertuck (1975). A second example of a two-factor return-generating process is Stone's (1974) two-index model, where individual security returns are linearly related to both equity and debt indices. Korkie (1974) presents an argument against Stone's model, whereas evidence in favor of it is presented by Martin and Keown (1977), Lloyd and Shick (1977), and Lynge and Zumwalt (1980).

14. A type of multiple-index model based on equation (8.38) was initially developed by Cohen and Pogue (1967).

15. For vector and matrix differentiation, refer to Appendix A7.3 in Chapter 7.

16. That is, $\begin{bmatrix} \alpha & I & \beta \end{bmatrix}' = \begin{bmatrix} \alpha_1 & \alpha_2 & \cdots & \alpha_n & \alpha_{n+1} \\ 1 & 1 & \cdots & 1 & 0 \\ \beta_1 & \beta_2 & \cdots & \beta_n & -1 \end{bmatrix}$ is a $(3 \times (n+1))$ matrix.

Non-Mean-Variance
Portfolios

CHAPTER 9

Non-Normal Distributions of Returns

Many portfolio-based finance theories utilize a mean-variance framework in which investors make decisions on the basis of means and variances of the rates of return. For example, the CAPM assumes all asset returns are normally distributed or investors have mean-variance preferences. Portfolio performance measures such as the Sharpe measure, the Treynor measure, and the Jensen measure are based on the two parameters of the normal distribution. However, there has been empirical evidence that asset returns are not normally distributed since Mandelbrot (1963), Fama (1965), and Blattberg and Gonedes (1974).[1] Researchers observe nonsymmetric, highly peaked, and longer-tailed (leptokurtic) characteristics in the empirical unconditional distribution of asset returns. Table 9.1 shows statistical results from normality tests of international stock market return distributions from 14 developed countries. Most of the countries show significantly positive skewness. In particular, skewness and kurtosis coefficients using weekly returns and monthly returns are quite different, even though skewness and kurtosis coefficients are pure index numbers that should remain invariant to the return measurement interval.[2] This evidence might be indicating that the returns are generated from several nonidentical distributions, such as a mixture of normal distributions.

In a dynamic economic environment, firms' investment and financing decisions will affect the systematic risk, expected return, and standard deviation of returns. For example, Boness, Chen and Jatusipitak (1974) find parameters shift after a capital structure change and Christie (1982) demonstrates that the standard deviation of a stock's return is an increasing function of both financial and operating leverage. Beaver's (1968) realized returns and Patell and Wolfson's (1981) *ex ante* assessments support an increase in the variance of stock returns around the announcement of quarterly earnings. Macro information shocks may also shift the level of interest rates and market risk premiums. Therefore, it is not surprising for the expected return and the risk dimensions of individual stocks and portfolios to change through time. Nonstationarity of mean and risk could cause the skewness, highly peaked, and longer-tailed (leptokurtic) characteristics in the empirical unconditional distribution of asset returns. This chapter presents several statistical distribution models that can capture the skewness and leptokurtic features of asset returns.

9.1 STABLE PARETIAN DISTRIBUTIONS

This distribution is defined by its characteristic function because its probability density is generally not known. Stable Paretian distributions are completely characterized by four parameters. The first parameter, denoted $\alpha \in (0, 2)$, is known as the

TABLE 9.1 Summary Statistics of International Stock Market Return Distributions

	Mean return		Variance		Skewness[a]		Kurtosis[a]		W-statistic		Prob < W[b]	
	Week	Month	Week	Month	Week	Month	Week	Month	Week	Month	Week	Month
Australia	0.176	0.767	0.152	3.021	0.199	28.799	3.351	531.676	0.986	0.957	0.75	0.05
Belgium	0.218	0.893	0.164	2.815	0.504	28.591	5.437	419.759	0.983	0.937	0.42	0.00
Canada	0.075	0.342	0.121	0.756	0.390	1.133	2.032	19.377	0.982	0.955	0.29	0.03
France	0.278	1.170	0.165	3.906	−0.017	42.870	3.083	889.654	0.986	0.958	0.69	0.05
Germany	0.248	1.052	0.159	2.153	−0.212	18.717	2.489	287.944	0.982	0.948	0.33	0.01
Hong Kong	0.550	2.210	0.212	1.140	0.354	2.368	4.647	65.767	0.975	0.955	0.03	0.03
Italy	0.044	−0.027	0.145	2.672	0.102	−3.563	3.179	268.171	0.974	0.944	0.01	0.01
Japan	0.042	0.250	0.126	2.429	0.241	9.454	4.091	212.333	0.973	0.932	0.01	0.00
Netherlands	0.243	1.024	0.052	0.926	0.021	−0.917	0.291	25.572	0.972	0.973	0.00	0.33
Singapore	0.409	1.607	0.323	0.934	1.052	2.006	14.101	26.943	0.960	0.951	0.00	0.02
Sweden	0.251	1.007	0.184	1.886	0.222	7.176	3.426	114.606	0.988	0.971	0.85	0.28
Switzerland	0.303	1.206	0.100	1.703	−0.163	−0.744	1.694	90.204	0.984	0.948	0.55	0.01
U.K.	0.170	0.692	0.079	1.083	0.035	0.816	1.125	47.455	0.979	0.970	0.15	0.25
U.S.	0.220	0.943	0.132	0.429	0.427	0.368	2.323	9.565	0.981	0.952	0.25	0.02

[a]Skewness and kurtosis represent the third and fourth central moments of the rates of return, respectively.

[b]If the probability (prob < W) is less than 0.10, the null hypothesis of normality cannot be supported at the ten percent level of significance.

Source: Adapted from Chunhachinda, Krishnan, Hamid, and Prakash, "Portfolio Selection and Skewness: Evidence from International Stock Markets," *Journal of Banking and Finance* 21 (1997): 143–167.

characteristic exponent and determines the membership of the particular distribution. For example, if $\alpha = 2$, then the random variable has a normal distribution, and if $\alpha = 1$, then the random variable has a Cauchy distribution. The second, third, and fourth parameters determine the location, dispersion, and symmetry of the random variable's distribution and, for a normal distribution, correspond to mean, standard deviation, and skewness (which, for the normal, is zero), respectively.

The normal distribution is one particular member of what is known as the family of stable Paretian distributions. The common characteristic of all members of this family is that they are invariant under addition, meaning that when random variables from a particular distribution are added together, the resulting random variable will have the same distribution. For example, if the returns on firm A and firm B are from Cauchy distributions (a particular membership of the stable Paretian distribution family), then the returns on any portfolio formed by combining A and B will also conform to the characteristics of the Cauchy distribution.

The reasonableness of invoking the central limit theorem to argue that returns are normally distributed can be questioned by noting that this theorem is applicable only when the distribution from which the sample is drawn has a finite standard deviation.[3] In particular, if daily returns come from a non-normal stable Paretian distribution (meaning $\alpha \neq 2$), then the central limit theorem cannot be invoked and the conclusion that monthly returns will be normally distributed cannot be drawn. Indeed, it has been argued conceptually that the monthly distribution for common stock returns is leptokurtic, meaning the distribution has more observations in the tails and center and fewer in the shoulders relative to the normal distribution. An illustration of such a distribution is shown in Figure 9.1. The reasoning behind this argument is that returns are affected by information, and information is generally in one of two categories—either large importance or small importance. Such a dichotomous information structure tends to generate either large or small returns. Essentially, returns are leptokurtic because information is leptokurtic.

Fama (1965), in a detailed empirical study of daily returns, found that observed returns were leptokurtic and concluded that a non-normal stable Paretian distribution fit the data better than a normal distribution.[4] An implication of his study is that the distribution for common stock returns has no finite standard deviation, suggesting that the central limit theorem–based argument for normality is inappropriate. Another implication is that even if investors have quadratic utility functions, they still cannot make decisions on the basis of means and standard deviations

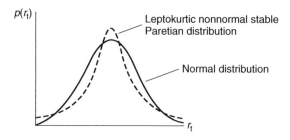

FIGURE 9.1 Normal and Leptokurtic Non-normal Stable Paretian Distributions

because standard deviations do not exist. However, by redefining the measure of risk, two-dimensional analysis of portfolios can still be performed. In this situation what is known as the semi-interquartile range can be used as the risk measure.[5] [6]

9.2   THE STUDENT'S *t*-DISTRIBUTION

The Student's *t* density function of asset returns, r_t, with location parameter μ, scale parameter H, and degrees of freedom v is represented by

$$f\left(r_t | \Theta\right) = \frac{\Gamma\left(\left(v+1\right)/2\right)\sqrt{H}}{\Gamma\left(v/2\right)\sqrt{\pi v}} \left[1 + \frac{H}{v}\left(r_t - \mu\right)^2\right]^{-(v+1)/2} \tag{9.1}$$

where $\Theta = \{\mu, H, v; -\infty < \mu < \infty, \; H > 0, \; v > 0\}$, μ is the mean value of r_t, and $\Gamma\left(\cdot\right)$ is the gamma function. The Student's-*t* distribution has the following properties: (1) $E\left(x\right) = \mu$ for $v > 1$, and undefined otherwise, and $\mathrm{Var}\left(x\right) = H^{-1}\left[v/\left(v-2\right)\right]$ for $v > 2$, and ∞ for $1 < v \leq 2$, (2) all moments of order $k < v$ are generally finite, (3) when $v = 1$, the Student's-*t* distribution is the Cauchy density function, and (4) as the degrees of freedom $v \to \infty$, the Student's-*t* distribution converges to the normal distribution. Because the Student's-*t* distribution is symmetric, the mean, median, and mode are the same. The skewness is zero for $v > 3$, and the kurtosis is $6/\left(v-4\right)$ for $v > 4$.

   Blattberg and Gonedes (1974) argued that the observed leptokurtic daily return distribution can be explained by an alternative to the non-normal stable Paretian distribution, the Student's-*t* distribution. Although able to explain the leptokurtosis observed by Fama (1965) in daily returns, the Student's-*t* distribution has a finite standard deviation. Thus, the central limit theorem can be applied to it and used to provide an argument that monthly returns are approximately normal. Furthermore, Blattberg and Gonedes, and later Fama (1976), argue that the empirical evidence on monthly returns suggests that normality is a reasonable approximation.

9.3   MIXTURES OF NORMAL DISTRIBUTIONS

In this distribution model, asset returns are normally distributed, but there is more than one such distribution per stock, meaning that the return distribution shifts through time and, thus, is not stationary.

9.3.1   Discrete Mixtures of Normal Distributions

Kon (1984) pointed out that the arguments for the Student's-*t* distribution or the stable Paretian distribution generally assume that asset returns are from the same distribution. Because there are good reasons to expect this distribution to be shifting or nonstationary, Kon investigated whether or not daily returns could be modeled as a discrete mixture of different normal distributions in which each return observation is viewed as a drawing from one of a finite number of normal distributions with some probability. The observations are not necessarily consecutive. He found they could be so modeled and, in a comparison with the Student's-*t* distribution, found the mixed distribution model to have more descriptive validity.

This view suggests that each return observation on a stock, r_t, has been generated by one of the following L distinct equations (or regimes):

$$r_t = \mu_1 + u_{1t} \qquad t \in I_1$$

$$r_t = \mu_2 + u_{2t} \qquad t \in I_2$$

$$\cdots$$

$$r_t = \mu_L + u_{Lt} \qquad t \in I_L$$

where μ_j is the mean of the return, r_t, in the j-regime $(j = 1, 2, \ldots, L)$, I_j is the homogeneous information set with T_j observations in each set. $\sum_{j=1}^{L} T_j = T$, u_{jt} is independently and identically normally distributed with a mean of zero and variance of σ_j^2, $0 < \sigma_j^2 < \infty$, $j = 1, 2, \ldots, L$. Define $\lambda_j = T_j/T$ as the proportion of observations associated with information set I_j. Thus, the probability density function for L regimes is described as

$$f(r_t|\Theta) = \sum_{j=1}^{L} \lambda_j \frac{1}{\sqrt{2\pi\sigma_j^2}} \exp\left\{-\frac{1}{2\sigma_j^2}(r_t - \mu_j)^2\right\} \tag{9.2}$$

where λ_j are the mixing probabilities, and the parameter vector is $\Theta = \{\mu_j, \sigma_j^2, \lambda_j\}$ for $j = 1, \ldots, L$.

9.3.2 Sequential Mixtures of Normal Distributions

Kim and Kon (1996, 1999) argued that relevant information that changes the risk-return structure is randomly released within some time interval, not at every moment, but in sequence. These information events translate into *sequential* discrete structural shifts for the mean and/or variance parameters in the time-series of security returns. To accommodate this sequential shift, they suggest a sequential mixture of normal distribution models in which asset returns are a sequence of stock returns that are normal variates with stationary mean or variance parameters up to a shift point. Define these as τ_1 return observations from regime 1. Thereafter, returns $\tau_1 + 1$ to τ_2 are a sequence of return observations from regime 2, and so forth, until the last sequence of return observations from $\tau_{K-1} + 1$ to τ_K is the K-th regime. The formulation of this model is as follows:

$$
\begin{array}{lll}
\text{Regime 1:} & r_t = \mu_1 + \varepsilon_{1t}, & t = 1, \ldots, \tau_1 \\
\text{Regime 2:} & r_t = \mu_2 + \varepsilon_{2t}, & t = \tau_1 + 1, \ldots, \tau_2 \\
& \vdots & \\
\text{Regime K:} & r_t = \mu_K + \varepsilon_{Kt}, & t = \tau_{K-1} + 1, \ldots, \tau_K (= T)
\end{array}
\tag{9.3}
$$

where μ_k is the mean of the return, r_t, in the k-regime $(k = 1, 2, \ldots, K)$ and ε_{kt} is the random error term of the k-th regime with mean 0 and variance $\sigma_{\varepsilon_k}^2$

$(k = 1, \ldots, K)$. The nonstationarity arises from observations that are drawn from a different population after each shift point.

The parameter vector to be estimated is $\Theta = \{\mu_k, \sigma_k^2, \tau_k\}$ for $k = 1, \ldots, K$. However, the key parameter to be estimated is τ_k, because μ_k and σ_k^2 can be estimated with the sample mean and variance after detecting the shift points, τ_k. The estimated shift points reflect announcement of information events such as merger and acquisition and information leakage. The estimation procedure is described in Kim (1991) and Kim and Kon (1996, 1999). They found that the sequential mixture specification has substantially more descriptive ability than the competing alternatives (normal distribution, Student's-t distribution, discrete mixture of normal distributions, and Poisson jump-diffusion process model).

9.4   POISSON JUMP-DIFFUSION PROCESS

Press (1968), Jarrow and Rosenfeld (1984), Ball and Torous (1985), and Akgiray and Booth (1986, 1987) provide some positive evidence on a Poisson jump-diffusion process for the distribution of stock returns. The Poisson jump-diffusion process for the distribution of stock returns consists of a geometric Brownian motion component and an independent compound Poisson process with normally distributed jump amplitudes. This Poisson jump-diffusion process can be expressed as follows:

$$\log \left(\frac{P_t}{P_{t-1}} \right) = \left(\alpha - \frac{1}{2}\sigma^2 \right) t + \sigma \, Z_t + \sum_{n=1}^{N_t} J_n \tag{9.3}$$

where P_t is the security price at time t, Z_t is a standard Brownian motion, N_t is a Poisson counting process with parameter $\lambda > 0$, J_n is a normal random variate with mean μ_J and variance σ_J^2 representing the logarithm of one plus the percentage change in security price caused by the n-th jump, α is the instantaneous conditional expected rate of return per unit of time for the Brownian motion part of the process, and σ^2 is the instantaneous conditional variance. The resulting probability density function of a security return is

$$f\left(r_t | \Theta\right) = \sum_{n=1}^{\infty} \frac{e^{-\lambda}\lambda^n}{n!} \phi \left(r_t | \mu + n\mu_J, \sigma^2 + n\sigma_J^2\right) \tag{9.4}$$

where $\mu = \alpha - (1/2)\,\sigma^2$, $\Theta = \{\mu, \ \sigma^2, \ \lambda, \ \mu_J, \ \sigma_J^2\}$, and $\phi\left(a|b\right)$ denotes a normal density function with mean a and variance b. This model is essentially an infinite mixture of normal distributions with parameter restrictions.

9.5   LOGNORMAL DISTRIBUTIONS

Logarithmic properties are applied in many ways in finance. Logarithmic utility and using natural logarithm to compute continuously compounded returns are useful applications for logarithms. Lognormal probability distributions are another beneficial application.

9.5.1 Specifications of Lognormal Distributions

One argument against normality is based on the concept of the investor's limited liability. There is a positive probability of achieving a return below any given value if returns are assumed to be normal. However, limited liability law means investors cannot lose more than the value of their investment. In other words, liability means that investors cannot earn less than −100 percent. Thus, on conceptual grounds it can be seen that normality and limited liability are inconsistent. Furthermore, although limited liability restricts how low returns can be, there are no limits on how high returns can be. That is, gains yielding rates of return in excess of 100 percent are not uncommon. This suggests that returns are likely to be generated by a positively skewed distribution.[7] As a result of limited liability and positive skewness, a lognormal distribution is often assumed to be more appropriate than a normal distribution in describing security returns.[8] Even though this skewness diminishes with the length of the differencing interval (that is, the holding period), positive skewness is still found in returns measured over periods as short as a month for both individual stocks and mutual funds.

When a probability distribution or a frequency distribution is positively skewed, its mean is larger than its median, and its median is larger than its mode. But it is not known which of these three measures of central tendency investors use in forming their expectations of the central or most likely rate of return. As a result, both the mean and variance statistics on which portfolio theory is based may be biased. To see this possible bias, let M denote the mode (or median) rate of return. If investors perceive M to be the central or most likely rate of return, so that they base their investment decisions on M instead of the mean, μ, then the difference $[\mu - M]$ measures bias. This bias affects the mean-squared error (MSE):

$$\begin{aligned}
\text{MSE}\,(r) &= E(r - M)^2 \\
&= E\{[r - E\,(r)] - [M - E\,(r)]\}^2 \\
&= E\left\{[r - E\,(r)]^2 + [M - E\,(r)]^2\right\} \\
&= \text{Var}\,(r) + \text{bias}^2
\end{aligned} \tag{9.5}$$

Equation (9.5) shows that the second statistical moment, $\text{Var}\,(r)$, differs from the mean-squared errors around M. It is possible that skewness causes such bias by causing investors to focus on M instead of $E\,(r)$.[9]

It also can be shown that even if μ is the measure of central tendency used by investors, skewness will nevertheless cause the alpha and beta statistics in the single-index market model, equation (8.1), to be biased and inconsistent. The problem is that portfolio theory and ordinary least-squares (OLS) regression both consider only the first two statistical moments. As result, skewness causes biases that depreciate the value of portfolio theory and OLS regression statistics.

Skewness can be reduced and even eliminated from many probability distributions by transforming the (positively skewed) holding period return to the continuously compounded return, as shown in equation (A1.7) of Chapter 1.

$$\dot{r}_t = \ln\left(\frac{P_t}{P_{t-1}}\right) = \ln\left(1 + r_t\right) \tag{9.6}$$

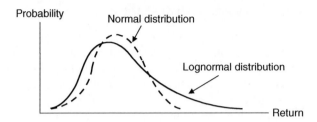

FIGURE 9.2 Normal and Lognormal Distributions

where $\dot{r}_t$ is the continuously compounded return and r_t is the holding period return.[10] If the continuously compounded return, $\dot{r}_t$, has a normal distribution with mean $\dot{\mu}$ and variance $\dot{\sigma}^2$ so that $\dot{r}_t \sim N\left(\dot{\mu}, \dot{\sigma}^2\right)$, then the holding period return (or discrete period return), $1 + r_t$ (or simply r_t), is said to have a *lognormal* distribution. Then, the mean and variance of $1 + r_t$ are denoted

$$E\left(1 + r_t\right) = \mu = \exp\left(\dot{\mu} + \frac{1}{2}\dot{\sigma}^2\right) \tag{9.7}$$

$$\text{Var}\left(1 + r_t\right) = \sigma^2 = \exp\left(2\dot{\mu} + 2\dot{\sigma}^2\right) - \exp\left(2\dot{\mu} + \dot{\sigma}^2\right)$$
$$= \mu^2\left[\exp\left(\dot{\sigma}^2\right) - 1\right] \tag{9.8}$$

The median of $1 + r_t$ is $\exp\left(\dot{\mu}\right)$, and the mode of $1 + r_t$ is $\exp\left(\dot{\mu} - \dot{\sigma}^2\right)$. In positively skewed distributions such as lognormal distributions, mean < median < mode. Figure 9.2 illustrates the lognormal and normal probability distributions of r_t and $\dot{r}_t$, respectively.

As shown in Figure 9.2, the logarithmic transformation "pulls in" the skewed positive tail of the distribution of asset returns and extends its truncated negative tail to minus infinity to create a more symmetrical (and hopefully more nearly normal) distribution. It is appropriate to use the lognormal probability distribution when the natural logarithm of returns has a normal distribution.

Because $\dot{r}_t$ is normally distributed, its measure of skewness (the third moment around its mean, equal to $E[(\dot{r}_t - \dot{\mu})^3]$) will be equal to zero. However, if r_t (or $1 + r_t$) is lognormally distributed, it will have a positive third moment. This moment, denoted κ, will be functionally related to $\dot{\mu}$ and $\dot{\sigma}^2$ as follows:

$$\kappa = \dot{\mu}^3\left[\left(\frac{\dot{\sigma}^2}{\dot{\mu}^2}\right)^3 + 3\left(\frac{\dot{\sigma}^2}{\dot{\mu}^2}\right)^2\right] \tag{9.9}$$

More generally, higher moments of r_t (or $1 + r_t$) will be functions of $\dot{\mu}$ and $\dot{\sigma}$, and thus the only parameters necessary to describe r_t are $\dot{\mu}$ and $\dot{\sigma}$. As a result, while being slightly reformulated, portfolio theory still involves only means and standard deviations when returns are lognormally distributed.

9.5.2 Portfolio Analysis under Lognormality

Assuming that returns are lognormally distributed does not negate the use of mean-variance analysis. If the assumption of normality is replaced by an assumption of

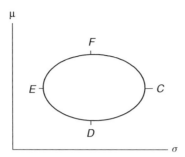

FIGURE 9.3A Opportunity Sets
in Risk-return Space (μ, σ) for
Noncompounded Returns

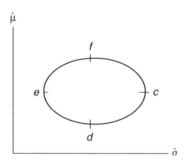

FIGURE 9.3B Opportunity Sets
in Risk-return Space $(\dot{\mu}, \dot{\sigma})$ for
Continuously Compounded
Returns

lognormality and investors are assumed to have utility functions displaying positive marginal utility of wealth (an assumption made in Chapter 4), then a modified form of the efficient frontier theorem is inappropriate. Figures 9.3A and 9.3B display ellipses within which the opportunity set of risky securities lies in (μ, σ) space and $(\dot{\mu}, \dot{\sigma})$ space, respectively.[11]

Continuously compounded returns, $\dot{r}_t$, can be converted to the standard unit normal variable

$$z_t = \frac{\dot{r}_t - \dot{\mu}}{\dot{\sigma}} \tag{9.10}$$

where z_t is normally distributed with mean 0 and variance 1, $N(0, 1)$. This conversion simplifies the derivation of the efficient frontier because the probability distribution of z_t is stable and the statistical relationships are well known. These conventions imply that $\dot{r}_t = \ln(1 + r_t) = \dot{\mu} + z_t \dot{\sigma}$, and that beginning wealth W_0 is related to terminal wealth W_T as shown in equation (9.11).

$$W_T = W_0(1 + r) = W_0 e^{\dot{r}} = W_0 e^{\dot{\mu} + z\dot{\sigma}} \tag{9.11}$$

Here the subscripts to r and z have been deleted for ease of exposition.

To maximize expected utility of terminal wealth, the investor will choose the portfolio that will maximize the expected utility equation (9.12),

$$E\left[U\left(W_T\right)\right] = \int_{-\infty}^{+\infty} U\left[W_0 \, e^{\dot\mu + z\dot\sigma}\right] f\left(z\right) dz \qquad (9.12)$$

because $z = g(\dot\mu, \dot\sigma)$, the portfolio owner's expected utility is a function of expected return $\dot\mu$ and risk $\dot\sigma$, measured using continuously compounded returns. The expected utility function, equation (9.12), is analyzed next to determine how risk and return affect expected utility.

The partial derivative of expected utility with respect to $\dot\mu$ will show the effect of maximizing return $\dot\mu$ for a given risk class $\dot\sigma$. Using the chain rule to take the partial derivative of equation (9.12) yields

$$\frac{\partial E\left[U\left(W_T\right)\right]}{\partial \dot\mu} = \left(\frac{\partial E\left[U\left(W_T\right)\right]}{\partial W_T}\right)\left(\frac{\partial W_T}{\partial \dot\mu}\right)$$

$$= \int_{-\infty}^{+\infty} \left(\frac{\partial U\left(W_T\right)}{\partial W_T}\right) W_T f\left(z\right) dz > 0 \qquad (9.13)$$

because $\left(\partial W_T / \partial \dot\mu\right) = W_T$. Equation (9.13) is positive because $\partial U\left(W_T\right)/\partial W_T$ is positive for investors who prefer more to less wealth, and $f(z)$, being a probability density function, can only take on positive values. Thus, for any given value of $\dot\sigma$ in Figure 9.3B, the investor will seek to maximize $\dot\mu$ in order to maximize expected utility. Graphically, Figure 9.3B shows that portfolios on the upper boundary of the ellipse between e and c dominate all other portfolios.

The partial derivative of expected utility with respect to $\dot\sigma$ will show the effect of minimizing $\dot\sigma$ for a given $\dot\mu$. Again, using the chain rule to take the partial derivative of equation (9.12) yields

$$\frac{\partial E\left[U\left(W_T\right)\right]}{\partial \dot\sigma} = \left(\frac{\partial E\left[U\left(W_T\right)\right]}{\partial W_T}\right)\left(\frac{\partial W_T}{\partial \dot\sigma}\right)$$

$$= \int_{-\infty}^{+\infty} \left(\frac{\partial U\left(W_T\right)}{\partial W_T}\right) W_T \, zf(z) \, dz \qquad (9.14)$$

Equation (9.14) is identical to equation (9.13) except the term z appears in the integrand. Because z is symmetrically distributed around zero and can therefore take on negative or positive values, and equation (9.13) was shown to be positive, equation (9.14) can be either negative or positive (or zero). This means that for a given level of $\dot\mu$, expected utility is maximized by either maximizing or minimizing $\dot\sigma$. That is,

$$\frac{\partial E\left[U\left(W_T\right)\right]}{\partial \dot\sigma} = \begin{cases} \text{positive} & \text{if } \left[\partial U\left(W_T\right)/\partial W_T\right] W_T \text{ is an increasing function} \\ 0 & \text{if } \left[\partial U\left(W_T\right)/\partial W_T\right] W_T \text{ is a constant} \\ \text{negative} & \text{if } \left[\partial U\left(W_T\right)/\partial W_T\right] W_T \text{ is a decreasing function} \end{cases}$$

$$(9.15)$$

The sign of $\partial E\left[U\left(W_T\right)\right]/\partial\dot\sigma$ will depend on the sign of the derivative of $\left[\partial U\left(W_T\right)/\partial W_T\right]W_T$, which equals

$$\frac{\partial\left[U'\left(W_T\right)\cdot W_T\right]}{\partial W_T} = U''\left(W_T\right)\cdot W_T + U'\left(W_T\right) = U'\left(W_T\right)\left[-\frac{U''\left(W_T\right)W_T}{U'\left(W_T\right)}+1\right]$$

$$= U'\left(W_T\right)\left[1 + R\left(W_T\right)\right] \qquad (9.16)$$

where $R\left(W_T\right) = W_T\left[-U''\left(W_T\right)/U'\left(W_T\right)\right]$ is the utility function's measure of relative risk aversion (RRA). We know

$$\frac{\partial E\left[U\left(W_T\right)\right]}{\partial\dot\sigma} = \begin{cases} \text{positive} & \text{if } R\left(W_T\right) > 1 \\ 0 & \text{if } R\left(W_T\right) > 1 \\ \text{negative} & \text{if } R\left(W_T\right) > 1 \end{cases} \qquad (9.17)$$

Thus, the sign of equation (9.17) will depend on the investor's wealth and utility function.[12] This means that, without additional information on W_T and function $U(\cdot)$, it is not possible to rule out any part of the upper boundary of the ellipse between e and c as being dominated by any other part.

The portfolios on the boundary of the ellipse between e and c must correspond to certain portfolios in (μ, σ) space. Once this correspondence is found, the efficient frontier when returns are lognormal can be identified. Equations (9.7) and (9.8) are the key to unraveling these relationships. Consider the ratio of equation (9.8) divided by equation (9.7).

$$\frac{\sigma}{\mu} = \left[\exp\left(\dot\sigma^2\right) - 1\right]^{1/2} \qquad (9.18)$$

From equation (9.18), it can be seen that

$$\mu = \frac{\sigma}{\left[\exp\left(\dot\sigma^2\right) - 1\right]^{1/2}} \qquad (9.19)$$

Equation (9.19) represents a straight line from the origin in (μ, σ) space that has a constant value of $\dot\sigma^2$ throughout its length. To further analyze the investment opportunities in (μ, σ) space from Figure 9.3A, a family of such constant $\dot\sigma^2$ lines is illustrated in Figure 9.4.

Taking the logarithm of equation (9.7) and solving it for $\dot\mu$ yields

$$\dot\mu = \ln\mu - 0.5\dot\sigma^2 \qquad (9.20)$$

If $\dot\sigma$ is a given value in equation (9.20), then $\dot\mu$ is made as large as possible by maximizing μ. This implies that moving out from the origin along any linear isoquant in Figure 9.4 to the point on the opportunity set with the highest attainable value of either μ or $\dot\mu$ will trace out the unique (μ, σ) efficient portfolio that corresponds to one $(\dot\mu, \dot\sigma)$ efficient portfolio. For example, on the ray OEY in Figure 9.4, portfolio Y has both the maximum $\dot\mu$ and the maximum μ along this isoquant. Tracing the maximum $\dot\mu$ portfolios at every value of $\dot\sigma$ in Figure 9.4 reveals that the curve PYFCN is the $(\dot\mu, \dot\sigma)$ efficient frontier. The existence of this efficient frontier implies

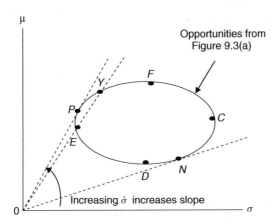

FIGURE 9.4 Analysis of (μ, σ) Opportunities in
Terms of $\dot{\mu}$ and $\dot{\sigma}$

that $\dot{\sigma}^2$ is a quantitative risk surrogate that may be used in place of the original σ^2
Markowitz risk measure.

Several interesting observations may be drawn with respect to the $(\dot{\mu}, \dot{\sigma})$ efficient
frontier. First, note that efficient portfolio f in Figure 9.3B is the portfolio with
the maximum expected return in the long run. That is, efficient portfolio f has the
maximum geometric mean rate of return, because $E\left[\ln\left(1 + r\right)\right] = \dot{\mu}$ is a geometric
mean return.[13] It also corresponds to the optimal portfolio for an investor with a
logarithmic utility function and will lie between E and F (the traditional efficient
frontier) in Figure 9.3A.[14] Second, note that the portion of the (μ, σ) efficient
frontier along the curve EP in Figure 9.4 is not $(\dot{\mu}, \dot{\sigma})$ efficient. That is, a part of
the traditional efficient frontier is no longer efficient if returns are lognormal. Third,
if a risk-free borrowing and lending rate exists, then there is no difference in the
efficient frontiers because the tangency points are identical. Finally, if unrestricted
short selling is permitted (but risk-free borrowing and lending are prohibited), then
the new efficient frontier will be a subset of the traditional efficient frontier. More
specifically, it will be an upper portion of the upper half of the hyperbola, because
it will no longer include a portion near the minimum variance portfolio. These last
two observations imply that the market portfolio will still lie on the traditional
efficient frontier as long as either unrestricted short selling is permitted or a risk-free
borrowing and lending rate exists. As a result, under these circumstances the CAPM
still holds if returns are lognormally distributed.

Restating the efficient frontier in $(\dot{\mu}, \dot{\sigma})$ space is worthwhile for several reasons.
First, the (μ, σ)-efficient frontier contains some undesirable portfolios in its highest
and lowest return sectors that are eliminated in the logarithmic transformation
to the $(\dot{\mu}, \dot{\sigma})$-efficient frontier. Second, the (μ, σ)-efficient frontier can ignore a
significant third moment. The $(\dot{\mu}, \dot{\sigma})$ analysis, however, includes and eliminates the
positive skewness of the discrete holding period returns in deriving the continuous-
time efficient frontier and is thus a superior decision-making process. Finally, the
$(\dot{\mu}, \dot{\sigma})$ analysis pinpoints the long-run wealth-maximizing portfolio, whereas this
maximum geometric mean return portfolio is not delineated by the (μ, σ) analysis.
The $(\dot{\mu}, \dot{\sigma})$-efficient portfolio with the highest expected return is the optimal choice
for investors wishing to maximize their terminal wealth.

9.6 CONCLUSIONS

The portfolio analysis is based on the assumption that asset returns are normally distributed with two parameters, mean and variance. However, empirical evidence shows that asset returns are not normally distributed. The empirical distribution of asset returns has nonsymmetric and leptokurtic characteristics. In other words, the distribution of asset returns is not characterized by the two parameters. This chapter has reviewed several non-normal probability distributions that are known to better capture the non-normal characteristics of asymmetry and leptokurtosis of asset returns.

NOTES

1. For an examination of daily stock return distributions for U.S. stocks, see Rachev, Stoyanov, Biglova, and Fabozzi (2005).
2. The skewness and kurtosis, which are the statistics most commonly used to test normality, are defined and measured by

$$
\text{Skewness} \equiv \gamma_1 = E\left[\left(\frac{r_t - \mu}{\sigma}\right)^3\right] = \frac{\mu_3}{\sigma^3}
$$

$$
= \frac{\left[\sum_{t=1}^{T}(r_t - \bar{r})^3/T\right]}{\left[\sum_{t=1}^{T}(r_t - \bar{r})^2/T\right]^{3/2}} = \frac{\sqrt{T}\sum_{t=1}^{T}(r_t - \bar{r})^3}{\left[\sum_{t=1}^{T}(r_t - \bar{r})^2\right]^{3/2}}
$$

$$
\text{Kurtosis} = \gamma_2 = E\left[\left(\frac{r_t - \mu}{\sigma}\right)^4\right] - 3 = \frac{\mu_4}{\sigma^4} - 3
$$

$$
= \frac{\left[\sum_{t=1}^{T}(r_t - \bar{r})^4/T\right]}{\left[\sum_{t=1}^{T}(r_t - \bar{r})^2/T\right]^2} - 3 = \frac{T\sum_{t=1}^{T}(r_t - \bar{r})^4}{\left[\sum_{t=1}^{T}(r_t - \bar{r})^2\right]^2} - 3
$$

where $\mu_k = E(r_t - \mu)^k$ is the k-th central moment, $\mu = E(r_t)$, and T is the sample size of time-series return observations. For normality, $\gamma_1 = 0$ and $\gamma_2 = 0$. The upper and lower one-percentile points in the distribution of the skewness statistic are 0.058 and -0.058, respectively. The upper and lower one-percentile points in the distribution of the excess kurtosis statistic are 0.13 and -0.11, respectively (see E. S. Pearson and H. O. Hartley, eds., 1966).
3. Of course, the mean must also be finite. See Fama (1976a, chap. 1) for a more detailed presentation of this counterargument.
4. It has been argued that the characteristic exponent α lies somewhere between 1.6 and 1.8.
5. The semi-interquartile range is equal to half the difference between the 0.75 and 0.25 fractiles of the cumulative probability distribution. For a summary on this form of two-dimensional portfolio analysis, see Fama and Miller (1972, chaps. 6 and 7).
6. Ortobelli, Rachev, and Fabozzi (2010) analyze portfolio selection problems with stable Paretian distributions.
7. As a practical matter, it can be counterargued that limited liability and positive skewness are unimportant when returns are measured over arbitrarily small intervals.

8. See Merton (1971) for a set of conditions under which portfolios will have lognormal returns when the component securities have lognormal returns.

9. For an interesting discussion of Tversky and Kahneman prospect theory and skewness, see Nicholas Barberis and Ming Huang, "Stocks as Lotteries: The Implications of Probability Weighting for Security Prices," American Economic Review 98, no. 5: 2066–2100.

10. See the appendix to Chapter 1 for a description and comparison of discrete and continuously compounded returns.

11. The use of ellipses here is for illustrative purposes only.

12. For example, if the investor has a logarithmic utility function, then $\partial E\left[U\left(W_T\right)\right]/\partial\dot{\sigma}=0$. In this situation, all portfolios with the same level of $\dot{\mu}$ will be equally desirable, regardless of their respective level of $\dot{\sigma}$.

13. Given that there are T observed returns on a security, the geometric mean of the security is defined as $\left[\left(1+r_1\right)\left(1+r_2\right)\cdots\left(1+r_T\right)\right]^{1/T}-1$. Take logs of the geometric mean and then find the expected value to obtain $E\left[\ln\left(1+r\right)\right]$.

14. If an investor has either a quadratic or logarithmic utility function, then his or her optimal portfolio will still be on the traditional efficient frontier even if returns have a lognormal distribution. See Elton and Gruber (1974b).

Non-Mean-Variance Investment Decisions

The mean-variance investment decision criterion is relevant when asset returns are normally distributed or investors' utility functions are quadratic.[1] In other words, the mean-variance approach holds in the circumstances that the two parameters, mean and variance, are sufficient to describe the investment environment. Therefore, when asset returns are not normally distributed or utility functions are not quadratic, other investment decision tools are needed.[2] This chapter introduces six other portfolio selection criteria: the geometric mean return (GMR) criterion, the safety-first criterion, value at risk (VaR), semivariance, stochastic dominance, and the mean-variance-skewness criterion. Although some of these criteria still use the first and second moment (mean and variance), they do not require a specific statistical distribution.

10.1 GEOMETRIC MEAN RETURN CRITERION

The geometric mean of past historical returns, $\bar{r}_g$, is defined as

$$\bar{r}_g = \left[(1 + r_1)(1 + r_2) \cdots (1 + r_T) \right]^{1/T} - 1$$

$$= \left[\prod_{t=1}^{T} (1 + r_t) \right]^{1/T} - 1 \tag{10.1}$$

Instead of adding together returns to obtain the mean return, one plus the holding period return is serially multiplied. In historical return observations we assume that each of the observations occurs equally likely, that is, with equal probability of $1/T$. Alternatively, when the probability of each return observation is p_j, the geometric mean return (GMR) is

$$\bar{r}_g = \prod_{j=1}^{S} (1 + r_j)^{p_j} - 1 \tag{10.2}$$

if we assume $\sum_{j=1}^{S} p_j = 1.0$.

For example, possible returns from an investment will be 15 percent, 5 percent, and −10 percent for the next period if the economy is in expansion, normal, and in recession, respectively. The probabilities of the expansion, normal, and recession economy for the next period are 0.3, 0.5, and 0.2, respectively. The GMR is

$$\bar{r}_g = (1 + 0.15)^{0.3}(1 + 0.05)^{0.5}(1 - 0.10)^{0.2} - 1 = 4.63\%$$

10.1.1 Maximizing the Terminal Wealth

In a multiperiod setting, it can be shown that the portfolio with the highest expected terminal value is the one with the highest expected GMR. This can readily be seen by noting that

$$E\left(W_T\right) = E\left[W_0\left(1 + r_1\right)\left(1 + r_2\right)\cdots\left(1 + r_T\right)\right]$$
$$= W_0\,E\left[\left(1 + \bar{r}_g\right)^T\right] \tag{10.3}$$

Because W_0 and T are constants, it can be shown that maximizing $E\left(W_T\right)$ is equivalent to maximizing E(GMR). Accordingly, the GMR criterion suggests selecting the portfolio at the beginning of each period that has maximum E(GMR) in order to maximize $E\left(W_T\right)$. Furthermore, this portfolio will be mean-variance efficient if either (1) returns are lognormally distributed, or (2) returns are normally distributed and investors have logarithmic utility functions.

10.1.2 Log Utility and the GMR Criterion

If an investor has a logarithmic utility function, then

$$E\left[U\left(W_T\right)\right] = E\left\{\ln\left[W_0\left(1 + r_1\right)\left(1 + r_2\right)\cdots\left(1 + r_T\right)\right]\right\} \tag{10.4a}$$
$$= \ln W_0 + E\left\{\ln\left[\left(1 + r_1\right)\left(1 + r_2\right)\cdots\left(1 + r_T\right)\right]\right\} \tag{10.4b}$$
$$= \ln W_0 + E\left[\ln\left(1 + \bar{r}_g\right)^T\right] \tag{10.4c}$$
$$= \ln W_0 + T\,E\left[\ln\left(1 + \bar{r}_g\right)\right] \tag{10.4d}$$

Because W_0 and T are constants, maximizing $E\left[U\left(W_T\right)\right]$ is equivalent to maximizing $E\left[\ln\left(1 + \bar{r}_g\right)\right]$. The portfolio that has the maximum value for $E\left[\ln\left(1 + \bar{r}_g\right)\right]$ will also have the maximum value for $E\left[\left(1 + \bar{r}_g\right)^T\right]$, so, choosing the portfolio with the maximum E(GMR) is mathematically equivalent to maximizing both $E\left[U\left(W_T\right)\right]$ and $E\left(W_T\right)$. Thus, the GMR criterion is also an expected utility-based criterion if investors have logarithmic utility functions.

A *myopic* single-period investment rule known as the maximum-expected-log (or MEL) rule has been described by Markowitz (1976), who argues that it is optimal in the long run. This rule is based on the GMR and it states that in each period t the investor should select that portfolio with the maximum expected value of $\ln\left(1 + r_t\right)$. Because equation (10.4b) can be rewritten as

$$E\left[U\left(W_T\right)\right] = \ln W_0 + E\left[\ln\left(1 + r_1\right)\right] + \cdots + E\left[\ln\left(1 + r_T\right)\right] \tag{10.5}$$

it can be seen that following the MEL rule is equivalent to maximizing $E\left[U\left(W_T\right)\right]$ and is therefore equivalent to maximizing the GMR. Although the MEL rule is an expected utility-maximizing rule if an investor has a logarithmic utility function, it is not an expected utility-maximizing rule for other types of utility functions, even though it maximizes expected terminal wealth. Accordingly, those investors who accept the use of utility theory in decision making reject the MEL rule as a general rule.

An investor who disregards past and future periods in making investment decisions for the current period is said to behave myopically. Using single-period analysis, as in Chapter 17, may thus be described as myopic economic behavior. Unfortunately, the phrase "myopic behavior" in everyday discussions connotes short-sighted behavior that is not good. In contrast, in a portfolio analysis context, delineating and selecting an optimal single-period efficient portfolio will be optimal multiperiod behavior and will maximize multiperiod expected utility under the following three conditions.

1. The investor has positive but diminishing utility of terminal wealth; that is,

$$U'\left(W_T\right) > 0 \text{ and } U''\left(W_T\right) < 0.$$

2. The investor has an isoelastic utility function (which has constant relative risk aversion).[3]
3. The single-period rates of return for securities are distributed according to a multivariate normal distribution and are independent of prior period returns.

These conditions simplify the mathematics sufficiently to prove that expected utility in the multiperiod case can be maximized by acting myopically.[4] For example, if the investor has a logarithmic utility function $U = \ln W_T$, where $W_T = W_0 \left(1 + r_1\right)\left(1 + r_2\right) \cdots \left(1 + r_T\right)$, then for any time t between 0 and T, the investor will act to maximize the derived utility function, which in this case is equivalent to maximizing $E\left[U\left(W_T\right)\right]$ or $E\left[\ln\left(1 + r_t\right)\right]$.

10.1.3 Diversification and the GMR

The previous section showed that selecting the portfolio with the greatest GMR is equivalent to maximizing the expected terminal wealth, $E\left(W_T\right)$, and, also, the expected utility, $E\left[U\left(W_T\right)\right]$, when the utility function is logarithmic. Another good feature of the geometric mean criterion in investment decision making is that the portfolio with the greatest GMR is usually a diversified portfolio. Suppose there are three stocks whose rates of return over five periods are given in Table 10.1. Among these three stocks, stock B provides the largest terminal wealth in five periods because it has the greatest GMR. Specifically, the investment of $1 in stocks A, B, and C will grow to $1(1 + 0.029)^5 = \$1.154, \$1(1 + 0.068)^5 = \$1.389$, and $\$1(1 + 0.030)^5 = \$1.159$, respectively. However, if an equally weighted (EW) portfolio is formed using these three stocks, the portfolio has a greater GMR than any of individual stocks. Specifically, the investment of $1 in the portfolio will grow to $1(1 + 0.126)^5 = \$1.810$. The reason for this result is that the GMR is greater when returns are less volatile. The GMR is smaller when there are extreme returns, although the arithmetic mean return is larger.

The approximate relation between the geometric mean and the arithmetic mean is

$$\bar{r}_g \approx \bar{r} - \frac{1}{2}\sigma^2 \tag{10.6}$$

TABLE 10.1 The GMR and Arithmetic Mean Return

Period	Stocks			EW portfolio
	A	B	C	
1	0.85	−0.25	−0.23	0.12
2	−0.50	0.70	0.18	0.13
3	0.42	−0.20	0.17	0.13
4	−0.45	0.70	0.15	0.13
5	0.60	−0.20	−0.05	0.12
Arithmetic avg. ($\bar{r}$)	0.184	0.150	0.044	0.126
Std. deviation (σ)	0.621	0.502	0.180	0.006
GMR ($\bar{r}_g$)	0.029	0.068	0.030	0.126

where $\bar{r}$ is the arithmetic mean.[5] Thus, the geometric mean is always less than or equal to the arithmetic mean. It is seen from equation (10.6) that the greater the volatility (σ^2), the less the GMR. Thus, the GMR is usually higher for well-diversified portfolios.

10.2   THE SAFETY-FIRST CRITERION

The Markowitz portfolio theory usually follows the mean-variance approach in which investors are assumed to choose among portfolios on the basis of a utility function defined in terms of the mean and variance of the portfolio return. In the mean-variance approach, however, the utility function is arbitrarily selected. Because of the arbitrary nature of utility functions, there were attempts to depart from the utility framework and invoke criterion based on more objective goals. One of these attempts is the safety-first criteria.

Safety-first criteria for portfolio selection are concerned only with the risk of failing to achieve a certain minimum target return or secure prespecified safety margins. The risk is commonly expressed as

$$\text{Prob}\left(r_p \leq r_L\right) \leq \alpha \tag{10.7}$$

where r_p is the return of portfolio p, r_L is a certain desired level of return below which the investor does not wish to fall, which is often referred to as the disaster level or the safety threshold, and α is an acceptable limit on the probability of failing to earn the minimally acceptable level of return, r_L.

10.2.1   Roy's Safety-First Criterion

Roy (1952) developed a safety-first criterion that seeks to minimize the probability of earning a disaster level of return, α in equation (10.7).[6] That is,

$$\text{Minimize   Prob}\left(r_p < r_L\right) \tag{10.8}$$

Roy's safety-first criterion implies that investors choose their portfolios by minimizing the loss probability for a fixed safety threshold called the floor return. Roy's criterion tries to control risk for a fixed return whereas Markowitz's mean-variance criterion offers a menu of positively related pairs of points having both the maximum local return and minimum local risk.

Table 10.2 shows 50 rates of return from four portfolios through 50 common time periods. These returns are sorted in ascending order in the table. Suppose that the investor does not wish returns to fall below −1 percent. The frequencies of the returns that fall below $r_L = -1\%$ are 8, 11, 7, and 6 out of 50 return observations for portfolios A, B, C, and D, respectively. That is, the probabilities that the return of each portfolio falls below $r_L = -1\%$ are 16 percent (=8/50), 22 percent (=11/50), 14 percent (=7/50), and 12 percent (=6/50) for portfolios A, B, C, and D, respectively. With respect to Roy's criterion, therefore, portfolio D is the best because it has the smallest probability to earn returns lower than the prespecified minimally acceptable level of return. Portfolios C, A, and B are the next best in order. That is, D > C > A > B. This preference ranking can differ from rankings based on a mean-variance approach such as the Sharpe ratio (to be explained further in Chapter 18). The Sharpe ratio, denoted S_p, is defined as the ratio of the excess return to the standard deviation.

$$S_p = \frac{\bar{r}_p - r_f}{\sigma_p} \tag{10.9}$$

Assuming the risk-free rate of return is $r_f = 0.012\%$, the Sharpe ratios of these four portfolios over 50 periods are 0.225, −0.110, 0.145, and 0.088, respectively. Thus, the ranking with respect to the Sharpe ratio is. A > C > D > B.

If the statistical distribution of returns can be characterized by mean and variance, Roy's safety-first criterion can be analyzed in a mean-variance context. For analytical convenience, we assume that returns are normally distributed. Then, the optimum portfolio is the one that has the smallest area of a left-hand side tail of the normal distribution. The probability in equation (10.8) can be transformed as

$$\text{Prob}\left(r_p < r_L\right) = \text{Prob}\left[\left(\frac{r_p - \text{E}\left(r_p\right)}{\sigma_p}\right) < \left(\frac{r_L - \text{E}\left(r_p\right)}{\sigma_p}\right)\right]$$

$$= \text{Prob}\left[Z < \left(\frac{r_L - \text{E}\left(r_p\right)}{\sigma_p}\right)\right] \tag{10.10}$$

where Z is a standard normal variate. Thus,

$$\text{Minimize } \text{Prob}\left(r_p < r_L\right) \equiv \text{Minimize } \text{Prob}\left[Z < \left(\frac{r_L - \text{E}\left(r_p\right)}{\sigma_p}\right)\right] \tag{10.11}$$

In Figure 10.1, the shaded area under the standard normal distribution indicates the probability that the return of a portfolio falls below the safety threshold level, r_L. The probability that a standard normal variate is less than $[r_L - \text{E}\left(r_p\right)]/\sigma_p$ can be easily calculated from the standard normal distribution table.

TABLE 10.2 Daily Returns from Four Stocks

Day	Unsorted original returns (%)				Sorted returns in ascending order (%)			
	A	B	C	D	A	B	C	D
1	0.80	0.40	−1.59	−0.34	−1.99	−4.31	−1.90	−2.59
2	0.04	1.54	1.51	1.11	−1.91	−3.10	−1.84	−1.49
3	5.38	−1.17	−1.90	−0.84	−1.74	−2.09	−1.59	−1.41
4	2.36	−0.46	−0.21	−1.28	−1.66	−1.43	−1.26	−1.28
5	−0.31	2.29	0.45	0.49	−1.55	−1.39	−1.24	−1.21
6	−1.99	−1.43	0.70	0.09	−1.37	−1.17	−1.11	−0.98
7	0.71	0.16	1.13	4.04	−1.26	−1.11	−1.02	−0.96
8	−1.74	−3.10	−1.84	−2.59	−1.10	−1.07	−0.73	−0.92
9	0.54	0.67	−0.04	1.64	−0.77	−1.06	−0.57	−0.84
10	−1.26	−0.57	0.50	−0.63	−0.74	−1.04	−0.51	−0.63
11	1.93	−0.61	0.11	0.77	−0.63	−1.03	−0.48	−0.62
12	1.46	1.68	1.49	2.44	−0.54	−0.82	−0.45	−0.56
13	0.18	0.11	0.76	0.94	−0.40	−0.75	−0.37	−0.42
14	1.65	0.95	2.03	1.33	−0.31	−0.65	−0.35	−0.41
15	0.07	−0.33	0.72	0.02	−0.30	−0.61	−0.24	−0.34
16	0.38	0.41	0.22	0.60	−0.30	−0.57	−0.21	−0.34
17	0.82	−1.39	−0.73	−1.49	−0.10	−0.54	−0.21	−0.21
18	0.92	0.79	0.61	0.51	−0.07	−0.46	−0.19	−0.21
19	−0.30	2.70	0.93	1.07	0.04	−0.45	−0.17	−0.06
20	2.00	0.81	0.33	0.06	0.07	−0.36	−0.04	−0.05
21	0.37	0.32	−0.37	0.16	0.17	−0.35	0.05	−0.05
22	−1.10	−0.82	−0.48	−0.42	0.18	−0.33	0.11	0.00
23	−0.54	−0.36	−0.45	−0.56	0.26	−0.33	0.17	0.00
24	1.08	1.77	0.98	1.50	0.27	−0.31	0.19	0.02
25	−0.10	0.36	−0.21	0.11	0.32	−0.22	0.22	0.02
26	−0.40	0.66	−0.51	0.11	0.37	−0.10	0.26	0.06
27	−1.91	−2.09	−1.24	−0.62	0.38	−0.01	0.27	0.06
28	0.65	0.27	0.52	−0.21	0.47	0.09	0.33	0.06
29	2.04	1.29	1.26	0.90	0.50	0.11	0.40	0.09
30	−0.77	−0.33	−0.57	0.45	0.53	0.16	0.44	0.11
31	0.17	−1.06	0.27	−0.98	0.54	0.27	0.45	0.11
32	0.50	−1.04	−0.24	0.06	0.54	0.32	0.50	0.16
33	−0.63	−0.65	−0.17	−0.21	0.55	0.36	0.52	0.16
34	−0.74	−1.11	−0.19	−0.96	0.65	0.40	0.55	0.45
35	0.47	−0.22	1.25	0.60	0.71	0.41	0.58	0.49
36	0.54	−0.54	0.74	0.00	0.71	0.44	0.61	0.51
37	−0.07	0.59	0.26	0.16	0.80	0.59	0.70	0.54
38	0.87	−4.31	0.19	1.07	0.82	0.59	0.72	0.60
39	−0.30	−0.75	−1.11	−1.41	0.87	0.61	0.74	0.60
40	0.27	−1.07	0.17	0.06	0.92	0.66	0.76	0.77
41	−1.66	−0.31	−1.02	−0.92	0.98	0.67	0.93	0.90
42	2.57	−0.01	0.40	−0.06	1.08	0.79	0.98	0.94
43	0.53	0.44	0.58	−0.41	1.46	0.81	0.99	1.07
44	0.98	0.09	0.99	0.00	1.65	0.95	1.13	1.07
45	0.32	−0.45	0.05	0.02	1.93	1.29	1.25	1.11
46	0.26	0.59	0.44	−0.05	2.00	1.54	1.26	1.33
47	0.55	0.61	1.33	−0.05	2.04	1.68	1.33	1.50
48	0.71	−0.35	−0.35	0.54	2.36	1.77	1.49	1.64
49	−1.37	−0.10	0.55	−0.34	2.57	2.29	1.51	2.44
50	−1.55	−1.03	−1.26	−1.21	5.38	2.70	2.03	4.04
Avg	0.31	−0.12	0.14	0.11				
Std dev	1.31	1.23	0.88	1.06				

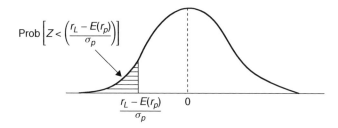

FIGURE 10.1 Probability the Return Falls Below r_L

EXAMPLE 10.1

The expected returns and standard deviations of the four portfolios from Table 10.2 are shown in Table 10.3. Assuming the returns of these portfolios are normally distributed and the threshold safety level or the floor return (r_L) is 3 percent, which portfolio is best with respect to Roy's safety-first criterion?

TABLE 10.3 Expected Return and Standard Deviation of Four Portfolios

	Portfolios			
	A	B	C	D
Expected return, $E(r_p)$	12%	10%	15%	10%
Standard deviation, σ_p	9%	4%	10%	8%
$\left[r_L - E(r_p)\right]/\sigma_p$	−1.00	−1.75	−1.20	−0.875
$\mathrm{Prob}\left[Z < \left(\frac{r_L - E(r_p)}{\sigma_p}\right)\right]$	0.1587	0.0401	0.1151	0.1908

The probability that the return of portfolio A is less than $r_L = 3\%$ is Prob $(Z < -1.00)$. From the standard normal distribution table, this probability is 0.1587. Similarly, the probabilities for portfolios B, C, and D are 0.0401, 0.1151, and 0.1908, respectively. The return from portfolio B has the smallest probability of falling below 3 percent and, thus, is the best with respect to Roy's criterion.

Roy's safety-first criterion is related to the Sharpe ratio. Minimizing the probability in equation (10.11) is equivalent to

$$\text{Minimize } \mathrm{Prob}\left[Z < \left(\frac{r_L - E(r_p)}{\sigma_p}\right)\right] \equiv \text{Minimize}\left[\frac{r_L - E(r_p)}{\sigma_p}\right]$$

$$\equiv \text{Maximize}\left[\frac{E(r_p) - r_L}{\sigma_p}\right] \qquad (10.12)$$

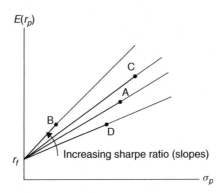

FIGURE 10.2 Sharpe's Criterion
Applied to Table 10.3

Thus, the optimum portfolio is the one with the greatest ratio $[E(r_p) - r_L]/\sigma_p$. Note that this decision criterion can be applied to any statistical distribution, as long as this distribution is characterized by only two parameters: mean and variance. The normality assumption of asset returns is not necessary. If the safety threshold r_L is replaced by the risk-free return r_f and we let the ratio be S_p, then

$$\text{Sharpe ratio} = S_p = \frac{E(r_p) - r_f}{\sigma_p} \tag{10.9}$$

Rewriting equation (10.9) yields

$$E(r_p) = r_f + S_p\sigma_p. \tag{10.13}$$

This is a straight line equation in $[\sigma_p, E(r_p)]$ space with an intercept r_f and slope S_p. Thus, the optimum portfolio is the one that has the greatest slope of the straight line originating r_f and passing through the portfolio. Figure 10.2 illustrates four lines representing portfolios A, B, C, and D in Table 10.3 of Example 10.1, respectively. The slope of the line indicates the desirability of the portfolio. The greater the slope, the more the desirability and the less probability that the return falls below the floor return. Portfolios lying on the same line are equally desirable, because they have the same slope. By combining the risk-free asset (with borrowing or lending at the risk-free rate) with a risky portfolio lying on the line, many equally desirable portfolios can be created. The line passing through r_f and point B has the highest slope; thus, portfolio B is most derirable. The remaining portfolio rankings are C > A > D.

10.2.2 Kataoka's Safety-First Criterion

Kataoka (1963) developed a safety-first criterion in which investors choose the portfolio with an insured return, r_L, as high as possible subject to the following constraint:[7] the probability that the portfolio return is no greater than the insured return must not exceed a predetermined level, denoted α.[8] In other words, the problem statement of Kataoka's safety-first criterion is

$$\text{Maximize } r_L$$

$$\text{subject to Prob}\left(r_p < r_L\right) \le \alpha \qquad (10.14)$$

EXAMPLE 10.2

Which portfolio is the most desirable among the four portfolios listed in Table 10.3 of Example 10.1 with respect to Kataoka's criterion, when $\alpha = 10\%$?

In Kataoka's criterion, investors choose the portfolio with the greatest insured return, r_L, under the constraint $\text{Prob}\left(r_p < r_L\right) \le 0.10$. By looking at the sorted returns in ascending order, we can observe that the insured return for portfolio A is -1.37 percent, because the frequency of portfolio A's returns being not greater than -1.37 percent is less than or equal to 5 out of 50 observations (or equivalently, 10 percent). That is, the constraint $\text{Prob}\left(r_A < -1.37\right) \le 0.10$ is satisfied. In this manner, we can find the insured levels of return satisfying the constraint for portfolios B, C, and D are -1.17 percent, -1.11 percent, and -0.98 percent, respectively. The maximum value among these insured levels of return is $L_D = -0.95$ percent. Thus, portfolio D is the best with respect to Kataoka's safety-first criterion, and portfolios C, B, and A are the next most desirable.

Like Roy's criterion, Kataoka's safety-first criterion can also be analyzed in a mean-variance approach, if the statistical distribution of returns can be characterized in terms of the mean and variance. The insured level of return, r_L, is the abscissa value below which the area under the statistical distribution is less than or equal to the predetermined level α. Figure 10.3 shows the insured level of return, r_L, when returns are normally distributed.

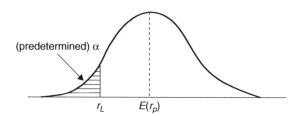

FIGURE 10.3 The Insured Level (r_L) Satisfying the Constraint $\text{Prob}(r_p < r_L) \le \alpha$

EXAMPLE 10.3

Table 10.3 presents the expected returns and standard deviations of four portfolios. Assume the portfolios' returns are normally distributed and the predetermined level of α is 5 percent. Which portfolio is the most desirable with respect to Kataoka's criterion?

The constraint can be transformed to

$$\text{Prob}\left(r_p < r_L\right) \leq \alpha \quad \Longleftrightarrow \quad \text{Prob}\left[Z \leq \left(\frac{r_L - E\left(r_p\right)}{\sigma_p}\right)\right] \leq \alpha \qquad (10.15)$$

Since $\alpha = 5\%$, the abscissa value in the standard normal distribution is $\left[r_L - E\left(r_p\right)\right]/\sigma_p = -1.645$. Thus, the insured level of return equals

$$r_L = E\left(r_p\right) + (-1.645) \times \sigma_p \qquad (10.16)$$

The insured level of return for portfolio A is

$$r_{L_A} = 12 + (-1.645) \times 9 = -2.805\%.$$

That is, the probability that portfolio A's return is less than -2.805 is at most 5 percent. Likewise, the insured levels of return for portfolios B, C, and D are

$$r_{L_B} = 10 + (-1.645) \times 4 = 3.42\%,$$

$$r_{L_C} = 15 + (-1.645) \times 10 = -1.45\%,$$

$$r_{L_D} = 10 + (-1.645) \times 8 = -3.16\%$$

At the same loss probability of $\alpha = 5\%$, the lowest possible acceptable returns for portfolios A, B, C, and D are -2.805 percent, 3.42 percent, -1.45 percent, and -3.16 percent, respectively. Thus, portfolio B is most desirable with respect to Kataoka's criterion, and portfolios C, A, and D are the next most desirable, in order of desirability.

Kataoka's safety-first criterion is also related to the traditional mean-variance approach in one circumstance. If the returns are normally distributed, then the constraint of equation (10.14) can be transformed as

$$\text{Prob}\left(r_p < r_L\right) \leq \alpha \quad \Longleftrightarrow \quad \left(\frac{r_L - E\left(r_p\right)}{\sigma_p}\right) \leq -z_\alpha \quad \Longleftrightarrow \quad r_L \leq E\left(r_p\right) - z_\alpha \sigma_p$$

$$(10.17)$$

where z_α is chosen so that $\text{Prob}\left(Z > z_\alpha\right) = \alpha$. Because investors want to make the insured level of return as large as possible, the last constraint in equation (10.17) becomes

$$r_L = E\left(r_p\right) - z_\alpha \sigma_p \qquad (10.18)$$

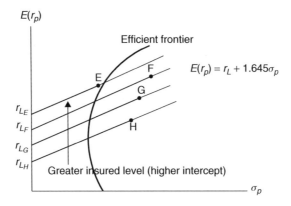

FIGURE 10.4 Karaoka's Safety-first Criterion

If $\alpha = 5\%$, then $z_\alpha = 1.645$, and equation (10.18) becomes

$$E\left(r_p\right) = r_L + 1.645\sigma_p \tag{10.19}$$

Figure 10.4 illustrates the parallel straight lines of equation (10.19) passing through portfolios E, F, G, and H in $\left[\sigma_p, E(r_p)\right]$ space, and they are in the investment opportunity set. These lines have the same slope of 1.645. Because the intercept indicates the insured level of return for each portfolio, portfolios locating on the straight line with the greater intercept are more desirable with respect to Kataoka's safety-first criterion. Thus, portfolio E is the best, because the straight line passing through the location of portfolio E has the highest intercept. Portfolios F, G, and H are the next best, respectively.

When Kataoka's safety-first criterion is contrasted with Roy's safety-first criterion in $\left[\sigma_p, E(r_p)\right]$ space, we see that Roy's criterion favors portfolios with a greater slope from the fixed intercept, whereas Kataoka's criterion prefers portfolios with the greatest intercept for a given slope.

10.2.3 Telser's Safety-First Criterion

Telser (1955) introduced another safety-first criterion three years after Roy's safety-first criterion.[9] His criterion assumes that investors maximize expected return, subject to the constraint that the probability of a return less than or equal to a prespecified minimum disaster level (r_L) does not exceed a given probability. Mathematically, Telser's criterion is expressed as

$$\text{Maximize } E(r_p)$$
$$\text{subject to Prob}\left(r_p \leq r_L\right) \leq \alpha \tag{10.20}$$

In the constraint of equation (10.20), the minimum disaster level, r_L, and the loss probability, α, are prespecified. Like equation (10.17), the constraint used in Telser's criterion of equation (10.20) can be reformulated as

$$E(r_p) \geq r_L + 1.645\sigma_p \tag{10.21}$$

Among the portfolios satisfying this constraint, the optimum portfolio with respect to Telser's criterion is the one with the greatest expected return.

EXAMPLE 10.4

Table 10.3 presents the expected returns and standard deviations from four portfolios. For this example, assume the portfolio's returns are normally distributed. If the minimum disaster level of return is $r_L = -2\%$ and the loss probability is $\alpha = 5\%$, which portfolio is the most desirable under Telser's criterion?

The constraints for the four portfolios are

$$E\left(r_A\right) \geq -2 + 1.645 \times 9 = 12.81\%,$$

$$E\left(r_B\right) \geq -2 + 1.645 \times 4 = 4.58\%,$$

$$E\left(r_C\right) \geq -2 + 1.645 \times 10 = 14.45\%,$$

$$E\left(r_D\right) \geq -2 + 1.645 \times 8 = 11.16\%.$$

The expected returns of portfolios A and D do not satisfy the constraint. The expected returns of portfolios B and C satisfy the constraint. We choose the portfolio that has the greatest expected return. Thus, portfolio C is most desirable with respect to Telser's safety-first criterion. Portfolio C is the second most desirable. Table 10.4 summarizes the statistics needed for Roy's, Kataoka's, and Telser's criteria.

TABLE 10.4 Three Safety-first Criteria for the Hypothetical Portfolios

	Portfolios			
	A	B	C	D
Expected return, $E(r_p)$	12%	10%	15%	10%
Standard deviation, σ_p	9%	4%	10%	8%
Roy's: Prob$\left\{Z \leq \left[\left(r_L - E(r_p)\right)/\sigma_p\right]\right\}$	0.1587	0.0401	0.1151	0.1908
Kataoka's: Insured return (r_L) with $\alpha = 5\%$	−2.85%	3.40%	1.90%	−1.30%
Telser's: $r_L + 1.645\sigma_p$ if $L = -2\%$	12.81%	4.58%	14.45%	11.16%

Like the two previous safety-first criteria, Telser's criterion can also be related to the traditional mean-variance approach under one circumstance. If the returns are normally distributed and there exists no risk-free asset, then the constraint in Telser's criterion can be illustrated as in Figure 10.5. Portfolios satisfying the constraint must lie in the shaded area, which is the intersection between the constraint and the opportunity set inside the mean-variance efficient frontier. Thus, the optimum portfolio is the one that has the greatest expected return among the portfolios located in the shaded region. In fact, the optimum portfolio will be on the mean-variance efficient frontier.

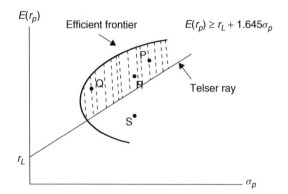

FIGURE 10.5 Telser's Safety-first Criterion without the Risk-free Asset

If a risk-free asset exists, the efficient frontier will equal the capital market line (CML). The intersection of the set satisfying the constraint and the opportunity set is the shaded area in Figure 10.6. Among the portfolios located in the shaded area, portfolio Q has the greatest expected return, at the intersection point of the Telser ray and the CML. Thus, portfolio Q is best with respect to Telser's criterion. The expected return of portfolio Q satisfies

$$r_L = E\left(r_Q\right) - z_\alpha \sigma_Q \tag{10.22}$$

Meanwhile, portfolio Q is on the CML and is formed by investing w_m in the market portfolio, m, and $\left(1 - w_m\right)$ in the risk-free asset. Thus, equation (10.22) can be rewritten as

$$r_L = \left[w_m E\left(r_m\right) + \left(1 - w_m\right) r_f\right] - z_\alpha \left(w_m \sigma_m\right) \tag{10.23}$$

Then,

$$w_m = \frac{r_L - r_f}{E\left(r_m\right) - r_f - z_\alpha \sigma_m} \tag{10.24}$$

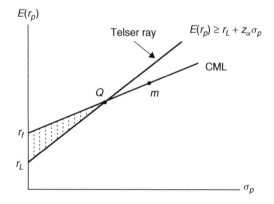

FIGURE 10.6 Telser's Safety-first Criterion with the Risk-free Asset

If the investor sets the loss probability (α) to be very small (i.e., very conservative), then z_α is large, and so the Telser ray will have a large positive slope and intersect the CML close to the point of the risk-free return. If the minimum disaster level of return (r_L) is close to the risk-free return, then the same result holds.

In summary, Kataoka's safety-first criterion contrasts with Roy's safety-first criterion in that the optimum portfolio with respect to Roy's criterion is the one with the smallest loss probability at a prespecified level of the insured return, r_L. And the optimum portfolio with respect to Kataoka's criterion is the one with the largest insured level of return at a prespecified level of loss probability, α. In Telser's criterion, both the insured return or the minimum disaster level of return and the loss probability are prespecified. Then, among the portfolios satisfying the prespecified r_L and α, the optimum portfolio is the one with the greatest expected return.

10.3   SEMIVARIANCE ANALYSIS

The dictionary definition of risk is "the chance of injury, damage, or loss." A financial loss that corresponds to this dictionary definition is a disappointing outcome in the left-hand tail of a probability distribution of single-period rates of return. Markowitz reformulated portfolio theory using only the disappointingly low returns to form a quantitative risk surrogate he called the semivariance.[10] When the probability distributions are symmetrically distributed, the implications of $[\sigma, E(r)]$ analysis are similar to the [semivariance, $E(r)$] results. However, when the probability distributions are skewed, the results from using the semivariance instead of the variance can differ significantly. This section reviews semivariance analysis.

10.3.1   Definition of Semivariance

The semivariance is a measure of dispersion of all observations that fall below some constant reference point (or threshold). Let the symbol h stand for a threshold or a benchmark return on the spectrum of possible one-period rates of return. The *semivariance* for the asset, denoted $\overline{\overline{\sigma}}_i^2$, is defined as

$$\overline{\overline{\sigma}}_i^2 = E\{\min[(r_i - h), 0]\}^2 \qquad (10.25)$$

The semivariance is estimated using historical return observations as follows

$$\overline{\overline{\sigma}}_i^2 = \frac{1}{T}\sum_{t=1}^{T}\{\min[(r_{it} - h), 0]\}^2$$

$$= \frac{1}{T}\sum_{t=1}^{T}(\overline{\overline{r}}_{it} - h)^2 \qquad (10.26)$$

where

$$\overline{\overline{r}}_{it} = \begin{cases} r_{it} & \text{if } r_{it} < h \\ h & \text{if } r_{it} \geq h \end{cases} \qquad (10.27)$$

For the continuous case, the semivariance for an asset i is:

$$\overline{\overline{\sigma}}_i^2 = \int_{-\infty}^{+\infty} \left\{ \min \left[(r_i - h), 0 \right] \right\}^2 f(r_i) \, dr_i$$

$$= \int_{-\infty}^{h} (r_i - h)^2 f(r_i) \, dr_i \qquad (10.28)$$

The semivariance is also called *lower partial moment*.[11] The *semideviation*, denoted $\overline{\overline{\sigma}}_i$, is

$$\overline{\overline{\sigma}}_i = \sqrt{\overline{\overline{\sigma}}_i^2} \qquad (10.29)$$

The riskless rate of return, the expected return, and zero are three commonly suggested values for h. Thus, the semivariance or the semideviation may measure the minimum acceptable rates of return for risky assets, $\overline{\overline{r}}_t = r_t < r_f$; worse-than-expected returns, $\overline{\overline{r}}_t = r_t < E(r)$; or negative returns, $\overline{\overline{r}}_t = r_t < 0$. More generally, any value may be assigned to h and the resulting statistics vary accordingly. Figure 10.7 illustrates the portion of an asset's probability distribution of single-period returns that might be used to calculate its semivariance. Only the shaded left-hand portion of the distribution shown in Figure 10.6 would be used to calculate the semivariance in equation series (10.25).

Using the semivariance as a risk measure requires redefining the dominant assets on the Markowitz efficient frontier to be:

- Those assets that have the minimum semivariance (semideviation) at each level of expected return, or conversely,
- Those assets that have the maximum expected return at each level of risk (as measured by either the semivariance or semideviation).

Figure 10.8 shows the Markowitz-efficient frontier in terms of the semideviation and expected return.

The single-period utility function that implies preference orderings for $[\overline{\overline{\sigma}}, E(r)]$ portfolios differs from the traditional utility function.

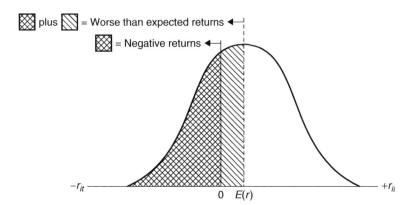

FIGURE 10.7 Probability Distribution of Returns Used to Calculate Semivariance if the Threshold Value h Equals $E(r)$ or Zero

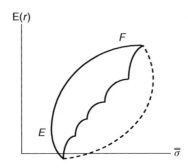

FIGURE 10.8 Efficient Set of
Portfolios in $[\overline{\overline{\sigma}}, \mathrm{E}(r)]$ Space

10.3.2 Utility Theory

The more traditional Markowitz-efficient portfolios in $[\sigma, \mathrm{E}(r)]$ space can be rationalized in terms of the single-period utility-of-returns function shown in equation
(10.30) if they are restricted to returns less than $(b/2c)$.

$$U(r) = br - cr^2 \quad \text{for } r < (b/2c) \tag{10.30}$$

The expected utility from this traditional quadratic function is derived in
equation (10.31).

$$\begin{aligned}
\mathrm{E}[U(r)] &= b\mathrm{E}(r) - c\mathrm{E}(r^2) \quad \text{for } b > c > 0 \\
&= b\mathrm{E}(r) - c\{\sigma^2 + [\mathrm{E}(r)]^2\} \\
&= b\mathrm{E}(r) - c\,\sigma^2 - c[\mathrm{E}(r)]^2 \\
&= f[\sigma, \mathrm{E}(r)]
\end{aligned} \tag{10.31}$$

where $[\partial f/\partial \mathrm{E}(r)] > 0$ and $[\partial f/\partial \sigma] < 0$. Some relevant findings about equation series
(10.31) discussed in Chapter 4 are reviewed here to contrast the utility functions
defined in terms of the semivariance and the variance.

Markowitz-efficient portfolios in mean-semivariance $[\overline{\overline{\sigma}}, \mathrm{E}(r)]$ space can be
rationalized in terms of the single-period utility of returns function shown in
equation (10.32).

$$U(r) = br - c\{\min[(r_t - h), 0]\}^2 \quad \text{for } c > 0 \tag{10.32}$$

Equation (10.32) is similar in some respects to the quadratic equation (10.30).
Equation (10.32) is quadratic for returns below h and linear in returns above
h. Figure 10.9 compares the utility functions from equations (10.31) and (10.32)
graphically.

The expected value of equation (10.32) is analyzed as follows.

$$\begin{aligned}
\mathrm{E}[U(r)] &= b\mathrm{E}(r) - c\,\mathrm{E}\{\min[(r_t - h), 0]\}^2 \\
&= b\mathrm{E}(r) - c\overline{\overline{\sigma}}^2 \\
&= g[\overline{\overline{\sigma}}, \mathrm{E}(r)]
\end{aligned} \tag{10.33}$$

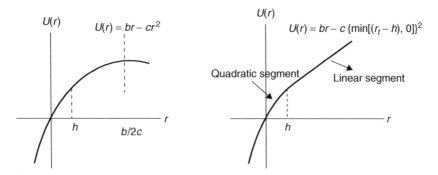

FIGURE 10.9 Comparison of Two Utility of Returns Functions

where

$$\frac{\partial g}{\partial E\,(r)} = b > 0 \quad \text{and} \quad \frac{\partial g}{\partial \overline{\overline{\sigma}}} = -2c\,\overline{\overline{\sigma}} < 0 \tag{10.34}$$

The effects that $E\,(r)$ and $\overline{\overline{\sigma}}$ have on expected utility equation (10.33) are shown in equation (10.34); these two partial derivatives have the same signs that $E\,(r)$ and σ, respectively, have on expected utility in equation (10.31). This means that an investor's indifference curves in $[\overline{\overline{\sigma}}, E\,(r)]$ space would be positively sloped and concave to the risk (measured on the $\overline{\overline{\sigma}}$) axis. The numerical values of the semideviation and the standard-deviation risk measures would differ for almost all assets, $\sigma_i \neq \overline{\overline{\sigma}}_i$. Nevertheless, the indifference maps in $[\sigma, E\,(r)]$ space and $[\overline{\overline{\sigma}}, E\,(r)]$ space can be expected to have similar shapes and orientations.

It would be difficult to assert generalities about preferences for the efficient frontiers generated from a given group of assets if the efficient frontiers were done in terms of both $[\sigma, E\,(r)]$ and $[\overline{\overline{\sigma}}, E\,(r)]$. If the utility function and the method of defining the efficient frontier were changed, it is highly likely that the portfolio that maximized expected utility would change too. However, cases may exist in which an investor with a given set of investment opportunities and an $f\,[\sigma, E\,(r)]$ expected utility function might select the same assets as another investor who has a $g\,[\overline{\overline{\sigma}}, E\,(r)]$ expected utility function. For example, if the value of h is identical to $E(r)$ and returns are symmetrically distributed, then $\overline{\overline{\sigma}}_i^2 = 0.5\sigma_i^2$ and the semivariance analysis yields the same results as the variance analysis.

Equations (10.32) and (10.33) rationalize the selection of Markowitz efficient portfolios in $[\overline{\overline{\sigma}}, E\,(r)]$ space that maximize expected utility. The following section discusses the derivation of the mean-semideviation $[\overline{\overline{\sigma}}, E(r)]$ efficient frontier.

10.3.3 Portfolio Analysis with the Semivariance

The objective of portfolio analysis with the semivariance is to delineate the set of portfolios that have the minimum semivariance at each level of the portfolio's expected return by varying the proportions of the investments in the portfolio.

The portfolio's expected return is the familiar weighted average return, equation (2.12).

$$E(r_p) = \sum_{i=1}^{N} w_i E\,(r_i) \tag{2.12}$$

The balance sheet identity, equation (2.11), is always present in Markowitz portfolio analysis.

$$1.0 = \sum_{i=1}^{N} w_i \tag{2.11}$$

The portfolio's semivariance, $\overline{\overline{\sigma}}_p^2$, is defined in equation series (10.35).[12]

$$\overline{\overline{\sigma}}_p^2 = E\{\min\left[\left(r_p - h\right), 0\right]\}^2$$

$$= E\left\{\min\left[\left(\sum_{i=1}^{N} w_i r_i - h\right), 0\right]\right\}^2 \tag{10.35}$$

Hogan and Warren (1972), Ang (1975), and Markowitz, Todd, Xu, and Yamane (1993) have shown that quadratic programming can be used to delineate a convex set of $[\overline{\sigma}, E(r)]$ efficient portfolios under the following three conditions:

1. The variance of returns is finite.
2. The portfolio's semivariance, equation (10.35), is continuously differentiable in the weight decision variable (w_i for all i).
3. The following first-order condition (namely, the gradient vector) is continuous in the weight decision variables.

$$\frac{\partial \overline{\overline{\sigma}}_i^2}{\partial w_i} = 2\,E\left\{\min\left[\left(r_p - h\right), 0\right]\right\} \tag{10.36}$$

These three conditions are met for a number of well-known probability distributions. So, it appears, numerical solutions can be computed without problems.

Computation of the semivariance efficient frontiers does not revolve around a symmetric variance-covariance matrix because the Markowitz cosemivariance is not symmetric, $\overline{\overline{\sigma}}_{ij} \neq \overline{\overline{\sigma}}_{ji}$, in most cases. Equation (10.37) defines the Markowitz cosemivariance, $\overline{\overline{\sigma}}_{ij}$, for a finite joint probability distribution of returns.

$$\overline{\overline{\sigma}}_{ij} = E\left\{\left(r_i - h\right)\left(\min\left[\left(r_j - h\right), 0\right]\right)\right\}$$

$$= E\left\{\left(r_i - h\right)\left(\overline{r}_j - h\right)\right\} \tag{10.37}$$

Equation (10.37) defines the *ex ante* Markowitz cosemivariance. Equation (10.37a) defines it in *ex post* terms.

$$\overline{\overline{\sigma}}_{ij} = \frac{1}{T} \sum_{t=1}^{T} \left(r_{it} - h\right)\left(\min\left[\left(r_{jt} - h\right), 0\right]\right)$$

$$= \frac{1}{T} \sum_{t=1}^{T} \left(r_{it} - h\right)\left(\overline{r}_{jt} - h\right) \tag{10.37a}$$

The Markowitz cosemivariance is the weighted average over all T pairs of r_{it} and r_{jt} that use only the paired values for which $r_{jt} < h$. The Markowitz cosemivariance may be zero if returns of asset i and asset j are independent or if all the returns of asset i exceed the value of h. When $i = j$, the cosemivariance equals the semivariance, $\overline{\overline{\sigma}}_{ij} = \overline{\overline{\sigma}}_i^2$.

The set of $[\bar{\bar{\sigma}}, E(r)]$-efficient portfolios will be identical to the set of $[\sigma, E(r)]$-efficient portfolios computed from the same investments if the following two conditions exist simultaneously:

1. The value of h equals $E(r)$ for every probability distribution. That is, the $E(r)$ is used as its own constant reference point.
2. All the probability distributions are symmetric, so that when the deviations from the mean are used, the variances will differ from the corresponding semivariances by a factor of two.

There is some doubt about the second point because some empirical skewness statistics show that modest skewness exists. Some econometricians would argue that this skewness is sample dependent and should be ignored because the unobservable skewness population parameters are probably zero. Other econometricians argue that skewness should not be ignored. These differing viewpoints raise the question of whether to use the variance or the semivariance.

Markowitz (1959) suggested the considerations of cost, convenience, familiarity, and the desirability of the portfolios as the criteria for selecting between the variance and the semivariance analysis. As computational costs diminish each year, the first two considerations diminish in importance. The third consideration is a temporary condition; a lack of familiarity with the semivariance can be overcome by a motivated student. Therefore, the fourth consideration, the desirability of the portfolios, seems to be the most important concern.

The desirability of the portfolios that can be obtained is of primary importance in deciding whether or not to use semivariance analysis. Various studies can be cited that suggest using semivariance.[13] However, if the probability distributions are sufficiently asymmetric to justify using the semivariance, it may be better to simply include skewness in the analysis and do portfolio analysis in three moments rather than use the semivariance. It may be advantageous to use three moments because the semivariance ignores the information contained in the right-hand tails of the probability distributions. But portfolio analysis in three moments does not ignore any data. Portfolio analysis using higher-order moments is examined in Section 10.4 of this chapter.

Estrada (2002, 2007) suggests a slightly different cosemivariance measure instead of using Markowitz's cosemivariance measure. Equations (10.38) and (10.39) define Estrada's cosemivariance for assets i and j, denoted $\bar{\bar{\sigma}}_{ij}$, in *ex ante* terms and *ex post* terms, respectively.

$$
\begin{aligned}
\bar{\bar{\sigma}}_{ij}' &= E\left\{\left(\min\left[(r_i - h), 0\right]\right)\left(\min\left[(r_j - h), 0\right]\right)\right\} \\
&= E\left\{(\bar{r}_i - h)(\bar{r}_j - h)\right\}
\end{aligned}
\tag{10.38}
$$

and

$$
\begin{aligned}
\bar{\bar{\sigma}}_{ij}' &= \frac{1}{T}\sum_{t=1}^{T}\left(\min\left[(r_{it} - h), 0\right]\right)\left(\min\left[(r_{jt} - h), 0\right]\right) \\
&= \frac{1}{T}\sum_{t=1}^{T}(\bar{r}_{it} - h)(\bar{r}_{jt} - h)
\end{aligned}
\tag{10.39}
$$

Unlike the Markowitz cosemivariance measure, equation (10.37), which is asymmetric in most cases, $\overline{\overline{\sigma}}_{ij} \neq \overline{\overline{\sigma}}_{ji}$, Estrada's cosemivariance measure is symmetric, $\overline{\overline{\sigma}}'_{ij} = \overline{\overline{\sigma}}'_{ji}$, in all cases. This difference in symmetry has two important implications for portfolio analysis. First, using Estrada's cosemivariance results in a symmetric variance-covariance matrix, whereas using Markowitz's cosemivariance usually results in an asymmetric variance-covariance matrix. Second, the semivariance is determined *endogenously* when the Markowitz cosemivariance is used. Because the value of any given Markowitz cosemivariance measure is not determined until computations involving $\overline{\overline{r}}_{it}$, $\overline{\overline{r}}_{jt}$, and h are completed for each cosemivariance value, the efficient frontier is determined endogenously by the values of these components. In contrast, the value of any given Estrada cosemivariance is invariant with respect to computations involving $\overline{\overline{r}}_{it}$, $\overline{\overline{r}}_{jt}$, and h. Thus, the efficient frontier that results is determined *exogenously*, because it is not dependent on any internal computations. In spite of these differences in symmetry and exogeneity, Estrada shows empirical evidence and argues that the semivariance of a portfolio computed with his cosemivariance is a close approximation to a portfolio computed with Markowitz's cosemivariance.[14] Essentially, Estrada argues that his cosemivariance provides a more convenient solution, and in addition, a solution that does not differ significantly from the traditional Markowitz semivariance solution.

10.3.4 Capital Market Theory with the Semivariance

Hogan and Warren (1974) derived a capital market line in $[\overline{\overline{\sigma}}, E(r)]$ space, denoted CML_d hereafter. Figure 10.10 illustrates the results.

The formula for the CML_d is

$$E\left(r_p\right) = r_f + \left[\frac{E\left(r_m\right) - r_f}{\overline{\overline{\sigma}}_m}\right]\overline{\overline{\sigma}}_p \qquad (10.40)$$

Equation (10.40) is an equilibrium portfolio pricing model in which the expected return from an efficient portfolio p equals the riskless rate, r_f, plus a risk premium. This risk premium equals the product of portfolio p's semideviation, $_p$, times the market price of risk, $\left[E\left(r_m\right) - r_f\right]/\overline{\overline{\sigma}}_m$, measured in terms of the semideviation.

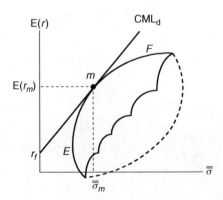

FIGURE 10.10   CML in $[\overline{\overline{\sigma}}, E(r)]$ Space

An asset pricing model for both individual securities and portfolios that is analogous to the security market line (SML) in $[\beta, E(r)]$ space is implicit in semivariance analysis. The SML for an asset i in terms of the cosemivariance, denoted SML_{cs}, is defined by equation (10.41).

$$E(r_i) = r_f + \left[E(r_m) - r_f\right]\overline{\overline{\beta}}_i \tag{10.41}$$

where

$$\overline{\overline{\beta}}_i = \frac{\overline{\overline{\sigma}}_{im}}{\overline{\overline{\sigma}}_m^2} = \frac{E\left\{(r_i - h)\left(\min\left[(r_m - h), 0\right]\right)\right\}}{E\left\{\min\left[(r_m - h), 0\right]\right\}^2}$$

$$= \frac{E(r_i - h)(\overline{r}_m - h)}{E(\overline{r}_m - h)^2} \tag{10.42}$$

This beta, $\overline{\overline{\beta}}_i$, is called the *downside beta*. Equation (10.41) is also called the *downside CAPM*. According to Estrada's definition of the cosemivariance in equation (10.38), the downside beta and the downside CAPM can be defined as

$$E(r_i) = r_f + \left[E(r_m) - r_f\right]\overline{\overline{\beta}}_i' \tag{10.43}$$

where

$$\overline{\overline{\beta}}_i' = \frac{\overline{\overline{\sigma}}_{im}'}{\overline{\overline{\sigma}}_m^2} = \frac{E\left\{\left(\min\left[(r_i - h), 0\right]\right)\left(\min\left[(r_m - h), 0\right]\right)\right\}}{E\left\{\min\left[(r_m - h), 0\right]\right\}^2}$$

$$= \frac{E(\overline{r}_i - h)(\overline{r}_m - h)}{E(\overline{r}_m - h)^2} \tag{10.44}$$

The downside SML, SML_{cs}, is depicted graphically in Figure 10.11.

All assets lying below the SML_{cs} are overpriced. Their expected returns are too low to adequately compensate investors for assuming the undiversifiable cosemivariance risk they entail. As a result, lack of demand for assets lying below the SML_{cs}

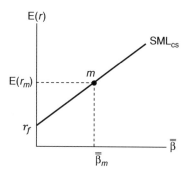

FIGURE 10.11   The SML from the Semivariance

tends to cause their market prices to fall and their expected returns to rise, as shown by the arrows in equation (10.45).

$$\text{E}(r) \uparrow = \frac{\text{E}(\text{capital gain or loss} + \text{cash dividend})}{\downarrow \text{Purchase price}} \qquad (10.45)$$

An opposite but symmetric line of reasoning will explain why those assets that plot above the SML_{cs} are underpriced in relation to their systematic cosemivariance risk. In general, the semivariance capital market theory implications are analogous to the mean-variance capital market theory of Chapters 6, 7, and 12.[15]

10.3.5 Summary about Semivariance

The semivariance is a quantitative risk surrogate that is comparable in some important respects to the variance. Similarly, the cosemivariance is analogous to the covariance of returns. However, it has not been possible to discern the superiority of one type of risk surrogate over another on behavioral grounds because risk aversion is personal, subjective, and therefore impossible to measure.

The economic implications of semivariance analysis are similar to those of the classical mean-variance theory. In fact, preliminary research suggests that there is a one-to-one correspondence between the efficient portfolios and asset prices implied by the different analyses based on the semivariance and the variance if the probability distributions are symmetric. The empirical evidence that has been published (for example, Chapter 14) suggests that the discrete one-period returns calculated over short differencing intervals and the continuously compounded returns may both be normally distributed. These suggestions of a normal probability distribution and the attendant similarities in the analysis diminish some researchers' interest in semivariance analysis. Semivariance research seems to progress slower than research on the classic mean-variance model, and if it does, the similarities may be the cause of these delays.[16]

Additional research is needed to clarify the role of semivariance analysis. Mathematical analysis is needed to delineate differences between the analogous semivariance and variance models. Empirical research is needed to document the existence of asymmetric probability distributions of basic financial random variables that cannot be readily transformed into symmetrically distributed variables. Research is needed to compare the results of semivariance analysis with portfolio analysis models based on mean-variance-skewness models. Portfolio analysis in three moments wastes less information than semivariance analysis, and thus may yield more optimal solutions in cases where the probability distributions are asymmetric.

10.4 STOCHASTIC DOMINANCE CRITERION

Portfolio analysis with stochastic dominance can be formulated differently to accommodate different utility functions.

10.4.1 First-Order Stochastic Dominance

A selection criterion called the *first-order stochastic dominance criterion* is a simple form of analysis that competes directly with Markowitz's mean-variance portfolio analysis. Stochastic dominance focuses on every bit of information in the probability distributions rather than simply focusing on the probability distributions' first two moments. As a result, stochastic dominance selection rules will occasionally yield portfolios that are more desirable than Markowitz-efficient portfolios.

When empirical distributions are non-normal, there exists the potential for serious conflicts between choices made by the stochastic dominance criterion and those made by the mean-variance criterion. Figure 10.12 shows the probability distributions for three risky investments. Uniform probability distributions are used to expedite the explanation, but stochastic dominance rules apply to any probability distribution. The expected returns on the three assets are $\mu_A = 5\%$, $\mu_B = 20\%$, and $\mu_C = 20\%$. Their standard deviations are $\sigma_A = 8.66\%$, $\sigma_B = 11.55\%$, and $\sigma_C = 14.43\%$, respectively.[17] Figure 10.13 graphically depicts these three assets on (σ, μ) space.

In the mean-variance portfolio analysis, assets A and B are efficient, while asset C is inefficient. However, inefficient asset C is more desirable than efficient asset A in some circumstances. The probability that asset A earns less than −5 percent is 1/6, while this probability for asset C is zero.[18] Or, the probability that asset A earns less than zero is 1/3, while this probability for asset C is only 1/10. For any given specific rate of return that is minimally tolerable, the chance of earning less than the specific rate of return is greater for asset A than for asset C. To investors who prefer more to less, asset C is more desirable than asset A, even though asset C is inefficient. This demonstrates that portfolio analysis that considers only the first two moments (mean and variance) may waste some information that could be used to maximize

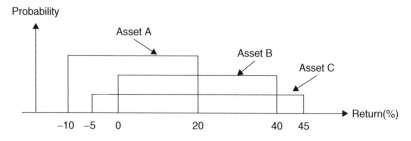

FIGURE 10.12 Uniform Probability Distributions for Three Assets' Returns

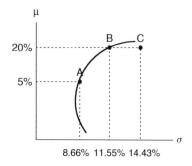

FIGURE 10.13 Three Assets in (σ, μ) Space

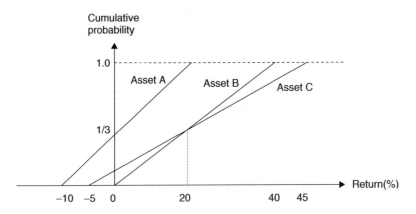

FIGURE 10.14 Cumulative Probability Distributions of Returns for Three Assets

investors' expected utility. Figure 10.14 illustrates the cumulative density function (cdf) or the cumulative distribution of the return for each of the three assets. Over all possible values of the returns, the cumulative probability that the return from asset A is less than a specific return is greater than the cumulative probability that the return from asset C is less than the specific return. In other words, the probability of earning less than any given amount of return from asset A is less than for asset C. In consideration of the downside risk, therefore, asset C is more desirable than asset A. Likewise, asset B is also more desirable than asset A.

In general, the cumulative probability distribution, $F(x)$, is defined as

$$F(r) = \text{Prob}(X \le r) = \int_{-\infty}^{r} f(x)\, dx \qquad (10.46)$$

where $f(r)$ is the probability density function (pdf) of asset returns. The cumulative distribution indicates the probability that an asset earns less than a certain level of return, x. Figure 10.15 illustrates the cumulative probability that the return is less than or equal to a given level of return (the shaded area) for that particular statistical distribution.

Figure 10.16 illustrates an example of the first-order stochastic dominance (FSD). The cumulative distribution for asset A lies below that for asset B for any given value of the return. It is said that asset A is more desirable than asset B in FSD.

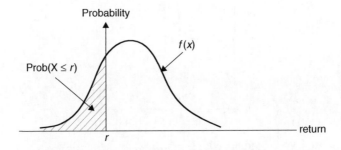

FIGURE 10.15 Cumulative Probability

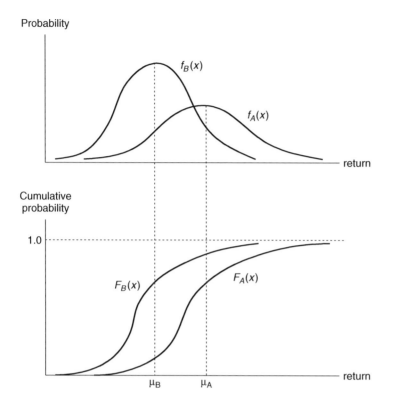

FIGURE 10.16 Illustrations of First-order Stochastic Dominance

FSD rule: Under the condition that investors prefer more to less (equivalently, $U'(r) > 0$), asset A dominates asset B in FSD if and only if $F_A(r) \leq F_B(r)$ or equivalently, $F_A(r) - F_B(r) \leq 0$ for all r with the strict inequality holding for at least one value of $r \in [a, b]$, where $F_A(\cdot)$ and $F_B(\cdot)$ are the cumulative distribution of the return of assets A and B, respectively, and a and b are the lower and upper bounds for r.

The economic interpretation of the FSD rule is that for all monotonic *nondecreasing* utility functions (i.e., $U'(r) > 0$), the expected utility from asset A is no less than that from asset B for *all* investors, irrespective of their attitudes toward risk (i.e., $E[U_A(r)] \geq E[U_B(r)]$). Furthermore, regardless of the assumptions about the utility functions, $F_A(r) \leq F_B(r)$ implies that the expected return of asset A is greater than or equal to the expected return from asset B [i.e., $E_A(r) \geq E_B(r)$ for positive r]. Note that the positive value restriction does not affect this implication because r can be simply replaced with $1 + r$. The proofs for these assertions are in the appendix to this chapter.

In fact, the following three statements are equivalent:

1. Asset A dominates asset B in FSD.
2. $F_A(r) \leq F_B(r)$, where $r \in [a, b]$.
3. $r_A =^{\text{dist}} r_B + \tilde{\upsilon}$, where a random variable $\tilde{\upsilon} \geq 0$. "$=^{\text{dist}}$" means that r_A and $r_B + \tilde{\upsilon}$ are equal *in distribution.*

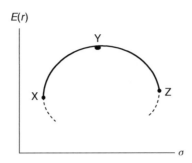

FIGURE 10.17 Efficient Set by
First-order Stochastic Dominance

The third statement means that if asset A dominates asset B in FSD, the expected return of asset A is at least as high as the expected return from asset B. However, the converse is not true.[19]

First-order stochastic dominance can be related to the mean-variance analysis if the returns are normally distributed. First-order stochastic dominance implies that investors prefer a higher expected return at any level of standard deviation. Thus, portfolios produced by first-order stochastic dominance lie on the upper part of the investment opportunity set. Figure 10.17 illustrates the efficient set by first-order stochastic dominance. Portfolios on the curve XYZ in Figure 10.16 have greater expected return than any other portfolio below the curve XYZ; thus, they are FSD-efficient. However, portfolios on the segment YZ are not mean-variance efficient, even though they are FSD-efficient.

EXAMPLE 10.5

Assets A and B have the outcomes with the associated probabilities shown in Table 10.5. Does asset A dominate asset B in FSD?

TABLE 10.5 Possible Outcomes of Two Assets

Asset A		Asset B	
Probability	Return	Probability	Return
1/4	4	1/4	3
1/4	5	1/4	4
1/4	7	1/4	6
1/4	8	1/4	7

The cumulative probabilities of the two assets are shown in Table 10.6.

EXAMPLE 10.5 (*Continued*)

TABLE 10.6 Cumulative Probabilities for Two Assets

Returns (x)	Cumulative probability Prob (r ≤ x)	
	A	B
3	0	1/4
4	1/4	2/4
5	2/4	2/4
6	2/4	3/4
7	3/4	1
8	1	1

Table 10.6 shows that the cumulative probability of the return from asset A is no greater than that from asset B for any value of the return. This fact is graphically shown in Figure 10.18. The cumulative distribution for asset B (solid line) never lies below that for asset A (dotted line). Thus, asset A dominates asset B in FSD.

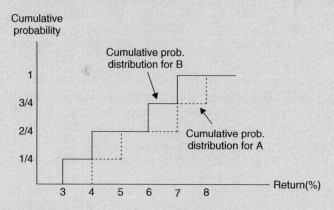

FIGURE 10.18 Cumulative Probability Distributions for Two Assets

10.4.2 Second-Order Stochastic Dominance

In the previous section's Figures 10.13 and 10.14, any preference between assets B and C cannot be made in first-order stochastic dominance because their cumulative distributions cross (overlap). Specifically, the probability of earning less than the return between −5 percent and 20 percent from asset B is lower than from asset C, whereas the probability of earning less than the return between 20 percent and 45 percent from asset C is lower than from asset B. In other words, asset B is more desirable than asset C over the low-return region, whereas asset C is more desirable than asset B over the high-return region. If the assumption of risk aversion is added to the FSD decision criterion, then a preference can be made between assets B and C. Risk-averse investors would be happier with a one percent increase from low returns than a one percent increase from high returns. Thus, asset B is more desirable than asset C to risk-averse investors. In this case, it is said that that asset B dominates asset C in second-order stochastic dominance (SSD).

SSD rule: Under the conditions that

1. investors prefer more to less (equivalently, $U'(r) > 0$),
2. investors are risk averse (equivalently, $U''(r) < 0$), and
3. the expected returns of assets A and B are equal [i.e., $E_A(r) = E_B(r)$], asset A dominates asset B in SSD if and only if

$$\int_a^r F_A(x)\,dx \le \int_a^r F_B(x)\,dx \text{ or equivalently, } \int_a^r [F_A(x) - F_B(x)]\,dx \le 0$$

for all r with the strict inequality holding for at least one value of $r \in [a,b]$, where a and b are the lower and upper bounds for r.

SSD implies that the expected utility from asset A exceeds or is equal to that from asset B (i.e., $E[U_A(r)] \ge E[U_B(r)]$) for all utility functions satisfying the conditions $U'(r) > 0$ and $U''(r) < 0$. See the end-of-chapter appendix for proof. The SSD rule can be applied when the cumulative probability distributions overlap as in Figure 10.14. However, the cumulative difference between the two cumulative probability distributions must remain nonnegative over the entire range of returns.

The relationship between the FSD and SSD efficient sets is that the SSD efficient set is a subset of the FSD efficient set. In other words, all the investments included in the SSD efficient set are also included in the FSD efficient set. However, the reverse does not hold. If asset A dominates asset B in SSD, then asset A also dominates asset B in FSD.

As with SSD, the following three statements are equivalent:

1. Asset A dominates asset B in SSD.
2. $E_A(r) = E_B(r)$ and $\int_a^b F_A(x)\,dx \le \int_a^b F_B(x)\,dx$, where $r \in [a,b]$.
3. $r_B =^{\text{dist}} r_A + \tilde{\varepsilon}$, with $E(\tilde{\varepsilon}|r_A) = 0$.

The third statement means that $\text{Var}(r_B) \ge \text{Var}(r_A)$, because $E(\tilde{\varepsilon}|r_A) = 0$ implies $\text{Cov}(r_A, \tilde{\varepsilon}) = 0$. Thus, if asset A dominates asset B in SSD, $E_A(r) = E_B(r)$ and $\text{Var}(r_B) \ge \text{Var}(r_A)$. However, the converse does not hold. Therefore, if one of the preceding three statements is satisfied, asset B is said to be more risky than asset A.[20]

Second-order stochastic dominance can be related to mean-variance analysis if returns are normally distributed. Portfolios on the segment XY in Figure 10.17 are SSD efficient because they satisfy the previous statements. Thus, the SSD-efficient set is equal to the mean-variance-efficient set if returns are normally distributed.

EXAMPLE 10.6

Assets A and B have the probabilistic outcomes shown in Table 10.7. Does asset A dominate asset B in SSD?

TABLE 10.7 Possible Outcomes of Two Assets

Asset A		Asset B	
Probability	Return	Probability	Return
1/4	4	1/4	3
1/2	5	1/4	4
1/4	8	1/4	6
		1/4	7

The cumulative probabilities and the accumulated values of the cumulative probabilities for the two assets are shown in Table 10.8.

TABLE 10.8 Cumulative Probabilities for Assets A and B

Returns (x)	Cumulative probabilities		Accumulations of cumulative probabilities	
	$F_A(x)$	$F_B(x)$	Cum $[F_A(x)]$	Cum $[F_B(x)]$
3	0	1/4	0	1/4
4	1/4	2/4	1/4	3/4
5	3/4	2/4	1	5/4
6	3/4	3/4	1 3/4	2
7	3/4	1	2 2/4	3
8	1	1	3 2/4	4

Table 10.8 shows that the cumulative probability for A is less than for B when the returns are three percent and four percent, but it is not less when the returns are five percent and six percent. This means that the cumulative distributions overlap. Figure 10.19 illustrates this intersection. In this case, the SSD rule cannot be applied.

Figure 10.20 depicts the accumulated cumulative probabilities for the two assets. The accumulated cumulative probability distribution for asset B (solid line) never lies below that for asset A (dotted line). Thus, asset A dominates asset B in SSD.

(Continued)

EXAMPLE 10.6 (*Continued*)

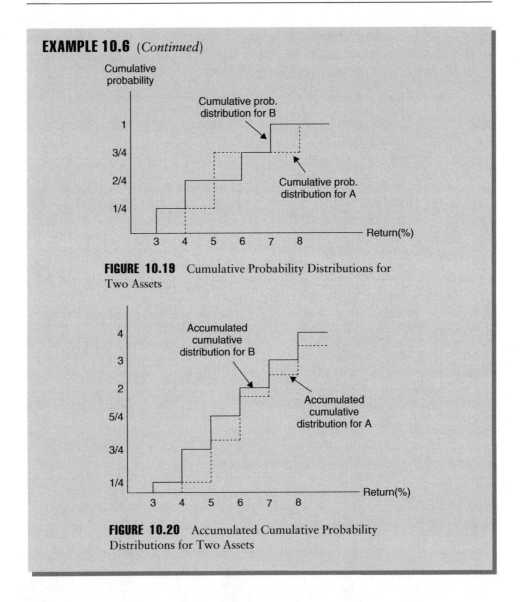

FIGURE 10.19 Cumulative Probability Distributions for Two Assets

FIGURE 10.20 Accumulated Cumulative Probability Distributions for Two Assets

10.4.3 Third-Order Stochastic Dominance

Any preference between two assets cannot be determined in SSD if the accumulations of the cumulative distributions for the two assets overlap. That is, if $\int_{-\infty}^{r} F_A(x)\, dx \leq \int_{-\infty}^{r} F_B(x)\, dx$ for some value of r, but $\int_{-\infty}^{r} F_A(x)\, dx > \int_{-\infty}^{r} F_B(x)\, dx$ for another value of r, then neither A nor B can be eliminated by SSD. To determine preferences between these assets by third-order stochastic dominance (TSD), it is necessary to assume that investors exhibit deceasing absolute risk aversion.

TSD rule: Under the conditions that

1. investors prefer more to less (equivalently, $U'(r) > 0$),
2. investors are risk averse (equivalently, $U''(r) < 0$),

3. investors exhibit deceasing absolute risk aversion (equivalently, $U'''(r) > 0$), and
4. the expected return of asset A is greater than or equal to that of asset B [i.e., $E_A(r) \geq E_B(r)$],

   asset A dominates asset B in TSD if and only if

   $\int_a^r \int_a^u F_A(x)\, dx\, du \leq \int_a^r \int_a^u F_B(x)\, dx\, du$, or equivalently,

   $\int_a^r \int_a^u [F_A(x) - F_B(x)]\, dx\, du \leq 0$ for all r, with the strict inequality holding for at least one value of $r \in [a, b]$, where a and b are the lower and upper bounds for r.

TSD implies that the expected utility from asset A is greater than or equal to that from asset B (i.e., $E[U_A(r)] \geq E[U_B(r)]$) for all utility functions satisfying the conditions $U'(r) > 0$, $U''(r) < 0$, and $U'''(r) > 0$. See the end-of-chapter appendix for proof. The TSD rule can be applied when the accumulated cumulative probability distributions overlap.

10.4.4 Summary of Stochastic Dominance Criterion

The stochastic dominance criteria consist of three forms, depending on the assumptions made regarding the investor's utility function. The FSD criterion requires the assumption $(\partial U / \partial r) > 0$. The SSD criterion requires the assumptions $(\partial U / \partial r) > 0$ and $(\partial^2 U / \partial r^2) < 0$. And the TSD criterion requires the assumptions $(\partial U / \partial r) > 0$, $(\partial^2 U / \partial r^2) < 0$, and $(\partial^3 U / \partial r^3) < 0$. Hence, the TSD efficient set is smaller than the SSD efficient set, which is smaller than the FSD efficient set. In other words, dominance by FSD implies dominance by SSD, and dominance by SSD implies dominance by TSD.

The advantages of selecting investments with stochastic dominance criteria instead of the mean-variance criteria are:

- Stochastic dominance orderings do not presume any particular form of probability distribution (namely, the normal distribution).
- The stochastic dominance criteria imply fewer restrictions on the investor's utility function.
- Undesirable portfolios, such as those on the lower section of the efficient frontier, can be eliminated from further consideration.
- The stochastic dominance selection criteria do not waste information about the probability distribution, every data point is considered. (Unfortunately, the fact that every data point needs to be considered is a deterrent in much empirical work).
- Investors with monotonically nondecreasing utility of wealth functions of any form will always obtain more expected utility from a stochastically dominant asset rather than a dominated one, but some Markowitz-efficient portfolios are not utility maximizers.

One shortcoming of the stochastic dominance criteria is that the stochastic dominance criterion involves pairwise comparisons of all alternatives. When there are many alternatives under consideration, the stochastic dominance criterion may not be feasible.[21] Another shortcoming of the stochastic dominance criteria is that it requires complete knowledge of every point in every asset's probability distribution.

This huge data requirement makes the stochastic dominance criteria impractical for much empirical work. Thus, while the theoretical logic of stochastic dominance is compelling, its usefulness is mostly academic.

10.5   MEAN-VARIANCE-SKEWNESS ANALYSIS

Whether skewness should be brought into portfolio analysis is a perennial question. The theoretical logic of portfolio analysis in three moments is undeniable. If skewness exists in either all or part of the probability distributions, this information should not be ignored.

10.5.1   Only Two Moments Can Be Inadequate

Skewness measures the asymmetry of a probability distribution. Skewness of returns, r_t, is defined by

$$\text{Skewness} = \text{E}\left[\left(\frac{r_t - \mu}{\sigma}\right)^3\right] = \frac{\mu_3}{\sigma^3}$$

$$= \frac{\left[\sum_{t=1}^{T}(r_t - \bar{r})^3/T\right]}{\left[\sum_{t=1}^{T}(r_t - \bar{r})^2/T\right]^{3/2}} = \frac{\sqrt{T}\sum_{t=1}^{T}(r_t - \bar{r})^3}{\left[\sum_{t=1}^{T}(r_t - \bar{r})^2\right]^{3/2}} \qquad (10.47)$$

Figure 10.21 shows a positively-skewed distribution. Positive skewness refers to an elongated tail on the right-hand side of the probability density distribution. Thus, the probability the mode occurs exceeds the probability of the median, and the probability the median occurs is greater than the probability of the mean. Investors like positive skewness, because the return is skewed toward high values and there is a small probability of large negative returns.[22] Note that the previously explained portfolio selection criteria such as the safety-first criterion, semivariance, and stochastic dominance emphasize downside risk, whereas the portfolio analysis with skewness considers upside potential.

Considerable empirical evidence documents the fact that common stock returns are positively skewed.[23] Table 9.1 presents the skewness statistics of international stock market return distributions of 14 developed countries; it shows that the stock returns from most countries exhibit positive skewness. Moreover, skewness is persistent.[24] Thus, empirical evidence weights in favor of considering skewness

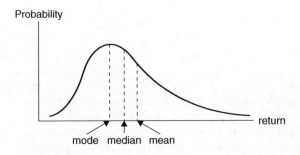

FIGURE 10.21   Positively Skewed Probability Distribution

in portfolio selection. If skewness is taken into account in portfolio selection, there are three parameters to be considered; mean, standard deviation, and skewness. In fact, the expected utility of a portfolio can be approximated by its mean return, its standard deviation, and its skewness, if it is assumed that returns come from an asymmetrical (but not lognormal) distribution.[25]

Let W_0 be the initial wealth invested in portfolio p. Then the wealth at the terminal time T, W_T, depends on the rate of return over the period r_p. That is, $W_T = W_0 (1 + r_p)$. Given an investor's utility function $U = f(W)$, the expected utility of the end-of-period wealth W_T can be approximated as

$$E[U(W_T)] \cong f[W_0(1 + \mu_p)] + \frac{f''[W_0(1 + \mu_p)]}{2!} W_0^2 \sigma_p^2$$

$$+ \frac{f'''[W_0(1 + \mu_p)]}{3!} W_0^3 \sigma_p^3 \operatorname{Skew}_p \qquad (10.48)$$

where $\mu_p = E(r_p)$ is the expected return of portfolio p and Skew_p is the skewness coefficient of the rate of return, r_p. Accordingly, the expected utility of portfolio p can be approximated by its expected return μ_p, standard deviation σ_p, and skewness Skew_p. Notice that $\operatorname{Skew}_p = E(r_p - \mu_p)^3 / \sigma_p^3$. Equation (10.48) is a Taylor series expansion; the derivation of equation (10.48) is described in this chapter's appendix A10.5.

It can be seen that investors will prefer more skewness to less if they have nonincreasing absolute risk aversion by noting that nonincreasing absolute risk aversion implies that

$$\frac{\partial}{\partial W_T}\left[-\frac{U''}{U'}\right] = \frac{-U'U''' + (U'')^2}{(U')^2} \leq 0 \qquad (10.49)$$

Thus, since $U' > 0$ due to nonsatiation, it is necessary that $U''' > 0$ in order for the investor to have nonincreasing absolute risk aversion. Given $U''' = f'''(W_T) = f'''[W_0(1 + r_p)] > 0$, the last term on the right-hand side of equation (10.48) can be rewritten as $(W_0^3 \sigma_p^3) \{f'''[W_0(1 + r_p)]/3!\}$, a positive quantity, times the skewness parameter, Skew_p. This means that larger Skew_p values imply higher levels of expected utility. Of course, if the skewness term is negligible, the expected utility can be represented as only the first and second moments.

10.5.2 Portfolio Analysis in Three Moments

W. H. Jean (1971, 1973) suggested how the first three statistical moments from assets' return probability distributions might determine prices and expected returns.[26] To represent this market situation graphically, Jean extended the two-dimensional $[\sigma, E(r)]$ analysis to three-dimensional $[\psi, \sigma, E(r)]$ space, where $\psi = [E(r_p - \mu_p)^3]^{1/3}$ represents the cube root of the third statistical moment of returns.[27] In other words, skewness equals ψ^3 / σ^3.

Generally, third-degree surfaces are shaped like the letter S. But, it is difficult to generalize in advance about exactly what shape the set of risky investment opportunities will assume. However, Jean has hypothesized that the convex hull shown in Figure 10.22 represents the relevant subset of the total set of investment

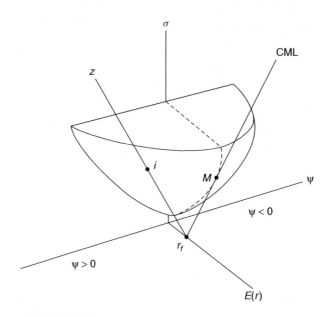

FIGURE 10.22 Investment Opportunities in $[\psi, \sigma, \mathrm{E}(r)]$
Space
Source: W.H. Jean, "More on Multidimensional Portfolio
Analysis," *Journal of Financial and Quantitative Analysis*,
June 1973.

opportunities in $[\psi, \sigma, \mathrm{E}(r)]$ space. The dashed line traces the $[\sigma, \mathrm{E}(r)]$ efficient
frontier if all assets' returns are symmetrically distributed. The classic capital market
line (CML) that exists in the absence of skewness extends from the riskless rate,
denoted r_f, up through the uniquely desirable market portfolio, denoted M, in the
$[\sigma, \mathrm{E}(r)]$ plane. However, when nonsymmetry is admitted to the analysis, the picture
becomes more complicated.

Because every investor presumably has a different utility function, they all have
different investment preferences in $[\psi, \sigma, \mathrm{E}(r)]$ space.[28] As a result, there is no
uniquely desirable risk asset such as the market portfolio in the three-dimensional
model—this is a major source of vagueness in the three-dimensional capital market
theory.

The expected return, risk, and cube root of the third moment of returns for any
risky portfolio p that may be constructed from a risky asset i, combined with the
risk-free asset, are defined in equations (10.50), (10.51) and (10.52), respectively.

$$\mu_p = w_i \mu_i + (1 - w_i) r_f \tag{10.50}$$

$$\sigma_p^2 = w_i^2 \sigma_i^2 \tag{10.51}$$

$$\psi_p = \sqrt[3]{E(r_p - \mu_p)^3} = \sqrt[3]{E(r_i - \mu_i)^3 w_i^3} = w_i \psi_i \tag{10.52}$$

Because, by definition, the riskless asset has risk and skewness of zero, $\sigma_f = 0$
and $\psi_f = 0$, portfolio p's risk and third moment are simple linear functions of the
risk and symmetry of risky asset i.[29] Equations (10.50), (10.51) and (10.52) form
the skeleton of capital market theory in $[\psi, \sigma, \mathrm{E}(r)]$ space.

10.5.3 Efficient Frontier in Three-Dimensional Space

Figure 10.22 illustrates the investment opportunity set in $[\psi, \sigma, \mathrm{E}\,(r)]$ space. It shows the location of a risky asset i. The line from the point r_f (indicating the location of the risk-free asset) up through point i to point z graphically represents the expected return, risk, and cube root of the third moment of the portfolio possibilities that can be constructed from asset i and r_f. Even if asset i has the maximum return in its risk class (that is, asset i is a Markowitz-efficient portfolio) for the value of its third moment, it will still not lie on the $[\sigma, \mathrm{E}\,(r)]$ efficient frontier, as illustrated in the two-dimensional projection shown in Figure 10.23.

The line $\overline{r_f iz}$ and the CML shown in Figures 10.23 and 10.24 are not the only investment opportunities. A line or ray from the riskless rate through any point in the set of risky investment opportunities shown in Figure 10.22 represents a feasible investment possibility. As a result, the complete set of feasible investments in $[\psi, \sigma, \mathrm{E}\,(r)]$ space is shaped like a cone, with its tip at point r_f, as shown in Figure 10.24. This cone envelops the set of risky investments shown in Figure 10.22. The cone extends infinitely far from point r_f if borrowing and lending are unrestricted. The cone of investment possibilities with borrowing and lending shown in Figure 10.24 is terminated to reflect the effects of margin requirements, credit restrictions, and short-selling limitations.

The surface of the cone in Figure 10.24 is composed of an infinite number of linear opportunity loci. Each of these lines is a CML analog in $[\psi, \sigma, \mathrm{E}\,(r)]$ space. When the CML analogs from Figure 10.24 are projected onto a two-dimensional $[\sigma, \mathrm{E}\,(r)]$ surface, some of them will dominate the CML, and some of them will be dominated by the CML, as shown in Figure 10.25.

The line $\overline{r_f iz}$ from Figures 10.22, 10.23, and 10.24 is dominated by the CML in $[\sigma, \mathrm{E}\,(r)]$ space. Nevertheless, an investor who had positive but diminishing marginal

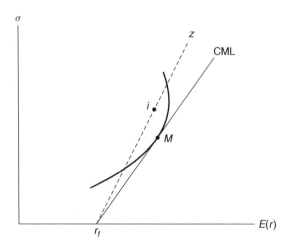

FIGURE 10.23 Investment Opportunities on the Line $\overline{r_f iz}$ Riz are Dominated by the CML in $[\sigma, \mathrm{E}\,(r)]$ Space
Source: W.H. Jean, "More on Multidimensional Portfolio Analysis," *Journal of Financial and Quantitative Analysis*, June 1973.

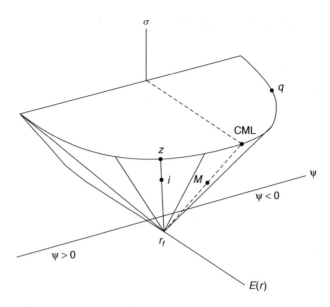

FIGURE 10.24   Cone of Investment Opportunities in
$[\psi, \sigma, \mathrm{E}\,(r)]$ Space with Borrowing and Lending at R
Source: W.H. Jean, "More on Multidimensional Portfolio
Analysis," *Journal of Financial and Quantitative Analysis,*
June 1973.

utility (that is, was greedy but risk-averse) might prefer an investment on the line
$\overline{r_f\textsc{i}\textsc{z}}$ over an investment on the CML if the opportunities on the line $\overline{r_f\textsc{i}\textsc{z}}$ are skewed
positively. A positive cube root of the third moment for the opportunities on the line
$\overline{r_f\textsc{i}\textsc{z}}$ could more than compensate for the expected returns on the line $\overline{r_f\textsc{i}\textsc{z}}$ that are
below the CML. In other words, the line $\overline{r_f\textsc{i}\textsc{z}}$ offers a long shot at a large return that
could entice some investors away from the opportunities on the CML; the CML has
higher average outcomes but less exciting possibilities for large returns.

The line $\overline{r_f\mu q}$ in Figure 10.25 is a CML analog from the surface of the cone in
Figure 10.24, but it dominates the CML in $[\sigma, \mathrm{E}\,(r)]$ space. Opportunity lines such
as the line $\overline{r_f\mu q}$ can exist in a $[\psi, \sigma, \mathrm{E}\,(r)]$ equilibrium if the cube root of their third
moments is negative. This negative skewness represents large probabilities of big
losses. As a result, risk-averse investors will require higher expected returns at any
given risk class to induce them to invest in the negatively skewed opportunities on
$\overline{r_f\mu q}$ instead of the symmetrically distributed opportunities on the CML.

The wealth-seeking risk-averse investor's preferences revealed by the choices
discussed in reference to Figure 10.26 can be represented formally as follows:

$$U = f\,(\text{wealth}), \quad f' > 0, \quad f'' < 0 \tag{10.53}$$

$$U = g\,(\text{return}), \quad g' > 0, \quad g'' < 0 \tag{10.54}$$

$$\mathrm{E}\,(U) = h\,[\psi, \sigma, \mathrm{E}\,(r)], \quad \frac{\partial h}{\partial \psi} > 0, \ \frac{\partial h}{\partial \sigma} < 0, \ \frac{\partial h}{\partial \mathrm{E}\,(r)} > 0 \tag{10.55}$$

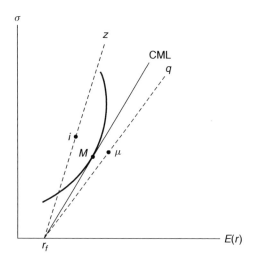

FIGURE 10.25   CML Dominates $\overline{r_f \imath z}$, and
$\overline{r_f \mu q}$ Dominates the CML in $[\sigma, \mathrm{E}\,(r)]$ Space
Source: W.H. Jean, "More on
Multidimensional Portfolio Analysis,"
*Journal of Financial and Quantitative
Analysis*, June 1973.

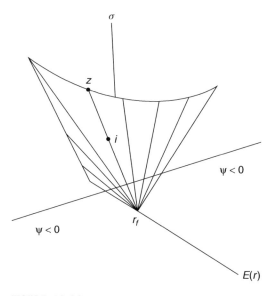

FIGURE 10.26   Efficient Frontier of Investments
in $[\psi, \sigma, \mathrm{E}\,(r)]$ Space
Source: W.H. Jean, "More on Multidimensional
Portfolio Analysis," *Journal of Financial and
Quantitative Analysis*, June 1973.

Further preference implications are as follows:

$$\frac{\partial \psi}{\partial \mu} \leq 0, \qquad \frac{\partial \psi}{\partial \sigma} \geq 0, \qquad \frac{\partial E(r)}{\partial \sigma} \geq 0 \qquad (10.56)$$

Convex utility surfaces possessing all the preferences shown in equations (10.53), (10.54), (10.55), and (10.56) can be generated from the logarithmic or power utility functions (that is, those possessing constant relative risk aversion, as discussed in Chapter 4). Thus, this analysis represents logical and realistic economic behavior.

Specifying the investors' utility functions as done in equations (10.53), (10.54), (10.55), and (10.56) allows the $[\psi, \sigma, E(r)]$-efficient frontier to be delineated. Efficient portfolios in three dimensions will be that portion of the cone in Figure 10.24 with:

- Maximum skewness for any given level of variance and expected rate of return.
- Minimum variance for any given level of skewness and expected rate of return.
- Maximum expected rate of return for any given level of skewness and variance.[30]

Figure 10.26 illustrates a subset of the surface of the cone of opportunities shown in Figure 10.24 that comprises the efficient portfolios in $[\psi, \sigma, E(r)]$ space. The $[\psi, \sigma, E(r)]$-efficient portfolios are also $[\text{skewness}, \sigma, E(r)]$ efficient because for any given values of $E(r)$ and σ, maximizing ψ is equivalent to maximizing skewness (namely, ψ^3/σ^3). Any point behind the efficient frontier is a dominated investment. Of course, what is an efficient investment in $[\psi, \sigma, E(r)]$ space may be inefficient when moments above the third are considered.

10.5.4 Undiversifiable Risk and Undiversifiable Skewness

It is well known from the mean-variance portfolio theory that the owner of any existing portfolio p should evaluate the risk increment to the portfolio when considering including a risky asset i. Equation (10.57) shows the formula for evaluating the risk of the revised portfolio, denoted rp.

$$\sigma_{rp}^2 = w_p^2 \sigma_p^2 + w_i^2 \sigma_i^2 + 2w_p w_i \sigma_{ip} \qquad (10.57)$$

where $w_p + w_i = 1.0$. Taking the cross partial derivative of σ_{rp}^2 with respect to asset i's weight and the old portfolio p's weight yields the covariance term shown in equation (10.58).

$$\frac{\partial^2 \left(\sigma_{rp}^2 \right)}{\partial w_i \partial w_p} = 2\sigma_{ip} \qquad (10.58)$$

The covariance σ_{ip} measures the increment the asset i will add to or detract from portfolio rp's risk as measured by σ_p. The covariance σ_{ip} is thus a measure of the undiversifiable risk increment. This covariance can be standardized by restating it as the asset i's beta coefficient with respect to portfolio p, as shown in equation (10.59).

$$\beta_{ip} = \frac{\sigma_{ip}}{\sigma_p^2} = \frac{\sigma_i \rho_{ip}}{\sigma_p} \qquad (10.59)$$

One of the insights from the mean-variance portfolio theory is that the systematic or undiversifiable risk that an individual security contributes to a portfolio can be more relevant in determining that asset's expected return and price than its total risk. This is also true where skewness is concerned, and, therefore, the systematic or undiversifiable portion of an asset's skewness is analyzed in the following paragraphs.

Equation (10.60) defines the third moment of the revised portfolio, denoted $M_3(r_{rp})$, if asset i is included in portfolio p.

$$
\begin{aligned}
M_3\left(r_{rp}\right) &= E\left[r_{rp} - E\left(r_{rp}\right)\right]^3 \\
&= w_i^3 M_3\left(r_i\right) + 3w_i^2 w_p E\left\{\left[r_i - E\left(r_i\right)\right]^2 \left[r_p - E\left(r_p\right)\right]\right\} \\
&\quad + 3w_i w_p^2 E\left\{\left[r_i - E\left(r_i\right)\right]\left[r_p - E\left(r_p\right)\right]^2\right\} + w_p^3 M_3\left(r_p\right)
\end{aligned}
\tag{10.60}
$$

Taking the cross partial derivative of $M_3\left(r_{rp}\right)$ in order to evaluate asset i's increment to the revised portfolio's third moment yields

$$
\begin{aligned}
\frac{\partial^2 M_3\left(r_{rp}\right)}{\partial w_i\, \partial w_p} &= 6w_i E\left\{\left[r_i - E\left(r_i\right)\right]^2 \left[r_p - E\left(r_p\right)\right]\right\} \\
&\quad + 6w_p E\left\{\left[r_i - E\left(r_i\right)\right]\left[r_p - E\left(r_p\right)\right]^2\right\}
\end{aligned}
\tag{10.61}
$$

The term $E\{[r_i - E(r_i)]^2 [r_p - E(r_p)]\}$ in equation (10.61) will always have the same sign as $M_3(r_{rp})$ because the quantity $[r_i - E\left(r_i\right)]^2$ is nonnegative. The sign of the term $\{[r_i - E(r_i)]^2 [r_p - E(r_p)]\}$ thus indicates whether including asset i will increase, not change, or decrease the third moment of portfolio p.

The quantity $E\left\{[r_i - E(r_i)][r_p - E(r_p)]^2\right\}$ in equation (10.61) gauges the skewness asset i tends to bring to portfolio p. This quantity can be converted into an index number, to expedite cross-sectional comparisons, by dividing $E\{[r_i - E(r_i)][r_p - E(r_p)]^2\}$ by the third moment of portfolio p, as shown next.

$$
\text{Coskewness} \equiv \gamma_{ip} = \frac{E\left\{\left[r_i - E\left(r_i\right)\right]\left[r_p - E\left(r_p\right)\right]^2\right\}}{E\left[r_p - E\left(r_p\right)\right]^3}
\tag{10.62}
$$

The quantity γ_{ip} is an index number called *coskewness*; it is for comparing the contribution of the i-th asset's skewness to the third moment of portfolio p. The sign of coskewness γ_{ip} will be greater than, equal to, or less than unity depending on whether asset i increases, does not change, or reduces the third moment of portfolio rp. Thus, γ_{ip} is an index (somewhat like the beta coefficient) of the asset i's systematic or undiversifiable skewness impact on portfolio rp. This gamma is additive, so that portfolio rp's gamma with respect to the market portfolio equals the sum of its assets' gammas, $\gamma_{pm} = \sum_i w_i \gamma_{ip}$, and the market portfolio's gamma equals unity.

Economic intuition suggests that an asset's total skewness or systematic skewness should be inversely related to its expected return—symbolically, $[\partial \mu / \partial M_3(r)] < 0]$. Empirical evidence tends to support this economic intuition. To estimate the coskewness of asset i, the following quadratic market model can be used.

$$
r_{it} = \alpha_i + \beta_i r_{mt} + \gamma_i r_{mt}^2 + \varepsilon_{it}
\tag{10.63}
$$

The estimate of the coefficient γ_i in the preceding quadratic market model indicates the estimate of the coskewness. Harvey and Siddique (2000) and Adesi, Gagliardini, and Urga (2004) found significant and negative coefficient of coskewness in most of the portfolios they considered. Cross-sectional regression (CSR) models are also used to examine the relation between returns and coskewness. Kraus and Litzenberger (1976), Harvey and Siddique (2000), and Smith (2006) cross-sectionally regressed portfolio returns on the estimated coskewness of the portfolios and also found a significant and negative coefficient on the coskewness variable.[31]

10.6 SUMMARY AND CONCLUSIONS

This chapter has analyzed several alternatives to the traditional mean-variance portfolio analysis, which assumes normality (sometimes, lognormality) of asset returns. The decision criterion of the traditional mean-variance portfolio analysis is a risk-return trade-off. In contrast, the theories introduced in this chapter do not assume a particular statistical distribution of returns and are not based on one specific risk-return trade-off. The safety-first criterion, semivariance analysis, and stochastic dominance criteria emphasize downside risk, whereas the portfolio analysis with skewness considers upside potential. These non-mean-variance approaches can also be applied when returns are normally distributed. In this case, many of these nontraditional approaches produce optimal portfolios that lie on the mean-variance efficient frontier.

APPENDIX A: STOCHASTIC DOMINANCE

This Appendix contains several mathematical proofs that were called for in Chapter 10.

A10.1 Proof for First-Order Stochastic Dominance

The expected utility of each asset's return is defined as

$$E\left[U\left(r_A\right)\right] = \int_a^b U\left(r\right)\,dF_A\left(r\right) \quad \text{and} \quad E\left[U\left(r_B\right)\right] = \int_a^b U\left(r\right)\,dF_B\left(r\right), \quad \text{(A10.1)}$$

where $F_A\left(\cdot\right)$ and $F_B\left(\cdot\right)$ are the cumulative distribution of the return of assets A and B, respectively, and the return $r \in [a,b]$. It is said that asset A dominates asset B in FSD if the expected utility of A's return is greater than the expected utility of B's return. That is, asset A dominates asset B in FSD if

$$\int_a^b U\left(r\right)\,dF_A\left(r\right) > \int_a^b U\left(r\right)\,dF_B\left(r\right) \quad \text{(A10.2)}$$

or equivalently

$$\int_a^b U\left(r\right)\,d\left[F_A\left(r\right) - F_B\left(r\right)\right] > 0 \quad \text{(A10.3)}$$

Using the integration by parts,

$$E\left[U\left(r_A\right)\right] - E\left[U\left(r_B\right)\right] = \int_a^b U\left(r\right)\, d\left[F_A\left(r\right) - F_B\left(r\right)\right]$$

$$= U\left(r\right)\left[F_A\left(r\right) - F_B\left(r\right)\right]_a^b - \int_a^b U'\left(r\right)\left[F_A\left(r\right) - F_B\left(r\right)\right]\, dr$$

Now, $F_A\left(b\right) = F_B\left(b\right) = 1$ and $F_A\left(a\right) = F_B\left(a\right) = 0$. Thus,

$$\int_a^b U\left(r\right)\, d\left[F_A\left(r\right) - F_B\left(r\right)\right] = -\int_a^b U'\left(r\right)\left[F_A\left(r\right) - F_B\left(r\right)\right]\, dr \qquad (A10.4)$$

If the right-hand term in equation (A10.4) is positive, asset A dominates asset B in FSD. Because $U'\left(r\right) > 0$, $\int_a^b U\left(r\right)\, d\left[F_A\left(r\right) - F_B\left(r\right)\right] > 0$, or, equivalently, $E\left[U\left(r_A\right)\right] - E\left[U\left(r_B\right)\right] > 0$, if $F_A\left(r\right) \leq F_B\left(r\right)$ for all r with the strict inequality holding for at least one value of r.

A10.2 Proof That $F_A\left(r\right) \leq F_B\left(r\right)$ Is Equivalent to $E_A\left(r\right) \geq E_B\left(r\right)$ for Positive r

Replacing the return r with $1 + r$ in the preceding equations does not affect the argument. Without loss of generality, thus, we still use the restriction that r is positive.

For positive values of a random variable r, the expected return is defined as

$$E\left(r\right) = \lim_{n \to \infty} \int_0^n r\, dF\left(r\right) \qquad (A10.5)$$

Using integration by parts,

$$\int_0^n r\, dF\left(r\right) = r\, F\left(r\right)\big|_0^n - \int_0^n F\left(r\right)\, dr$$

$$= n\, F(n) - \int_0^n F\left(r\right)\, dr$$

$$= -n\left[1 - F\left(n\right)\right] + \int_0^n \left[1 - F\left(r\right)\right]\, dr \qquad (A10.6)$$

However, $n\left[1 - F\left(n\right)\right] = n\int_n^\infty f\left(r\right)\, dr < \int_n^\infty r f\left(r\right)\, d = 0$ as $n \to \infty$. Thus, $\lim_{n \to \infty} n\left[1 - F\left(n\right)\right] = 0$. From equations (A10.5) and (A10.6),

$$E\left(r\right) = \int_0^\infty \left[1 - F\left(r\right)\right]\, dr \qquad (A10.7)$$

Therefore, if $F_A\left(r\right) \leq F_B\left(r\right)$, then $E_A\left(r\right) \geq E_B\left(r\right)$ for positive r. Figure A10.1 graphically shows the expected value of the return. The shaded portion is the area

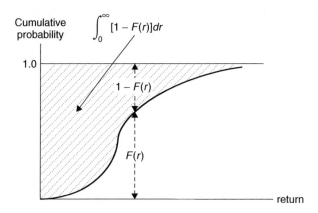

FIGURE A10.1   Expected Value of a Random Variable
and its Cumulative Distribution

under the curve $1 - F(r)$ and it equals $\int_0^\infty [1 - F(r)]\, dr$. Thus, the shaded area is the
expected value of the return.

A10.3   Proof for Second-Order Stochastic Dominance

For the second-order stochastic dominance, we also need to prove that the expected
utility of the return on asset A is greater than or equal to that of the return on asset
B under certain conditions. From the proof of the first-order stochastic dominance,
we have

$$E\left[U\left(r_A\right)\right] - E\left[U(r_B)\right] \equiv \int_a^b U\left(r\right)\, d\left[F_A\left(r\right) - F_B\left(r\right)\right] = -\int_a^b U'\left(r\right)\left[F_A\left(r\right) - F_B\left(r\right)\right]\, dr$$
$$\text{(A10.4)}$$

We need to prove that the preceding equation is positive under the SSD criteria.
Integration by parts of the right-hand side of equation (A10.4) gives

$$-\int_a^b U'\left(r\right)\left[F_A\left(r\right) - F_B\left(r\right)\right] dr$$

$$= -U'\left(r\right)\int_a^r \left[F_A\left(x\right) - F_B\left(x\right)\right] dx\Big|_a^b + \int_a^b U''\left(r\right)\int_a^r \left[F_A\left(x\right) - F_B\left(x\right)\right] dx\, dr$$

$$= -U'\left(b\right)\int_a^b \left[F_A\left(x\right) - F_B\left(x\right)\right] dx$$

$$+ \int_a^b U''\left(r\right)\int_a^r \left[F_A\left(x\right) - F_B\left(x\right)\right] dx\, dr \qquad\qquad \text{(A10.8)}$$

The first term on the right-hand side in equation (A10.8) becomes

$$\int_a^b \left[F_A\left(x\right) - F_B\left(x\right)\right] dx = \int_a^b \left[1 - F_B\left(x\right)\right] dx - \int_a^b \left[1 - F_A\left(x\right)\right] dx$$
$$= E_B\left(r\right) - E_A\left(r\right)] = 0$$

Thus,

$$E\left[U\left(r_A\right)\right] - E\left[U\left(r_B\right)\right] = -\int_a^b U'\left(r\right)\left[F_A\left(r\right) - F_B\left(r\right)\right] dr$$

$$= \int_a^b U''\left(r\right)\int_a^r \left[F_A\left(x\right) - F_B\left(x\right)\right] dx\, dr \qquad \text{(A10.9)}$$

If the inequality $\int_a^r F_A\left(x\right) dx \leq \int_a^r F_B\left(x\right) dx$ holds, then the right-hand side in equation (A10.9) is positive, because $U''^{(r)} < 0$ by definition. Therefore, $E\left[U\left(r_A\right)\right] \geq E\left[U\left(r_B\right)\right]$. The proof is completed.

A10.4 Proof for Third-Order Stochastic Dominance

In the proof of the second-order stochastic dominance, we have equation (A10.9). For the third-order stochastic dominance, we need to prove that the right-hand side of equation (A10.9) is positive under the TSD criteria. Integration by parts for the right-hand side of equation (A10.9) gives

$$\int_a^b U''\left(r\right)\int_a^r \left[F_A\left(x\right) - F_B\left(x\right)\right] dx\, dr = U''\left(b\right)\int_a^u\int_a^b \left[F_A\left(x\right) - F_B\left(x\right)\right] dx\, du$$

$$- \int_a^b U'''\left(r\right)\int_a^r\int_a^u \left[F_A\left(x\right) - F_B\left(x\right)\right] dx\, du\, dr$$

$$\text{(A10.10)}$$

Because $E_A\left(r\right) \geq E_B\left(r\right)$, the term in equation (A10.10), $\int_a^b \left[F_A\left(x\right) - F_B\left(x\right)\right] dx\, du$, is negative, and $U''\left(b\right) < 0$ by definition. Thus, the first term on the right-hand side is positive. Because $U'''\left(r\right) > 0$ by definition, the second term on the right-hand side is also positive if $\int_a^r\int_a^u F_A\left(x\right) dx\, du \leq \int_a^r\int_a^u F_B\left(x\right) dx\, du$. Therefore, $E\left[U\left(r_A\right)\right] \geq E\left[U\left(r_B\right)\right]$. The proof is completed.

APPENDIX B: EXPECTED UTILITY AS A FUNCTION OF THREE MOMENTS

Let an investor's utility function be $U = f\left(W\right)$. By using a Taylor's series expansion, an investor's utility function is represented as

$$U\left(W_T\right) = f\left(\mu_{w_T}\right) + f'\left(\mu_{w_T}\right)\left(W_T - \mu_{w_T}\right) + \frac{f''\left(\mu_{w_T}\right)}{2!}\left(W_T - \mu_{w_T}\right)^2$$

$$+ \frac{f'''\left(\mu_{w_T}\right)}{3!}\left(W_T - \mu_{w_T}\right)^3 + \sum_{n=4}^{\infty}\left[\frac{f^{(n)}\left(\mu_{w_T}\right)}{n!}\left(W_T - \mu_{w_T}\right)^n\right] \qquad \text{(B10.1)}$$

where W_T is the amount of wealth at the terminal time T, $\mu_{w_T} = E\left(W_T\right)$ is the expected wealth at the terminal time, and $f^{(n)}\left(\cdot\right)$ is the n-th derivative function. By taking the expectations on both sides of equation (B10.1), the expected utility is

$$E\left[U\left(W_T\right)\right] = f\left(\mu_{w_T}\right) + \frac{f''\left(\mu_{w_T}\right)}{2!}E\left[\left(W_T - \mu_{w_T}\right)^2\right] + \frac{f'''\left(\mu_{w_T}\right)}{3!}E\left[\left(W_T - \mu_{w_T}\right)^3\right]$$

$$+ \sum_{n=4}^{\infty}\left[\frac{f^{(n)}\left(\mu_{w_T}\right)}{n!}E\left[\left(W_T - \mu_{w_T}\right)^n\right]\right] \tag{B10.2}$$

Assuming the fourth and higher-order terms are approximately zero, the expected utility becomes a function of the mean, variance, and skewness of W_T. That is,

$$E\left[U\left(W_T\right)\right] \cong f\left(\mu_{w_T}\right) + \frac{f''\left(\mu_{w_T}\right)}{2!}\sigma_{w_T}^2 + \frac{f'''\left(\mu_{w_T}\right)}{3!}\sigma_{w_T}^3\left(\text{Skew}_{w_T}\right) \tag{B10.3}$$

where $\sigma_{w_T}^2 = E[(W_T - \mu_{w_T})^2]$ is the variance of W_T or the second moment of W_T around the mean, $\sigma_{w_T}^3 = E[(W_T - \mu_{w_T})^2]$ is the third moment of W_T around the mean, and $\text{Skew}_{w_T} = E[(W_T - \mu_{w_T})^3]/\sigma_{w_T}^3$ is the skewness coefficient of W_T.

Because $W_T = W_0\left(1 + r_p\right)$, the expected utility can be represented as

$$E\left[U\left(W_T\right)\right] \cong f\left[W_0\left(1 + \mu_p\right)\right] + \frac{f''\left[W_0\left(1 + \mu_p\right)\right]}{2!}W_0^2\sigma_p^2$$

$$+ \frac{f'''\left[W_0\left(1 + \mu_p\right)\right]}{3!}W_0^3\sigma_p^3\left(\text{Skew}_p\right) \tag{B10.4}$$

where Skew_p is the skewness coefficient of the rate of return, r_p. Accordingly, the expected utility of portfolio p can be approximated by its mean return μ_p, its standard deviation σ_p, and its skewness.

NOTES

1. Markowitz (1959) showed that nonquadratic utility functions can be locally approximated with a quadratic utility function. Thus, he argued that the assumption of quadratic utility function is not critical.
2. Leland (1999) showed that when the assumptions of normality and the mean-variance preferences are violated, the CAPM and its risk measures are invalid; the market portfolio is mean-variance inefficient and the CAPM alpha mismeasures the investment performance.
3. The isoelastic utility function is described in Section 4.8.3 of Chapter 4.
4. A stationary portfolio policy can be defined as one in which the same proportions are invested in each asset at the beginning of every period. In a multiperiod setting, such a policy means that at the beginning of each period the investor simply reweights his or her portfolio to have the original proportions. Mossin (1968) has shown that such a policy is optimal if, in addition to the three conditions listed here, a fourth condition is added. This fourth condition is that the distribution of returns must be stationary.
5. For proof, see Young and Trent (1969).
6. See A. D. Roy, "Safety First and the Holding of Assets," *Econometrica* 20 (1952): 431–449.

7. See S. Kataoka, "A Stochastic Programming Model," *Econometrica* 31 (1963): 181–196.
8. Ding and Zhang (2009) establish a risky asset pricing model based on risky funds that is similar to the CAPM.
9. See L. G. Tesler, "Safety First and Hedging," Rev. Econ. Stud. 23 (January 1955–1956): 1–16.
10. The semivariance is calculated from only the disappointingly low returns; the best investment outcomes do not enter the computations. Harry M. Markowitz, *Portfolio Selection* (New York: John Wiley & Sons, 1959), chap. 9.
11. See Bawa (1975) and Bawa and Lindenberg (1977) for the development of a mean-lower partial moment asset pricing model, and Price, Price, and Nantell (1982) for a test of this model.
12. For the continuous case, the portfolio's semivariance is:

$$\overline{\overline{\sigma}}_i^2 = \int_{-\infty}^{h} \left(r_p - h \right)^2 f\left(r_p \right) dr_p$$

13. A representative but not exhaustive list of references that consider various aspects about semivariance analysis include the following: J.P. Quirk and R. Saposnik, "Admissibility and Measurable Utility Functions," *Review of Economic Studies*, February 1962, 140–146; and R. O. Swalm, "Utility Theory Insights into Risk Taking," *Harvard Business Review*, November–December 1966, 123–136. Further, see J. C. T. Mao, "Models of Capital Budgeting, E-V versus E-S," *Journal of Financial and Quantitative Analysis*, January 1970, 657–675. Also see Javier Estrada, "Mean-Semivariance Optimization: A Heuristic Approach," *Journal of Applied Finance* 18, no. 1 (Spring–Summer 2008): 57–72.
14. For additional discussion of cosemivariance-based efficient frontiers and numerical examples, see Javier Estrada, "Mean-Semivariance Optimization: A Heuristic Approach," *Journal of Applied Finance* 18, no. 1 (Spring–Summer 2008): 57–72.
15. Stone wrote a monograph and a paper in which he showed that the semivariance, the standard deviation, the mean absolute deviation, utility theory, and other forms of risk analysis are special cases of a general three-parameter risk measure that he devised. For a brief summary, see Bernell K. Stone, "A General Class of Three-Parameter Risk Measures," *Journal of Finance*, June 1973, 675–685. The monograph by Stone is titled *Risk, Return and Equilibrium: A General Single-Period Theory of Asset Selection and Capital Market Equilibrium* (Cambridge, MA: The MIT Press, 1970).
16. Eugene F. Fama suggested using the normal distribution. See Chapters 1, 2, and 3 of Fama's book, *Foundations of Finance* (New York: Basic Books, 1976).
17. The expected return of a variable uniformly distributed between a and b is $\mu = \left(a + b \right) /2$, and its variance is $\sigma^2 = \left(b - a \right)^2 /12$.
18. The cumulative probability distribution for the uniform distribution over the interval $[a,b]$ is Prob $\left(r_i \leq x \right) = (x - a) / (b - a)$.
19. See Huang and Litzenberger (1988) for further discussion.
20. See also Huang and Litzenberger (1988) for further discussion.
21. Levy and Kroll (1976, 1978) extended the stochastic dominance criterion by allowing the riskless borrowing and lending. Their extended SD rule provides a sharper decision relative to the standard SD rule; hence a smaller efficient set is obtained.
22. Arditti (1967) showed that a utility function that has positive but diminishing marginal utility and also exhibits nonincreasing absolute risk aversion in the Pratt-Arrow sense has a preference for positive skewness.
23. For empirical evidence of skewness, see Francis (1975), Simkowitz and Beedles (1978), Singleton and Wingender (1986), Lau, Wingender, and Lau (1989), Muralidhar (1993),

Defusco, Karelis, and Muralidhar (1996), Chunhachinda, Krishnan, Hamid, and Prakash (1997), Kim and Kon (1996, 1999), and Prakash, Chang, and Pactwa (2003).

24. See Singleton and Wingender (1986), Muralidhar (1993), Defusco, Karelis, and Muralidhar (1996), and Sun and Yan (2003).

25. For an individual with a cubic utility function, this would be an exact ranking procedure. However, such utility functions have certain undesirable properties regarding, for example, risk aversion. Thus, it is probably better to motivate the mean-variance-skewness model by viewing it as a reasonable approximation for investors facing nonsymmetric return distributions (excepting the lognormal case). It has been shown by Arditti (1967) that investors who have nonincreasing absolute risk aversion will have a preference for positive skewness, thus it makes sense for investors facing nonsymmetric return distributions to pay attention to not only mean and variance but also skewness.

26. For the multidimensional asset pricing models, see Ingersoll (1975) and Kraus and Litzenberger (1976).

27. The skewness of a portfolio is not a weighted average of the skewness of the component securities. Like variance, it depends on the covariances between securities.

28. Research with stochastic dominance decision rules has developed techniques for eliminating a subset of the investments that are dominated. However, the stochastic dominance models cannot select a single most desirable investment opportunity because they involve no utility function, either implicitly or explicitly (see Whitmore, 1970).

29. Equation (10.71) is derived from the formula for the third moment of a portfolio of two assets.

$$\psi_p^3 = w_i^3 E[r_i - E\,(r_i)]^3 + 3w_i^2\,(1-w_i)\,E\left\{[r_i - E\,(r_i)]^2\left[r_f - E\left(r_f\right)\right]\right\}$$

$$+\,3w_i(1-w_i)^2 E\left\{[r_i - E\,(r_i)]\left[r_f - E\left(r_f\right)\right]^2\right\} + (1-w_i)^3 E\left[r_f - E\left(r_f\right)\right]^3$$

$$= w_i^3 E[r_i - E\,(r_i)]^3$$

because $r_f - E\left(r_f\right) = 0$.

30. Decreasing absolute risk aversion in the Pratt-Arrow sense (see Chapter 4) is necessary to generate skewness preference.

31. Christie-David and Chaudhry (2001) considered the coskewness (the third moment) as well as the cokurtosis (the fourth moment) and found that the second, third, and fourth moments are all important in explaining future returns.

CHAPTER 11

Risk Management: Value at Risk

Value at risk (VaR) is a useful tool for assessing the financial risk in a portfolio of risky assets, and it is widely used to manage portfolio risk. After various financial disasters during 1993–1995, many banks began to adopt VaR as a key tool to manage market risk. The Basel Committee on Banking Supervision also adopted VaR as the international standard for regulatory purposes.[1] Basel II defines three major components of risk that a financial institution will face: credit risk, operational risk, and market risk. The preferred approach to measure the market risk is VaR. Nonfinancial industries such as energy, agriculture, and airline industries also use VaR for risk management.

11.1 VAR OF A SINGLE ASSET

Many portfolio managers interested in estimating the potential maximum loss over a given planning horizon at some given confidence level use VaR. VaR is the maximum expected loss that will not be exceeded with a specified probability over a predetermined time horizon. For example, with a 95 percent (equals $1 - \alpha$) confidence level, VaR should exceed 5 percent (equals α) of the total number of observations in the distribution. Popular choices of the confidence level are 95 percent and 99 percent, but the choice is arbitrary.

The formal definition of VaR, expressed in percentage terms, is

$$\text{Prob}\left(r_i \leq \text{VaR}\right) = \alpha \tag{11.1}$$

where r_i is the return from asset i. Figure 11.1 illustrates VaR for the case in which the returns have a statistical probability distribution that is known or can be estimated.

From a statistical point of view, the VaR estimation entails the estimation of a quantile of the distribution of returns. Suppose a bank calculates the VaR on a portfolio of $1 million over a horizon of one day with a 95 percent confidence level. This can be interpreted to mean that, on average, in 95 trading days out of 100, the loss on the portfolio will not exceed $1 million over a single trading day, but on five trading days in 100 (that is, in the worst scenarios), these days' trading losses can be expected to exceed $1 million. The user is free to specify any trading horizon and any frequency of loss (namely, α).

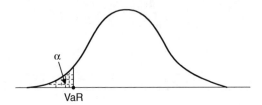

FIGURE 11.1 VaR in a Probability Distribution

The definition of VaR in equation (11.1) can be transformed as

$$\text{Prob}\left(r_i \leq \text{VaR}\right) = \alpha \quad \Longleftrightarrow \quad \text{Prob}\left[Z \leq \left(\frac{\text{VaR} - \mu_i}{\sigma_i}\right)\right] = \alpha \qquad (11.2)$$

where $\mu_i = E\left(r_i\right)$ is the expected return (or mean) of r_i, σ_i is the standard deviation of the return r_i, and $Z = \left[\left(r_i - \mu_i\right)/\sigma_i\right]$ is a standardized variable of r_i. Therefore, in percentage terms, VaR over a unit period with $(1 - \alpha)$ confidence level is expressed as

$$\text{VaR} = \mu_i - z_\alpha \sigma_i \qquad (11.3)$$

where z_α is such that $\text{Prob}\left(Z > z_\alpha\right) = \alpha$. For example, if the return is normally distributed, $z_\alpha = 1.645$ for a 95 percent confidence level ($\alpha = 5\%$) and $z_\alpha = 2.326$ for a 99 percent confidence level ($\alpha = 1\%$). The distribution of r_i or Z can be any statistical distribution that is characterized by two parameters, μ_i and σ_i. Note that the mean and standard deviation are computed with returns measured over the unit period. For instance, if the unit period is a day, then the mean and standard deviation should be estimated using daily returns. If the return of an asset is normally distributed with mean of 0.31 percent per day and standard deviation of 1.31 percent per day, then the VaR (in percentage terms) with 95 percent confidence level is: $\text{VaR} = \mu_i - z_\alpha = 0.31 - 1.645 \times 1.31 = -1.845\%$. If one million dollars are invested, then the VaR over a single day is $-\$18,450$. In other words, with 95 percent confidence (or in 95 trading days out of 100), the loss on this investment will not exceed $18,450 over the next day. But, with probability of 5 occurrences out of 100 (in case of the worst scenario), the loss could exceed $18,450 over the next day. Hereafter, we simply interpret VaR as the expected (or potential) maximum loss.

Because VaR represents a loss, we can denote VaR in percentage (or return VaR) terms, assuming the mean, μ_i, is zero, as

$$\text{VaR} = z_\alpha \sigma_i \qquad (11.4)$$

by dropping the minus sign. Because VaR is usually computed for short periods of time such as a day, the mean is close to zero. Thus, the assumption for the mean of zero in computing VaR could be acceptable. Although μ_i is not zero, VaR from equation (11.4) still can be used by adjusting later for the mean. If returns have an identical and independent normal distribution, the variance of the return over T

days equals T times the variance of the one-day variance. Thus, the VaR over the next T days is

$$\text{VaR}(T) = \mu_i T - z_\alpha \sigma_i \sqrt{T} \qquad (11.5)$$

where VaR (T) is VaR over the next T days. In the preceding example, the VaR in percentage term over the next week (five trading days) will be

$$\text{VaR}(5) = 0.31 \times 5 - 1.645 \times 1.31 \times \sqrt{5} = -3.269\%$$

Thus, VaR with 95 percent confidence level from the $1 million investment over the next week is $-\$32,690$. In other words, if the worst scenario happens, the expected maximum loss from this $1 million investment over the next week is expected to be $ 32,690. Assuming μ_i is zero, the T-day VaR can also be denoted

$$\text{VaR}(T) = z_\alpha \sigma_i \sqrt{T} = \text{VaR}(1) \times \sqrt{T} \qquad (11.6)$$

where VaR $(1) = z_\alpha \sigma_i$ is a unit period VaR. By multiplying the dollar amount invested in asset i, W, by this VaR in percentage terms, we obtain VaR in dollars (or dollar VaR). That is,

$$\text{VaR} = z_\alpha \sigma_i W \qquad (11.7)$$

The VaR statistic has three components: a time period (T), a confidence level (α), and a loss percentage (a quantile of the distribution of returns; $\mu_i - z_\alpha \sigma_i$). The VaR approach is contrasted with the safety-first criterion in that the safety-first criterion considers the trade-off between the expected return and the worst tolerable outcome, whereas the VaR approach considers only the size of the worst tolerable outcome that can occur with a designated probability α over a specified time horizon.

11.2 PORTFOLIO VAR

When individual risky assets are combined into a portfolio, the variance of the portfolio consists of the variances and covariances of individual assets and, typically, there is a reduction in the variance as the number of assets increases. When risk is measured by VaR, we observe similar characteristics in the portfolio's risk. Thus, we do an analysis for portfolio VaR in this section that is similar to the analysis of a portfolio's variance in the early chapters.

The portfolio rate of return is defined as

$$r_{pt} = \sum_{i=1}^{N} w_i r_i \qquad (11.8)$$

where N is the number of assets. Based on equation (11.8), the variance of this portfolio rate of return is denoted as

$$\sigma_p^2 = w' \Sigma w \qquad (11.9)$$

where $w' = (w_1, w_2, \ldots, w_N)$ is an $(N \times 1)$ weight vector, and Σ is a $(N \times N)$ covariance matrix. The portfolio variance in terms of dollar amount is $\sigma_p^2 W^2$, where W is the total dollars invested. The portfolio VaR is

$$\text{Portfolio VaR} = \text{VaR}_p = z_\alpha \sigma_p W \qquad (11.10)$$

Like the portfolio variance, the portfolio VaR can also be related to the individual VaRs. When $N = 2$, the square of the portfolio VaR is

$$\begin{aligned} \text{VaR}_p^2 &= \left(z_\alpha \sigma_p W\right)^2 = z_\alpha^2 \left[w_1^2 \sigma_1^2 + w_2^2 \sigma_2^2 + 2w_1 w_2 \rho_{12} \sigma_1 \sigma_2\right] W^2 \\ &= \left(z_\alpha \sigma_1 W_1\right)^2 + \left(z_\alpha \sigma_2 W_2\right)^2 + 2\rho_{12} \left(z_\alpha \sigma_1 W_1\right)\left(z_\alpha \sigma_2 W_2\right) \\ &= \text{VaR}_1^2 + \text{VaR}_2^2 + 2\rho_{12} \text{VaR}_1 \text{VaR}_2 \\ &\leq \left(\text{VaR}_1 + \text{VaR}_2\right)^2 \qquad (11.11) \end{aligned}$$

where $W_i = w_i W$ is the dollar amount invested in asset i and w_i is the proportion invested in asset i for $i = 1, 2$. Thus, the portfolio VaR is less than or equal to the sum of the individual assets' VaRs. That is, there is a risk-reducing diversification effect in the portfolio's VaR:

$$\text{VaR}_p \leq \text{VaR}_1 + \text{VaR}_2 \qquad (11.12)$$

The equality holds when the returns of two assets are perfectly positively correlated: $\rho_{12} = +1$. The previous case with $N = 2$ can be extended to the general case:

$$\text{VaR}_p \leq \sum_{i=1}^{N} \text{VaR}_i \qquad (11.13)$$

EXAMPLE 11.1

There are two assets, A and B, whose standard deviations are 3 percent and 8 percent, respectively. The correlation coefficient between the returns of these two assets is -0.20. If \$6 million and \$4 million are invested in assets A and B, respectively, what is the portfolio VaR with 95 percent confidence level?

First, we need to compute the standard deviation of the portfolio.

$$\sigma_p = \left[(0.6)^2(0.03)^2 + (0.4)^2(0.08)^2 + 2(0.6)(0.4)(-0.2)(0.03)(0.08)\right]^{1/2}$$

$$= 0.03343 \text{ or } 3.343\%$$

Thus, the portfolio VaR is

$$\text{VaR}_p = z_\alpha \sigma_p W = 1.645 \times 0.03343 \times \$10 \text{ million} = \$549{,}932$$

This portfolio VaR is less than the sum of two individual VaRs. The individual assets' VaRs are

$$\text{VaR}_A = z_\alpha \sigma_A W_A = 1.645 \times 0.03 \times \$6 \text{ million} = \$296{,}100$$

$$\text{VaR}_B = z_\alpha \sigma_B W_B = 1.645 \times 0.08 \times \$4 \text{ million} = \$526{,}400$$

11.3   DECOMPOSITION OF A PORTFOLIO'S VAR

Rather than looking at the portfolio VaR as a whole, it is better to examine the marginal contribution of the individual portfolio components to the portfolio's VaR, the proportion of a portfolio's VaR that can be attributed to a particular portfolio component, and the change in a portfolio's VaR from a newly added position.

11.3.1   Marginal VaR

When the overall VaR is given as a number, we need information regarding how we alter the portfolio mix in order to mitigate the overall risk exposure of the portfolio. To do this, we need a measure of the marginal contribution of the individual portfolio component to the portfolio VaR. The marginal VaR of an individual asset is a measure of how much the portfolio VaR (the total portfolio risk) is changed from taking an additional dollar of exposure to the asset. Thus, the marginal VaR of an asset i is defined as

$$\text{Marginal VaR}_i = \frac{\partial \left(\text{VaR}_p \right)}{\partial W_i} \tag{11.14}$$

where W_i is the dollar amount invested in asset i (equals $w_i W$). As a portfolio management tool, this is more useful than the instrument's isolated risk. The marginal contribution of an individual asset i to the portfolio's variance from one additional unit of investment in that asset is measured by differentiating the portfolio variance with respect to the weight of asset i. For instance, if the portfolio's variance is denoted as

$$\sigma_p^2 = \sum_{i=1}^{N} \sum_{j=1}^{N} w_i w_j = \begin{bmatrix} w_1^2 \sigma_{11} + w_1 w_2 \sigma_{12} + w_1 w_3 \sigma_{13} + \cdots + w_1 w_N \sigma_{1N} \\ + w_2 w_1 \sigma_{21} + w_2^2 \sigma_{22} + w_2 w_3 \sigma_{23} + \cdots + w_2 w_N \sigma_{2N} \\ \vdots \qquad\qquad \vdots \qquad\qquad \vdots \\ + w_i w_1 \sigma_{i1} + w_i w_2 \sigma_{i2} + w_i w_3 \sigma_{i3} + \cdots + w_i w_N \sigma_{iN} \\ \vdots \qquad\qquad \vdots \qquad\qquad \vdots \\ + w_N w_1 \sigma_{N1} + w_N w_2 \sigma_{N2} + w_N w_3 \sigma_{N3} + \cdots + w_N^2 \sigma_{NN} \end{bmatrix},$$

then the partial derivative of the portfolio's variance with respect to the i-th weight variable is shown next in an expanded form

$$\frac{\partial \sigma_p^2}{\partial w_i} = \begin{bmatrix} + w_1 \sigma_{1i} \\ + w_2 \sigma_{2i} \\ \vdots \\ + w_i \sigma_{i1} + w_i \sigma_{i2} + \cdots + 2 w_i \sigma_{ii} + \cdots + w_i \sigma_{iN} \\ \vdots \\ + w_N \sigma_{Ni} \end{bmatrix}$$

$$= 2 w_1 \sigma_{1i} + 2 w_2 \sigma_{2i} + \cdots + 2 w_N \sigma_{Ni}$$

$$= 2 w_i \sigma_i^2 + 2 \sum_{\substack{j=1, \\ j \neq i}}^{N} w_j \sigma_{ij} = 2 \sum_{j=1}^{N} w_j \sigma_{ij} = 2 \sigma_{ip} \tag{11.15}$$

where σ_{ip} is the covariance of returns between the asset i and the portfolio. Because $\partial \sigma_p^2 / \partial w_i = (2\sigma_p)(\partial \sigma_p / \partial w_i)$, equation (11.15) reduces to

$$\frac{\partial \sigma_p}{\partial w_i} = \frac{\sigma_{ip}}{\sigma_p} \tag{11.16}$$

Note that if portfolio p is the market portfolio, then $\partial \sigma_p / \partial w_i = \beta_i \sigma_p$, where β_i is the market beta. Thus, the market beta also can be interpreted as a measure of the marginal contribution of the asset to the market risk. In the same vein, from equation (11.16), the marginal VaR of an asset i from one additional dollar of investment is

$$\text{Marginal VaR}_i = \frac{\partial \left(z_\alpha \sigma_p W\right)}{\partial \left(w_i W\right)}$$

$$= z_\alpha \left(\frac{\sigma_{ip}}{\sigma_p}\right) \tag{11.17}$$

If portfolio p is the market portfolio, then we obtain the relation between an asset's marginal VaR and its total VaR.

$$\text{Marginal VaR}_i = z_\alpha \beta_i \sigma_p = \text{VaR}_p \times \left(\frac{\beta_i}{W}\right) \tag{11.18}$$

Because it is defined as a ratio of the dollar amounts, the marginal VaR has no standardized units.

When investors want to reduce a portfolio's VaR, they should decrease their position in a portfolio component with a large marginal VaR number, because this component contributes a large amount of risk. The marginal VaR is useful for identifying the best candidates for risk reduction.

11.3.2   Incremental VaR

The incremental VaR measures the change in portfolio VaR when a new position is added to the portfolio; it measures the new asset's potential impact on the total VaR. It differs from the marginal VaR in that the marginal VaR measures an impact on the portfolio VaR by changing one additional dollar exposure of an *existing* portfolio component, whereas the incremental VaR measures an impact on the portfolio VaR from changing the position of a portfolio component. For the incremental VaR, the amount added or subtracted can be large. For example, consider a portfolio consisting of 100 assets. The portfolio manager is considering changing three stocks at once by increasing these investments by $100, $150, and $80, respectively. In this case, the portfolio manager might be interested in how much the portfolio VaR would be changed. This is the incremental VaR. In contrast, if the portfolio manager is interested in how much the portfolio VaR would be changed by adding an additional $1 to one asset, then the manager needs to measure the marginal VaR.

Computing the incremental VaR requires "repricing" the portfolio VaR before and after the change in the position. The difference in the portfolio VaR between after and before the change in the position is the incremental VaR. Let a be a vector of new positions. Then, the marginal VaR is defined as

$$\text{Incremental VaR } (a) = \text{VaR}_{p+a} - \text{VaR}_p \tag{11.19}$$

where VaR_{p+a} is the new portfolio VaR after new positions are added to the portfolio. Jorion (2001) shows that the incremental VaR is approximated as

$$\text{Incremental VaR } (a) \approx \sum_{i=1}^{L} \text{Marginal VaR}_i \times a_i \tag{11.20}$$

where marginal VaR_i is the marginal VaR of asset i, a_i is the changed dollar amount invested in asset i, and L is the number of assets whose positions have been changed. However, if the amount of the change a_i is relatively large, the preceding approximation may not work well.

11.3.3 Component VaR

The component VaR of an asset is the decomposed portion of the portfolio VaR created by including one asset in the portfolio; parts of it can be attributed to each of the portfolio components. The sum of all component VaRs equals the portfolio VaR. Thus, the component VaR of an asset indicates the contribution of the asset to the total VaR. The component VaR measures how much the portfolio VaR would change if a particular component were deleted from the portfolio. By definition, $\text{VaR}_p = \sum_{i=1}^{N} (\text{component VaR}_i)$. From equation (11.18),

$$\text{VaR}_p = \sum_{i=1}^{N} w_i \left(\beta_i \text{VaR}_p \right)$$

$$= \sum_{i=1}^{N} w_i \left[W \times \left(\text{Marginal VaR}_i \right) \right]$$

$$= \sum_{i=1}^{N} \left[W_i \times \left(\text{Marginal VaR}_i \right) \right] \tag{11.21}$$

where $W_i = w_i W$ is the dollar amount invested in asset i. Therefore, the component VaR of an asset i is

$$\text{Component VaR}_i = w_i \beta_i \text{VaR}_p \quad \text{or} \quad W_i \times \left(\text{Marginal VaR}_i \right) \tag{11.22}$$

Thus, the marginal VaR of an asset i can also be obtained from

$$\text{Marginal VaR}_i = \frac{\text{Component VaR}_i}{W_i} \tag{11.23}$$

EXAMPLE 11.2

A summary of Example 11.1 is shown in Table 11.1. The portfolio VaR was $549,900.

TABLE 11.1 Summary of Two Assets from Example 11.1

	A	B	Portfolio $(w_A = 0.6, w_B = 0.4)$
Standard deviation (σ_i)	3%	8%	3.343%
Investment amount (W_i)	$6 million	$4 million	$10 million
Investment weight (w_i)	0.6	0.4	1.00
VaR	$296,100	$526,400	$549,900

The correlation coefficient between the returns of assets A and B is -0.20.

1. What is the component VaR of each asset?

   To compute the component VaR, we need to compute β_i. Because $\sigma_{ip} = \sum_{j=1}^{N} w_j \sigma_{ij}$,

   $$\beta_1 = \frac{\sigma_{1p}}{\sigma_p^2} = \frac{\sum_{j=1}^{2} w_j \sigma_{1j}}{\sigma_p^2} = \frac{(0.6)(0.03)^2 + (0.4)(-0.2)(0.03)(0.08)}{\sigma_p^2} = 0.31138$$

   $$\beta_2 = \frac{\sigma_{2p}}{\sigma_p^2} = \frac{\sum_{j=1}^{2} w_j \sigma_{2j}}{\sigma_p^2} = \frac{(0.6)(-0.2)(0.03)(0.08) + (0.4)(0.08)^2}{\sigma_p^2} = 2.03293$$

   From equation (11.22), the component VaRs of assets A and B are, respectively,

   $$\text{Component VaR}_1 = w_1 \beta_1 \text{VaR}_p = 0.6 \times 0.31138 \times \$549,900 = \$102,737$$

   $$\text{Component VaR}_2 = w_2 \beta_2 \text{VaR}_p = 0.4 \times 2.03293 \times \$549,900 = \underline{\$447,163}$$

   Total $549,900

2. What is the marginal VaR of each asset?

   From equation (11.23), the marginal VaRs of assets A and B are, respectively,

   $$\text{Marginal VaR}_A = \$103,737/\$6 \text{ million} = 0.01729$$

   $$\text{Marginal VaR}_B = \$447,163/\$4 \text{ million} = 0.11179$$

   The preceding results for the marginal VaR indicate that when $1 additional cash is invested in asset A, the portfolio's VaR is increased by $0.01729. For asset B, the analogous increase in the portfolio's VaR is

EXAMPLE 11.2 (*Continued*)

$0.11179. Thus, when the investment in asset B is decreased, there is more reduction in the portfolio's VaR than with asset A.

3. If we purchase an additional $10,000 worth of asset A by selling $10,000 worth of asset B, what is the change in the portfolio VaR or the incremental VaR?

   From equation (11.20), the incremental VaR is approximately

$$\text{Incremental VaR } (a) \approx 0.01729 \times \$10,000 + 0.11179 \times (-\$10,000)$$

$$= -\$945$$

Thus, after the position in the two assets is changed, the portfolio VaR is decreased by $945.

11.4   OTHER VARS

The fundamental VaR model can be extended.

11.4.1   Modified VaR (MVaR)

In Section 11.1 the standard definition of VaR with $(1 - \alpha)$ confidence level is expressed as

$$\text{VaR} = \mu_i - z_\alpha \sigma_i \qquad (11.3)$$

where z_α is such that $\text{Prob}\,(Z > z_\alpha) = \alpha$. In fact, z_α is the distance between the mean of the distribution and the VaR in terms of standard deviation. If returns are assumed to be normally distributed, $z_\alpha = 1.645$ for a 95 percent confidence level ($\alpha = 5\%$) and $z_\alpha = 2.326$ for a 99 percent confidence level ($\alpha = 1\%$). However, there is ample empirical evidence against the assumption that returns are normally distributed. When returns are non-normally distributed, we need to account for non-normality and modify the standard (Gaussian) VaR. A simple way to account for non-normality is the Cornish-Fisher expansion, which adjusts the VaR in terms of skewness and excess kurtosis. Skewness is a measure for the amount of asymmetry in the return distribution, and kurtosis is a measure for the thickness of the tails of the return distribution relative to those of the normal distribution.[2] By using the Cornish-Fisher expansion, the modified VaR is expressed as

$$\text{VaR} = \mu_i - z_\alpha^{\text{cf}} \sigma_i$$

where

$$z_\alpha^{\text{cf}} = z_\alpha + \frac{1}{6} \left(z_\alpha^2 - 1 \right) \gamma_1 + \frac{1}{24} \left(z_\alpha^3 - 3z_\alpha \right) \gamma_2 - \frac{1}{36} \left(2z_\alpha^3 - 5z_\alpha \right) \gamma_1^2$$

γ_1 is the skewness, and γ_2 is the excess kurtosis. When skewness and excess kurtosis are zero, which is the case under normality, the modified VaR equals the standard Gaussian VaR.

11.4.2 Conditional VaR (CVaR)

Whereas VaR measures the expected maximum loss over a given horizon under normal market conditions at a given confidence level, conditional VaR (CVaR) is the expected (probability-weighted average) loss conditional on the loss being equal to or greater than the VaR. In other words, CVaR is the expected loss in a normal market once the market moves beyond normal limits. Figure 11.2 illustrates CVaR.

In contrast to VaR that is a description about only one particular point in the tail part of the distribution, CVaR is a comprehensive measure of the a part of the tail.[3] CVaR is also known as expected shortfall, tail VaR, and expected tail loss.

If returns are normally distributed, CVaR can also be estimated by using the first two moments of the return distribution as

$$\text{CVaR} = \mu_i - z_\alpha^m \sigma_i$$

where

$$z_\alpha^m = \frac{\exp\left(-z_\alpha^2/2\right)}{\alpha\sqrt{2\pi}}$$

At the 95 percent confidence level, $z_\alpha^m \approx 2.06$.[4] For example, for an asset whose returns are normally distributed with mean return of 8 percent and standard deviation of 15 percent, the VaR and CVaR of this asset are VaR $= -16.75$ percent and CVaR $= -22.9$ percent at the 95 percent confidence level. This -22.9 percent is the average tail loss when a loss exceeds the threshold of the worst fifth percentile of the return distribution.

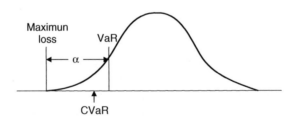

FIGURE 11.2 Conditional VaR

11.5 METHODS OF MEASURING VAR

There is more than one way to estimate a portfolio's VaR.

11.5.1 Variance-Covariance (Delta-Normal) Method

The variance-covariance method assumes the distributional form of the return or the market factors, and variances-covariances are computed based on some assumed probability distribution. Thus, this first method is a parametric approach.[5] A multivariate normal distribution is commonly assumed. The VaRs in the previous sections are simple examples of the variance-covariance method, assuming that return observations of the assets are available and the variances and covariances can be computed easily. In reality, however, there are cases for which the return observations are insufficient to compute variances and covariances. For example, maybe the instruments are not traded on an organized exchange. For these cases, we identify the market factors affecting the value of the asset and use the variances and covariances of the market factors to obtain the variance of the asset. The procedure to compute the VaR for these cases is discussed next.

Consider a U.S. bank that enters a long position in a six-month Great Britain pound (GBP) forward contract to receive £10 million in exchange for $15 million in six months. The forward exchange rate is $1.50/£ in this example. We explain the step-by-step procedure to obtain the VaR for this contract using the variance-covariance method.

Step 1: Risk Mapping The first step is to identify the market factors and the simpler, standardized instruments that are related to the market factors, and to map the asset (the GBP forward contract) onto the standardized instruments.

The positions that the U.S. bank takes from the six-month GBP forward contract are as follows. The U.S. bank will receive £10 million and will pay in return $15 million in six months. This is equivalent to the U.S. bank taking a long position in a six-month GBP-denominated zero-coupon bond with face value of £10 million and a short position in a six-month USD-denominated zero-coupon bond with face value of $15 million. The value of the long position in the GBP-denominated zero-coupon bond depends on the six-month GBP interest rate, and the value of the short position in the USD-denominated zero-coupon bond depends on the six-month USD interest rate. Each interest rate is the discount rate for the GBP- or USD-denominated face value for the six-month period. Moreover, the U.S. bank will have a cash position of £10 million in six months. The value of this cash position will depend on the spot GBP/USD exchange rate in six months.

In this case, from the perspective of a U.S. bank, three standardized positions will be used: (1) a six-month USD-denominated zero-coupon bond whose value is exposed only to the six-month USD spot interest rate, (2) a six-month GBP-denominated zero-coupon bond whose value is exposed only to the six-month GBP spot interest rate, and (3) a spot position in the GBP whose value (in dollars) is exposed to the spot exchange rate. Therefore, there are three market factors: the six-month USD interest rate (r_{USD}), the six-month GBP interest rate (r_{GBP}), and the spot dollar/pound exchange rate (S_x).

Step 2: Computing the Variance-Covariance of Changes in the Market Factors In the second step, it is necessary to assume the distribution of changes in the market factors. A multivariate normal distribution is usually assumed with means of zero for a short period of time such as a single trading day. The variances and covariances of changes in the market factors can be computed using historical data of the market factors. The correlation coefficients between the changes in the market factors are also computed.

Step 3: Delta-Normal Method After estimating the variances and covariances of changes in the market factors, we determine the variances and covariances of changes in the value of the standardized positions. The standard deviations of changes in the value of standardized positions are determined by multiplying the standard deviations of changes in the market factors by the sensitivities of changes in the standardized positions to changes in the market factors. For example, if the value of a single position (V) is changed by 1.5 percent for a 1 percent change in the market factor f that solely affects the value of the position, then the standard deviation of changes in the value of the position is *approximately* 1.5 times as large as the standard deviation of changes in the market factor. We call this sensitivity *delta* (Δ). Mathematically,

$$\text{Change in V} = \Delta \times \text{change in } f$$

or $\qquad\qquad\qquad\qquad dV = \Delta \times df \qquad\qquad\qquad\qquad\qquad$ (11.24)

where $\Delta = \partial V / \partial f$ is the first partial derivative of V with respect to f.[6] For instance, if this is the position in a fixed income security, and the market factor is the market interest rate, then the sensitivity Δ indicates the dollar duration, and Δ / V is the duration. Equation (11.24) represents a linear relation between the change in the market factor and the change (in dollars) in the value of the position. Equation (11.24) can be rewritten as

$$dV = \left(\Delta \times f\right)\left(\frac{df}{f}\right) \qquad\qquad\qquad (11.25)$$

Here, $\Delta \times f$ is the change amount (in dollars) in the value of the position for a change of the market factor by df, and $\left(df/f\right)$ is the percentage change in the market factor, f (i.e., the market factor return). The standard deviation of dV is equal to $\Delta \times f$ times the standard deviation of the percentage change in the market factor. The dollar VaR of the position is, therefore,

$$\text{VaR} = z_\alpha \left(\Delta \times f\right) \sigma_f \qquad\qquad\qquad (11.26)$$

where σ_f is the standard deviation of $\left(df/f\right)$. This is the *delta-normal* method. Of course, the return VaR can also be easily obtained by slightly transforming equation (11.25) into

$$\frac{dV}{V} = \Delta \left(\frac{f}{V}\right)\left(\frac{df}{f}\right) \qquad\qquad\qquad (11.27)$$

Thus, the return VaR is

$$\text{VaR} = z_\alpha \Delta \left(\frac{f}{V}\right) \sigma_f \qquad\qquad\qquad (11.28)$$

The delta-normal method is valid when the change of the market factor or the underlying variable is very small. However, when its change is relatively large, the approximation by the delta-normal method [equation (11.24) or equation (11.25)] could produce a significant error. In this case, it is necessary to consider an additional term to reduce the error; the gamma term, which is the second-order term in the Taylor series expansion. This method is the *delta-gamma* method. The appendix of this chapter explains the delta-gamma method. However, here we explain the measurement of VaR by using only the delta-normal method, assuming the change in the market factor is small.

By using the delta-normal method, we can extend the single-factor and single-position case of equation (11.25) to a set of multiple positions or a portfolio. Suppose that a portfolio consists of N standardized positions and the value of each position depends only on a particular market factor. Then, the change in the value of the portfolio, dV_p, is denoted

$$dV_p = \sum_{i=1}^{N} \Delta_i \left(df_i\right) \tag{11.29}$$

where $V_p = \sum_{i=1}^{N} V_i$ is the value of the portfolio, V_i is the value of the position i, and $\Delta_i = \partial V_p/\partial f_i = \partial V_i/\partial f_i$ because $\partial V_j/\partial f_i = 0$ for $j \neq i$. Here the value of each position is assumed to depend on only one corresponding market factor. The change in the value of the position can also be approximated when the value of each position depends on K relevant market factors. Equation (A11.3) in the end-of-chapter appendix expresses this more rigorously.

By transforming equation (11.29) slightly, the change in the value of the portfolio (or the portfolio return) can be represented by

$$dV_p = \sum_{i=1}^{N} \left(\Delta_i f_i\right) \left(\frac{df_i}{f_i}\right) = \sum_{i=1}^{N} q_i r_i \tag{11.30}$$

where $q_i = \Delta_i f_i$ and $r_i = df_i/f_i$ is the percentage change in the market factor or the market factor return. The variance of the dollar change in the value of the portfolio is

$$\mathrm{Var}\left(dV_p\right) = q' \Sigma q \tag{11.31}$$

and the dollar VaR of the portfolio is

$$\mathrm{VaR} = z_\alpha \left(q' \Sigma q\right)^{\frac{1}{2}} \tag{11.32}$$

where $q' = (q_1, q_2, \ldots, q_N)$ and Σ defines the variance-covariance matrix of the market factor returns.

The return VaR can also be obtained by transforming equation (11.30);

$$\frac{dV_p}{V_p} = \sum_{i=1}^{N} \left(\frac{\Delta_i}{V_i}\right) f_i \left(\frac{V_i}{V_p}\right) \left(\frac{df_i}{f_i}\right) \tag{11.33}$$

The term $\left(\frac{\Delta_i}{V_i}\right) f_i \left(\frac{V_i}{V_p}\right)$ in the preceding equation indicates the percentage change in the value of the position i (i.e., the rate of retun on the portfolio i), and (V_i/V_p) is the weight of the position i in the portfolio. We can rewrite equation (11.33) as

$$\frac{dV_p}{V_p} = \sum_{i=1}^{N} \left(\frac{q_i}{V_p}\right) \left(\frac{df_i}{f_i}\right) = \sum_{i=1}^{N} q_i^* r_i \tag{11.34}$$

where $q_i^* = q_i/V_p$.

Step 4: Computing the Portfolio Variance and VaR Based on equation (11.34), the variance of the percentage change in the value of the portfolio is

$$\text{Var}\left(\frac{dV_p}{V_p}\right) = q^{*'}\Sigma q^*$$ (11.35)

where $q^{*'} = (q_1^*, q_2^*, \ldots, q_N^*)$, and the return VaR of the portfolio is

$$\text{VaR} = z_\alpha \left(q^{*'}\Sigma q^*\right)^{1/2}$$ (11.36)

In summary, the variance-covariance method (or the delta-normal method) assumes the forms of the probability distribution of changes in the market factors are known. And, estimates of the means, variances, and covariances of these changes must be computed. The computation of the VaR is relatively analytical and straightforward in this method. However, there are some drawbacks to this method. First, if returns are not normally distributed, the computed VaR may under- or overestimate the true VaR. For example, if the probability distribution of returns has fat tails, the actual VaR would be higher than the computed VaR. As shown in Chapter 9's Table 9.1, empirical evidence rejects the normality assumption for stock returns. Second, if the variances and covariances change over time, the estimated variances and covariances could result in the computation of erroneous VaRs. Unfortunately, this nonstationarity of the parameters is common. Third, this method is subject to the estimation error for the parameters, even though the parameters are stationary. Fourth, to use the delta-normal or delta-gamma method, the relation between the value of the portfolio (or a single instrument) and the relevant market factors should be given in a closed-form solution. Otherwise, the differentiation is not possible, and thus the portfolio variance cannot be represented by the variance-covariance of the market factors.

To overcome the first weakness of the variance-covariance method, we can assume non-normal distribution such as a mixture of normal distributions, log-normal distributions, Student's-t distributions, or Poisson jump-diffusion process. These distributions are explained in Chapter 9. To overcome the second weakness, various methods have been suggested to estimate variances and covariances by allowing them to change over time. And, several methods of estimating time-varying volatilities are introduced in the next section.

11.5.2 Historical Simulation Method

The historical simulation method is a simple, nonparametric approach to estimating a portfolio's VaR. In this approach, hypothetical time series of profits or losses from the portfolio are generated, and the VaR of the portfolio is estimated from this hypothetical times series data. The way to generate hypothetical time series outcomes for a portfolio is laborious, but not mathematical. The portfolio of interest is employed to process actual historical time series data from the market factors or the underlying variables, while the portfolio analyst tabulates the changes in the value of the portfolio that would have occurred in each period. If there are 100 time series observations of historical data from the relevant market factors, then 100 hypothetical changes in the value of the portfolio can be generated. After sorting these 100 hypothetical values of the change into descending order, we choose the 95th (or 99th) value as the VaR of the portfolio with a 95 percent (99 percent) confidence interval.

A more detailed explanation of the historical simulation method is provided by using the example of the six-month GBP forward contract (to receive £10 million in exchange for $15 million) used in the previous section. First, we identify the market factors that are relevant to the value of the forward contract. As mentioned previously, this forward contract can be treated as a portfolio of two positions: a short position in the six-month USD-denominated zero-coupon bond with a face value of $15 million and a long position in the six-month GBP-denominated zero-coupon bond with a face value of £10 million. The identified market factors are the six-month USD interest rate, the six-month GBP interest rate, and the spot dollar/pound exchange rate.

Second, we obtain historical times series data of the three market factors for the most recent N days. It would be better to use a large and diverse sample of historical time series data to form a finer distribution of changes.

Third, we run the portfolio (the forward contact) through the historical time series data of the market factors. Hypothetical daily mark-to-market profits and losses from the forward contract are tabulated. The USD mark-to-market value of the combined position is obtained through

$$\left[\frac{£10 \text{ million}}{1 + r_{\text{GBP}}(180/360)}\right] \times (\$/£ \text{ exchange rate}) - \left[\frac{\$15 \text{ million}}{1 + r_{\text{USD}}(180/360)}\right]$$

For example, at $t = 0$ (today), suppose that the values of the market factors (the USD interest rate, the GBP interest rate, and the spot dollar/pound exchange rate) are 3 percent, 5 percent, and $1.5151/£, respectively.[7] Thus, the current mark-to-market value of the position or the portfolio is $2,896.83. Table 11.2 summarizes the first five days of simulated returns. Suppose we calculate a sample of N changes in the mark-to-market value of the positions.

Fourth, we use the N changes in the mark-to-market value of the portfolio to construct a distribution of the changes (in dollars). Then, we select the 5 percentile value (the loss) from the left (or the 5 percentile from the bottom of the array sorted in descending order). This is the VaR value that has a 95 percent confidence interval.

TABLE 11.2 Mark-to-Market Values of the Six-Month GBP Forward Contract

Day	r_{USD} (%)	r_{USD} (%)	Spot exchange rate	Value of the combined position ($) ($V_p$)	Change in V_p ($) ($\Delta V_p$)
	3.00	5.00	1.5151	2,896.83	n.a.
1	3.04	5.01	1.5148	2,870.34	−26.50
2	2.97	4.91	1.5146	2,769.04	−101.30
3	2.88	4.90	1.5152	2,848.50	79.46
4	3.04	5.09	1.5155	3,015.92	167.42
5	3.10	5.10	1.5150	2,966.38	−49.55
⋮	⋮	⋮	⋮	⋮	⋮

If an investor takes a single position and its historical time series data are available, it is very simple to find the VaR. For example, Table 10.2 lists 50 daily returns of portfolio A. This portfolio's VaR for a single trading day with a 90 percent confidence level is a return of −1.55 percent (i.e., the fifth-lowest return among 50 arrayed return observations). This VaR means that −1.55 percent is the worst loss that this portfolio is likely to suffer during all but very exceptional days (in 1 out of 10 days).

In summary, the historical simulation does not assume any distributional form of returns or changes of market factors and does not involve the estimation of any parameters for the market factors. Thus, this method is a nonparametric approach. This method is popular and relatively easy to use. According to Perignon and Smith (2006), 73 percent of the financial institutions that disclose their VaR method use the historical simulation method. However, this method also has some weakness. First, the implicit assumption of this method is that past time series data contains forward-looking information that represents plausible future scenarios. If this assumption isnt true, the VaR obtained from the simulation could misjudge the risk profile of the position or the portfolio. Second, reasonably long historical time series data for all relevant market factors should be used to obtain a diverse and representative sample. Third, if there is an increasing (decreasing) trend in volatility over the historical time period, the computed VaR will underestimate (overestimate) the actual VaR, because all historical time series data points are equally weighted. This last weakness could be alleviated by putting more weight on the more recent data points.

11.5.3 Monte Carlo Simulation Method

The Monte Carlo simulation method of computing the VaR is similar to the historical simulation method in many respects. However, it is different from the historical simulation method in one main aspect. Rather than using the historical time series data of market factors to compute the value of the portfolio, the Monte Carlo simulation method uses values of the market factors simulated from presumed statistical distributions. The most commonly assumed distribution is a multivariate normal distribution. Pseudo-random number generators are used to generate tens of thousands of hypothetical values of market factors, and hypothetical changes in the value of the portfolio are computed. These tens of thousands values of the changes are compiled into a distribution. The 5 percentile value from the bottom of the array is the VaR with a 95 percent confidence interval.

The Monte Carlo simulation method is most flexible and powerful. This method can incorporate nonlinearities in the portfolio's value with respect to the underlying market factors and can incorporate other irregularities in the data, such as fat tails and nonstationarity of the parameters. However, if the number of underlying market factors increases and the structure of their comovements becomes more complicated, then the Monte Carlo simulation method becomes more difficult to run and could produce erroneous VaR estimates.

Which Method Should Be Chosen?   Which one of the three methods of calculating VaR is the best? Each method has its advantages and disadvantages. The answer depends on their ability to assess the risks of the target assets (especially complex portfolios containing many derivatives), ease of implementation, flexibility in analyzing the effect of the changes in the assumptions, and so on. Risk managers should choose the method of calculating VaR by considering which dimension they find most important.

11.6   ESTIMATION OF VOLATILITIES

In the VaR measurements, the most important input variables are the volatility (or the standard deviation) and correlation, because measures of VaR depend on the quality of the volatility input. Financial volatility may not be directly observable, and volatility should be estimated using a certain known price process. In this section, we introduce several methods of estimating volatilities. Because financial time series show that volatility seems to cluster in a predictable fashion, volatility estimation methods tend to be designed to capture the time-varying phenomenon of volatility. This volatility clustering means that after periods of persistent high volatility, periods of persistent low volatility follow, and vice versa. The predictability of volatility has important implications in risk management, because risk managers are interested in forecasting these potential losses.

Before proceeding to the introduction of the volatility-measuring methods, one noteworthy fact is that the correct calculation of covariances between asset returns is also important in measuring portfolio VaRs. Unfortunately, not as much research has been done to find the best method for calculating covariances as for calculating volatilities.

11.6.1   Unconditional Variance

The unconditional variance is estimated by assuming that the financial time series is stationary, and its variance is constant. Thus, the unconditional variance of returns is estimated as

$$\sigma^2 = \frac{1}{T} \sum_{t=1}^{T} \left(r_t - \bar{r} \right)^2 \qquad (11.37)$$

where r_t is the rate of return at time t, and $\bar{r}$ is the sample mean. This variance estimate is used for a volatility forecast for the next day. This method will be valid when returns are identically and independently distributed (*iid*). Because low- frequency data such as monthly or quarterly returns somewhat satisfy the *iid* condition, the unconditional variance estimate could be used to estimate the VaR for the next month or quarter.

11.6.2   Simple Moving Average

This method is simple and widely used. The volatility is estimated by rolling over an estimation window of fixed length and taking the average of squared returns over the estimation window. That is,

$$\sigma_t^2 = \frac{1}{M} \sum_{j=1}^{M} r_{t-j}^2 \qquad (11.38)$$

where M is the length of the estimation window. This method produces a one-period-ahead volatility estimate, because the volatility at time t is estimated using the return observations available up to time $t - 1$. By rolling over the estimation window day by day, the volatility forecast is updated every day by adding a new observation and dropping the oldest observation from the estimation window. Because the implicit assumption of this method is that the mean is zero (or very close to zero), this method can be valid for high-frequency data such as intraday returns or daily returns.

11.6.3 Exponentially Weighted Moving Average

The exponentially weighted moving average (EWMA) method became popular after RiskMetrics of J.P. Morgan used it successfully in introducing their analytical VaR methodology. Rather than assigning the uniform equal weight to each of the squared returns, as in the rolling moving average method, this method assigns more weight to the recent information and less weight to the past information. The volatility for day t is estimated through

$$\sigma_t^2 = \sum_{j=0}^{\infty} w_j r_{t-1-j}^2 \tag{11.39}$$

where $w_j = \lambda^j / \sum_{j=0}^{\infty} \lambda^j$, and λ is a parameter called the *decay factor* $(0 < \lambda < 1)$. This volatility estimate for day t is the weighted average of the squared returns available up to day $t - 1$. Equation (11.39) can be rewritten as

$$\sigma_t^2 = (1 - \lambda) \left[r_{t-1}^2 + \lambda r_{t-2}^2 + \lambda^2 r_{t-3}^2 + \cdots \right] \tag{11.40}$$

Thus, the weight of past observations decreases exponentially, and recent observations receive greater importance in forecasting the next-day volatility. The value of λ can be optimally determined according to a particular purpose. RiskMetrics used the value $\lambda = 0.94$ for daily financial time series data and went backward 75 data points in their estimation horizon.[8]
Equation (11.39) can also be rewritten as

$$\sigma_t^2 = \lambda \sigma_{t-1}^2 + (1 - \lambda) r_{t-1}^2 \tag{11.41}$$

The volatility forecast for day t is also obtained by the weighted average of the volatility for day $t - 1$ and the squared return of day $t - 1$ with the weight of λ. Equation (11.41) indicates that the RiskMetrics method is a special case of a GARCH model, called IGARCH (1,1). GARCH models are the topic of the next section.

11.6.4 GARCH-Based Volatility

One of the most widely-used approaches in modeling financial volatility is the autoregressive conditional heteroscedasticity (ARCH) or generalized ARCH (GARCH) model developed by Engel (1982) and Bollerslev (1986). These models are designed to capture time-varying volatility and volatility clustering. In GARCH models, the volatility of the current error term (or the return) is considered to be a function of the volatilities of the past error terms and the squared error terms.

The rate of return at time t with mean zero and variance σ_t^2 is denoted as

$$r_t = \sigma_t \varepsilon_t, \quad \text{where} \quad \varepsilon_t \sim N(0,1) \tag{11.42}$$

The volatility process is assumed as

$$\sigma_t^2 = a_0 + \sum_{j=1}^{p} a_j \sigma_{t-j}^2 + \sum_{j=1}^{q} b_j r_{t-j}^2 \tag{11.43}$$

This is the GARCH(p,q) model. In the GARCH(1,1) model, the volatility for day t is represented as

$$\sigma_t^2 = a_0 + a_1 \sigma_{t-1}^2 + b_1 r_{t-1}^2 \tag{11.44}$$

The RiskMetrics volatility estimate of equation (11.41) is a special case of the GARCH(1,1) with the restriction of $a_1 + b_1 = 1$ and $a_0 = 0$.[9] As seen in equation (11.43), the GARCH models are appropriate in the circumstance that squared returns are autocorrelated. Although some financial time series data are weakly autocorrelated, the squared time series data tend to show a strong autocorrelation. This situation causes a phenomenon called *volatility clustering*. GARCH-type models are popular in modeling volatility of financial time series.

Although the common assumption of the distributional form of the return or the error term is a normal distribution, the other distributions such as the Student's-t distribution, a mixture of normals, or a lognormal distribution can be assumed to capture fat tails. Many variants of the preceding standard GARCH model have been suggested. Some of the GARCH-type models tend to fit a particular financial time series better.[10]

11.6.5 Volatility Measures Using Price Range

The price range is the difference between the high and low prices. Many studies use the price range information to improve volatility estimation. There are many versions for estimating volatility using the price range. This section introduces the price range-based volatility estimators.[11]

Assuming the asset price follows a continuous random walk with constant diffusion, Parkinson (1980) suggested a range-based estimator for volatility. We define

$$D_t = \ln H_t - \ln L_t, \tag{11.45}$$

where H_t and L_t are the highest and lowest prices observed duing day t, respectively. Alizadeh, Brandt, and Diebold (2002) and Brandt and Diebold (2006) point out that the log price range of equation (11.45) is superior as a volatility proxy to log absolute or squared returns for two reasons. First, the log range-based estimate appears more robust to microstructure noise such as the bid-ask bounce. Second, the log range is very well approximated as a normal variate; $D_t \sim N(0.43 + \ln \sigma_t, 0.29^2)$. For instance, Parkinson (1980) shows that the expected value of the squared range is

$$E(D_t^2) = 4\,\sigma^2 \ln 2$$

The range-based estimate of unconditional variance is, therefore,

$$\sigma^2 = \frac{1}{4\ln 2}\frac{1}{T}\sum_{t=1}^{T} D_t^2 \tag{11.46}$$

Equation (11.46) suggests that the Parkinson daily volatility estimator is

$$\sigma_{t,P}^2 = \frac{1}{4\ln 2} D_t^2 \tag{11.47}$$

The daily variance estimate σ_t^2 can be used as the volatility forecast for the next day, $t+1$.

The Parkinson estimator for daily volatility of equation (11.47) uses two data points, the highest and lowest price during the day. In addition to these two data points, Garman and Klass (1980) use two additional data points for their volatility estimator: the opening and closing prices. By assuming a diffusion process with zero drift for stock price, they suggest several volatility methods. Among these, the best analytic scale-invariant volatility estimator is

$$\sigma_{t,GK}^2 = 0.511\left(u_t - d_t\right)^2 - 0.019\left[c_t\left(u_t + d_t\right) - 2u_t d_t\right] - 0.383 c_t^2 \tag{11.48}$$

where

$$u_t = \ln H_t - \ln O_t, \quad d_t = \ln L_t - \ln O_t, \quad c_t = \ln C_t - \ln O_t \tag{11.49}$$

H_t is the highest price during day t, L_t is the lowest price during day t, O_t is the opening price on day t, and C_t is the closing price on day t.

Rogers and Satchell (1991) also suggest a volatility estimator using price ranges by allowing nonzero drift in the diffusion process for stock price. Their estimator is

$$\sigma_{t,RS}^2 = u_t\left(u_t - c_t\right) + d_t\left(d_t - c_t\right) \tag{11.50}$$

The Parkinson estimator $(\sigma_{t,P}^2)$ of equation (11.47), the Garman and Klass estimator $(\sigma_{t,GK}^2)$ of equation (11.48), and the Rogers and Satchell estimator $(\sigma_{t,RS}^2)$ of equation (11.50) are obtained by using price information (highest, lowest, opening, closing prices) for the single day t. These estimators can be used for the volatility forecast for the next day $t+1$, $\hat{\sigma}_{t+1}^2$. Of course, the volatility forecast for the next day $t+1$, $\hat{\sigma}_{t+1}^2$, can also be obtained by taking the average of these past n volatility estimates. For example, the volatility forecast by the Rogers and Satchell estimator is

$$\hat{\sigma}_{t+1,RS}^2 = \frac{1}{n}\sum_{j=t-(n-1)}^{t} \sigma_{j,RS}^2 \tag{11.51}$$

The volatility forecast by the Parkinson and Garman and Klass estimators are similarly defined.

Yang and Zhang (2000) devise an estimator that combines the classical estimator and the Rogers-Satchell estimator. They show that their estimator is unbiased and independent of the drift term. Their volatility forecast for the next day $t + 1$ is

$$\sigma^2_{t+1,YZ} = \sigma^2_{t+1,o} + k\sigma^2_{t+1,c} + (1 - k)\sigma^2_{t+1,RS} \tag{11.52}$$

where

$$\sigma^2_{t+1,o} = \frac{1}{(n-1)} \sum_{j=t-(n-1)}^{t} (o_j - \bar{o})^2, \quad \sigma^2_{t+1,c} = \frac{1}{(n-1)} \sum_{j=t-(n-1)}^{t} (c_j - \bar{c})^2,$$

$$o_j = \ln O_j - \ln C_{j-1}, \quad c_j = \ln C_j - \ln O_j, \quad \bar{o} = \frac{1}{n} \sum_{j=t-(n-1)}^{t} o_j, \quad \bar{c} = \frac{1}{n} \sum_{j=t-(n-1)}^{t} c_j$$

and k is a constant. Yang and Zhang (2000) suggest setting the value of k as

$$k = 0.34 / \left[1 + \frac{n+1}{n-1}\right].$$

11.6.6 Implied Volatility

The volatility measures discussed so far are based on historical data. However, historical data may not be enough to provide the best volatility forecast of future risks, because it contains only past information. In contrast, option trading data contains forward-looking information. Thus, the implied volatility obtained from option trading data may have important information for future risks that historical data lacks.

By setting the price of an option pricing model equal to the market price of an existing option, that option's volatility parameter can be backed out of the pricing model. More specifically, the model price of a European call option at time t, C_t, from the Black-Scholes option pricing formula is

$$C_t = S_t N(d_1) - Ke^{-rT} N(d_1) \tag{11.53}$$

where S_t is the underlying asset price, K is the strike price, r is the continuously compounded risk-free rate of return, T is the time to maturity of the option in years, $N(d_1)$ is the cumulative standard normal distribution function, and

$$d_1 = \frac{\ln(S_t/K) + (r + \sigma^2/2)T}{\sigma\sqrt{T}}, \quad d_2 = d_1 - \sigma\sqrt{T}$$

By replacing the model price C_t in equation (11.53) with the observed market price of an existing call option, we can solve this equation with respect to the volatility parameter σ by an iterative method, because the other variables, S_t, K, r, and T can be discovered unambiguously.[12] The value of σ backed out of equation (11.53) is called the *implied volatility*, because it is implied by the values of the other parameters and the Black-Scholes option pricing formula.

To measure marketwide implied volatilities using index options, the Chicago Board Options Exchange (CBOE) introduced the implied volatility index, known as VXO, in 1993. This volatility index was a measure of the implied market volatility computed from 30-day S&P 100 index at-the-money options. In 2003, the CBOE replaced this volatility measure by launching a newer volatility index known as VIX, also called a *fear index* in the media. The new VIX is computed from S&P500 index call and put options over a wide range of strike prices and provides estimates of the implied volatility of the S&P 500 index over the next 30 days. VIX is independent of any model and no longer relies on the Black-Scholes model. After the exceptionally successful example of CBOE, other exchanges across the world developed their own respective volatility indexes.[13]

There are advantages of using the implied volatility. First, the implied volatility may convey forward-looking information about the underlying asset. Second, as long as the traded price of the underlying asset is available, the implied volatility can be computed. Thus, high-frequency implied volatilities can be obtained any time the market is open. There are also disadvantages. First, an implied volatility estimate depends on the choice of the option pricing model. Thus, if the option pricing model is incorrectly specified, the computed implied volatility would provide misleading assessments of future risks. If markets are efficient and the option pricing model is correctly specified, implied volatilities computed from options on the same underlying asset with the same expiration date should be identical, even with different strike prices. However, empirical studies show that the implied volatility computed from the Black-Scholes option pricing model exhibits a peculiar pattern across strike prices (known as a *volatility smile*). Second, implied volatilities obtained from deep-in-the-money or deep-out-of-the-money options tend to be higher than those obtained from at-the-money options on the same underlying asset. Third, if there is no closed-form solution for an option, it would be difficult to obtain the implied volatility. To overcome this disadvantage, however, several model-free methods have been suggested.[14] Fourth, there are measurement problems in implied volatilities. The measurement problems are mainly caused by nonsynchronous trading. More specifically, the timing of the closing prices of the option and the underlying asset may differ. For example, for infrequently traded options, the last trade of the option may occur prior to the last trade of the day. Transaction costs are another source of the measurement errors. Fifth, if there are no actively traded options on the asset, it is not possible to estimate its implied volatility.

There has been a debate about the predictive power of the historical volatility and the implied volatility for future volatility.[15] Early studies generally showed that the historical volatility provides a better forecast for future volatility than the implied volatility.[16] In contrast, recent studies report evidence that the implied volatility is more informationally efficient in forecasting future volatility than the historical volatility.[17] Because the comparison results could be sensitive to the research setting such as the choice of options, the choice of the option pricing model, the frequency of market data, and the sample period, this issue is still being debated.

11.7 THE ACCURACY OF VAR MODELS

Before implementing a VaR model to predict risk, risk managers should first consider the following key parameters: the distribution of returns (for parametric methods), the method of measuring VaR, the method of measuring volatility, the model of volatility, and so on. There are also many smaller parameters within each method.

For example, if a simple moving average method is chosen to estimate volatility, there are many choices for the length of the estimation window. In other words, there are too many assumptions about the input parameters. Various VaR models can be constructed from a combination of these parameters. Risk managers can construct a particular VaR model for an asset or a whole institution by determining the parameters and implement that VaR model to manage risk. To ensure successful risk management, risk managers should regularly check if the VaR model being used is performing properly—a process called *model validation*. Moreover, there is now growing pressure from regulators, investors, creditors, senior management, and credit rating agencies to provide information regarding the accuracy of the VaR models being used. Model validation can be carried out with widely used tools such as backtesting and stress testing. In this section, we introduce these model validation tools to assess the accuracy and performance of one or more VaR models.

11.7.1 Back-Testing

Standard back-tests of a VaR model compare the observed portfolio loss for a given horizon with the expected loss obtained from the VaR model. In a simple back-test, the number or percentage of times that the actual portfolio returns fall outside the VaR number is compared with the confidence level used. For instance, if a portfolio has a daily VaR of $1 million at the 99 percent confidence level, this means that the portfolio has a 1 percent chance of experiencing a loss of at least $1 million over a single-day horizon under normal market conditions. Over 250 days (approximately one year of trading days), we would expect to see (1% of 250 days equals) 2.5 exceptional days when the portfolio's loss exceeds the VaR number of $1 million. If we observe more (less) than 2.5 days out of 250 days that the actual loss exceeds $1 million, the VaR number tends to be underestimated (overestimated). Thus, the VaR model needs to be revised.[18]

In a statistical sense, 2.5 days are the average of the exceptional days in many 250-day experiments. Because the backtest is a statistical technique, it is subject to estimation error. Therefore, we need a statistical test to determine how many exceptional days are sufficient to reject the validity of the VaR number (the null hypothesis). Kupiec (1995) suggested a test to determine if the observed frequency of exceptional days is consistent with the frequency of the expected exceptional days. The number of exceptions x follows a binomial probability distribution with mean of αT (α is the significance level, $\alpha = 0.01$; T is the number of trading days over the testing horizon, $T = 250$) and variance of $\alpha (1 - \alpha) T$. When T is large, from the central limit theorem,

$$z = \frac{x - \alpha T}{\sqrt{\alpha (1 - \alpha) T}} \approx N(0, 1) \tag{11.54}$$

If the standard normal variate z falls within a certain confidence interval (say, 95%), then we do not reject the null hypothesis (the validity of the VaR number). In the 1996 Basel rules allowing a 5 percent Type I error, up to four exceptions are acceptable for the VaR over a 250-day horizon at the 99 percent confidence level.

A more sophisticated way of backtesting is to examine both the frequency and the size of expected losses. This can provide an indication of how well the model captures the frequency of exceptions as well as the size of the expected loss beyond the VaR number. The size of the expected loss is known as the expected tail loss (ETL).[19]

11.7.2 Stress Testing

VaR numbers indicate the expected potential losses under normal market conditions. If some extreme event such as the Asian financial crisis in 1997, the Long-Term Capital Management (LTCM) affair of 1998, or the subprime mortgage crisis of 2006–2013 occurs, the actual losses can be far beyond the VaR number, and risk management tools based on the VaR will break down.[20] To overcome the limitations of the VaR approaches, the Basel Committee requires firms to perform stress testing to complement the results of their VaR analyses. The purpose of stress tests is to determine the losses that might occur under unlikely but plausible circumstances and to provide useful information about a firm's risk exposure that VaR methods can easily miss because VaR models focus on normal market risks rather than the risks associated with rare or extreme events. Whereas the VaR is a probabilistic measure, stress testing is a nonstatistical risk measure and the loss estimate cannot be associated with a theoretically derived probability.

Essentially, stress testing is a scenario analysis used to investigate the effects of extreme market conditions. Scenarios do not have probabilities attached to them. Typically, scenario analyses begin with a set of hypothetical large movements in key variables, such as 5 to 10 standard deviation moves in market factors. After determining a set of scenarios, the next step is to determine the changes in the prices of all component instruments in the portfolio and the impact on the value of the portfolio. The final step is to prepare some contingency plans for certain scenarios. In reality, there is no standard way to conduct stress testing and no common criteria to set up scenarios. Scenario analysis techniques vary widely across firms and risk managers.[21] A common stress-testing procedure is to allow one or a few key market factors to move by an exceptionally large amount while the other market factors move in their usual way. In other words, the procedure is to shock a key market factor and then examine the predicted impact on the value of the modeled portfolio.[22]

Stress tests can be problematic. The most obvious problem is subjectivity. Because stress tests depend on scenarios contrived by the stress tester, the value of stress testing depends critically on the choice of scenarios, and this makes it difficult to assess the results of a stress test objectively. Another problem is that the results of stress tests are difficult to interpret because they give us no idea of the probabilities of the events concerned. Suppose a risk manager has the results of stress testing obtained under an extremely unlikely scenario. What kind of action should be taken to deal with this information? The results may be almost irrelevant, because the risk manager would not be able to take expensive precautionary measures against events that may be too improbable to worry about. In fact, if we have two sets of separate risk estimates—probabilistic estimates such as VaR, and the loss estimates produced by stress tests—it will be difficult to combine them. Therefore, it would be better to work with these estimates somewhat independently of each other, and use one estimate to check for prospective losses that the other estimation procedure missed. There is also the problem that it is difficult to check the accuracy of stress-test procedures. In other words, they are difficult to backtest. The common stress testing procedure that gives a shock to a key market factor also has the problem that it ignores the correlations between the stressed prices and the other prices that may change during a stress.

11.8   SUMMARY AND CONCLUSIONS

As the volatility of financial markets has substantially increased in recent years, financial institutions have become more vulnerable to the shocks caused by this volatility than in previous years. Accordingly, practitioners, researchers, and regulators have begun to design and develop more sophisticated risk management tools. VaR has become the standard measure used to quantify financial risk. This chapter presented the methods of computing VaR, the implication of a certain value of VaR, and the real applications of VaR. This chapter also presented various methods of measuring volatility.

APPENDIX: THE DELTA-GAMMA METHOD

The delta-normal method is valid when the change of the market factor or the underlying variable is very small. However, when its change is relatively large, it could produce a significant amount of error. In order to improve the quality of the linear approximation, it is necessary to add an additional term in the Taylor series expansion of the valuation function.

If the portfolio is a single position, then

$$dV = \left(\frac{\partial V}{\partial f}\right) df + \frac{1}{2}\left(\frac{\partial^2 V}{\partial f^2}\right)(df)^2 + \cdots \tag{A11.1}$$

or

$$dV = \Delta\, df + \frac{1}{2}\Gamma(df)^2 + \cdots \tag{A11.2}$$

where $\Delta = \partial V/\partial f$ and $\Gamma = \partial^2 V/\partial f^2$. If the value of a single position depends on K market factors, the change in the value of the position is represented by the Taylor series expansion as

$$dV = \Delta'\,(df) + \frac{1}{2}(df)'\,\Gamma\,(df) \tag{A11.3}$$

where $\Delta' = \left(\frac{\partial V}{\partial f_1}, \frac{\partial V}{\partial f_2}, \ldots, \frac{\partial V}{\partial f_K}\right)$ is a $(K \times 1)$ vector of deltas, $df = (df_1, df_2, \ldots, df_K)$ is a $(K \times 1)$ vector of the changes in the K market factors, and Γ is a $(K \times K)$ symmetric matrix of gammas; $\Gamma = \{\Gamma_{i,j}\}_{i,j=1,\ldots,K}$, in which $\Gamma_{i,j} = \partial^2 V/\partial f_i \partial f_j$.

By dropping the third-order and higher terms in the Taylor series expansion, we can rewrite equation (A11.2) as

$$dV = \Delta f\left(\frac{df}{f}\right) + \frac{1}{2}\Gamma f^2\left(\frac{df}{f}\right)^2 \tag{A11.4}$$

or

$$dV = \Delta fr + \frac{1}{2}\Gamma f^2 r^2 \tag{A11.5}$$

where $r = df/f$ is the rate of return on the market factor. If the rate of return, r, is normally distributed with mean of zero and variance σ^2, its odd-numbered moments will all be zero. Thus, the variance of dV is

$$\text{Var}\,(dV) = \Delta^2 f^2 \sigma^2 + \frac{1}{2}\Gamma^2 f^4 \sigma^4 \qquad (A11.6)$$

Note that $E\left(r^4\right) = 3\sigma^4$, $\text{Var}\left(r^2\right) = 2\sigma^4$, and $\text{Cov}\left(r, r^2\right) = 0$. Then, the dollar VaR is

$$\text{VaR} = z_\alpha \left(\Delta^2 f^2 \sigma^2 + \frac{1}{2}\Gamma^2 f^4 \sigma^4 \right)^{1/2} \qquad (A11.7)$$

and the return VaR is

$$\text{VaR} = z_\alpha \left[\left(\frac{\Delta}{V} \right)^2 f^2 \sigma^2 + \frac{1}{2}\left(\frac{\Gamma}{V} \right)^2 f^4 \sigma^4 \right]^{1/2} \qquad (A11.8)$$

If the portfolio consists of N positions or assets, assuming that the value of each position depends on only one corresponding market factor, then

$$
\begin{aligned}
dV &= \sum_{i=1}^{N} \left[\Delta_i\, df_i + \frac{1}{2}\Gamma_i (df_i)^2 \right] \\
&= \sum_{i=1}^{N} \left[\Delta_i f_i \left(\frac{df_i}{f_i} \right) + \frac{1}{2}\Gamma_i f_i^2 \left(\frac{df_i}{f_i} \right)^2 \right] \\
&= \sum_{i=1}^{N} \left[\Delta_i f_i r_i + \frac{1}{2}\Gamma_i f_i^2 r_i^2 \right] \qquad (A11.9)
\end{aligned}
$$

where $r_i = df_i/f_i$ is the rate of return on the i-th position, which is assumed to be normally distributed with mean of zero and variance σ_i^2. For simplicity, we rewrite equation (A11.9) as

$$dV = \sum_{i=1}^{N} \left[q_i r_i + Q_i r_i^2 \right] \qquad (A11.10)$$

where $q_i = \Delta_i f_i$ and $Q_i = \frac{1}{2}\Gamma_i f_i^2$. Then, the variance of dV is

$$
\begin{aligned}
\text{Var}\,(dV) &= \text{Var}\left(\sum_{i=1}^{N} q_i r_i \right) + \text{Var}\left(\sum_{i=1}^{N} Q_i r_i^2 \right) \\
&= q'\Sigma q + Q'\Omega Q \qquad (A11.11)
\end{aligned}
$$

where $q' = (q_1, q_2, \dots, q_N)$, $Q' = (Q_1, Q_2, \dots, Q_N)$, and Ω is the $(N \times N)$ variance-covariance matrix of r_i^2; that is, $\Omega = \{2\sigma_{ij}^2\}_{i,j=1,\dots,N}$. Note that $\text{Cov}\left(r_i^2, r_j^2\right) = 2\sigma_{ij}^2$. The dollar VaR is

$$\text{VaR} = z_\alpha \left(q'\Sigma q + Q'\Omega Q \right)^{1/2} \qquad (A11.12)$$

The percentage change in the value of the portfolio is, from equation (A11.10),

$$\frac{dV}{V} = \sum_{i=1}^{N} \left[q_i^* r_i + Q_i^* r_i^2 \right] \tag{A11.13}$$

where

$$q_i^* = \left(\frac{\Delta_i}{V} \right) f_i = \left(\frac{\Delta_i}{V_i} \right) w_i f_i, \qquad Q_i^* = \frac{1}{2} \left(\frac{\Gamma_i}{V_i} \right) w_i f_i^2, \qquad w_i = \frac{V_i}{V}$$

Note that if position i is a fixed income security, (Δ_i / V_i) indicates the duration and (Γ_i / V_i) measures convexity. Then, the variance of the portfolio return is

$$\operatorname{Var}\left(\frac{dV}{V} \right) = q^{*'} \Sigma q^* + Q^{*'} \Omega Q^* \tag{A11.14}$$

where $q^{*'} = (q_1^*, q_2^*, \ldots, q_N^*)$, $Q' = (Q_1^*, Q_2^*, \ldots, Q_N^*)$. So, the return VaR is

$$\text{VaR} = z_\alpha \left(q^{*'} \Sigma q^* + Q^{*'} \Omega Q^* \right)^{1/2} \tag{A11.15}$$

NOTES

1. The Basel II accord uses three pillars: (1) minimum capital requirement (to address risk), (2) supervisory review process, and (3) market discipline requirements. The first pillar deals with maintenance of regulatory capital calculated for three major components of risk that a financial institution will face: credit risk, operational risk, and market risk.
2. See Stoyanov, Rachev, Racheva-Yotova, and Fabozzi (2011) for fat-tailed models for risk estimation.
3. For desirable properties of CVaR, see Rockafellar and Uryasev (2000) and Pflug (2000).
4. For CVaR for the case of non-normality, see Huang, Zhu, Fabozzi, and Fukushima (2010) and Xiong and Idzorek (2011).
5. Parametric approaches assume a distribution of the target variable, and thus, parameters of the distribution are involved.
6. If this is the position in a call option (C), then the market factor is the underlying stock price (S), and $\Delta = \partial C / \partial S$ is the call option's delta.
7. The spot exchange rate is calculated from the spot-forward parity; that is, forward exchange rate = (spot exchange rate) $\times E^{(0.03-0.05) \times \left(\frac{6}{12} \right)}$.
8. RiskMetrics Group, *RiskMetrics—Technical Documents* (New York: J.P. Morgan, 1996).
9. The GARCH with the restriction of $\Sigma_{j=1}^{p} a_j + \Sigma_{j=1}^{q} b_j = 1$ is called the integrated GARCH, IGARCH(p,q).
10. For comparison among various GARCH-type models, see Kim and Kon (1994) and Hentschel (1995). Also, see Poon and Granger (2003) for a literature review for various GARCH models.
11. See Brownlees and Gallo (2010) for comparison of volatility measures.
12. For the case of an at-the-money call option, Brenner and Subrahmanyam (1988) derived an approximation to the implied volatility $\sigma \sqrt{t} \approx \sqrt{2\sigma} (C_t / S_t)$ for $S_t = K e^{-rT}$. Corrado and Miller (1996) derived a more general formula for the implied volatility.

13. Siriopoulos and Fassas (2009) present a list of volatility indexes across the world.
14. For model-free estimation of implied volatilities, see Dupire (1994), Neuberger (1994), Carr and Madan (1998), Demeterfi, Derman, Kamal, and Zou (1999a, 1999b), Britten-Jones and Neuberger (2000), and Jiang and Tian (2005).
15. See Poon and Granger (2003) for a literature review of historical volatility and implied volatility.
16. See Day and Lewis (1992), Lamoureux and Lastrapes (1993), and Canina and Figlewski (1993).
17. See Day and Lewis (1993), Christensen and Prabhala (1998), and Szakmary, Ors, Kim, and Davidson (2003).
18. Berkowitz and O'Brien (2002) examined the accuracy and the performance of the VaR models of six large U.S. commercial banks.
19. See Jorion (2007, p.131) for the computation of the ETL.
20. Yet another newspaper columnist has been predicting the end of the sub-prime mortgage crisis nearly every month since 2008. None of these forecast has been valid and, in truth, progress is small.
21. Kupiec (1998) attempts to formalize the stress-testing procedure.
22. This stress-testing procedure is somewhat similar to the sensitivity analysis that allows a variable to move but the other variables to remain fixed.

Asset Pricing Models

CHAPTER 12

The Capital Asset Pricing Model

After Markowitz developed the two-parameter portfolio analysis model, researchers began investigating the stock market implications that would occur if all investors used the Markowitz two-parameter model to make their investment decisions.[1] As a result of these investigations, what is referred to as the capital asset pricing model (CAPM) was developed. The CAPM is also called the security market line (SML). This Nobel prize–winning theory is not the only theory that could be called a capital market theory, but for the purposes of this chapter we will refer to it as such. A similar but different capital market theory that takes place in continuous time will be presented in Chapter 15.

12.1   UNDERLYING ASSUMPTIONS

Capital market theory is based on the assumptions underlying portfolio analysis, because the theory is essentially an accumulation of the logical implications of portfolio analysis. The initial portfolio theory assumptions are:

1. Investors in capital assets (defined as all terminal-wealth-producing assets) are risk-averse one-period expected-utility-of-terminal-wealth maximizers. Equivalently, investors are risk averse and maximize their expected utility of returns over a one-period planning horizon.
2. Investors find it possible to make their portfolio decisions solely on the basis of the mean and standard deviation of the terminal wealth (or, equivalently, rates of return) associated with the alternative portfolios.
3. The mean and standard deviation of terminal wealth (or, equivalently, rates of return) associated with these portfolios are finite numbers that exist and can be estimated or measured.
4. There are a collection of assumptions that underlie most economic theories. All capital assets are infinitely divisible, meaning that fractions of shares can be bought or sold. Investors are assumed to be price takers (instead of price setters). Finally, taxes and transactions costs are assumed to be nonexistent.

Investors who conform to the preceding assumptions will prefer Markowitz-efficient portfolios over inefficient portfolios. Bearing these investors in mind, it is possible to begin to discuss capital market theory. A fairly exhaustive list of the additional assumptions necessary to generate the theory follows.

5. There is a single risk-free interest rate at which all borrowing and lending takes place.
6. All assets, including human capital, are marketable.
7. Capital markets are perfect, meaning that (a) all information is freely and instantly available to everyone (transparency prevails), (b) no margin requirements exist, and (c) investors have unlimited opportunities to borrow, lend, or sell assets short.
8. Investors all have *homogeneous expectations* over the same one-period investment horizon, and they all have the same perceptions regarding each security's *ex ante* expected return, variance, and covariance during the universal planning horizon. These uniform perceptions are sometimes called *idealized uncertainty*.

The reader who is unaccustomed to economic analysis is probably confused and discouraged by a theory that begins with a list of unrealistic assumptions. Such should not be the case. These assumptions are necessary only to get started and will be relaxed in the next chapter. The assumptions provide a concrete foundation upon which a theory can be derived by applying the forces of logic, intuition, and mathematics. Without these assumptions, the analysis would degenerate into a polemic discussion. Discussions of which historical facts, what folklore, and which institutions were significant, what their relationships were, and what conclusions might be reached by a "reasonable man" are not very productive. Such thinking usually gets bogged down.

Traditionally, economists base their analysis on assumptions that are as few and as simple as possible. Then a theory is derived with conclusions and implications that are incontestable, given the assumptions. Subsequently, the assumptions are relaxed one at a time in order to determine what can be expected in more realistic circumstances.

12.2   THE CAPITAL MARKET LINE

The capital asset pricing model (CAPM) is based on a concept known as the capital market line (CML), illustrated in Figure 12.1.[2] Two important features of the CML are the market portfolio and separation, which are discussed next.

12.2.1   The Market Portfolio

Imagine a capital market in equilibrium. In this equilibrium all investors' optimal portfolio choices have been aggregated into one huge *market portfolio*, denoted m, and, supply equals demand for every asset. After aggregating all investors' optimal portfolio choices, the market portfolio must contain every marketable asset in the proportion w_i, where

$$w_i = \frac{\text{total market value of asset } i}{\text{total market value of all assets in the market}}$$

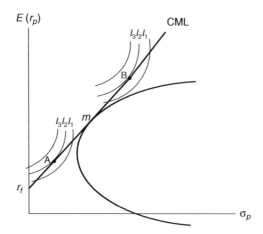

FIGURE 12.1 Risk-return Indifference Curves and the CML

The reason all marketable assets must be contained in m is that if some asset were not included in m, no one would own that asset and, as a result, the market would not be completely clear.[3] In this equilibrium, r_f must be the interest rate that equates the supply and demand for loanable funds.

The *market portfolio* is a unanimously desirable risky portfolio containing all risky securities in the proportions in which they are supplied in equilibrium. Accordingly, the return on the market portfolio is the weighted average of the returns of all securities in the market. Unfortunately, the market portfolio cannot actually be observed—because it does not really exist. In theory, the market portfolio contains all assets—that is, commodities, art objects, stocks, bonds, real estate, and so on. Thus, commonly used stock market indexes (like the S&P 500 index) are imperfect substitutes for the theoretical market portfolio. We could try to create a closed system by arbitrarily restricting capital market theory to, for example, the New York Stock Exchange (NYSE) listed common stocks. In this hypothetical case the market portfolio would be completely observable. But there is no apparent logic for making such a large restriction because most investors would be better off to expand their set of candidate assets to include non-NYSE securities. After pondering the difference between the (countably infinite) theoretical market portfolio and its commonly observed (relatively tiny) surrogates, it becomes apparent that the divergence is considerable.

12.2.2   The Separation Theorem

Assumptions 5, 6, and 7 imply that all investors face the linear efficient frontier called the CML in Figure 12.1. Homogeneous expectations (assumption 8) ensure that all investors will envision efficient frontiers identically. However, because they have different utility functions, they will have different preferences that lead them to select different portfolios from the efficient frontier. These portfolios will involve a long or short position in the risk-free asset (that is, either borrowing or lending at r_f). Thus, all investors are concerned with just m, the market portfolio, and the riskless interest rate, r_f. This observation is the basis for the *two-fund theorem*, which is also referred to as the *separation theorem.*

The separation theorem is based on the previous eight assumptions. It states that if we let $n + 1$ denote the total number of securities in existence (the last of which is the risk-free security), there exists a pair of efficient portfolios that are independent of investors' preferences, and all investors will be indifferent between choosing their personal optimal portfolios from among the original $n + 1$ securities or from the two efficient portfolios.[4] One of these portfolios contains only the riskless security, and the other portfolio contains the n risky assets.[5]

The separation theorem implies that all investors, whether timid or aggressive, should hold the same mix of risky securities in their optimum portfolio. Then, after they select their optimal portfolio, they should use borrowing or lending at the risk-free interest rate r_f to attain their preferred risk class. This conclusion differs substantially from the ever-popular financial interior decorator concept of portfolio management, which asserts that the portfolio manager should skillfully design a portfolio to match the client's personality. According to the interior decorating idea, a timid investor's portfolio would contain a completely different set of securities from an aggressive investor's portfolio. In contrast, the separation theorem suggests that both investors should both own portfolio m and differ only in the way they finance it.

Another way to view the separation theorem is to imagine that the optimal *investment decision*, which is to buy the market portfolio, is the decision made first. Next, the investor must decide how to finance his/her decision to purchase m. The *finance decision* is to determine whether to lend or borrow at the risk-free interest rate r_f. Note that the investment decision could be made days before the finance decision is completed and the purchase is consummated; this time difference highlights the *separation* between the finance and investment decisions.

12.2.3   Efficient Frontier Equation

Assuming homogeneous expectations, the eighth assumption, guarantees that all investors face the same efficient frontier and that efficient frontier consists of linear combinations of r_f and m. This linear efficient frontier is referred to as the capital market line (CML). The equation for the CML can be derived quite simply, because the vertical intercept is r_f and the slope can be derived by dividing the vertical distance between m and r_f by the horizontal distance between m and r_f. Thus, the CML equation is

$$E\left(r_p\right) = r_f + \left[\frac{E\left(r_m\right) - r_f}{\sigma_m}\right]\sigma_p \tag{12.1}$$

where $E\left(r_p\right)$ and σ_p denote the expected return and standard derivation of any efficient portfolio p.

12.2.4   Portfolio Selection

Figure 12.1 graphically depicts the CML: It is the dominant efficient frontier facing investors. Each individual investor will select their personal optimal portfolio from the CML by finding the tangency point between their indifference curves and the

CML. Two such optimal portfolios are shown in Figure 12.1 and are denoted *A* and *B*. Portfolio *A* represents a portfolio consisting of roughly 50 percent lending at the risk-free rate and a 50 percent long position in the market portfolio. Portfolio *B*, representing a more aggressive but still risk-averse investor, consists of borrowing at the risk-free rate an amount equal to about 50 percent of the investor's own funds and investing these borrowed funds, plus the investor's own initial equity funds, in the market portfolio.

12.3   THE CAPITAL ASSET PRICING MODEL

The capital asset pricing model (CAPM) includes the preceding list of assumptions, numerous greedy investors who always prefer more to less, a risk-averse attitude that is shared in varying degrees by all investors, and the implications of the aforementioned items.

12.3.1   Background

Thus far in this chapter the analysis has determined that the expected return of an efficient portfolio is a linear function of its standard deviation of return. The implication this has for the determination of equilibrium rates of return for individual securities (or inefficient portfolios) is considered in this section.

Investors wanting to earn high average rates of return must take high risks and endure the associated loss of sleep, the possibility of ulcers, and the chance of bankruptcy. The question to which we now turn is: Should investors worry about total risk, undiversifiable risk, diversifiable risk, or all three?

Utility theory suggests that *investors should seek investments that have the maximum expected return in their risk class.* Happiness from investing is presumed to be derived from the expected utility function: $E(U) = f[\sigma, E(r)]$. The investment preferences of wealth-seeking, risk-averse investors represented by this function cause them to maximize their expected utility (or, equivalently, happiness) by (1) maximizing their expected return in any given risk class [because $\partial E(U)/\partial E(r) > 0$], or conversely, (2) minimizing their total risk at any given rate of expected return [because $\partial E(U)/\partial\sigma < 0$]. In selecting individual assets, it turns out that investors will not be particularly concerned with the asset's total risk, σ. Equation (8.3) in Chapter 8 shows the statistical partition of an asset's total risk into its systematic and unsystematic components. The unsystematic portion of total risk can be easily diversified away by holding a portfolio of different randomly selected securities.[6] Systematic risk is not so easy to eliminate. Systematic risk affects all stocks in the market and is undiversifiable. Therefore, portfolio theory suggests that only the undiversifiable (or systematic) risk is worth avoiding.[7]

In the search for individual assets that will minimize their portfolio's risk exposure at a given level of expected return, investors tend to focus on each asset's *undiversifiable (or systematic) risk.* They will bid up the prices of assets with low systematic risk (that is, low beta coefficients). In contrast, assets with high beta coefficients will experience low demand and market prices that are low relative to assets' income. Stated differently, assets with high (low) levels of systematic risk will tend to have high (low) expected returns. An asset with high (low) systematic risk should experience high (low) expected returns to induce investors to assume this undiversifiable risk. The equilibrium rate of return for zero systematic risk equals the risk-free interest rate. The CAPM is a relationship in which the expected rate of return of the i-th asset is a linear function of that asset's systematic risk as represented by β_i. Equation (12.2) summarizes many of the implications of the CAPM succinctly in a single equation.

$$E(r_i) = r_f + [E(r_m) - r_f]\beta_i \qquad (12.2)$$

where

β_i = the independent variable representing systematic risk of i-th asset, it determines the dependent variable

$E(r_i)$ = the expected rate of return for asset i, the dependent variable

r_f = the riskless rate of return,[8] and

$[E(r_f) - r_f]$ = the market risk premium.

Each *expected return* from the CAPM can be interpreted as the *risk-adjusted discount rate, cost of capital, equilibrium rate of return*, or *capitalization rate* that investors should expect to earn for bearing that amount of systematic risk.

Systematic or undiversifiable risk is the main factor risk-averse investors should consider in deciding whether a security yields enough rate of return to induce them to buy it. Other factors, such as diversifiable risk, the glamor of the stock, and the company's financial ratios, are important only to the extent they affect the security's risk and return. The CAPM graphically represents the trade-off of systematic risk for returns that investors expect and are entitled to receive. This implies that the CAPM is an *asset-pricing model*.

12.3.2 Derivation of the CAPM

This section presents a mathematical derivation of the CAPM by Sharpe (1964). Other derivation procedures by Lintner (1965a) and Huang and Litzenberger (1988) are presented in the end-of-chapter appendix.

Imagine a portfolio p that consists of a proportion w_i invested directly in an arbitrary asset i and a proportion $(1 - w_i)$ invested in the market portfolio m. Note that w_i represents excess demand for asset i, since the market portfolio already contains asset i in equilibrium. This portfolio will lie somewhere on the curve im', illustrated in Figure 12.2. The exact location of this portfolio depends on the magnitude of w_i. Because i is contained in m, p contains varying amounts of money invested in asset i at various points along the curve im'. Thus, the market portfolio excluding asset i, denoted m', must be on an extension of the curve im' past m. Furthermore, the curve im' must be tangent to the efficient frontier EF at point m, because m is just a linear combination of i and m'.

Portfolio p will have an expected return and standard deviation equal to

$$E(r_p) = w_i E(r_i) + (1 - w_i) E(r_m) \qquad (12.3)$$

and

$$\sigma_p = \left[w_i^2 \sigma_i^2 + (1 - w_i)^2 \sigma_m^2 + 2w_i (1 - w_i) \sigma_{im} \right]^{1/2} \qquad (12.4)$$

As w_i changes, $E(r_p)$ and σ_p will change as follows:

$$dE(r_p)/dw_i = E(r_i) - E(r_m) \qquad (12.5)$$

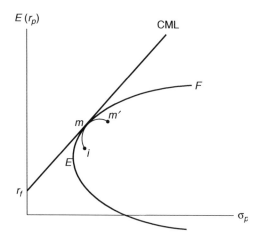

FIGURE 12.2 Opportunity Set for
Combinations of *i* and *m*

and

$$d\sigma_p/dw_i = \left[w_i\sigma_i^2 - (1-w_i)\,\sigma_m^2 + (1-2w_i)\,\sigma_{im} \right]/\sigma_p \qquad (12.6)$$

Now the change in $E\left(r_p\right)$ relative to a change in σ_p can be calculated by dividing equation (12.5) by equation (12.6) as shown next.

$$\frac{dE\left(r_p\right)}{d\sigma_p} = \frac{\left[E\left(r_i\right) - E\left(r_m\right)\right]\sigma_p}{w_i\sigma_i^2 - (1-w_i)\,\sigma_m^2 + (1-2w_i)\,\sigma_{im}} \qquad (12.7)$$

Equation (12.7) can be interpreted as the slope of the curve im'. In equilibrium, there is no excess demand for asset *i*. Thus, when $w_i = 0$ in equation (12.7) (implying that $\sigma_p = \sigma_m$), the slope of the curve equals

$$\left.\frac{dE\left(r_p\right)}{d\sigma_p}\right|_{w_i=0} = \frac{\left[E\left(r_i\right) - E\left(r_m\right)\right]\sigma_p}{\sigma_{im} - \sigma_m^2} \qquad (12.8)$$

Furthermore, the slope of the curve im' when $w_i = 0$ must be the same as the slope of the CML, because the CML is tangent to the efficient frontier EF at *m* and the efficient frontier EF is tangent to im' at *m*. From equation (12.1), the slope of the CML can be seen to be equal to $\left[E\left(r_m\right) - r_f\right]/\sigma_m$. Equating the slope of the CML to the slope of the curve im' at *m* results in

$$\frac{E\left(r_m\right) - r_f}{\sigma_m} = \frac{\left[E\left(r_i\right) - E\left(r_m\right)\right]\sigma_p}{\sigma_{im} - \sigma_m^2} \qquad (12.9)$$

or, after simplification,

$$E\left(r_i\right) = r_f + \left[\frac{E\left(r_m\right) - r_f}{\sigma_m^2}\right]\sigma_{im} \qquad (12.10)$$

Equation (12.10) is referred to as the capital asset pricing model (CAPM) or the security market line (SML). Equations (12.3) through (12.10) explain the theoretical derivation of this Nobel prize–winning asset pricing model.

The CAPM indicates that, in equilibrium, every asset will have an expected return that is linearly related to its covariance with the market portfolio. Furthermore, this relationship will be positive, because $\left[E\left(r_m\right) - r_f\right]/\sigma_m^2$ is positive. If an asset i has a covariance with m of zero, $\sigma_{im} = 0$, then it will have an expected return equal to r_f, even though it may have a nonzero standard deviation. Thus, the covariance of an asset's return with the market portfolio's return, not its variance of return, determines an asset's expected return and is therefore the relevant measure of the asset's risk.[9] Using the definition of the beta for asset i, $\beta_i = \sigma_{im}/\sigma_m^2$, the CAPM equation (8.10) can be equivalently rewritten as

$$E\left(r_i\right) = r_f + \left[E\left(r_m\right) - r_f\right]\beta_i \qquad (12.2)$$

In this form, the equilibrium relationship between risk and expected return involves β_i instead of σ_{im}. However, β_i and σ_{im} differ only by a factor of σ_m^2, and σ_m^2 is the same for all assets in the market. Thus, both β_i and σ_{im} are referred to as the systematic risk of asset i, because the only difference between the CAPM in equation (12.10) and the CAPM in equation (12.2) is in the units used to measure the same undiversifiable risk. Figure 12.3 depicts the CAPM or the security market line (SML). In the CAPM equation of (12.2), the riskless rate of return, r_f, indicates the intercept of the SML. The market risk premium, $\left[E\left(r_m\right) - r_f\right]$, measures the slope of the SML.

For the CAPM, note that the point where $\beta_i = 1$ is equivalent to $\sigma_{im} = \sigma_m^2$ and that any security with an expected return equal to $E\left(r_m\right)$ will have $\beta_i = 1$. Furthermore, any security with an expected return greater than $E\left(r_m\right)$ will have $\beta_i > 1$, and any security with an expected return less than $E\left(r_m\right)$ will have $\beta_i < 1$. Hence $\beta_i = 1$ provides a convenient partition of securities into what are referred to as defensive and aggressive securities. Those securities with $\beta_i < 1$ are called defensive securities and those securities with $\beta_i > 1$ are called aggressive securities.

Of interest in the derivation of both the CML and the CAPM is the observation that the ability to make unrestricted short sales (assumption 4) is not critical. If, for example, no short sales were allowed, then all investors would still face the

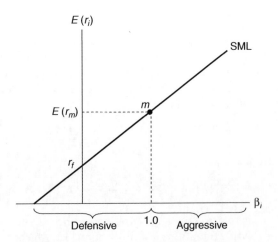

FIGURE 12.3 The Capital Asset Pricing Model (CAPM) or Security Market Line (SML)

same linear efficient frontier that originated at r_f and was tangent to the Markowitz efficient frontier, as illustrated on Figure 12.2. The separation theorem would still exist and the derivation of the CAPM would be exactly the same. Thus, the existence of a risk-free borrowing and lending rate, as long as the rates are the same, is sufficient to derive the CAPM, regardless of short-sale restrictions.

12.4   OVER- AND UNDER-PRICED SECURITIES

The CAPM has security price implications illustrated in Figure 12.4. Points between the CAPM and the vertical axis, such as point L, represent securities whose current prices are lower than they would be in equilibrium. Thus, points such as L represent securities with unusually high expected returns for the amount of systematic risk they bear. Because they have unusually high expected returns, there will be strong demand for them. This means that investors will bid their purchase prices up until their equilibrium rate of return is driven down onto the CAPM at L'.

For example, consider a stock whose estimated end-of-period price is $E(P_1)$. Given its current price P_0 and assuming that no dividends will be paid this period, its initial expected return $E(r)$ is equal to $\left[E(P_1) - P_0\right]/P_0 = \left[E(P_1)/P_0\right] - 1$. Having P_0 be too low can be seen to be equivalent to having $E(r)$ be too high, meaning that $E(r) > r_f + \left[E(r_m) - r_f\right]\beta$. The resulting bidding up of P_0 will lower $E(r)$ and will continue to lower $E(r)$ until the following equilibrium is reached: $E(r) = r_f + \left[E(r_m) - r_f\right]\beta$. In other words, all securities positioned above the SML are underpriced.

Similarly, securities represented by points between the CAPM and the horizontal axis represent securities whose prices are too high. This means that securities such as H do not offer sufficient levels of expected return to induce rational investors to accept the amount of systematic risk they bear. As a result, H's price will fall due to a lack of demand. Furthermore, it will continue falling until it is low enough so that the security's expected return is on the CAPM at H'. Then the capital loss will cease and an equilibrium will emerge until a change in the firm's systematic risk, a change

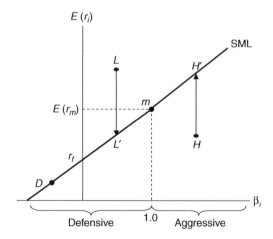

FIGURE 12.4   The Capital Asset Pricing Model (CAPM), or Security Market Line (SML), with Security Price Implications

in expected returns, or some other change causes another disequilibrium. More generally, all securities positioned below the SML are overpriced. After considering the effect the CAPM can have on the market prices of all assets, it is easy to see why it is called an asset pricing model.

12.5   THE MARKET MODEL AND THE CAPM

The market model and the CAPM have certain links to each other.[10] The market model is an important part of the return-generating model and is based on the simple assumption that security returns conform to a multivariate normal distribution. As discussed in Chapter 8, this model can be expressed algebraically as

$$r_i = \alpha_i + \beta_i r_m + \varepsilon_i \tag{8.1}$$

where the regression slope coefficient is $\beta_i = \text{cov}(r_i, r_m)/\sigma_m^2$. The CAPM is an equilibrium model that explains expected returns over one holding period and is based on the assumptions given in the early pages of this chapter. The CAPM was shown to be equal to

$$E(r_i) = r_f + [E(r_m) - r_f]\beta_i \tag{12.2}$$

Given the expected return on the market $E(r_m)$, the market model of equation (8.1) expresses a security's expected return as

$$E(r_i) = \alpha_i + \beta_i E(r_m) \tag{12.11}$$

In comparing equations (12.2) and (12.11), it can be seen that if the CAPM is valid, then

$$\alpha_i = \beta_i(1 - r_f) \tag{12.12}$$

As will be shown next, the CAPM is typically converted from an *ex ante* model to an *ex post* or empirical model by merging it with a return-generating model.[11]

By assuming that the multivariate normal distribution of returns is stationary over time, equation (12.2) can be modified by adding time subscripts. Furthermore, it can be noted from equation (12.11) that $\alpha_i = E(r_i) - \beta_i E(r_m)$. Substituting this expression for α_i into the time-subscripted version of equation (8.1) results in a form of the market model that can be viewed as a return-generating model,

$$r_{it} = E(r_i) + \beta_i[r_{mt} - E(r_m)] + \varepsilon_{it} \tag{12.13}$$

Substituting the expression for $E(r_i)$ [as shown in a time-subscripted version of equation (12.2)] into equation (12.13) results in

$$r_{it} = r_{ft} + \beta_i(r_{mt} - r_{ft}) + \varepsilon_{it} \tag{12.14}$$

Now, rearranging equation (12.14) and adding an intercept term, the following *ex post* version of the CAPM is created:

$$r_{it} - r_{ft} = \alpha_i + \beta_i(r_{mt} - r_{ft}) + \varepsilon_{it} \tag{12.15}$$

Taking the expected value of equation (12.15) and rearranging terms indicates that the intercept term α_i is equal to

$$\alpha_i = \left[E\left(r_i\right) - r_f\right] - \beta_i \left[E\left(r_m\right) - r_f\right] \tag{12.16}$$

Equation (12.16) suggests that the term $\beta_i \left[E\left(r_m\right) - r_f\right]$ must be equal to $E\left(r_i\right) - r_f$ in the CAPM. Accordingly, the true value of α_i is zero and sample estimates of it should not be significantly different from zero if the CAPM is valid and stationary over time.

Finally, if equation (12.15) is applied to sample data for a given stock that has been generated by the CAPM, then the estimated values of α_i and β_i will be biased in opposite directions if r_{ft} and r_{mt} are correlated over time.[12] However, empirical studies indicate that estimates of β_i derived from the market model and the CAPM are quite similar in magnitude.[13] Thus, the conceptual problem of using the market model to estimate β_i when the CAPM is assumed to be valid does not create any serious empirical problems.

12.6   SUMMARY AND CONCLUSIONS

The capital asset pricing model is a major paradigm in the field of finance. Building on Markowitz's two-parameter portfolio analysis model, several path-breaking researchers developed this model during the 1960s. The theory's necessary assumptions include homogeneous expectations, perfect markets, and the existence of a risk-free borrowing and lending rate. After making these (and other) assumptions, the capital market line can be derived and the separation theorem can be proven. The result is that each investor will choose his or her optimal portfolio from combining two portfolios: one consisting of the risk-free asset and the other consisting of the market portfolio. Evaluation of individual securities in this setting leads to the revelation that a security's expected return is a positive linear function of its beta (or covariance) with the market portfolio, a relationship that is referred to as the capital asset pricing model.

This chapter presents formulas and graphs representing the CAPM. These diagrams and equations are the final results of the Nobel prize–winning financial economists who developed the CAPM. Their genius insights and the various forms of mathematical analysis used to derive the CAPM and win the Nobel prizes are summarized in the appendix to this chapter.[14]

APPENDIX: DERIVATIONS OF THE CAPM

A12.1   Other Approaches

Several approaches for deriving the CAPM exist.

A. Lintner's Derivation   Lintner (1965) presented another derivation of the CAPM. Given the investment opportunity set (under the curve ABF) containing all risky assets, and, the risk-free asset illustrated in Figure A12.1, wealth-maximizing

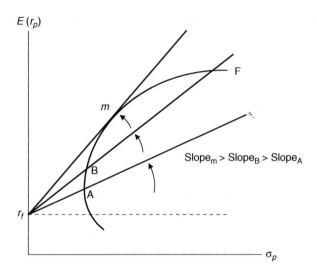

FIGURE A12.1 Combining the Risk-free Asset with Risky Assets

investors will want to maximize the slope of the straight line passing through the risk-free rate of return, r_f. Maximizing the slope of the straight line (θ) indicates that investors maximize their expected return at a given level of risk or minimize the risk at a given level of expected return. Thus, the following formulation can be set up:

$$\text{Maximize } \theta = \frac{E(r_p) - r_f}{\sigma_p} \tag{A12.1}$$

$$= \frac{\sum_{i=1}^{n} w_i [E(r_i) - r_f]}{\left[\sum_{i=1}^{n} w_i^2 \sigma_i^2 + \sum_{i=1}^{n} \sum_{\substack{j=1 \\ j \neq i}}^{n} w_i w_j \sigma_{ij}\right]^{1/2}}$$

In order to obtain the maximum value of θ, we take the first derivative with respect to the weight w_i ($i = 1, \ldots, n$) and set it equal to zero. The solution to the preceding maximization problem is equivalent to finding the simultaneous solution of the following n simultaneous equations

$$\frac{\partial \theta}{\partial w_1} = 0$$

$$\frac{\partial \theta}{\partial w_2} = 0$$

$$\vdots \tag{A12.2}$$

$$\frac{\partial \theta}{\partial w_n} = 0$$

Specifically, the *i*-th derivative equation is written as

$$\frac{\partial \theta}{\partial w_i} = \left(\frac{1}{\sigma_p} \right) \left[E\left(r_i\right) - r_f - \lambda \left(w_i \sigma_i^2 + \sum_{\substack{j=1 \\ j \neq i}}^{n} w_j \sigma_{ij} \right) \right] = 0 \qquad \text{(A12.3)}$$

where $\lambda = \left(\left[E\left(r_p\right) - r_f \right] \right) / \sigma_p^2$. Equation (A12.3), which is the necessary and sufficient condition for the unique (global) maximum, can be rewritten as

$$E\left(r_i\right) - r_f = \lambda \left(w_i \sigma_i^2 + \sum_{\substack{j=1 \\ j \neq i}}^{n} w_j \sigma_{ij} \right) \qquad \text{(A12.4)}$$

However, the term in parentheses on the right-hand side of equation (A12.4) equals the covariance between asset *i* and the portfolio *p* that contains the asset. That is,[15]

$$w_i \sigma_i^2 + \sum_{\substack{j=1 \\ j \neq i}}^{n} w_j \sigma_{ij} \equiv \sigma_{ip} \qquad \text{(A12.5)}$$

If the portfolio *p* contains all assets in the market, then the portfolio *p* equals the market portfolio *m*. Therefore, equation (A12.4) becomes the CAPM equation below:

$$E\left(r_i\right) - r_f = \left[\frac{E\left(r_m\right) - r_f}{\sigma_m^2} \right] \sigma_{im}$$

$$= \left[E\left(r_m\right) - r_f \right] \beta_i \qquad \text{(A12.6)}$$

Solving the *n* simultaneous equations of equation (A12.2) provides the solution for the optimal risky portfolio (or the tangent portfolio) *m*.

B. Hwang and Litzenberger's Approach   Huang and Litzenberger (1988) presented another approach to derive the CAPM. Suppose a risk-averse investor *i* has the initial wealth W_{i0} at time $t = 0$. At the beginning $(t = 0)$, this investor invests W_{ij} in risky asset j $(j = 1, 2, \ldots, n)$ and the remaining $\left(W_{i0} - \Sigma_{j=1}^{n} W_{ij} \right)$ in the riskless asset. Suppose also that the rates of return of risky assets $\left(r_1, r_2, \ldots, r_n \right)$ are multivariate normally distributed. After one period $(t = 1)$, the investor's wealth is

$$\tilde{W}_{i1} = \left(W_{i0} - \sum_{j=1}^{n} W_{ij} \right) \left(1 + r_f \right) + \sum_{j=1}^{n} W_{ij} \left(1 + r_j \right)$$

$$= W_{i0} \left(1 + r_f \right) + \sum_{j=1}^{n} W_{ij} \left(r_j - r_f \right) \qquad \text{(A12.7)}$$

Thus, this investor's choice problem is to maximize his or her utility at the end of the period with respect to the investments in risky assets (W_{ij}). That is,

$$\text{Maximize } E\left[U_i\left(\tilde{W}_{i1}\right)\right]$$

$$= \text{Maximize } E\left[U_i\left(W_{i0}\left(1+r_f\right) + \sum_{j=1}^{n} W_{ij}\left(r_j - r_f\right)\right)\right] \qquad \text{(A12.8)}$$

where $U_i\left(\cdot\right)$ is a risk-averse utility function. Because U is strictly increasing concave, the first-order necessary and sufficient conditions for the existence of the solution in equation (A12.8) are

$$E\left[U_i'\left(\tilde{W}_{i1}\right)\left(r_j - r_f\right)\right] = 0 \quad \text{for all } j \qquad \text{(A12.9)}$$

where U_i' is the first derivative of the utility function U_i. with respect to W_{ij}.

By using the definition of a covariance,

$$\text{Cov}\left[U_i'\left(\tilde{W}_{i1}\right), r_j - r_f\right] = E\left[U_i'\left(\tilde{W}_{i1}\right) - E\left\{U_i'\left(\tilde{W}_{i1}\right)\right\}\right]\left[\left(r_j - r_f\right) - E\left(r_j - r_f\right)\right]$$

$$= E\left[U_i'\left(\tilde{W}_{i1}\right)\left(r_j - r_f\right)\right] - E\left[U_i'\left(\tilde{W}_{i1}\right)\right] E\left[r_j - r_f\right]$$

$$= 0 - E\left[U_i'\left(\tilde{W}_{i1}\right)\right] E\left[r_j - r_f\right]$$

Therefore,

$$\text{Cov}\left[U_i'\left(\tilde{W}_{i1}\right), r_j\right] = -E\left[U_i'\left(\tilde{W}_{i1}\right)\right] E\left[r_j - r_f\right] \qquad \text{(A12.10)}$$

When two random variables X and Y are bivariate normally distributed and g is differentiable and satisfies some regularity conditions, we have

$$\text{Cov}\left[g\left(X\right), Y\right] = E\left[g'\left(X\right)\right] \text{Cov}\left(X, Y\right) \qquad \text{(A12.11)}$$

Equation (A12.11) implies that because $\tilde{W}_{i1}$ and r_j are bivariate normally distributed, equation (A12.10) can be written as

$$E\left[U_i'\left(\tilde{W}_{i1}\right)\right] E\left[r_j - r_f\right] = -E\left[U''\left(\tilde{W}_{i1}\right)\right] \text{Cov}\left(\tilde{W}_{i1}, r_j\right)$$

$$\Rightarrow \left(\frac{1}{\theta_i}\right) E\left[r_j - r_f\right] = \text{Cov}\left(\tilde{W}_{i1}, r_j\right) \qquad \text{(A12.12)}$$

where $\theta_i = -E[U''(\tilde{W}_{i1})]/E[U_i'(\tilde{W}_{i1})]$, which is the i-th investor's absolute risk aversion (ARA). Summing equation (A12.12) over all investors i and rearranging yields

$$E\left[r_j - r_f\right] = \left(\sum_i \theta_i^{-1}\right)^{-1} \text{Cov}\left(\tilde{W}_{m1}, r_j\right)$$

$$= W_{m0}\left(\sum_i \theta_i^{-1}\right)^{-1} \text{Cov}\left(r_m, r_j\right) \qquad \text{(A12.13)}$$

where $\tilde{W}_{m1} = \Sigma_i \tilde{W}_{i1} = W_{m0}\left(1 + r_m\right)$. Here $\tilde{W}_{m1}$ indicates the sum of the end-period wealth of all investors or the market wealth at the end of the period, W_{m0} is the initial market wealth, and r_m is the rate of return on the market. Because equation (A12.13) holds for individual assets, it must hold for the market portfolio. That is, for the market portfolio m,

$$E\left[r_m - r_f\right] = W_{m0}\left(\sum_i \theta_i^{-1}\right)^{-1} Cov\left(r_m, r_m\right)$$

$$\Rightarrow W_{m0}\left(\sum_i \theta_i^{-1}\right)^{-1} = \frac{E\left[r_m - r_f\right]}{Var\left(r_m\right)} \qquad (A12.14)$$

Substituting equation (A12.14) into (A12.13) yields

$$E\left(r_j - r_f\right) = E\left(r_m - r_f\right)\left[\frac{Cov\left(r_m, r_j\right)}{Var\left(r_m\right)}\right]$$

Equivalently,
$$E\left(r_j\right) = r_f + \left[E\left(r_m\right) - r_f\right]\beta_j \qquad (12.2)$$

This shows how Huang and Litzenberger derived the same CAPM.

A12.2 Tangency Portfolio Research

The way of identifying the tangency portfolio (or optimal risky portfolio), which is at point m on Figure A12.1, has been already described in equation (A7.15) of Chapter 7. This section presents a different way of identifying the tangency portfolio. For each asset i, the necessary and sufficient condition for the unique maximization is described as in equation (A12.4). Thus, the necessary and sufficient condition for the maximization for all assets $(i = 1, \ldots, n)$ is the following n simultaneous equation system:

$$E\left(r_1\right) - r_f = x_1\sigma_1^2 + x_2\sigma_{12} + x_3\sigma_{13} + \cdots + x_{1n}\sigma_{1n}$$

$$E\left(r_2\right) - r_f = x_1\sigma_{21} + x_2\sigma_2^2 + x_3\sigma_{23} + \cdots + x_n\sigma_{2n}$$

$$E\left(r_3\right) - r_f = x_1\sigma_{31} + x_2\sigma_{32} + x_3\sigma_3^2 + \cdots + x_n\sigma_{3n} \qquad (A12.15)$$

$$\vdots$$

$$E\left(r_n\right) - r_f = x_1\sigma_{n1} + x_2\sigma_{n2} + x_3\sigma_{n3} + \cdots + x_n\sigma_n^2$$

where $x_i = \lambda w_i$. In matrix form, the preceding n simultaneous equations system of (A12.15) becomes

$$\left(\mu - r_f l\right) = \Sigma\, x \qquad (A12.16)$$

where $\mu = \left[E\left(r_1\right)\ E\left(r_2\right)\ \cdots\ E\left(r_n\right)\right]'$ is the $(n \times 1)$ expected return vector, $l = (1\ 1\ \cdots\ 1)'$ is the n-vector of ones, Σ is the $(n \times n)$ variance-covariance matrix, and $x = (x_1\ x_2\ \cdots\ x_n)'$ is the $(n \times 1)$ solution vector. Thus, the solution of equation (A12.16) is

$$x = \Sigma^{-1}\left(\mu - r_f l\right) \qquad (A12.17)$$

Because the x vector is a transformed variable, the optimal weights for the optimal risky portfolio, w, are obtained by standardizing the transformed variable. The standardization can be done in two ways according to the definition of short sales. First, by the standard definition of short sales, that is, $\Sigma_{i=1}^{n} w_i = 1$, the actual optimal weight is obtained from $w_i = x_i / \Sigma_{i=1}^{n} x_i$. That is,

$$w = \frac{x}{x'l} \tag{A12.18}$$

This is the final solution for the optimal risky portfolio or the tangency portfolio, m.

Substituting equation (A12.17) for x in equation (A12.18) yields

$$w = \frac{\Sigma^{-1}\left(\mu - r_f l\right)}{\left(\mu - r_f l\right)' \Sigma^{-1} l}$$

$$= \frac{\Sigma^{-1}\left(\mu - r_f l\right)}{\mu' \Sigma^{-1} l - r_f l' \Sigma^{-1} l}$$

$$= \frac{\Sigma^{-1}\left(\mu - r_f l\right)}{A - r_f C} \tag{A12.9}$$

In fact, the optimal weight of equation (A12.19) is exactly the same as equation (A7.15) in Chapter 7.

Lintner (1965), however, defines alternatively the short sales from the standard definition. When an investor sells short a particular stock, the proceeds from the short sale are deposited in escrow, and in addition, an amount equal to the initial margin requirements must be deposited in the escrow. All the cash deposits are held until the short position is covered. According to Lintner's definition, therefore, the short sale is not a source of funds, but a use of funds. Because $w_i < 0$ for short sales, the proportion of the funds invested in the short sale is $|w_i|$. That is, $\Sigma_{i=1}^{n} |w_i| = 1$. The actual optimal weights are therefore obtained by standardizing in equation (A12.20):

$$w_i = \frac{x_i}{\sum_{i=1}^{n} |x_i|} \tag{A12.20}$$

EXAMPLE A12.1

Suppose the riskless rate of return is 5 percent, and consider three securities whose expected returns and variance-covariances are given as follows:

$$\mu = \begin{pmatrix} \mu_1 \\ \mu_2 \\ \mu_3 \end{pmatrix} = \begin{pmatrix} 7 \\ 9 \\ 12 \end{pmatrix} \quad \text{and} \quad \Sigma = \begin{pmatrix} \sigma_1^2 & \sigma_{12} & \sigma_{13} \\ \sigma_{21} & \sigma_2^2 & \sigma_{23} \\ \sigma_{32} & \sigma_{32} & \sigma_3^2 \end{pmatrix} = \begin{pmatrix} 16 & 12 & -9 \\ 12 & 20 & 6 \\ -9 & 6 & 25 \end{pmatrix}$$

EXAMPLE A12.1 (*Continued*)

Then, the (3×3) simultaneous equations from equation (A12.15) are as follows:

$$7 - 5 = 15x_1 + 12x_2 - 9x_3$$
$$9 - 5 = 12x_1 + 20x_2 + 6x_3$$
$$12 - 5 = -9x_1 + 6x_2 + 25x_3$$

The solution for the transformed variable of the preceding equations is described as

$$x = \begin{pmatrix} x_1 \\ x_2 \\ x_3 \end{pmatrix} = \begin{pmatrix} 16 & 12 & -9 \\ 12 & 20 & 6 \\ -9 & 6 & 25 \end{pmatrix}^{-1} \begin{pmatrix} 7 - 5 \\ 9 - 5 \\ 12 - 5 \end{pmatrix} = \begin{pmatrix} 1.4053 \\ -0.9471 \\ 1.0132 \end{pmatrix}$$

By the standard definition of short sales, because $w_i = x_i / \Sigma_{i=1}^{n} x_i$, the weights for the optimal risky portfolio or the tangency portfolio are

$$w_1 = \frac{x_1}{\sum_{i=1}^{3} x_i} = \frac{1.4053}{1.4053 + (-0.9471) + 1.0132} = 0.9551$$

$$w_2 = \frac{x_2}{\sum_{i=1}^{3} x_i} = \frac{-0.9471}{1.4053 + (-0.9471) + 1.0132} = -0.6437$$

$$w_3 = \frac{x_3}{\sum_{i=1}^{3} x_i} = \frac{1.0132}{1.4053 + (-0.9471) + 1.0132} = 0.6886$$

By Lintner's definition of short sales, because $w_i = x_i / \sum_{i=1}^{n} |x_i|$, the weights for the optimal risky portfolio are

$$w_1 = \frac{x_1}{1.4053 + |-0.9471| + 1.0132} = \frac{1.4053}{3.3656} = 0.4174$$

$$w_2 = \frac{x_2}{1.4053 + |-0.9471| + 1.0132} = \frac{-0.9471}{3.3656} = -0.2814$$

$$w_3 = \frac{x_1}{1.4053 + |-0.9471| + 1.0132} = \frac{1.0132}{3.3656} = 0.3010$$

NOTES

1. See Jack Treynor, "How to Rate Management of Investment Funds," *Harvard Business Review* 43 (1965): 63–75; William Sharpe, "Capital Asset Prices: A Theory of Market Equilibrium under Conditions of Risk," *Journal of Finance* 19 (1964): 425–442; John Lintner, "Security Prices, Risk, and the Maximal Gains from Diversification," *Journal of Finance*, December 1965, 587–615; Jan Mossin, "Security Pricing and Investment

Criteria in Competitive Markets," *American Economic Review* 59, no. 5 (1969): 749–756; and E. F. Fama, "Risk, Return, and Equilibrium: Some Clarifying Comments," *Journal of Finance*, March 1968, 29–39.

2. The CML was first introduced by William Sharpe, "Capital Asset Prices: A Theory of Market Equilibrium under Conditions of Risk," *Journal of Finance* 19 (1964): page 426, Figure 1. This classic article is reprinted in William F. Sharpe, Editor, *William F. Sharpe: Selected Works*, World Scientific Publishing Company Inc., 2012, ISBN-10: 9814329959, ISBN-13: 978–9814329958, 692 pages.

3. Excess demand would not equal zero in this case, where excess demand is defined as demand less supply. See Fama (1971) for a discussion of market-clearing conditions for the market portfolio. An important problem related to separation and market-clearing conditions is known as *aggregation*. If investors have initial endowments of securities, then initial prices affect the size of their initial wealth. This means that the derivation of equilibrium initial prices is complicated when such prices are dependent on investors' levels of initial wealth. Rubinstein (1974) and Brennan and Kraus (1978) present an analysis of aggregation, defined as the situation where equilibrium prices can be expressed in terms that are independent of allocations of initial wealth.

4. Consider three versions of the separation theorems. The initial version of the theorem by Tobin (1958) differs from the version stated here by not requiring the two funds to be the same for all investors. The reason for this difference is due to the fact Tobin did not invoke the homogeneous expectations assumption in his analysis. His version simply stated that an investor should consider putting his or her money in two funds, one consisting of the risk-free asset and one consisting of only risky assets. However, the latter fund need not be the same for all investors. A second, but related, definition of separation states that separation occurs if, for n assets, the investor's optimal portfolio can be formed by investing in k funds, where $k < n$, and where the composition of the k funds is independent of the investor's initial wealth position. Cass and Stiglitz (1970) have linked this definition of separation to the types of utility functions that investors possess. In particular, they have shown that this type of separation occurs if the "risk tolerance" of the investor is a linear function of terminal wealth W_T. Here, an investor's risk tolerance, denoted $T(W_T)$, is defined to be equal to the reciprocal of the investor's measure of absolute risk aversion, $-U''(W_T)/U'(W_T)$. Algebraically, risk tolerance is a linear function of terminal wealth if $T(W_T) = a + bW_T$, because the quadratic, power, logarithmic, and negative exponential utility functions have this property. An important insight is that if (1) investors have a linear risk tolerance utility function, (2) the term b in this linear risk tolerance function (sometimes referred to as cautiousness) is the same for all investors, and (3) investors have homogeneous expectations, then the two-fund separation (that is, $k = 2$) exists for any arbitrary multivariate return distribution. Ross (1978b) has approached separation from a third angle, examining the kinds of multivariate return distributions that will yield two-fund types of separation for arbitrary utility functions. He assumes that investors have homogeneous expectations. An important finding is that separation depends not so much on the marginal distributions of the individual securities as it does on the correlations between the various securities.

5. Of course, there are other pairs of portfolios that could replace these two and for which the separation theorem would still hold. However, these other pairs would simply be linear combinations of the two funds mentioned in the theorem.

6. John Evans and S. H. Archer, "Diversification and the Reduction of Dispersion: An Empirical Analysis," *Journal of Finance*, December 1968, 761–767; W.H. Wagner and S. Lau, "The Effect of Diversification on Risk," *Financial Analysts Journal*, November–December 1971, 52; Edwin J. Elton and Martin J. Gruber, "Risk Reduction and Portfolio Size: An Analytical Solution," *Journal of Business* 30, no. 4 (October 1977): 415–437.

7. Both the systematic and unsystematic portions of total risk must be considered by *undiversified investors*. Entrepreneurs who have their entire net worth invested in one

business, for example, can be bankrupt by a piece of bad luck that could be easily averaged away in a diversified portfolio. Poorly diversified investors should not treat the diversifiable risk lightly. Only well-diversified investors can afford to ignore diversifiable risk.

8. Fischer Black has suggested a model in which it is not necessary to assume the existence of a riskless rate; see Fischer Black, "Capital Market Equilibrium with Restricted Borrowing," *Journal of Business*, July 1972, 444–454. In Black's model the riskless interest rate is replaced by a portfolio that has a beta equal to zero but still has some small amount of variance. The *zero-beta portfolio* is uncorrelated with the market portfolio, so that its total risk and its unsystematic risk are identical and both are positive quantities. The zero-beta portfolio is created by holding risky securities and leveraging and selling short. Some preliminary empirical estimates of the rates of return on the zero-beta portfolio have been published; see F. Black, M. C. Jensen, and M. Scholes, "The Capital Asset Pricing Model: Some Empirical Tests," *Studies in the Theory of Capital Markets*, M. C. Jensen, ed. (New York: Praeger, 1972). Professor Gordon Alexander has shown an algorithm which could be used to obtain estimates of the returns from zero-beta portfolio: Gordon Alexander, "An Algorithmic Approach to Deriving the Minimum Variance Zero-Beta Portfolio," *Journal of Financial Economics*, March 1977.

9. This relationship also holds if i is defined as a portfolio instead of an individual asset. In this case, σ_{im} is simply the weighted average of the covariances of the component securities with m (that is, $\sigma_{im} = \Sigma_{j=1}^{n} w_j \sigma_{ij}$, where w_j is the weighted of asset j in the portfolio).

10. Markowitz first introduced this model at pages 98–100 (including footnote 1) of *Portfolio Selection* (New York: John Wiley & Sons, 1959). Stapleton and Subrahmanyam (1983) discuss the relationship between the CAPM and the market model where the independent variable in the market model is the market portfolio. Markowitz (1984) also discusses the relationship between the CAPM and the market model; however, he defines the independent variable in the market model to be an underlying unobservable factor that may be approximated by an index.

11. See Blume and Husic (1973) for a discussion of the identification of the correct return-generating process.

12. See Roll (1969) or Miller and Scholes (1972, 54–56) for details.

13. Miller and Scholes (1972, 56) argue that r_{ft} and r_{mt} are correlated over time but that the standard deviation associated with r_{ft} is so small that the covariance between r_{ft} and r_{mt} is practically zero, and thus the market model beta and CAPM beta should be very close in magnitude for any given security.

14. Readers mastering the explanations of this chapter's graphs and formulas can discuss the CAPM and read the chapters that follow without delving into this chapter's appendix.

15. The covariance of asset i with the portfolio p containing the asset is, by definition, $\text{Cov}(r_i, r_p) \equiv \sigma_{ip} = E\{[r_i - E(r_i)][r_p - E(r_p)]\} = E\{[r_i - E(r_i)][\Sigma w_j r_j - \Sigma w_j E(r_j)]\} = \Sigma_{j=1}^{n} w_j E\{[r_i - E(r_i)][r_j - E(r_j)]\} = \Sigma_{j=1}^{n} w_j \sigma_{ij}$. Note that $\sigma_{ii} = \sigma_i^2$.

CHAPTER 13

Extensions of the Standard CAPM

The CAPM presented in Chapter 12 is based on a large number of unrealistic assumptions. In this chapter and several chapters that follow, some of these assumptions are aligned to be more similar to conditions existing in the "real world."[1] This chapter begins by reconsidering the assumptions regarding risk-free borrowing and lending, homogeneous expectations, perfect markets, and asset marketability. Then, the assumption that investors are one-period expected-utility-of-terminal-wealth maximizers is relaxed by looking at some multiperiod models. Later, in Chapter 16, several assumptions are removed simultaneously and replaced by one simple assumption. Chapter 16 derives the arbitrage pricing model and considers what happens when security returns are generated by several different risk factors.

13.1   RISK-FREE BORROWING OR LENDING

One of the assumptions underlying the CAPM is that investors can lend and borrow an unlimited amount of money at a single riskless rate of interest. This assumption is clearly unrealistic. In the real world, it would not be difficult to lend an unlimited amount of money at the riskless rate, but almost no one can borrow at that same riskless rate of interest. Investors must borrow at a greater interest rate than the rate at which they lend (for instance, deposit savings at a bank) if money lenders are to survive. More critically, in a strict sense a truly riskless asset may not exist in the real world. This section examines how our models are changed by making more realistic assumptions about the riskless rate of interest.

13.1.1   The Zero-Beta Portfolio

Consider a situation where all the CAPM assumptions are maintained except one. Suppose the fifth assumption (that there is a single risk-free interest rate at which all borrowing and lending can take place) is abandoned. As a result, neither risk-free borrowing nor risk-free lending is permitted. Because limited short selling of risky assets is still permitted, every investor faces the same minimum variance boundary—the hyperbola (in $[\sigma, E(r)]$ space). Furthermore, every investor will be selecting an optimal portfolio from the upper half (positively sloped part) of that boundary, the efficient frontier. Black (1972) suggested an equilibrium asset pricing model called the zero-beta CAPM to accommodate these circumstances.

Chapter 7 noted that any portfolio on the efficient frontier could be represented as a linear combination of two arbitrarily chosen portfolios on the minimum variance boundary (of efficient frontier portfolios), say, p_1 and p_2. Because the homogenous expectations assumption implies the minimum variance boundary is the same for all investors, the optimal portfolio for any investor can be viewed as a linear combination of p_1 and p_2. Thus, the separation theorem will still hold, because p_1 and p_2 can be viewed as two portfolios in which any investor can invest. Although all investors can hold a linear combination of two portfolios on the minimum variance boundary, the proportion of the two portfolios that are selected can differ to accommodate each investor's different risk and return preferences.

As mentioned previously, the market portfolio m is the weighted sum of combinations held by all investors. Because each linear combination is on the minimum variance boundary, the market portfolio also is on the minimum variance boundary. These facts were shown more formally elsewhere.[2]

If the market portfolio m is efficient, but neither risk-free borrowing nor risk-free lending is permitted, what happens to the CAPM? Clearly, the classic CAPM model, equation (12.2), cannot hold if r_f ceases to exist. However, an analogous form of the CAPM can be derived. Every efficient frontier portfolio, except for the global minimum variance portfolio, has its own unique counterpart frontier portfolio with which it has a zero covariance. This portfolio is called *zero-covariance* (or *zero-beta*) *portfolio*. Because the market portfolio is an efficient frontier portfolio, it has a unique zero-covariance portfolio. This chapter's appendix A12.1 explains the characteristics of the zero-covariance portfolio.

Figure 13.1 depicts the location of the zero-covariance portfolio of the market portfolio. Extending a horizontal dashed line through the intercept, this line's intersection with the hyperbola occurs at point Z in Figure 13.1. This portfolio has an expected return of $E(r_z)$ and lies on the inefficient portion of the minimum variance boundary. Thus, portfolio Z exists and its returns are uncorrelated with those of m. Accordingly, Z is typically referred to as the *minimum-variance zero-beta portfolio*. The separation theorem noted that all investors could be viewed as purchasing a portfolio comprised of p_1 and p_2, two different portfolios on the minimum variance boundary. If we assume m and Z are the two portfolios p_1 and p_2, then in equilibrium, the holdings of Z must net out to zero and the holdings of m must net out to m.

The covariance of an efficient portfolio p and any risky portfolio q is expressed as

$$\sigma_{pq} = w'_q \Sigma w_p \tag{13.1}$$

By using the expressions of the optimal weight w_p in equation (7.4b), we have

$$\sigma_{pq} = w'_q \Sigma \left(\lambda \Sigma^{-1} \mu + \gamma \Sigma^{-1} l \right) = \lambda E(r_q) + \gamma \tag{13.2}$$

because $w'_q \mu = E(r_q)$ and $w'_q l = 1$. Because the market portfolio m is an efficient portfolio, the covariance term σ_{pq} in equation (13.2) can be replaced with σ_{mq}. Then, the expected return on the risky portfolio q is expressed as

$$E(r_q) = -\frac{\gamma}{\lambda} + \frac{1}{\lambda}\sigma_{mq} \tag{13.3}$$

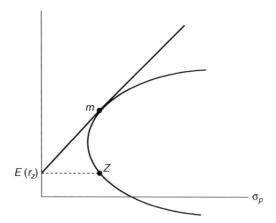

FIGURE 13.1 The Market Portfolio and
Zero-beta Portfolio

By using the expressions for λ and γ from equations (7.14) and (7.15), the expected return on the risky portfolio q is

$$E(r_q) = \left[\frac{AE(r_m) - B}{CE(r_m) - A}\right] + \left[\frac{D}{CE(r_m) - A}\right]\sigma_{mq} \qquad (13.4)$$

By using some algebra, equation (13.4) becomes

$$E(r_q) = \left[\frac{A}{C} - \frac{D/C^2}{E(r_m) - A/C}\right] + \left[E(r_m) - \left(\frac{A}{C} - \frac{D/C^2}{E(r_m) - A/C}\right)\right]\left(\frac{\sigma_{mq}}{\sigma_m^2}\right) \quad (13.5)$$

From equation (A13.2) in the appendix to this chapter, the expected return on the zero-beta portfolio is

$$E(r_z) = \frac{A}{C} - \frac{D/C^2}{E(r_m) - A/C} \qquad (13.6)$$

By defining $\beta_q = \sigma_{mq}/\sigma_m^2$ in equation (13.5), we obtain the equation for the expected return on a risky asset q:

$$E(r_q) = E(r_z) + \left[E(r_m) - E(r_z)\right]\beta_q \qquad (13.7)$$

Equation (13.7) is sometimes referred to as the two-factor model or the zero-beta version of the CAPM (or simply the *zero-beta CAPM*), because in equilibrium all security returns are a linear function of two factors, $E(r_z)$ and $E(r_m)$. The asset pricing implications of this model are the same as in the earlier version, despite the removal of r_f, as long as unrestricted short selling is permitted; expected returns are still a linear function of beta, where the role of r_f has been replaced by $E(r_z)$.

13.1.2   No Risk-Free Borrowing

Suppose that lending (investing) at a risk-free rate is allowed, but no risk-free borrowing is permitted. In this situation investors face a linear efficient frontier up to a tangency point T, beyond which the efficient frontier coincides with the hyperbola of equation (A7.2). Thus, a three-fund separation theorem exists, because every investor will consider the risk-free asset as one fund and the hyperbola as being a linear combination of two other funds, p_1 and p_2. The market portfolio m will still be efficient, and the zero-beta version of the CAPM will still be valid.

Recognizing that the market portfolio m is efficient, the zero-beta version of the CAPM must hold because it depends solely on the recognition that m is efficient. Because m is above T on the hyperbola in Figure 13.2, and $E(r_z)$ and r_f represent the vertical intersections of lines tangent to m and T, respectively, it follows that $E(r_z) > r_f$. Furthermore, while the zero-beta version of the CAPM was shown to hold for any security or portfolio when no risk-free lending or borrowing was allowed, we now see that it still holds for any risky security or any portfolio comprised of only risky securities. This follows because the risk-free asset has a $\beta = 0$ but has a return of $r_f < E(r_z)$, even though Z also has a $\beta = 0$. Thus, combining r_f with any risky asset will produce a portfolio with a beta that does not have an expected return as indicated by the zero-beta CAPM.

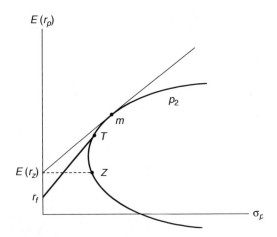

FIGURE 13.2 Relationship Between the Tangency Portfolio, the Market Portfolio, and its Zero-beta Portfolio

13.1.3   Lending and Borrowing Rates Can Differ

The real world borrowing rate (r_{fB}) must be above the risk-free lending rate (r_{fL}) if banks are going to survive. The efficient frontier for this situation is depicted in Figure 13.3. Investors face a linear efficient frontier from the risk-free lending rate r_{fL} to a tangency portfolio T_L on the hyperbola. Then they face a curved segment of the hyperbola from T_L to T_B. T_B is the tangency point corresponding to the risk-free borrowing rate r_{fB}. Above T_B the efficient frontier is again linear. Thus, a four-fund

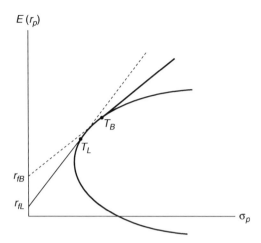

FIGURE 13.3 Efficient Frontier with Different Risk-free Rates

separation theorem exists in that every investor will consider r_{fB}, r_{fL}, p_1 and p_2. However, m is still efficient and the zero-beta CAPM is still valid.

In order to show that the market portfolio m is efficient, the previous analysis is extended by letting V_{iB} and V_{iL} denote scalars equal to the value of the investment that investor i either borrows at rate r_{fB} or lends at rate r_{fL}, respectively (thus, $V_{iB} \le 0$ and $V_{iL} \ge 0$). Let $\boldsymbol{w}_i^*$ be an $(n+2) \times 1$ vector in which the last two cells, denoted w_{iB} and w_{iL}, represent the proportion borrowed and lent at rates r_{fB} and r_{fL}, respectively (thus, $w_{iB} \le 0$ and $w_{iL} \ge 0$). If $\boldsymbol{w}_i$ is defined as

$$\boldsymbol{w}_i = \frac{\left(\boldsymbol{w}_i^* - w_{iB}\boldsymbol{l}_B - w_{iL}\boldsymbol{l}_L\right)}{\left(1 - w_{iB} - w_{iL}\right)}$$

where $\boldsymbol{l}_B$ and $\boldsymbol{l}_L$ are $(n+2) \times 1$ zero-vectors except for entries of 1 in rows $n+1$ and $n+2$, respectively, then the market portfolio has a weight vector of

$$\boldsymbol{w}_m = \sum_{i=1}^{L} \left[\boldsymbol{w}_i \left(\frac{V_i^{**}}{\sum_{i=1}^{L} V_i^{**}} \right) \right] \tag{13.8}$$

where $V_i^{**} = V_i - V_{iB} - V_{iL}$. Here V_i is the total value of the investment of investor i. Because aggregate risk-free borrowing must equal aggregate risk-free lending, note that $\sum_i \left(V_{iB} + V_{iL} \right) = 0$ and $\sum_i V_i^{**} = \sum_i V_i$, where the summations are over all L investors. Again, it can be seen that

$$\boldsymbol{w}_m = \boldsymbol{w}_{p1} \left[\frac{\sum_{i=1}^{L} \alpha_i V_i^*}{\sum_{i=1}^{L} V_i^*} \right] + \boldsymbol{w}_{p2} \left[1 - \left(\frac{\sum_{i=1}^{L} \alpha_i V_i^*}{\sum_{i=1}^{L} V_i^*} \right) \right] \tag{13.9}$$

where $\boldsymbol{w}_i$ is a linear combination of p_1 and p_2. Thus, by choosing p_1 to correspond to T_L and p_2 to correspond to T_B, m can be seen to be efficient and to lie between T_L

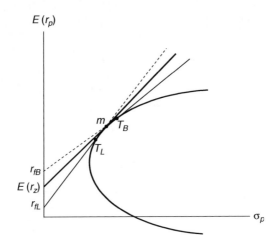

FIGURE 13.4   Zero-beta CAPM Under Different
Borrowing and Lending Risk-free Rates

and T_B on the hyperbola. Furthermore, given that m is efficient, the zero-beta CAPM must hold for all risky securities. Finally, note that due to the vertical intercepts of the tangency lines at T_L, m, and T_B, it follows that $r_{fL} < E(r_z) < r_{fB}$, as seen in Figure 13.4.

The existence of the CAPM (or the zero-beta CAPM) depends basically on the market portfolio being an efficient portfolio. This requires either unrestricted short selling or the existence of a risk-free asset; without either requirement, the market portfolio will not be identifiable and the CAPM will not exist (see Roll, 1977; Ross, 1977a; and Fama, 1976, chap. 8).

13.2   HOMOGENEOUS EXPECTATIONS

Expectations may be homogeneous in two separate respects: (1) the length of the investment horizon, and (2) the equality of investors' perceptions of a given security's risk and return statistics. These two aspects will be examined separately next.

13.2.1   Investment Horizons

CAPM assumption 8 in Section 12.1 of Chapter 12 states that investors have identical investment horizons. It is more realistic to assume that different investors have different horizons. Gilster (1983), expanding on Gressis, Philippatos, and Hayya (1976), relaxes this assumption and shows that in the absence of a risk-free asset, the composition of the efficient frontier is the same for any investment horizon. The addition of equal risk-free borrowing and lending rates coupled with unrestricted short selling will result in a linear CAPM.[3] However, this linearity is destroyed if short selling is restricted.

Merton (1973), in analyzing asset pricing in a continuous-time framework, has found that under certain conditions the single-period discrete-time CAPM is still valid. This means that the CAPM holds regardless of the length of an individual investor's horizon. However, because Merton's model is a multiperiod model, further discussion of that model is postponed until Chapter 15.

13.2.2   Multivariate Distribution of Returns

CAPM assumption 8 also states that investors have identical perceptions regarding the multivariate probability distributions of returns for the assets. More specifically, it is assumed that all investors have the same perceptions regarding means, variances, and covariances of returns for any given asset. Relaxing this assumption can be viewed as a consequence of relaxing the assumption that all investors freely and instantly receive all information, part (a) of assumption 7. If all investors do not have the same information, then (at least initially) they will not have the same perceptions, meaning that different investors will have different perceptions regarding the probability distribution.[4]

Lintner (1969) was the first to explore the impact of heterogeneous expectations on asset pricing. Assuming that investors had negative exponential utility functions, Lintner demonstrated that the composition (that is, weighting) of the risky portion of an investor's optimal portfolio will generally be unique, depending on the set of risk aversion parameters for all investors in the market as well as their probability assessments regarding asset returns.[5] Thus, with heterogeneous expectations, the separation theorem no longer holds, and investors no longer consider just the risk-free asset and the market portfolio. Nevertheless, market equilibrium still prevails where the variables are complex weighted averages of all investors' expectations. This means that the CAPM holds from the viewpoint of a representative investor, even though individual investors disagree on individual securities' expected returns and betas.

In Lintner's model all information is exogenous because current prices are not used to form or alter expectations. This has been criticized on the grounds that it is not consistent with the concept of rationality. That is, investors ought to make use of not only their own information, but also the information contained in current prices. This approach to examining heterogeneous expectations has been introduced by Grossman (1976) and Grossman and Stiglitz (1976). In their rational expectations approach, investors have different amounts of information that they use to form their initial expectations and trading strategies. Then, investors realize that current market prices tell them something about other investors' information. Accordingly, they revise their expectations and trading strategies. Ultimately, market-clearing prices will reflect all underlying information and no investor will have an incentive to change his or her expectations and trading strategy based on these prices. Thus, in equilibrium information and expectations are endogenous.

Later, Grossman and Stiglitz (1980) considered the implications of having information that is costly to acquire. Assuming there are two types of investors, informed and uninformed, Grossman and Stiglitz initially show that an equilibrium market-clearing price cannot exist. The reason is that if market prices reveal the information of the informed to the uninformed, then the uninformed would get the same benefits of knowing this information but without incurring the associated costs. However, the informed would realize this and would thus find it advantageous to switch to being uninformed. In turn, this means that nobody would bother to become informed. Then, in the final analysis, everyone would have an incentive to gather information because abnormal returns could be earned from that information. As a result, investors will gather information, leading us back to the initial situation where prices reveal the information of the informed.

Grossman and Stiglitz provide a way out of this conundrum. The key is to introduce an additional source of uncertainty into the model, such as having a random supply of the risky assets. This means that market clearing prices are noisy signals in that they do not fully reveal all the information that is known by the informed investors. Instead, the market clearing price for a given security now reflects both information and supply, and the uninformed investor cannot be sure of their relative effects. An equilibrium will now exist, where some investors are informed and some are uninformed. This is because if some uninformed (informed) investors switch to become informed (uninformed), then prices become less (more) noisy and reveal more (less) information, meaning informed (uninformed) investors would find it advantageous to switch back to become uninformed (informed). As a result, in equilibrium, informed investors have higher costs relative to uninformed investors. However, their higher information costs would be just offset by their higher returns, leaving nobody with an incentive to switch. In this situation, market prices could be described as partially aggregating information instead of fully aggregating information.

Diamond and Verrecchia (1981) derive an equilibrium asset pricing model in this situation and show that Lintner's model is a special case where the amount of uncertainty in the supply of risky assets is very large. Admati (1985) expands on their work and shows that investors still make their decisions in mean-variance space. However, each investor has a unique assessment of the magnitude of the parameters of the CAPM, because each investor has a unique benchmark portfolio that is efficient and plays the role of the market portfolio. Each investor's market portfolio is unique because prices are not fully revealing and thus the investor's expectations are dependent on his or her own unique information.

13.3 PERFECT MARKETS

Combining CAPM assumptions 4 and 7 in Section 12.1 of Chapter 12 is equivalent to assuming perfect markets exist. This section considers omitting assumptions 4 and 7 to create imperfect markets. The effect of restricting the availability of information is equivalent to assuming heterogeneous expectations. This was discussed in the preceding section. Market imperfections such as margin requirements, together with having different borrowing and lending rates, have also been discussed. This section explores market imperfections such as taxes, transactions costs, indivisibility, and price competition.

13.3.1 Taxes

The assumption of perfect markets implies that personal income and capital gains taxes are nonexistent.[6] It is more realistic to assume that these taxes exist and that their tax rates are different. Brennan (1970) explored a situation where, in addition to differential tax rates, investors have homogeneous expectations in regard to before-tax returns while dividend yields are known with certainty.[7] If investors have different tax rates and choose optimal portfolios based on their after-tax returns, this is equivalent to heterogeneous after-tax expectations where differences in investors' expectations have a given structure.

Brennan's after-tax CAPM assumes that the dividend yield (dividends divided by price) on each asset is known with certainty and is taxed at a constant rate that is different for each investor. This tax rate is also applicable to the interest earned on the risk-free asset. Capital gains are also taxed at a constant rate, but that rate is different for each investor. The capital gain tax rate is generally lower than the dividend yield tax rate. The resulting expected return on a risky asset is given by

$$E(r_j) = r_f + \{[E(r_j) - r_f] - \tau(\delta_m - r_f)\}\beta_j + \tau(\delta_j - r_f) \qquad (13.10)$$

where δ_m is the dividend yield on the market portfolio, δ_j is the dividend yield for stock j, and τ is a tax factor that is a complex function of investors' tax rates and wealth. The value of τ can reasonably be expected to be positive. The derivation of the CAPM with the same taxes as equation (13.10) is in appendix A13.2 to this chapter.[8]

Thus, before-tax expected returns are a function not only of the security's beta, but also of the security's dividend yield. Accordingly, before-tax expected returns will be positively related to dividend yields and, in reflecting this additional dimension, the Brennan tax version of the CAPM is frequently referred to as the security market plane (on the three-dimensional space of the expected return, beta, and dividend yield). Figure 13.5 illustrates equation (13.10).

Note that if the capital gains and dividend tax rates are equal, then $\tau = 0$ in equation (13.10) and the three-dimensional security market plane reduces to the familiar two-dimensional security market line (the standard CAPM). In this situation every investor's after-tax linear efficient frontier will have the same tangency portfolio. In particular, the after-tax linear efficient frontier will be located at a vertical distance of $\tau_i E(r_{p_i})$ below the before-tax linear efficient frontier, where τ_i is the tax rate applicable to both capital gains and dividend income for investor i, and $E(r_{p_i})$ is the expected return for investor i's efficient portfolio p. Thus, while its composition is the same for all investors, the location of the after-tax efficient frontier is investor-specific when the capital gains and dividend tax rates are equal.

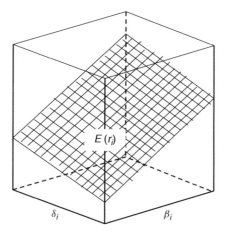

FIGURE 13.5 Security Market Plane of Brennan's CAPM with Taxes

While equation (13.10) describes the equilibrium asset pricing relationship for individual assets, the risky portion of an individual investor's optimal portfolio will be unique if he or she is in a unique tax bracket. That is, the hyperbola representing the minimum variance boundary of risky assets and the corresponding linear efficient frontier, when determined on a before-tax basis, are identical for all investors due to the assumption that they have homogeneous expectations regarding the distribution of before-tax returns. However, investors will be choosing their optimal portfolios on the basis of after-tax returns which, due to different tax rates, differ between investors. Thus, the location and shape of the after-tax hyperbola will differ from investor to investor. The after-tax risk-free rate will also differ, being less than or equal to the before-tax rate for all investors. As a result, the linear after-tax efficient frontier will also be investor specific and is likely to involve larger positions in those assets in which the investor has a comparative tax advantage. For example, because corporate investors are taxed relatively lightly on dividend income, corporate investors are likely to invest more heavily in high-dividend-yield securities and less in low-dividend-yield securities than are investors with high levels of taxable income. In summary, firms will have owners (investors) who are attracted by the firm's dividend payout policy. This tendency of particular investors to hold securities of firms with certain dividend payout policies is typically referred to as the *dividend clientele effect*.

13.3.2 Transaction Costs

If the assumption of no transaction costs is dropped, it can be surmised that the CML and CAPM would have bands on both sides, as shown in Figures 13.6 and 13.7.

Within these bands, it would not be profitable for investors to buy and sell securities and generate the price revisions necessary to attain equilibrium, because the transaction costs would consume the profit that induces such trading. As a result, the markets would never reach the theoretical equilibrium as described by the CAPM, even if the other simplifying assumptions were retrained. Furthermore, investors need not diversify over all securities to obtain portfolios within the banded

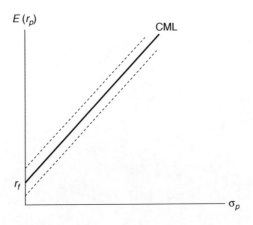

FIGURE 13.6 Transaction Costs Obscure CML

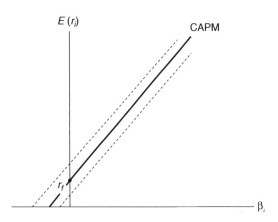

FIGURE 13.7   Transaction Costs Obscure CAPM

CML. Nevertheless, given their small relative size, transaction costs will not have a substantial impact on equilibrium prices and returns.

13.3.3   Indivisibilities

If assets are not infinitely divisible (that is, if partial shares could not be bought or sold), then it can be conjectured that the CAPM would degenerate. However, given the presence of a large number of wealthy investors (for example, financial institutions), consideration of indivisibilities is not likely to have a notable impact on the CAPM.

Levy (1978) examined the CAPM when the perfect market conditions of both perfect indivisibility and no transaction costs are relaxed by assuming that investor k holds stocks of n_k firms, where n_k can be very small. In this situation, the asset-pricing measure of the risk of a security is a weighted average of each investor's measure of the security's systematic risk. For stocks that are held by many investors, the CAPM can be viewed as an approximate equilibrium model; otherwise, a stock's variance is a more relevant measure of its risk.

13.3.4   Price Competition

Assuming investors are *price takers* allows the impact of their individual behavior on asset prices to be ignored. However, there are certain investors who, due to their size, may be able to affect equilibrium asset prices by their own trading activity. Lindenberg (1979) explored this issue by using oligopoly theory to conclude that sellers' supply decisions are made in consideration of their likely impact on market prices. In particular, he assumes there are two types of investors—price takers and price affecters—where the distinction between the two has to do with the impact of their individual trades on prices.

The initial result of having these two types of investors is that the price affecters will not hold the market portfolio. Instead, the risky portion of their optimal portfolio will be investor specific and will depend on, among other things, their initial holdings of each security. In contrast, price takers will all hold the same risky portfolio (levered up or down with risk-free borrowing and lending, depending on their utility functions). This risky portfolio will be equal to the market portfolio less the aggregate holdings of the price affecters. This implies that those securities held in greater than market proportions by the price affecters will have higher values than predicted by the CAPM. In turn, this means that in equilibrium the following three-factor CAPM exists:

$$E(r_j) = r_f + \lambda_1 \beta_{jm} + \lambda_2 \beta_{js} \qquad (13.11)$$

where $\beta_{jm} = \sigma_{jm}/\sigma_m^2$ and $\beta_{js} = \sigma_{js}/\sigma_s^2$. Here m and s denote the market portfolio and the aggregate price affecters' portfolio, and the terms λ_1 and λ_2 can be viewed as the market prices of risk relating to m and s, respectively. As can be seen in equation (13.11), this means that the expected return on asset j in the presence of price affecters may be either greater or less than its expected return in their absence. Similar to Brennan's tax version of the CAPM shown in Figure 13.5, equilibrium asset returns are based on two factors, resulting in a three-dimensional security market plane. The three dimensions are the expected returns and the two beta coefficients, β_{jm} and β_{js}.

13.4   UNMARKETABLE ASSETS

CAPM assumption 6 states that all assets are marketable, implying that the opportunity set of portfolios is the same for all investors. However, investors typically hold claim to certain assets that are not marketable. Examples of these illiquid assets include human capital, Social Security, and pensions. Human capital is an asset that produces returns in the form of wages and salaries; it cannot be physically separated from the person involved, and because slavery is prohibited, it cannot be sold. Social Security and pensions provide the person with cash flows over certain years of his or her life and cannot, by law, be sold to another person. Although these assets are clearly not marketable, they are nevertheless relevant when investors are seeking to identify their optimal portfolios.

Mayers (1972) has examined the asset pricing implications of introducing nonmarketable assets into the CAPM. If the world is divided up into marketable and unmarketable assets, then Mayers's CAPM is

$$E(r_j) = r_f + \frac{[E(r_m) - r_f]}{\left[\text{Var}(r_m) + \left(\frac{P_N}{P_m}\right)\text{Cov}(r_N, r_m)\right]} \cdot \left[\text{Cov}(r_j, r_{m+N}) + \left(\frac{P_N}{P_m}\right)\text{Cov}(r_j, r_N)\right]$$

(13.12)

where
   P_m is the total market value of all marketable assets,
   P_N is the total market value of all nonmarketable assets,
   r_N is the one-period rate of return of nonmarketable assets,

$$r_{m+N} = \left(P_m/P_{m+N}\right)r_m + \left(P_N/P_{m+N}\right)r_N, \text{ and } P_{m+N} = P_m + P_N$$

The proof of equation (13.12) may be found in section A13.3 in the appendix to this chapter.

Several interesting observations can be made about Mayers's CAPM. First, investors face different efficient frontiers and, therefore, the separation theorem is no longer valid. Mayers's CAPM provides a compelling explanation of why investors do not all hold the same risky portfolio. Second, a linear equilibrium asset pricing relationship still exists after unmarketable assets are introduced. Third, the relevant measure of an asset's risk depends not only on its covariance with the market portfolio m but, also, on its covariance with the portfolio of unmarketable assets N. However, these two measures of risk, $\text{Cov}\,(r_j, r_m)$ and $\text{Cov}\,(r_j, r_N)$, can be collapsed into one measure. To elaborate, note that equation (13.12) can be rewritten as

$$E(r_j) = r_f + \frac{\left[E(r_m) - r_f\right]}{\left[(P_m/P_{m+N})\,\text{Var}(r_m) + (P_N/P_{m+N})\,\text{Cov}\,(r_N, r_m)\right]} \times \text{Cov}\,(r_j, r_{m+N})$$

(13.13)

Thus, the systematic risk of a marketable asset can be expressed as its covariance with an overall index consisting of both marketable and nonmarketable assets. Fourth, the slope of the CAPM, known as the *market price of risk*, is changed by the presence of nonmarketable assets. The traditional CAPM has a slope term of $\left[E(r_m) - r_f\right]/\text{Var}(r_m)$, while the slope term in equation (13.13) can be rewritten as $\left[E(r_m) - r_f\right]/\text{Cov}\,(r_m, r_{m+N})$.[9] Fifth and last, Mayers has shown that his model can be used to indicate the effect that missing assets have on tests of the traditional CAPM.[10] That is, imagine that the assets in m are observed and included in the tests, whereas those in N are observed but are excluded from the tests. In this situation, examination of equation (13.13) reveals that ignoring the effect of the nonmarketable assets in N will present obstacles in testing the traditional CAPM.[11]

13.5   SUMMARY AND CONCLUSIONS

The CAPM rests on a number of assumptions that are made to simplify the model building. Relaxation of some of these assumptions was shown here to have no effect on the CAPM as long as it could still be demonstrated that the market portfolio was mean-variance efficient. Generally, this will occur if either unrestricted short selling is allowed or a risk-free borrowing and lending rate exists.

Certain assumptions, when relaxed, lead to equilibrium asset pricing relationships that can differ from the traditional CAPM. Two examples of this are the introduction of differential taxes on dividends and capital gains, and the recognition that certain assets are nonmarketable. In these situations, the concept of two-fund separation no longer applies. Instead, different investors face different efficient frontiers. However, equilibrium asset pricing equations still exist and indicate that each asset has two risk measures that determine its expected return. Accordingly, the CAPM is sometimes referred to as the security market plane instead of the security market line.

APPENDIX: DERIVATIONS OF A NON-STANDARD CAPM

This appendix describes the derivation of the zero-beta portfolio and its characteristics. Also, the derivation of Brennan's (1970) after-tax CAPM and Mayers's (1972) CAPM for nonmarketable securities is presented.

A13.1   The Characteristics of the Zero-Beta Portfolio

Equation (A7.2) in the appendix to Chapter 7 noted that the minimum variance boundary was a hyperbola (in $[\sigma, E(r)]$ space) that could be expressed as

$$\sigma_p^2 = \frac{C}{D}\left[E(r_p) - \frac{A}{C}\right]^2 + \frac{1}{C} \tag{A7.2}$$

where $E(r_p)$ and σ_p denote, respectively, the expected return and standard deviation of an efficient portfolio p and A, C, and D are constants and are defined in equation (7.16). In fact, equation (A7.2) expresses a relationship between the expected return and variance of an efficient portfolio. Furthermore, the covariance of an efficient portfolio p and any risky portfolio q is expressed as

$$\sigma_{pq} = \frac{C}{D}\left[E(r_p) - \frac{A}{C}\right]\left[E(r_q) - \frac{A}{C}\right] + \frac{1}{C} \tag{A7.5}$$

Suppose there is a frontier portfolio Z that has a zero covariance with the market portfolio. Based on equation (A7.5), the covariance between this portfolio and the market portfolio m is

$$\sigma_{zm} = \frac{C}{D}\left[E(r_z) - \frac{A}{C}\right]\left[E(r_m) - \frac{A}{C}\right] + \frac{1}{C} \tag{A13.1}$$

When the expected return on portfolio Z equals

$$E(r_z) = \frac{A}{C} - \frac{D/C^2}{\mu_m - A/C} \tag{A13.2}$$

the covariance between portfolios m and Z, σ_{zm}, equals zero. That is, portfolio Z is a zero-covariance (or zero-beta) portfolio of the market portfolio m. This zero-covariance portfolio Z is unique, because its expected return $E(r_z)$ is uniquely determined. Note that any efficient portfolio has its own unique zero-covariance portfolio. However, the global minimum variance portfolio does not have a zero-covariance portfolio, because its covariance with the zero-covariance portfolio is $1/C$, which is strictly positive, never zero.

The zero-covariance portfolio Z is inefficient, because its expected return is even lower than the expected return of the global minimum variance portfolio; that is,

$$E(r_z) = \frac{A}{C} - \frac{D/C^2}{E(r_m) - A/C} < E\left(r_{MVP}\right) = \frac{A}{C}$$

because $D = BC - A^2 > 0$ from equation (7.16) and $E(r_m) > A/C$. Section A7.1 of the appendix to Chapter 7 explains the characteristics of the global minimum variance portfolio.

The slope of the tangent line passing through the efficient portfolio p on the hyperbola of equation (A7.2) is calculated as

$$\frac{\partial E(r_p)}{\partial \sigma_p} = \left(\frac{\partial E(r_p)}{\partial \sigma_p^2}\right)\left(\frac{\partial \sigma_p^2}{\partial \sigma_p}\right)$$

$$= \left(\frac{2C\left[E(r_p) - A/C\right]}{D}\right)^{-1}(2\sigma_p)$$

$$= \frac{D\sigma_p}{CE(r_p) - A} \tag{A13.3}$$

Because the slope of the line is known, the intercept of the tangent line is calculated as

$$E(r_p) - \left(\frac{\partial E(r_p)}{\partial \sigma_p}\right)\sigma_p = E(r_p) - \left(\frac{D\sigma_p}{CE(r_p) - A}\right)\sigma_p$$

$$= \frac{A}{C} - \frac{D/C^2}{E(r_p) - A/C} \tag{A13.4}$$

Since the market portfolio m is an efficient portfolio, the slope and intercept of the tangent line passing through point m are obtained by replacing subscript p with m in equations (A13.3) and (A13.4), respectively. The intercept is exactly the same as the expected return on the zero-covariance portfolio of equation (A13.2).

A13.2 Derivation of Brennan's After-Tax CAPM

Brennan's (1970) after-tax CAPM assumes that the dividend yield on each stock j, denoted δ_j, is known with certainty and is taxed at a constant rate of τ_{di} for investor i. This tax rate is also applicable to the interest earned on the risk-free asset. Capital gains for investor i are taxed at the constant rate of τ_{gi}. Thus, investor i's after-tax return on security j and the risk-free asset can be expressed as

$$r_{ji}^A = \left(r_j - \delta_j\right)\left(1 - \tau_{gi}\right) + \delta_j\left(1 - \tau_{di}\right) \tag{A13.5}$$

and
$$r_{fi}^A = r_f\left(1 - \tau_{di}\right) \tag{A13.6}$$

respectively. From equations (A13.5) and (A13.6), it can be seen that

$$r_{ji}^A - r_{fi}^A = \left(r_j - r_f\right)\left(1 - \tau_{gi}\right) - \left(\delta_j - r_f\right)\left(\tau_{di} - \tau_{gi}\right) \tag{A13.7}$$

$$\text{Cov}\left(r_{ji}^A, r_{ki}^A\right) = \left(1 - \tau_{gi}\right)^2 \text{Cov}\left(r_j, r_k\right)$$

$$= \left(1 - \tau_{gi}\right)^2 \sigma_{jk} \tag{A13.8}$$

$$\text{Var}\left(r_{ji}^A\right) = \left(1 - \tau_{gi}\right)^2 \sigma_j^2 \tag{A13.9}$$

In Section 7.1 of Chapter 7, it was shown that the minimum variance boundary of risky assets was a hyperbola (when risk was measured by standard deviation). This hyperbola, when combined with a risk-free asset, resulted in a linear efficient frontier for the investor that was tangent to the hyperbola at a point denoted T. In Brennan's after-tax model, investors select their optimal portfolios by using the settings shown in Chapter 7 on an after-tax basis. Thus, investors will have an optimal portfolio that is a combination of the risk-free asset and some investor-specific risky tangent portfolio, denoted T_i for investor i. Assuming that markets will clear and equilibrium will exist, the CML-like structure facing each investor will be unique and can be expressed as

$$E\left(r_{p_i}^A\right) = r_{fi}^A + \left(\frac{E\left(r_{Ti}^A\right) - r_{fi}^A}{\sigma_{Ti}^A}\right)\sigma_{pi}^A \qquad (A13.10)$$

where $E\left(r_{p_i}^A\right)$ and σ_{pi}^A denote the after-tax expected return and standard deviation on efficient portfolio p for investor i. Using equations (A13.5) through (A13.9) allows equation (A13.10) to be rewritten as

$$E\left(r_{p_i}^A\right) = r_f\left(1 - \tau_{di}\right) + \left[\frac{\left(E\left(r_{T_i}\right) - r_f\right)\left(1 - \tau_{gi}\right) - \left(\delta_{Ti} - r_f\right)\left(\tau_{di} - \tau_{gi}\right)}{\sigma_{Ti}\left(1 - \tau_{gi}\right)}\right]\sigma_{pi}^A \qquad (A13.11)$$

When the market reaches equilibrium, each investor will believe that assets are priced so that an after-tax SML holds where T replaces the role of the market portfolio as shown in Chapter 12. Thus, to investor i, individual risky assets are priced according to

$$E\left(r_{ji}^A\right) = r_{fi}^A + \left[\frac{E\left(r_{T_i}^A\right) - r_{fi}^A}{\text{Var}\left(r_{Ti}^A\right)}\right]\text{Cov}\left(r_{Ti}^A, r_{ji}^A\right) \qquad (A13.12)$$

Substituting from equations (A13.5) through (A13.9) into equation (A13.12) and simplifying results in

$$\left[E(r_j) - r_f\right]\left(1 - \tau_{gi}\right) - \left(\delta_j - r_f\right)\left(\tau_{di} - \tau_{gi}\right) = \left[\frac{E\left(r_{T_i}^A\right) - r_{fi}^A}{\sigma_{Ti}^2}\right]\text{Cov}\left(r_{Ti}, r_j\right) \qquad (A13.13)$$

Dividing equation (A13.13) by $\left(1 - \tau_{gi}\right)$ results in

$$\left[E(r_j) - r_f\right] - \left(\delta_j - r_f\right)\left(\frac{\tau_{di} - \tau_{gi}}{1 - \tau_{gi}}\right) = \left[\frac{E\left(r_{T_i}^A\right) - r_{fi}^A}{\sigma_{Ti}^2\left(1 - \tau_{gi}\right)}\right]\text{Cov}\left(r_{Ti}, r_j\right) \qquad (A13.14)$$

Letting V_i denote the invested amount of investor i, equation (A13.14) can be multiplied by V_i and then simplified to

$$\left(V_i/\lambda_i\right)\left[E(r_j) - r_f\right] - \left(V_i/\lambda_i\right)\left(\delta_j - r_f\right)\left(\frac{\tau_{di} - \tau_{gi}}{1 - \tau_{gi}}\right) = V_i\text{Cov}\left(r_{Ti}, r_j\right) \qquad (A13.15)$$

where $\lambda_i = [E(r^A_{T_i}) - r^A_{f_i}]/[\sigma^2_{T_i}(1 - \tau_{g_i})]$. Summing equation (A13.15) over all L investors results in

$$\sum_{i=1}^{L} (V_i/\lambda_i) [E(r_j) - r_f] - \sum_{i=1}^{L} (V_i/\lambda_i) (\delta_j - r_f) \left(\frac{\tau_{di} - \tau_{gi}}{1 - \tau_{gi}} \right) = \sum_{i=1}^{L} V_i \text{Cov} (r_{T_i}, r_j)$$

(A13.16)

Remembering that the assumptions are (1) investors have homogeneous expectations regarding before-tax returns, (2) the sum of all investors' investment V_i is equal to the current value M of the market portfolio (because net borrowing = 0), and (3) each investor's risky portion of his or her optimal portfolio consists of a unique tangency portfolio with return r_{T_i}, it follows that

$$\sum_{i=1}^{L} V_i \text{Cov} (r_{T_i}, r_j) = M \sum_{i=1}^{L} \text{Cov} \left(\frac{V_i r_{T_i}}{M}, r_j \right)$$

$$= M \text{Cov} (r_m, r_j)$$

(A13.17)

Thus, equation (A13.16) can be rewritten as

$$\sum_{i=1}^{L} (V_i/\lambda_i) [E(r_j) - r_f] - \sum_{i=1}^{L} (V_i/\lambda_i) (\delta_j - r_f) \left(\frac{\tau_{di} - \tau_{gi}}{1 - \tau_{gi}} \right) = M \text{Cov} (r_m, r_j)$$ (A13.18)

or

$$[E(r_j) - r_f] - \tau (\delta_j - r_f) = H \text{Cov} (r_m, r_j)$$ (A13.19)

where

$$H = M/ \left[\sum_{i=1}^{L} (V_i/\lambda_i) \right]$$

and

$$\tau = \left(\frac{H}{M} \right) \left\{ \sum_{i=1}^{L} \left(\frac{V_i}{\lambda_i} \right) \left(\frac{\tau_{di} - \tau_{gi}}{1 - \tau_{gi}} \right) \right\}$$

Solving equation (A13.19) for H and letting j be the market portfolio m results in

$$H = \left[(E(r_j) - r_f) - \tau (\delta_j - r_f) \right] /\text{Cov} (r_m, r_j)$$

$$= \left[(E(r_m) - r_f) - \tau (\delta_m - r_f) \right] /\sigma^2_m$$

(A13.20)

Substituting equation (A13.20) into equation (A13.19) and rearranging results in Brennan's taxable-returns version of the CAPM,

$$E(r_j) = r_f + \left\{ \left[(E(r_m) - r_f) - \tau (\delta_m - r_f) \right] /\sigma^2_m \right\} \times \text{Cov} (r_m, r_j) + \tau (\delta_j - r_f)$$

(A13.21)

or

$$E(r_j) = r_f + \left\{ \left[E(r_m) - r_f \right] - \tau (\delta_m - r_f) \right\} \beta_j + \tau (\delta_j - r_f)$$ (A13.22)

The value of τ can reasonably be expected to be positive because it is generally observed that $0 < \tau_{gi} < \tau_{di} < 1$. The exact value of τ depends on tax rates as well as the investor's investable wealth and utility functions.

A13.3 Derivation of Mayers's CAPM for Nonmarketable Assets

Each investor i has an expected utility function $\overline{U}_i$ that is expressed in terms of a portfolio's expected end-of-period dollar value E_i and dollar variance S_i, where

$$E_i = \sum_{j=1}^{n} w_{ij}\overline{R}_j + \overline{R}_i^N - \left(1 - r_f\right)D_i \tag{A13.23}$$

and

$$S_i = \sum_{j=1}^{n}\sum_{k=1}^{n} w_{ij}w_{jk}\text{Cov}\left(R_j, R_k\right) + \text{Var}\left(R_i^N\right) + 2\sum_{j=1}^{n} w_{ij}\text{Cov}\left(R_i^N, R_j\right) \tag{A13.24}$$

where w_{ij} denotes the proportion of the total market value of firm j held by investor i; R_j is the end-of-period dollar value of firm j; n denotes the number of firms; R_i^N is the end-of-period dollar value of investor i's nonmarketable assets; r_f is the risk-free rate of return (where appropriate, the lowercase letter r will indicate rate of return while the uppercase letter R will indicate dollar returns); D_i is the current dollar value of the debt of investor i. A bar above an uppercase letter indicates an expected value. Here the investor's initial investable wealth V_i is equal to

$$V_i = \sum_{j=1}^{n} w_{ij}P_i - D_i \tag{A13.25}$$

where P_i is the current dollar value of firm j. Investors are assumed to have homogeneous expectations over the multivariate distribution of R_j's. All of the other CAPM assumptions given in Section 12.1 of Chapter 12 (except assumption 6) are maintained. Mayers (1973) has also considered the case where the risk-free asset does not exist. Analogous to the Black model, his results are essentially unchanged except that a zero-covariance asset now plays the role of the risk-free asset.

In this situation the investor will choose values of w_{ij} and D_i that maximize $\overline{U}_i$. This can be done by forming the Lagrangian objective function,

$$\text{Max}\ \overline{U}_i + \lambda_i\left[V_i - \sum_{j=1}^{n} w_{ij}P_j + D_i\right] \tag{A13.26}$$

and differentiating it with respect to w_{ij} and D_i. The result is the following $n + 1$ equations: for $j = 1, \ldots, n$,

$$\left(\frac{\partial\overline{U}_i}{\partial E_i}\right)\overline{R}_j + 2\left(\frac{\partial\overline{U}_i}{\partial S_i}\right)\left[\sum_{k=1}^{n} w_{ik}\text{Cov}\left(R_j, R_k\right) + \text{Cov}\left(R_i^N, R_j\right)\right] - \lambda_i P_j = 0 \tag{A13.27}$$

and

$$-\left(1 + r_f\right)\left(\frac{\partial\overline{U}_i}{\partial E_i}\right) + \lambda_i = 0 \tag{A13.28}$$

Solving equation (A13.28) for λ_i, substituting that value into equation (A13.27), and then simplifying results in

$$\left(\frac{\partial S_i}{\partial E_i}\right) = -2\left[\frac{\sum_{k=1}^{n} w_{ik}\mathrm{Cov}\left(R_j, R_k\right) + \mathrm{Cov}\left(R_i^N, R_j\right)}{\overline{R}_j - \left(1 + r_f\right)P_j}\right], \quad j = 1, \ldots, n \quad (A13.29)$$

Equation (A13.29) indicates investor i's marginal rate of substituting of risk for return. Because $\partial S_i / \partial E_i$ must have the same value of any two securities j and l in the investor's optimal portfolio, it follows that

$$\frac{\sum_{k=1}^{n} w_{ik}\mathrm{Cov}\left(R_j, R_k\right) + \mathrm{Cov}\left(R_i^N, R_j\right)}{\overline{R}_j - \left(1 + r_f\right)P_j} = \frac{\sum_{k=1}^{n} w_{ik}\mathrm{Cov}\left(R_l, R_k\right) + \mathrm{Cov}\left(R_i^N, R_l\right)}{\overline{R}_l - \left(1 + r_f\right)P_l}$$

$$(A13.30)$$

Furthermore, because in equilibrium equation (A13.30) will hold for each investor, both sides can be summed over all L investors,

$$\sum_{i=1}^{L}\left[\frac{\sum_{k=1}^{n} w_{ik}\mathrm{Cov}\left(R_j, R_k\right) + \mathrm{Cov}\left(R_i^N, R_j\right)}{\overline{R}_j - \left(1 + r_f\right)P_j}\right]$$

$$= \sum_{i=1}^{L}\left[\frac{\sum_{k=1}^{n} w_{ik}\mathrm{Cov}\left(R_l, R_k\right) + \mathrm{Cov}\left(R_i^N, R_l\right)}{\overline{R}_l - \left(1 + r_f\right)P_l}\right] \quad (A13.31)$$

Noting that $\sum_{i=1}^{L} w_{ik} = 1$, equation (A13.31) simplifies to

$$\frac{\sum_{k=1}^{n}\mathrm{Cov}\left(R_j, R_k\right) + \sum_{i=1}^{L}\mathrm{Cov}\left(R_i^N, R_j\right)}{\overline{R}_j - \left(1 + r_f\right)P_j} = \frac{\sum_{k=1}^{n}\mathrm{Cov}\left(R_l, R_k\right) + \sum_{i=1}^{L}\mathrm{Cov}\left(R_i^N, R_l\right)}{\overline{R}_l - \left(1 + r_f\right)P_l}$$

$$(A13.32)$$

or $\quad \dfrac{\mathrm{Cov}\left(R_j, R_m\right) + \mathrm{Cov}\left(R_N, R_j\right)}{\overline{R}_j - \left(1 + r_f\right)P_j} = \dfrac{\mathrm{Cov}\left(R_l, R_m\right) + \mathrm{Cov}\left(R_N, R_l\right)}{\overline{R}_l - \left(1 + r_f\right)P_l} \quad (A13.33)$

because $\sum_{k=1}^{n} R_k = R_m$ and $\sum_{i=1}^{L} R_i^N = R_N$. Continuing, equation (A13.33) will be unaltered if both the numerator and denominator of one side are summed over all n securities (note that this is equivalent to setting R_l equal to R_m). Performing this summation on the RHS results in

$$\frac{\mathrm{Cov}\left(R_j, R_m\right) + \mathrm{Cov}\left(R_N, R_j\right)}{\overline{R}_j - \left(1 + r_f\right)P_j} = \frac{\sum_{l=1}^{n}\left[\mathrm{Cov}\left(R_l, R_m\right) + \mathrm{Cov}\left(R_N, R_l\right)\right]}{\sum_{l=1}^{n}\left[\overline{R}_l - \left(1 + r_f\right)P_l\right]} \quad (A13.34)$$

or

$$\frac{\mathrm{Cov}\left(R_j, R_m\right) + \mathrm{Cov}\left(R_N, R_j\right)}{\overline{R}_j - \left(1 + r_f\right)P_j} = \frac{\mathrm{Var}(R_m) + \mathrm{Cov}\left(R_N, R_m\right)}{\overline{R}_m - \left(1 + r_f\right)P_m} \quad (A13.35)$$

where P_m denotes the total current market value of all marketable securities. Noting that

$$\mathrm{Cov}\left(R_j, R_m\right) = P_j P_m \mathrm{Cov}\left(r_j, r_m\right), \mathrm{Cov}\left(R_N, R_j\right) = P_N P_j \mathrm{Cov}\left(r_N, r_j\right),$$

$$\mathrm{Var}(r_m) = P_m^2 \mathrm{Var}(r_m), \mathrm{Cov}\left(R_N, R_m\right) = P_N P_m \mathrm{Cov}\left(r_N, r_m\right),$$

$$\overline{R}_j = P_j\left(1 + \mu_j\right), \overline{R}_m = P_m\left(1 + \mu_m\right)$$

equation (A13.31) can be rewritten in terms of rates of return as

$$\frac{P_j\left[P_m \mathrm{Cov}\left(r_j, r_m\right) + P_N \mathrm{Cov}\left(r_N, r_j\right)\right]}{P_j\left[1 + \mu_j - \left(1 + r_f\right)\right]} = \frac{P_m\left[P_m \mathrm{Var}(r_m) + P_N \mathrm{Cov}\left(r_N, r_m\right)\right]}{P_m\left[1 + \mu_m - \left(1 + r_f\right)\right]} \quad \text{(A13.36)}$$

or

$$\frac{P_m \mathrm{Cov}\left(r_j, r_m\right) + P_N \mathrm{Cov}\left(r_N, r_j\right)}{\mu_j - r_f} = \frac{P_m \mathrm{Var}(r_m) + P_N \mathrm{Cov}\left(r_N, r_m\right)}{\mu_m - r_f} \quad \text{(A13.37)}$$

Finally, solving equation (A13.37) for $\overline{r}_j$ yields Mayers's CAPM,

$$\mu_j = r_f + \frac{\left[\mu_m - r_f\right]}{\left[\mathrm{Var}(r_m) + \left(\frac{P_N}{P_m}\right) \mathrm{Cov}\left(r_N, r_m\right)\right]} \cdot \left[\mathrm{Cov}\left(r_j, r_{m+N}\right) + \left(\frac{P_N}{P_m}\right) \mathrm{Cov}\left(r_j, r_N\right)\right]$$

$$\text{(A13.12)}$$

NOTES

1. This chapter provides a mathematically rigorous explanation of what happens when the simplifying assumptions underlying the CAPM are relaxed. This chapter is of primary interest to professors of finance and economics, and to graduate students. This chapter is not required to read the chapters that follow.
2. Let w_i denote the $(n \times 1)$ weight vector of n assets for the optimal portfolio of investor i, and let V_i denote the dollar value (a scalar) invested in the optimal portfolio by investor i. If there are L investors in the market,

$$w_m = \frac{\sum_{i=1}^{L} w_i V_i}{\sum_{i=1}^{L} V_i} = \sum_{i=1}^{L}\left[w_i\left(\frac{V_i}{\sum_{i=1}^{L} V_i}\right)\right] \quad (1)$$

where w_m is the $(n \times 1)$ weight vector of n assets for the market portfolio m. Because w_i is the weight vector for investor i's efficient portfolio, it can be expressed as a linear combination of w_{p1} and w_{p1}; the weight vectors for p_1 and p_2 are:

$$w_i = \alpha_i w_{p1} + \left(1 - \alpha_i\right) w_{p2} \quad (2)$$

Substituting equation (2) into equation (1) yields

$$w_m = \sum_{i=1}^{L}\left[\left(\alpha_i w_{p1} + \left(1 - \alpha_i\right) w_{p2}\right)\left(\frac{V_i}{\sum_{i=1}^{L} V_i}\right)\right] \quad (3)$$

rearranging,

$$w_m = w_{p1} \left[\frac{\sum_{i=1}^{L} \alpha_i V_i}{\sum_{i=1}^{L} V_i} \right] + w_{p2} \left[1 - \left(\frac{\sum_{i=1}^{L} \alpha_i V_i}{\sum_{i=1}^{L} V_i} \right) \right] \qquad (4)$$

Note that the two terms in brackets on the right-hand side of equation (4) sum to one and therefore can be viewed as weights. Because they are multiplied by the weight vectors of two portfolios on the minimum variance boundary, the market portfolio itself must be on the minimum variance boundary. The market portfolio can be shown to be efficient by virtue of being on the upper half of this boundary. Because p_1 and p_2 can be any two portfolios on the minimum variance boundary, let them be efficient portfolios with expected returns equal to the lowest and highest values chosen by the L different investors. Selecting p_1 and p_2 in this fashion means that for all investors $0 \leq \alpha_i \leq 1$ and thus $0 \leq \left(\sum_{i=1}^{L} \alpha_i V_i / \sum_{i=1}^{L} V_i \right) \leq 1$, where the summation is over all L investors. This means that m must lie on that segment of the minimum variance boundary between p_1 and p_2. By selection, p_1 and p_2 are segments of the efficient frontier. Thus, m is an efficient portfolio.

3. Gilster (1983) also points out that his results require an assumption that portfolio returns are stationary and serially independent.

4. Barry (1978) and Brown (1979) have analyzed the impact that recognition of estimation risk has on the CAPM. Assuming that investors have the same degree of estimation risk and that estimation risk is similar across securities, they concluded that the basic predictions of the CAPM were unaffected. However, when estimation risk was allowed to differ across securities, Barry and Brown (1985) found that these basic predictions were affected.

5. Lintner also argued that his conclusions hold if investors have quadratic utility functions.

6. Alternatively, as mentioned earlier, these taxes can be allowed to exist but must be equal and symmetric with respect to gains and losses.

7. Litzenberger and Ramaswamy (1979) have extended this model by assuming there are both margin and income constraints on borrowing together with a progressive taxation scheme. Singer (1979) extended Brennan's model by having endogenous tax rates.

8. Theoretical counterarguments to Brennan's tax version of the CAPM have been raised by Black and Scholes (1974), Miller and Scholes (1978), and Schaefer (1982).

9. If P_N/P_m is approximately zero, then both the systematic risk of a security, $\text{Cov}(r_j, r_{m+N})$, and the market price of risk, $[E(r_m) - r_f]/\text{Cov}(r_m, r_{m+N})$, will be essentially unaltered by the consideration of nonmarketable assets, and in an approximate sense the traditional CAPM will hold. In the limiting case when $P_N/P_m = 0$, Mayers's CAPM reduces exactly to the standard CAPM.

10. Mayers's CAPM can also be viewed as a model where a certain set of assets have such large transactions costs that trading in them is prohibitively expensive. Accordingly, Mayers's CAPM offers some insight into the issue of transactions costs. Mayers (1976) has also shown how his model can be used to examine the issue of market segmentation.

11. Research on the effect of excluding assets in tests of the CAPM has been conducted by Stambaugh (1982, 1983) and Kandel (1984).

CHAPTER 14

Empirical Tests of the CAPM

The capital asset pricing model (CAPM) states that the expected return from a risky asset is positively and linearly related to its beta. Although many extended models of the CAPM, described in Chapter 12, support a linear relationship between the expected return and beta, other models, including the multiperiod asset pricing model to be described in Chapters 15 and 16, suggest that systematic risks other than beta are needed to explain the expected return. That is, other models suggest that beta is not the sole source of systematic risk. Moreover, the expected return may be associated with the standard deviation or with some firm characteristics such as firm size and financial ratios. These alternative risk measures create the need to test how well the CAPM fits empirical data. There are two approaches to testing the validity of asset pricing models: time-series tests and cross-sectional regression tests.

14.1   TIME-SERIES TESTS OF THE CAPM

Black, Jensen, and Scholes (1972) first introduced time-series tests to examine restrictions on the intercept term of market model regressions. They considered the following regression model for asset i:

$$r_{it} - r_{ft} = \alpha_i + \beta_i \left(r_{mt} - r_{ft} \right) + \varepsilon_{it} \qquad t = 1, \ldots, T \qquad (14.1)$$

Equation (14.1) is identical to regression equation (8.5). If the CAPM is valid, the intercept term α_i should be zero for all assets. That is, the CAPM implies that the intercept estimate, $\hat{\alpha}_i$, should not be statistically significantly different from zero for all individual assets or portfolios.

Simply examining the estimates of α_i, however, could introduce bias and/or inefficiencies in the tests, because the residual errors of the time-series market model are correlated within certain groups of stocks, as shown by King (1966) and others. To reduce this problem, Black, Jensen, and Scholes (1972) (hereafter BJS) used a method of grouping stocks into portfolios. However, if stocks are assigned to portfolios randomly, then the portfolio betas will tend to be clustered about one. Because maximum possible cross-sectional dispersion in the sizes of the portfolio betas was desired, BJS used the individual stock betas estimated by equation (14.1) to rank the stocks and then formed 10 portfolios of stocks that were grouped into risk deciles.

Although this procedure will produce a range of portfolio betas, it also introduces selection bias into the analysis. This bias occurs because those stocks in the high (low) beta portfolio will tend to have positive (negative) measurement errors. That is, stocks will be in the high (low) beta decile either because their beta has been estimated correctly and they belong in this decile, or, because their beta has been overestimated (underestimated) and the stock belongs in a lower (higher) decile, resulting in a net positive (negative) measurement error in the portfolio. This would cause α_i to be biased in the opposite direction. That is, the intercept estimate of the high (low) beta portfolio tends to be negatively (positively) biased. To avoid this selection bias, BJS calculated the rate of return on each portfolio in the following sixth year (that is, the year following the five-year period during which individual betas were calculated and the decile portfolios formed). BJS proceeded to update the procedure one year at a time, resulting in a set of monthly returns from 1931 to 1965 for each of the 10 portfolios. Thus, the composition of the portfolios changed from one five-year estimation period to the next. These portfolio returns are called *post-ranking* returns, whereas returns used to estimate individual stocks' beta are called *pre-ranking* returns.

After BJS calculated 35 years of monthly (post-ranking) returns for each of the 10 portfolios, they were able to undertake time-series tests of the CAPM by estimating α_i and β_i in equation (14.1) for each of the 10 beta portfolios for the entire 35-year (420-month) sample period. Table 14.1 presents a summary of the estimation results. Over a wide range of portfolio betas, it can be noted that α_i and β_i are inversely related. The data in Table 14.1 suggests that high-beta stocks tend to earn less than expected and low-beta stocks tended to earn more than expected.

Table 14.1 indicates that the CAPM does not hold, because the intercept estimates of portfolios 2 and 9 ($\hat{\alpha}_2$ and $\hat{\alpha}_9$) are significantly different from zero at a 5 percent significance level. The intercept estimate of the lowest beta portfolio ($\hat{\alpha}_{10}$) is also significantly different from zero at a 10 percent significance level. Rather than performing individual t-tests, as above, a simultaneous test of the null hypothesis H_0: $\alpha_1 = \alpha_2 = \cdots = \alpha_{10} = 0$ can also be performed. By assuming that the residual returns of test assets in equation (14.1) follow a multivariate normal

TABLE 14.1 Time-Series Test Results by Black, Jensen, and Scholes (1972)

Beta portfolio	Monthly excess return $(\bar{r}_p - \bar{r}_f)$	Beta $(\hat{\beta}_p)$	Intercept $(\hat{\alpha}_p)$ ($\times 100$)	R^2
high	0.0213	1.561	−0.083 (−0.43)	0.963
2	0.0177	1.384	−0.194 (−1.99)	0.988
3	0.0171	1.248	−0.065 (−0.76)	0.988
4	0.0163	1.163	−0.017 (−0.25)	0.991
5	0.0145	1.057	−0.054 (−0.87)	0.992
6	0.0137	0.923	0.059 (0.79)	0.983
7	0.0126	0.853	0.046 (0.71)	0.985
8	0.0115	0.753	0.081 (1.18)	0.979
9	0.0109	0.629	0.197 (2.31)	0.956
low	0.0091	0.499	0.201 (1.87)	0.898

*t-statistics in parentheses from two-tailed tests.
Source: Black, Fischer, Michael C. Jensen, and Myron Scholes, "The Capital Asset Pricing Model: Some Empirical Tests," in *Studies in the Theory of Capital Markets*, ed. Michael C. Jensen. (New York: Praeger, 1972) 79–121.

distribution with a mean vector of zero and covariance matrix Σ, Gibbons, Ross, and Shanken (1989) (GRS) suggest the following test statistic for the simultaneous test, which is an F-statistic with degrees of freedom N and $(T - N - 1)$:

$$F_{\text{GRS}} = \left[\frac{T(T - N - 1)}{N(T - 2)} \right] \left(\frac{\hat{\alpha}_p' \hat{\Sigma}^{-1} \hat{\alpha}_p}{1 + \hat{\theta}_p^2} \right) \tag{14.2}$$

where

$T =$ number of time-series return observations,
$N =$ number of test assets ($N = 10$ in the case of the BJS time-series tests) ($N < T$),
$\hat{\alpha}_p' = (\hat{\alpha}_1, \hat{\alpha}_2, \ldots, \hat{\alpha}_N)$,
$\hat{\Sigma} =$ covariance matrix of the residual returns,
$\hat{\theta} = (\bar{r}_m - \bar{r}_f) / s_m$,
$\bar{r}_m - \bar{r}_f =$ average excess market return,
$s_m =$ standard deviation of excess market returns $(r_{mt} - r_{ft})$.

Thus, a large value of the test statistic in equation (14.2), F_{GRS}, ensures the rejection of the validity of the CAPM.

In fact, the CAPM predicts that the market portfolio is mean-variance efficient. Therefore, the test for the validity of the CAPM is equivalent to the test for the mean-variance efficiency of the market portfolio. According to Roll (1977), however, this hypothesis cannot be tested because the true market portfolio cannot be observed.[1] In this circumstance, the practically possible empirical tests of the CAPM are narrowed to test if a given proxy for the market portfolio is a valid surrogate; that is, to test if a given market proxy is mean-variance efficient. The mean-variance efficiency test for a given market proxy is equivalent to testing the null hypothesis H_0: $\alpha_i = 0$ for $i = 1, \ldots, N$. Note that N is the number of test assets.

The GRS test statistic in equation (14.2) is one of the most frequently used test statistics in testing the mean-variance efficiency of a given market proxy. To test the mean-variance efficiency of the CRSP equal-weighted index, Gibbons, Ross, and Shanken (1989) used the same 10 beta-sorted portfolios as test assets that BJS used in Table 14.1.[2] They reported the F-statistic of 0.96, which has a p-value of 0.48, indicating that the *ex ante* efficiency of the CRSP equal-weighted index cannot be rejected.[3] In other words, if this index is taken as the true market portfolio, then the Sharpe-Lintner version of the CAPM cannot be rejected.[4]

14.2 CROSS-SECTIONAL TESTS OF THE CAPM

Cross-sectional tests of the CAPM examine whether actual returns of assets are cross-sectionally linearly related with their actual betas. These tests estimate the intercept and slope coefficient of the following cross-sectional regression model:

$$\bar{r}_i - \bar{r}_f = \gamma_0 + \gamma_1 \hat{\beta}_i + \varepsilon_i, \qquad i = 1, \ldots, N \tag{14.3}$$

where $\bar{r}_i - \bar{r}_f$ denotes the average excess rate of return for asset i over a particular time period, and $\hat{\beta}_i$ is the beta of asset i estimated with the time-series market model. The estimated beta is used as an explanatory variable instead of the true beta, because the true beta is unknown. In equation (14.3), each data observation corresponds to an individual asset. In fact, cross-sectional tests of the CAPM are usually performed with a two-pass methodology. In the first pass, betas are estimated from the market model using time-series return observations. In the second pass, these estimated betas are used as the regressor in cross-sectional regressions. If the CAPM is valid, the following finding should hold:

- The intercept term, γ_0, should not be significantly different from zero.
- The slope coefficient on the beta, γ_1, should be positive and equal to the market risk premium $(\bar{r}_m - \bar{r}_f)$.
- Beta should be the only variable that explains returns of risky assets. When other variables such as idiosyncratic risk or firm characteristics are added into the cross-sectional regression equation, these variables should have no explanatory power. That is, the coefficient on these variables should not be significantly different from zero.

Cross-sectional tests of the CAPM are more complicated than time-series tests due to some econometric problems introduced from using estimated betas instead of the true betas and time-varying attributes of the market risk premium. Three important works in cross-sectional tests are described next.

14.2.1 Black, Jensen, and Scholes's (1972) Tests

Black, Jensen, and Scholes (1972) also conduct cross-sectional tests of the CAPM by using 10 beta decile portfolios described in Section 14.1. The cross-sectional regression model they estimate is

$$\bar{r}_i - \bar{r}_f = \gamma_0 + \gamma_1 \hat{\beta}_i + \varepsilon_i, \qquad i = 1, \ldots, 10 \qquad (14.4)$$

The beta of each portfolio is estimated using the whole sample of time-series return observations, which assumes the beta is stationary over the entire sample period. The average excess return of each portfolio is also computed using returns over the entire sample period. The estimation results of equation (14.4) over the 35-year period (from January 1931 to December 1965) and four subperiods are shown in Table 14.2.

TABLE 14.2 Cross-Sectional Test Results by Black, Jensen, and Scholes (1972)

Test period	$\hat{\gamma}_0$	$t(\hat{\gamma}_0)$	$\hat{\gamma}_1$	$\bar{r}_m - \bar{r}_f$ $(= \gamma_1)$	$t(\gamma_1 - \hat{\gamma}_1)$
Jan 1931–Dec 1965	0.0036	6.52	0.0108	0.0142	6.53
Jan 1931–Sep 1939	−0.0080	−4.45	0.0304	0.0220	−4.91
Oct 1939–Jun 1948	0.0044	3.20	0.0107	0.0149	3.23
Jul 1948–Mar 1957	0.0078	7.40	0.0033	0.0112	7.98
Apr 1957–Dec 1965	0.0102	18.89	−0.0012	0.0088	19.61

*t-statistics are from two-tailed tests.
Source: F. Black, M. Jensen, and M. Scholes, "The Capital Asset Pricing Model: Some Empirical Tests," in *Studies in the Theory of Capital Markets*, ed. M. C. Jensen (New York: Praeger, 1972), 79–121.

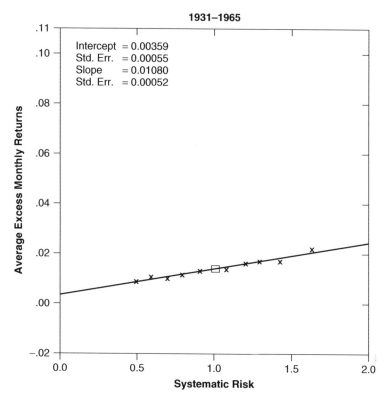

FIGURE 14.1 Average Monthly Excess Returns Versus Beta for the 35-Year Period of 1931–1965 for 10 Portfolios
Source: F. Black, M. Jensen, and M. Scholes, "The Capital Asset Pricing Model: Some Empirical Tests," in *Studies in the Theory of Capital Markets*, ed. M. C. Jensen (New York: Praeger, 1972), Figure 1, p. 94.

The cross-sectional test results in Table 14.2 are graphically depicted in Figure 14.1. Each cross in Figure 14.1 represents the beta and average excess rate of return for one of the 10 portfolios. The small square near the center of the 10 crosses represents the risk (that is, $\beta = 1$) and average excess return for the market proxy used by BJS. The straight line in Figure 14.1 is an empirical estimate of the CAPM prepared with regression equation (14.3). This long-run average CAPM may be considered to be the best empirical estimate of the equilibrium CAPM developed by BJS because it uses both bull and bear market periods in measuring the market's average tendencies.

When shorter sample periods are used to determine the cross-sectional regression estimates of the *ex post* CAPM, it sometimes assumes positions that surprise students who have not considered all the implications of capital market theory for the dynamic disequilibria characterized by short-run buying and selling. Figure 14.2 and Table 14.2 show empirical estimates of the *ex post* CAPM that BJS prepared from four different sample periods of 105 months each. The CAPM from the April 1957 to December 1965 sample slopes downward. This empirically estimated *ex post* CAPM slopes downward because the sample period contained market declines in 1957, 1960, 1962 and 1965. During bearish periods the high-beta stocks experienced the

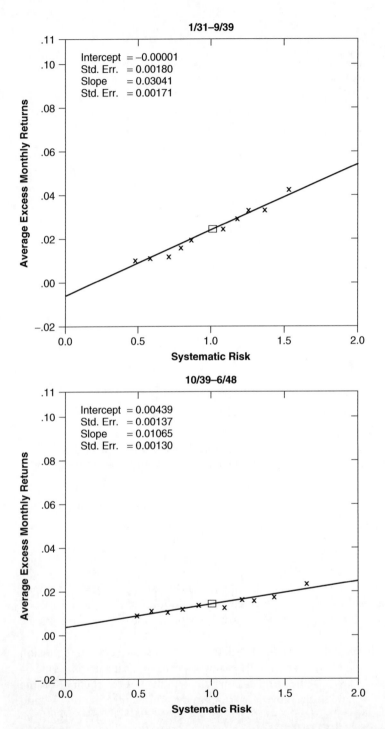

FIGURE 14.2 Empirical Estimates of the Security Market Line (SML) for the Subperiods for the 10 Portfolios
Source: F. Black, M. Jensen, and M. Scholes, "The Capital Asset Pricing Model: Some Empirical Tests," in *Studies in the Theory of Capital Markets*, ed. M. C. Jensen (New York: Praeger, 1972), Figures 2, 3, 4, and 5, pp. 96–97.

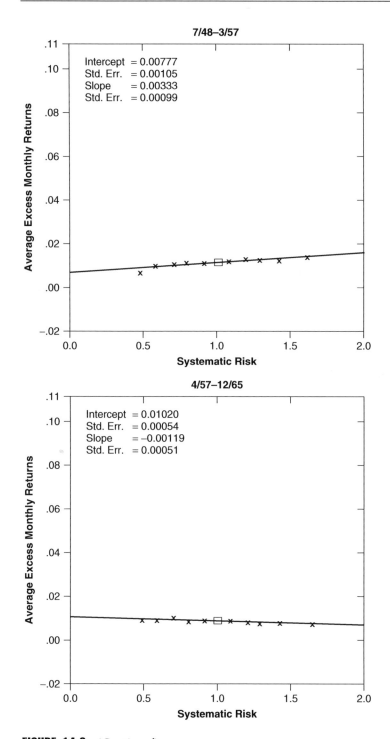

FIGURE 14.2 (*Continued*)

lowest rates of return, and this pulled down their average return below what was earned by the less risky low-beta stocks. Conversely, in bullish sample periods, such as occurred from January 1931 to September 1939 (following the Great Crash of 1929), the empirically estimated *ex post* CAPM slopes steeply upward because the high-beta stocks experienced the highest average rates of return. If shorter time periods were employed to empirically estimate the *ex post* CAPM, their intercept and slope coefficients would vary even more dramatically than those shown in Figure 14.2.

Analysis of the data in Table 14.2 reveals that for three of the four subperiods and for the entire sample period, the estimate of γ_0 is significantly greater than zero and the estimate of γ_1 is significantly less than $(\bar{r}_m - \bar{r}_f)$. These results suggest that the intercept and slope terms in equation (14.3) are, relative to the CAPM, too high and too low, respectively. In other words, the time-series tests show that on average low-beta stocks earn more than the CAPM suggests, and high-beta stocks earn less than the CAPM suggests.

BJS argue that these results are to be expected if the zero-beta version of the CAPM from Section 13.1.1 of Chapter 13 is valid. If the zero-beta version of the CAPM is valid, then the following returns-generating model is appropriate:

$$r_{it} - r_{Zt} = \alpha_i^* + \beta_i^* \left(r_{mt} - r_{Zt} \right) + \varepsilon_{it}^* \qquad (14.5)$$

where r_{Zt} is the return on the zero-beta portfolio and α_i^* is expected to equal zero if the zero-beta CAPM is valid. Assuming equation (14.5) is the correct model implies that the intercept term in equation (14.1) has an expected value of

$$\alpha_i = \left(\bar{r}_Z - \bar{r}_f \right) \left(1 - \beta_i \right) \qquad (14.6)$$

where $\bar{r}_Z$ and $\bar{r}_f$ are the mean returns of the zero-beta portfolio and the risk-free rate over the sample period, respectively. Thus, for time-series tests, if $\bar{r}_Z > \bar{r}_f$, then high-beta portfolios will tend to have negative estimated α's and low-beta portfolios will tend to have positive estimated α's. Furthermore, the cross-sectional tests of equation (14.4) imply that the intercept and slope parameters, γ_0 and γ_1, should have true values of $\bar{r}_Z - \bar{r}_f$ and $\bar{r}_m - \bar{r}_Z$, respectively. And, in addition, the value of $\bar{r}_m - \bar{r}_f$ is implied by the traditional CAPM. Hence, in the cross-sectional tests, if $\bar{r}_Z > \bar{r}_f$, then γ_0 will be positive and γ_1 will be less than $\bar{r}_m - \bar{r}_f$. An interpretation of Tables 14.1 and 14.2 and Figure 14.1 and 14.2 is that $\bar{r}_Z$ is not stationary over the 35-year test period, being less than $\bar{r}_f$ in the first subperiod and successively greater than $\bar{r}_f$ in the following subpeiods. BJS conclude by rejecting the traditional version of the CAPM and suggesting that the data are consistent with the zero-beta version of the CAPM. However, BJS readily admit that they have not conducted a direct test of the latter model and suggest that the data are also consistent with other versions of the CAPM (such as Mayers's version).[5]

14.2.2 Fama and MacBeth's (1973) Tests

Fama and MacBeth (1973) (hereafter FM) investigated the CAPM by estimating the following cross-sectional regression (CSR) equation for each month t using 20 portfolios of NYSE-listed stocks:

$$r_{it} = \gamma_{0t} + \gamma_{1t}\hat{\beta}_{it-1} + \gamma_{2t}\hat{\beta}_{it-1}^2 + \gamma_{3t}\hat{s}_{it-1} \left(\hat{\varepsilon}_i \right) + \eta_{it}, \qquad i = 1, \ldots, N \qquad (14.7)$$

where r_{it} denotes the return on portfolio i in month t, $\hat{\beta}_{it-1}$ is the estimated beta for portfolio i in month $t - 1$ by using return observations available up to month $t - 1$, $\hat{s}_{it-1}(\hat{\varepsilon}_i)$ is the estimated residual standard deviation for portfolio i in month $t - 1$ using residual returns from the market model, and η_{it} is the random error term. $\hat{\beta}_{it-1}$ and $\hat{s}_{it-1}(\hat{\varepsilon}_i)$ are obtained from first-pass regressions. That is, the beta of each portfolio is estimated from the market model using time-series return observations available up to month $t - 1$. The residuals are obtained simultaneously from the market model. Then, the residual standard deviation of each portfolio is computed using these residuals. In fact, $\hat{\beta}_{it-1}$ is a predictive beta. Each month over the test period, the cross-sectional regression model of equation (14.7) is estimated. Thus, estimates of the CSR coefficients, $\hat{\gamma}_{0t}$, $\hat{\gamma}_{1t}$, $\hat{\gamma}_{2t}$, and $\hat{\gamma}_{3t}$, are obtained each month. Fama and MacBeth regard the averages of these estimated values ($\bar{\hat{\gamma}}_0$, $\bar{\hat{\gamma}}_1$, $\bar{\hat{\gamma}}_2$, and $\bar{\hat{\gamma}}_3$) as the ultimate estimates of the risk premiums, γ_0, γ_1, γ_2, and γ_3. t-statistics for testing the null hypothesis that $\gamma_j = 0$ for $j = 0, 1, 2, 3$ are

$$t\left(\bar{\hat{\gamma}}_j\right) = \frac{\bar{\hat{\gamma}}_j}{s\left(\hat{\gamma}_j\right)/\sqrt{T}} \tag{14.8}$$

where $s\left(\bar{\hat{\gamma}}_j\right)$ is the standard deviation of the estimated gamma coefficient $\hat{\gamma}_{jt}$, and T is the number of the estimated gamma coefficients.

The hypotheses to be tested are

- Linearity: $\gamma_{2t} = 0$. The relationship between risk and return is linear. If the hypothesis is true, then the coefficient on the squared beta term should not be significantly different from zero.
- Beta is the only relevant measure of risk: $\gamma_{3t} = 0$. If this hypothesis is true, then the coefficient on the non-β variables should not be significantly different from zero.
- The relationship between risk and return is positive: $\gamma_{1t} > 0$. If this hypothesis is true, then the coefficient on the beta variable should be significantly greater than zero.

These three hypotheses are consistent with both the traditional and zero-beta versions of the CAPM, and thus are viewed by FM as fundamental tests of mean-variance asset pricing models. A more specific hypothesis that can be tested is that the true value of γ_{0t} is equal to the risk-free rate. Alternatively, the zero-beta version of the CAPM can be tested by hypothesizing that the true value of γ_{0t} is greater than the risk-free rate.

Certain aspects of FM's methodology are analogous to those of BJS. The FM data consists of all stocks traded on the NYSE during the period January 1926–June 1968. Although it might seem that equation (14.7) could be tested on a sample of individual stocks, the recognition that β and $s(\varepsilon)$ cannot be observed directly and must be estimated separately led FM to perform their tests on portfolios, where measurement errors are less severe. Desiring a range of portfolio betas, FM estimated individual stock betas using the market model over a "portfolio formation period," usually consisting of seven years of monthly data.[6] Ranking the stocks by the magnitude of their estimated betas, FM formed 20 arrayed portfolios. Then, the betas and residual standard deviations of the portfolios were estimated over a subsequent five-year estimation period.[7] Next, the returns on each portfolio were calculated monthly over a subsequent four-year testing period. After each year of the testing period, the portfolio betas and residual standard deviations were reestimated by adding that year to the estimation period. The portfolio formation, estimation, and testing periods were set up using nonoverlapping samples. Thus, the returns in the first year of the testing period were matched with the estimated β and $s(\varepsilon)$ from the previous five years (see Panel A in Table 14.3); the returns for the second year were matched with the estimated β and $s(\varepsilon)$ from the previous six years (see Panel B); the returns for the third year were matched with the estimated β and $s(\varepsilon)$ from the previous seven years (see Panel C); and, the returns for the fourth year were matched with the estimated β and $s(\varepsilon)$ from the previous eight years (see Panel D). Upon completion of a four-year test period, the portfolio formation period, estimation period, and test period were all advanced by four years and the process was repeated.

This procedure resulted in a testing period of 402 months from January 1935 to June 1968, along with monthly estimates of the portfolio betas and residual standard deviations, where the latter two values were based on previous data and thus were, in a sense, lagged values. With this set of data, FM estimated equation (14.7) for each month, resulting in a set of 402 estimates of $\hat{\gamma}_{0t}$, $\hat{\gamma}_{1t}$, $\hat{\gamma}_{2t}$, and $\hat{\gamma}_{3t}$. Using these estimated values, the average values and their simple t-tests were computed in order to test the various hypotheses.

Table 14.3 reports FM cross-sectional test results. Panel A of Table 14.3 indicates that for the entire period and two of the three subperiods, the average slope coefficient on the squared beta variable ($\overline{\hat{\gamma}}_2$) was not significantly different from zero.[8] Furthermore, the average slope coefficient on the residual standard deviation ($\overline{\hat{\gamma}}_3$) was not significantly different from zero in any of the three subperiods or the entire period. Panels B and C support these conclusions. Thus, it appears safe to conclude that the risk-return relationship is linear and that nonsystematic risk is unimportant in asset pricing. Having reached this conclusion, Panel D, based on equation (14.7), presents the most accurate tests of γ_0 and γ_1, because the estimates are derived without being affected by the presence of either the $\hat{\beta}_{it-1}^2$ or $\hat{s}_{it-1}(\hat{\varepsilon}_i)$ terms. Here it can be seen that for the entire period and two of the three subperiods γ_0 and γ_1 are significantly positive. At this stage in the analysis, the data appear to be consistent with both the traditional and zero-beta versions of the CAPM, because beta appears to be the relevant measure of risk and the risk-return relationship appears to be both linear and positive.

Also reported in Panel D of Table 14.3 are the average values of $\hat{\gamma}_{0t} - r_{ft}$ and $r_{mt} - r_{ft}$ over the entire test period and three subperiods. If the traditional version of the CAPM is valid, then the average value of $\hat{\gamma}_{0t} - r_{ft}$ (i.e., $\overline{\hat{\gamma}}_0 - \overline{r}_f$) should not be significantly different from zero, and the average value of $r_{mt} - r_{ft}$ (i.e., $\overline{r}_m - \overline{r}_f$) should correspond to $\overline{\hat{\gamma}}_1$, which is the market risk premium estimate. Unfortunately, for the entire period and all of the subperiods, $\overline{\hat{\gamma}}_0 - \overline{r}_f$ is positive and is significant for the entire period and one of the subperiods. Thus, it appears that the empirical version of the CAPM has an intercept above the risk-free rate of return, r_f, as was also found by BJS. Furthermore, although no statistical test was conducted, it can be seen that $\overline{r}_m - \overline{r}_f$ is notably greater than $\overline{\hat{\gamma}}_1$ over the entire test period and in each of the subperiods. Again, like BJS, it appears that the empirical version of the CAPM

TABLE 14.3 Fama and MacBeth's (1973) Summary of Cross-Sectional Regression Test Results

Period	$\bar{\gamma}_0$	$\bar{\gamma}_1$	$\bar{\gamma}_2$	$\bar{\gamma}_3$	$\bar{\gamma}_0 - \bar{r}_f$	$\bar{r}_m - \bar{r}_f$
Panel A:						
1935–6/1968	0.0020 (0.55)	0.0114 (1.85)	−0.0026 (−0.86)	0.0516 (1.11)		
1935–1945	0.0011 (0.13)	0.0118 (0.94)	−0.0009 (−0.14)	0.0817 (0.94)		
1946–1955	0.0017 (0.44)	0.0209 (2.39)	−0.0076 (−2.16)	−0.0378 (−0.67)		
1956–6/1968	0.0031 (0.59)	0.0034 (0.34)	−0.0000 (−0.00)	0.0960 (1.11)		
Panel B:						
1935–6/1968	0.0049 (1.92)	0.0105 (1.79)	−0.0008 (−0.29)			
1935–1945	0.0074 (1.39)	0.0079 (0.65)	0.0040 (0.61)			
1946–1955	−0.0002 (−0.07)	0.0217 (2.51)	−0.0087 (−2.83)			
1956–6/1968	0.0069 (1.56)	0.0040 (0.42)	0.0013 (0.29)			
Panel C:						
1935–6/1968	0.0054 (2.10)	0.0072 (2.20)		0.0198 (0.46)		
1935–1945	0.0017 (0.26)	0.0104 (1.41)		0.0841 (1.05)		
1946–1955	0.0110 (3.78)	0.0075 (1.47)		−0.1052 (−1.89)		
1956–6/1968	0.0042 (1.28)	0.0041 (0.96)		0.0633 (0.79)		
Panel D:						
1935–6/1968	0.0061 (3.24)	0.0085 (2.57)			0.0048 (2.55)	0.0130 (4.28)
1935–1945	0.0017 (0.26)	0.0104 (1.41)			0.0037 (0.82)	0.0195 (2.54)
1946–1955	0.0110 (3.78)	0.0075 (1.47)			0.0078 (3.31)	0.0103 (2.60)
1956–6/1968	0.0042 (1.28)	0.0041 (0.96)			0.0034 (1.39)	0.0095 (2.92)

*Numbers in parentheses indicate t-statistic.

Source: E. F. Fama and J. D. MacBeth, "Risk, Return, and Equilibrium: Empirical Tests," *Journal of Political Economy* 81 (1973): 607–636.

has a lower slope than implied by the risk-free version of the CAPM. In summary, FM's test results, like those of BJS, are consistent with the zero-beta version of the CAPM.[9] They are also consistent, however, with other versions of the CAPM.

It is worthwhile to note that the number of test (post-ranking) portfolios (N) in the previous studies is arbitrarily determined. Black, Jensen, and Scholes (1972) chose $N = 10$, whereas Fama and MacBeth (1973) did $N = 20$. The smaller the number of test portfolios is (i.e., the more the number of individual stocks in a portfolio), the less the measurement error in estimated betas and the less severe the errors-in-variables (EIV) problem. However, the smaller number of test portfolios also reduces the test power in the CSR tests due to the loss of information. There is an apparent trade-off between the measurement error and the test power. Therefore, when the CAPM tests are performed using portfolios, there is an issue regarding what is the optimal number of test portfolios. Also, there is another issue regarding how to form test portfolios. There are many characteristics used to sort individual stocks into portfolios such as beta, firm size, earnings-price ratio, and so on. The test results could be sensitive to the portfolio formation method. These issues are inevitable in the two-pass test methodology. To avoid these issues, individual stocks rather than portfolios should be used in the CSR tests. In this case, however, the test results are subject to the largest EIV bias, although test power is the strongest. Kim (1995, 1997) suggested a method of correcting for EIV bias for the use of individual stocks. His method is described in Section 14.3.1.

14.2.3 Fama and French's (1992) Tests

Fama and French (1992) published a study on the cross-sectional relationship between average returns and betas and reported evidence that is inconsistent with the CAPM. Their testing methodology is similar to Fama and MacBeth (1973). The CSR model estimated is, for each month t,

$$r_{it} = \gamma_{0t} + \gamma_{1t}\hat{\beta}_i + \gamma_{2t}\text{Char}_{i,t-1} + \eta_{it}, \qquad i = 1, \dots, N \qquad (14.9)$$

where $\hat{\beta}_i$ is the estimated beta of firm i using the full sample period, and $\text{Char}_{i,t-1}$ is a characteristic value (such as firm size or book-to-market) of firm i available up to month $t - 1$. Fama and French conduct the CSR test using individual stocks rather than using portfolios. In fact, the estimated beta variable in equation (14.9) is the full-period post-ranking beta of a size-β portfolio that is allocated to each stock contained in the portfolio. The reason they use portfolio betas instead of individual stock betas is that the measurement error of the beta variable can be alleviated. The authors seem to be implicitly suggesting portfolio betas adequately represent the attributes of individual stock betas of portfolio member stocks. To separate the effect of beta from firm size in average stock returns and to increase the test power, they formed size-β portfolios. In June of each year, all NYSE stocks are sorted by firm size (a stock's closing price times number of shares outstanding) to determine the NYSE decile breakpoints for firm size. All NYSE, AMEX, and Nasdaq stocks are then allocated into one of 10 size portfolios based on the NYSE breakpoints.[10] After constructing 10 size-sorted portfolios, they subdivide each size portfolio into 10 portfolios on the basis of pre-ranking betas for individual stocks. The pre-ranking betas are estimated using 24 to 60 monthly returns (as available) from the five years before July of year y. The β-breakpoints within each size decile are determined by using only NYSE stocks. After assigning firms into one of the 100 size-β portfolio in

June of year y, the equally-weighted monthly returns of the portfolios for the next 12 months from July of year y to June of year $y + 1$ are computed. Thus, portfolios are rebalanced every year. Then, they estimate portfolios' betas using the full sample (July 1963 to December 1990) of post-ranking returns on each of the 100 size-β portfolios.

Fama and French (1992) use three different firm characteristic variables; natural logarithm of firm size on June of year y ($\ln V_{t-1}$), natural logarithm of the ratio of book value of common equity to market value of common equity measured at the end of year $y - 1$ ($\ln BM_{t-1}$ or book-to-market), and earnings-price ratio [If earnings are positive, E(+)/P equals the ratio of earnings to stock price and E/P dummy equals 0. If earnings are negative, E(+)/P equals 0 and E/P dummy equals 1]. In order for the CAPM to be valid, only the average slope coefficient on the beta variable ($\hat{\bar{\gamma}}_1$) is positive and significantly different from zero, while the average slope coefficient on the firm characteristic variable ($\hat{\bar{\gamma}}_2$) should not be different from zero.

TABLE 14.4 Fama and French's (1992) Cross-Sectional Regression Test Results (July 1963 to December 1990)

$\hat{\beta}$	$\ln V_{t-1}$	$\ln BM_{t-1}$	E/P dummy	E(+)/P
0.15 (0.46)				
	−0.15 (−2.58)			
−0.37 (−1.21)	−0.17 (−3.41)			
		0.50 (5.71)		
			0.57 (2.28)	4.72 (4.57)
	−0.11 (−1.99)	0.35 (4.44)		
	−0.13 (−2.47)	0.33 (4.46)	−0.14 (−0.90)	0.87 (1.23)

*Numbers in parentheses indicate t-statistic.
Source: Adapted from E. Fama and K. R. French, "The Cross-Section of Expected Stock Returns," *Journal of Finance* 47 (1992): 129–176.

Table 14.4 reports time-series averages of the slope coefficients from month-by-month Fama and MacBeth (1973) cross-sectional regressions of equation (14.9). The test results show that unlike Fama and MacBeth (1973), market beta does not help explain average stock returns for January 1963 – December 1990. For example, the average slope coefficient on the estimated beta alone ($\hat{\beta}$) is 0.15 percent per month, with a t-statistic of 0.46, and it is even negative when firm size is included in the model. Contrary to the prediction by the CAPM, however, the firm characteristic variables help explain the cross-section of average stock returns. That is, the average slope coefficient on the firm size variable is negative and significantly different from zero, and the average slope coefficient on the book-to-market variable is positive and significantly different from zero.[11] This negative relation between firm size and average stock returns and this positive relation between book-to-market and average stock returns are persistent regardless of the other variables included in the model.[12]

14.3 EMPIRICAL MISSPECIFICATIONS IN CROSS-SECTIONAL REGRESSION TESTS

Fama and French's (1992) results could be quite damaging to the CAPM (both the standard and zero-beta versions). Fama and French (1992) received a great deal of attention from both practitioners and academics. A popular U.S. newspaper published articles displaying headlines such as "Beta is dead!" However, a number of researchers have criticized their work. First, their results, like all other results using the Fama and MacBeth two-pass test methodology, are subject to the so-called EIV problem. More specifically, Fama and French's EIV problem is that the slope coefficient on the beta variable is measured with error and, as a result, is underestimated. At the same time, the slope coefficient on the firm characteristic variable is overestimated (see Kim, 1995, 1997). Second, like most studies using estimated betas, Fama and French arbitrarily used five years of data in estimating betas, presuming that betas are stationary over the period. However, there is much evidence that beta is not stationary. For example, Schaefer, Brealey, Hodges, and Thomas (1975) compared several random beta coefficient models with a constant beta coefficient model and found that the random walk and first-order autoregressive models outperformed the constant beta model. Therefore, the nonstationarity of beta should be accommodated in some way when estimating betas. Third, the result with book-to-market may be due to a statistical fallacy like survivorship bias (or hindsight bias).[13] Fourth, the beta estimate is sensitive to the investment horizon or return measurement interval.[14] Handa, Kothari, and Wasley (1989) and Kothari, Shanken, and Sloan (1995) report that average returns are positively related to beta when annual return data, rather than monthly return data, are used to estimate beta. There is no compelling reason for preferring either monthly data over annual data, or vice versa. Therefore, Fama and French's results should not be viewed as the final word. In this section, among the empirical misspecification issues, we discuss (a) the EIV bias issue, which may be one of the most serious issues in the CSR tests within the Fama and MacBeth two-pass methodology, and, (b) the issue of the sensitivity of beta to the return measurement interval.

14.3.1   The Errors-in-Variables Problem

As mentioned in the previous section, the CSR tests performed with the Fama and MacBeth (1973) traditional two-pass estimation methodology are subject to the EIV problem because the true beta is unknown. An estimated beta is used instead as an explanatory variable in the cross-sectional regression. That is, in the first pass, beta estimates are obtained from separate time-series regressions from the market model for each asset, and in the second pass, the slope coefficients (the gammas) are estimated cross-sectionally by regressing asset returns on the estimated betas. Therefore, the explanatory variable in the CSR is measured with error. The EIV problem is one of the most serious problems in the CSR tests that affect the CAPM test results.

The CSR model for estimating the return-risk relation at a specific time t is

$$r_{it} = \gamma_{0t} + \gamma_{1t}\beta_{it} + \eta_{it}, \qquad \text{for } i = 1, \ldots, N \qquad (14.10)$$

where β_{it} is the true beta for asset i at time t. Because β_{it} is unobservable, the estimated beta, $\hat{\beta}_{it-1}$, is used as a proxy for the true beta. Thus, the CSR model actually estimated is

$$r_{it} = \gamma_{0t} + \gamma_{1t}\hat{\beta}_{it-1} + \eta_{it}, \qquad \text{for } i = 1, \ldots, N \qquad (14.11)$$

The explanatory variable, therefore, is measured with error:

$$\hat{\beta}_{it-1} = \beta_{it} + \xi_{i,t-1} \tag{14.12}$$

where $\xi_{i,t-1}$ is the measurement error with mean of zero and variance of $\sigma^2_{\xi_{t-1}}$.

In this case, the market risk premium (the price of risk) in equation (14.11), γ_{1t}, is underestimated. That is, the market risk premium estimate of equation (14.11) is lower than the true value of the market risk premium, γ_{1t}. We can show this in the following way:

$$E\left(\hat{\gamma}_{1t}\right) - \gamma_{1t} = -\frac{1}{1+\tau}\left[1 - \frac{2}{(N-1)}\frac{\tau^2}{(1+\tau)^2}\right]\gamma_{1t} + O\left(N^{-2}\right) \tag{14.13}$$

where $\tau = \sigma^2_{\beta_t}/\sigma^2_{\xi_{t-1}}$ and $O\left(N^{-2}\right)$ is the term containing all remaining terms with order less than or equal to N^{-2}. The term $O\left(N^{-2}\right)$ goes to zero for a moderate size of N. Note that $\sigma^2_{\beta_t}$ and $\sigma^2_{\xi_{t-1}}$ are the cross-sectional variance of β_{it} and $\xi_{i,t-1}$, respectively. Because the right-hand term of equation (14.13) is negative, $\hat{\gamma}_{1t}$ is negatively biased and thus γ_{1t} is underestimated under traditional least squares estimation. The underestimation of γ_{1t} leads to an overestimation of the intercept term γ_{0t}.

In order to examine whether a firm characteristic such as firm size explains the cross-section of stock returns, the firm characteristic variable is included in the CSR equation of (14.11):

$$r_{it} = \gamma_{0t} + \gamma_{1t}\hat{\beta}_{it-1} + \gamma_{2t}V_{i,t-1} + \eta_{it}, \qquad \text{for } i = 1, \dots, N \tag{14.14}$$

where $V_{i,t-1}$ is the firm size variable of firm i at time $t-1$ measured without error. In this case, the underestimation of γ_{1t} is even more severe. The slope coefficient on the size variable, γ_{2t}, is more negatively biased than the true value of the coefficient. Analytically, the biases of the least squares estimates of γ_{1t} and γ_{2t} are

$$E\left(\hat{\gamma}_{1t}\right) - \gamma_{1t} = -\left[\frac{1}{1+\tau\left(1-\rho^2_{\hat{\beta}V}\right)}\right]\gamma_{1t} + O\left(N^{-1}\right) \tag{14.15}$$

$$E\left(\hat{\gamma}_{2t}\right) - \gamma_{2t} = \left(\frac{\sigma_{\hat{\beta}V}}{\sigma^2_V}\right)\left[\frac{1}{1+\tau\left(1-\rho^2_{\hat{\beta}V}\right)}\right]\gamma_{1t} + O\left(N^{-1}\right) \tag{14.16}$$

$$= \left(\frac{\sigma_{\hat{\beta}V}}{\sigma^2_V}\right)\left[E\left(\hat{\gamma}_{1t}\right) - \gamma_{1t}\right] + +O\left(N^{-1}\right)$$

where $\sigma_{\hat{\beta}V}$ $(\rho_{\hat{\beta}V})$ is the cross-sectional covariance (correlation coefficient) between the estimated beta ($\hat{\beta}_{it-1}$) and the firm size variable ($V_{i,t-1}$), σ^2_V is the cross-sectional variance of the firm size variable, and $O\left(N^{-1}\right)$ is the term containing all remaining terms with order less than or equal to N^{-1}.

Equation (14.15) now shows that after including the firm size variable, γ_{1t} is underestimated even more, because the magnitude of negative bias in equation (14.15) is greater than that in equation (14.13), because $\rho^2_{\hat{\beta}V}$ is always less than one.

At the same time, equation (14.16) shows that the traditional least squares coefficient estimate of the firm size variable, $\hat{\gamma}_{2t}$ is negatively biased, as long as the estimated beta and the firm size are negatively correlated. It is empirically well documented that these two variables are negatively correlated. In other words, the CSR coefficient associated with the firm size variable is estimated more negatively than its true value under the traditional least squares estimation procedure. Therefore, the explanatory power of the firm size variable has been overestimated in previous empirical studies. The extent of the overestimation depends on the magnitude of the correlation coefficient between these two variables. The greater the negative correlation, the more severe the overestimation of the coefficient associated with firm size.

Equation (14.16) also indicates that if the estimated beta and the second explanatory variable measured without error are positively correlated, the traditional least squares coefficient estimate on the second variable is positively biased. An example of this case is the book-to-market equity ratio; it is empirically observed that this variable is positively correlated with the estimated beta. When the book-to-market equity ratio is included as the second variable in equation (14.14), instead of the firm size variable, the least squares estimate of γ_{2t} is positively (upward) biased; that is, the average value of the slope coefficient on the book-to-market variable is greater than the true value of γ_{2t}. Therefore, the explanatory power of the book-to-market equity ratio for average stock returns reported by Fama and French (1992) is also exaggerated under the traditional Fama and MacBeth two-pass methodology.

The biases of the least squares estimators of γ_{1t} and γ_{2t} described in equations (14.13), (14.15), and (14.16) could be eliminated if T-consistent beta estimates are used ($\tau \to \infty$ as $T \to \infty$, because $\sigma^2_{\xi_{t-1}} \to 0$), or if a finite set of well-diversified portfolios can be constructed ($\tau \to \infty$ as $\sigma^2_{\xi_{t-1}} \to 0$). Here, T is the time series sample size used in estimating the beta. A T-consistent estimator means that the estimator of a parameter converges to the true value of the parameter as T gets larger. However, concerns about changing risk premium parameters and beta nonstationarity limit the length of the time-series T that can be used. Similarly, the construction of a finite set of well-diversified portfolios is difficult in practice. Thus, it is not practically possible to eliminate the biases by the use of T-consistent estimators. Under these circumstances, an N-consistent gamma estimator is needed to asymptotically remove the biases. Here, N is the number of assets used in the CSR estimation. The N-consistent estimator means that the estimator of a parameter converges to the true value of the parameter as N increases for a given time-series sample size T.

Kim (1995) suggested a closed-form solution for an N-consistent estimation method of correcting for the EIV bias.[15] In order to examine the behavior of the N-consistent estimator, Kim formed various numbers of size-β portfolios; that is, $N = 9$ (3×3), 16 (4×4), 25 (5×5), 49 (7×7), 64 (8×8), 100 (10×10), 196 (14×14), 289 (17×17), and 400 (20×20). In addition to these size-β portfolios, he also considered individual stocks as test assets; he used all NYSE/AMEX stocks and all NYSE/AMEX/Nasdaq stocks. Size-β portfolios are formed as in Fama and French (1992). He used the weighted least squares (WLS) method for the CSR estimation.

Table 14.5 reports the CSR estimation results with Kim's correction for the EIV bias when the number of time-series return observations used to estimate betas (T) is fixed at five years (or 60 monthly observations) for all stocks. As the number of

TABLE 14.5 Kim's (1995) CSR Results with and without the Correction for the EIV Bias (July 1936 to December 1991)

Portfolio size (N)	EIV-Corrected Results			Uncorrected Results		
	$\hat{\gamma}_0$	$\hat{\gamma}_1$	$\hat{\gamma}_2$	$\hat{\gamma}_0$	$\hat{\gamma}_1$	$\hat{\gamma}_2$
9 (= 3×3)	0.452 (3.29)	0.530 (1.92)		0.503 (3.82)	0.476 (1.78)	
16 (= 4×4)	0.471 (3.48)	0.506 (1.86)		0.523 (4.03)	0.450 (1.71)	
25 (= 5×5)	0.462 (3.44)	0.515 (1.89)		0.522 (4.08)	0.449 (1.72)	
49 (= 7×7)	0.418 (3.06)	0.552 (2.01)		0.492 (3.82)	0.471 (1.82)	
64 (= 8×8)	0.407 (3.00)	0.564 (2.07)		0.487 (3.83)	0.475 (1.85)	
100 (= 10×10)	0.394 (2.82)	0.573 (2.08)		0.498 (3.89)	0.456 (1.80)	
196 (= 14×14)	0.360 (2.47)	0.599 (2.14)		0.502 (3.95)	0.438 (1.78)	
289 (= 17×17)	0.299 (1.99)	0.671 (2.33)		0.512 (4.11)	0.425 (1.79)	
400 (= 20×20)	0.231 (1.43)	0.752 (2.52)		0.525 (4.26)	0.413 (1.80)	
NYSE/AMEX	0.230 (1.42)	0.766 (2.59)		0.564 (5.06)	0.375 (1.76)	
NYSE/AMEX/NASDAQ	0.207 (1.40)	0.809 (2.63)		0.578 (5.22)	0.368 (1.76)	
9 (= 3×3)	1.097 (4.98)	0.190 (0.65)	−0.086 (−2.77)	0.503 (3.82)	0.476 (1.78)	−0.089 (−2.87)
16 (= 4×4)	1.017 (4.92)	0.212 (0.75)	−0.074 (−2.48)	0.523 (4.03)	0.450 (1.71)	−0.078 (−2.62)
25 (= 5×5)	1.076 (5.27)	0.188 (0.67)	−0.084 (−2.88)	0.522 (4.08)	0.449 (1.72)	−0.089 (−3.05)
49 (= 7×7)	1.001 (4.89)	0.240 (0.85)	−0.079 (−2.72)	0.492 (3.82)	0.471 (1.82)	−0.086 (−2.99)
64 (= 8×8)	1.023 (5.06)	0.228 (0.81)	−0.083 (−2.85)	0.487 (3.83)	0.475 (1.85)	−0.091 (−3.14)
100 (= 10×10)	0.988 (4.37)	0.252 (0.91)	−0.080 (−2.76)	0.498 (3.89)	0.456 (1.80)	−0.089 (−3.10)
196 (= 14×14)	0.901 (4.37)	0.300 (1.06)	−0.070 (−2.47)	0.502 (3.95)	0.438 (1.78)	−0.087 (−3.07)
289 (= 17×17)	0.833 (3.90)	0.337 (1.29)	−0.068 (−2.39)	0.512 (4.11)	0.425 (1.79)	−0.095 (−3.38)
400 (= 20×20)	0.683 (2.86)	0.515 (1.64)	−0.059 (−2.28)	0.525 (4.26)	0.413 (1.80)	−0.100 (−3.52)
NYSE/AMEX	0.609 (2.58)	0.644 (1.94)	−0.057 (−2.16)	0.564 (5.06)	0.375 (1.76)	−0.105 (−3.95)
NYSE/AMEX/NASDAQ	0.566 (2.52)	0.704 (2.14)	−0.054 (−2.03)	0.578 (5.22)	0.368 (1.76)	−0.103 (−3.92)

*Numbers in parentheses indicate *t*-statistic.

Source: Adapted from D. Kim, "The Errors-in-Variables Problem in the Cross-Section of Expected Stock Returns," *Journal of Finance* 50 (1995): 1605–1634.

portfolios (N) increases, the risk premium estimate ($\hat{\bar{\gamma}}_1$) with the correction for the EIV bias increases in magnitude and becomes more positively significant. Because the N-consistent estimation is applied, the risk premium estimate with all individual stocks (with the largest N) would have the smallest bias and be closest to the true value of the risk premium. This approach also leads to a smaller value of the intercept estimate ($\hat{\bar{\gamma}}_0$) when N increases. The intercept estimate turns out insignificant when all individual stocks are used. Even in the presence of the firm size variable, the risk premium estimate is still positively significant when using all individual stocks. Without the correction for the EIV bias, however, the risk premium estimate is insignificant, as in the previous studies, and the intercept estimate is strongly significant. Here, the left-hand side variable in the CSR of equations (14.11) and (14.14) is the asset return in excess of the risk-free rate of return.

The previous results were obtained by assuming that all assets (portfolios or individual assets) have the same length of beta estimation period (T) of five years. This assumption would be valid for the case of the estimation by portfolios because all portfolios have no missing return observations over the whole period. However, it could induce a selection bias in the case of the estimation by individual stocks because individual stocks having observations less than the predetermined beta estimation period of five years are excluded from the CSR estimation. By allowing the beta estimation period to be different across individual assets, Kim (1997) estimated the CSR models of equations (14.11) and (14.14) through an iterative method by using all individual stocks whose return observations are available for at least 24 months up to 60 months. The estimation results over the period July 1963–December 1993 are reported in Table 14.6. With correcting for the EIV bias, the risk premium estimate is positively significant and the intercept estimate is insignificant, when the beta is the lone explanatory variable in the model. Even in the presence of firm size and book-to-market, the risk premium estimate is still positively significant. Firm size is no longer significant, although book-to-market is still significant. The above results somewhat support the validity of the CAPM. Thus, Kim (1995, 1997) argued that Fama and French's (1992) results may have been exaggerated because of their

TABLE 14.6 Kim's (1997) CSR Results with and without the Correction for the EIV Bias for Various Stocks (July 1963 to December 1993)

EIV-Corrected results				Uncorrected results			
Intercept	$\hat{\beta}$	$\ln V_{t-1}$	$\ln BM_{t-1}$	Intercept	$\hat{\beta}$	$\ln V_{t-1}$	$\ln BM_{t-1}$
−0.011	0.935			0.428	0.379		
(−0.06)	(2.40)			(2.97)	(1.51)		
0.376	0.818	−0.058		1.030	0.203	−0.101	
(1.37)	(2.02)	(−1.55)		(4.31)	(0.86)	(−2.70)	
−0.027	0.977		0.197	0.500	0.319		0.222
(−0.13)	(2.40)		(3.52)	(3.35)	(1.29)		(3.81)
0.221	0.875	−0.031	0.160	1.025	0.153	−0.089	0.134
(0.77)	(2.10)	(−0.84)	(3.51)	(4.24)	(0.67)	(−2.40)	(2.97)

*Numbers in parentheses indicate t-statistic.
Source: Adapted from D. Kim, "A Reexamination of Firm Size, Book-to-Market, and Earnings-Price in the Cross-Section of Expected Stock Returns," *Journal of Financial and Quantitative Analysis* 32 (1997): 463–489.

failure to correct for the EIV problem, even though there is a misspecification in the CAPM related to book-to-market.

14.3.2 Sensitivity of Beta to the Return Measurement Intervals

The CAPM assumes that all investors are single-period expected-utility-of-terminal-wealth maximizers. There is no particular restriction on the length of the holding period (investment horizon) as long as it is the same for all investors. This period can be one day, one month, one year, or even longer. In empirical tests, the investment horizon is arbitrarily selected, because the true investment horizon is unknown. Miller and Scholes (1972), Handa, Kothari, and Wasley (1989), and Kothari, Shanken, and Sloan (1995) use annual return data, implicitly assuming that investors' investment horizon is one year. Roll (1969) uses weekly data, whereas Friend and Blume (1970), Black, Jensen, and Scholes (1972), Fama and MacBeth (1973), Fama and French (1972), and many others use monthly return data. The reason that monthly returns are most popular in empirical tests is simply that the use of monthly returns can avoid some econometric problems (e.g., the nonsynchronous problem, serial correlation) in statistical inferences and provides a sufficient number of observations.

According to the length of the true investment horizon, investors' risk aversion is different, and the risk-return relation changes. Thus, the risk measurement or beta should be sensitive to the length of the investment horizon. Levhari and Levy (1977) analytically showed beta sensitivity to the return measurement interval. They presented a relationship between beta with n-period investment horizon and beta with one period:

$$\beta(n) = \frac{\sum_{i=0}^{n-1} a_i \beta_1^{n-i} (1+\theta)^i}{\sum_{i=0}^{n-1} a_i} \tag{14.17}$$

where $\beta(n)$ is the beta measured with n-period returns, β_1 is the beta measured with one-period returns,

$$a_i = \binom{n}{i} (\sigma_m^2)^{n-i} [E(r_m^2)]^i$$

$$\theta = (\beta_1 - 1) \left[\frac{E(r_m) - r_f}{E(r_m)} \right]$$

$E(r_m)$ and σ_m^2 are the one-period expected return and variance of the market portfolio, and r_f is the one-period risk-free rate of return. It can be shown from equation (14.17) that

$$\beta(n) = \beta_1 \text{ for a stock with } \beta_1 = 1 \text{ (neutral stock)}$$
$$\beta(n) > \beta_1 \text{ for a stock with } \beta_1 > 1 \text{ (aggressive stock)} \tag{14.18}$$
$$\beta(n) < \beta_1 \text{ for a stock with } \beta_1 < 1 \text{ (defensive stock)}^{[16]}$$

Equation (14.18) indicates that as the length of return measurement interval (i.e., investment horizon) increases, n-period beta for a stock with one-period beta greater than one ($\beta_1 > 1$) increases, while n-period beta for a stock with one-period beta less than one ($\beta_1 < 1$) decreases. The reason that beta changes with the return measurement interval is that an asset's covariance with the market and the market's variance do not change proportionately as the return measurement interval is changed.

Handa, Kothari, and Wasley (1989) showed how beta estimates of 20 size portfolios change with the length of the return measurement interval (n). Their results are reported in Table 14.7. For small-sized portfolios (aggressive stocks), beta estimates increase monotonically with the length of the return measurement interval, whereas for large-sized portfolios (defensive stocks), beta estimates decrease monotonically with the length of the return measurement interval. As a result, the cross-sectional spread in betas is wider when annual returns are used than when monthly returns are used.

To examine the sensitivity of the explanatory power of betas and the firm size effect, Handa, Kothari, and Wasley (1989) performed the CSR tests by using betas estimated with monthly returns and annual returns within the Fama and MacBeth two-pass framework. The CSR equation they estimated is

$$r_{pt} = \gamma_{0t} + \gamma_{1t}\hat{\beta}_{p,t-1}(m) + \gamma_{2t}\hat{\beta}_{p,t-1}(a) + \gamma_{3t}\log\left(MV_{p,t-1}\right) + \eta_{pt} \qquad (14.19)$$

TABLE 14.7 Beta Estimates of 20 Size Portfolios with Various Return Measurement Intervals

Size portfolio	Return measurement interval							
	Day	Week	Month	2-month	3-month	4-month	6-month	Year
Smallest	0.99	1.18	1.41	1.53	1.51	1.57	1.60	1.66
2	1.02	1.13	1.27	1.33	1.37	1.42	1.41	1.38
3	1.04	1.12	1.23	1.29	1.32	1.35	1.31	1.31
4	1.08	1.13	1.18	1.17	1.21	1.21	1.20	1.18
5	1.08	1.11	1.14	1.17	1.16	1.17	1.19	1.16
6	1.10	1.10	1.11	1.11	1.12	1.15	1.14	1.22
7	1.09	1.10	1.08	1.08	1.08	1.11	1.11	1.10
8	1.10	1.10	1.04	1.05	1.06	1.07	1.09	1.10
9	1.09	1.08	1.03	1.01	1.03	1.02	1.01	1.04
10	1.05	1.05	1.00	0.99	0.99	0.97	0.98	0.94
11	1.03	1.02	0.99	0.99	0.99	0.96	0.97	1.00
12	0.98	0.96	0.96	0.94	0.94	0.93	0.94	0.97
13	0.96	0.95	0.92	0.89	0.88	0.88	0.88	0.88
14	0.97	0.93	0.91	0.88	0.88	0.88	0.87	0.87
15	0.95	0.91	0.88	0.87	0.86	0.85	0.86	0.83
16	0.93	0.90	0.85	0.82	0.81	0.79	0.79	0.79
17	0.90	0.87	0.81	0.80	0.77	0.74	0.73	0.72
18	0.90	0.85	0.79	0.77	0.76	0.71	0.73	0.70
19	0.86	0.79	0.71	0.68	0.66	0.63	0.62	0.59
Largest	0.90	0.78	0.69	0.63	0.61	0.58	0.58	0.56
Average	1.00	1.00	1.00	1.00	1.00	1.00	1.00	1.00

Source: P. Handa, S. P. Kothari, and C. Wasley, "The Relation between the Return Interval and Betas: Implications for the Size Effect," *Journal of Financial Economics* 23 (1989): 79–100.

TABLE 14.8 Cross-Sectional Regression Test Results using Monthly and Annual Betas

Period	Months	$\hat{\gamma}_0$ (intercept)	$\hat{\gamma}_1$ (monthly beta)	$\hat{\gamma}_2$ (annual beta)	$\hat{\gamma}_3$ (firm size)
		Panel A: Using monthly betas			
1941–1982	504	0.0300 (3.40)	0.0006 (0.13)		−0.0015 (−3.14)
1941–1954	168	0.0056 (0.05)	0.0160 (2.08)		0.0000 (0.02)
1955–1968	168	0.0254 (2.21)	0.0042 (0.72)		−0.0015 (−2.46)
1969–1982	168	0.0640 (3.13)	−0.0185 (−2.31)		−0.0031 (−2.67)
		Panel B: Using annual betas			
1941–1982	504	0.0109 (1.60)		0.0083 (3.62)	−0.0006 (−1.39)
1941–1954	168	0.0171 (1.48)		0.0092 (2.10)	−0.0010 (−1.28)
1955–1968	168	0.0141 (1.58)		0.0078 (2.32)	−0.0008 (−1.48)
1969–1982	168	0.0015 (0.10)		0.0078 (1.91)	0.0001 (0.07)

Source: P. Handa, S. P. Kothari, and C. Wasley, "The Relation between the Return Interval and Betas: Implications for the Size Effect," *Journal of Financial Economics* 23 (1989): 79–100.

where $\hat{\beta}_{p,t-1}(m)$ is the monthly beta estimate for portfolio p and $\hat{\beta}_{p,t-1}(a)$ is the annual beta estimate for portfolio p. The CSR estimation results presented in Table 14.8 indicate that the risk premium associated with monthly beta is indistinguishable from zero and firm size has a reliable negative relation with returns (in panel A). However, when annual betas and firm size are in the model, the average coefficient on annual betas ($\hat{\gamma}_2$) is reliably positive and size is no longer significant in any period considered. Kothari, Shanken, and Sloan (1995) also reported that average stock returns do indeed reflect substantial compensation for beta, provided that betas are measured at the annual intervals. This evidence is consistent with the joint hypothesis that the CAPM is descriptively valid and portfolio returns increase when annual betas are used.

14.4 MULTIVARIATE TESTS

Unlike the BJS tests and the Fama and MacBeth tests, multivariate tests consider the interaction between returns of test assets. Betas and risk premium are usually simultaneously estimated in multivariate tests. However, the problem of conducting multivariate tests is that when the number of test assets is large relative to the length of time series, multivariate tests cannot be performed. To perform a multivariate test, therefore, portfolios must be formed as test assets, and individual assets cannot be used in the test.

14.4.1 Gibbons's (1982) Test

Gibbons (1982) developed an alternative methodology for testing the CAPM that focused on the link between the market model and the CAPM. He assumed that the market model is true. That is, the return on asset i is a linear function of a market portfolio proxy:

$$r_{it} = \alpha_i + \beta_i r_{mt} + \varepsilon_{it} \tag{14.20}$$

The market model of equation (14.20) is merely a statistical statement rather than one derived from financial theory. Equation (14.20) implies

$$E(r_{it}) = \alpha_i + \beta_i E(r_{mt}) \tag{14.21}$$

The CAPM requires the following expected return-risk relationship across all assets at a point in time,

$$E(r_{it}) = \gamma + \beta_i [E(r_{mt}) - \gamma] \tag{14.22}$$

where γ is either the risk-free rate of return, r_f, or the expected return on the zero-beta portfolio, $E(r_Z)$. Gibbons (1982) points out that the Black model implies the following constraint on the intercept of the market model:

$$\alpha_i = \gamma(1 - \beta_i) \tag{14.23}$$

for all assets. Equation (14.23) is the basis of Gibbons's test.

Gibbons uses equation (14.23) as a null hypothesis and the following equation as the alternative hypothesis:

$$\alpha_i \neq \gamma(1 - \beta_i) \tag{14.24}$$

Two sets of estimators for α_i and β_i can be calculated for each asset, one set under the null hypothesis H_0: $\alpha_i = \gamma(1 - \beta_i)$ and another set under the alternative hypothesis H_A: $\alpha_i \neq \gamma(1 - \beta_i)$. If the null hypothesis is true, Gibbons shows how a multivariate estimation scheme based on a technique known as a "seemingly unrelated regression model" (SURM) can be used to estimate this set of β_i's and γ (and therefore the set of α_i's). Gibbons emphasizes that the advantage of his approach over Fama and MacBeth's (1973) two-pass methodology is that β and γ do not need to be estimated sequentially, but can be estimated simultaneously. This means that the EIV problem encountered by the use of the estimated betas rather than the use of the true betas in the cross-sectional regression tests can now be avoided. In fact, Gibbons linearizes the nonlinear constraint of equation (14.23) in order to estimate β_i's and γ under the null hypothesis. As Shanken (1992) points out, the advantage of Gibbons's approach is apparently lost in linearizing the constraint of equation (14.23), because the resulting estimator turns out to be a second-pass regression estimator and thus still subject to the EIV problem. If the alternative hypothesis is true, then simple regression with the market model can be used to estimate a set of α_i's and β_i's. Based on these two sets of estimators, Gibbons develops a likelihood ratio test (LR test) to see if the two sets of estimators are close to each other.[17] If they are, then the null hypothesis is accepted; otherwise, the null hypothesis is rejected.

Gibbons analyzed 10 different five-year periods from January 1926 through December 1975 using monthly returns on NYSE-listed stocks to conduct his tests. After estimating the beta for each security using a given five-year period, the securities were ranked by their estimated betas and put into one of 40 portfolios. Then the same five years of data were used to conduct the LR test. In five of the ten periods the LR test rejected the CAPM at the 0.05 level of significance. Furthermore, for three of the remaining five periods the CAPM was nearly rejected. Thus, Gibbons concluded that to the extent that his market index was an adequate proxy, the data were inconsistent with both the risk-free and zero-beta versions of CAPM.

14.4.2   Stambaugh's (1982) Test

Although Gibbons (1982) appears to have improved on the statistical methodology, his test results could be sensitive to incorrect specification of the market index portfolio that is the proxy for the true market portfolio. Roll and Ross (1994) show that even small departures of the market index portfolio from *ex post* market efficiency can easily lead to empirical results that show no cross-sectional relationship between beta and average returns. Because Gibbons used a proxy for the market index and ended up rejecting the CAPM, we still do not know if the CAPM is actually valid and he simply used a poor proxy, or if the CAPM is simply an invalid model.

Stambaugh (1982) tested to see if inferences about the CAPM could be reversed by changing market indexes. Four different composite indexes were used. These indexes consisted of various combinations of indexes of returns from common stocks, corporate bonds, U.S. government bonds, Treasury bills, residential real estate, house furnishings, and automobiles. The period from February 1953–December 1976 was broken into four approximately equal subperiods for testing purposes.

Forming 40 beta-based portfolios of common stocks in a manner similar to Gibbons and conducting a "Lagrangian multiplier test" (LM test) of equation (14.23), as well as Gibbons's LR test, Stambaugh found that the two tests gave opposite results. Pursuing the matter further, Stambaugh noted that in a simulation study Gibbons's LR test did not conform closely to its limiting distribution and tended to reject the null hypothesis of equation (14.23) too often when the number of securities (or in this case, portfolios) being analyzed was moderately large in relation to the length of time-series.[18]

Dividing the 40 portfolios into two groups of 20 and again conducting the two tests on each group separately, Stambaugh found that for both groups of portfolios both tests do not reject the null hypothesis. Furthermore, these results were virtually unaffected by how broad a market index was used. Although this is not a rigorous examination of the two tests, it does appear to be safer to draw conclusions from the LM test than from the LR test in that the LM test appears to conform more closely to its limiting distribution. On this basis, for the 40 portfolios of common stocks, the evidence is consistent with the risk-free rate and a significantly positive relationship between beta and average return. However, other tests utilizing other types of assets and forming common stock portfolios by other means gave mixed results regarding the validity of the CAPM. He also found that even when common stocks represent only 10 percent of the value of the whole portfolio (including common stocks, corporate bonds, U.S. government bonds, Treasury bills, residential real estate, house furnishings, and automobiles), inferences about the CAPM are virtually identical to those obtained with a stocks-only market index (i.e., the CRSP market index).

14.4.3   Jobson and Korkie's (1982) Test

Similar to Stambaugh (1982), Jobson and Korkie (1982) noted that Gibbons's (1982) LR test tends to reject the null hypothesis of equation (14.23) too often when the number of securities is large. In particular, for the sample size and number of observations used by Gibbons, this tendency was found to exist. After making certain adjustments to the LR test, Jobson and Korkie no longer rejected the null hypothesis (the validity of the CAPM) in three of the four time periods tested, consistent with Stambaugh's results.

14.4.4   Shanken's (1985) Test

Shanken (1985) developed a cross-sectional regression test (CRST) of the CAPM. Because Shanken's CSRT has a close relation to the Hotelling T^2 test whose exact distribution is known, he proposed the T^2 distribution as a useful approximation to the exact distribution of the CSRT after a simple adjustment for errors in the estimation of beta. Shanken showed that the three test statistics, the LR test, the LM test, and his CSR test, are exact transformations of one another: There is really just one test, and all three test statistics have the same asymptotic chi-squared distribution. In an empirical application of the CSRT, Shanken reported that the CRSP equal-weighted index is inefficient.

14.4.5   Generalized Method of Moment (GMM) Tests

The CAPM tests previously discussed require some regularities of return observations. These regularities are normality of asset returns or error terms in equation (14.1), homoscedasticity and serial uncorrelation of error terms, and stationarity of the parameters. However, there is ample empirical evidence that actual asset returns hardly satisfy these regularities. That is, asset returns are not normally distributed and are serially correlated in some cases, and the mean and variance of asset returns are not stationary. Therefore, the test statistics designed and estimated by assuming that the regularities are satisfied could mislead the test results. In this circumstance, Hansen (1982) and Hansen and Singleton (1982) suggested a generalized method of moment (GMM) estimation which is robust to the violation of those regularities. The GMM estimation can also accommodate the inclusion of instrumental variables, which is needed to capture a dynamic feature of beta and risk premium.

Many researchers applied the GMM estimation to test the validity of the CAPM.[19] Using the GMM estimation, Harvey (1989) finds that the Sharpe-Lintner version of the static CAPM is unable to capture the dynamic behavior of asset returns such as time-varying betas and market risk premium, and Jagannathan and Wang (1996) report that a conditional version of the CAPM outperforms the static (unconditional) CAPM. However, Kan and Robotti (2009) report that there is little evidence that conditional and intertemporal CAPM-type specification outperform the simple static (unconditional) CAPM.

14.5   IS THE CAPM TESTABLE?

In 1977, Richard Roll published an article that took exception to all previously published tests of the CAPM. While arguing that the CAPM is testable in principle, Roll (1997, 129–130) also argued that "no correct and unambiguous test of the theory has appeared" and that "there is practically no possibility that such a test can be accomplished in the future." The logic behind his assertion is based on the observation that there is only one potentially testable hypothesis associated with the CAPM, which is that the true market portfolio is a mean-variance efficient portfolio. All other hypotheses (such as there being a linear relationship between beta and expected return) can be shown to be redundant, given the main hypothesis. Furthermore, this main hypothesis cannot be tested because the true market portfolio cannot be observed. The reason it cannot be observed is because it must include all risky assets (tangible and intangible) that can be held by investors. It would include stocks, bonds, real estate, privately held businesses, collectibles, and human capital. Some of these assets are barely traded or not traded at all.[20]

The use of proxies for the true market portfolio in empirical tests, as had been the case thus far, is unacceptable according to Roll because (1) they might be efficient when the true market portfolio is inefficient, thus leading the researcher to falsely accept the CAPM, or (2) they might be inefficient when the true market portfolio is efficient, thus leading the researcher to falsely reject the CAPM. Although proxies are frequently used in testing various economic theories, the point is that even a slight departure from efficiency in the market portfolio can lead to a large departure from the expected return-beta relationship, which would negate the practical usefulness of the model (see also Roll and Ross, 1994). Furthermore, because there is only one testable hypothesis, the lack of complete data cannot be overcome with various indirect tests.[21] The upshot is that based on past tests of the CAPM, it is impossible to know what to conclude regarding the viability of the CAPM. It is important to recognize, however, that Roll's critique does not reject the CAPM per se; it only rejects its empirical testability.

14.6   SUMMARY AND CONCLUSIONS

Because the true market portfolio cannot be observed, an adequate test of the CAPM has yet to be performed. Nevertheless, as Markowitz (1983) has noted, sensible practical use of portfolio analysis and the CAPM does not depend on the success of this empirical research. In practice, proxies such as the S&P 500 are used to stand in for the true market portfolio. At this point, tests of the CAPM break down to examining the expected return-beta relation and to testing the efficiency of the market proxy. If we can find a market proxy that makes alpha values, on average, uniformly zero at acceptable levels of significance, then this market proxy can be assumed sufficiently close to the true, unobservable market portfolio and can be used in portfolio analysis.

NOTES

1. This issue is further to be discussed in Section 14.5 of this chapter.
2. The CRSP refers to Center for Research in Security Prices at the University of Chicago. The CRSP Equal-Weighted index is a market index containing all U.S. stocks traded in New York Stock Exchange, American Stock Exchange, and Nasdaq, where each stock has an equal weight.
3. There have been efforts to identify a better proxy for the market portfolio, and there has been a debate about which market proxy is superior. The CRSP value-weighted portfolio has been the most frequently used proxy for the market portfolio. Arnott, Hsu, and Moore (2005) reported that portfolios weighted by fundamental measures of company size such as assets, dividends, sales, earnings, and employees resulted in better Sharpe

ratios than could be obtained with the traditional market value weighted portfolio. On the other hand, Perold (2007) and Blitz and Swinkels (2008) argued that portfolios weighted by fundamental measures of company size do not necessarily outperform market value weighted portfolios. More recently, Francis, Hessel, Wang, and Zhang (2010) found that repurchase weighted portfolios and total payout weighted portfolios are superior to portfolios weighted by dividends in terms of excess returns and Sharpe ratios.

4. The Black (1972) version of the CAPM is contrasted because it has the return of the zero-beta portfolio in the equation instead of the return of the risk-free asset, r_f.

5. Sharpe and Cooper (1972) conducted a similar study at about the same time as BJS, and had similar results. Roll (1977, 136) describes a study by Pettit and Westerfield (1974) as also being similar to BJS.

6. These stock betas are called pre-ranking betas.

7. These portfolios are called post-ranking portfolios, and betas estimated using the post-ranking portfolio returns are called post-ranking betas.

8. FM also conducted their t-tests on even smaller subperiods; those results were consistent with what is reported here.

9. Foster (1978a) replicated this study over a 528-month test period of January 1931–December 1974 using both an equal-weighted and a value-weighted index in order to see if the results were affected by the choice of the index used. Little difference was noted.

10. Fama and French (1992) used nonfinancial firms only.

11. The negative relation between firm size and stock returns was already well known before Fama and French (1992). Banz (1981) and Reinganum (1981) first documented this size or small-firm effect. Later, Keim (1983), Reinganum (1983), and Blume and Stambaugh (1983) showed that the size effect occurs virtually entirely in January; it is called the January effect.

12. The earnings-price ratio variables alone are positively significant (see Basu, 1983). However, their significance disappears when the firm size and book-to-market variables are included in the model.

13. Kothari, Shanken, and Sloan (1995) argued that Fama and French's (1992) results regarding book-to-market are subject to survivorship bias, because several years of the surviving firms' historical data were included, but nonsurviving firms' data were not included, when the accounting database Fama and French used added firms to the database. Thus, they argued that the book-to-market of Fama and French is exaggerated. However, Kim (1997) later reexamined the book-to-market effect after filling in the non-surviving firms' accounting data and found that the book-to-market effect was still significant. Davis, Fama and French (2000) also found that the book-to-market effect is as strong for 1929 to 1963 as for the period Fama and French originally studied.

14. Levhari and Levy (1977) analytically show that the return measurement interval plays a crucial role and has a great impact on the beta estimate in that the beta estimate of aggressive stocks (usually high-beta stocks) increases with the return measurement interval, while the beta estimate of defensive stocks (usually low-beta stocks) decreases with the return measurement interval.

15. Kim's method directly corrects for the bias and produces the consistent estimate of risk premium, whereas Shanken (1992) provides an EIV correction for the standard errors of the risk premium estimate.

16. For a stock with $\beta_1 > 1$, $\theta > 0$ and $\left[\sum_{i=0}^{n-1} a_i (1+\theta)^i / \sum_{i=0}^{n-1} a_i\right] > 1$. Because $\beta_1^{n-i} \geq \beta_1$ for $i = 0, 1, \ldots, n-1$, $\beta(n) > \beta_1$. For a stock with $\beta_1 < 1$, $\theta < 0$ and $\left[\sum_{i=0}^{n-1} a_i (1+\theta)^i / \sum_{i=0}^{n-1} a_i\right] < 1$. Because $\beta_1^{n-i} \leq \beta_1$ for $i = 0, 1, \ldots, n-1$, $\beta(n) < \beta_1$.

17. Gibbons verified via simulation that the LR test is adequate when dealing with five assets (or, in this case, portfolios). Of interest is that Stambaugh (1982), as will be discussed shortly, apparently has found that as the number of assets increases from five, the LR test tends to reject equation (14.23) too frequently.

18. In a later study, Stambaugh (1983) noted that this problem occurs when there are more than 10 securities (or portfolios).

19. See Hansen, Heaton, and Luttmer (1995), Hansen and Jagannathan (1997), Jagannathan, Kubota, and Takehara (1998), Campbell and Cochrane (2000), Lettau and Ludvigson (2001), Hodrick and Zhang (2001), Dittmar (2002), Farnsworth, Ferson, Jackson, and Todd (2002), and Kim, Kim, and Min (2011), among others.

20. For an attempt at measuring the world market portfolio, see Ibbotson, Siegel, and Love (1985). If the market portfolio is narrowly construed to include only equity shares, then a stock market index can be used as the market portfolio in empirical tests. As a result, the CAPM must be viewed as a partial equilibrium model. In other words, the CAPM is now restricted to just the stock market, and a particular one at that, such as the NYSE, and has no further implications. It is a partial equilibrium model because it only explains diversification among common stocks and has asset pricing implications for only common stocks. All other possible investments are exogenous to this narrowly defined capital market theory—that is, it only rationalizes a partial or single-market (namely, a stock market) equilibrium. Accordingly, the partial equilibrium view can be criticized as being ad hoc, because the implied market segmentation is arbitrary. Of course, if one chooses to ignore this criticism, then Roll's research suggests that only one test can be undertaken—namely, to see if the stock market index at hand is mean-variance efficient.

21. The fact that frequently used proxies are highly correlated with each other does not mean that the choice of a proxy is unimportant. Roll shows that there exists a proxy that has a correlation coefficient of 0.895 with the proxy used by Black, Jensen, and Scholes (1972) and, had it been used, this proxy would have completely supported the traditional CAPM. For an interesting discussion on proxies, see Jacob and Pettit (1984, Chapter 11 appendix).

CHAPTER **15**

Continuous-Time Asset Pricing Models

Although the CAPM has been a backbone in the modern finance theory, it is still subject to theoretical criticism because of the assumptions on which the model is based. One of the assumptions subject to criticism is that the CAPM is a static single-period model. That is, all investors have the same holding period. As stated by Merton (1973), implicitly, this means that the trading horizon (defined as the minimum length of time between successive trades), the decision horizon (defined as the length of time between decisions regarding investing), and the planning horizon (defined as the time interval in the investor's utility function) are all assumed to be equal to each other and to be of the same length for all investors. Critics argue that investors make their investment decisions intertemporally by maximizing their multiperiod utility of lifetime consumption, rather than choosing their portfolios according to the Markowitz mean-variance criterion to maximize their single-period utility.[1] Merton (1973) also argues that if we would expect that preferences and future investment opportunity sets are state dependent, an equilibrium model accommodating portfolio selection behavior for an intertemporal utility maximizer is needed, which will be different from the model for a single-period utility maximizer such as the CAPM.

Whereas some researchers, such as Jensen (1969), Lee (1976), Levhari and Levy (1977), and Gilster (1983), have explored the implications for the CAPM of investors having disparate horizons, another approach has been to develop a continuous-time version of the CAPM, which is, by nature, intertemporal. Three assumptions generally common to such a version are (1) investors can trade continuously; (2) asset prices are stochastic processes and the unanticipated portion of their returns (defined as the actual return less its expected return) is a martingale; and (3) these stochastic processes can be described as diffusion processes with continuous sample paths, meaning that prices have a lognormal distribution and returns are serially independent and identically distributed through time. This chapter presents two such intertemporal models: the intertemporal CAPM (ICAPM) and the consumption-based CAPM (CCAPM).

15.1 INTERTEMPORAL CAPM (ICAPM)

Merton (1973) derived a version of the CAPM by assuming that trading in assets takes place continuously over time, asset returns are lognormally distributed, and investors maximize their expected utility at each time for lifetime consumption.

Merton argues that when there is stochastic variation in investment opportunities, there will be risk associated with innovations in the state variables that describe the investment opportunities. One of the state variables that is directly observable is the interest rate. By assuming that a single state variable such as the interest rate is sufficient to describe changes in the investment opportunity set, Merton suggests the intertemporal capital asset pricing model (ICAPM).

If the risk-free interest rate is constant (nonstochastic), the investment opportunity set is also constant, and investors will hold portfolios chosen from two funds: the risk-free asset and the market portfolio (m). That is, all investors will be indifferent between choosing portfolios made from the original individual assets or choosing these two funds. In this case, the equilibrium returns will satisfy

$$E\left(r_i\right) = r_f + \left[E\left(r_m\right) - r_f\right]\beta_i \tag{15.1}$$

where m is the market portfolio, and $\beta_i = \sigma_{im}/\sigma_m^2$. Equation (15.1) is the continuous-time analog to the security market line of the classical CAPM. This is exactly the same as the CAPM except that instantaneous rates of return (i.e., continuously compounded returns) are used instead of rates of returns over discrete time intervals (i.e., holding period returns) and the distribution of returns is lognormal instead of normal. Hence, the additional assumption of a constant investment opportunity set is a sufficient condition for investors to behave as if they were single-period maximizers and for the equilibrium relation specified by the CAPM to be relevant.

However, the assumption of a constant investment opportunity set is not consistent with the fact that the interest rate is changing stochastically over time. If the risk-free interest rate is changing stochastically over time, investors will face another risk caused by unfavorable shifts in the opportunity set. In this circumstance, investors will hold portfolios chosen from three funds: the so-called risk-free asset, the market portfolio (m), and a portfolio (N) whose return is perfectly negatively correlated with the stochastic risk-free rate of return. The first and second funds (the stochastic risk-free asset and the market portfolio) provide investors with an instantaneously efficient risk-return frontier. The third fund (portfolio N) allows investors to hedge against risk caused by unfavorable intertemporal shifts in the efficient frontier (the investment opportunity set). All investors' optimal portfolios can be represented as a linear combination of the three mutual funds (portfolios). Again, all investors will be indifferent between choosing portfolios from among the original individual assets or from choosing these three funds. In this case, the equilibrium returns will satisfy

$$E\left(r_i\right) = r_f + \left[E\left(r_m\right) - r_f\right]\beta_i^{(m)} + \left[E\left(r_N\right) - r_f\right]\beta_i^{(N)} \tag{15.2}$$

where

$$\beta_i^{(m)} = \frac{\beta_{im} - \beta_{iN}\beta_{Nm}}{1 - \rho_{Nm}^2}$$

$$\beta_i^{(N)} = \frac{\beta_{iN} - \beta_{im}\beta_{Nm}}{1 - \rho_{Nm}^2}$$

$$\beta_{jk} = \frac{\text{Cov}\left(r_j, r_k\right)}{\text{Var}\left(r_k^2\right)}$$

and N is the portfolio whose returns are perfectly negatively correlated with the stochastic risk-free rate of return. Note that all returns in equation (15.2) are instantaneous (continuously compounded) returns. Even though an asset may have no correlation with the market portfolio (that is, $\rho_{im} = 0$), it still will not typically have an expected return equal to r_f as the traditional CAPM would suggest. Only if both $\rho_{im} = 0$ and $\rho_{iN} = 0$ will an asset have an expected return equal to r_f.

Richard (1979) has extended Merton's work by allowing there to be S sources of uncertainty (state variables) in the opportunity set instead of just the risk-free rate.[2] These sources of uncertainty influence the magnitude of the risk-return parameters of the assets, μ_i and σ_i, thereby causing the investment opportunity set to shift intertemporally. This leads him to replace Merton's three-fund theorem with an $S + 2$ funds theorem, meaning that any investor will be indifferent between choosing from the set of original assets or a set of $S + 2$ funds. These funds consist of the stochastic risk-free asset, the market portfolio, and S hedging portfolios constructed to insulate the investor from each of the S sources of uncertainty.

15.2   THE CONSUMPTION-BASED CAPM (CCAPM)

This section introduces an intertemporal model called the consumption-based CAPM (CCAPM).

15.2.1   Derivation

Rubinstein (1976), Lucas (1978), and Breeden (1979) suggest a different approach to obtain investors' equilibrium expected return. They assume investors maximize the expected value of a time-additive and state-independent lifetime utility function, they have homogeneous beliefs concerning the characteristics of asset returns, and there is a single consumption good. More specifically, let an investor (or a representative agent) have the intertemporal objective of maximizing an expected utility that depends only on the current and future consumption:

$$Q = \underset{C_t}{\text{Max}} \, E_t \left[\sum_{t=0}^{\infty} \delta^t \, U\left(c_t\right) \right] \tag{15.3}$$

where $E_t[\cdot]$ is the expectation operator at time t, δ is the time preference discount factor $(0 < \delta < 1)$, and $U(c_t)$ is the utility of consumption at time t, c_t. We assume the utility function is time separable, which means that utility at a particular date depends only on consumption at that same date, and satisfies $U'(\cdot) > 0$ and $U''(\cdot) < 0$. We also assume this investor can trade freely in asset i.

The first-order condition for maximization is

$$\frac{\partial Q}{\partial c_t} = E_t \left[\delta^t U'\left(c_t\right) + \delta^{t+1} U'\left(c_{t+1}\right) \left(\frac{\partial c_{t+1}}{\partial c_t} \right) \right] = 0 \tag{15.4}$$

From equation (15.4), we have

$$U'\left(c_t\right) = \delta \, E_t \left[U'\left(c_{t+1}\right) \left(-\frac{\partial c_{t+1}}{\partial c_t} \right) \right] \tag{15.5}$$

Here, $-\left(\partial c_{t+1}/\partial c_t\right)$ indicates the increased amount of consumption at time $t+1$ when the consumption at time t is decreased by \$1. This savings of \$1 at time t is invested in a risky asset at the rate of return r_{t+1}, and so the consumption in the next period is increased by \$$(1 + r_{t+1})$. Thus,

$$-\frac{\partial c_{t+1}}{\partial c_t} = 1 + r_{t+1} \tag{15.6}$$

Plugging (15.6) into (15.5) yields

$$U'\left(c_t\right) = \delta\, E_t\left[\, U'\left(c_{t+1}\right)\left(1 + r_{t+1}\right)\right] \tag{15.7}$$

Equation (15.7) can be rewritten as

$$E_t\left[\,\left(1 + r_{t+1}\right) M_{t+1}\right] = 1 \tag{15.8}$$

where

$$M_{t+1} = \frac{\delta\, U'\left(C_{t+1}\right)}{U'\left(C_t\right)} \tag{15.9}$$

which is the *stochastic discount factor (SDF)* or *pricing kernel*. This indicates the marginal rate of substitution of current for future consumption.

The implication of the first-order condition of equation (15.7) is as follows: This investor's optimal consumption and portfolio plan is constructed so that he or she equates the utility loss from a reduction in current consumption to the additional gain in (discounted) consumption in the next period. More specifically, a \$1 reduction in consumption today reduces utility by $U'\left(c_t\right)$, but results in an expected payout of \$$(1 + r_{t+1})$ in the next period from \$1 of investment. When this expected payoff is spent on the next period's consumption, the extra (discounted) utility per \$1 in the next period is $\delta\, U'\left(c_{t+1}\right)$. Hence, the total extra expected (discounted) utility in the next period is $\delta\, U'\left(c_{t+1}\right)\left(1 + r_{t+1}\right)$.

By using $E\left(xy\right) = E\left(x\right) E\left(y\right) + Cov\left(x,y\right)$ and $Cov\left(g\left(x\right),y\right) = E[g'\left(x\right)]\, Cov(x,y)$ for a differentiable function g, equation (15.7) can be written as

$$\begin{aligned}
U'\left(c_t\right) &= \delta\left[E_t\left(U'\left(c_{t+1}\right)\right) E_t\left(1 + r_{t+1}\right) + Cov\left\{U'\left(c_{t+1}\right),\left(1 + r_{t+1}\right)\right\}\right] \\
&= \delta\left[E_t\left(U'\left(c_{t+1}\right)\right) E_t\left(1 + r_{t+1}\right) + E_t\left[U''\left(c_{t+1}\right)\right] Cov\left\{c_{t+1},\left(1 + r_{t+1}\right)\right\}\right]
\end{aligned} \tag{15.10}$$

From equation (15.8), the expected return from the risky asset is expressed as

$$E_t\left(1 + r_{t+1}\right) = \left(\frac{U'\left(c_t\right)}{\delta\, E_t\left[U'\left(c_{t+1}\right)\right]}\right) + \gamma\, Cov\left\{c_{t+1},\left(1 + r_{t+1}\right)\right\} \tag{15.11}$$

where $\gamma = -\left(E_t\left[U''\left(c_{t+1}\right)\right]/E_t\left[U'\left(c_{t+1}\right)\right]\right)$ measures Arrow-Pratt absolute risk aversion. Equation (15.11) implies the expected return on a risky asset depends on the covariance of an asset's payoff with consumption. That is, the greater the covariance of an asset's payoff with consumption, the greater the expected return should be.

When there is no consumption-related risk (i.e., the covariance term equals zero in equation (15.11)), the expected return should equal the risk-free return. Thus, the first term on the right-hand side of equation (15.11), $\{U'(c_t)/\delta\, E_t\,[U'(c_{t+1})]\}$, must be equal to the risk-free rate of return. In fact, this term equals a reciprocal of the pricing kernel of equation (15.9). Thus, the risk-free rate of return equals a reciprocal of the pricing kernel or the stochastic discount factor.

15.2.2   The Consumption-Based CAPM with a Power Utility Function

The form given in equation (15.11) is simply a general relation between an asset's expected return and its covariance with consumption. To provide a specific form of asset pricing models, we need to specify a utility function. A widely-accepted utility function is the one that exhibits constant relative risk aversion (CRRA) with a coefficient of relative risk aversion of γ. This is a time-separable power utility function defined as

$$U(c_t) = \frac{c_t^{1-\gamma}}{1-\gamma}$$

Then, the first-order condition of equation (15.7) can be rewritten as

$$\frac{1}{\delta} = E_t\left[(1+g_{c,t+1})^{-\gamma}(1+r_{t+1})\right] \tag{15.12}$$

where $g_{c,t+1} = (c_{t+1} - c_t)/c_t$ is the growth rate in consumption. By taking a Taylor's approximation around $\gamma = 0$, we obtain[3]

$$(1+g_{c,t+1})^{-\gamma}(1+r_{t+1}) \cong \left(1 - \gamma\, g_{c,t+1} + \frac{1}{2}\gamma(1+\gamma)g_{c,t+1}^2\right)(1+r_{t+1})$$

$$\approx 1 + r_{t+1} - \gamma\, g_{c,t+1} - \gamma\, g_{c,t+1} r_{t+1} + \frac{1}{2}\gamma(1+\gamma)g_{c,t+1}^2$$

assuming $r_{t+1}\, g_{c,t+1}^2 \approx 0$ (the third or higher order of the term is assumed to equal zero).

Thus, equation (15.12) becomes

$$\frac{1}{\delta} \cong 1 + E(r_{t+1}) - \gamma\, E(g_{c,t+1}) - \gamma\, E(r_{t+1})\, E(g_{c,t+1}) - \gamma\, \text{Cov}(r_{t+1}, g_{c,t+1})$$

$$+ \frac{1}{2}\gamma(1+\gamma)\left\{[E(g_{c,t+1})]^2 + \text{Var}(g_{c,t+1})\right\} \tag{15.13}$$

Assuming a sufficiently short time period, as is possible with continuous time models, the terms $[E(g_{c,t+1})]^2$ and $E(r_{t+1})\, E(g_{c,t+1})$ go toward zero. Thus, equation (15.11) yields

$$E(r_{t+1}) \cong \frac{1}{\delta} - 1 + \gamma\, E(g_{c,t+1}) + \gamma\, \text{Cov}(r_{t+1}, g_{c,t+1}) - \frac{1}{2}\gamma(1+\gamma)\,\text{Var}(g_{c,t+1})$$

$$\tag{15.14}$$

For a risk-free asset, equation (15.14) reduces to

$$E\left(r_f\right) \cong \frac{1}{\delta} - 1 + \gamma \, E\left(g_{c,\,t+1}\right) - \frac{1}{2}\gamma\left(1+\gamma\right) \mathrm{Var}\left(g_{c,\,t+1}\right) \tag{15.15}$$

Subtracting equation (15.15) from equation (15.14) yields

$$E\left(r_{t+1}\right) - r_f = \gamma \, \mathrm{Cov}\left(r_{t+1}, g_{c,\,t+1}\right)$$

or

$$E\left(r_{t+1}\right) = r_f + \lambda\, \beta_{c,\,t+1} \tag{15.16}$$

where $\lambda = \gamma\, \mathrm{Var}(g_{c,\,t+1})$ is the market price of consumption risk, and $\beta_{c,\,t+1} = \mathrm{Cov}(r_{t+1}, g_{c,\,t+1})/\mathrm{Var}(g_{c,\,t+1})$ is the consumption beta.

Equation (15.16) implies that an asset's risk premium depends on the covariance between the asset's return and the (aggregate) consumption growth rate. This is the *consumption-based CAPM (CCAPM)*. The intuition is that if an investor holds assets, he can sell some of the assets to finance consumption when his current income is low. Thus an individual asset is more desirable if its returns are expected to be high when consumption is low (because more can be invested). However, if its returns are expected to be high when consumption is high (because less can be invested), the asset is less desirable and more risky, and, thus, the investor demands a larger risk premium to hold it.

The formulation of the consumption-based CAPM can be generalized. In the previous derivation of the CCAPM, if the utility is a function of an uncertain amount of total (marketwide) wealth instead of consumption, the CCAPM of equation (15.16) becomes the standard CAPM, because the consumption growth rate, $g_{c,\,t+1}$, is equivalent to the rate of return on the market portfolio. Cochrane (1991) also derives the production-based CAPM by using producers and production functions in the place of consumers and utility functions, which are used in deriving the consumption-based CAPM. The marginal rate of substitution of consumption in equation (15.9) is substituted as the marginal rate of transformation of capital. The empirical evidence finds generally little support for the CCAPM. However, Jagannathan and Wang (2007) recently provide evidence supporting the CCAPM when consumption betas are computed using consumption growth based on the fourth quarter.

15.3   CONCLUSIONS

Breeden's 1979 consumption-based asset pricing model offers better research possibilities than competing asset pricing models based on the (impossible to measure) market portfolio (or any surrogate for the market portfolio that might be contrived). Under certain conditions, Breeden's consumption-based model is equivalent to a multibeta model that allows an asset's price to depend on a number of different state variables. Stulz (1981) was sufficiently impressed with Breeden's model that he used it to develop an impressive international capital asset pricing model (international CAPM).

Preceding Breeden (1981), Solnik (1974a, 1974b) also developed a respectable international CAPM, which is similar in form to this chapter's standard (continuous-time) intertemporal capital asset pricing model (ICAPM) of equation (15.1). Solnik tested his model using daily data from eight European countries and the United

States and found weak empirical support for the model. Grauer, Litzenberger, and Stehle (1976) developed an international CAPM that assumed identical tastes across countries. Stehle (1977) went on to improve on Solnik's work and reported weak empirical evidence supporting his changes.

Stulz (1981) increased the generality of Solnik's (1974) international CAPM by allowing different countries to temporarily experience different consumption opportunities, until arbitrage once again equalized them. Stulz also expanded the consumption opportunity set to include the present consumption opportunities, the prices of the present opportunities, and the future prices of the present opportunities. He assumed that, although the commodities could not be traded, all the assets could be traded. Stulz used this model to show that, while always remaining in equilibrium, the forward exchange rate should be inversely proportional to the covariance of the changes in the exchange rate. And the forward exchange rate should also be inversely proportional to the covariance of changes in the real world consumption rate.

APPENDIX: LOGNORMALITY AND THE CONSUMPTION-BASED CAPM

The derivation for the consumption-based CAPM (CCAPM) of equations (15.13) through (15.16) does not require any particular distributional form for the rate of investment return (r) and the consumption growth rate (g). If the rate of investment return and the consumption growth rate are *lognormally* distributed, the Taylor's approximation is not needed.

A15.1   Lognormality

When a random variable X is lognormally distributed,

$$\log X \sim N\left(\mu, \sigma^2\right)$$

Then, its mean and variance are given by

$$E\left(X\right) = \exp\left(\mu + \frac{1}{2}\sigma^2\right) \quad \text{and} \quad \operatorname{Var}\left(X\right) = \exp\left(2\mu + \sigma^2\right)\left[\exp\left(\sigma^2\right) - 1\right]$$

Therefore, it has the property that

$$\log E\left(X\right) = \mu + \frac{1}{2}\sigma^2 = E\left(\log X\right) + \frac{1}{2}\operatorname{Var}\left(\log X\right) \tag{A15.1}$$

A15.2   The Consumption-Based CAPM with Lognormality

We assume that the rate of investment return (r) and the consumption growth rate (g) are lognormally distributed. By taking the natural logarithm on both sides of equation (15.12) and using the lognormality of equation (A15.1), we have

$$-\log \delta = E_t\left[-\gamma \log\left(1 + g_{c,t+1}\right) + \log\left(1 + r_{t+1}\right)\right]$$

$$+ \frac{1}{2}\operatorname{Var}\left[-\gamma \log\left(1 + g_{c,t+1}\right) + \log\left(1 + r_{t+1}\right)\right] \tag{A15.2}$$

We let $\dot{r}_{t+1} = \log\left(1 + r_{t+1}\right)$ and $\dot{g}_{c,t+1} = \log\left(1 + g_{c,t+1}\right)$.

Note that the rate of return and consumption growth rate are both *continuously compounded*. Then, equation (A15.2) can rewritten as

$$E_t\left(\dot{r}_{t+1}\right) = -\log\delta + \gamma\, E_t\left(\dot{g}_{c,t+1}\right) - \frac{1}{2}\text{Var}\left(\dot{r}_{t+1}\right) + \frac{1}{2}\gamma^2\text{Var}\left(\dot{g}_{c,t+1}\right)$$
$$- \gamma\,\text{Cov}\left(\dot{r}_{t+1},\dot{g}_{c,t+1}\right) \tag{A15.3}$$

For a risk-free asset, equation (A15.3) reduces to

$$E_t\left(\dot{r}_f\right) = -\log\delta + \gamma\, E_t\left(\dot{g}_{c,t+1}\right) + \frac{1}{2}\gamma^2\text{Var}\left(\dot{g}_{c,t+1}\right) \tag{A15.4}$$

Subtracting equation (A15.4) from equation (A15.3) yields

$$E_t\left(\dot{r}_{t+1} - \dot{r}_f\right) + \frac{1}{2}\text{Var}\left(\dot{r}_{t+1}\right) = \gamma\,\text{Cov}\left(\dot{r}_{t+1},\dot{g}_{c,t+1}\right)$$

or

$$E\left(\dot{r}_{t+1}\right) + \frac{1}{2}\text{Var}\left(\dot{r}_{t+1}\right) = \dot{r}_f + \lambda\,\dot{\beta}_{c,t+1} \tag{A15.5}$$

where $\lambda = \gamma\,\text{Var}\left(\dot{g}_{c,t+1}\right)$ is the market price of consumption risk, and $\dot{\beta}_{c,t+1} = \text{Cov}\left(\dot{r}_{t+1},\dot{g}_{c,t+1}\right)/\text{Var}\left(\dot{g}_{c,t+1}\right)$ is the (continuously compounded version of the) consumption beta. The consumption beta here is estimated by regressing continuously compounded returns on continuously compounded growth rates of consumption. On the other hand, the consumption beta in equation (15.16) is estimated by using single-period gross simple returns and consumption growth rates. The variance term on the left-hand side of equation (A15.5), $(1/2)\,\text{Var}\left(\dot{r}_{t+1}\right)$, is a Jensen's inequality adjustment arising from the fact that expectations of log returns are used.

NOTES

1. Fama (1970) has shown, however, that though an investor faces a multiperiod problem, in his consumption-investment decision for any period the consumer's behavior is indistinguishable from that of a risk averter who has a one-period horizon, if preferences and future investment opportunity sets are not state dependent. That is, under certain conditions, intertemporal portfolio maximization can be treated as if the investor had a single-period utility function.
2. As stated by Richard (1979), examples of these sources of uncertainty might include the growth rate in the money supply, prices of industrial goods, disposable income, and wage rates.
3. The Taylor series expansion of a function $f(x)$ that is infinitely differentiable in a neighborhood of a number a is

$$f(x) = f(a) + \frac{f'(a)}{1!}(x-a) + \frac{f''(a)}{2!}(x-a)^2 + \frac{f'''(a)}{3!}(x-a)^3 + \cdots.$$

In particular, when $a = 0$, the series is

$$f(x) = f(0) + \frac{f'(0)}{1!}x + \frac{f''(0)}{2!}x^2 + \frac{f'''(a)}{3!}x^3 + \cdots.$$

Thus,

$$\left(1 + g_{c,t+1}\right)^{-\gamma} = 1 - \gamma\, g_{c,t+1} + \frac{\gamma\,(1+\gamma)}{2}g_{c,t+1}{}^2 - \frac{\gamma\,(1+\gamma)\,(2+\gamma)}{6}g_{c,t+1}{}^3 + \cdots.$$

By assuming the third or higher order of $g_{c,t+1}$ equals zero,

$$\left(1 + g_{c,t+1}\right)^{-\gamma} \approx 1 - \gamma\, g_{c,t+1} + \frac{\gamma\,(1+\gamma)}{2}g_{c,t+1}{}^2.$$

CHAPTER 16

Arbitrage Pricing Theory

Although the principal topic of this book is portfolio analysis and the CAPM, it should be kept in mind that academic acceptance of the CAPM as the premier asset pricing paradigm is less than universal. The arbitrage pricing theory (APT), formulated by Ross (1976, 1977b), is considered as an alternative pricing model like Breeden's consumption-based CAPM and Merton's intertemporal CAPM. APT is less restrictive than the CAPM in that it applies in both the single-period and multiperiod settings. Furthermore, it is based on fewer and more realistic assumptions. APT only requires us to assume that markets are perfectly competitive and investors' utility functions are monotonically increasing and concave.[1] The CAPM assumptions of quadratic utility functions and/or normally distributed returns are not necessary in deriving the asset pricing equation of APT.

16.1   ARBITRAGE CONCEPTS

Arbitrage is a trading strategy that exploits the mispricing of two or more assets. If the prices of some securities are not properly aligned, for instance, it is possible to earn risk-free profits by simultaneously trading the mispriced assets. Two or more securities that are economically equivalent should have the same expected return. If the expected returns are not equal, the economic *law of one price* states that profitable arbitrage is possible. To generate a risk-free profit from misaligned prices, arbitrageurs purchase a long position in the cheaper security that is financed by using the cash proceeds from a short position in the more expensive one. Next, we consider several examples of arbitrage; the discussion is streamlined by ignoring transaction costs. Realistically speaking, transaction costs kill many deals that offer only moderate profits.

   Illustration 1: Gold is a fungible commodity that is traded around the world. Suppose one ounce of gold is traded at \$1,000 in New York while it is also trading at £630 in London. If we assume the exchange rate between the U.S. dollar and the British pound is \$1.6/£, the law of one price is violated because gold is traded at higher price in London than in New York. An arbitrageur could profit from these misaligned prices by selling short one ounce of gold in London for £630, because £630 times \$1.6/£ equals \$1,008—which is \$8 above the \$1,000 price of gold in New York. To earn a quick profit the arbitrageur should start by borrowing an ounce of physical gold in London from an anonymous third party. Without delay, the borrowed gold is sold for £630 in London. Then, the arbitrageur quickly phones

New York with an order to buy one ounce of gold bullion at a purchase price of $1,000 (before the price changes disadvantageously). This purchased gold is used to repay the ounce of gold that was borrowed in London. This series of transactions leaves the arbitrageur holding $8 of profit without taking any risk (because perfectly hedged long and short positions offset each other's price changes), and, without investing any of the arbitrageur's personal funds.

If illustration 1 fails to excite you, consider transacting in tons instead of ounces.

Illustration 2: Suppose the per-ounce spot price of gold is $1,000, and the six-month futures price of gold is $1,025. Assume the risk-free interest rate is 4 percent, and that there are no gold storage costs. Under these circumstances, the futures price is high relative to the spot price, because the spot-futures parity formula tells us that after we figure in the interest expense needed to finance an inventory of gold for six months, the appropriate futures price should be $1,020.20 (which is $4.80 less than the $1,025 futures price).

$$\text{Appropriate futures price, } F_0 = \$1,000 \times e^{0.04 \times (1/2)} = \$1,020.20$$

An arbitrageur could start to work earning an arbitrage profit by selling one short futures contract at the relatively high price of $1,025 and, simultaneously, buying a long futures position in the spot market at the relatively low price of $1,000 per ounce. While establishing this imperfect hedge, the arbitrageur borrows $1,000 at 4 percent interest rate for six months to provide cash with which to finance an ounce of gold that is carried in inventory for six months. When the short futures contract matures, the arbitrageur delivers the ounce of stored gold to the owner of the short position for a price of $1,025. The arbitrageur uses this $1,025 to pay off the borrowings of $1,020.20 (= $1,000 \times e^{0.04 \times (1/2)}$). Thus, the arbitrageur is left holding an arbitrage profit of $4.80 (=$1,025 − $1,020.20) per ounce without investing any personal funds and without taking any risks that were not hedged away.

Illustration 3: Exchange-traded funds (ETFs) are investment funds traded on stock exchanges, like stocks. Most ETFs are indexed to some index. The oldest and most popular ETF is the Standard & Poor's Depository Receipt (SPDR, pronounced "spider") that is indexed to the S&P500 index. SPDRs (ticker: SPY) are actively traded on the New York Stock Exchange (NYSE). Standard & Poor's Corporation recomputes the net asset value (NAV) of the S&P500 index every 15 seconds during the hours that the stock exchanges are open.[2] Consider arbitrage opportunities involving SPDRs and the underlying S&P500 index.

Because the Investment Company Act of 1940 requires mutual funds to buy and sell their shares at their NAV per share, there are few arbitrage profits to be earned from mutual funds that are indexed to the S&P500. In contrast, the ETFs that are listed and traded on organized stock exchanges trade like shares of stock, and their market prices fluctuate freely. In particular, the market prices of SPDRs that invest only in the 500 stocks in the S&P500 index sometimes fluctuate above or below their NAV. Differences between the market prices of an indexed ETF and the simultaneous NAV of its underlying index are called *tracking errors*. Tracking errors violate the *law of one price*. And market prices that violate the law of one price provide opportunities to earn arbitrage profits. For example, when the market price of an ETF that is indexed to the S&P500 index (or any other index) rises above its NAV, arbitrage profits can be earned from positive tracking errors like those illustrated next.

Market price of a SPDR at time t	$1,000
Less: NAV per share of the SPDR at time t	$980
Equals: Positive tracking error at time t	+ $20

When positive tracking errors exist, arbitrage profits can be earned from selling short X dollars' worth of SPDRs, because SPDRs are temporarily overpriced. At the same time, spend a total of X dollars to buy 500 long positions for each of the 500 stocks that comprise the S&P500 index. To offset the short SPDR position, the 500 long stock positions should be purchased in exactly the same proportions they have in the S&P500 index. Regardless of whether the value of the S&P500 index rises or falls, these offsetting long and short pricing pressures are likely to reduce the SPDR's positive tracking error to zero within a very short time, earn arbitrage profits for the arbitrageur, and correct the temporary violation of the law of one price.[3]

Illustration 4: When the market price of an ETF that is indexed to the S&P500 index (or any other index) temporarily falls below its NAV, arbitrage profits can be earned from the negative tracking error illustrated next.

Market price of a SPDR at time t	$980
Less: NAV per share of the same SPDR at time t	$1,000
Equals: Negative tracking error at time t	− $20

When negative tracking errors exist, arbitrage profits can be earned from buying long X dollars' worth of SPDRs, which are temporarily underpriced. At the same time, open 500 short stock positions with a total market value of X dollars in each of the 500 stocks that comprise the S&P500 index. To offset the long SPDR position, the 500 short stock positions should be in the same proportions the 500 stocks have in the S&P500 index. Regardless of whether the value of the S&P500 index rises or falls, these offsetting long and short pricing pressures should quickly reduce the SPDR's negative tracking error to zero, earn arbitrage profits for the arbitrageur, and correct the temporary violation of the law of one price.

Illustration 5: Suppose that the expected return on the market portfolio is $E(r_m) = 9\%$, the risk-free rate of return is $r_f = 4\%$, and the well-diversified portfolio A has a beta of $\beta_A = 0.8$ and an expected return of $E(r_A) = 10\%$. Portfolio A's expected return of 10 percent creates an opportunity to earn arbitrage profits. Figure 16.1 illustrates the location of portfolio A in $[\beta, E(r)]$ space.

The one-factor security market line (SML, or CAPM) implies that the required (equilibrium) rate of return on portfolio A should be: $E(r_i) = r_f + \beta[E(r_M) - r_f] = 4\% + 0.80 \times (9\% - 4\%) = 8\%$. Because investors can earn 10 percent from portfolio A and this is 2 percent more than equilibrium expected return of 8 percent, portfolio A is underpriced. To earn 2 percent of arbitrage profit, an arbitrageur should buy a long position worth $1 of underpriced portfolio A. Without using the arbitrageur's personal funds, the dollar needed to purchase A can be obtained with the proceeds from a short sale of $1 worth of a new portfolio the arbitrageur

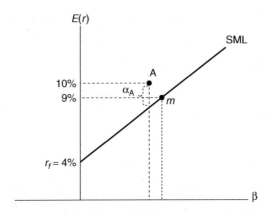

FIGURE 16.1   An Arbitrage Opportunity with a
One-factor Security Market Line

constructs by borrowing 20 percent of $1 at the risk-free asset and short selling
an amount of the market portfolio equal to 80 percent of $1.[4] This new short
portfolio's 20 percent and 80 percent weights in the risk-free asset and the market
portfolio are selected so it has the same beta of 0.8 and the same expected return of
8% as portfolio A. The net return from the combination of a long position in the
mispriced portfolio A and a short position in the new portfolio is:

$$\$1 \times \left(10\% \text{ from A}\right) - \$1 \times (0.2 \times 4\% + 0.8 \times 9\% = 8\%)$$

$$= 10\cent - 8\cent = 2\cent \text{ per } \$1 \text{ or } 2\%$$

To better understand the lucrative nature of the preceding arbitrage transaction,
think of undertaking a $100 million arbitrage position (A) without investing a
cent of your own funds, and (B) without taking any risks. The dollar net profit is
$2 million, and with no money invested (a denominator of zero), the arbitrageur's
rate of return is positive infinity. This return might be earned within a few hours or
a few days.

Illustration 6: Suppose two well-diversified portfolios, A and B, have betas of
1.5 and 0.6, and expected returns of 12 and 9 percent, respectively. The risk-free rate
of return is 5 percent. To see how an arbitrage profit opportunity exists, consider a
third portfolio consisting of portfolios A and B combined with the weights $-2/3$ +
$5/3 = 1.0$, respectively.

$$w_A = \frac{-\beta_B}{\beta_A - \beta_B} = \frac{-0.6}{1.5 - 0.6} = -\frac{2}{3} \quad \text{and} \quad w_B = \frac{\beta_A}{\beta_A - \beta_B} = \frac{1.5}{1.5 - 0.6} = \frac{5}{3}$$

To achieve these portfolios, an arbitrageur buys a long position in portfolio B
with a weight of 5/3 and sells short portfolio A, which is represented by the negative
weight of $-2/3$. These proportions add up to 1.0, and result in a portfolio, p,
which has a beta of zero, $[(-2/3 \text{ in A}) \times 1.5 + (5/3 \text{ in B}) \times 0.6] = 0$. A zero beta
portfolio is riskless and its expected return should equal the risk-free return of
5 percent. However, this mispriced portfolio's (disequilibrium) expected return is
$(-2/3 \text{ in A}) \times 12\% + (5/3 \text{ in B}) \times 9\% = 7$ percent. This riskless portfolio earns

TABLE 16.1 A Procedure of Earnings Arbitrage Profits

Transaction	Initial cash flow	Ending cash flow	Beta
Sell short the risk-free asset	+$100	−$105	0
Buy long position in *p*	−$100	+$107	$(-2/3) \times 1.5 + (5/3) \times 0.6 = 0$
Sum	$0	+$2	0

2 percent more than the risk-free return. Thus, a profitable arbitrage transaction can be achieved by selling short the risk-free asset (borrowing at the risk-free rate of 5 percent) and investing the proceeds to buy a long position in the portfolio. This transaction generates a profit of $2 per $100 of invested funds. These results are summarized in Table 16.1.

The previous illustrations 1 through 4 show cases of *risk-free arbitrage*, also called *deterministic arbitrage*. Risk-free arbitrage achieves an arbitrage profit by taking a long position in an underpriced security and a simultaneous short position in an overpriced security. The arbitrage profit is earned as buying the long position in the underpriced security bids up its price. And, at the same time, more arbitrage profit is earned as selling short the overpriced security creates selling pressure that drives down its price. When the prices of the underpriced security and the overpriced security converge, the economic *law of one price* is fulfilled and the arbitrage profit opportunities cease to exist. In contrast to illustrations 1 through 4, illustrations 5 and 6 show examples of the *statistical arbitrage* in which arbitrage profits are not achieved through single transactions. Statistical arbitrage is based on the expected values of multiple assets that earn arbitrage profits from multiple transactions.[5] It differs from deterministic arbitrage in which a (sure) risk-free profit can be obtained through single transactions.

Opportunities to earn arbitrage profits from misaligned prices that violate the law of one price are temporary situations that typically vanish within a few minutes. Arbitrageurs are more sophisticated, they move faster, and they have more money to invest than the average investor. As a result, when an arbitrageur discovers misaligned prices that violate the law of one price, the profit-making activities of the arbitrageur quickly bring misaligned prices in line with the law of one price.

16.2 INDEX ARBITRAGE

Index arbitrage is currently the most popular trading strategy for exploiting arbitrage. It is possible to perform profitable index arbitrage on many different security price indexes. Thousands of stock indexes and thousands of bond indexes in the U.S. generate enough revenue for their creators (such as S&P and Moodys) to pay the cost of maintaining and updating them and still be profitable. The Standard & Poor's 500 index (S&P500) appears to be the most profitable: It generates millions of dollars of annual income from licensing fees for the Standard & Poor's Corporation. Over 100 mutual funds are indexed to (are managed with the goal of mimicking) the S&P500 index. The Chicago Mercantile Exchange (CME) lists and trades futures contracts on the S&P500 index that are among the most frequently traded futures contracts in the world. The CME also lists and trades put and call options on the S&P 500 index that generate extremely large daily volumes of transactions. In addition, over a dozen ETFs, including the SPDR, are also indexed to the S&P500.

In futures and stock markets, absent market frictions such as transaction costs, the law of one price should hold. But, occasionally this law is temporarily violated during the life of a futures contract. Then, a breif opportunity exists to make a riskless arbitrage profit equal to the difference between the actual and theoretical futures price.

16.2.1   Basic Ideas of Index Arbitrage

Index arbitrage is a strategy designed to make an arbitrage profit from temporary discrepancies between the actual price of an index and the price of a futures contract on that index. It is analogous to illustration 2 in the previous section if the underlying asset is an index instead of gold.[6]

From the spot-futures parity, the relationship between the futures price and spot price of an index at time t is

$$F_t = S_t e^{(r-q)(T-t)} \quad \text{(Spot–futures parity)}$$

where F_t = futures price of an index that will mature in T years, S_t = spot price of an index; that is, the current level of the index at time t, r = risk-free interest rate (continuously compounded; annualized), T = time to maturity (in years), and q = dividend yield (continuously compounded and annualized).[7]

In the preceding spot-futures parity equation the theoretically fair futures price is $S_t e^{(r-q)(T-t)}$. If the actual futures price does not equal the theoretical fair futures price, an opportunity to earn arbitrage profit emerges. If the actual futures price is higher than the fair futures price (namely, $F_t > S_t e^{(r-q)(T-t)}$), this means the current futures price is overpriced relative to the spot price of the index. When this happens, a profit-maximizing arbitrageur quickly sells the index futures contract short and, at the same time, buys a long position in the index. These trades create a fully hedged (riskless) position for the arbitrageur, until the maturity of the futures contract. At maturity, the futures price changes to F_T from F_t, and the spot price changes to S_T from S_t. One of the few certainties in futures markets is that the futures price and the spot price will converge at maturity, $F_T = S_T$. Thus, if the futures contract's market price before its maturity date (and, therefore, before convergence) is above its delivery price at maturity (that is, $F_T < F_t$), the gain from the short position in the index futures contract will be large enough to cover the loss from the long position in the spot market and the carrying cost (that is, the risk-free interest rate minus cash dividend yield). If the futures contract's market price before its maturity date (and, therefore, before convergence) is below the delivery price at maturity (specifically, $F_T > F_t$), the loss from the short position in the index futures contract is smaller than the gain from the long position in the spot market, after deducting the cost of carry. In other words, regardless of whether the futures price increases or decreases to F_T at maturity after taking the hedged position the arbitrageur earns risk-free arbitrage profits.

In contrast, if the actual futures price is lower than the fair futures price (that is, $F_t < S_t e^{(r-q)(T-t)}$), this means that, relative to the spot price of the index, the current futures contract is underpriced. A greedy arbitrageur will perform a valuable service for society by rapidly buying a long position in the underpriced futures contract on the index and simultaneously selling short the stocks that comprise the index. These trades accomplish two good results. First, they tend to align the misaligned prices. Second, they also create a fully hedged riskless position for the arbitrageur, which lasts until the futures contract matures. In addition, the clever arbitrageur earns risk-free arbitrage profits, regardless of whether the futures price increases or decreases. To be specific about the paragraphs above, buying or selling securities to offset a short or a long position in a securities market index means buying or selling the securities in the index in proportion to their weights in the index.[8]

16.2.2 Index Arbitrage and Program Trading

As mentioned in the previous section, when the actual futures price does not equal the fair futures market price for the underlying goods, an arbitrage opportunity occurs. For example, when the actual futures price is higher than the fair futures price, the overpriced index futures contract is sold short and the underlying stock index portfolio is bought (to create a long position) to complete a riskless arbitrage profit opportunity. Executing this trade involves *simultaneously* purchasing all of the component stocks of the index according to the weight of each stock in the index to duplicate the index. Such a trade of all component stocks at once is known as a *program trade*, because a computer program must be used to execute such large transactions instantly.[9]

The decision to execute a program trade is based on the premium or spread, which is the difference between the S&P 500 index futures contract's fair value for the underlying 500 stocks minus the current (spot) price of the S&P 500 index. This spread usually ranges between $5.00 to −$5.00, and slowly decays or rises as the S&P 500 futures contract approaches expiration. When the spread difference rises to a certain positive level, program trades are activated. Large institutional traders then buy the component stocks in the S&P 500 index on the NYSE and sell short the S&P 500 index futures contract on the CME. When the spread difference drops to a predefined negative level, program trades are activated and large institutional traders enter trades to reverse the spread to zero.

16.2.3 Use of ETFs for Index Arbitrage

In practice, index arbitrage profits can be difficult to earn. The first difficulty lies in the high transaction costs. Trading all of the component stocks in an index involves high transaction costs. The second is illiquidity. If some stocks are not liquid enough, their trading prices could be significantly different from the price that arbitrageurs originally intended to trade. Thus, it could be difficult to execute trades on all of the component stocks simultaneously. A third difficulty is the restriction on short sales of stocks. While futures can be shorted on a downtick, some individual stocks cannot be shorted on a downtick, making it impossible to execute an arbitrage strategy that requires selling short the component stocks in the index. A fourth potential problem lies with the tracking errors. To reduce transaction costs and to overcome illiquidity, some arbitrageurs buy or sell a subset of the component stocks in the index in hopes of mimicking the whole index portfolio. In this case, ETFs can be employed to reduce the tracking errors.

Using ETFs can overcome some of the difficulties of executing an index arbitrage strategy that requires short selling stocks or trading all the component stocks in the index simultaneously. ETFs are investment funds that are listed and traded on stock exchanges, like shares of stock. Most ETFs are index funds that invest in the same securities underlying a particular stock market index, and they attempt to replicate the performance of the index as closely as possible. Trading an ETF is economically equivalent to trading simultaneously all the component stocks in the underlying index. The first benefit from using ETFs is that transaction costs on the portfolio are smaller than the cost of trading all the component stocks separately. Second, most ETFs are highly liquid. For instance, both the S&P 500 index futures contract and the SPDR (the oldest ETF indexed to the S&P500 index) are highly liquid and continuously trade in large volumes. Third, the short selling restrictions are much less severe when trading ETFs. The uptick rule does not apply to ETFs as it does to individual equities. Fourth, the tracking errors should be minimal when trading S&P500 futures against SPDRs, because the SPDR has the same composition and weights as the S&P 500 index. As a result of these benefits, using ETFs can expedite the execution of index arbitrage on the S&P500 index.

16.3 THE ASSET PRICING EQUATION

Expensive goods are typically hoarded and, in contrast, inexpensive goods are more likely to be squandered. More generally, in a capitalistic society resources are allocated by their market prices. This kind of resource allocation system makes it important to eliminate violations of the law of one price and eliminate any other arbitrary aspects in the price formation processes. Financial economists have studied the role of arbitrage in forming market prices. By exploring the ramifications of widespread arbitrage activity, financial economists have developed an APT that models the resulting price formation system for a nation that enjoys free markets.

The APT begins by assuming that asset returns are governed by a linear return-generating process similar to the multiple-index models discussed in Chapter 8.[10] In particular, any asset i is assumed to have returns that are generated by the following process:

$$r_{it} = a_i + \beta_{i1} r_{p_1,t} + \beta_{i2} r_{p_2,t} + \cdots + \beta_{iK} r_{p_K,t} + \epsilon_{it} \qquad (16.1)$$

where a_i is a constant for asset i, β_{ik} is the factor loading (or factor beta) of asset i on the k-th factor $(k = 1, \ldots, K)$, $r_{p_k,t}$ denotes the return on the k-th factor portfolio, and ϵ_{it} is the mean-zero random error term for asset i, representing unexplained residual or idiosyncratic risk. Note that the factor loading β_{ik} is interpreted as a measure of asset i's sensitivity to the k-th risk factor, or, stated differently, a measure of the systematic risk of asset i with respect to the k-th factor. The variables in equation (16.1) satisfy the following conditions: $E\left(\epsilon_{it}\epsilon_{jt}\right) = 0$ for $i \neq j$ and $E\left(\epsilon_{it} r_{p_k,t}\right) = 0$, meaning that the error term for any security is uncorrelated with any factor or the error term of any other security, and homoscedasticity prevails or, symbolically, $E\left(\epsilon_{it}^2\right) = \sigma_{\epsilon_i}^2$.

In deriving the APT asset pricing equation, first note that taking the expected value of equation (16.1) yields

$$E\left(r_i\right) = a_i + \beta_{i1} E\left(r_{p_1,t}\right) + \beta_{i2} E\left(r_{p_2,t}\right) + \cdots + \beta_{iK} E\left(r_{p_K,t}\right) \qquad (16.2)$$

Subtracting equation (16.2) from equation (16.1) and rearranging results in

$$r_{it} = E\left(r_i\right) + \beta_{i1}f_{1t} + \beta_{i2}f_{2t} + \cdots + \beta_{iK}f_{Kt} + \epsilon_{it} \qquad (16.3)$$

where $f_{kt} = r_{p_k,t} - E\left(r_{p_k,t}\right)$ is a mean-zero *risk factor*. While APT states that asset returns are generated by K independent risk factors, also referred to as indexes or factor portfolios, it is important to recognize that APT does not specify a numerical value for K or what the indexes represent. All we know is that K must be notably less than the number of risky securities in order to be able to obtain a mathematical solution.

16.3.1 One Single Factor with No Residual Risk

When asset returns are related to a single factor with no residual risk, factor equation (16.4) represents this situation:

$$r_{it} = E\left(r_i\right) + \beta_i f_t \qquad (16.4)$$

We consider a portfolio, p, consisting of two assets whose nonzero systematic risks are β_i and β_j $(\beta_i \neq \beta_j)$, their investment weights are w_i and w_j, respectively, and, $w_i + w_j = 1$. This portfolio's return is

$$
\begin{aligned}
r_{pt} &= w_i\left[E\left(r_i\right) + \beta_i f_t\right] + w_j\left[E\left(r_j\right) + \beta_j f_t\right] \\
&= w_i\left[E\left(r_i\right) - E\left(r_j\right)\right] + E\left(r_j\right) + \left[w_i\left(\beta_i - \beta_j\right) + \beta_j\right]f_t \qquad (16.5)
\end{aligned}
$$

The last term in equation (16.5), $\left[w_i\left(\beta_i - \beta_j\right) + \beta_j\right]f_t$, is the component containing risk because the risk factor f_t is in the last term. Therefore, if we choose the weight,

$$w_i = \frac{-\beta_j}{\beta_i - \beta_j} \qquad (16.6)$$

the return on the portfolio is certain. To avoid earning any arbitrage profits, the return on the portfolio should equal the risk-free rate of return. That is,

$$w_i\left[E\left(r_i\right) - E\left(r_j\right)\right] + E\left(r_j\right) \equiv r_f \qquad (16.7)$$

Note that the systematic risk of the portfolio is zero. That is, $\beta_p = w_i\beta_i + w_j\beta_j = \left[-\beta_j/\left(\beta_i - \beta_j\right)\right]\beta_i + \left[\beta_i/\left(\beta_i - \beta_j\right)\right]\beta_j = 0$. Substituting equation (16.6) into equation (16.7) yields

$$\frac{E\left(r_i\right) - r_f}{\beta_i} = \frac{E\left(r_j\right) - r_f}{\beta_j} \qquad (16.8)$$

Equation (16.8) implies that the ratios of the excess return to risk should be equal for all assets, to ensure that no profitable arbitrage opportunities exist. If we let this ratio be a constant, λ, then

$$E\left(r_i\right) = r_f + \beta_i\lambda \qquad (16.9)$$

is an equilibrium one-factor asset pricing model. APT refers to λ, and as the *factor risk premium* and requires it to equal the expected excess return on a portfolio with the factor loading equal to one ($\beta = 1$).

16.3.2 Two Factors with No Residual Risk

When asset returns are related with two factors and no residual risk, the factor model of equation (16.3) becomes

$$r_{it} = E(r_i) + \beta_{i1}f_{1t} + \beta_{i2}f_{2t} \tag{16.10}$$

As in the previous case, we consider a three-asset portfolio, p. The return on this portfolio is

$$r_{pt} \equiv \sum_{i=1}^{3} w_i r_{it} = \sum_{i=1}^{3} w_i E(r_i) + \left(\sum_{i=1}^{3} w_i \beta_{i1}\right) f_{1t} + \left(\sum_{i=1}^{3} w_i \beta_{i2}\right) f_{2t} \tag{16.11}$$

If we choose the three assets' weights for portfolio p such that

$$\sum_{i=1}^{3} w_i \beta_{i1} = 0 \quad \text{and} \quad \sum_{i=1}^{3} w_i \beta_{i2} = 0 \tag{16.12}$$

then the return on this portfolio is certain. In order to guarantee that no profitable arbitrage opportunities exist, the portfolio's return should equal the risk-free rate of return. That is,

$$\sum_{i=1}^{3} w_i E(r_i) = r_f \tag{16.13}$$

The three conditions in equations (16.12) and (16.13) can be written as

$$\begin{pmatrix} E(r_1) - r_f & E(r_2) - r_f & E(r_3) - r_f \\ \beta_{11} & \beta_{21} & \beta_{31} \\ \beta_{12} & \beta_{22} & \beta_{32} \end{pmatrix} \begin{pmatrix} w_1 \\ w_2 \\ w_3 \end{pmatrix} = \begin{pmatrix} 0 \\ 0 \\ 0 \end{pmatrix} \tag{16.14}$$

If the inverse of the coefficient matrix in equation (16.14) exists, the unique solution for the weights is $w = (w_1, w_2, w_3)' = (0, 0, 0)'$.[11] This violates the condition that the sum of the weights equals one: $\sum_{i=1}^{3} w_i = 1$. The necessary condition for $\sum_{i=1}^{3} w_i = 1$ is that at least one of the weights should not equal zero. To have such a solution, the inverse of the coefficient matrix should not exist. In other words, the coefficient matrix in equation (16.14) must be singular (or its determinant must be zero). In a singular matrix, vectors (row or column) are said to be *linearly dependent*, and any row (or column) vector is represented as a linear combination of the other remaining row (or column) vectors.[12] So, the first row can be represented as a linear combination of the last two rows. Thus, the i-th component of the first row can be written as a linear combination of the i-th component of the last two rows.

$$E(r_i) = r_f + \lambda_1 \beta_{i1} + \lambda_2 \beta_{i2} \tag{16.15}$$

where λ_1 and λ_2 are known as the factor risk premiums related to the first and second factors, respectively. This is an equilibrium two-factor asset pricing model. See the end-of-book Appendix C to learn more about linear dependence in a matrix.

The interpretation of the factor premiums λ_1 and λ_2 is that if we choose the weights such that $\sum_{i=1}^{3} w_i \beta_{i1} = 1$ and $\sum_{i=1}^{3} w_i \beta_{i2} = 0$, then from equation (16.15), we can show that the expected excess return on a portfolio equals λ_1, where $\sum_{i=1}^{3} w_i E(r_i) - r_f = \lambda_1$. In fact, this portfolio has unit sensitivity (a beta of one) to the first factor and zero sensitivity (a beta of zero) for the other factor. That is,

$$
\begin{aligned}
r_{p_1,t} &= \sum_{i=1}^{3} w_i E(r_i) + \left(\sum_{i=1}^{3} w_i \beta_{i1} \right) f_{1t} + \left(\sum_{i=1}^{3} w_i \beta_{i2} \right) f_{2t} \\
&= E(r_{p_1,t}) + f_{1t}
\end{aligned}
\tag{16.16}
$$

Similarly, λ_2 is the expected excess return on a portfolio whose weights are determined from $\sum_{i=1}^{3} w_i \beta_{i1} = 0$ and $\sum_{i=1}^{3} w_i \beta_{i2} = 1$. This portfolio has unit sensitivity to the second factor and zero sensitivity to the other factor. That is,

$$
\begin{aligned}
r_{p_2,t} &= \sum_{i=1}^{3} w_i E(r_i) + \left(\sum_{i=1}^{3} w_i \beta_{i1} \right) f_{1t} + \left(\sum_{i=1}^{3} w_i \beta_{i2} \right) f_{2t} \\
&= E(r_{p_2,t}) + f_{2t}
\end{aligned}
\tag{16.17}
$$

Therefore, the equilibrium two-factor model of equation (16.15) can be rewritten as

$$
E(r_i) = r_f + \left(\bar{\delta}_1 - r_f \right) \beta_{i1} + \left(\bar{\delta}_2 - r_f \right) \beta_{i2}
\tag{16.18}
$$

where $\bar{\delta}_k = E(r_{p_k,t})$ for $k = 1, 2$.

16.3.3 *K* Factors with No Residual Risk

This is a simple extension of the previous two-factor case. The factor model of equation (16.3) is expanded to become

$$
r_{it} = E(r_i) + \beta_{i1} f_{1t} + \beta_{i2} f_{2t} + \cdots + \beta_{iK} f_{Kt}
\tag{16.19}
$$

As in the two-factor case, we consider a portfolio, p, consisting of $K+1$ assets. Then, the return on this portfolio is described as

$$
r_{pt} = E(r_{pt}) + \left(\sum_{i=1}^{K+1} w_i \beta_{i1} \right) f_{1t} + \left(\sum_{i=1}^{K+1} w_i \beta_{i2} \right) f_{2t} + \cdots + \left(\sum_{i=1}^{K+1} w_i \beta_{iK} \right) f_{Kt}
\tag{16.20}
$$

where $E(r_{pt}) = \sum_{i=1}^{K+1} w_i E(r_i)$. If we choose the weights of the $(K+1)$ assets for portfolio p such that

$$
\sum_{i=1}^{K+1} w_i \beta_{i1} = 0, \quad \sum_{i=1}^{K+1} w_i \beta_{i2} = 0, \quad \ldots, \quad \sum_{i=1}^{K+1} w_i \beta_{iK} = 0
\tag{16.21}
$$

then the return on this portfolio is certain. To eliminate any profitable arbitrage opportunities, the portfolio's return should equal the risk-free rate of return. That is,

$$
\sum_{i=1}^{K+1} w_i E(r_i) = r_f
\tag{16.22}
$$

The preceding $(K+1)$ conditions in equations (16.21) and (16.22) can be written in matrix form as

$$
\begin{pmatrix}
E(r_1)-r_f & E(r_2)-r_f & \cdots & E(r_{K+1})-r_f \\
\beta_{11} & \beta_{21} & \cdots & \beta_{K+1,1} \\
\vdots & \vdots & \ddots & \vdots \\
\beta_{1K} & \beta_{2K} & \cdots & \beta_{K+1,K}
\end{pmatrix}
\begin{pmatrix}
w_1 \\ w_2 \\ \vdots \\ w_{K+1}
\end{pmatrix}
=
\begin{pmatrix}
0 \\ 0 \\ \vdots \\ 0
\end{pmatrix}
\tag{16.23}
$$

As in the previous section, if the inverse of the coefficient matrix in equation (16.23) exists, the unique solution for the weights is $w = (w_1, w_2, \ldots, w_{K+1})' = (0,0,\ldots,0)'$. This violates the condition that the sum of the weights equals one. To satisfy this condition, at least one of the weights should not equal zero, and the inverse of the coefficient matrix should not exist. In other words, the coefficient matrix in equation (16.23) must be singular, and any row (or column) vector is represented as a linear combination of the other remaining row (or column) vectors. Therefore, the first row can be represented as a linear combination of the last K rows. That is, the i-th component of the first row can be written as

$$
E(r_i) = r_f + \lambda_1\beta_{i1} + \lambda_2\beta_{i2} + \cdots + \lambda_K\beta_{iK}
\tag{16.24}
$$

where λ_k is known as the factor risk premium related with the k-th factor. As in the two-factor case, equation (16.24) can be rewritten as

$$
E(r_i) = r_f + (\bar\delta_1 - r_f)\beta_{i1} + (\bar\delta_2 - r_f)\beta_{i2} + \cdots + (\bar\delta_K - r_f)\beta_{iK}
\tag{16.25}
$$

where $\bar\delta_k = E(r_{p_k,t})$ for $k = 1, 2, \ldots, K$

16.3.4 K Factors with Residual Risk

In the previous three subsections, we considered simplified cases in which the risky assets had no residual risk. It is more realistic to consider risky assets that have residual risk. When residual risk is considered, a residual term is added to equation (16.19) to obtain the following K-factor model

$$
r_{it} = E(r_i) + \beta_{i1}f_{1t} + \beta_{i2}f_{2t} + \cdots + \beta_{iK}f_{Kt} + \epsilon_{it}
\tag{16.3}
$$

Consider portfolio p, consisting of n assets. The return on this portfolio is

$$
r_{pt} = E(r_{pt}) + \left(\sum_{i=1}^{n} w_i\beta_{i1}\right)f_{1t} + \cdots + \left(\sum_{i=1}^{n} w_i\beta_{iK}\right)f_{Kt} + \sum_{i=1}^{n} w_i\epsilon_{it}
\tag{16.26}
$$

where $E(r_{pt}) = \sum_{i=1}^{n} w_i E(r_i)$. Assume an arbitrage portfolio consisting of these n assets is so well diversified that

$$
\sum_{i=1}^{n} w_i\epsilon_{it} \cong 0
\tag{16.27}
$$

which means this arbitrage portfolio has approximately zero residual (diversifiable) risk included in its returns. If we choose the weights for the n assets in the arbitrage portfolio such that

$$
\sum_{i=1}^{n} w_i\beta_{ik} = 0 \text{ for } k = 1, \ldots, K
\tag{16.28}
$$

then this portfolio is *approximately* riskless. A riskless arbitrage portfolio should have $w_i \approx 1/n$, and n should be chosen to be a large number. According to the law of large numbers, because the error terms, ϵ_{it}, are mutually uncorrelated, the number of assets for the arbitrage portfolio, n, should be large enough for the weighted average of the error terms to approach zero. In other words, for an appropriately large value of n, the residual variance is diversified away, as shown in equation (16.29).

$$r_{pt} = E\left(r_{pt}\right) + \left(\sum_{i=1}^{n} w_i \beta_{i1}\right) f_{1t} + \cdots + \left(\sum_{i=1}^{n} w_i \beta_{iK}\right) f_{Kt} \qquad (16.29)$$

As in the previous case, the equilibrium asset pricing model can be written as

$$E\left(r_i\right) = r_f + \lambda_1 \beta_{i1} + \lambda_2 \beta_{i2} + \cdots + \lambda_K \beta_{iK} \qquad (16.30)$$

or

$$E\left(r_i\right) = r_f + \left(\bar{\delta}_1 - r_f\right) \beta_{i1} + \left(\bar{\delta}_2 - r_f\right) \beta_{i2} + \cdots + \left(\bar{\delta}_K - r_f\right) \beta_{iK} \qquad (16.31)$$

where $\bar{\delta}_k = E\left(r_{p_k,t}\right)$ is the expected return on a factor portfolio that has unit sensitivity to the k-th factor and no sensitivity to all other factors. Algebraically, this means that $\sum_{i=1}^{n} w_i \beta_{ik} = 1$ and $\sum_{i=1}^{n} w_i \beta_{ih} = 0$ for $h = 1, \ldots, k-1, k+1, \ldots, K$. The factor portfolio is a well-diversified portfolio and its returns track innovations in the sources of macroeconomic risk.

From equation (16.31), it can be seen that an asset's risk premium is simply a linear combination of the various factor risk premiums. Equations (16.30) and (16.31) are two different representations of the asset pricing implications of APT; they show that an asset's expected return equals the sum of the set of factor sensitivities for that asset. Equation (16.1) can also be viewed as a multivariate regression equation of the variable r_{it} on a set of K independent variables $(r_{p_1,t}, \ldots, r_{p_K,t})$ that are not collinear. Thus, the factor sensitivities can be interpreted as

$$\beta_{ik} = \frac{\text{Cov}\left(r_{it}, r_{p_k,t}\right)}{\text{Var}\left(r_{p_k,t}\right)} \qquad (16.32)$$

and an asset's return can be viewed as being based on the covariances of the asset's return with the various risk factors. Intuitively, an asset's current price and expected return are determined by the asset's sensitivity to various unique risks. Graphically, all assets would plot on what is known as a hyperplane, where each axis of the hyperplane (except the axis measuring expected returns) measures a particular sensitivity to some risk factor.

16.4 ASSET PRICING ON A SECURITY MARKET PLANE

The APT has security-price implications illustrated in Figure 16.2. The plane $\overrightarrow{r_f aEb}$ indicates the equilibrium pricing equation of the APT represented by equation (16.30) or (16.31) when the number of risk factors is two. Points above the plane $\overrightarrow{r_f aEb}$ represent securities that are underpriced. For example, security U is underpriced because its price is lower than it should be in equilibrium. Points such as U represent securities with unusually high expected returns for the amount of systematic risks they bear (namely, β_1 and β_2 in Figure 16.2). Because security U has an unusually

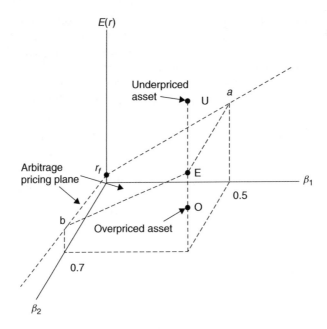

FIGURE 16.2 APT Plane for a Two-factor Model

high expected return, it will experience strong investor demand. Investors will bid up the purchase price of security U until its anticipated return is driven down onto the APT plane at point E in Figure 16.2.

The preceding arguments about underpricing are similar to those in Section 12.4 of Chapter 12. When the estimated end-of-period price of a stock is $E(P_1)$ and its current price is given as P_0, its initial expected return $E(r)$ is equal to $[E(P_1) - P_0]/P_0 = [E(P_1)/P_0] - 1$, assuming that no cash dividends are paid. If the price P_0 is too low, this is equivalent to having $E(r)$ too high, meaning that $E(r) > r_f + \lambda_1\beta_1 + \lambda_2\beta_2$. In this case, excess demand will bid up the price P_0 and lower $E(r)$ until the following equilibrium is achieved: $E(r) = r_f + \lambda_1\beta_1 + \lambda_2\beta_2$. In other words, all securities positioned above the APT plane are underpriced.

EXAMPLE 16.1

Assume the riskless rate of return is 4 percent. Consider a well-diversified portfolio, U, with a factor beta on the first factor of $\beta_{U1} = 0.5$, and factor beta on the second factor of $\beta_{U2} = 0.7$. This portfolio is expected (or anticipated) to earn 2 percent for a subsequent period. The APT pricing equation states 10.2 percent should be the expected return from portfolio U.

$$E(r_U) = r_f + \lambda_1\beta_1 + \lambda_2\beta_2 = r_f + (\bar\delta_1 - r_f)\beta_{U1} + (\bar\delta_2 - r_f)\beta_{U2}$$
$$= 4\% + (8\% - 4\%) \times 0.5 + (10\% - 4\%) \times 0.7$$
$$= 4\% + 2\% + 4.2\% = 10.2\%$$

EXAMPLE 16.1 (*Continued*)

The amount of underpricing is the difference between the expected (or anticipated) return and the equilibrium return. It is $12\% - 10.2\% = 1.8\%$. This underpriced investment opportunity will motivate profit-seeking investors to bid the price of portfolio U up until its expected return is reduced to its equilibrium expected return at point E in Figure 16.2. Note that the risk premium for this portfolio is 6.2 percent (=2 percent + 4.2 percent).

Inverse but symmetric logic suggests that securities located below the APT plane represent securities whose current prices are too high. This means that securities such as O are overpriced. Security O offers insufficient levels of expected return to induce rational investors to accept the amount of systematic risk they bear. As a result, O's price will fall due to a lack of investor demand. The price of O will continue falling until its expected return is on the APT plane at point E in Figure 16.2. More generally, all securities positioned below the APT plane are overpriced.

16.5 CONTRASTING APT WITH CAPM

The APT is more general and robust than the CAPM because (1) the equilibrium returns of assets from the APT are dependent on many factors, not just one; (2) the APT makes no rigid assumptions about investors' utility functions (only risk aversion is required); and (3) the CAPM requires that the market portfolio be mean-variance efficient, while the APT does not require anything special from the market portfolio.

Suppose that asset returns are generated by the market model, meaning that $K = 1$ in equation (16.1). In other words, there is only one risk factor in the return-generating process. If this factor is the true market portfolio, then $\bar{\delta}_1 = E\left(r_m\right)$ and equation (16.31) simplifies to the well-known standard CAPM,

$$E\left(r_i\right) = r_f + \left[E\left(r_m\right) - r_f\right]\beta_{i1} \tag{16.33}$$

Thus, the CAPM can be derived under the less rigorous assumptions of the APT by simply assuming that there is only one risk factor in the return-generating process and that this factor corresponds to the true market portfolio. Note that if this factor is not the true market portfolio, the one-factor APT will not equal the CAPM.

Alternatively, it is interesting to explore the implications of assuming that there is only one factor and that this factor is not the true market portfolio. Consider some proxy market portfolio that is well diversified (for example, the S&P 500 index). Again, equation (16.31) reduces to

$$E\left(r_i\right) = r_f + \left[E\left(r_{mp}\right) - r_f\right]\beta_{i1} \tag{16.34}$$

where $\bar{\delta}_1 = E\left(r_{mp}\right)$ denotes the expected return on the proxy market portfolio. In this situation expected returns are linearly related to the proxy market portfolio's expected returns. This proxy market portfolio must be mean-variance efficient.

It is noteworthy to mention that even if more than one factor $(K > 1)$ is in the return-generating process of equation (16.1), the CAPM can still hold. Even when the CAPM holds, it is still possible for asset returns to be generated by one or more multifactor models. Suppose that asset returns are generated by the K-factor return-generating process of equation (16.1). Then, the equilibrium model for this return generating process is

$$E\left(r_i\right) = r_f + \lambda_1 \beta_{i1} + \lambda_2 \beta_{i2} + \cdots + \lambda_K \beta_{iK} \qquad (16.30)$$

Because the CAPM is a static equilibrium model, it holds for all securities as well as the K arbitrage portfolios used in the return-generating process. Thus, the equilibrium excess return on each of the arbitrage portfolios is described by the CAPM as

$$\lambda_k = \beta_{p_k}\left[E\left(r_m\right) - r_f\right] \quad \text{for } k = 1, \dots, K \qquad (16.35)$$

where β_{p_k} is the *factor beta* of the k-th arbitrage portfolio, r_{p_k}. Substituting equation (16.35) into equation (16.30) yields

$$E\left(r_i\right) = r_f + b_i\left[E\left(r_m\right) - r_f\right] \qquad (16.36)$$

where $b_i = \beta_{i1}\beta_{p_1} + \beta_{i2}\beta_{p_2} + \cdots + \beta_{iK}\beta_{p_K}$. This implies that if the market beta of asset i is defined as $\sum_{k=1}^{K}\beta_{ik}\beta_{p_k}$, its expected return is priced by the CAPM, even though its returns are generated from a multifactor return-generating process. Thus, the CAPM cannot be rejected even if more than one factor is found to be important in asset pricing.

16.6   EMPIRICAL EVIDENCE

Although the APT seems more robust than the CAPM in many aspects, it has two problems. First, the theory contains no clue about the number of factors, K. Second, even if the number of factors were known, the task of identifying the risk factors is daunting.

One major effort to find the number of the factors (K) was conducted by Roll and Ross (1980). They used daily returns for all NYSE and AMEX listed securities from July 3, 1962, through December 31, 1972, and followed a two-step procedure. First, K orthogonal factors were estimated, together with a matrix of coefficients β_{ik}, called *factor loadings*. In the setting where both the risk factors (f_{kt}) and the factor loadings are unknown in the return-generating process of equation (16.3), the factors and factor loadings are estimated using a multivariate statistical procedure called *factor analysis*. Also estimated in this step were the expected returns for the securities. Second, using the previously estimated expected returns and factor loadings, cross-sectional tests of APT based on equation (16.30) were conducted.

Roll and Ross divided their sample into 42 groups of 30 securities per group and applied their two-step procedure to each group. Examining the results from the 42 groups, they concluded that there were at least three and probably four risk factors that are important in asset pricing. They also concluded that it was unlikely that there were five or more important factors. Brown and Weinstein (1983) also found evidence that the data for common stock returns were consistent with the existence of three factors, and were generally in conflict with five or seven factor representations of APT.[13]

Roll and Ross (1980) also tested to see if securities' variances were a significant factor in explaining their expected returns, because they should not be important if APT is valid. This is because the diversifiable component of a security's return (ε_{it}) can be eliminated by forming a randomly diversified portfolio and, thus, the only contribution to a portfolio's risk would be made by its factor loadings. The authors found that despite the high correlation between variances and expected returns, variance did not contribute to the explanatory power of APT, thereby providing additional empirical support for APT.

In later studies, Chen, Roll, and Ross (1986) and Roll and Ross (1984a) identified four economic factors that influence either the future cash flows from a security or the value of these cash flows to the investor. These factors, denoted f_{kt} in equation (16.3), represent unanticipated changes in the following four economic variables:

1. Inflation (this influences the level of discount rate and the future cash flows).
2. Industrial production (this measures business activity).
3. Default risk premium [this is the yield spread between high-grade (Aaa) and low-grade (Baa) corporate bonds; it is a measure of the degree of risk aversion implicit in pricing).
4. Term premium (this is the slope of the yield curve and it is equal to the difference in long-term government bond returns and Treasury bill rates; it measures the unanticipated return on long-term bonds and captures the effect of changes in the business cycle).

Chen, Roll, and Ross noted that the emergence of these factors was not surprising, because in terms of dividend discount models of stock valuation, the first two factors affect the numerator (that is, expected cash flows) and the last two factors affect the denominator (that is, the discount rate) of the present value equation. The return-generating process that Chen, Roll, and Ross tested is

$$r_{it} = a_i + \beta_{i1}\text{IP}_t + \beta_{i2}\text{EI}_t + \beta_{i3}\text{UI}_t + \beta_{i4}\text{Default}_t + \beta_{i5}\text{Term}_t + \epsilon_{it} \qquad (16.37)$$

where   IP is the percentage change in industrial production,
           EI is the percentage change in expected inflation,
           UI is the percentage change in unanticipated inflation,
           Default is the default risk premium, and
           Term is the term structure premium.

Another important contribution to identifying the risk factors was made by Fama and French (1993). By using firm characteristics rather than macroeconomic variables, they construct a model to explain returns on both stocks and bonds. The factors are constructed from empirical evidence on firm characteristic variables that seem to predict average returns well and, therefore, may be capturing risk premiums. The model Fama and French suggested is

$$r_{it} - r_f = \beta_{i1}\left(r_{mt} - r_f\right) + \beta_{i2}\text{SMB}_t + \beta_{i3}\text{HML}_t + \epsilon_{it} \qquad (16.38)$$

where

$$r_m = \text{the return on the market portfolio,}$$
SMB (small minus big) = the return from a portfolio containing small stocks minus the return from a portfolio containing large stocks,

HML (high minus low) = the return from a portfolio containing stocks with
                       high book to-market price ratio minus the return
                       from a portfolio containing stocks with low
                       book-to-market price ratios.

In fact, SMB and HML are zero-investment arbitrage portfolios. The model
of equation (16.38) is now well known as the Fama and French three-factor
model. Because the three factors used in the model are factor portfolios, when the
intercept term is allowed, the intercept of equation (16.38) is a measure of portfolio
performance called Jensen's alpha. This model can be used as either an asset
pricing model or to measure portfolio performance. Note, however, that because the
macroeconomic factors used in equation (16.37) are not portfolios, this model cannot
be directly used as an asset pricing model or to measure portfolio performance.[14]

16.7   COMPARING THE APT AND CAPM EMPIRICALLY

A direct comparison of the APT and the CAPM was conducted by Chen (1983).
He compared the performance of the APT with that of the CAPM in a variety of
ways using daily data from 1963 to 1978. First, the factor loadings from the APT
were estimated by using factor analysis, and the market betas for the CAPM were
estimated as time-series regressions. Then, the following cross-sectional regression
models of stock returns on the factor loadings $(\hat{\beta}_{i1}, \ldots, \hat{\beta}_{iK})$ or market betas $(\hat{\beta}_{im})$
were estimated:

$$r_i = \lambda_0 + \lambda_1 \hat{\beta}_{i1} + \lambda_2 \hat{\beta}_{i2} + \cdots + + \lambda_K \hat{\beta}_{iK} + \varepsilon_i \text{ (APT)} \qquad (16.39)$$

$$r_i = \lambda_0 + \lambda_1 \hat{\beta}_{im} + + \eta_i \text{ (CAPM)} \qquad (16.40)$$

Here, ε_i and η_i are typical error terms. Interestingly, the simple correlation
coefficient between the estimated market betas, $\hat{\beta}_{im}$, and the estimated first factor
loading, $\hat{\beta}_{i1}$, was found to be roughly 0.95, regardless of the market index used to
estimate the market beta. Continuing, a test of the null hypothesis that $\lambda_1 = \lambda_2 =
\cdots = \lambda_K = 0$ for equation (16.39) was conducted. The null hypothesis was rejected,
suggesting that the stocks did not all have the same expected return.

A second test by Chen involved the following cross-sectional regression:

$$r_i = \alpha \hat{r}_{i,\text{APT}} + (1 - \alpha) \hat{r}_{i,\text{CAPM}} + e_i \qquad (16.41)$$

where the values of $\hat{r}_{i,\text{APT}}$ and $\hat{r}_{i,\text{CAPM}}$ are the expected return of stock i generated
by the APT and the CAPM, respectively. The values of $\hat{r}_{i,\text{APT}}$ and $\hat{r}_{i,\text{CAPM}}$ are fitted
returns obtained from the cross-sectional regression of equations (16.39) and (16.40),
respectively. If the estimate of α is close to zero, this would support the CAPM over
the APT. On the other hand, if the estimate of α is close to one, this is viewed as
support for the APT relative to the CAPM. Every version of this test produced an
estimate of α that was in excess of 0.9, thereby suggesting that the APT fits the data
better and is a more realistic model than the CAPM.

A third test by Chen was to cross-sectionally regress the CAPM residuals, $\hat{\eta}_i$, on
the APT factor loadings, and to cross-sectionally regress the APT residuals, $\hat{\varepsilon}_i$, onto

the CAPM market betas. These two cross-sectional regressions are as follows:

$$\hat{\eta}_i = \lambda_0 + \lambda_1 \hat{\beta}_{i1} + \lambda_2 \hat{\beta}_{i2} + \cdots + \lambda_K \hat{\beta}_{iK} + \xi_i \qquad (16.42)$$

$$\hat{\varepsilon}_i = \lambda_0 + \lambda_1 \hat{\beta}_{im} + v_i \qquad (16.43)$$

Both residuals, $\hat{\eta}_i$ and $\hat{\varepsilon}_i$, are estimates of the random error terms for stock i estimated using equations (16.40) and (16.39), respectively. The purpose of this test was to see if there was any information about expected returns in the random error terms of either model. If a particular model is valid, its random error term should behave like white noise. The results suggested that, in most cases, the CAPM was not able to explain the APT residuals. Chen argued that the CAPM was misspecified and the APT was able to pick up the return not captured by the CAPM.

Finally, Chen's fourth test was to see if, in general, either the variance of a firm's stock returns or the firm's size was related to the firm's stock return after removal of the portion of the firm's return that was explained by the APT. The results were negative and suggested that neither firm variance nor firm size has any significant explanatory power after risk is adjusted for with the APT. Thus, two of the empirical anomalies related to the CAPM appear to be explained by APT.[15] These findings can be construed as evidence against the CAPM.

16.8   CONCLUSIONS

The APT is more general and more robust than the CAPM, and its derivation requires fewer assumptions than the CAPM. However, the critical weakness of the APT is that the number of factors and their identities are not specified in the model. Finding the appropriate number of factors and their identities has been one of the central subjects in asset pricing models research. Fama and French's (1993) three-factor model, described in the previous section, is currently widely recognized in industry and academia as one of the APT models that explain data relatively well among many competing models. However, because this three-factor model also does not explain satisfactorily some of the empirical anomalies that arise with the CAPM, efforts to find a better model should be pursued.[16]

NOTES

1. Theoretical extensions and refinements to Ross's APT have been made by Connor (1981), Huberman (1982), Chamberlain (1983), Chamberlain and Rothschild (1983), Chen and Ingersoll (1983), Dybvig (1983), Grinblatt and Titman (1983a), Stambaugh (1983b), and Ingersoll (1984); Merton (1977) has compared APT with his continuous-time version of the CAPM.

2. The net asset value (NAV) per share equals the net aggregate market value of a mutual fund portfolio divided by the total number of outstanding shares in the mutual fund.

$$\text{NAV} = \frac{(\text{Market value of total assets at } t - \text{Fund's total liabilities at } t)}{(\text{Total number of shares outstanding at time } t)}$$

The SEC requires all U.S. mutual funds to compute and publish their NAV daily, and sell and redeem their shares only at their current NAV. In contrast, U.S. law permits

ETFs and closed-end investment companies to be bought and sold at premiums above
and discounts below their NAV.

3. The administrative problems inherent in quickly transacting 500-securities trades is
routinely dealt with by using a computer program to execute a program trade. Program
trading is discussed in Chapter 20.

4. It is interesting to note that the $1 of borrowed funds mentioned previously could,
alternatively, be obtained by issuing a new $1 security that had the same expected return
and beta as the newly constructed portfolio.

5. In the hedge fund industry, statistical arbitrage refers to a particular trading strategy that
utilizes short-term mean-reversion of stock prices. It is a heavily computational technique
of equity trading that involves large numbers of securities, very short holding periods,
data mining, and statistical methods. It also involves automated trading systems called
algorithmic trading, which is the use of computer programs for entering trading orders
with the computer algorithm deciding on aspects of the order such as the timing, price,
or quantity of the order without human intervention. A special class of algorithm trading
is high-frequency trading (HFT), in which computers make decisions to initiate buy and
sell orders based on information that is computed electronically, before human traders
are capable of processing the information they observe.

6. Unlike commodity futures, index futures contracts are always settled in cash.

7. To learn more about the spot-futures parity, see John Hull, *Options, Futures, and Other
Derivatives* (Prentice Hall, 2008).

8. Interestingly, the S&P 500 index is constructed to be a free-float capitalization-weighted
index. This means that the weight of each stock is determined by the size of its free-float
market capitalization [={(total number of shares outstanding) − (number of locked-in
shares)} × (price per share)]. Taking such precautions in constructing the index ensures
that a liquid market exists in which to trade the shares in the index.

9. Program trade is a generic term used to describe a type of trading in securities, usually
consisting of baskets of 15 or more stocks with a combined value of at least $1
million. With this broad definition, the New York Stock Exchange (NYSE) reported that
program trading accounts for about 30 percent and as high as 46.4 percent of the trading
volume on that exchange every day over the period from 2004 to 2006. However, Neal
(1993) found that only 47.5 percent of all trades by program trading by 1992 were
related to stock index arbitrage. Other reasons for program trading were liquidation of
portfolios, portfolio realignment, and a variety of other trading strategies. Nonetheless,
these historical percentages show the importance of program trading at the NYSE.

10. See Sharpe (1985, chap. 8) for a discussion of the relationship between multiple-index
models and APT.

11. If the inverse of the coefficient matrix exists, the solution for the weights in equation
(16.14) is written as

$$\begin{pmatrix} w_1 \\ w_2 \\ w_3 \end{pmatrix} = \begin{pmatrix} E(r_1) - r_f & E(r_2) - r_f & E(r_3) - r_f \\ \beta_{11} & \beta_{21} & \beta_{31} \\ \beta_{12} & \beta_{22} & \beta_{32} \end{pmatrix}^{-1} \begin{pmatrix} 0 \\ 0 \\ 0 \end{pmatrix}$$

If the inverse matrix in the preceding equation exists (that is, the determinant of the
coefficient matrix is not zero), then all weights are zeros.

12. Consider a linear equation system: $Ax = x_1 a_1 + x_2 a_2 + \cdots + x_n a_n$, where A is an $(n \times n)$
coefficient matrix, $x = (x_1, x_2, \ldots, x_n)'$ is an $(n \times 1)$ vector, and a_j is the j-th $(n \times 1)$
vector in the matrix A. If there exists a nonzero vector $x \neq 0$, such that $x_1 a_1 + x_2 a_2 +
\cdots + x_n a_n = 0$, then provided none of $a_1, a_2, \ldots, a_n$ is null, those vectors are said to be
linearly dependent. This means that one vector can be represented by a linear combination
of the other vectors. In this case, the matrix A is said to be *singular* and its determinant
equals zero.

13. The testable implications of the APT have been questioned by Shanken (1982) and Dhrymes, Friend, and Gultekin (1984). In particular, Shanken (1982) argues that the APT is inherently more susceptible to empirical verification than the CAPM. See Dybvig and Ross (1985c) and Roll and Ross (1984b) for replies to Shanken and Dhrymes et al., respectively. Shanken (1985) provides a response to Dybvig and Ross, while Dhrymes, Friend, Gultekin, and Gultekin (1985) extend Dhrymes, Friend, and Gultekin and provide a response to Roll and Ross. Other papers discussing various aspects of empirical testing of APT include Kryzanowski and To (1983) and Cho, Elton, and Gruber (1984).

14. Besides Fama and French (1993), there have been many efforts to identify the risk factors. Among these, Carhart (1997) suggested a four-factor model including the Fama and French three factors and a factor that is designed to capture the price momentum effect by Jegadeesh and Titman (1993). Pastor and Stambaugh (2003) suggested a model including a liquidity factor, Kim (2006) suggested a two-factor model including the market factor and a factor capturing earnings uncertainty risk, and Kim and Qi (2010) suggested a model including a factor of earnings quality information.

15. As noted by Schwert (1983), this is a common explanation of empirical anomalies that have been uncovered using some kind of a CAPM-based model. That is, such anomalies are viewed as evidence that the CAPM is misspecified, rather than as evidence of inefficient markets. Indeed, it can be argued that the best way to test any asset pricing model is to see if a factor not in the model is related systematically to returns.

16. Fama and French's (1993) three-factor model fails to explain only a few examples, including the momentum effect (see Fama and French, 1996) and the January effect (see Kim, 2006).

Implementing the Theory

Portfolio Construction and Selection

If the capital asset pricing model (CAPM) is valid, then selecting an investor's optimal portfolio will consist of determining his or her utility function and choosing the appropriate mix of the risk-free asset and market portfolio. All securities would be priced so they plot exactly on the CAPM (also known as the security market line or SML), and there would be no overvalued or undervalued securities. In this situation, it can be said that current security prices fully reflect all information and that security markets are efficient. Note that in this situation, no investor is expected to earn abnormal returns, where abnormal return is defined as a return that is greater than normal for the amount of risk borne by the investor.

17.1 EFFICIENT MARKETS

West (1975) provided a general interpretation of the notion of efficient markets. It is generally accepted that a major economic goal is to have *allocationally efficient markets*. That is, it is desirable to have capital channeled to where it can do the most good. This will occur when those economic units with the most promising investment opportunities get the necessary funds. In order to have allocationally efficient markets, it is necessary to have both internally and externally efficient markets. Internal (or operational) efficiency refers to the cost and speed of transacting. External (or pricing) efficiency refers to prices that adjust to new information quickly and in an unbiased fashion. Fama's (1970b) classifications of efficiency, discussed next, are concerned with external efficiency; accordingly, subsequent references to efficiency will refer to external efficiency.

17.1.1 Fama's Classifications

Expanding on the notion of externally efficient markets, Fama (1970b) provided three classifications of efficiency that depend on the set of information used at time t, denoted θ_t.

A market is efficient with respect to θ_t if it is impossible to have expected economic profits (that is, abnormal expected returns, adjusted for risk and transactions costs) by trading on the basis of θ_t.

The three classifications of efficiency are:

1. *Weak-form efficiency*, which constrains θ_t to the set of past price and return data (some people include trading volume in θ_t)

2. *Semistrong-form efficiency*, which constrains θ_t to the set of publicly available information (which includes the set of past prices)
3. *Strong-form efficiency*, which does not constrain θ_t at all, defining it to be the set of all information, public or private

As you can see by Fama's classification scheme, as one moves from weak-form to semistrong-form to strong-form efficiency, the set of information expands.

17.1.2   Formal Models

Efficient markets can be linked to stock price and return behavior by time-series models of stock prices and returns. Four such models receiving attention are the fair-game model, the martingale model, the submartingale model, and the random walk model. Consider first the fair-game model, where p_t denotes the stock price of a firm at time period t and r_t denotes the return from a share of its stock from $t-1$ to t. For ease of exposition, dividends are assumed to be nonexistent. Descriptively, a *fair-game model* says that it is impossible to use information θ_t to estimate abnormal expected returns. If ε_{t+1} is defined as

$$\varepsilon_{t+1} = r_{t+1} - E\left(r_{t+1}\right) \qquad (17.1)$$

then $E\left(\varepsilon_{t+1}|\theta_t\right) = 0$ if returns are a fair game. This simply means that the expected returns, given information set θ_t, equal the expected returns without the information set. (Note, however, that this does not mean expected returns are zero or positive—they could be negative.[1]) In application to the CAPM, this means that the set of information θ_t will not provide the investor with an expected return other than that given by the CAPM. Thus, tests of efficiency can be conducted by using various implications of the CAPM to see if abnormal returns can be earned based on each one of the three definitions of θ_t.

The martingale, submartingale, and random walk models are all special cases of the fair-game model. A martingale model, applied to prices, states that given an information set θ_t, the best estimate of tomorrow's price p_{t+1} is today's price p_t.

$$\mathrm{E}\left(p_{t+1}|\theta_t\right) = p_t \qquad (17.2a)$$

A submartingale model simply replaces the equality in equation (17.2a) with a greater than or equal to sign:

$$\mathrm{E}\left(p_{t+1}|\theta_t\right) \geq p_t \qquad (17.2b)$$

Because $\mathrm{E}\left(r_{t+1}|\theta_t\right) = \left[\mathrm{E}\left(p_{t+1}|\theta_t\right) - p_t\right]/p_t$, martingale and submartingale models can be rewritten in terms of returns, respectively, as

$$\mathrm{E}\left(r_{t+1}|\theta_t\right) = 0 \qquad (17.3a)$$

and

$$\mathrm{E}\left(r_{t+1}|\theta_t\right) \geq 0 \qquad (17.3b)$$

Thus, if prices follow a martingale, tests of efficiency can be conducted simply by checking to see if above-zero returns can be earned based on each of the three definitions of θ_t. On the other hand, if prices follow a submartingale, then these tests require a model of normal returns, simply observing positive returns is not sufficient to conclude markets are inefficient. Because prices are generally expected to rise over time, the submartingale is generally regarded as a better model. However, for short time intervals (that is, intervals from t to $t+1$), the martingale may be a reasonable approximation.[2]

The random walk model states that prices follow a random walk if changes in prices are independent and identically distributed. That is,

$$f\left(\Delta p_{t+1}|\theta_t\right) = f\left(\Delta p_{t+1}\right) \qquad (17.4\text{a})$$

and

$$f\left(\Delta p_{t+1}\right) = f\left(\Delta p_t\right) \qquad (17.4\text{b})$$

where $\Delta p_{t+1} = p_{t+1} - p_t$ and $f(\cdot)$ denotes the probability distribution of price changes. In this model, the distribution of price changes is unaffected by θ_t and is the same from one period to the next. Although it is not proper to do so, statistically speaking, the random walk model is frequently stated in terms of returns:[3]

$$f\left(r_{t+1}|\theta_t\right) = f\left(r_{t+1}\right) \qquad (17.5\text{a})$$

and

$$f\left(r_{t+1}\right) = f\left(r_t\right) \qquad (17.5\text{b})$$

This means that the parameters of the distribution of returns are constant through time and are unaffected by any information set, θ_t. However, empirical evidence suggests that the random walk properties of returns (or price changes) are too restrictive; accordingly, the submartingale model is typically used as the model of price behavior in tests of external efficiency.

The fair game model, submartingale model, and CAPM can be linked together in the following fashion. If prices are assumed to come from a submartingale model, then for returns to be a fair game the following must hold:

$$E\left(r_{t+1}\right) = E\left(r_{t+1}|\theta_t\right) \geq 0 \qquad (17.6)$$

Furthermore, the CAPM states that

$$E\left(r_{t+1}\right) = r_{ft+1} + \left[E\left(r_{mt+1} - r_{ft+1}\right)\right]\beta \geq 0 \qquad (17.7)$$

Thus, if the CAPM is valid and a security's return follows a submartingale model, then for any information set θ_t the best estimate of its expected return is based on the CAPM. In other words, θ_t does not provide any information of value. CAPM-based tests of efficiency are, therefore, really joint tests of the CAPM being valid and markets being efficient.

Proceeding to tests of market efficiency, we ask: What does the evidence regarding common stocks suggest? Without detailing the multitude of tests performed, suffice it to say that markets appear to be weak-form efficient but not strong-form efficient.[4] However, a controversy exists as to whether or not markets are semistrong-form efficient. Although most tests based on public information fail to find evidence of inefficiencies, there are a few tests that appear to have found such evidence. Let us assume that some inefficiencies appear to exist or, more important, that investors believe such inefficiencies exist. In this situation let us see how portfolio theory can be normatively implemented in managing a portfolio of common stocks, along with a risk-free asset (such as Treasury bills), so as to outperform a naive buy-and-hold strategy of comparable risk.

17.2 USING PORTFOLIO THEORIES TO CONSTRUCT AND SELECT PORTFOLIOS

The procedures outlined in Chapters 6 and 7 present a method for utilizing portfolio theory in the construction and selection of a portfolio and are appropriate if it is assumed that the underlying multivariate distribution of returns is stationary.[5] Of course, if the CAPM is believed to be valid, then there is no need to utilize these procedures, because an investor will be concerned only with a mix of the risk-free asset and market portfolio. However, there remains one situation to be considered. Namely, what should the investor do if he or she believes the underlying multivariate distribution of returns is not stationary and that the CAPM is not completely valid? In this situation, if the investor believes identifiable inefficiencies exist and, therefore, the CAPM is not completely valid, it is still possible to use the CAPM to provide a framework for portfolio construction and selection, revision, and evaluation (the latter are discussed in Chapter 18). Here we concentrate on the application of portfolio theory to a risk-free asset, such as Treasury bills, and some common stocks. The model discussed next is unabashedly normative and is based on the work of Ambachtsheer (1972), Treynor and Black (1973), Ferguson (1975), and Sharpe (1978), as well as others.

In implementing portfolio theory, the portfolio manager must consider how it relates to the areas of security analysis, market timing, and diversification. *Security analysis* involves the forecasting of price movements of individual common stocks and is frequently referred to as selectivity or "microforecasting." *Market timing*, also known as "macroforecasting," involves forecasting general stock market price movements. Analysis of diversification involves identification of the degree to which the prices of various securities covary.

All three of these areas can be linked to specific parameters of the following CAPM-based return-generating model:

$$r_{it} - r_f = \alpha_i + \beta_i \left(r_{mt} - r_f\right) + \varepsilon_{it} \tag{17.8}$$

Here ε_{it} is an error term with an expected value of zero and a variance of $\sigma_{\varepsilon_i}^2$. Note that with this model, over the next time period the expected return of a security, $E(r_i)$, given the expected return of the market, $E(r_m)$, is equal to

$$E(r_i) = \alpha_i + r_f + \beta_i \left[E(r_m) - r_f\right] \tag{17.9}$$

In equation (17.9), α_i represents the abnormal return for security i, because its expected normal return according to the CAPM is equal to $r_f + \beta_i \left[E(r_m) - r_f\right]\}$.

TABLE 17.1 Portfolio Construction and Selection Decision Matrix

Selection ability	Market timing ability	
	Good	Poor
Good	Active management	Active management
	1. Concentrate portfolio in securities with $\alpha_i > 0$	1. Concentrate portfolio in securities with $\alpha_i > 0$
	2. Shift portfolio beta based on market forecast	2. Keep portfolio beta at desired long-term value
Poor	Active management	Passive management
	1. Hold diversified portfolio	1. Hold diversified portfolio
	2. Shift portfolio beta based on market forecast	2. Keep portfolio beta at desired long-term value

Source: Adapted from K. Ambachtsheer, "Portfolio Theory and the Security Analysis," *Financial Analysts Journal* 28 (November–December 1972): 53–57.

Graphically α_i can be viewed as being equal to the vertical distance between the point $[\beta_i, E(r_i)]$ and the SML. In equilibrium the expected value of α_i is zero.

Selectivity, timing, and diversification can be linked to the parameters α_i, β_i, and ε_i in equation (17.8), respectively. In regard to selectivity and timing, Table 17.1 provides a convenient means of summarizing the portfolio construction and selection decisions.

If the portfolio manager has good selectivity (that is, microforecasting) ability he or she will want to take long positions in those securities with $\alpha_i > 0$ and, if permitted, take short positions in those securities with $\alpha_i < 0$. The size of the position will depend on the magnitude of not only α_i but also $\sigma_{\varepsilon_i}^2$. In the absence of selectivity ability, the portfolio manager will be concerned with maintaining a diversified portfolio.

Good market timing (that is, macroforecasting) ability means that the larger the forecast of $E(r_m) - r_f$, the higher the portfolio's beta should be. Inability suggests that the portfolio manager should simply keep the portfolio beta at its desired long-term average.

The motivation behind these suggested courses of action lies in equations (17.8) and (17.9). Because the return on a portfolio (r_p) equals $\Sigma w_i r_i$, it can be seen that

$$E\left(r_p\right) - r_f = \alpha_p + \beta_p \left[E(r_m) - r_f\right] \tag{17.10}$$

where $\alpha_p = \Sigma w_i \alpha_i$ and $\beta_p = \Sigma w_i \beta_i$.[6] Furthermore,

$$\sigma_p^2 = \sum_i \sum_j w_i w_j \beta_i \beta_j \sigma_m^2 + \sum_i w_i^2 \sigma_{\varepsilon_i}^2$$

$$= \beta_p^2 \sigma_m^2 + \sigma_{\varepsilon_p}^2 \tag{17.11}$$

if it is assumed that $\text{Cov}\left(\varepsilon_i, \varepsilon_j\right) = 0$ when $i \neq j$, because this implies that $\sigma_{\varepsilon_p}^2 = \Sigma w_i^2 \sigma_{\varepsilon_i}^2$. Equation (17.10) shows that the portfolio will have an abnormal return (α_p) that is a weighted average of the individual securities' abnormal returns (α_i). Because the portfolio beta (β_p) is simply a weighted average of the individual securities' betas (β_i), it can also be seen that if there is a forecast that $E(r_m)$ will be notably larger than r_f, then having a portfolio with a large beta will mean that the portfolio has a larger expected return. The firms' betas are also of concern in diversification because they affect the level of the portfolio's variance (σ_p^2), as shown in equation (17.11).

17.3 SECURITY ANALYSIS

It was noted in Figure 12.4 that if a security did not lie on the CAPM (or the SML), it was either overvalued or undervalued. If the asset plots above the CAPM, then it was viewed as being undervalued, because for its level of risk, it had an expected return greater than suggested by the CAPM. Similarly, if a security was located below the CAPM, it was viewed as being overvalued, because for its level of risk, it had an expected return less than the corresponding CAPM equilibrium value. As mentioned earlier, α_i denotes the vertical distance between a security's expected return, $E(r_i)$, and its "equilibrium" level of expected return as suggested by the CAPM, an amount equal to $r_f + \beta_i \left[E(r_m) - r_f \right]$. Thus, algebraically,

$$\alpha_i = E(r_i) - \left\{ r_f + \beta_i \left[E(r_m) - r_f \right] \right\} \tag{17.12}$$

By rearranging equation (17.12), equation (17.9) can be derived. We can see that if $\alpha_i > 0$ $(\alpha_i < 0)$, then the security will plot above (below) the CAPM and hence is presumed to be undervalued (overvalued). Thus, the security analyst should be concerned with accurate estimation of α_i.

The link of security analysis to α_i can be illustrated with a simple example. Assume that stock i has a current price of p_{i0} and, according to the CAPM, its equilibrium expected rate of return is $E(r_i)$. Ignoring dividends, this means that the end-of-period expected price $E\left(p_{i1}\right)$ can be expressed as a function of p_{i0} and $E(r_i)$,

$$E\left(p_{i1}\right) = p_{i0} \left[1 + E(r_i) \right] \tag{17.13}$$

because by definition $E(r_i) = \left[E\left(p_{i1}\right) - p_{i0} \right] / p_{i0}$. Now imagine that the security analyst has noted that the current stock price p_{i0} is too low (that is, the stock is currently undervalued) and should instead be p_{i0}^*.[7] Assuming that the market will recognize and correct this discrepancy, the end-of-period price should not be $E\left(p_{i1}\right)$, but $E\left(p_{i1}^*\right) = p_{i0}^* \left[1 + E(r_i) \right]$. Thus, the total expected return for this security is not $E(r_i)$ but an amount equal to $\left[E\left(p_{i1}^*\right) - p_{i0} \right] / p_{i0}$, denoted $E\left(r_i^*\right)$. Remembering that $E(r_i)$ denotes an equilibrium expected rate of return equal to $r_f + \beta_i \left[E(r_m) - r_f \right]$, we can link $E\left(r_i^*\right)$ and $E(r_i)$ as follows:

$$
\begin{aligned}
E\left(r_i^*\right) &= \left[E\left(p_{i1}^*\right) - p_{i0} \right] / p_{i0} \\
&= \left[\left\{ E\left(p_{i1}^*\right) - E\left(p_{i1}\right) \right\} + \left\{ E\left(p_{i1}\right) - p_{i0} \right\} \right] / p_{i0} \\
&= \alpha_i + E(r_i) \\
&= \alpha_i + r_f + \beta_i \left[E(r_m) - r_f \right]
\end{aligned}
\tag{17.14}
$$

where $\alpha_i = \left[E\left(p_{i1}^*\right) - E\left(p_{i1}\right) \right] / p_{i0}$ is the abnormal expected return on stock i.

Closely related to the estimation of α_i is the estimation of $\sigma^2_{\varepsilon_i}$, the residual variance. This parameter can be viewed as an estimate of the security analyst's uncertainty about the estimate of α_i, because ε_i has an expected value of zero. And $\sigma^2_{\varepsilon_i}$ is also important for diversification purposes.

In estimating α_i and $\sigma^2_{\varepsilon_i}$, the security analyst should be supplied with estimates of $E(r_m)$ and r_f. Because there are generally several analysts working for a portfolio manager, it is logical to have the portfolio manager provide these analysts with such estimates. Otherwise, it is likely that the security analysts would employ their own unique estimates of $E(r_m)$ and r_f, which, in turn, would affect their estimates of α_i and $\sigma^2_{\varepsilon_i}$. By using one set of estimates, the security analysts will all be assuming the same behavior of the market.

17.4 MARKET TIMING

The expected return of a portfolio was shown in equation (17.10) to depend on not only the accurate estimation of each security's α_i, but also the accurate estimation of each security's β_i and macroeconomic forecasts of $E(r_m)$ and r_f. Market timing refers to changing the portfolio's composition based on the latter two forecasts. Because, for all practical purposes, the forecast of r_f is known with certainty, market timing basically refers to the forecast of $E(r_m)$ relative to r_f.

The greater (smaller) the value of the quantity $E(r_m) - r_f$, the greater (smaller) the beta of the portfolio should be for portfolio managers engaged in market timing. This will, in turn, result in a greater expected return for the portfolio. Changing the beta of the portfolio can be accomplished in one of three ways. First, the proportion of the portfolio invested in the risk-free asset can be raised (thereby lowering β_p) or lowered (thereby raising β_p), depending on the market forecast. Here the relative composition of the risky portion of the portfolio remains fixed while the risky portfolio's overall proportion varies in lockstep with alterations in the risk-free asset proportion (because the two proportions have to sum to 1). Second, while the proportion of the portfolio invested in the risk-free asset is kept constant, the composition of the risky portion of the portfolio can be altered.[8] For example, if the goal is to raise β_p, then low-beta stocks can be sold and replaced with high-beta stocks. Third, use some combination of the two previous methods.

As in selectivity, timing decisions require not only a forecast of the market return but also a measure of the confidence in that forecast. The standard deviation of market returns (σ_m) is a component of the portfolio's variance and thus lends itself to this purpose. Accordingly, in making timing decisions the forecaster must estimate both $E(r_m)$ and σ_m.[9] Also important are the forecast of r_f and the estimation of β_i.

17.4.1 Forecasting Beta

Estimation of the betas of individual common stocks is important to portfolio managers because, as mentioned earlier, depending on the portfolio manager's market timing ability, she or he will want either to keep the portfolio beta at a fixed value or to alter it based on the magnitude of the quantities $E(r_m) - r_f$

and σ_m. One method for estimating beta is based on the market model, described in Chapter 8 as

$$r_{it} = \alpha_i + \beta_i r_{mt} + \varepsilon_{it} \qquad (17.15)$$

where estimates of α_i, β_i, and the variance of ε_{it} can be obtained by OLS regression programs available on most computer systems. Because equation (17.15) is a time-series model, historical returns that are widely available can be used.

Blume (1971), in the first major study of beta coefficients, examined all NYSE-listed common stocks over the 42-year period from July 1926 through June 1968.[10] Using the market model, he estimated the beta coefficient for each stock over each of six consecutive seven-year periods. The average coefficient of determination for the six estimation periods, in chronological order, was 0.51, 0.49, 0.36, 0.32, 0.25, and 0.28, suggesting a general decline in the explanatory power of the market model. Next, Blume calculated the correlation coefficient between the set of beta coefficients from each estimation period and the set of beta coefficients from the next estimation period. For the resulting five comparisons, the correlation coefficients were, in chronological order, 0.63, 0.62, 0.59, 0.65, and 0.60, suggesting that historical value of beta has limited forecasting value.[11]

In a test of the hypothesized tendency of beta coefficients to drift toward their mean value of 1, Blume cross-sectionally regressed the set of beta coefficients for one estimation period ($\hat{\beta}_{it}$) on the set of beta coefficients in the previous estimation period ($\hat{\beta}_{it-1}$),

$$\hat{\beta}_{it} = \gamma_0 + \gamma_1 \hat{\beta}_{it-1} + \varepsilon_{it}, \qquad \text{for } i = 1, \ldots, N \qquad (17.16)$$

The results are displayed in Table 17.2. As can be seen from the table, the intercept terms range from 0.265 to 0.526 and the slope terms range from 0.489 to 0.750. Thus, in testing the accuracy of using *ex post* betas as a forecast of future values, the evidence suggests that there is a tendency for beta to drift toward its mean value of one.[12] Generally, the coefficients displayed in Table 17.2 suggest that betas estimated in one period that are greater (less) than one will, in the next period, still be greater (less) than one but will have drifted closer to the value of one. For example, when betas estimated over the period 7/1961–6/1968 (period t)

TABLE 17.2 Measurement of Drift for Beta Coefficients
$\beta_{it} = \gamma_0 + \gamma_1 \hat{\beta}_{it-1} + \varepsilon_{it}$

Time period		$\hat{\gamma}_0$	$\hat{\gamma}_1$
t	$t-1$		
7/1933–6/1940	7/1926–6/1933	0.320	0.714
7/1940–6/1947	7/1933–6/1940	0.265	0.750
7/1947–6/1954	7/1940–6/1947	0.526	0.489
7/1954–6/1961	7/1947–6/1954	0.343	0.677
7/1961–6/1968	7/1954–6/1961	0.399	0.546

Source: Adapted from Marshall Blume, "On the Assessment of Risk," *Journal of Finance* 26 (March 1971): 1–10.

are regressed on betas estimated over the period 7/1954–6/1961 (period $t-1$), the following estimated equation was obtained:

$$\hat{\beta}_{it} = 0.399 + 0.546\, \hat{\beta}_{it-1} \qquad (17.17)$$

If we wish to forecast the beta for any stock for the next period 7/1968–6/1975 (period $t+1$), the forecasted beta for the period $t+1$ will be $0.399 + 0.546$ times the beta over the period t. If the beta for period t is 2.0, then the forecasted beta for period $t+1$ would be $0.399 + 0.546 \times 2.0 = 1.491$, which is lower than the previous period's beta. If the beta for period t is 0.5, then the forecasted beta for period $t+1$ would be $0.399 + 0.546 \times 0.5 = 0.672$, which is greater than the previous period's beta. These examples document the tendency of betas to regress toward their mean value of one.

Vasicek (1973) subsequently suggested a Bayesian technique for adjusting individual security betas. In particular, information from a base period is used to estimate the cross-sectional distribution of individual security betas. The beta estimate of an individual stock i over the base period t and its variance are denoted $\hat{\beta}_{it}$ and $\sigma^2_{\hat{\beta}_i}$.[13] Next, the cross-sectional average and variance of the estimated betas of all individual stocks are denoted $\overline{\beta}$ and σ^2_{β}.[14] The following Bayesian estimate of beta can be calculated:

$$\beta_{it+1} = h_i\overline{\beta} + (1 - h_i)\,\hat{\beta}_{it} \qquad (17.18)$$

where

$$h_i = \frac{\sigma^2_{\hat{\beta}_i}}{\sigma^2_{\beta} + \sigma^2_{\hat{\beta}_i}} \qquad (17.19)$$

As can be seen, because the sum of two weights equals 1, this adjusted beta is a weighted average of the cross-sectional average of the betas, $\overline{\beta}$, and the historical beta estimate, $\hat{\beta}_{it}$. The weight placed on each beta term depends on the degree of the precision of the beta term. The more precise the historical beta estimate (i.e., the smaller the $\sigma^2_{\hat{\beta}_i}$), the more weight is given to the term of the historical beta estimate. This is a Bayesian procedure. The mean of the posterior distribution of beta (or the posterior beta), β_{it+1}, is a weighted average of the mean of the prior distribution of beta (or the prior beta), $\overline{\beta}$, and the sample beta, $\hat{\beta}_{it}$. The weights are determined by the variance of the prior distribution of beta, σ^2_{β}, and the variance of the sample beta, $\sigma^2_{\hat{\beta}_i}$. Because $\overline{\beta} \cong 1$, the Bayesian technique can be viewed as a second method of adjusting for the tendency of beta to drift toward 1.

Vasicek noted a similar technique used by Merrill Lynch, Pierce, Fenner & Smith Inc. (hereafter ML). In particular, the ML estimate is

$$\hat{\beta}_{it} = (1 - k) + k\hat{\beta}_{it-1} \qquad (17.20)$$

where k is a constant for all stocks. Comparing equation (17.20) with equation (17.16), it can be seen that the two are equivalent if γ_0 is constrained to equal $1 - \gamma_1$. Thus, k can be estimated in a manner analogous to Blume but with a constraint on the intercept term. That is, two nonoverlapping adjacent estimation periods can be used to get two sets of betas, and then the more recent estimates can be regressed on the previous estimates.

Comparing the ML estimator with the Bayesian estimator reveals that the ML estimator uses the same weights for all securities, whereas the Bayesian technique uses weights specific to each security (due to the $\sigma^2_{\hat{\beta}_i}$ term). Thus, the ML technique can be viewed as a special case of the Bayesian technique where it is assumed that $\overline{\beta} \cong 1$ and $\sigma^2_{\hat{\beta}_i}$ is the same for all securities.

Empirical tests of these estimators have been conducted by Klemkosky and Martin (1975) and Euback and Zumwalt (1979). The results of these studies suggest that for individual securities, the adjusted estimators (Blume, Bayesian, and ML) are valuable in improving the accuracy of the forecasts. In particular, estimates of high or low betas are notably enhanced by the use of these techniques. However, the differences between them do not appear to be substantial, which is not surprising, because these adjusted estimators are all similar.

Given that beta coefficients are nonstationary, two additional approaches to forecasting beta have been pursued. The first approach has been to try to identify that model of nonstationarity which best characterizes beta. The second approach seeks to identify those financial variables that are most closely linked to beta and thereby allow one to forecast beta by using the most recent values of these financial variables.

17.4.2   Nonstationarity of Beta

There are various models for capturing nonstationarity of beta. First, the Theil (1971) model states that, for an asset i,

$$\beta_{it} = \beta_i + \varepsilon_{it} \tag{17.21}$$

where ε_{it} is a normally distributed random error term with a mean of zero. Thus, with this model each period's beta for a given stock is an observation of a normally distributed random variable with a mean of β_i. Tests of this model have been conducted by Fabozzi and Francis (1978), Alexander and Benson (1982), and Bos and Newbold (1984), with mixed results.

The random walk model states that

$$\beta_{it} = \beta_{it-1} + \varepsilon_{it} \tag{17.22}$$

where ε_{it} is a normally distributed random error term. With this model, each period's beta for a given stock is equal to what it was last period plus a random shock. Sunder (1980) tested this model on individual common stocks and found that when a large number of observations was used (for example, 300 observations of monthly returns), the model fit the data quite well. However, when using smaller numbers of observations (for example, 75 observations of monthly returns), the results were much weaker.[15]

A first-order autoregressive process for beta states that

$$\beta_{it} = \rho\,\beta_{it-1} + (1 - \rho)\,\overline{\beta}_i + \varepsilon_{it} \tag{17.22a}$$

where ρ is known as the auto correlation coefficient (with a value between -1 and $+1$), $\overline{\beta}_i$ is the mean value, and ε_{it} is a typical mean-zero random shock term.[16]

Ohlson and Rosenberg (1982) noted that this model implies that the random shock term affects next period's beta in that β_{it-1} includes the value of ε_{it-1}. Arguing that there should be a purely random term with no carry-forward effect, they modified equation (17.22) by adding a second shock term with zero mean. Using the CRSP (Center for Research in Security Prices, located at the University of Chicago) equal-weighted NYSE-based market index as the dependent variable and the CRSP value-weighted NYSE-based market index as the independent variable, Ohlson and Rosenberg estimated ρ to be equal to 0.9875 using 50 years of monthly data. In view of this high level of autocorrelation, they rejected both the Theil and random walk models. Ohlson and Rosenberg left unaddressed the question of what form of the autoregressive model was optimal for shorter time intervals.

Schaefer, Brealey, Hodges, and Thomas (1975) compared all three random coefficient models with a constant coefficient model. They found that for the periods 1926–1935 and 1936–1945 the random walk and first-order autoregressive models were superior for a sample of NYSE-listed common stocks using monthly data. However, they were unable to determine which of these two models was superior over either time period. When the period 1946–1955 was examined, firms were found to have had random betas, but it could not be determined which one of the three models best fit the data. The periods 1956–1965 and 1966–1971 did not provide strong evidence indicating that firms had random betas. The authors concluded their study by noting that such tests of the stationarity of individual common stock betas contain large estimation errors, thereby making it difficult to make strong statements about the form of the nonstationarity.

Bos and Newbold (1984) similarly compared all three random coefficient models on NYSE-listed common stocks using monthly data over the period 1970–1979. Initial evidence indicated that the constant-coefficient models could be rejected for a majority of the stocks. Further evidence indicated that the parameter ρ in equation (17.22) was fairly symmetrically distributed around a value of zero, but that the distribution was not tightly clustered. This, the authors argue, can be construed as a failure to find strong evidence against the Theil model. However, the authors caution that their tests of the hypothesis that $\rho = 0$ may not be very powerful.

In summary, beta does appear to be a random coefficient. However, it appears that more testing is necessary before any specific random coefficient model can be used with confidence in estimating individual security beta coefficients. In particular, comparisons of the forecasting ability of the various adjusted beta techniques need to be conducted.

Kim (1993) suggested a different type of beta nonstationarity model, assuming that the beta is stationary over a period (regime) until a structural shift point, and then the beta changes to another level after the structural shift point.[17] Specifically, the formulation of his sequential beta nonstationarity model is as follows (subscript i for an asset is omitted):

$$\text{Regime } 1 : r_t = \alpha_1 + \beta_1 r_{mt} + \varepsilon_{1t}, \qquad t = 1, \ldots, \tau_1$$

$$\text{Regime } 2 : r_t = \alpha_2 + \beta_2 r_{mt} + \varepsilon_{2t}, \qquad t = \tau_1 + 1, \ldots, \tau_2$$

$$\vdots$$

$$\text{Regime } K : r_t = \alpha_K + \beta_K r_{mt} + \varepsilon_{Kt}, \qquad t = \tau_{K-1} + 1, \ldots, \tau_K$$

where ε_{kt} is the random error term of the k-th regime with mean 0 and variance $\sigma^2_{\varepsilon_k}$ ($k = 1, \ldots, K$). The preceding formulation assumes that the parameters of the market model ($\alpha_k, \beta_k,$ and $\sigma^2_{\varepsilon_k}$) change after the structural shift point, τ_k. Thus, the beta is assumed to change in a stepwise way rather than changing gradually at every time point. Kim developed a statistical procedure to sequentially estimate the structural shift points of the beta. He found that the length of the beta stationarity period is related to firm size and the magnitude of beta. He also found that the average length of the beta stationarity period is about 54 months when a 5 percent significance level is applied in detecting the structural shift points. These results provide some support for the currently widely used arbitrary choice of five years in estimating betas, assuming that betas are stationary over this five-year period.[18]

17.4.3   Determinants of Beta

As mentioned previously, another approach to forecasting beta involves establishing the relationship between it and fundamental financial variables or macroeconomic variables. Research has indicated that some of the factors that cause beta to change are such characteristics as changes in the firm's fundamentals (such as financial leverage, operating leverage, cash dividend yield, and earnings growth) or changes in macroeconomic conditions.

Early work in this area was done by Beaver, Kettler, and Scholes (1970), hereafter denoted BKS.[19] Using data on 307 firms for the period 1947–1956, they estimated the parameters of the following regression model:

$$\hat{\beta}_{it} = \gamma_0 + \gamma_1 P_{it} + \gamma_2 G_{it} + \gamma_3 V_{it} + \varepsilon_{it} \tag{17.23}$$

where P_{it} denotes the payout ratio for firm i in period t, G_{it} denotes the growth rate in total assets for firm i in period t, and V_{it} is a measure of earnings variability for firm i in period t. The estimated coefficients of equation (17.23) were positive for γ_0, γ_1, and γ_3, and negative for γ_2. In sign, these estimates were consistent with the a priori expectations of BKS. Next, BKS compared the estimated value of $\gamma_0 + \gamma_1 P_{it} + \gamma_2 G_{it} + \gamma_3 V_{it}$ with $\hat{\beta}_{it}$ as estimators of β_{it+1}, where β_{it+1} was firm i's beta coefficient over the next period 1957–1965. The mean squared error of the former and latter estimators was 0.089 and 0.093, respectively, suggesting that the former approach to estimating *ex ante* betas was marginally superior.[20]

Based on BKS and other studies, Rosenberg and Guy (1976a, 1976b) and Rosenberg and Marathe (1975, 1976) have suggested a prediction rule for developing beta estimates for individual securities. Essentially, the analyst begins with the industry average betas and modifies them by adding on the appropriate adjustment factors to obtain a beta prediction for an individual firm's stock.[21] The resulting adjusted beta estimate is, arguably, a better estimate than the firm's own historical OLS beta. The problem with this procedure is that the proper adjustments for all possible changes and combinations of changes must be estimated econometrically. Perhaps that is why various investment services provide beta forecasts for use by portfolio managers.[22]

Ferson and Schadt (1996) and Ferson and Harvey (1999) assume that a firm's expected return and risk changes according to the change of macroeconomic and business conditions. Under this assumption, the following linear return-generating process is suggested

$$r_{it} = \alpha_{it-1}\left(Z_{t-1}\right) + \beta_{it-1}\left(Z_{t-1}\right)r_{mt} + \varepsilon_{it} \tag{17.24}$$

where $\mathrm{E}\left(\varepsilon_{it}|Z_{t-1}\right) = 0$, and Z_{t-1} is an $L \times 1$ vector of mean zero information variables known at time $t-1$. Equation (17.24) is a time-varying market model in which the intercept and slope coefficients α_i and β_i are conditional on the information set available up to time $t-1$, Z_{t-1}. Assuming that the parameters are a linear function of the information set,

$$\beta_{it-1}\left(Z_{t-1}\right) = b_{i0} + b_{i1}'Z_{t-1} \tag{17.25}$$

and

$$\alpha_{it-1}\left(Z_{t-1}\right) = a_{i0} + a_{i1}'Z_{t-1} \tag{17.26}$$

Substituting the parameters in equation (17.24) with equations (17.25) and (17.26) yields

$$
\begin{aligned}
r_{it} &= \left(a_{i0} + a_{i1}'Z_{t-1}\right) + \left(b_{i0} + b_{i1}'Z_{t-1}\right)r_{mt} + \varepsilon_{it} \\
&= a_{i0} + a_{i1}'Z_{t-1} + b_{i0}r_{mt} + b_{i1}'\left(Z_{t-1}r_{mt}\right) + \varepsilon_{it}
\end{aligned} \tag{17.27}
$$

Equation (17.27) may be interpreted as an unconditional multiple factor model, where the market portfolio is the first factor, and the lagged information variables and the product of the market and the lagged information variables are additional factors. The parameters, a_{i0}, a_{i1}, b_{i0}, and b_{i1}, can be estimated by estimating the regression model of equation (17.27). Then, the fitted beta value is obtained from

$$\hat{\beta}_{it-1}\left(Z_{t-1}\right) = \hat{b}_{i0} + \hat{b}_{i1}'Z_{t-1} \tag{17.28}$$

and it can be used as a forecast of the next period beta, β_{it}.

For the information variables, Ferson and Schadt (1996) and Ferson and Harvey (1999) suggest (1) one-month Treasury bill yield, (2) dividend yield of the Standard & Poor's 500 index, (3) the spread between Moody's Baa and Aaa corporate bond yields (the default premium), and (4) the spread between a 10-year and a one-year Treasury bond yield (term premium, or slope of the yield curve).

17.5 DIVERSIFICATION

Chapter 8 discussed the implications for diversification of the market model and two forms of multiple-index models. It was noted that a key assumption of the market model was that the correlation between the error terms of any two securities was zero. The multiple-index models could, however, allow for the error terms of two securities in the same industry to be correlated while assuming that the error terms of two securities in different industries are uncorrelated. The implications for diversification are different for these models, depending on how many indexes were appropriate to describe security returns.[23] With the market model, diversification of any sort would be expected to provide a reduction in the risk of the portfolio, whereas with the multiple-index models, diversification across industries has more risk reduction potential than diversification within an industry.

17.5.1   Simple Diversification

Evans and Archer (1968) have shown that portfolios of randomly selected securities (that is, simply diversified portfolios) have risk that decreases to a minimum level equal, asymptotically, to the risk of the market portfolios, as the portfolio's size is increased. Figure 17.1 depicts the nature of this relationship, and was prepared as follows.

At the start a data bank of semiannual rates of return from January 1958–July 1967 for 470 NYSE firms was stored in the memory of a computer; a random number generator was used to select individual securities from the data bank that were to be formed into equal-weighted portfolios. Initially 60 securities were selected and treated as one-stock portfolios in calculating the average of their individual standard deviation of returns.

Then 120 securities were selected and formed into 60 two-stock portfolios. At this point the standard deviation of returns was calculated for each of the 60 two-stock portfolios and then the average of these 60 standard deviations was calculated. This process of generating 60 portfolios and calculating their average standard deviation was subsequently repeated for portfolios of size 3, 4, 5,..., 38, 39, and 40 securities, respectively. Figure 17.1 is a graph with the average standard deviation of returns plotted for each of these 40 different portfolio sizes. As can be seen from the figure, on average most of the gains from diversification in terms of risk reduction were achieved by the time the portfolio had roughly 10 to 15 securities in it. Portfolios containing more than 100 different stocks should be prepared to defend themselves from charges of superfluous diversification.

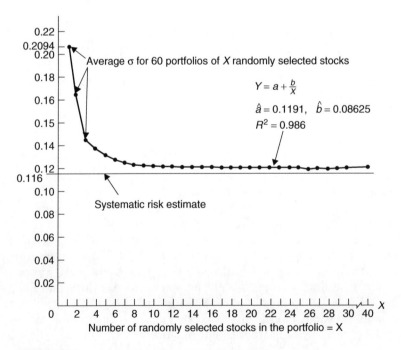

FIGURE 17.1   Simple Diversification Reduces Risk

Simple diversification reduces a portfolio's total risk by allowing the independent random errors (that is, the unsystematic risk) from the individual securities to average out to zero as *n* gets large, leaving only the systematic risk. Lintner says (1965b, p. 589; words in brackets added):

> *Apart from negatively correlated stocks, all the gains from diversification come from "averaging over" the independent components of the returns and risks of individual stocks. Among positively correlated stocks, there would be no gains from diversification if independent variations [that is, unsystematic risk] were absent.*

Simple diversification ignores covariances and, thus, does not explicitly consider the systematic risk of the portfolio. It seems reasonable to expect the portfolio beta to equal one because securities have betas distributed around one. Furthermore, on average, the portfolios will be well diversified across various industries. Thus, as the number of securities in a portfolio (*n*) increases), the variance of the portfolio, σ_p^2, should asymptotically approach σ_m^2 when randomly selected securities are included. Indeed, this was what Evans and Archer observed.

In an extension of the Evans and Archer study, Upson, Jessup, and Matsumoto (1975), hereafter UJM, point out that it is also important to look at the standard deviation of the distribution of mean returns over the sample period for each portfolio size. That is, in the Evans and Archer study, for each portfolio, its mean return and standard deviation of returns were calculated over the sample period and then the average of the standard deviations was calculated for each portfolio size. UJM argue that it is also important to consider not only the average of the individual portfolio standard deviations, but also the standard deviation of the distribution of the mean returns in order to reflect how close a naively diversified portfolio comes to achieving the average market return. Following a procedure similar to Evans and Archer, UJM find that portfolios of 8, 16, 32, and 128 securities have a standard deviation of the distribution of mean returns that is 35 percent, 25 percent, 17 percent, and 8 percent of the standard deviation of the distribution of mean returns for one-stock portfolios, respectively. UJM conclude that portfolio managers should diversify among more than 16 stocks, and that diversifying among even 30 or more stocks can be worthwhile in terms of risk reduction.[24]

17.5.2 Timing and Diversification

Earlier it was mentioned that portfolio managers wishing to engage in market timing should seek to alter the beta of their portfolio in a direction dependent on the market forecast. Three methods of altering beta were mentioned. The first, altering the percentage of funds in the risk-free asset and a given risky portfolio, has no diversification implications. This is because the resulting portfolio will still have a standard deviation of returns that is dependent on the standard deviation of the risky portfolio and the proportion of funds invested in it. The second method, altering the percentage of funds in high-beta securities vis-à-vis low-beta securities, can have diversification implications. The third method involves combining the first two methods.

Much evidence exists suggesting that there is a positive correlation between measures of systematic (β_i) and unsystematic ($\sigma_{\varepsilon_i}^2$) risk. This means that portfolios with higher betas will have greater amounts of unsystematic risk. Accordingly, high-beta portfolios should not be as well diversified as low-beta portfolios if both contain a similar number of securities. Klemkosky and Martin (1975a) tested this hypothesis by examining 350 securities over the 120-month period from July 1963 to June 1973. First, Klemkosky and Martin estimated β_i and $\sigma^2_{\varepsilon_i}$ for each stock over this 120-month period and then regressed the set of beta estimates on the set of residual variances:

$$\hat{\beta}_i = \gamma_0 + \gamma_1 \hat{\sigma}^2_{\varepsilon_i} + \eta_i \qquad (17.29)$$

The coefficient γ_1 was found to be significantly positive at the 0.01 level, thereby confirming the Miller and Scholes (1972) observation.

Second, Klemkosky and Martin formed equal-weighted portfolios for sizes ranging from 2 through 25 securities. For any given portfolio size n, the portfolios were formed by arraying the securities in descending order according to their estimated beta and then putting the first n securities into the first portfolio, the second n securities into the second portfolio, and so on. Thus, the total number of portfolios of size n was approximately equal to $350/n$. For each portfolio, its variance was calculated in two ways. First, portfolio returns were calculated by equal weighting and then the portfolio variance was calculated directly $(\hat{\sigma}^2_p)$. Second, the portfolio variance was calculated using the RHS of equation (17.11) with equal weights $(\hat{\beta}^2_p \sigma^2_m)$. The difference between the two (expressed as a percentage of the directly calculated portfolio variance) should represent the effect on diversification of ignoring group effects, because the latter procedure assumes that the residuals are not correlated between firms. For any given portfolio size, the following statistic was calculated as a measure of unsystematic or residual variance (RVAR):

$$\text{RVAR}_p = \hat{\sigma}^2_p - \hat{\beta}^2_p \sigma^2_m \qquad (17.30)$$

where $\hat{\sigma}^2_p$ is the directly calculated portfolio variance and $\hat{\beta}^2_p \sigma^2_m$ is the estimate of systematic risk of the portfolio. Next, Klemkosky and Martin ran the following regression for all portfolios of a given size:

$$\hat{\beta}_p = \gamma_0 + \gamma_1 \text{RVAR}_p + \eta_p \qquad (17.31)$$

The correlation coefficient increased from 0.726 to 0.899 for equation (17.31) as n increased from 2 to 25.

Third, Klemkosky and Martin divided all the portfolios of each size into quartiles based on $\hat{\beta}_p$. Then, the average values of RVAR_p were calculated for those portfolios in the upper and lower quartiles and were denoted RVAR_H and RVAR_L, respectively. Klemkosky and Martin observed that for any portfolio size, RVAR_H was always greater than RVAR_L and the ratio $\text{RVAR}_H/\text{RVAR}_L$ tended to increase as portfolio size increased (although the difference between RVAR_H and RVAR_L tended to decrease).

Thus, it appears that a substantially greater number of stocks are required in a high-beta portfolio in order to achieve the same level of risk reduction as in a low-beta portfolio. The implication is that given a choice for how to engage in market timing, the portfolio manager is better off using the method whereby the percentage of funds invested in the risk-free asset is altered.

17.5.3 International Diversification

In the discussion of diversification, only domestic common stocks have been considered so far. An interesting aspect of diversification is provided by foreign stocks.[25] A strict interpretation of the CAPM indicates that the market portfolio should be internationally diversified. Restricting our view to just U.S. stocks implies that capital markets are segmented. As Lessard (1974, 1976) has noted, if markets are fully integrated, diversifying internationally (relative to national diversification) will allow the investor to reduce the portfolio's unsystematic risk. However, if markets are segmented, the potential gains from international diversification might be even greater. This is because some of the systematic risk, when measured using a national market portfolio, will become unsystematic due to the expansion of the market portfolio to include foreign stocks. Evidence presented by Lessard and others suggests that while a world index is important in explaining individual security returns, country factors are also extremely important.

The major complication in the consideration of foreign stocks is the presence of exchange rate risk.[26] Not only is the future price of a foreign security uncertain but, in addition, the rate of exchange to convert this potential transaction price (and any cash dividends) into the investor's home currency is also uncertain. This can be seen by letting $x_{c,t}$ denote the exchange rate at time t between the currency of country c and the U.S dollar, for example, expressed as dollars per foreign currency unit, and by letting $r_{c,it}$ denote the rate of return from firm i located in country c over time period t. Thus, by definition,

$$r_{c,it} = \frac{\left(p_{c,it} - p_{c,it-1}\right) + d_{c,it}}{p_{c,it-1}} \tag{17.32}$$

where $p_{c,it}$ denotes the stock price of firm i located in country c over time period t, and $d_{c,it}$ denotes the dividend per share received on this stock over time period t. From the perspective of a U.S. investor, the rate of return on this stock can be expressed by converting the parameters on the RHS of equation (17.32) into U.S. dollars. Doing so results in

$$r_{US,it} = \frac{\left(p_{c,it} + d_{c,it}\right)\left(x_{c,t}\right) - p_{c,it-1}\left(x_{c,t-1}\right)}{p_{c,it-1}\left(x_{c,t-1}\right)} \tag{17.33}$$

or, by simplifying,

$$r_{US,it} = \left[\left(1 + r_{c,it}\right)\left(1 + r_{x,t}\right)\right] - 1 \tag{17.34}$$

$$= r_{c,it} + r_{x,t} + r_{c,it}r_{x,t}$$

where $r_{x,t} = \left(x_{c,t} - x_{c,t-1}\right)/x_{c,t-1}$, which can be viewed as the rate of return on the exchange rate. Here, $r_{US,it}$ is the aggregate rate of return on stock i to the U.S. investor.

As can be seen from equation (17.34), the rate of return $r_{US,it}$ has three components. The first component, $r_{c,it}$, is what an investor would earn if he or she were a citizen in country c and bought a share of the stock of firm i at time $t-1$ and sold it at time t. The second component, $r_{x,t}$, is the rate of return on changes in the exchange rate. That is, it represents what one would earn if he or she converted a given amount of U.S. dollars to the currency of country c at time $t-1$ and held this currency until time t, at which time it was converted back into U.S. dollars. The third component is simply a cross-product of the previous two and represents the effect the change in the exchange rate has had on the security's capital gain or loss (and dividends). In sum, it can be seen that international investing involves both price risk and exchange rate risk.

In a study paralleling Evans and Archer (1968), Solnik (1974a) examined the diversification implications of international investing. In particular, he examined over 300 European stocks, in addition to a sample of U.S. stocks, on a weekly basis from 1966 to 1971. Numerous portfolios of various sizes were randomly formed using only U.S. stocks and then using both U.S. and European stocks. For the latter portfolios, Solnik initially assumed that exchange rate risk would be completely hedged, meaning that he assumed $r_{x,t} = 0$ in equation (17.34), when he calculated U.S. returns for European socks. Later, Solnik removed this assumption and calculated U.S. returns using the actual values of $r_{x,t}$ during the sample time period.

Figure 17.2 presents Solnik's results. The vertical axis is based on the average variance of the individual common stocks in his sample and represents the ratio of the average variance of portfolios of a given size to this base. As can be seen in the diagram, substantial benefits can be achieved by diversifying internationally, regardless of whether or not exchange risk is hedged.[27] Note that the gains from international diversification are similar whether or not the exchange risk is hedged.

A second method for analyzing at the effect of international diversification on portfolio risk is to examine the location of the efficient frontier when such diversification takes place in comparison to its location when only domestic diversification takes place. A classic study in this area was conducted by Levy and Sarnat (1970).

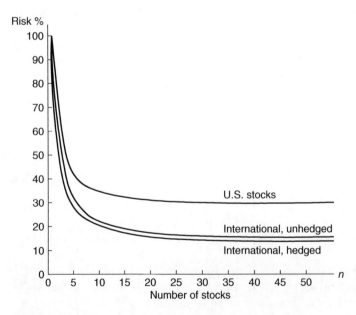

FIGURE 17.2   International Diversification
Source: B. Solnik, "Why Not Diversify Internationally Rather Than Domestically?"
Financial Analysts Journal 30, no. 4 (July–August 1974): Figure 11, p. 51.

These authors examined annual rates of return, converted to U.S. dollars, for national stock market indexes of 28 countries from the period 1951–1967. Using these data, average rates of return as well as variances and covariances were estimated and the tangency portfolios with the relevant efficient frontier were identified for risk-free rates of return of 2 percent, 3 percent, 4 percent, and 6 percent (short selling was prohibited). The composition of these tangency portfolios is shown in Table 17.3, together with their mean rates of return and standard deviations.

Keeping in mind that the U.S. market index had a mean rate of return of 12.1 percent as well as a standard deviation of 12.1 percent, it can be seen from Table 17.3 that notable gains from international diversification were available to U.S. investors. In particular, substantial risk reduction could have been accomplished by international diversification. The benefits from international diversification in terms of the Sharpe ratio are also shown in Table 17.4. The Sharpe ratio is a measure of risk-adjusted performance defined as the ratio of the excess return to risk and is calculated as $(\bar{r}_p - r_f)/\sigma_p$. Table 17.4 shows that the Sharpe ratios of the tangency portfolios with international diversification are substantially greater than those of the U.S. market index only. These results indicate that international diversification improves the risk-return trade-off for U.S. investors.

Besides international diversification, global asset allocation also provides better opportunities for profit and hence improves the risk-return trade-off for U.S. investors. Odier and Solnik (1993) prepared Figure 17.3, which illustrates the efficient frontier for U.S. stocks and several international stocks for the 1980–1990

TABLE 17.3 Composition of Tangency Portfolios

	Risk-free rates			
	2%	3%	4%	6%
United States	0.366	0.410	0.428	0.511
Japan	0.147	0.167	0.176	0.209
Latin and South America	0.195	0.160	0.141	0.032
Western Europe	0.057	0.070	0.090	0.120
Others	0.235	0.193	0.165	0.128
Total weights	1.000	1.000	1.000	1.000
Tangency portfolio (*p*):				
Mean return ($\bar{r}_p$)	0.095	0.105	0.110	0.125
Standard deviation (σ_p)	0.057	0.064	0.068	0.084

Source: Adapted from Levy and Sarnat, "International Diversification of Investment Portfolios," *American Economic Review* 4 (1970): 668–675. Table 17.4 has the same source.

TABLE 17.4 The Sharpe Ratios [$= (\bar{r}_p - r_f)/\sigma_p$] for Tangency Portfolios from Table 17.3 and for the U.S. Market Index

	Risk-free rates			
	2%	3%	4%	6%
Tangency portfolio (*p*)	1.316	1.172	1.029	0.774
U.S. market index ($\bar{r}_{us} = 0.121$, $\sigma_{us} = 0.121$)	0.837	0.752	0.669	0.504

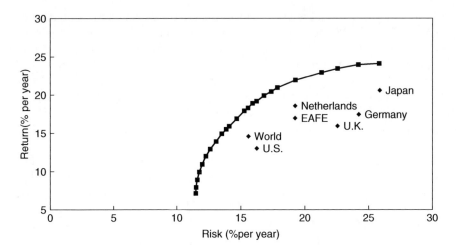

FIGURE 17.3 Efficient Frontier for U.S. and Global Stocks (U.S. Dollar, 1980–1990)
Source: Adapted from Odier and Solnik, "Lessons for International Asset Allocation,"
Financial Analysts Journal 49 (1993 Mar/Apr): 63–77.

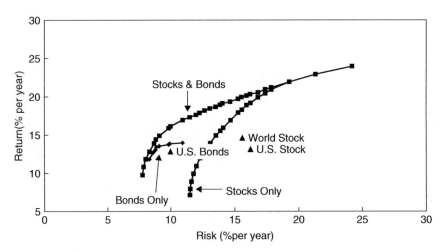

FIGURE 17.4 Efficient Frontier for U.S. Stocks, Global Stocks, and U.S. Bonds (U.S. Dollar,
1980–1990)
Source: Adapted from Odier and Solnik, "Lessons for International Asset
Allocation,"*Financial Analysts Journal* 49 (1993 Mar/Apr): 63–77.

period. The U.S. stock market has a return of 13.3 percent per year and a standard
deviation of 16.2 percent per year over this period. Other countries' stock markets
have greater return and risk. Figure 17.3 shows that international diversification of
the U.S. stock portfolio could greatly improve return without a large increase in the
portfolio's risk. Specifically, at the same risk level as the U.S. stock portfolio (16.2%),
a global stock portfolio would achieve 19 percent annualized return, compared with
13.3 percent return of the U.S. portfolio.

    If bonds are added into the international stock portfolios, the diversification
benefit can be even greater. Figure 17.4 illustrates the efficient frontiers for global

and U.S. stocks only, for U.S. bonds only, and for the combined stocks and bonds. This figure shows clearly that the efficient frontier for the combined stocks and bonds dominates the efficient frontiers for stocks only and for bonds only. Thus, global asset allocation can significantly enhance international investors' risk-return trade-off.

17.6 CONSTRUCTING AN ACTIVE PORTFOLIO

After discussing selectivity, market timing, and diversification, it is useful to consider how the investor should go about constructing and selecting an optimal portfolio. Again, the situation considered here involves only common stocks and a risk-free asset (such as Treasury bills) as potential investments. Because the "true" market portfolio remains unidentified, the Standard & Poor's 500 is used as a proxy.

As mentioned earlier, if the investor is not interested in either selectivity or market timing, then portfolio construction and selection are straightforward. The investor simply buys and holds proportions of the risk-free asset and the market portfolio that are determined by where the investor's highest utility isoquant is tangent to the CML. Because the investor is not interested in market timing, the location of the CML will be based on the current risk-free rate and the consensus opinion about the expected return and variance of the market portfolio, where the latter opinions are not expected to vary over time. The investor may want to readjust the proportions periodically as the risk-free rate changes or as his or her risk preferences change. Essentially, a buy-and-hold strategy is called for, and the investor is said to be following a passive investment strategy.

If interested only in market timing, the investor would plot the CML based on his or her own estimates of r_f, μ_m, and σ_m. Then the optimal proportions of the risk-free asset and market portfolio would be determined by the tangency point between the investor's indifference utility curve and the CML. Periodically, the estimates of r_f, μ_m, and σ_m should be updated, resulting in the location of the CML shifting. This shifting necessitates that the investor adjust the proportions invested in the risk-free asset and market portfolio. In this situation the investor is said to be following one form of an active investment strategy. The difference between this and a passive investment strategy is the frequency with which revisions are made in the estimates of r_f, μ_m, and σ_m.

The situation where the investor is interested in selectivity, with or without an interest in market timing, introduces a second form of an active investment strategy. One CAPM-based approach is that of Treynor and Black (1973), which focuses on the use of equation (17.8).[28] As stated by Treynor and Black, this approach assumes that the investor is attempting to profit from expectations that differ from the market consensus. They further assume the market is sufficiently large so that the investor's trades do not affect market prices. Transactions costs are ignored and unconstrained short selling is permitted. With this approach security analysts provide estimates of α_i, β_i, and $\sigma_{\varepsilon_i}^2$ for each of the n securities under consideration. Estimates of r_f, μ_m, and σ_m could also be provided by an in-house macroeconomics forecasting group. Frequent revision of these parameters is appropriate if the investor desires to engage in market timing.

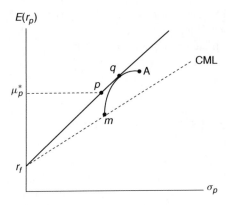

FIGURE 17.5   Constructing an Active
Portfolio

Consider the case where an actively managed portfolio, denoted A, is combined
with a market index portfolio (m) and the risk-free asset. The market index portfolio
is probably passively managed. The actively managed portfolio A consists of K
individual assets. In this case, we determine the optimal weights for K assets in
portfolio A to minimize the portfolio risk at a given level of expected return.
Figure 17.5 illustrates an optimal risky portfolio, p, when an active portfolio A is
added to a passively-managed market portfolio m and the risk-free asset. Portfolio p
is determined by minimizing its variance at a prespecified level of expected return μ_p^*.

We let the fraction of wealth invested in asset i (contained in portfolio A), the
market portfolio, and the risk-free asset be denoted by w_i, w_m, and w_f, respectively,
to construct the combined portfolio p. So,

$$w_A + w_m + w_f = 1 \qquad (17.35)$$

where $w_A = \sum_{i=1}^{K} w_i$. The combined portfolio p's return is denoted

$$
\begin{aligned}
r_{pt} &= \sum_{i=1}^{K} w_i r_{it} + w_m r_{mt} + w_f r_f \\
&= \sum_{i=1}^{K} w_i \left[r_f + \alpha_i + \beta_i \left(r_{mt} - r_f \right) + \varepsilon_{it} \right] + w_m r_{mt} + w_f r_f \\
&= \sum_{i=1}^{K} w_i \alpha_i + \left[w_f + \sum_{i=1}^{K} w_i \left(1 - \beta_i \right) \right] r_f + \left(w_m + \sum_{i=1}^{K} w_i \beta_i \right) r_{mt} + \sum_{i=1}^{K} w_i \varepsilon_{it}
\end{aligned}
$$
$$(17.36)$$

Then the expected return and variance of portfolio p are equal to

$$E\left(r_p \right) = \sum_{i=1}^{K} w_i \alpha_i + \left[w_f + \sum_{i=1}^{K} w_i \left(1 - \beta_i \right) \right] r_f + \left(w_m + \sum_{i=1}^{K} w_i \beta_i \right) E(r_m) \qquad (17.37)$$

and

$$\sigma_p^2 = \left(w_m + \sum_{i=1}^{K} w_i \beta_i \right)^2 \sigma_m^2 + \sum_{i=1}^{K} w_i^2 \sigma_{\varepsilon_i}^2 \qquad (17.38)$$

respectively. The expected return of the portfolio can be rewritten by observing that $w_f = 1 - w_m - \left(\sum_{i=1}^{K} w_i \right)$ and then making the appropriate substitution for w_f in equation (17.37), resulting in

$$E(r_p) = \sum_{i=1}^{K} w_i \alpha_i + \left[1 - w_m - \sum_{i=1}^{K} w_i \beta_i \right] r_f + \left(w_m + \sum_{i=1}^{K} w_i \beta_i \right) E(r_m) \qquad (17.39)$$

If we now define $w_{K+1} = w_m + \sum_{i=1}^{K} w_i \beta_i$, equations (17.38) and (17.39) can be rewritten as

$$E(r_p) = \sum_{i=1}^{K} w_i \alpha_i + \left(1 - w_{K+1} \right) r_f + w_{K+1} E(r_m) \qquad (17.40)$$

$$\sigma_p^2 = w_{K+1}^2 \sigma_m^2 + \sum_{i=1}^{K} w_i^2 \sigma_{\varepsilon_i}^2 \qquad (17.41)$$

In order to determine the location and composition of the efficient frontier, a quadratic programming (QP) problem that seeks to minimize the variance of portfolio p expressed in equation (17.41) subject to the linear constraint in equation (17.40) needs to be solved for various levels of μ_p.[29] For an arbitrary level of μ_p, say μ_p^*, this means the following Lagrangian can be formed:

$$L = w_{K+1}^2 \sigma_m^2 + \sum_{i=1}^{K} w_i^2 \sigma_{\varepsilon_i}^2 - 2\lambda \left[\sum_{i=1}^{K} w_i \alpha_i + \left(1 - w_{K+1} \right) r_f + w_{K+1} E(r_m) - \mu_p^* \right] \qquad (17.42)$$

where λ is a Lagrangian multiplier. The first-order conditions for a minimum are

$$\frac{\partial L}{\partial w_i} = 2 w_i \sigma_{\varepsilon_i}^2 - 2\lambda \alpha_i = 0, \qquad i = 1, \dots, K \qquad (17.43)$$

and

$$\frac{\partial L}{\partial w_{K+1}} = 2 w_{K+1} \sigma_m^2 - 2\lambda \left[E(r_m) - r_f \right] = 0 \qquad (17.44)$$

Simplifying these equations results in

$$w_i = \frac{\lambda \alpha_i}{\sigma_{\varepsilon_i}^2}, \qquad i = 1, \dots, K \qquad (17.45)$$

and

$$w_{K+1} = \frac{\lambda \left[E(r_m) - r_f \right]}{\sigma_m^2} \qquad (17.46)$$

Substituting equations (17.45) and (17.46) into equation (17.40) and solving for λ results in

$$\lambda = \frac{\left(\mu_p^* - r_f\right)}{\left[\left(E(r_m) - r_f\right)^2/\sigma_m^2 + \sum_{i=1}^{K}\left(\alpha_i^2/\sigma_{\varepsilon_i}^2\right)\right]} \tag{17.47}$$

By substituting equation (17.47) into equation (17.45), it can be seen that the investor will be making a direct investment in each one of the K securities in an amount equal proportionately to

$$w_i = \left\{ \frac{\left(\mu_p^* - r_f\right)}{\left[\left(E(r_m) - r_f\right)^2/\sigma_m^2 + \sum_{i=1}^{K}\left(\alpha_i^2/\sigma_{\varepsilon_i}^2\right)\right]} \right\} \left(\frac{\alpha_i}{\sigma_{\varepsilon_i}^2}\right) \tag{17.48}$$

Note that, generally speaking, the larger the abnormal return (α_i) is, or the more certain the investor is of that abnormal return (that is, the smaller unsystematic risk $\sigma_{\varepsilon_i}^2$), the greater the direct investment in security i. Furthermore, these weights can be positive or negative, depending on whether α_i is positive or negative. Of course, if certain securities were not analyzed, and thus had $\alpha_i = 0$, then their weights w_i would equal zero. Indeed, if the investor were not interested in selectivity, then $\alpha_i = 0$ for all securities, resulting in $w_i = 0$ for all securities and leaving the investor with the decision of how to allocate his or her funds between the risk-free asset and the market portfolio.

The overall optimal portfolio for the investor can be thought of as consisting of investments in three portfolios, where these portfolios are the risk-free asset, the market portfolio, and the actively-managed portfolio A, which consists of the sum of the previously mentioned direct investments. The total share of wealth held in these direct investments will consist of

$$w_A \equiv \sum_{i=1}^{K} w_i = \left\{ \frac{\left(\mu_p^* - r_f\right)}{\left[\left(E(r_m) - r_f\right)^2/\sigma_m^2 + \sum_{i=1}^{K}\left(\alpha_i^2/\sigma_{\varepsilon_i}^2\right)\right]} \right\} \left\{ \sum_{i=1}^{K} \frac{\alpha_i}{\sigma_{\varepsilon_i}^2} \right\} \tag{17.49}$$

Normalizing the weights given in equation (17.48) by dividing them by equation (17.49) results in

$$w_i^\circ \equiv \frac{w_i}{\sum_{i=1}^{K} w_i} = \frac{\left(\alpha_i/\sigma_{\varepsilon_i}^2\right)}{\sum_{i=1}^{K}\left(\alpha_i/\sigma_{\varepsilon_i}^2\right)} \quad \text{for } i = 1, \ldots, K \tag{17.50}$$

Thus, the sum of the direct investments w_i can be construed to be an investment in an active portfolio that consists of these K securities with the proportions shown in equation (17.50). That is, an active portfolio can be formed by investing the relative proportions given in equation (17.50) into the K risky assets, with the aggregate proportion in this portfolio being equal to $\sum_{i=1}^{K} w_i$. Note that $\sum_{i=1}^{K} w_i^\circ = 1$ and $\sum_{i=1}^{K} w_i = 1 - w_f - w_m$. An interesting observation on equation (17.50) is that the relative proportions for the active portfolio are independent of μ_p^*, the market parameters $E(r_m)$ and σ_m, and r_f, and the investor's attitudes toward risk and return. However, equation (17.49) indicates this is not true for the overall proportions $\sum_{i=1}^{K} w_i$.

The proportion invested in the market portfolio m can be calculated by remembering that $w_m = w_{K+1} - \sum_{i=1}^{K} w_i \beta_i$, and then substituting the values for w_{K+1} and w_i given in equations (17.45) and (17.46), respectively, into this expression [in doing so, the value for λ given in equation (17.47) would also be utilized]. Algebraically, this equivalent to

$$
w_m = w_{K+1} - \sum_{i=1}^{K} w_i \beta_i
$$

$$
= \lambda \left\{ \frac{[E(r_m) - r_f]}{\sigma_m^2} - \sum_{i=1}^{K} \left(\frac{\beta_i \alpha_i}{\sigma_{\varepsilon_i}^2} \right) \right\}
$$

$$
= \left\{ \frac{(\mu_p^* - r_f)}{\left[(E(r_m) - r_f)^2 / \sigma_m^2 + \sum_{i=1}^{K} (\alpha_i^2 / \sigma_{\varepsilon_i}^2) \right]} \right\} \times \left\{ \frac{[E(r_m) - r_f]}{\sigma_m^2} - \sum_{i=1}^{K} \left(\frac{\beta_i \alpha_i}{\sigma_{\varepsilon_i}^2} \right) \right\}
$$

$$(17.51)$$

The investment weight of the risk-free asset is

$$
w_f = 1 - w_A - w_m
$$

$$
= 1 - \lambda \left\{ \frac{[E(r_m) - r_f]}{\sigma_m^2} + \sum_{i=1}^{K} \left(\frac{(1 - \beta_i) \alpha_i}{\sigma_{\varepsilon_i}^2} \right) \right\}
$$

$$
= 1 - \left\{ \frac{(\mu_p^* - r_f)}{\left[(E(r_m) - r_f)^2 / \sigma_m^2 + \sum_{i=1}^{K} (\alpha_i^2 / \sigma_{\varepsilon_i}^2) \right]} \right\} \left\{ \frac{[E(r_m) - r_f]}{\sigma_m^2} + \sum_{i=1}^{K} \left(\frac{(1 - \beta_i) \alpha_i}{\sigma_{\varepsilon_i}^2} \right) \right\}
$$

$$(17.52)$$

In summary, the efficient portfolio p can be constructed with the investment weights of portfolio A, the market portfolio, and the risk-free asset from equations (17.49), (17.51), and (17.52), respectively. Portfolio A is constructed with the investment weights of individual assets from equation (17.50)—or equivalently, equation (17.53).

The tangency portfolio can be viewed as a blending of an active portfolio, described in equation (17.50), and a market portfolio, which can be viewed as a passive portfolio. Figure 17.5 shows this tangency portfolio q. The relative proportions invested in the two portfolios to create the tangency portfolio can be calculated by taking their proportions in the efficient portfolio with return of μ_p^* and normalizing them. The (normalized) proportions in the active portfolio A and the market portfolio m will equal

$$
\overset{\circ}{w}_A = \frac{w_A}{w_m + w_A} = \frac{\sum_{i=1}^{K} w_i}{w_m + \sum_{i=1}^{K} w_i}
$$

$$(17.53)$$

and

$$
\overset{\circ}{w}_m = \frac{w_m}{w_m + w_A} = \frac{w_m}{w_m + \sum_{i=1}^{K} w_i}
$$

$$(17.54)$$

respectively. Using equations (17.49), (17.51), and (17.53), the optimal weight of the active portfolio A to construct the tangency portfolio q in Figure 17.5 is

$$
\overset{\circ}{w}_A = \left(\sum_{i=1}^{K} \frac{\alpha_i}{\sigma_{\varepsilon_i}^2} \right) \Bigg/ \left\{ \frac{[E(r_m) - r_f]}{\sigma_m^2} + \sum_{i=1}^{K} \left(\frac{(1 - \beta_i) \alpha_i}{\sigma_{\varepsilon_i}^2} \right) \right\}
$$

$$(17.55)$$

$$
\overset{\circ}{w}_m = 1 - \overset{\circ}{w}_A
$$

$$(17.56)$$

Thus, the expected return of the tangency portfolio q is described as

$$E\left(r_q\right) = w_A^\circ E\left(r_A\right) + w_m^\circ E(r_m) \tag{17.57}$$

After the tangency portfolio has been determined, the efficient portfolio can also be constructed by combining the tangency portfolio and the risk-free asset, because the entire efficient frontier consists of a linear combination of the risk-free asset and the tangency portfolio. The determination of the weights for the tangency portfolio and the risk-free asset will depend on the investor's attitude toward risk and return, as indicated by his or her utility function. Or, if the investor's target expected return is given as μ_p^*, the weights for the tangency portfolio and the risk-free asset are also determined by solving the following equation with respect to w_q.

$$\mu_p^* = w_q E\left(r_q\right) + \left(1 - w_q\right) r_f \tag{17.58}$$

Note that in equation (17.58) μ_p^* is given, $E\left(r_q\right)$ is determined from equation (17.57), and the risk-free rate of return is also given.

In summary, portfolio construction and selection can be thought of as the following six steps:

1. Estimate α_i, β_i and $\sigma_{\varepsilon_i}^2$ in the market model of equation (17.8).
2. Compute the (normalized) weights of individual assets to be contained in the active portfolio as shown in equation (17.50).
3. Compute the expected return of the active portfolio with the weights from step 2).
4. Determine the (normalized) weights of the active portfolio and the market portfolio for the tangency portfolio using equations (17.55) and (17.56). This step involves blending the active portfolio with the passive market portfolio to determine the tangency portfolio.
5. Determine the weights of the tangency portfolio and the risk-free asset by examining the investor's utility function (or the given target expected return). Only in this last step does the investor's attitude toward risk and return come into play.
6. Determine the actual (un-normalized) weights of the active portfolio and the market portfolio for the target portfolio. Also, determine the actual weights of the individual assets contained in the active portfolio for the target portfolio.

Equations (17.49), (17.50), (17.51), (17.52), and (17.55) determine the investment weights for the active portfolio, the market portfolio, and the risk-free asset, and they have the summation of the terms containing the parameters α_i, β_i, and $\sigma_{\varepsilon_i}^2$ over K individual assets. This summation can be substituted with the term containing the corresponding parameters of the market model for the active portfolio under the certain circumstance. When the residual error terms from the market model are independent across K individual assets [i.e., $\text{Cov}\left(\varepsilon_{it}, \varepsilon_{jt}\right) = 0$ for $i \neq j$ and so $\sigma_{\varepsilon_A}^2 = \sum_{i=1}^K w_i^2 \sigma_{\varepsilon_i}^2$], the following equalities hold:

$$\sum_{i=1}^K \frac{\alpha_i}{\sigma_{\varepsilon_i}^2} = \frac{\alpha_A}{\sigma_{\varepsilon_A}^2}, \qquad \sum_{i=1}^K \frac{\beta_i \alpha_i}{\sigma_{\varepsilon_i}^2} = \frac{\beta_A \alpha_A}{\sigma_{\varepsilon_A}^2}, \qquad \sum_{i=1}^K \frac{\alpha_i^2}{\sigma_{\varepsilon_i}^2} = \frac{\alpha_A^2}{\sigma_{\varepsilon_A}^2} \tag{17.59}$$

where α_A, β_A, and $\sigma^2_{\varepsilon_A}$ are the parameters of the market portfolio for the active portfolio A,

$$r_{At} - r_f = \alpha_A + \beta_A \left(r_{mt} - r_{ft}\right) + \varepsilon_{At} \qquad (17.60)$$

See the end-of-chapter appendix of this chapter for proof of equation (17.59). When the equalities in equation (17.59) hold, the investment weights for portfolio A, individual assets, the market portfolio, and the risk-free asset can be rewritten as follows:

$$w_A = \left\{ \frac{\left(\mu^*_p - r_f\right)}{\left[\left(E(r_m) - r_f\right)^2 / \sigma^2_m + \left(\alpha^2_A / \sigma^2_{\varepsilon_A}\right)\right]} \right\} \left(\frac{\alpha_A}{\sigma^2_{\varepsilon_A}}\right) \qquad (17.49a)$$

$$w^\circ_i \equiv \frac{w_i}{\sum_{i=1}^K w_i} = \frac{\alpha_i / \sigma^2_{\varepsilon i}}{\alpha_A / \sigma^2_{\varepsilon A}}, \qquad i = 1, \ldots, K. \qquad (17.50a)$$

$$w_m = \left\{ \frac{\left(\mu^*_p - r_f\right)}{\left[\left(E(r_m) - r_f\right)^2 / \sigma^2_m + \left(\alpha^2_A / \sigma^2_{\varepsilon_A}\right)\right]} \right\} \times \left\{ \frac{\left[E(r_m) - r_f\right]}{\sigma^2_m} - \frac{\beta_A \alpha_A}{\sigma^2_{\varepsilon_A}} \right\} \qquad (17.51a)$$

$$w_f = 1 - \left\{ \frac{\left(\mu^*_p - r_f\right)}{\left[\left(E(r_m) - r_f\right)^2 / \sigma^2_m + \left(\alpha^2_A / \sigma^2_{\varepsilon_A}\right)\right]} \right\} \left\{ \frac{\left[E(r_m) - r_f\right]}{\sigma^2_m} + \frac{\left(1 - \beta_A\right)\alpha_A}{\sigma^2_{\varepsilon_A}} \right\} \qquad (17.52a)$$

$$w^\circ_A = \left(\frac{\alpha_A}{\sigma^2_{\varepsilon_A}}\right) \Bigg/ \left\{ \frac{\left[E(r_m) - r_f\right]}{\sigma^2_m} + \frac{\left(1 - \beta_A\right)\alpha_A}{\sigma^2_{\varepsilon_A}} \right\} \qquad (17.55a)$$

Here, $w_A + w_m + w_f = 1$. If the residual error terms from the market model are not cross-sectionally independent [i.e., $\text{Cov}\left(\varepsilon_{it}, \varepsilon_{jt}\right) \neq 0$], the equalities in equation (17.59) do not hold.

When information about individual assets contained in the active portfolio is unknown but information of the active portfolio as a whole is known, the previous substituted equations (17.49a) through (17.55a) should be used to determine the investment weights. Suppose that an investor wants to allocate his or her wealth into a hedge fund (A), an index fund (m), and Treasury bill (f). In this case, the investor cannot be expected to know much about the individual assets in the hedge fund. The composition of the hedge fund must be regarded as given. Thus, the investor needs to determine the optimal allocation in the hedge fund, the index fund, and the Treasury bill. Their optimal weights can be determined by equations (17.49a), (17.51a), and (17.52a), respectively.

EXAMPLE 17.1

Suppose there are five stocks to be actively managed and a passively managed market index, the S&P500. The mean return and variance of the S&P500 index are $E(r_m) = 0.0089$ and $\sigma^2_m = 0.000616$, and the risk-free rate of return

(Continued)

EXAMPLE 17.1 (*Continued*)

is $r_f = 0.0024$. In this example, we determined the optimal weights for these five stocks to achieve a given target expected return of $\mu_p^* = 0.012$.

> Step 1. We estimate the parameters α_i, β_i, and $\sigma_{\varepsilon i}^2$ in the market model for each of the five stocks. The estimates are shown in Table 17.5.

TABLE 17.5 Basic Characteristics for Five Stocks and S&P500

	Stocks contained in the active portfolio A					S&P500
	1	2	3	4	5	
Mean return, $E(r_i)$	0.0096	0.0196	0.0077	0.0113	0.0144	0.0089
Alpha, α_i	0.0018	0.0119	−0.0019	0.0056	0.0032	0.0000
Beta, β_i	0.845	0.805	1.109	0.497	1.361	1.000
Residual variance, $\sigma_{\varepsilon i}^2$	0.0029	0.0022	0.0017	0.0012	0.0019	–

> Step 2. We compute the (normalized) weights of individual assets to be contained in the active portfolio through equation (17.50). Note that $w_A = \sum_{i=1}^{5}\left(\alpha_i/\sigma_{\varepsilon_i}^2\right) = 11.263$. The (normalized) weights for the five stocks for the active portfolio A are shown in Table 17.6.

TABLE 17.6 Investment Weights for Five Stocks for the Active Portfolio A

	Investment weights for stocks contained in the active portfolio A					$\sum_{i=1}^{5} \overset{\circ}{w_i}$
	1	2	3	4	5	
$\overset{\circ}{w_i}$	0.055	0.480	−0.099	0.414	0.150	1.000

> Step 3. Compute the expected return of the active portfolio A based on the weights obtained in step 2.

$$E\left(r_A\right) = \sum_{i=1}^{5} \overset{\circ}{w_i}\, E(r_i) = (0.055)\,(0.0096) + \cdots + (0.150)\,(0.0144)$$

$$= 0.0160$$

> Step 4. For the tangency portfolio, determine the (normalized) weights of the active portfolio and the index portfolio using equations (17.55) and (17.56).

$$\overset{\circ}{w_A} = \left[\sum_{i=1}^{K} \frac{\alpha_i}{\sigma_{\varepsilon_i}^2}\right] \Bigg/ \left\{\frac{\left[E(r_m) - r_f\right]}{\sigma_m^2} + \sum_{i=1}^{K}\left(\frac{(1-\beta_i)\alpha_i}{\sigma_{\varepsilon_i}^2}\right)\right\}$$

$$= 11.263/\,(10.552 + 3.017) = 0.830$$

$$\overset{\circ}{w_m} = 1 - \overset{\circ}{w_A} = 1 - 0.830 = 0.170$$

EXAMPLE 17.1 (*Continued*)

Then, the expected return of the tangency portfolio is

$$E\left(r_q\right) = w_A^\circ E\left(r_A\right) + w_m^\circ E(r_m) = 0.830 \times 0.0160 + 0.170 \times 0.0089$$
$$= 0.0148$$

Step 5. Determine the weights of the tangency portfolio (w_q) and the risk-free (w_f) at a given level of the target expected return. Because the target expected return is $\mu_p^* = 0.012$, set

$$\mu_p^* = w_q E\left(r_q\right) + w_f r_f \Rightarrow 0.012 = w_q\left(0.0148\right) + \left(1 - w_q\right)\left(0.0024\right).$$

Solving the preceding equation with respect to w_q, we obtain $w_q = 0.774$ and

$$w_f = 1 - w_q = 0.226.$$

Step 6. Determine the actual weights of the active portfolio and the market portfolio for the target portfolio. Because the tangency portfolio is composed of the active portfolio and the index portfolio with the weights $w_A^\circ = 0.830$ and $w_m^\circ = 0.170$, the actual weights of the two portfolios are determined by allocating the total weight assigned to the tangency portfolio, according to $w_A^\circ = 0.830$ and $w_m^\circ = 0.170$. Their actual weights are

$$w_m = w_q w_m^\circ = (0.774)(0.170) = 0.132 \text{ and}$$
$$w_A = w_q w_A^\circ = (0.774)(0.830) = 0.642$$

Likewise, the actual weights for the five stocks are determined by allocating the total weight assigned to the active portfolio, $w_A = 0.642$, according to the normalized weights of the five stocks presented in Table 17.6. That is, the actual weights of the five stocks are determined by $w_i = w_A w_i^\circ$ for $i = 1, \ldots,$ 5. Thus,

$$w_1 = 0.642 \times 0.055 = 0.035, \quad w_2 = 0.642 \times 0.480 = 0.308$$

$$w_3 = 0.642 \times (-0.099) = -0.064,$$

$$w_4 = 0.642 \times 0.414 = 0.266, \quad w_5 = 0.642 \times 0.150 = 0.096.$$

EXAMPLE 17.2

What are the actual weights of the active portfolio, the index portfolio, and the risk-free asset, if the target expected return changes to $\mu_p^* = 0.010$?

As long as the composition of the active portfolio is unchanged, the tangency portfolio is the same. Thus, the steps 1 through 4 are the same.

(*Continued*)

EXAMPLE 17.2 (*Continued*)

Because the target return is earned from investing in the tangency portfolio and the risk-free asset,

$$\mu_p^* = w_q E\left(r_q\right) + w_f r_f \Rightarrow 0.010 = w_q\,(0.0148) + \left(1 - w_q\right)(0.0024).$$

Solving the preceding equation with respect to w_q, we obtain yields $w_q = 0.613$ and $w_f = 1 - w_q = 0.387$. Thus, the actual weights for the index portfolio and the active portfolio are $w_m = w_q w_m^{\circ} = (0.613)\,(0.170) = 0.104$, and $w_A = w_q w_A^{\circ} = (0.613)\,(0.830) = 0.509$.
The actual weights of the five stocks are

$$w_1 = 0.509 \times 0.055 = 0.028, \qquad w_2 = 0.509 \times 0.480 = 0.244$$

$$w_3 = 0.509 \times (-0.099) = -0.050,$$

$$w_4 = 0.509 \times 0.414 = 0.211, \qquad w_5 = 0.509 \times 0.150 = 0.076.$$

Before long, the arrival of new information will necessitate revising the optimal portfolio.

17.7   PORTFOLIO REVISION

After an optimal portfolio is selected and funds are invested, the need for portfolio revision arises almost immediately. The investment proportions that define an optimum portfolio (w_{it} for $i = 1, 2, \ldots, n$ assets) become suboptimal even if the investor's investment needs and wishes are identical over time because (1) cash dividends and interest income increase cash holdings, (2) some assets' actual weights wander away from their optimal values because of changing market prices, (3) of the risk classes of some assets change, and (4) some expected returns vary. Most these changes cause the set of investment opportunities (including the efficient frontier), as well as the location (in mean-variance space) of the current portfolio, to shift incrementally minute by minute. Thus, optimal portfolios need revising soon after they are purchased. This revision is necessary even if the portfolio owner's utility function is isoelastic (so that it is independent of the owner's level of wealth) and the owner experiences no change in preferences (so that the indifference map in risk-return space is stable). This situation is represented graphically in Figure 17.6.

17.7.1   Portfolio Revision Costs

In Figure 17.6 an initial portfolio at point C was selected from the opportunity set bounded by BCD based on the indifference map in risk-return space. Then a better opportunity set, denoted $EFHG$, subsequently became available. If there were a risk-free rate, it too could shift over time, resulting in changes in the location of the linear efficient frontier as well as in the composition of the tangent portfolio. Using the same indifference map, the portfolio manager could maximize expected utility

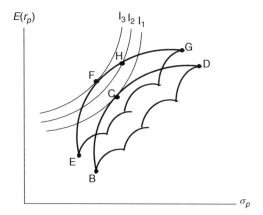

FIGURE 17.6 Known Indifference Map and
Changing Investment Opportunities

by revising portfolio *C* to become portfolio *F*. Purchasing the initial portfolio and later making the needed changes requires explicit knowledge of the indifference map. This approach can be suggested as a practical policy only if the person who owns the portfolio can consistently articulate sufficiently detailed investment objectives to allow the indifference map to be constructed. If the portfolio is owned by a group of people (for example, a mutual fund) or managed by a committee, it will be nearly impossible to delineate the preferences of the relevant group because community or social welfare functions cannot be derived.[30] Different people do not desire the same portfolio, because each person probably has a unique set of indifference curves. For example, a timid investor might initially prefer a portfolio nearer to *B* while an aggressive investor might simultaneously prefer a portfolio nearer to *D* in Figure 17.6. Investors select the point where their highest-valued indifference curve is just tangent to the current efficient frontier in order to maximize their expected utility. Clearly, not all points on the efficient frontier yield the same expected utility to an investor. Therefore, a portfolio with multiple owners, such as a mutual fund, should not be content just to be efficient. If a mutual fund was originally at point *C* but over time changed to point *F*, some shareholders in that fund might sell their shares. They then might buy shares in a different fund that would place them closer to point *H*, which is in the same risk class as *C*, but has higher expected return and could be even more desirable than *F*.

Mutual fund shareholders, in general, do not desire a fund that changes risk classes over time. This is because shareholders can come closer to maximizing their expected utility if their mutual fund buys efficient portfolios over time that are in some desired risk class. Thus, the objective of managing a portfolio with multiple owners becomes one of simply maximizing expected return in a "preferred risk habitat." In the initial formation of such a portfolio, management should select and publicize the risk class in which they plan to maintain the portfolio so that investors whose preferences concur will be attracted to investing and ownership. It appears that this is what is occurring (as a first approximation) when some mutual funds promote themselves as aggressive growth funds, while some competing income funds can succeed by stressing the receipt of cash dividend income and limited risk exposure.

Although the manager of a portfolio that has multiple owners can usually maximize the owners' expected utility by seeking to maximize the portfolio's expected return in some preferred risk habitat, other problems related to portfolio revision arise. The portfolio revision process is further complicated by certain costs that economists call market imperfections, because they keep supply and demand from functioning smoothly. Some market imperfections that cause the "real world" to differ from an economically idealistic model include the following revision costs:

- Commissions for buying and selling securities
- Transfer taxes for buying and/or selling securities
- Capital gains taxes that must be paid when capital gains are realized
- Other revision costs, which include:
    - Data analysis expenses, such as those incurred in performing security analysis
    - Portfolio construction and selection costs, such as computer expenses
    - Professional and clerical salaries for the portfolio manager's staff

As a result of these unavoidable cash outlays, portfolio revision should not be done too frequently. Instead, portfolio revision should be undertaken on a limited basis using some objective cost-benefit criterion to determine when it is profitable to revise.

17.7.2 Controlled Transition

Smith (1971) has suggested a policy he called "controlled transition" to manage a multiperiod portfolio. Smith's controlled transition procedure is less costly than a procedure of completely revising the portfolio as it periodically becomes inefficient. The policy of complete transition entails recomputation of the efficient frontier each time the security analyst's latest expectations indicate that the currently held portfolio is suboptimal. The resulting revision will probably entail liquidating at least part of the portfolio and reinvesting the proceeds. Such a policy will typically result in significant revision costs.

In contrast to complete transition, Smith's policy of controlled transition is a heuristic policy that will tolerate suboptimal portfolios on a continuing basis and will result in fewer portfolio revisions. This transition process proceeds as follows.

First, the weights of each security currently held, along with the corresponding number of shares, are determined. These can be denoted by vectors w_0 and N_0, respectively, with the values for individual securities being denoted w_0^i and n_0^i, respectively. Second, the weights and share numbers of the target portfolio needs to be identified. These are denoted w_* and N_* (or individually w_*^i and n_*^i), respectively. Here the target portfolio is the new optimal portfolio that, in the absence of market imperfections, would be selected by the portfolio manager.

Depending on the circumstances, this may be the portfolio on the new efficient frontier that has the same standard deviation as the currently held portfolio. If risk-free borrowing and lending are available, it may be the corresponding new tangent portfolio.[31] Third, each security that has $n_0^i - n_*^i \neq 0$ is evaluated marginally in terms of its impact on the portfolio's expected return and revision costs. This is accomplished in the following three steps:

1. For stock i (assuming $n_0^i - n_*^i \neq 0$), the change from n_0^i to n_*^i is evaluated by assuming it is the only change made in the portfolio. New portfolio weights, denoted w_*^i, are calculated. The dollar increase in the resulting portfolio's expected value is calculated as $M\left[E\left(w_1^i\right) - E\left(w_0^i\right)\right] = B_1^i$, where M denotes the current market value of the portfolio weights and E is an expected return operator. The notation w_1^i indicates that in the first iteration, the number of shares of only security i (n_1^i) has changed from the initial holdings of n_0^i.[32] Thus, $E\left(w_1^i\right)$ and $E\left(w_0\right)$ denote the expected return of the portfolios associated with the weight vectors w_1^i and w_0^i, respectively. The dollar costs of this revision are also calculated and are denoted C_1^i. This procedure is repeated for each stock that has $n_0^i - n_1^i \neq 0$.
2. The benefit-cost ratio B_1^i/C_1^i is calculated for each i. The ratio with the maximum value indicates the first revision to be made. If this maximum value is less than one, then no revisions are to be made, because marginal costs exceed marginal benefits. Accordingly, the procedure ends.
3. Treat the "pseudo" portfolio identified in step 2 as if it were the currently held portfolio. Repeat step 1, calculating new weights w_2^i and new values of B_2^i and C_2^i. Repeat step 2, and if the maximum B_2^i/C_2^i is greater than 1, make that revision and again go back to step 1 and perform another iteration. The maximum cost-benefit ratio in step 2 will eventually decline to less than one. At that point, the final optimal portfolio will have been identified. This portfolio will be held until it is time for the next periodic revision, at which time it will be similarly reevaluated.

Figure 17.7 shows a currently held inefficient portfolio at point A. Assuming that σ_A is the desired risk class, portfolio B is the target portfolio (if a risk-free asset

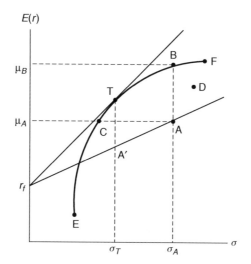

FIGURE 17.7 Portfolio Revision Possibilities with Controlled Transition

is assumed to exist, then T is the target). The impact of inserting new securities one by one into inefficient portfolio A is determined by calculating the resulting portfolios' expected returns and risks as the candidate securities are introduced and evaluated. Of these portfolio revisions, the one that offers the largest expected marginal net benefit should be selected at each iteration. As long as these expected benefits are positive, successive iterations are continually made until ultimately either B is reached or further benefits become nonpositive.

One problem that exists with this procedure, assuming that r_f does not exist, is that certain changes may increase both the expected return and risk of the portfolio. Any changes resulting in a new dominant portfolio within the triangular figure bounded by ABC in Figure 17.7 will be preferred by all risk-averse investors. However, following Smith's procedure, the resulting new portfolio may be outside this region, such as point D, and may not be preferred to A by risk-averse investors. Of course, assuming that r_f exists means that any change that creates a portfolio plotting above the line r_fA is desirable, because borrowing and lending can be employed to form a portfolio in the same risk class as A. That is, in Figure 17.7, lending an appropriate amount of money at r_f, combined with purchasing D, will result in a new portfolio plotting directly above A.

Fisher (1975) provided a somewhat similar approach to portfolio revision by having the portfolio manager use estimates of each security's risk parameters, together with the current portfolio's composition, to solve for the estimates of the expected returns of the individual securities that would make the current portfolio mean-variance efficient. With this information, the portfolio manager can compare his or her expected return estimates with the previous input statistics and alter the current portfolio one security at a time, where the sequential order of changes is based on the size of the discrepancies in expected returns. In the process the transactions costs incurred by each change could be considered. When the transactions costs from the last change under consideration are greater than the corresponding benefits, no further changes are considered.

17.7.3 The Attainable Efficient Frontier

As a result of portfolio revision costs, it is not possible for a revised portfolio to attain the true efficient frontier along the curve ECBF in Figure 17.8. Instead, the attainable efficient frontier along the curve $E'C'B'F'$ represents optimum portfolios that can be obtained realistically. The vertical difference between the unconstrained efficient frontier curve ECBF and the attainable efficient frontier $E'C'B'F'$ equals the revision costs stated as a percentage of the portfolio's total assets.

In situations such as the one depicted in Figure 17.8, current portfolio A should be revised to attain point B'. In contrast, if the current portfolio is A'', no revisions should be made, even though A'' is inefficient relative to the unconstrained efficient frontier. Portfolio revisions should occur as often as they are possible according to the controlled transition policy: This may be a month, a quarter, or perhaps even longer after an optimum portfolio is originally purchased.[33] There is no single optimum time schedule for portfolio revision.

17.7.4 A Turnover-Constrained Approach

Schreiner (1980) argues that revision models based on dollar amounts of revision costs are "impractical as to both computation and implementation." Furthermore,

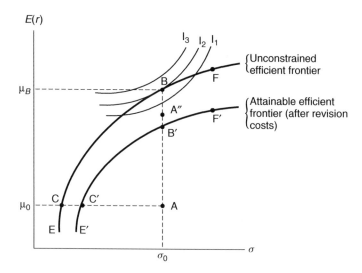

FIGURE 17.8 Portfolio Revision Possibilities with an Attainable Efficient Frontier

the use of approximations can be complex. As an alternative, he proposes a different approach that is based on the concept of turnover rate (defined as the smaller of purchases or sales during a period, divided by the average value of the portfolio over the period). Mathematically, the portfolio turnover rate (PTR) can be expressed as:

$$\text{PTR} = \frac{(P + S - NI)/2}{(\text{NAV}_B + \text{NAV}_E)/2} \tag{17.61}$$

where P denotes total purchases of securities during the period, S denotes total sales of securities during the period, NI denotes the absolute net value of any cash inflow or outflow to the portfolio during the period, and NAV_B and NAV_E denote the beginning-of-period and end-of-period net asset values (NAV) of the portfolio, respectively.[34]

The turnover approach of Schreiner involves constraining the portfolio turnover rate when the decision on the composition of a new optimal portfolio is made. For example, given a revised expected return vector and variance-covariance matrix, the Markowitz model efficient portfolio with expected return of μ_p^* will be the solution w^* to the following quadratic programming (QP) problem:

$$\text{Minimize } w'\Sigma w \tag{17.62}$$

$$\text{subject to } w'E = \mu_p^*$$

$$w'l = 1$$

$$\text{PTR} \leq B$$

$$w \geq 0$$

where Σ is the covariance matrix of assets, w is the weight vector, E is the expected return vector, l is the vector of ones, and B is the upper bound on the portfolio turnover rate; otherwise, this problem is identical to the problem stated in Chapter 6.

The turnover constraint can be expressed as follows, letting w_i^- denote the known current inefficient portfolio weight for security i, and I_i denote a binary variable that assumes a value of $+1$ when $w_i > w_i^-$ and -1 when $w_i < w_i^-$ (w_i is simply the element in row i of w),

$$\frac{1}{2}\left[\sum_{i=1}^{n} I_i\left(w_i - w_i^-\right)\right] \leq B \qquad (17.63)$$

Incorporating this constraint into problem (17.62) is complicated by the fact that the value of I_i depends on the solution for w_i. However, Schreiner shows how this can readily be handled in utilizing Markowitz's (1959, App. A) critical line algorithm.

Because the amount of portfolio turnover is closely linked to the amount of the associated revision costs, by constraining turnover the portfolio manager is, in effect, constraining revision costs. Noting that the solution to problem (17.62) can easily be determined, Schreiner advocates finding the set of solutions for varying levels of B. Then the portfolio manager can estimate the dollar amount associated with the actual turnover corresponding to each level of B. The determination of the optimal revised portfolio can ultimately be based on consideration of the dollar amount of revision costs and the dollar value of the portfolio, as well as expected returns and standard deviations of returns.

17.8   SUMMARY AND CONCLUSIONS

The discrete-time single-period mean-variance portfolio selection model was shown to be applicable in a multiperiod setting under certain circumstances. Two alternative multiperiod portfolio objectives were considered: (1) maximize the expected utility of terminal wealth of a portfolio from which no intermediate withdrawals or deposits were made, and (2) maximize the expected utility of a series of consumption-investment decisions that occur over several periods. The first multiperiod portfolio objective can be achieved by selecting myopic single-period efficient portfolios if it is assumed that (a) the investor has positive but diminishing marginal utility of wealth, (b) the investor has an isoelastic utility function, and (c) the single-period rates of return are normally distributed and independent of prior period returns.

In order to achieve the second multiperiod portfolio objective by acting myopically, the following assumptions must be added: (d) The consumer-investor's tastes are not affected by the state of the world, (e) the consumer-investor acts as if future consumption and investment opportunities are known, and (f) the utility of consumption in every period is separable from the utility of consumption in other periods.

The nature of these last three assumptions undermines somewhat the conclusions that can be drawn from the more general consumption-investment problem. However, in an approximate sense these assumptions suggest that mean-variance analysis is a useful procedure for single-period and multiperiod portfolio management problems.

Transactions costs were taken into consideration and, combined with the necessity of revising portfolios to maintain optimality, these market imperfections were shown to preclude attainment of the true efficient frontier. However, a policy of controlled revision to maximize a portfolio's expected return in some preferred risk class was suggested as a practical procedure that can maintain near-optimality over multiple periods. Alternatively, a second practical procedure that constraints portfolio turnover was suggested as a means of maintaining near-optimality.

APPENDIX: PROOFS FOR SOME RATIOS FROM ACTIVE PORTFOLIOS

This appendix provides proofs that some ratio from an active portfolio equals the sum of the ratios of the individual assets contained in the active portfolio.

A17.1   Proof for $\alpha_A/\sigma_{\varepsilon_A}^2 = \sum_{i=1}^{K} (\alpha_i/\sigma_{\varepsilon_i}^2)$

The intercept (or the Jensen measure) of the market model for portfolio A is the weighted average of the intercepts of all individual assets contained in the portfolio. That is, $\alpha_A = \sum_{i=1}^{K} (w_i\alpha_i)$. We let

$$H = \sum_{i=1}^{K} \frac{\alpha_i}{\sigma_{\varepsilon_i}^2} \tag{A17.1}$$

Then, from equations (17.50) and (A17.1),

$$\alpha_A = \sum_{i=1}^{K} w_i\alpha_i = \sum_{i=1}^{K} \left[\frac{(\alpha_i/\sigma_{\varepsilon_i}^2)}{H}\right]\alpha_i = \left(\frac{1}{H}\right)\sum_{i=1}^{K}\left(\frac{\alpha_i^2}{\sigma_{\varepsilon_i}^2}\right) \tag{A17.2}$$

because the weight for asset i equals $w_i = (\alpha_i/\sigma_{\varepsilon_i}^2)/H$ from equation (17.50). Assuming that the residuals are independent across securities, the residual variance from the market model for portfolio A is

$$\sigma_{\varepsilon_A}^2 = \sum_{i=1}^{K} w_i^2\sigma_{\varepsilon_i}^2 = \sum_{i=1}^{K}\left[\frac{(\alpha_i/\sigma_{\varepsilon_i}^2)}{H}\right]^2\sigma_{\varepsilon_i}^2 = \left(\frac{1}{H^2}\right)\sum_{i=1}^{K}\left(\frac{\alpha_i^2}{\sigma_{\varepsilon_i}^2}\right) \tag{A17.3}$$

Thus, the ratio of α_A to $\sigma_{\varepsilon_A}^2$ is

$$\frac{\alpha_A}{\sigma_{\varepsilon_A}^2} = H = \sum_{i=1}^{K} \frac{\alpha_i}{\sigma_{\varepsilon_i}^2} \tag{A17.4}$$

A17.2   Proof for $(\alpha_A\beta_A/\sigma_{\varepsilon_A}^2) = \sum_{i=1}^{K} (\alpha_i\beta_i/\sigma_{\varepsilon_i}^2)$

From equation (A17.2), we have

$$\alpha_A\beta_A = \left(\sum_{i=1}^{K} w_i\alpha_i\right)\left(\sum_{i=1}^{K} w_i\beta_i\right) = \left(\sum_{i=1}^{K}\left[\frac{(\alpha_i/\sigma_{\varepsilon_i}^2)}{H}\right]\alpha_i\right)\left(\sum_{i=1}^{K}\left[\frac{(\alpha_i/\sigma_{\varepsilon_i}^2)}{H}\right]\beta_i\right)$$

$$= \left(\frac{1}{H^2}\right)\left[\sum_{i=1}^{K}\left(\frac{\alpha_i^2}{\sigma_{\varepsilon_i}^2}\right)\right]\left[\sum_{i=1}^{K}\left(\frac{\alpha_i\beta_i}{\sigma_{\varepsilon_i}^2}\right)\right] \tag{A17.5}$$

Thus, using equations (A17.5) and (A17.3),

$$\frac{\alpha_A \beta_A}{\sigma_{\varepsilon_A}^2} = \sum_{i=1}^{K} \left(\frac{\alpha_i \beta_i}{\sigma_{\varepsilon_i}^2} \right) \qquad (A17.6)$$

It can be similarly shown that

$$\frac{\alpha_A \left(1 - \beta_A \right)}{\sigma_{\varepsilon_A}^2} = \sum_{i=1}^{K} \left(\frac{\alpha_i \left(1 - \beta_i \right)}{\sigma_{\varepsilon_i}^2} \right) \qquad (A17.7)$$

A17.3   Proof for $\left(\alpha_A^2 / \sigma_{\varepsilon_A}^2 \right) = \sum_{i=1}^{K} \left(\alpha_i^2 / \sigma_{\varepsilon_i}^2 \right)$

Similar to equation (A17.5),

$$\alpha_A^2 = \left(\sum_{i=1}^{K} w_i \alpha_i \right)^2 = \left(\sum_{i=1}^{K} \left[\frac{\left(\alpha_i / \sigma_{\varepsilon_i}^2 \right)}{H} \right] \alpha_i \right)^2$$

$$= \left(\frac{1}{H^2} \right) \left[\sum_{i=1}^{K} \left(\frac{\alpha_i^2}{\sigma_{\varepsilon_i}^2} \right) \right]^2 \qquad (A17.8)$$

Using equations (A17.8) and (A17.3) results in

$$\frac{\alpha_A^2}{\sigma_{\varepsilon_A}^2} = \sum_{i=1}^{K} \left(\frac{\alpha_i^2}{\sigma_{\varepsilon_i}^2} \right) \qquad (A17.9)$$

NOTES

1. See Feller (1968, 249).
2. There is another model of stock prices that has been linked to discounted dividend models of stock prices. This model, called a *martingale model with drift d*, has $E\left(p_{t+1} | \theta_t \right) = \left(1 + d \right) p_t$ or, equivalently, $E\left(r_{t+1} | \theta_t \right) = d$ (see Samuelson, 1973).
3. Returns cannot follow a random walk if prices do because an intertemporally constant distribution of price changes implies a changing distribution of returns.
4. The evidence for weak-form efficiency has to do with tests of mechanical trading rules based on past price data and tests about the statistical nature of price changes and returns. See Fama (1970b) for a summary. The primary evidence against strong-form efficiency has to do with the returns earned by insiders. See Copeland and Weston (1984, chap. 10) for details. For an interesting discussion of the testability of market efficiency as defined by Fama (1970b), see LeRoy (1976) and Fama (1976b).
5. It is logical to assume that the more observations used to estimate the variance-covariance matrix and expected return vector, the greater the likelihood that nonstationarity exists in the data. Thus, although more data are preferred, there is a limit imposed by the estimation errors introduced by nonstationarity. Early research by Gonedes (1973), for example, suggested that roughly seven years of monthly data be used. However, in order to have a nonsingular variance-covariance matrix, there must be more observations per security than the number of securities being evaluated. Thus, if 100 securities are to

be evaluated, at least 101 periodic observations are required. It might seem convenient simply to use weekly observations over seven years instead of monthly observations, but this introduces the potential problem of nonsynchronous trading (see Scholes and Williams, 1977; Dimson, 1979; and Fowler and Rorke, 1983). For a further discussion, together with a simple test for stationarity, see Roll (1981).

6. All summations are over i from one to n where n denotes the number of risky securities being considered.

7. The value of p_{i0}^* (or p_{i1}^*) could be determined by the use of a dividend discount model (see Fouse 1976, 1977; and Lanstein and Jahnke, 1979).

8. This can have implications for diversification, however, which will be discussed later in this chapter. For a discussion of market timing strategies, see Grant (1978).

9. For an evaluation of the accuracy of one set of market forecasts, see Lakonishok (1980). For alternative methods of forecasting market returns, see Morgan (1978), Merton (1980), and Smith (1982). Merton also presents an admittedly simple estimation model for σ_m^2.

10. A similar study was conducted by Levy (1971).

11. These are product–moment correlation coefficients; rank-order correlation coefficients produced similar values. Blume (1971) also calculated the correlation coefficients using the betas of portfolios of stocks and noted a striking increase in their magnitude. For example, for portfolios of 10 securities the correlation coefficient ranged from 0.89 to 0.94, and for portfolios of 50 securities it ranged from 0.98 to 0.99. For further analysis, see Alexander and Chervany (1980).

12. In a subsequent paper, Blume (1975) noted that this tendency of beta to drift toward one was not due to order bias, which was described in Chapter 13 and referred to the tendency of high (low) estimated betas to have positive (negative) measurement error. Francis (1979) argued that the primary cause of a change in an asset's beta is a change in the correlation of the asset's returns with the market portfolio's returns.

13. The variance of the OLS beta estimate, $\text{Var}\left(\hat{\beta}_i\right)$, is estimated as $\hat{\sigma}_{\varepsilon_i}^2 / \sum \left(r_{mt} - \bar{r}_m\right)^2$; $\hat{\sigma}_{\varepsilon_i}^2$ is the estimator of the residual variance from the market model and the summation is over the estimation period.

14. These two parameters can be viewed, in Bayesian parlance, as the prior information available.

15. At the 0.05 level of significance, 52 percent of the tests conducted over two 300-month periods indicated that the associated firms had Markov betas; similarly, 15 percent of the tests conducted over eight 75-month periods indicated that the associated firms had Markov betas.

16. Note that if $\rho = 1$, this model collapses to the random walk model, and if $\rho = 0$, then it collapses to the Theil model.

17. Fabozzi and Francis (1977) suggested another beta nonstationarity model specifying that a firm's beta assumed one of two values, depending on whether the market was currently bullish or bearish. The authors found no substantive evidence to support this model. Later, Francis and Fabozzi (1979) modified this model to see if a firm's beta was related to the contemporaneous phase of the business cycle and found some, albeit weak, evidence of an association between the two. Other research in this area has been done by Francis (1975), Gooding and O'Malley (1977), and Kim and Zumwalt (1979).

18. Kim and Kon (1996, 1999) also examined nonstationarity of mean return and variance of individual stocks.

19. Beaver, Kettler, and Scholes (1970) related the beta of a stock to seven fundamental firm variables. These variables are dividend payout, asset growth, leverage, liquidity, asset size (total assets), earnings variability (standard deviation of the earnings-price ratio), and accounting beta (the slope coefficient of the time-series regression of the earnings-price ratios of the firm on the average of earnings-price ratios of the market. To

relate fundamental variables to the beta, Thompson (1976) reviewed 43 variables, while Rosenberg and Marathe (1975) reviewed 101 variables.

20. Since BKS, there have been several studies that investigate the link between various accounting risk measures (dubbed ARMs) and beta. Elgers and Murray (1982) present a study and cite some of the more prominent studies. Foster (1978b, Chap. 9) also cites some of the more prominent studies, such as Thompson (1976).

21. Fabozzi and Francis (1979a) have also shown how industry factors, together with certain financial ratios, are determinants of beta.

22. See Harrington (1983) for a description and evaluation of these forecasts. Schneller (1983) suggests that for well-diversified portfolios, it probably is not cost effective to purchase and use these "better betas."

23. The argument for decomposing the error term of the market model into two components to capture the extra market covariance risk (as discussed in Chapter 8) can be viewed as an argument in support of multiple-index models (see Rosenberg and Marathe, 1976).

24. For other interesting extensions of Evans and Archer, see Wagner and Lau (1971) and the contrasting articles by Johnson and Shannon (1974) and Bloomfield, Leftwich, and Long (1977). Elton and Gruber (1977) argue that significant reductions in risk can be obtained by adding stocks beyond 15 to a portfolio.

25. Another interesting aspect of diversification is to consider the addition of securities other than common stocks, such as corporate bonds and preferred stocks.

26. There are also political risks associated with investing in foreign stocks. These risks include such things as exchange controls and expropriation, and are not considered here.

27. Jacquillat and Solnik (1978) compared investing in U.S.-based multinational firms with investing in foreign firms in terms of their relative effects on portfolio risk. They found that these multinationals performed similarly to "uninternational" U.S. firms and, thus, were incapable of providing the investor with risk-reduction benefits comparable to foreign firms. However, Agmon and Lessard (1977) have a contradictory view and argue that U.S. investors should consider multinationals when diversifying their portfolios.

28. Because it is assumed in using equation (17.8) that $\mathrm{Cov}\left(\varepsilon_{it}, \varepsilon_{jt}\right) = 0$ if $i \neq j$, the existence of industry or group effects is ignored here. Frankfurter and Phillips (1980) present a method for portfolio construction and selection that does consider such effects.

29. The initial objective is to determine the composition of the tangency portfolio. Thus, any level of expected return that is greater than the risk-free rate will suffice for this purpose, because the resulting efficient portfolio will simply be a mix of the tangency portfolio and risk-free asset.

30. For a discussion of the problems associated with the construction of group preference orderings, the interested reader is directed to Henderson and Quandt (1980, particularly sec. 11.6).

31. In Figure 17.7, the target portfolios corresponding to these two sets of circumstances are B and T, respectively, where A is the currently held portfolio.

32. In turn, this means that all elements of the proportion vector have changed. Furthermore, if the number of shares n_1^i has increased, Smith's procedure implicitly assumes that the necessary funds are gotten by borrowing at the risk-free rate; similarly, if the number of shares n_1^i has decreased, the excess funds are implicitly assumed to be invested at the risk-free rate.

33. See Johnson and Shannon (1974) for a study presenting empirical evidence that revising an efficient portfolio each quarter results in significantly better performance than buying and holding an initially efficient portfolio. However, Bloomfield, Leftwich, and Long (1977) take issue with this finding.

34. Schreiner noted that this definition of PTR is in accord with the method prescribed by the SEC for use by mutual funds.

CHAPTER 18

Portfolio Performance Evaluation

Most professional money managers provide material that describes their portfolio services in a flattering manner. Potential investors should beware of such promotional materials. Investors should investigate before they invest.

An abundance of widely accepted folklore is used in the investments industry. When erroneous beliefs are discredited and folklore is replaced with scientific methods portfolio analysis will advance. In the meantime, loanable funds will be misallocated and research expenditures will be squandered on charlatans.

To evaluate the investment performance of portfolios, we introduce Nobel Prize–winning economic models. Then, empirical data from mutual funds is used to populate the economic models with data and demonstrate how to analyze the successes and failures of professional investment managers. The performances of *open-end investment companies* are evaluated. *Mutual funds*, as they are nicknamed, are studied because (1) their advertisements promising investors the benefit of "professional money management" raise questions as to whether the services are worth their price, and (2) the Investment Company Act of 1940 and the Securities Exchange Commission (SEC) require that mutual funds' data be made readily accessible to the public. U.S. securities law is based on the legal concept of "full disclosure". The phrase full disclosure refers to the idea that financial transparency will reduce deception and facilitate better allocation of the nation's resources. No other country in the world requires as much transparency from its financial services industry as the United States.

18.1 MUTUAL FUND RETURNS

The first step in evaluating the performance of open-end investment companies is to calculate their one-period rates of return. The returns from mutual fund shares are computed from their net asset value per share (NAV). NAV is an important concept, because U.S. securities law requires that all (open-end) mutual fund shares must be purchased and sold at their NAV per share. A portfolio's NAV per share at time t is defined as

$$\text{NAV}_t = \frac{\text{Market value of all assets at } t - \text{Portfolio's total liabilities at } t}{\text{Number of shares outstanding at time } t} \qquad (18.1)$$

Because most mutual funds do not use financial leverage (borrowing), portfolios' liabilities are usually very close to zero (namely, some utility bills, rent, the payroll) when stated as a percentage of the assets managed. U.S. securities laws mandating full disclosure (transparency) require every U.S. mutual fund to compute its NAV every business (trading) day and distribute it free to newspapers for publishing.

Mutual fund investors receive three types of income from their shares: (1) unrealized gains or losses on securities carried forward (not yet liquidated) in the portfolio—this appears as a change in the fund's (NAV) for period t; (2) disbursements of interest and cash dividends from securities in the fund's portfolio to the fund's investors during period t; and (3) disbursements to investors of capital gains realized when securities are sold during period t. The holding period return (HPR) from a mutual fund share, denoted HPR_t, is calculated as follows.

$$\text{HPR}_t = \frac{\left(\text{NAV}_t - \text{NAV}_{t-1}\right) + d_t + g_t}{\text{NAV}_{t-1}} \tag{18.2}$$

where $\text{NAV}_t - \text{NAV}_{t-1}$ = change in the fund's net asset value per share (NAV) for time period t, this is unrealized gains and losses that show up in a mutual fund's book value

d_t = disbursements of interest and cash dividends for period t

g_t = disbursements of capital gains realized when securities are sold for period t

The numerator contains the investor's income. The quantity $\left(\text{NAV}_t - \text{NAV}_{t-1}\right)$ may be positive or negative; it measures the change in one share's net asset value per share (unrealized changes in the book value of assets not sold) during the holding period. The denominator equals the purchase price at the beginning of the holding period, NAV_{t-1}. These portfolio HPRs are equivalent to the HPRs from common stocks defined by equation (1.1).

18.2 PORTFOLIO PERFORMANCE ANALYSIS IN THE GOOD OLD DAYS

Long before mutual funds were legally formalized by the Investment Company Act of 1940, it was recognized that most diversified investment portfolios performed better during bull market periods than they did when bear market conditions prevailed. To smooth over the alternating bull-bear market effects, some financial analysts tabulated the average rates of return computed over a "representative sample period" for a list of candidate portfolios. The most proficient financial analysts defined a *representative sample period* to be long enough to include both bullish years and bearish years. After the average rates of return from different mutual funds were tabulated and compared, the financial analyst would usually recommend investing in the portfolios that earned the highest *average* rate of return. The most proficient portfolio analysts bragged that their investment advice was better advice than the advice from the myopic investment advisors who simply recommended investing in the portfolio that earned the highest rate of return last year. This one-parameter (rate of return) investment management procedure constituted the prevailing wisdom until 1952, when Markowitz introduced a new portfolio theory that considered both the rate of return and scientific risk estimates.[1] However, even after 1952, millions of investors that are unaware of Markowitz portfolio theory still endeavor to invest in the portfolio that had the highest rate of return last year.

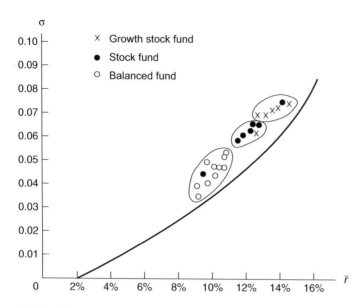

FIGURE 18.1 Farrar's Efficient Frontier Computed from 23 Mutual Funds

During the early 1960s Donald Farrar published one of the first empirical studies of Markowitz's revolutionary new portfolio theory.[2] Farrar used Markowitz's new portfolio theory to consider return and risk together in the same graph. Farrar gathered monthly historical observations from 1946 to 1956 on 23 mutual funds, tabulated the rates of return for each portfolio, computed average return and risk statistics for each mutual fund, and then delineated the Markowitz efficient frontier that could be derived from these 23 data points. Figure 18.1 shows that all of the 23 mutual funds lie near, but not on, the Markowitz-efficient frontier. Farrar reported:

> *The plots do seem to follow closely along the frontier of optimal portfolios. Even more encouraging, however, is the tendency of the funds to cluster along the boundary in almost perfect groups of balanced funds, stock funds, and growth funds, respectively.*[3]

Farrar's scientific findings were among the first to pinpoint the fact that none of the mutual funds performed in an impressive (Markowitz-efficient) manner. In 1965 Fama reported that rankings of 39 mutual funds' annual rates of return from year to year over 11 consecutive years appeared to be arrayed randomly from year to year.[4] Francis and Archer (1971) opined that none of the mutual funds were on the efficient frontier because they diversified superfluously.[5] Francis and Archer also observed that, although Farrar's analysis was impressive, it failed to produce a scientific ranking procedure that could be used to array the mutual funds in a risk-adjusted return framework. During the 1960s Jack L. Treynor, William F. Sharpe, and Michael C. Jensen filled this void by producing different scientific performance-ranking procedures.

18.3   CAPITAL MARKET THEORY ASSUMPTIONS

Financial economists require the assumptions listed next to help them develop the capital market theory presented in the preceding chapters. All the following assumptions are combined to create the capital market line (CML) and the security market line (SML), and the Treynor, Sharpe, and Jensen portfolio performance evaluation models introduced in this chapter.

- All market assets are infinitely divisible. This means that fractional shares of every asset may be purchased.
- Homogeneous expectations, also called *idealized uncertainty*, prevail. This assumption means that all investors visualize the same expected return, risk, and correlation statistics for each and every asset.
- An infinite amount of money can be borrowed or lent at one risk-free rate of interest.
- All investors use the same one-period investment horizon when making their investment decisions. As a result, capital market theory models only cover one time period.
- Taxes, commission expenses, and all the other transaction charges that are commonly charged for buying and selling securities do not exist. This is sometimes euphemistically referred to as the frictionless markets assumption.
- Inflation is zero and no change in the level of market interest rates is anticipated. Stated differently, the nation's central bank always pursues optimal monetary policies.
- The capital markets are in a static equilibrium in which supply equals demand for every asset and every liability.
- Lying on the Markowitz efficient frontier is a market portfolio that contains all assets in the world in the proportions in which they exist. All investors want to invest in this uniquely desirable portfolio (because it has the maximum attainable Sharpe ratio).

Some readers may become discouraged with a capital market theory that is rife with unrealistic assumptions. Actually, these assumptions are valuable contributors to the analysis, not liabilities. The assumptions provide a foundation on which a theory can be derived by applying the forces of economic logic and mathematics. Without these simplifying assumptions, the analysis would probably degenerate into inconclusive arguments. Given these assumptions, a capital market theory is derived that has incontestable conclusions and implications. As Milton Freidman has pointed out, the final test of a theory should be its predictive power, not the realism of its simplifying assumptions.[6] Nevertheless, it is comforting to know that when we discard some of the unrealistic simplifying assumptions, the theory or model retains impressive predictive powers.

18.4   SINGLE-PARAMETER PORTFOLIO PERFORMANCE MEASURES

As mentioned previously, in an effort to measure various aspects of the performance of investment portfolios, various models have been proposed.[7] The more sophisticated suggestions sought to take both the risk and the rate of return from a portfolio into consideration. Jack Treynor, William Sharpe, and Michael Jensen have developed models for portfolio performance measurement that consider both risk and return simultaneously and, at the same time, allow the desirability of the candidate portfolios to be ranked. In other words, each of the following models develops one ordinal number that can be used to unambiguously rank the performance of any number of different mutual funds and other investment portfolios.

18.4.1 Sharpe's Reward-to-Variability Ratio

William Sharpe extended a linear risk-return modeling technique developed earlier by a Nobel laureate named James Tobin.[8] Sharpe's model analyzes empirical statistics like the hypothetical data shown in Table 18.1. Sharpe's portfolio performance model won a Nobel Prize, too.

Sharpe subtracts from each fund's average rate of return, $\bar{r}$, an estimate of the riskless interest rate, r_f. The portion of the average holding period return (HPR) above the riskless interest rate is called a *risk premium*. The risk premium is also called an *excess return* because it measures the additional return the investor earns for investing in assets that have more than zero risk. Sharpe divided each portfolio's risk premium by the standard deviation of its returns, σ, a measure of the portfolio's total risk. Let S_p denote this ratio of risk premium per unit of risk from portfolio p.[9]

$$S_p = \frac{\text{Excess return (or risk premium)}}{\text{Total risk}} = \frac{\bar{r}_p - r_f}{\sigma_p} \qquad (18.3)$$

Sharpe's index of desirability was developed to compare and rank investment portfolios from different risk classes that have different average rates of return. Sharpe's ratio collapses both the risk and the return statistics into a single index number, S_p, that is suitable for ranking purposes. Table 18.2 contains the calculations of the Sharpe ratios for some of the hypothetical portfolios in Table 18.1. Forward-looking portfolio analysis can be accomplished by substituting the expected return and expected risk statistics, denoted $E(r)$ and $E(\sigma)$, in place of the historical values $\bar{r}$ and σ in equation (18.3).

Sharpe's reward-to-risk ratio for a risky asset measures the slope of a straight line in $(\sigma, \bar{r})$ space. Figure 18.2 illustrates the Sharpe ratios for three portfolios in

TABLE 18.1 Summary Statistics for Five Hypothetical Mutual Funds, or Similar Investment Portfolios

Portfolio	Average return $(\bar{r}_p)$	Standard deviation (σ_p)	Beta (β_p)	Correlation coefficient with the market
Alpha (A)	7%	3%	0.4	0.89
Beta (B)	10%	8%	1.0	0.91
Gamma (G)	11%	6%	0.8	0.90
Delta (D)	15%	13%	1.4	0.95
Epsilon (E)	18%	15%	1.6	0.88
S&P 500 (m)	12%	9%	1.0	1.00
Riskless rate (r_f)	3%	0%	0.0	0.00

TABLE 18.2 Calculating Sharpe's Ratios for Three Portfolios in Table 18.1

Portfolio	Sharpe ratio
Gamma (G)	$S_G = \dfrac{\bar{r}_G - r_f}{\sigma_G} = \dfrac{11 - 3}{6} = 1.33$
Delta (D)	$S_D = \dfrac{\bar{r}_D - r_f}{\sigma_D} = \dfrac{15 - 3}{13} = 0.92$
Epsilon (E)	$S_E = \dfrac{\bar{r}_E - r_f}{\sigma_E} = \dfrac{18 - 3}{15} = 1.00$
S&P 500 (m)	$S_m = \dfrac{\bar{r}_m - r_f}{\sigma_m} = \dfrac{12 - 3}{9} = 1.00$

Tables 18.1 and 18.2. The Figure shows that investors would prefer to invest in Gamma (G) to Epsilon (E) because combinations of G and the riskless asset give greater returns for the same level of risk than combinations of E and the riskless asset. Similarly, E is preferred to D. Thus, Gamma (G) is the most desirable investment, in terms of the Sharpe reward-to-risk ratio. Symbolically, $S_G > S_E > S_D$.

If Standard & Poor's 500 is viewed as a proxy for the market portfolio, its reward-to-risk ratio will proxy for the slope of the CML over the evaluation period. Any portfolio that plots above (below) the CML, thereby outperforming (underperforming) the market portfolio on a risk-adjusted basis, will have a reward-to-variability ratio greater (less) than the ratio for the market portfolio, as approximated by Standard & Poor's 500. Thus, S_p can also be used to measure performance relative to a simple-minded (no investment skill involved) benchmark like the S&P 500 Index. In the preceding example, in terms of the Sharpe ratio, portfolio G outperformed the market (m), portfolio D underperformed the market, and portfolio E performed just as well as the market.

Sharpe went on to calculate the Sharpe ratios for 34 mutual funds. Think of the Dow Jones Industrial Average (DJIA) as representing a naive buy-and-hold

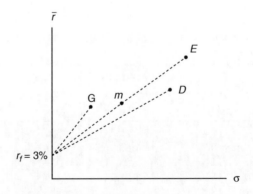

FIGURE 18.2 Illustration of Sharpe's Ranking Technique

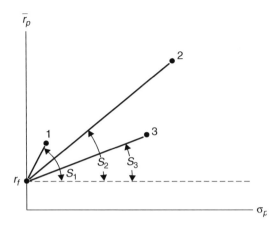

FIGURE 18.3 Reward-to-risk Ratios can be Used to Rank Portfolios from Different Risk Classes

investment strategy: Thinking this way allows us to use the DJIA as a standard of comparison for evaluating the performance of the actively managed professional portfolios. The introduction of Sharpe's model was exciting, and Sharpe's mutual fund findings were also interesting. He reported that the average Sharpe ratio for the 34 funds was 0.633, which is considerably below the 0.667 for the DJIA. Of the 34 funds that were analyzed, only 11 did better than (outperformed) the DJIA in Sharpe's ranking. Figure 18.3 shows how Sharpe's ratio is used to rank the performance of portfolios that are in different risk classes.

If a superior mutual fund existed, Sharpe was not able to detect it. Most of the 30 mutual funds earned an average return that is a little below that which would be achieved by investing in a portfolio made up from the 30 stocks in the DJIA. After deducting commissions and taxes, the net return the typical mutual fund pays to its shareholders is below what the investor could have averaged by naively buying and holding a mutual fund that indexed itself to a stock market index.

When Sharpe's findings were first published in 1966, some investors were naively swallowing the advertisements published by the mutual funds that proclaimed they achieved superior returns because they were actively managed by professional money managers. When Sharpe showed scientific evidence that, on average, a large proportion of the professionally managed mutual funds do not perform as well as a naive buy-and-hold strategy, many people were surprised. Some people erroneously jumped to the conclusion that Sharpe's financial findings must be incorrect. Sharpe's findings, that most mutual funds cannot outperform a naive buy-and-hold strategy, have been supported by other (unbiased) scholarly studies. As suggested earlier by Figure 18.1, none of the mutual funds discussed are Markowitz-efficient. Other models that were designed to evaluate investment performance scientifically are the topic of the remainder of this chapter.[10]

18.4.2 Treynor's Reward-to-Risk Ratio

In 1965, Jack Treynor suggested regressing the holding period returns (HPRs) from mutual funds, denoted r_p, onto the contemporaneous returns from a market index, denoted r_m.[11] That is, he suggested estimating the following model:

$$r_{pt} = \alpha_p + \beta_p r_{mt} + \varepsilon_{pt} \quad \text{for} \quad t = 1, \ldots, T \quad (18.4)$$

where α_p and β_p are the intercept and slope coefficients for portfolio p, and the regression's unexplained residuals for time period t are represented by ε_{pt}. Treynor called this regression line the characteristic line. More recently, the name "characteristic line" has been generalized to sometimes refer to regressions using excess returns, as will be shown in equation (18.10).

As mentioned in Chapter 12, the regression slope coefficient (β_p) in equation (18.4) is referred to as the portfolio's beta and is a measure of the *ex post* systematic risk of the portfolio, meaning that it is a measure of the historical responsiveness of the portfolio to changes in the market index. Furthermore, a portfolio's beta is the weighted average of the beta coefficients of the securities in the portfolio. Symbolically,

$$\beta_p = \text{Cov}\left(r_{pt}, r_{mt}\right)/\sigma_m^2 \quad (18.5)$$

$$= \sum_{i=1}^{n} w_i \left[\text{Cov}\left(r_{it}, r_{mt}\right)/\sigma_m^2\right]$$

$$= \sum_{i=1}^{n} w_i \beta_i$$

Thus, portfolios classified as balanced funds would generally have lower betas than growth funds because the "balanced funds" tend to hold securities that have lower betas.

Treynor's reward-to-volatility ratio, denoted T_p for portfolio p, utilizes a portfolio's beta to measure risk. Treynor's index of portfolio desirability is defined in equation (18.6).

$$T_p = \frac{\text{Excess return (or risk premium)}}{\text{Portfolio's beta}} = \frac{\bar{r}_p - r_f}{\beta_p} \quad (18.6)$$

Treynor's investment-ranking device is illustrated in Table 18.3, which contains the calculations of the Treynor ratios for the hypothetical portfolios in Table 18.1. Treynor's ranking device is illustrated in Figure 18.4.

Because $T_G > T_E > T_D$, portfolio G is the best performer among the three portfolios. Note that T_p measures the slope of a straight line from the riskless interest rate, r_f, to portfolio p in $(\beta, \bar{r})$ space. Because T_p measures the slope of a straight line from r_f to portfolio p in $(\beta, \bar{r})$ space, portfolio G has the greatest slope, portfolio E has the second greatest slope, and portfolio D has the least slope. Any portfolio that has T_p greater (less) than the Treynor ratio for the market portfolio outperformed (underperformed) the market portfolio and would plot above (below) the capital asset pricing model (CAPM) (or SML). Thus, a useful benchmark for T_p is the value of $T_m = (\bar{r}_m - r_f)$ for a market proxy, calculated over the same evaluation period used for portfolio p. Figure 18.4 shows that, in terms of the Treynor ratio, portfolios G and E outperformed the market, and portfolio D underperformed the market.

TABLE 18.3 Calculating Treynor's Ratios for Three Portfolios from Table 18.1

Portfolio	Treynor ratio
Gamma (G)	$T_G = \dfrac{\bar{r}_G - r_f}{\beta_G} = \dfrac{11 - 3}{0.8} = 10.00$
Delta (D)	$T_D = \dfrac{\bar{r}_D - r_f}{\beta_D} = \dfrac{15 - 3}{1.4} = 8.57$
Epsilon (E)	$T_E = \dfrac{\bar{r}_E - r_f}{\beta_E} = \dfrac{18 - 3}{1.6} = 9.38$
S&P 500 (*m*)	$T_m = \dfrac{\bar{r}_m - r_f}{\beta_m} = \dfrac{12 - 3}{1} = 9.00$

Sharpe's ratio is a portfolio-ranking tool that has no asset-pricing implications. Sharpe's ratio should not be used to assess the performance of individual stocks, bonds, and other individual investments because the individual assets contain undisclosed amounts of diversifiable (non-beta) risk. This diversifiable risk is included in the total risk for the Sharpe ratio. Diversifiable risk and total risk both have no asset-pricing implications. In contrast, the beta used in Treynor's model measures only undiversifiable risk, and undiversifiable risk does have asset-pricing implications.

Initially, Treynor presented his portfolio-ranking device without any reference to its asset-pricing implications.[12] Then, in an unpublished manuscript, Treynor laid out the asset-pricing implications of his portfolio-ranking device. In a later paper Treynor coauthored with Fischer Black, they explained how Treynor's model could be used to analyze common stocks.[13] Treynor's later papers show that it is logical to substitute the subscript *i* for individual shares of stock in place of the subscript *p* used to represent portfolios in the preceding paragraphs that describe Treynor's model.

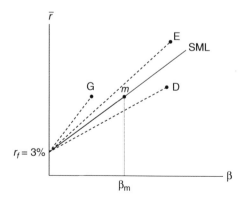

FIGURE 18.4 Illustration of Treynor's Ranking Technique

18.4.3 Jensen's Measure

Michael Jensen (1968, 1969) also developed a one-parameter portfolio performance measure.[14] Like Treynor's measure, Jensen's measure is based on the asset-pricing implications of the CAPM. The formula for the CAPM is

$$E\left(r_p\right) = r_f + \left[E\left(r_m\right) - r_f\right]\beta_p \qquad (18.7)$$

Jensen rearranged the preceding CAPM (or SML) formula by replacing the expected returns with historical average (realized) returns to obtain the following.

$$\alpha_p = \bar{r}_p - \left[r_f + \left(\bar{r}_m - r_f\right)\beta_p\right] \qquad (18.8)$$

Because the first term on the right-hand side of equation (18.8) represents portfolio p's realized return and the term in the square brackets represents the return from the CAPM, it can be seen that the difference between the portfolio's realized performance and the CAPM performance, denoted α_p, measures the desirability of portfolio p. The CAPM is shown graphically in Figure 18.5 together with two hypothetical portfolios (or individual assets such as stocks or bonds) represented by points 1 and 2.

The α_p, which is sometimes referred to as *Jensen's alpha*, measures the vertical distance that portfolio p's realized return lies above or below the CAPM (or SML). Thus, positive values of Jensen's alpha represent portfolios with positive abnormal returns, such as α_1 in Figure 18.5. These portfolios *outperform* the market proxy used in equations (18.7), (18.8), (18.9), and (18.10). The negative value of Jensen's alpha for portfolio 2 indicates that portfolio 2 *underperforms* the market proxy; it offers a poor return for the amount of systematic risk in that portfolio. Table 18.4 contains the calculations of Jensen's alpha for the hypothetical portfolios in Table 18.1. The computations in Table 18.4 reveal that portfolios G and E outperformed the market by 0.8 percent and 0.6 percent, respectively, and portfolio D underperformed the market by 0.6 percent.

Because Jensen's alpha measures only vertical deviations from the *ex post* CAPM (but, in a sense, ignores the risk dimension), it alone is not sufficient to rank

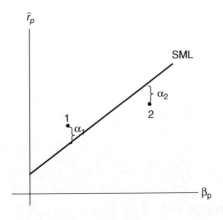

FIGURE 18.5 Jensen's Measure

TABLE 18.4 Calculating Jensen's Alpha for Three Portfolios in Table 18.1

Portfolio	Jensen's alpha
Definition of α_p	$\alpha_p = \bar{r}_p - \left[r_f + \left(\bar{r}_m - r_f \right) \beta_p \right]$
Gamma (G)	$\alpha_G = 11 - [3 + (12 - 3) \times 0.8] = +0.8\%$
Delta (D)	$\alpha_D = 15 - [3 + (12 - 3) \times 1.4] = -0.6\%$
Epsilon (E)	$\alpha_E = 18 - [3 + (12 - 3) \times 1.6] = +0.6\%$

portfolios. Nevertheless, Jensen's alpha can be used for performance evaluation relative to a market proxy. The reason for this lies in what is known as leverage bias. Consider the two portfolios A and B with $\alpha_B > \alpha_A$ and $\beta_B > \beta_A$ illustrated in Figure 18.6. In this situation, homemade leverage (that is, more borrowing at r_f), combined with an investment in A, creates a new portfolio A' that has $\beta_B = \beta_{A'}$ and $\alpha_{A'} > \alpha_A$. Note that the Treynor measures of A and B represent the slopes of the T_A and T_B lines in Figure 18.6. Despite the lower Jensen's alpha for portfolio A, its Treynor measure is greater than that of portfolio B, $T_A > T_B$. Thus, A is a better portfolio than B because, for any given beta, an appropriate combination of A with the riskless asset can give a larger Jensen's alpha than any combination of B and the riskless asset.

The CAPM equation (18.7) can be rearranged as follows:

$$E\left(r_p\right) - r_f = \left[E\left(r_m\right) - r_f \right] \beta_p \qquad (18.9)$$

Jensen removes the expectation operators from equation (18.9), adds time subscripts, adds a regression error term, ε_{pt}, and inserts a regression intercept term,

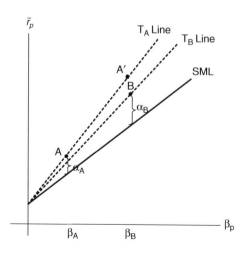

FIGURE 18.6 Jensen's Alpha and the Treynor Measure

denoted α_p, to create equation (18.10):

$$r_{pt} - r_{ft} = \alpha_p + \beta_p \left(r_{mt} - r_{ft} \right) + \varepsilon_{pt} \tag{18.10}$$

This is the excess return version of the market model of equation (8.1) in Chapter 8. The regression intercept term, α_p, is Jensen's alpha. Jensen suggests measuring α_p by fitting regression equation (18.10) for $t = 1, 2, \ldots, T$ time periods (for example, $T = 60$ months).[15] The slope coefficient, β_p, is called Jensen's beta coefficient and measures the *ex post* systematic risk of the portfolio. Equation (18.10) is simply an *ex post* version of the *ex ante* model.

The estimate of the portfolio's *ex post* systematic risk, β_p, from equation (18.10) will typically differ, but only slightly, from the estimate of the portfolio's *ex post* systematic risk determined by using the market model of equation (8.1) or (8.5). This is because Jensen's beta equals $\text{Cov}\left[\left(r_{pt} - r_{ft} \right), \left(r_{mt} - r_{ft} \right) \right] / \text{Var}\left(r_{mt} - r_{ft} \right)$, while the market model's beta equals $\text{Cov}\left[r_{pt}, r_{mt} \right] / \text{Var}\left(r_{mt} \right)$. If the risk-free rate of return is constant over the estimation period, these two betas will be exactly equal. Empirically, the variance of the risk-free rate is not zero, but it is small enough so that there is little notable difference between the two betas.

Forward-looking (*ex ante*) portfolio analysis can be accomplished by substituting the expected return in place of the historical values, $\bar{r}$, in equation (18.8). Then, the *ex ante* version of Jensen's alpha is defined as

$$\alpha_p = E\left(r_p \right) - \left[r_f + \left(E\left(r_m \right) - r_f \right) \beta_p \right] \tag{18.11}$$

Assets with positive α_p locate above the SML and are *underpriced*. They offer a high subsequent expected return relative to the equilibrium returns represented by the CAPM. Because investors would expect to earn higher return from the assets with positive Jensen's alphas than the equilibrium return on the CAPM, rational investors prefer these assets. Thus, strong demand will bid up their prices until their subsequent expected return is driven downward onto the equilibrium SML (or CAPM). This price movement will stop when the expected return equals the equilibrium return. Symmetric but reverse logic explains assets with negative α_p; they are located below the SML and are *overpriced*. These overpriced assets do not offer sufficient return to induce rational investors to accept their level of systematic risk. As a result, selling pressure will push their prices downward. Their market prices will continue to fall until purchase prices are low enough to allow the subsequent expected return to rise up to the equilibrium SML (or CAPM). All assets with Jensen's alpha of zero are located on the equilibrium line SML; they are *fairly priced*. Note that we use the term "outperformed" or "underperformed" according to the positive or negative value of the *ex post* version of Jensen's alpha in equation (18.8), because the *ex post* version of Jensen's alpha measures the past performance of assets. In contrast, the *ex ante* version of Jensen's alpha of equation (18.11) measures the forward-looking performance of assets, and thus we use the different but analogous terms "underpriced" or "overpriced."

One additional point is worth noting. For measuring Jensen's alpha, the equilibrium rate of return can also be measured by other asset-pricing models; for instance, the arbitrage pricing theory (APT).

18.4.4 Information Ratio (or Appraisal Ratio)

Jobson and Korkie (1984) presented an interesting alternative use of Jensen's alpha. They identified the incremental contribution in performance made by adding new assets to an optimal portfolio. They showed that the maximum change in a portfolio's Sharpe measure from the addition of new assets is a simple function of Jensen's alpha and the residual variance from the market model. Consider the case where an actively managed portfolio, A, is added to an index portfolio, *m*, that may be passively managed. This case is illustrated in Figure 18.7.

Then, the squared Sharpe ratio of a risky optimal portfolio *q* constructed using portfolios A and *m* is denoted

$$S_q^2 = S_m^2 + \left[\frac{\alpha_A}{\sigma_{\varepsilon_A}} \right]^2 \qquad (18.12)$$

where α_A and σ_{ε_A} are the intercept and the standard deviation of the residuals from the market model regression of portfolio A's excess return on the excess returns from the index portfolio *m* given by

$$r_{At} - r_{ft} = \alpha_A + \beta_A \left(r_{mt} - r_{ft} \right) + \varepsilon_{At} \qquad (18.13)$$

Equation (18.12) shows that the incremental contribution of the actively-managed portfolio to the optimal risky portfolio *q*'s Sharpe ratio is determined by the ratio of its Jensen's alpha to its residual standard deviation. This ratio is called the *information ratio* or *appraisal ratio*. The mathematical proof for equation (18.12) is given in the end-of-chapter appendix. The best asset addition is the one that achieves the greatest adjusted Jensen measure $[\alpha_A^2/\sigma_{\varepsilon_A}^2]$. Thus, investment candidates may be ranked according to the magnitude of their information ratio.

Suppose *n* mutual funds and a market index portfolio *m* are to be evaluated using excess returns for *T* periods. Arraying the *n* funds by their Sharpe ratios can indicate the best to worst performance over the sample period. Assume that only one of the *n* funds can be purchased. On the other hand, arraying the same funds by

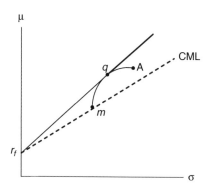

FIGURE 18.7 Managing an Active Portfolio

the adjusted Jensen measure, $\alpha_A^2/\sigma_{\varepsilon_A}^2$, $A = 1, \ldots, n$, indicates the funds making the best to worst additions to the index portfolio m. Once again, assume only one of the n funds can be purchased and combined optimally with the index portfolio m. Using the adjusted Jensen measure will maximize the Sharpe ratio of the combined optimal risky portfolio.

The active portfolio consists of K individual assets. The information ratio of the active portfolio, $\alpha_A/\sigma_{\varepsilon_A}$, is maximized when the investment weight in each asset is proportional to the ratio; $\alpha_i/\sigma_{\varepsilon_i}^2$. Normalizing this weight gives us the weight in each asset in the active portfolio, denoted as

$$w_i = \frac{\left(\alpha_i/\sigma_{\varepsilon_i}^2\right)}{\sum_{i=1}^{K}\left(\alpha_i/\sigma_{\varepsilon_i}^2\right)} \tag{17.50}$$

The procedure to obtain the optimal weights of equation (17.50) is described in Section 17.6 of Chapter 17.

18.4.5 M^2 Measure

While the Sharpe ratio can be used to rank portfolios, the interpretation of its value may be difficult for some investors to understand. When comparing the Sharpe ratios of two funds, inexperienced investors might feel it is difficult to recognize how much one fund is economically better than the other fund, although the funds can be ranked using the Sharpe ratio. Modigliani and Modigliani (1997) proposed a somewhat different measure of risk-adjusted performance, called M^2, that they believe will be more easily understood by investors. Like the Sharpe ratio, M^2 is based on the *ex post* CML. M^2 is equivalent to the average return the fund would have achieved if it had the same total risk as the benchmark market index. The fund with the highest M^2, like the fund with the highest Sharpe ratio, is interpreted as the fund with the highest return for any given risk class.

Consider the managed portfolio p in Figure 18.8. The Sharpe ratio of this portfolio is higher than that of the market portfolio m. But, it might not be easy to interpret how much portfolio p outperformed the market. Suppose portfolio p is mixed with the riskless asset to construct an adjusted portfolio p^* that has the same risk level as the market portfolio. Thus, portfolio p^* has the same standard deviation as the market portfolio. Portfolios p and p^* are equivalent with respect to the Sharpe ratio. Because the market portfolio and portfolio p^* have the same standard deviation, we can compare their performance directly by simply comparing their returns. The M^2 is the vertical distance between two locations, p^* and m in Figure 18.8. That is,

$$M^2 = \bar{r}_{p^*} - \bar{r}_m \tag{18.14}$$

$$= \left(S_p - S_m\right)\sigma_m$$

where S_p and S_m are the Sharpe ratios of portfolios p and m, respectively.

Table 18.5 contains the calculations of the M^2 for the hypothetical portfolios in Table 18.1. It shows that portfolio G outperformed the market by 2.97 percent, while portfolio D underperformed the market by 0.72 percent, evaluated at the same level of risk as the market portfolio.

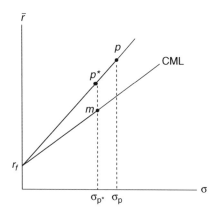

FIGURE 18.8 Illustration of M^2

TABLE 18.5 Calculating the M^2 for the Three Portfolios in Table 18.1

Portfolio	Sharpe ratio	M^2
		$M_p^2 = \left(S_p - S_m\right)\sigma_m$ *defined*
Gamma (G)	1.33	$M_G^2 = (1.33 - 1.00) \times 9\% = 2.97\%$
Delta (D)	0.92	$M_D^2 = (0.92 - 1.00) \times 9\% = -0.72\%$
Epsilon (E)	1.00	$M_E^2 = (1.00 - 1.00) \times 9\% = 0.00\%$
S&P 500 (m)	1.00	n.a.

18.5   MARKET TIMING

If a portfolio manager can foresee a bull market ahead, the manager should shift the portfolio's assets into high-beta stocks to maximize the portfolio's capital gains. If a bear market is foreseen, the portfolio manager should lower the portfolio's beta by liquidating equity securities and holding cash, selling stock short, selling stock index futures short, writing calls on a stock market index, buying puts on a stock market index, investing in bonds, or shifting into lower-beta stocks before the stock market falls. Ideally, the portfolio beta and the slope of the characteristic line will be higher when the market is about to go up (in a bull market), and lower when the market is about to fall (in a bear market). Figure 18.9 defines the market as a bull market if the market return is greater than the riskless interest rate, $r_{mt} - r_f > 0$, and as a bear market if the market return is lower than the riskless interest rate, $r_{mt} - r_f < 0$. A portfolio with such an adept portfolio manager would have the curvilinear characteristic line shown in Figure 18.9. In other words, a portfolio manager that can correctly time the stock market should have a characteristic line with $\partial^2 r_p / \partial r_m^2 > 0$.

In an effort to determine if any mutual fund managers were able to predict the timing of the stock market's alternating bull and bear markets, Treynor and Mazuy (1966) reformulated the linear characteristic line in equation (18.10) to be the

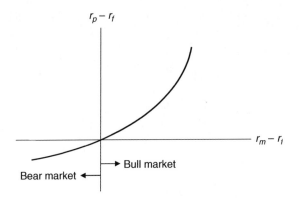

FIGURE 18.9 Curvilinear Characteristic Line for a
Portfolio Manager that can Time the Market

quadratic characteristic line in equation (18.15).[16] Equation (18.15) uses multiple regression to regress a portfolio's excess returns onto simultaneous excess returns from the stock market and the market's excess return squared.

$$r_{pt} - r_f = \alpha_p + \beta_p \left(r_{mt} - r_f \right) + \gamma_p \left(r_{mt} - r_f \right)^2 + \varepsilon_{pt} \qquad (18.15)$$

The regression intercept term is α_p, and β_p and γ_p are regression coefficients on the excess returns from the market index and the market's excess returns squared, respectively. Equation (18.15) is a time-series regression like the characteristic line in equation (18.10), but with a second-order explanatory variable, r_{mt}^2, added to capture any curvilinear relation between portfolio p and the market that might exist. This version of a characteristic line can be viewed as a tool to evaluate a portfolio manager's ability to make *timing decisions* by examining the coefficient on the squared term, γ_p.

18.5.1   Interpreting the Market Timing Coefficient

Three values of the market timing coefficient γ_p in equation (18.15) are noteworthy.

1. *Negative γ_p coefficient.* Suppose a portfolio manager erroneously forecasted the market would rise and, therefore, erroneously moved the portfolio's investments into high-beta assets to obtain the most benefit from the forecasted upturn. If the market actually moved down, the inept portfolio manager's γ_p coefficient would be negative. In this case, the quadratic characteristic line would not be concave toward the asset return axis, as shown in Figure 18.9. Instead, it would be concave toward the market return axis.

2. *Zero γ_p coefficient.* If a portfolio manager has no ability to forecast the market's turns, γ_p will equal zero. The γ_p term would not have to precisely equal zero to indicate a lack of market timing skill; if it is not significantly different from zero in a statistical sense, it is considered to be a zero γ_p coefficient even if it has some nonzero value.

3. *Positive γ_p coefficient.* Adept market timing decisions cause a portfolio's characteristic line to have positive γ_p values, as illustrated in Figure 18.9.

Treynor and Mazuy estimated equation (18.15) using 10 annual returns for 57 mutual funds—25 growth funds and 32 balanced funds. They reported that γ_p was not significantly different from zero for all of the 57 mutual funds except one. One fund's γ_p coefficient was marginally above zero, so its characteristic line displayed slightly discernible curvature upward. Because the value of γ_p that fits the returns best was zero for the other 56 mutual funds, it seems appropriate to say that curvilinear equation (18.15) reduces to the simple linear regression equation (18.10). This absence of γ_p coefficients that were significantly larger than zero is statistical evidence suggesting that none of the 57 portfolios examined by Treynor and Mazuy were managed by people who could forecast stock market turns. Thus, the classic linear characteristic line is more descriptive of their performance than the curvilinear model.

A similar methodology for a test of whether a portfolio manager has market timing ability was proposed by Henriksson and Merton (1981). They consider an alternative *ex post* version of equation (18.10) for measuring the market timing ability. The authors assume that market timers forecast either $r_{mt} > r_{ft}$ or $r_{mt} \leq r_{ft}$.[17] Their model uses $\gamma(t)$ to denote a variable representing the portfolio manager's market forecast at the beginning of period t, where $\gamma(t) = 1$ means the forecast is that $r_{mt} > r_{ft}$ and $\gamma(t) = 0$ means the forecast is that $r_{mt} \leq r_{ft}$.

18.5.2 Henriksson and Merton's Model

Henriksson and Merton assume that there are two target levels of systematic risk that are dependent on the $\gamma(t)$ coefficient of equation (18.15). That is, if $\gamma(t) = 1$, then the portfolio will be adjusted to a high level of beta and if $\gamma(t) = 0$, then the portfolio will be adjusted to a low level of beta. The following ordinary least squares (OLS) regression model can thus be used to estimate the separate contributions of selectivity and timing:

$$r_{pt} - r_{ft} = \alpha_p + \beta_p \left(r_{mt} - r_{ft} \right) + \varphi_p D_t \left(r_{mt} - r_{ft} \right) + \varepsilon_{pt} \qquad (18.16)$$

where D_t is a dummy variable such that

$$D_t = \begin{cases} 0 & \text{if } r_{mt} > r_{ft} \\ -1 & \text{if } r_{mt} \leq r_{ft} \end{cases} \qquad (18.17)$$

The coefficient φ_p expresses the portfolio manager's timing ability. If the manager has no ability, then $\varphi_p = 0$. Because φ_p is estimated using a time-series regression, a simple t-test of the null hypothesis $H_0 : \varphi_p = 0$ can be conducted to see if φ_p was significantly positive. It is noteworthy that a significant negative value would imply that timing would have been valuable if the manager had done just the opposite of what was actually done.[18] Furthermore, the term α_p in equation (18.16) expresses the portfolio manager's ability to select good investments, and its estimated value can also be subjected to a t-test of the null hypothesis $H_0 : \alpha_p = 0$.[19] Stated differently, α_p can be evaluated as Jensen's alpha.

Henriksson (1984) applied equation (18.16) to a sample of 116 mutual funds for the period January 1968–June 1980.[20] Tests conducted at the 0.05 level indicated that there were 11 positive and 8 negative estimated values of α_p that were statistically significant, and 3 positive and 9 negative estimated values of φ_p that were significant. These results indicate that there was little evidence that portfolio managers successfully engaged in either market timing or selectivity during this period. Further support for this observation was provided when the observation period was divided into two subperiods. Within each subperiod, results similar to the overall period were observed and, interestingly, there was no apparent relationship in the magnitudes of the estimated parameters for the first subperiod when compared to the second subperiod.

18.5.3 Descriptive Comments

The Sharpe and Treynor's portfolio ranking models of equations (18.3) and (18.6) measure an investor's stock-picking skills. The Treynor and Mazuy model and the Henriksson and Merton model cannot be used to rank the performance of different investment managers. They are different and important measures of investment management ability. The Treynor and Mazuy model of equation (18.15) and the Henriksson and Merton model of equation (18.16) measure an investor's ability to forecast the market's turning points. Jensen's alpha is another portfolio-ranking model. The Jensen measure can be used to rank the stock-picking ability of portfolio managers, but it differs significantly from the Sharpe and Treynor portfolio ranking models.

The portfolio evaluation procedures of Merton-Henriksson seem to be subject to the Roll critique [described in Section 14.1] because their procedure is based on the CAPM. However, it is noteworthy to mention that a counterargument against Roll's critique was put forth by Henriksson (1984). He argued that portfolio managers are not attempting to forecast the true market portfolio's returns. Instead, it can be argued that they are more concerned with just those equities traded on a particular stock market (for example, the New York Stock Exchange), and, thus, the timing should be tested relative to a specific market index. According to Peterson and Rice (1980), the choice of the proxy for the market portfolio is relatively unimportant. It seems reasonable, then, to use the Sharpe measure to gauge overall performance and the Treynor-Mazuy and Merton-Henriksson procedures to gauge timing performance.

18.6 COMPARING SINGLE-PARAMETER PORTFOLIO PERFORMANCE MEASURES

At this point, two questions arise. First, are the different investment performance measures similar? Second, is one of the investment performance measures better than the others?

18.6.1 Ranking Undiversified Investments

Sharpe's reward-to-variability ratio uses total risk (measured by the standard deviation of returns) to measure portfolio risk. In contrast, Jensen's differential return and Treynor's reward-to-volatility ratio use systematic beta risk as their measure of portfolio risk. Which measure of risk is more appropriate depends on the situation. Sharpe's model is satisfactory for ranking portfolios and other diversified investments. But Sharpe's model is not suitable for ranking the desirability of individual stocks, bonds, and other undiversified assets. Individual assets' total risk contains unsystematic risk that has no asset-pricing implications in portfolio theory and, thus, the presence of diversifiable risk limits the use of Sharpe's model. Treynor's measure considers systematic risk and is suitable for evaluating the performance of both individual assets and diversified portfolios. Jensen's measure is another beta-based tool and it is also useful for evaluating the performance of both individual assets and diversified portfolios too. If a highly diversified portfolio is being evaluated, it is possible that there will not be much difference in the rankings from the Sharpe, Treynor, and Jensen measures, because there will be so little unsystematic risk present in a highly diversified portfolio.

18.6.2 Contrasting the Three Models

The Sharpe, Treynor, and Jensen portfolio performance measures are all positive linear transformations of each other under certain plausible circumstances. CAPM equation (18.7) can be applied to any asset (or portfolio), and, if all assets are correctly priced, all $[\beta_i, E(r_i)]$ pairs will fit the model. To recognize explicitly that not all assets (and thus portfolios) are located on the CAPM, Jensen adds a constant term, denoted α_p, and rewrites the theoretical SML model as

$$\bar{r}_p - r_f = \alpha_p + (\bar{r}_m - r_f)\,\beta_p \qquad (18.18)$$

where α_p is a measure of disequilibrium for portfolio p. Note that if $\alpha_p = 0$, then portfolio p is correctly priced.

Treynor's one-parameter portfolio performance measure, T_p, is obtained by dividing both sides of (18.18) by the beta coefficient to obtain equation (18.19).

$$T_p = \frac{\bar{r}_p - r_f}{\beta_p} = \frac{\alpha_p}{\beta_p} + (\bar{r}_m - r_f) \qquad (18.19)$$

Equation (18.19) shows that Treynor's measure is a linear transformation of Jensen's measure, α_p, because $(\bar{r}_m - r_f)$ is a constant. Sharpe's measure may be derived from equation (18.18) by noting that $\beta_p = (\rho_{pm}\sigma_p\sigma_m)/\sigma_m^2$, as shown by

$$\bar{r}_p - r_f = \alpha_p + (\bar{r}_m - r_f)\left(\frac{\rho_{pm}\sigma_p\sigma_m}{\sigma_m^2}\right) \qquad (18.20)$$

For well-diversified portfolios, $\rho_{pm} \cong 1$. Dropping the unitary correlation coefficient and dividing equation (18.20) by σ_p yields Sharpe's measure:

$$S_p = \frac{\bar{r}_p - r_f}{\sigma_p} \cong \frac{\alpha_p}{\sigma_p} + \left(\frac{\bar{r}_m - r_f}{\sigma_m}\right) \qquad (18.21)$$

Because the last term, $(\bar{r}_m - r_f)/\sigma_m$, is made up of exogenous constants, it is a constant too. Thus, the Sharpe measure is shown to be a linear transformation of Jensen's alpha. That is, $S_p = \alpha_p/\sigma_p + (\text{constant})$.

Finally, T_p and S_p can linked to each other by remembering that $T_p = (\bar{r}_p - r_f)/\beta_p$ and substituting $(\rho_{pm}\sigma_p\sigma_m)/\sigma_m^2$ for β_p. This results in $T_p = \left[(\bar{r}_p - r_f)/\rho_{pm}\sigma_p\right]\sigma_m$, so that if portfolio p is a well-diversified portfolio, $\rho_{pm} \cong 1$ and

$$T_p = S_p\sigma_m \tag{18.22}$$

indicating that the Treynor measure and the Sharpe measure are approximately linear transformations of each other.

In 1966, just before Jensen contrived his alpha measure, Sharpe examined the empirical relationship between the Treynor measure and the Sharpe ratio.[21] Measuring 34 mutual funds over the same sample period, Sharpe reported that the simple correlation between the Sharpe and Treynor measures was 0.40. After ranking the 34 mutual funds by both measures, Sharpe found a rank correlation between the Sharpe and Treynor rankings of 0.97. Because the preceding algebra showed that the Treynor measure and the Sharpe ratio are linear transformations of the Jensen measure, it seems likely that the three portfolio performance measures will yield similar rankings if the same mutual funds are compared over the same sample period.

18.6.3   Survivorship Bias

When using the Sharpe, Treynor, and Jensen portfolio performance measures to evaluate empirical mutual fund data, the results will almost surely be influenced by survivorship bias. Most empirical evaluations of mutual fund data are based on historical data. *Ex post* sample data is typically composed of only those mutual funds that survived until the end of the sample period. Weak mutual funds that failed to survive throughout the sample period are omitted from the study because their sample data is incomplete. Omitting the mutual funds that failed during the sample period means that only the surviving mutual funds get compared and contrasted. Compared to the population of all mutual funds that existed throughout a mutual fund study, the sample composed of only survivors can be expected to yield upward-biased average returns and downward-biased risk statistics. Survivorship bias will make performance statistics gathered from surviving mutual funds appear to be more attractive than the unobservable parameters that represent a larger sample that includes the failed funds.[22]

18.7   THE INDEX OF TOTAL PORTFOLIO RISK (ITPR) AND THE PORTFOLIO BETA

The relationship between a portfolio's systematic risk (beta) and its total risk (standard deviation) may be seen more clearly in terms of a ratio called the *index of total portfolio risk* (ITPR), which equals the ratio of the standard deviation of portfolio p to the standard deviation of the market portfolio m (or a market index), σ_p/σ_m. The relationship between the ITPR and the systematic risk β_p is developed from equation (18.23a), the variance decomposition equation derived from the characteristic line.

$$\underbrace{\sigma_p^2}_{\text{Total risk}} = \underbrace{\beta_p^2\sigma_m^2}_{\text{Systematic risk}} + \underbrace{\sigma_{\varepsilon p}^2}_{\text{Unsystematic risk}} \tag{18.23a}$$

If portfolio p is efficient, by the definition of efficiency, its diversifiable variance must be zero, $\sigma^2_{\varepsilon p} = 0$. This allows equation (18.23a) to be simplified to represent an efficient portfolio as shown next.

$$\sigma^2_p = \beta^2_p \sigma^2_m + 0 \tag{18.23b}$$

The relation between β_p and ITPR for efficient portfolios is derived by dividing both sides of equation (18.23b) by σ^2_m and taking the square root.

$$\text{ITPR} = \frac{\sigma_p}{\sigma_m} = \beta_p \tag{18.24}$$

The same relation between portfolio p's beta and its ITPR for *efficient* portfolios can be derived more simply by manipulating the definition of the beta coefficient, as shown next.

$$\beta_p = \frac{\text{Cov}\left(r_{pt}, r_{mt}\right)}{\text{Var}\left(r_{mt}\right)} = \frac{\rho_{pm}\sigma_p\sigma_m}{\sigma^2_m} = \frac{\sigma_p}{\sigma_m}, \qquad \text{because } \rho_{pm} = 1 \tag{18.25}$$

Again, we see that β_p equals the ITPR for an efficient portfolio. But, this relationship is different for an inefficient (dominated) portfolio that contains diversifiable risk, $\sigma^2_{\varepsilon p}$.

$$\text{ITPR}^2_p = \frac{\sigma^2_p}{\sigma^2_m} = \frac{\beta^2_p \sigma^2_m + \sigma^2_{\varepsilon p}}{\sigma^2_m} > \beta^2_p \tag{18.26a}$$

Taking the square root yields:

$$\text{ITPR}_p = \frac{\sigma_p}{\sigma_m} > \beta_p \tag{18.26b}$$

Figure 17.1 shows that naive diversification can reduce portfolio risk to the undiversifiable level. Figure 17.1 and equation (18.24) both show that when the diversifiable risk is zero, $\sigma_p = \sigma_m$, and the index of total portfolio risk (ITPR) equals unity, $\text{ITPR}_p = \beta_p = 1$. When a portfolio's risk is above the market's systematic level, $\beta_p > 1$ and $\sigma_p > \sigma_m$. Symmetrically, when $\beta_p < 1$ then $\sigma_p < \sigma_m$ for an efficient portfolio. Summarizing, the $\text{ITPR}_p = \sigma_p/\sigma_m = \beta_p$ when portfolio p is efficient. If a portfolio manager is doing an average job of finding undervalued securities, that portfolio's average return and beta should plot on the SML (or CAPM). But if a portfolio manager's average and beta plot between the SML and the $E(r)$ axis, that portfolio manager is a superior stock picker. Conversely, a portfolio that is located below the SML is picking overvalued securities—that is, it is picking losers.

Figure 18.10 shows in $[\beta, E(r)]$ space that portfolio Q lies between the SML and the vertical axis and it earned a higher return (r_2) than what is appropriate (r_1) for its level of systematic risk (β_Q). In spite of portfolio Q's adept stock picking, portfolio Q in Figure 18.10 is a dominated portfolio in $[\sigma, E(r)]$ space. In other words, portfolio Q would be located below the CML in $[\sigma, E(r)]$ space. Portfolio Q would have an even worse average return if its manager were not so adept at picking

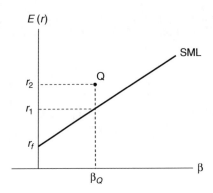

FIGURE 18.10   Security Market Line (SML)

winners. Figure 18.11 shows that for its level of total portfolio risk, as measured by ITPR $= \sigma_Q/\sigma_m$, portfolio Q had a return below what is appropriate (r_3), as measured by the CML (namely, $r_2 < r_3$). The apparent paradox between portfolio Q's returns in Figures 18.10 and 18.11 is resolved in Figure 18.11. The multiaspect portfolio performance evaluation tools in Figure 18.11 resolve the paradox by showing that portfolio Q's manager picked winners but did not diversify well. Thus, it can be concluded that the manager of portfolio Q is good at stock picking and bad at diversifying.[23]

A portfolio manager's investment objective need not necessarily be to purchase only a Markowitz-efficient portfolio. A Markowitz-efficient investor might want to buy shares in portfolio Q in an effort to reap its abnormally high return. If so, that investor must combine shares of Q with shares of other assets (perhaps, to create a portfolio of portfolios) to minimize risk. When multiple criteria are appropriate, the more discriminating tools introduced previously are necessary for portfolio performance evaluation.

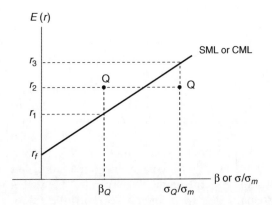

FIGURE 18.11   Tools for Evaluating Portfolio Performance

18.8 MEASUREMENT PROBLEMS

The one-parameter portfolio measures, when applied to mutual funds, suggest that most investors would be better off investing in an index fund (that is, a passively managed portfolio that corresponds to the market portfolio). These portfolio performance measures have been criticized on the following issues:

1. *The borrowing and lending rates are different*: It is not realistic to assume that the risk-free borrowing and lending rates are equal because the latter rate must be less than the former rate for investors if banks are to survive. Assuming that the rates are equal results in an excessively high benchmark for high-risk portfolios, because a low risk-free lending rate (for example, U.S. Treasury bills) is used for r_f.[24] All three of the portfolio performance measures discussed previously have this serious flaw that exerts a bias against selecting high-risk portfolios. As mentioned here and discussed in Chapter 13, the borrowing and lending rates available in the real capital markets differ. This inconvenient fact causes the CML and SML to become nonlinear (for example, see Figures 13.3 and 13.4). The nature of these nonlinearities implies lower-equilibrium expected returns for the high-risk portfolios than indicated by the theoretical CML and SML. Because none of the three portfolio-evaluation models discussed earlier makes adjustments for this, they all tend to be biased against high-risk portfolios.[25]
2. *Selection of an appropriate benchmark index*: Maintaining an index fund is not as easy as it may seem and, as a result, index funds may not be a fair benchmark. For example, reinvesting cash dividends, meeting the clients' withdrawal requests, deducting the management fees, and transactions costs cause index funds to have tracking error (that is, not mimic their target index perfectly).[26]
3. *Performance evaluation period*: While the actual realized return can be measured precisely, it is only an estimate of the true capability of the portfolio manager. Only over many observations (that is, with a sample that is large enough to be representative) can we get an accurate assessment of the portfolio manager's true capability, thereby letting us distinguish luck from skill in measuring performance. However, the client may not be willing to wait a long time (until a representative sample accumulates) before making a decision.[27]
4. *Nonstationarity of portfolio return distribution*: The one-parameter performance measures assume certain stationarity properties that do not actually exist. For example, mutual funds may alter their betas depending on market conditions, as suggested in Chapter 17. Changing investment policies changes Jensen's beta in equation (18.10). Thus, its ordinary least squares estimate is biased, which, in turn, means that Jensen's measure is biased, too.
5. *Measurement of the market portfolio's returns*: There will be errors in measuring the unobservable market portfolio's returns. Such errors, even when minor, can have a major impact on the measurement of portfolio performance. Indeed, all of these criticisms can be interpreted to mean that improper benchmarks are being used with any of the three one-parameter portfolio measures.

The next section discusses the last two issues in greater detail.

18.8.1   Measurement of the Market Portfolio's Returns

Roll's (1977) critique for empirical tests of the CAPM, discussed in Chapter 14, argues that, for all practical purposes, the CAPM is not empirically testable. The reason for this was the inability to measure accurately the true market portfolio's returns and the problems associated with the use of a proxy. Roll (1978) has continued this line of inquiry by investigating the use of Treynor and Jensen CAPM-based measures of portfolio performance. He reports that these measures are ambiguous, not robust, and capable of being manipulated with seemingly innocuous changes in their computation. One of the major problems with these measures has to do with the market portfolio.

Consider a situation where there are several portfolios to be ranked in terms of their performance. Assume that over the evaluation period the composition of these portfolios has been fixed and that both the expected return vector and the variance-covariance matrix have been stationary. In order to rank the portfolios with either the Treynor or Jensen measure, a market portfolio needs to be identified. Roll shows that if a mean-variance efficient portfolio is used, then all the portfolios will be tied for the same rank. If, however, an inefficient portfolio is used, depending on the composition of this portfolio, any ranking is possible. Thus, Roll concludes that these portfolio performance measures are useful not for evaluating portfolio performance, but instead for determining if the market proxy is mean-variance efficient.

To elaborate, imagine that some portfolio managers have what Roll refers to as a "perfect ability" to select *ex ante* mean-variance efficient portfolios, and the remaining portfolio managers have less-than-perfect ability, meaning that the latter group selects inefficient portfolios. The choice of an inefficient market proxy means that some managers with perfect ability could be ranked lower than some managers with less-than-perfect ability, while a different proxy could reverse these rankings. Unfortunately, there is no clear way to determine which ranking is correct.[28]

The logic behind Roll's argument lies in the relationship between market proxies and the estimation of beta. In particular, a mean-variance inefficient proxy for the market portfolio can be found that will produce a beta for a portfolio of any desired magnitude, and hence any desired measure of performance can be produced. In an example, Roll shows that two different proxies whose returns have a correlation coefficient of 0.897 will produce two sets of rankings for 15 hypothetical portfolios that have a rank-order correlation coefficient of only 0.0036, suggesting that the rankings are unrelated to each other.[29]

Roll generalizes his criticism of the Treynor and Jensen measures by first examining what happens when the composition of each portfolio is allowed to change over time while maintaining the stationarity assumption. In this situation, his negative conclusions are reinforced. Furthermore, introducing nonstationarity in the expected return vector and variance-covariance matrix does not change his conclusions either. Again, a portfolio manager who has "perfect ability" and acts appropriately can have his or her performance viewed as inferior if an inefficient market proxy is used.[30]

One implication of Roll's criticism is that Sharpe's measure is still useful because it does not require the identification of a proxy for the market portfolio.[31] However, Miller and Gehr (1978) have shown that Sharpe's measure is biased. Because the bias is solely a function of the number of return intervals (T) in the evaluation period,

Jobson and Korkie (1981a) have shown that an approximately unbiased estimator of a fund's performance can be calculated as

$$S_p^* = S_p \left[\frac{T}{(T + 0.75)} \right] \quad (18.27)$$

where S_p is the biased measure as shown in equation (18.3). As can be seen in equation (18.27), the adjustment for bias for a large sample is relatively minor, but is more pronounced for a smaller value of T. Also note that the bias does not affect the rankings of a set of portfolios, assuming that T is the same for all of them.

Jobson and Korkie also indicated that any two funds, say A and B, can be tested to see if there is a statistically significant difference in their performance over some evaluation period by calculating

$$Z = \frac{(S_B - S_A)}{\sqrt{\theta}} \quad (18.28)$$

where θ is calculated as

$$\theta = \left(\frac{1}{T} \right) \left[\frac{1}{2} \left[S_A^2 + S_B^2 - S_A S_B \left(1 + \rho_{AB}^2 \right) \right] + 2 \left(1 - \rho_{AB} \right) \right] \quad (18.29)$$

and S_A and S_B are the Sharpe measures of funds A and B, respectively, and ρ_{AB} is the correlation coefficient between returns on funds A and B. The test statistic Z in equation (18.28) is approximately normally distributed with a mean of zero and a standard deviation of one in large sample sizes and is well behaved in smaller sample sizes.[32] For example, if over 60 months portfolios A and B have $\bar{r}_A - r_f = 1.5$ percent, $\bar{r}_B - r_f = 0.5$ percent, $\sigma_A = 3$ percent, $\sigma_B = 7$ percent, and $\sqrt{\theta} = 0.190$, then $Z = [(0.5/7) - (1.5/3)]/0.190 = -2.26$, which indicates that A outperformed B significantly using a 95 percent confidence interval.[33]

Peterson and Rice (1980) empirically investigated Roll's argument that the CAPM-based measures of portfolio performance give ambiguous portfolio performance evaluations. Quarterly returns for 15 mutual funds were calculated over two five-year observation periods, 1967–1971 and 1972–1976. Four commonly used market portfolio proxies were utilized: the DJIA, the Standard & Poor's 500 Stock index, and two indexes representing an equal-weighted and value-weighted index of all NYSE-listed common stocks. Three-month Treasury bill rates were used for the quarterly risk-free rates over both evaluation periods. Using the four different indexes, the Treynor measure and a modified version of the Jensen measure were calculated for each fund over both of the evaluation periods; the Sharpe measure was also calculated for each fund over both periods.

Peterson and Rice found that for either the Treynor or modified Jensen measure, the choice of market proxy made little difference in ranking the performance of the portfolios. Furthermore, the Sharpe measure produced rankings that were quite similar to both the Treynor and Jensen rankings. Thus, practically speaking, the choice of an index or measure does not appear to affect the relative rankings of the portfolios. Peterson and Rice also noted that these findings were true in both of the evaluation periods (although the rankings were not the same from one period to the next).

18.8.2   Nonstationarity of Portfolio Return Distributions

The composition of a managed portfolio will change over time due to decisions involving selectivity, timing, or both. Even in the absence of these decisions, the proportions invested in the various securities will change (unless a rebalancing strategy is followed) as the securities' returns are realized. This means that even if the expected return vector and variance-covariance matrix are stationary, portfolio returns will be observations from a nonstationary distribution. Using simple regression in order to calculate either Jensen's or Treynor's measure can introduce bias into the measure and distort any test of statistical significance. Recognizing this, various authors have developed models of performance evaluation that allow for nonstationarity. One such model was developed by Merton (1981) and Henriksson and Merton (1981).

Building on the work of Fama (1972) and Jensen (1972), Merton and Henriksson developed a statistical test based on the CAPM that permits identification and separation of the gains due to timing skills from the gains due to selectivity skills.[34] As shown in Chapter 17, a return-generating model based on the CAPM can be represented algebraically as

$$r_{pt} - r_{ft} = \alpha_p + \beta_p \left(r_{mt} - r_{ft} \right) + \varepsilon_{pt} \tag{17.8}$$

where $E \left(\varepsilon_{pt} | r_{mt} \right) = 0$ and $E \left(\varepsilon_{pt} \right) = 0$. The preceding model has been shown by Jensen (1972) and Grant (1977) to be inadequate for measuring the separate contributions of market timing and selectivity. By considering an alternative *ex post* version of equation (17.8) for measuring these separate contributions, Henriksson and Merton suggested the model of equation (18.16) to include a term for testing the managers' market timing ability and to accommodate the nonstationarity of beta. The use of Henriksson and Merton's model was described in Section 18.5.

An interesting alternative version of the model shown in equation (18.16) was developed by Kon and Jen (1978, 1979). In its simplest form, Kon and Jen assume that the portfolio manager sets the portfolio beta at one of two alternative levels based on his or her market forecast. Thus, portfolio returns will belong to one of two regimes,

$$r_{pt} - r_{ft} = \begin{cases} \alpha_{1p} + \beta_{1p} \left(r_{mt} - r_{ft} \right) + \varepsilon_{1,pt}, & t \in T_1 \tag{18.17a} \\ \\ \alpha_{2p} + \beta_{2p} \left(r_{mt} - r_{ft} \right) + \varepsilon_{2,pt}, & t \in T_2 \tag{18.17b} \end{cases}$$

where T_1 and T_2 are the two sets of subperiods corresponding to the time periods when beta is set at one of its two target levels, and $\varepsilon_{1,pt}$ and $\varepsilon_{2,pt}$ are normally distributed error terms with variances of $\sigma_{\varepsilon_1}^2$ and $\sigma_{\varepsilon_2}^2$, respectively. Kon and Jen further assume that there is an unknown probability λ_i that portfolio manager p will choose regime i ($i = 1, 2$) in any period t. This leads to a key distinction in the models of Merton-Henriksson and Kon-Jen. The former test to see if there is a correspondence between the observed value of $r_{mt} - r_{ft}$ and the beta chosen by the portfolio manager, whereas the latter do not test for such a correspondence. That is, D_t, which is defined in equation (18.17), is specified by Henriksson and Merton but is treated as an unknown by Kon and Jen, meaning that for any t, D_t may be zero or -1, regardless of the magnitude of $\left(r_{mt} - r_{ft} \right)$. Accordingly, Henriksson and

Merton's model can be viewed as testing for timing ability, while Kon and Jen's model can be viewed as testing for the existence of timing activities (which may or may not be successful).

Using a sample of 49 mutual funds and their net monthly returns from January 1960 to December 1971, Kon and Jen (1979) found that only 12 funds were best characterized by a single regime. Of the 37 other funds, 27 were best characterized as having two regimes, as shown in equations (18.17a) and (18.17b), while 10 funds had three regimes. Focusing on the two-regime model, it should be kept in mind that if $\alpha_{1p} \neq \alpha_{2p}$ or $\beta_{1p} \neq \beta_{2p}$ or $\sigma_{1p} \neq \sigma_{2p}$, then the fund could be characterized as having more than one regime (and an analogous statement can be made for three regimes). Continuing, Kon and Jen found that among the 27 two-regime funds, 15 funds had $\hat{\beta}_{1p} \neq \hat{\beta}_{2p}$, 11 funds had $\hat{\alpha}_{1p} \neq \hat{\alpha}_{2p}$, and 15 funds had $\hat{\sigma}_{1p} \neq \hat{\sigma}_{2p}$, where the tests were conducted at the 0.05 level of significance. Of the 10 three-regime funds, nine had at least two different $\hat{\beta}$'s, six had at least two different $\hat{\alpha}$'s, and six had at least two different $\hat{\sigma}$'s. Thus, Kon and Jen concluded that for many mutual funds it was more likely that the data were generated by a mixture of two or three regimes rather than one regime, as initially implied by Jensen.[35] Furthermore, the existence of multiple levels of beta suggests that a large number of funds engage in timing activities.[36]

Subsequently, Kon (1983) extended his analysis of mutual funds to examine both timing and selectivity performance. His sample consisted of 37 mutual funds whose net returns were calculated over the period January 1960 to June 1976. Of the 37 funds, 25 were found to have two regimes, and 12 were found to have three regimes. Using certain statistical procedures, Kon was able to assign each month of the observation period to a particular regime for each fund, thereby enabling him to evaluate the overall timing performance for the 37 funds. Eleven funds indicated positive timing performance, and as many as five of these funds had performance that was statistically significant. Furthermore, 23 of the funds had positive selectivity performance, with as many as five being statistically significant. Overall, there were six funds with positive performances in both timing and selectivity, whereas 22 funds exhibited a trade-off between the two activities. The remaining nine funds had negative performances in both timing and selectivity. Combining timing and selectivity performance measure, 22 funds had positive investment performance and the remaining 15 funds were negative, once again providing evidence that is consistent with the efficient market hypothesis.[37] Kon concluded that most portfolio managers could improve their performance if they focused more on the one activity—timing or selectivity—at which they are best.

18.9 DO WINNERS OR LOSERS REPEAT?

Whether the winners (or the losers) in one period remain winners (or losers) in a subsequent period has been a classical issue in research on persistence of performance for last 40 years. The research results falls into two groups: one group that does not find performance persistence, and the other group that does.

In the classical research by Jensen (1968), who examined the performance of 115 mutual funds over the period from 1945 to 1964, no evidence for persistence was found. After Jensen (1968), several studies also found the same conclusion.

Kritzman (1983) examining fixed-income funds, Dun and Theisen (1983) examining 201 institutional portfolios over the period 1973–1982, and Elton, Gruber, and Rentzler (1990) examining 51 publicly offered commodity funds over the period 1980–1988 found no evidence for performance persistence.

Several other studies, however, found that performance does persist. Grinblatt and Titman (1992) examining 157 mutual funds over the period 1975–1984, Lehmann and Modest (1987) examining 130 mutual funds over the period 1968–1982, and Hendricks, Patel, and Zeckhauser (1993) examining 165 equity mutual funds over the period 1974–1988 found evidence for performance persistence.

The research results on performance persistence just discussed can involve one or both of the following issues.

Statistical problems: All of the preceding portfolio performance models use parametric statistics that are designed to enable the researcher to make informative probabilistic statements. In order to use these models, certain statistical conditions and assumptions must be met.

Survivorship bias: The preceding portfolio performance models typically use sample data that is composed of mutual funds that are survivors. Mutual funds that fail during the sample period are dropped from the sample because they provide incomplete sample data.

In particular, Brown, Goetzmann, Ibbotson, and Ross (1992) showed that survivorship bias could significantly affect the results of performance persistence. They demonstrated in numerical examples that the effect caused by survivorship bias can be strong enough to generate the appearance of significant persistence.

Goetzmann and Ibbotson (1994) suggested an approach to portfolio performance evaluation that sidesteps the problems above. The Goetzmann and Ibbotson study focuses on determining whether the best performing portfolios are able to repeat their high level of performance year after year. This is an important question because winning the performance derby is what interests investors.

Goetzmann and Ibbotson's database consisted of monthly holding period returns from a sample of several hundred mutual funds over a 13-year period. The returns were computed after deducting the mutual funds' management fees, but front-end load fees, exit fees, and taxes were not taken into count.[38] All cash flows from the mutual funds were reinvested in the funds every month. The mutual funds' returns were measured over a two-year within-sample period for the years 1976–1977 to predict the out-of-sample performance for the subsequent two-year period, 1978–1979. Similarly, Goetzmann and Ibbotson used the prior two years' performances to predict the subsequent two-year performances for the periods 1980–1981, 1982–1983, 1984–1985, and 1986–1987. All of the funds that existed for each two-year interval were included in the computations. The aggregate sample included some mutual funds that did not survive throughout the sample period; thus, survivorship bias was not an issue. Every mutual fund was categorized as either a winner or a loser, according to whether the fund ranked above or below that two-year sample's median return.

Table 18.6 shows two-way tables of winners and losers for each two-year subsample. The summary of eight years (1978 to 1985, inclusive) of results is shown

TABLE 18.6 Two-Way Tables of Ranked Mutual Fund Returns over Successive Two-Year Periods

		1978–1979 Winners	1978–1979 Losers			1980–1981 Winners	1980–1981 Losers
1976–1977	Winners	84	54	1978–1979	Winners	110	41
	Losers	50	88		Losers	38	113
		1982–1983 Winners	1982–1983 Losers			1984–1985 Winners	1984–1985 Losers
1980–1981	Winners	63	96	1982–1983	Winners	104	62
	Losers	96	63		Losers	71	95
		1986–1987 Winners	1986–1987 Losers			Combined successive winners	Results period losers
1984–1985	Winners	125	72	Initial winners		486 (59.9%)	325 (40.1%)
	Losers	72	125	Initial losers		327 (40.3%)	484 (59.7%)

Source: William N. Goetzmann and Roger G. Ibbotson, "Do Winners Repeat?" *Journal of Portfolio Management* 20, no. 10 (Winter 1994): 9–18.

in the lower right-hand corner of the table. Measured over all subsamples, the table shows that if a mutual fund was classified as a winner (loser) in a two-year sample, there is about a 60 percent chance it will be a winner (loser) again in the next two-year sample. Table 18.6 also shows that this repeat-winners pattern occurred in four out of the five two-year subsamples. While the tendency for winners to repeat their good performances is noticeable, it is far from guaranteed. In particular, when the 1980–1981 rankings were used to predict the 1982–1983 rankings, the repeat-winners phenomenon was reversed.

It could be argued that high-return mutual funds continued to have high-ranking returns year after year because they were high-risk funds, not because they were winners. To overcome this objection, Goetzmann and Ibbotson replicated their study using risk-adjusted returns. Equation (18.8) was used to compute Jensen's alphas over successive two-year intervals and thereby generate risk-adjusted return measures for each subsample. To the extent that Jensen's alphas are appropriate risk-adjusted return measures, the SML suggests that any persistence in the ranking of mutual funds' alphas results from differences in management skill. To investigate this possibility, the mutual funds were categorized as winners or losers depending on whether their Jensen's alpha was above or below, respectively, the period's median alpha. Table 18.7 shows two-way tables of winners and losers for each two-year subsample. As with the preceding table, the combined results are shown in the lower right-hand corner of Table 18.7. The results in Table 18.7 provide further support for the repeat-winners hypothesis. The winner-loser breakdowns in all five subsamples and the aggregate sample are consistent with the persistence hypothesis.

The simplicity of the two-way tables is delightful. The hypothesis that is tested is not based on a complicated theory. No statistical assumptions about the underlying

TABLE 18.7 Two-Way Tables of Ranked Alphas over Successive Two-Year Subsamples

		1978–1979 Winners	1978–1979 Losers			1980–1981 Winners	1980–1981 Losers
1976–1977	Winners	83	55	1978–1979	Winners	105	44
	Losers	52	86		Losers	40	109
		1982–1983 Winners	1982–1983 Losers			1984–1985 Winners	1984–1985 Losers
1980–1981	Winners	83	75	1982–1983	Winners	85	73
	Losers	75	83		Losers	73	85
		1986–1987 Winners	1986–1987 Losers			Combined successive winners	Results period losers
1984–1985	Winners	126	49	Initial winners		482 (62.0%)	296 (38.0%)
	Losers	45	130	Initial losers		285 (36.6%)	493 (63.4%)

Source: William N. Goetzmann and Roger G. Ibbotson, "Do Winners Repeat?" *Journal of Portfolio Management* 20, no. 10 (Winter 1994): 9–18.

data are necessary to use two-way tables. And, because each two-way table spans four years, some mutual funds that failed later in the eight-year aggregate period were included in the earliest years of the study. In other words, the aggregate eight-year sample included an ever-changing list made up of both survivors and failures. And the two-way tables are so easy to understand that few investors have trouble comprehending the results.

To substantiate the findings reported in Tables 18.6 and 18.7, Goetzmann and Ibbotson reformulated their study in several different ways. First, they examined the subset of their funds called growth funds, to see if the repeat-winner phenomenon might result from some particular mixtures of stocks and bonds within the portfolios. Using the same investigative procedures reported previously, Goetzmann and Ibbotson found that the results reported in Tables 18.6 and 18.7 were equally true for the growth funds. Second, Goetzmann and Ibbotson reformulated their study in terms of one-year subsamples instead of two-year subsamples. Using the one-year subsamples provided supported the repeat-winners hypothesis, but the shorter subsamples yielded weaker support than the two-year subsamples. Third, Goetzmann and Ibbotson shortened the length of their subsamples to increase the number of observations, even though the shorter intervals contain more statistical noise. They used one-month subsamples. The monthly results were also supportive of the repeating winners hypothesis. Fourth, Goetzmann and Ibbotson reformulated their methodology using three-year subsamples and 4×4 classification tables (instead of the 2×2 tables of Tables 18.6 and 18.7). They did not employ subsamples in excess of three years because the mutual fund manager might change or the fund's strategy might change over subsamples of much greater length. The raw returns and the alphas displayed in four-way tables uniformly suggest that quartile rankings from three-year subsamples have predictive power for quartile ranking in the next three-year period. Although these results could be due to risk factors that were omitted, timing strategies, or fee-related considerations, they are consistent with the repeat-winner hypothesis.[39]

Burton Malkiel (1995) published a study of equity mutual fund data from 1971 to 1991 that was critical of research suggesting it is possible to detect funds that will probably enjoy superior performance in the future. Malkiel argued that while the repeat-winners phenomenon was observable during the 1970s, this phenomenon was not present during the 1980s. However, Gruber (1996) also examined 260 equity mutual funds over the period 1985–1994 and found significant persistence that, he argued, explained the growth in active mutual funds. Malkiel controlled for risk by using the CAPM, while Gruber controlled for size, book-to-market, and bond market effects.

Carhart (1997) studied mutual fund data from 1962–1993 for evidence of persistent mutual fund performance. He reports that "funds with high returns last year have higher-than-average expected returns next year, but not in the years thereafter..." Carhart finds a strong tendency for losers to persist. He concludes that mutual funds that perform worst usually continue their bad performances for years.

Despite that the data have been intensively analyzed in many different approaches, the results of the last 40 years of research on performance persistence are at best mixed. The connection between past historical performance and future performance may be weak.

18.10   SUMMARY ABOUT INVESTMENT PERFORMANCE EVALUATION

Before 1952 investment performance evaluation consisted, primarily, of computing the rates of returns earned by different candidate portfolios and selecting the portfolio with the highest historical rate of return. If risk was discussed at all, it was not a sophisticated or analytical discussion. Things changed in 1952, when Harry Markowitz introduced portfolio theory to the world.[40] This chapter reviews investment performance evaluation tools that were introduced after 1952, beginning with Donald Farrar's 1962 analysis of 23 mutual funds that included both return and risk together in the same graph, Figure 18.1.

In 1965 Jack Treynor introduced the first one-parameter portfolio performance tool that is based on Markowitz's two-parameter portfolio theory.[41] Treynor created a two-parameter model that considers the rate of return and risk and collapses them into a single (one-parameter) index number that can be used to rank the performance of both individual assets and diversified portfolios. Equation (18.6) defines Treynor's performance measure and Figure 18.4 illustrates the model. Treynor's model is based on the simple regression model Treynor referred to as the characteristic line, equation (18.4). Treynor's model is the first of four different single-parameter investment performance tools introduced in this chapter that is based on Markowitz portfolio theory; coincidently, all four models were introduced during the 1960s.[42]

Early in 1966 William Sharpe published a portfolio performance measure that can be used to rank the desirability of an assortment of different mutual funds that are investment candidates.[43] Sharpe's risk premium per unit of risk formula is defined by equation (18.3) and illustrated in Figure 18.2; the model is based on total risk. As discussed previously, total risk is the sum of diversifiable risk plus undiversifiable risk. In Markowitz portfolio theory, diversifiable risk is void of asset-pricing implications, and therefore, the Sharpe ratio has no asset-pricing implications. Nevertheless, it is a very useful and popular tool for ranking the performance of mutual funds and other portfolios.

Later in 1966, Jack Treynor, with the aid of Kay Mazuy, published another insightful portfolio performance evaluation model.[44] After Treynor introduced the linear characteristic line, equation (18.4), in 1965, Treynor and Mazuy introduced a curvilinear characteristic line, equation (18.15), in 1966. Unlike any other scientific portfolio performance evaluation tool, the Treynor-Mazuy curvilinear characteristic line measures the ability of a portfolio manager to forecast the stock market's turning points. Figure 18.9 illustrates the Treynor and Mazuy characteristic line for the special case of a portfolio manager who has a valuable ability to time the market. While the ability of the Treynor-Mazuy 1966 model to measure market-timing skills is a valuable and unique portfolio performance evaluation tool, the model cannot be used to rank the desirability of candidate portfolios. Treynor's 1965 model is his investment-ranking tool.

Michael Jensen's doctoral dissertation at the University of Chicago was published in 1968 and it is the fourth portfolio performance evaluation tool that was published during the 1960s; it, too, is based on Markowitz portfolio theory.[45] Jensen begins with Sharpe's single-index regression model, equation (18.4), which is identical to Treynor's linear characteristic line, and reformulates this time-series simple regression model. Jensen reformulated the simple regression model to include a new regression intercept term. Equation (18.10) is the regression model that includes Jensen's alpha as the regression intercept. Figure 18.6 shows two different Jensen's alphas illustrated with the SML. Jensen's alpha is a risk-adjusted rate of return measure that can be used to rank the desirability of individual stock and bond investments and, also, diversified portfolios, like mutual funds.

Although the Treynor, Sharpe, and Jensen portfolio ranking models are each uniquely different, they are all useful in a similar ways. If they were all used to rank the desirability of (50, or 500, or 5,000) different mutual funds, their rankings would differ. But their rankings would be sufficiently similar that they would all have high positive rank correlation coefficients with each other.

In 1994 Goetzmann and Ibbotson showed how to adapt simple two-way and four-way classification tables to evaluate the performance of mutual funds.[46] The performance hypothesis they tested is not based on Markowitz portfolio theory. No complex statistical assumptions are necessary to use the tables. And the eight year sample of mutual funds is an ever-changing list made up of both survivors and failures—not just survivors. Unfortunately, the two-way and four-way tables cannot be used to rank the investment candidates or isolate portfolios with superior or inferior market-timing skills. But Goetzmann and Ibbotson were able to demonstrate that mutual funds performing best (worst) in one time period usually performed best (worst) in the following time interval. Research-oriented investors are lucky to have such a large menu of tools with which to evaluate the investment candidates.[47]

APPENDIX: SHARPE RATIO OF AN ACTIVE PORTFOLIO

This appendix proves equation (18.12), which shows a gain with respect to the Sharpe ratio can be obtained by managing an active portfolio.

A18.1   Proof that $S_q^2 = S_m^2 + [\alpha_A / \sigma(\varepsilon_A)]^2$

The tangency portfolio q in Figure 18.7 is composed of the active portfolio A and the index portfolio m. The optimal weights for portfolios A and m are given in equations (17.55) and (17.56) in Chapter 17, by using equation (17.59), as

$$w_A^\circ = \left(\frac{1}{\lambda}\right)\left(\frac{\alpha_A}{\sigma_{\varepsilon_A}^2}\right) \tag{A18.1}$$

$$w_m^\circ = \left(\frac{1}{\lambda}\right)\left(\frac{\mu_m - r_f}{\sigma_m^2} - \frac{\alpha_A \beta_A}{\sigma_{\varepsilon_A}^2}\right) \tag{A18.2}$$

where $\lambda = \left[(\mu_m - r_f)/\sigma_m^2\right] + \left[(1 - \beta_A)\alpha_A/\sigma_{\varepsilon_A}^2\right]$. Note that the active portfolio A consists of K individual assets. Then, the expected excess return on the tangency portfolio q is described as

$$\mu_q - r_f = w_m^\circ(\mu_m - r_f) + w_A^\circ(\mu_A - r_f) \tag{A18.3}$$
$$= \left(\frac{1}{\lambda}\right)\left\{\left(\frac{\mu_m - r_f}{\sigma_m^2} - \frac{\alpha_A \beta_A}{\sigma_{\varepsilon_A}^2}\right)(\mu_m - r_f) + \left(\frac{\alpha_A}{\sigma_{\varepsilon_A}^2}\right)[\alpha_A + \beta_A(\mu_m - r_f)]\right\}$$

because $\mu_A = \alpha_A + r_f + \beta_A(\mu_m - r_f)$. Rearranging equation (A18.3) results in

$$\mu_q - r_f = \left(\frac{1}{\lambda}\right)\left[\left(\frac{\mu_m - r_f}{\sigma_m}\right)^2 + \frac{\alpha_A^2}{\sigma_{\varepsilon_A}^2}\right] \tag{A18.4}$$

The variance of the tangency portfolio q is also described as

$$\sigma_q^2 = w_m^{\circ 2}\sigma_m^2 + w_A^{\circ 2}\sigma_A^2 + 2w_m^\circ w_A^\circ \sigma_{Am}$$
$$= \left(\frac{1}{\lambda}\right)^2\left[\left(\frac{\mu_m - r_f}{\sigma_m^2} - \frac{\alpha_A \beta_A}{\sigma_{\varepsilon_A}^2}\right)^2\sigma_m^2 + \left(\frac{\alpha_A}{\sigma_{\varepsilon_A}^2}\right)^2(\beta_A^2\sigma_m^2 + \sigma_{\varepsilon_A}^2)\right.$$
$$\left. + 2\left(\frac{\mu_m - r_f}{\sigma_m^2} - \frac{\alpha_A \beta_A}{\sigma_{\varepsilon_A}^2}\right)\left(\frac{\alpha_A}{\sigma_{\varepsilon_A}^2}\right)\beta_A \beta_m \sigma_m^2\right]$$
$$= \left(\frac{1}{\lambda}\right)^2\left[\left(\frac{\mu_m - r_f}{\sigma_m}\right)^2 + \frac{\alpha_A^2}{\sigma_{\varepsilon_A}^2}\right] \tag{A18.5}$$

because $\sigma_A^2 = \beta_A^2\sigma_m^2 + \sigma_{\varepsilon_A}^2$ and $\beta_m = 1$ from the single-index model of equation (18.13). Thus, using equations (A18.4) and (A18.5), the squared Sharpe ratio of a risky portfolio q is

$$S_q^2 = \left(\frac{\mu_q - r_f}{\sigma_q}\right)^2 = \left(\frac{\mu_m - r_f}{\sigma_m}\right)^2 + \frac{\alpha_A^2}{\sigma_{\varepsilon_A}^2}$$

$$= S_m^2 + \left[\frac{\alpha_A}{\sigma(\varepsilon_A)}\right]^2$$

NOTES

1. Harry M. Markowitz, "Portfolio Selection," *Journal of Finance* 7, no. 1 (1952): 89. Reprinted by Harry M. Markowitz, Editor, *Harry Markowitz Selected Works*, World Scientific Publisher, Singapore, 2010, 693 pages, Volume 1.
2. Donald E. Farrar reformulated his prize-winning doctoral dissertation and other research into a book titled *The Investment Decision under Uncertainty* (Englewood Cliffs, NJ: Prentice-Hall, 1962).
3. Ibid., 74.
4. Eugene F. Fama, "Behavior of Stock Prices," *Journal of Business*, 1965, Table 18, page 93.
5. J. C. Francis and S. H. Archer, *Portfolio Analysis* (Englewood Cliffs, NJ: Prentice-Hall, 1971): 157–171.
6. Milton Freidman, "The Methodology of Positive Economics," *Essays in Positive Economics* (Chicago: University of Chicago Press, 1935): 3–43.
7. A list of the classic models touched on in this chapter includes James Tobin, "Liquidity Preference as Behavior towards Risk," *Review of Economic Studies* 26, no. 1 (February 1958): 65–86; Donald E. Farrar, *The Investment Decision under Uncertainty* (Englewood Cliffs, NJ: Prentice-Hall, 1962); Jack L. Treynor, "How to Rate Management of Investment Funds," *Harvard Business Review*, January–February 1965, 63–75; William F. Sharpe, "Mutual Fund Performance," *Journal of Business*, January 1966, 119–138; and Michael C. Jensen, "The Performance of Mutual Funds in the Period 1945–1964," *Journal of Finance*, May 1968, 389–416.
8. James Tobin, "Liquidity Preference as Behavior towards Risk," *Review of Economic Studies* 26, no. 1 (February 1958): 65–86.
9. William F. Sharpe, "Mutual Fund Performance," *Journal of Business*, January 1966, 119–138. Reprinted by William F. Sharpe, Editor, *William F. Sharpe: Selected Works*, World Scientific Publishing Company Inc., 2012, ISBN-10: 9814329959, ISBN-13: 978-9814329958, 692 pages.
10. These conclusions align with the classic empirical studies by Michael C. Jensen and more recent findings. See M. C. Jensen, "The Performance of Mutual Funds in the Period 1945–1964," *Journal of Finance*, May 1968, 389–416 and M. C. Jensen, "Risk, the Pricing of Capital Assets, and the Evaluation of Investment Portfolios," *Journal of Business*, April 1969, 167–185.
11. Jack L. Treynor, "How to Rate Management of Investment Funds," *Harvard Business Review*, January–February 1965, 63–67.
12. Ibid.
13. Jack Treynor and Fischer Black, "How to Use Security Analysis to Improve Portfolio Selection," *Journal of Business* 46 (January 1973): 66–86.
14. Michael C. Jensen, "The Performance of Mutual Funds in the Period 1945–1964," *Journal of Finance*, May 1968, 389–416 and "Risk, the Pricing of Capital Assets, and the Evaluation of Investment Portfolios," *Journal of Business* 42 (April 1969): 167–247.

15. Because α_p is a regression intercept term, it was suggested by Jensen that a simple t–test be used to judge whether or not the portfolio's performance was statistically significantly different from zero. However, such a statistical test has been criticized for being too weak to detect good performance, where good performance means earning, say, 2 percent or 3 percent more per year than the market on a risk-adjusted basis (see, for example, Good, Ferguson, and Treynor, 1976; Hodges and Brealey, 1973; Murphy, 1977). Furthermore, Jensen (1972) and Grant (1977) have shown that α_p (and β_p) is biased if the fund is engaged in timing activities. Finally, it should be noted that Jensen applied his technique to a sample of mutual funds, but was later criticized on several grounds by Mains (1977).

16. J. L. Treynor and K. K. Mazuy, "Can Mutual Funds Outguess the Market?" *Harvard Business Review*, July–August 1966, 131–166.

17. Jensen (1972) assumed that the market timer forecasted the level of return on the market and that the bivariate distribution of forecasted market returns and actual market returns was normal. The result was that the market timer's forecasting ability could be measured by the correlation coefficient of this bivariate distribution. However, if attempts at selectivity were also being made, the contributions of timing and selectivity could not be separated.

18. The estimated values of β_p and $(\beta_p - \varphi_p)$ should not be interpreted as estimates of the target levels of beta; such an interpretation is accurate only if the forecasts were perfectly accurate.

19. Henriksson and Merton (1981) note that when testing for forecasting ability, all returns should be measured before deducting management fees.

20. Alternative versions of equation (18.16) have been tested by Fabozzi and Francis (1979b), Alexander and Stover (1980), and Chang and Lewellen (1984), with results consistent with Henriksson's results.

21. William F. Sharpe, "Mutual Fund Performance," *Journal of Business*, January 1966, 119–138. See Figure 4 and its discussion.

22. See Philippe Jorion and William N. Goetzmann, "Global Stock Markets in the Twentieth Century," *Journal of Finance* 54, no. 3 (June 1999): 978. Also see Stephen J. Brown, William J. Goetzmann, and Stephen Ross, "Survival," *Journal of Finance* 50 (1995): 853–873. And see Burton G. Malkiel, "Returns from Investing in Equity Mutual Funds, 1971–1991," *Journal of Finance* 50, no. 2 (June 1995): 553. Malkiel provides empirical estimates that survivorship bias is about 150 basis points per year in traditional mutual fund studies.

23. The model for simultaneously evaluating different aspects of a portfolio's performance is discussed more fully by E. F. Fama in "Risk and Evaluation of Pension Fund Portfolio Performance," *Measuring the Investment Performance of Pension Funds* (Park Ridge, IL: Bank Administration Institute, 1968) and also "Components of Investment Performance," *Journal of Finance*, June 1972, 551–567. Both these articles are reprinted as readings 27 and 28 in *Modern Developments in Investment Management*, edited by J. Lorie and A. Brealey (New York: Praeger Press, 1972).

24. See Friend and Blume (1970) and Klemkosky (1973).

25. This problem was first pointed out by Irwin Friend and Marshall Blume, "Measurement of Portfolio Performance under Uncertainty," *American Economic Review*, September 1970. Also see R. C. Klemkosky, "The Bias in Composite Performance Measures," *Journal of Financial and Quantitative Analysis*, June 1973, 505–514.

26. See Good, Ferguson, and Treynor (1976).

27. Grubel (1979) argues that because successful portfolio managers tend to change jobs frequently, most past tests of performance, having focused on portfolios rather than managers, do not provide insight into either the ability of the managers or the efficient market hypothesis.

28. An interesting problem [discussed by Levy (1984)] that has a similar effect involves varying the investment horizon. Such variations will affect the estimated size of beta,

thereby changing not only the sizes of the Treynor and Jensen measures of performance but also their performance rankings. Dybvig and Ross (1985a, 1985b) analyzed a situation where an uninformed observer attempts to measure the performance of portfolio managers that may have had superior information. Similar to Roll, they find that, in general, any ranking is possible.

29. Furthermore, these two inefficient proxies have correlation coefficients with an efficient portfolio of 0.982 and 0.920.

30. The effect of errors in measurement of the benchmark portfolio on performance evaluation is explained in more detail in Roll (1980, 1981). While a procedure for identifying and correcting for benchmark errors is also presented by Roll, he recognizes that it may be difficult to use, because most portfolios contain a large number of securities which, by their sheer number, complicate his procedure.

31. Two other useful procedures that are immune from Roll's criticism are the geometric mean procedure and Cornell's (1979) comparison period procedure. The geometric mean procedure, as the name suggests, simply evaluates performance on the basis of the magnitude of the geometric mean return earned by a portfolio over an evaluation period. In Chapter 12 it is mentioned that investors with logarithmic utility functions who wanted to maximize expected terminal wealth over multiple periods should choose the portfolio with maximum geometric mean return at the beginning of each period. Thus, the procedure is appropriate for investors in such a situation. Cornell's procedure estimates individual securities' expected returns from a period prior to the evaluation period, and then uses these estimates to determine the portfolio's period-by-period expected return from which the actual return is subtracted in order to determine its risk-adjusted abnormal return.

32. However, the power of the Z statistic in detecting differences in performance with monthly data is low, and thus requires either large differences or many observations. Jobson and Korkie have also developed a chi-square test statistic to test for the equivalence of performance of any number of portfolios.

33. Jobson and Korkie (1981a) also show that Treynor's measure is biased and that test statistics based on it are neither well behaved nor powerful.

34. Their model can be generalized to any multifactor return structure.

35. Similar findings were observed when an estimate of the zero-beta portfolio return, r_{zt}, was used instead of the riskless rate of return, r_{ft}, in equations (18.17a) and (18.17b).

36. Alexander, Benson, and Eger (1982) argue that if common stock betas approximately follow a random walk process [that is, if $\beta_t = \beta_{t-1} + \varepsilon_t$, where ε_t is a random error term with $E(\varepsilon_t) = 0$] and mutual funds do not engage in timing decisions, then mutual fund betas will themselves approximately follow a random walk process. Thus, a potential problem in drawing conclusions from Kon and Jen's test results is that some funds may have actually had random walk betas, yet Kon and Jen's test may have indicated they had two or three betas, thereby leading to the false conclusion that they did engage in timing activities.

37. This finding is consistent with Kon and Jen (1979) and Mains (1977), where it was noted that the average value of α_p, calculated over all funds and all regimes, was slightly positive. The results of these tests suggest that mutual funds are, on average, able to beat the market on a risk-adjusted basis, but not by a substantial amount. Williams (1980), Ambachtsheer (1974, 1977), Ambachtsheer and Farrell (1979), and Farrell (1982) argue that the organizational design of professional money managers is as important as their predictive abilities in trying to earn abnormal returns. Thus, one interpretation of the performance of mutual funds is that their organizational design is often inadequate.

38. For a discussion of mutual funds' fees see, Miles Livingston and Edward S. O'Neal, "The Cost of Mutual Fund Distribution Fees," *The Journal of Financial Research* 11, no. 2 (Summer 1998): 205–218.

39. For research findings that support Goetzmann and Ibbotson's results see Mark Grinblatt and Sheridan Titman, "The Persistence of Mutual Fund Performance," *Journal of Finance* 47 (1992):1977–1984. Also, see Darryll Hendricks, Jayendu Patel, and Richard Zeckhauser, "Hot Hands in Mutual Funds: Short-Run Persistence of Relative Performance, 1974–1988," *Journal of Finance* 48, 93–130.

40. Harry Markowitz, "Portfolio Selection," *Journal of Finance*, March 1952, 77–91.

41. Jack L. Treynor, "How to Rate Management of Investment Funds," *Harvard Business Review*, January–February 1965, 63–75.

42. Jack Treynor also suggested another approach to portfolio selection. Jack Treynor and Fischer Black, "How to Use Security Analysis to Improve Portfolio Selection," *Journal of Business*, January 1973.

43. William F. Sharpe, "Mutual Fund Performance," *Journal of Business*, January 1966, 119–138.

44. J. L. Treynor and K. K. Mazuy, "Can Mutual Funds Outguess the Market?" *Harvard Business Review*, July–August 1966, 131–166.

45. Michael C. Jensen, "The Performance of Mutual Funds in the Period 1945–1964," *Journal of Finance*, May 1968, 389–416.

46. William N. Goetzmann and Roger G. Ibbotson, "Do Winners Repeat?" *Journal of Portfolio Management*, 20, no. 10 (Winter 1994).

47. Fred D. Arditti (1971) suggested a three-parameter portfolio performance system that considers the first three moments: "Another Look at Mutual Fund Performance," *Journal of Financial and Quantitative Analysis*, June 1971. Francis argued that although skewness was theoretically relevant, it could not be measured empirically with sufficient reliability to justify considering it: "Skewness and Investors' Decisions," *Journal of Financial and Quantitative Analysis*, March 1975. C. G. Martin published an independent study supporting Francis's findings in the *Review of Business and Economic Research* titled, "Ridge Regression Estimates of Ex Post Risk-Return Trade-Off on Common Stock," Spring 1978, 1–15.

CHAPTER 19

Performance Attribution

Markowitz portfolio theory is discussed at length in finance textbooks and finance classes around the world, and several Nobel prizes have been awarded (to Markowitz himself, and to professors Tobin and Sharpe) for achievements rooted in Markowitz portfolio theory. But time goes on, and recently newer investment models and concepts have emerged. Chapters 19 and 20 explore a few financial developments that emerged after Markowitz portfolio theory was decades old. These new ideas are not completely independent of Markowitz portfolio theory. These concepts, models, and institutions coexist and are tangential to Markowitz's venerable theory. In view of the importance of Markowitz portfolio theory, and also the importance of these newer developments, it is worthwhile to consider how they interact. After reviewing the new developments, we ponder the possibility that they might have a symbiotic relationship with, or might conflict in some way with, Markowitz portfolio theory. Chapter 19 begins this inquiry by exploring portfolio performance attribution. Chapter 19 is an extension of Chapter 18 that reflects what some portfolio managers are doing today.

The manager of a hedge fund that is a fund of funds might use portfolio performance attribution to select acquisitions. Or a mutual fund, or other portfolio, manager who is considering retaining money management services (of someone who might even be a competitor) might employ portfolio performance attribution tools. And, of course, any investor who is comparison shopping may benefit from portfolio performance attribution.

When a portfolio manager's performance is evaluated, the managed portfolio's returns are generally compared with the returns of some reference or benchmark portfolio. The difference between the portfolio's return and the benchmark's return is the portfolio manager's excess return that results from active management. The purpose of portfolio performance attribution is to figure out how selected portfolios earn their excess returns.

There are generally three forms of performance attribution. The first one is factor model analysis in which a particular factor model (or an asset pricing model) is used. In this analysis, the excess return is attributed to the portfolio manager's selection ability and market timing ability. The second one is return-based style analysis proposed by Sharpe (1992). In this analysis, a managed portfolio's returns are separated into two components: one attributable to style and the other attributable to selection. The third one is return decomposition-based analysis. This analysis attributes the excess return to the asset allocation effect, the security (or sector) selection effect, and an interaction effect.

19.1   FACTOR MODEL ANALYSIS

Based on the CAPM, a traditional approach to measure the *selection* ability of a portfolio manager is to regress the excess returns of a managed fund $(r_{pt} - r_f)$ on the simultaneous excess market returns $(r_{mt} - r_f)$. That is, assuming that the market beta (or slope coefficient) is constant over time, the intercept coefficient of equation (19.1) indicates return from security selectivity:

$$r_{pt} - r_f = \alpha_p + \beta_p(r_{mt} - r_f) + \varepsilon_{pt} \tag{19.1}$$

This is the excess return version of the simpler market model of equation (8.1) described in Chapter 8. If a portfolio manager has superior abilities in predicting the performance of individual securities in the portfolio by observing each security's selection signals, the portfolio manager will earn a positive abnormal return, and the intercept coefficient (Jensen's alpha) will turn out to be positive, $\alpha_p > 0$. Otherwise, the portfolio manager will earn a negative abnormal return, and the intercept coefficient will turn out to be negative, $\alpha_p < 0$. Thus, the intercept coefficient α_p measures a portfolio manager's selection ability to pick the best securities.

In the preceding equation, the market beta is assumed to be invariant through time. However, the market beta (or systematic risk measure) can be time-varying. There may be two reasons that the market beta of a portfolio is time-varying. First, if structural shifts in systematic risk of individual securities occur, the market beta of the portfolio containing those securities will capture some of this variance. Second, if the fund manager attempts to time the market factor $(r_{mt} - r_f)$ based on timing signals, there will be a dynamic shift in the systematic risk sensitivities. In fact, it would be difficult in practice to separate these two reasons. Therefore, when we measure the timing ability of the fund manager, we assume that the first reason does not result in time-varying market betas. That is, we assume that there are no structural shifts in systematic risk of individual securities.

If a portfolio manager's market timing attempts (i.e., forecasts about the movement of the market factor, $r_{mt} - r_f$) are reflected in movements in the portfolio risk sensitivities, the risk sensitivities can be represented as

$$\beta_{pt} = \overline{\beta}_p + \delta_{r_{mt}-r_f} \tag{19.2}$$

where $\overline{\beta}_p$ is the average or target beta of the portfolio, and $\delta_{r_{mt}-r_f}$ is the forecast about the movement of the market factor and $E(\delta_{r_{mt}-r_f}) = 0$. If $r_{mt} > r_f$ is forecasted, $\delta_{r_{mt}-r_f}$ would be positive, and if $r_{mt} < r_f$ is forecasted, $\delta_{r_{mt}-r_f}$ would be negative. If the forecast $\delta_{r_{mt}-r_f}$ is a linear function of the market factor, and equation (19.2) replaces the slope coefficient in equation (19.1), then the return of the managed portfolio is represented as

$$r_{pt} - r_f = \alpha_p + \overline{\beta}_p(r_{mt} - r_f) + \gamma_p(r_{mt} - r_f)^2 + \varepsilon_{pt} \tag{19.3}$$

This is the same as the quadratic regression equation (18.15) whose linear characteristic line Treynor and Mazuy (1966) reformulated to test the timing ability of the portfolio manager. In the absence of market timing ability, the coefficient on the variable $(r_{mt} - r_f)$ will be the target beta of the portfolio, and the coefficient on the squared term $(r_{mt} - r_f)^2$, γ_p, will be zero. However, if the portfolio manager has market timing ability, γ_p will be positive. Within the analytical framework in equation (19.3), the coefficient γ_p can be used to measure a portfolio manager's market timing ability to predict general market price movements. Section 18.5 of Chapter 18 further explains the implication of the market timing ability coefficient, γ_p.

If additional factors other than the market factor are involved in generating a portfolio's returns, a multifactor model is needed to measure the selection ability and timing ability of a portfolio manager. These additional factors could represent some investment style characteristics. Besides timing the market factor, the portfolio managers may be timing some other factors. If these factors are the size and value factors, portfolio managers change the sensitivity of portfolio returns to size and value factors according to their forecasts about the movement of those factors. They increase (decrease) the sensitivity (or factor beta) during the periods when small firms are expected to outperform (underperform) big firms, and high book-to-market equity firms are expected to outperform (underperform) low book-to-market equity firms.

To measure the selection ability and the previously mentioned timing abilities of a portfolio manager, the Fama and French (1993) three-factor model can be used.

$$r_{pt} - r_f = \alpha_p + \beta_{p1}(r_{mt} - r_f) + \beta_{p2}\text{SMB}_t + \beta_{p3}\text{HML}_t$$
$$+ \gamma_{p1}(r_{mt} - r_f)^2 + \gamma_{p2}\text{SMB}_t^2 + \gamma_{p3}\text{HML}_t^2 + \varepsilon_{pt} \qquad (19.4)$$

where SMB (small minus big) is the return from a portfolio containing small stocks minus the return from a portfolio containing large stocks, and HML (high minus low) is the return from a portfolio containing stocks with high book-to-market ratios minus the return from a portfolio containing stocks with low book-to-market ratio.

The preceding model assumes that timing signals used by portfolio managers to forecast a factor are orthogonal to the other factors. This model is simply an extension of the one-factor-based model of equation (19.3). The intercept coefficient α_p (or Jensen alpha) also measures selection ability.[1] The slope coefficient γ's in equation (19.4) measure factor timing ability. If the portfolio manager possesses market timing ability, size timing ability, and value timing ability, γ_{p1}, γ_{p2}, and γ_{p3} will be nonzero, respectively.

Other factors can also be used to test other timing ability. For example, to test macroeconomic timing ability, the mimicking portfolio for the macroeconomic variable can be included in the model.

19.2 RETURN-BASED STYLE ANALYSIS

Nobel laureate William Sharpe (1992) proposed a return-based style analysis to analyze asset allocation. Sharpe defines asset allocation as the allocation of an investor's portfolio across a number of major asset classes. After defining a set of asset classes, a procedure for measuring exposure to variations in returns of asset classes is determined. In this analysis, a managed portfolio's returns are regarded to behave as if the portfolio were invested in these asset classes or benchmarks. Next, it is possible to determine how effectively portfolio managers have performed their functions and the extent to which value has been added through active management. The effectiveness of the investor's overall asset allocation can be measured by comparing the managed portfolio's actual returns with the returns from a set of asset classes. Here, the composition of the asset classes reveals the portfolio manager's style.

To effectively accomplish all these tasks of style analysis, an asset class factor model can be used. Suppose that K factor (mimicking) portfolios drive the return of an asset i. The linear factor model is

$$r_{it} = a_i + \beta_{i1}r_{F_1,t} + \beta_{i2}r_{F_2,t} + \cdots + \beta_{iK}r_{F_K,t} + \varepsilon_{it} \tag{19.5}$$

where r_{it} is the return of the asset i during time period t, r_{F_k} represents the return of the portfolio mimicking the k-th factor $(k = 1, 2, \ldots, K)$, ε_{it} represents the residual return of asset i with mean zero, and β_{ik} represents the sensitivity (or exposure) of the asset return to the k-th factor portfolio. The sum of the intercept term and the residual term, $a_i + \varepsilon_{it}$, represents the nonfactor component of the return on asset i. The key assumptions in the preceding factor model are that the residual return (or the nonfactor component) is uncorrelated with the returns from the factors $\left[\text{i.e.}, E\left(\varepsilon_{it}r_{F_k}\right) = 0 \text{ for } k = 1, 2, \ldots, K\right]$, and the residual term for one asset is also uncorrelated with that of every other asset $\left[\text{i.e.}, E\left(\varepsilon_{it}\varepsilon_{jt}\right) = 0 \text{ for } i \neq j\right]$.

In the model of equation (19.5), each factor represents the return on an asset class or style, and the sensitivities (β_{ik}) are required to sum to 1. The return on an asset i is actually the return of a portfolio invested in the K asset classes plus a nonfactor component. The sum of the sensitivity times the factor return $(\beta_{i1}r_{F_1,t} + \beta_{i2}r_{F_2,t} + \cdots + \beta_{iK}r_{F_K,t})$ can be termed as the return attributable to *style* and the nonfactor component $(a_i + \varepsilon_{it})$ as the return attributable to *selection*. Thus, the Sharpe approach in equation (19.5) separates the return into two main components: style and selection. In fact, the term $\beta_{i1}r_{F_1,t} + \beta_{i2}r_{F_2,t} + \cdots + \beta_{iK}r_{F_K,t}$ indicates the return of a passive portfolio with the same style. The objective of style analysis is to delineate the style (or determine the exposures of the asset classes) that minimizes the variance of the difference between the return on the target fund (r_{it}) and the term attributable to style $(\beta_{i1}r_{F_1,t} + \beta_{i2}r_{F_2,t} + \cdots + \beta_{iK}r_{F_K,t})$. This difference is called the fund's *tracking error*, and its variance the fund's *tracking variance*.

Sharpe (1992) suggested an example of asset classes (or factors) to use for style analysis. Table 19.1 shows 12 asset classes and the associated (market capitalization-weighted) indexes. Each index represents a style or strategy that could be followed. These 12 asset classes are assumed to cover the institutional universe of U.S. equities. The first five asset classes (1–5) are related to U.S. fixed-income securities, the next four asset classes (6–9: value, growth, medium size, and small size) are related to U.S. equities, and the last three asset classes (10–12) are related to foreign bonds and equities.

Sharpe (1992) estimated the multiple regression model of equation (19.5) by using 60 monthly returns from the Trustees' Commingled U.S. Portfolio (an open-end mutual fund) over the period from January 1985 through December 1989 for the dependent variable and monthly returns of the 12 indexes over the same period for the independent variables. Table 19.2 provides the estimation results. The unconstrained regression column shows the multiple regression estimation results (in percentage) of equation (19.5) *without* any constraints on the slope coefficients.

TABLE 19.1 Asset Classes for a Style Analysis

	Name of asset class	Description	Index used
1	Bills	Cash-equivalents with less than 3 months to maturity	Salomon Brothers' 90-day Treasury Bill Index
2	Intermediate-Term Government Bonds	Government bonds with less than 10 years to maturity	Lehman Brothers' Intermediate-Term Government Bond Index
3	Long-Term Government Bonds	Government bonds with more than 10 years to maturity	Lehman Brothers' Long-Term Government Bond Index
4	Corporate Bonds	Corporate bonds with ratings of at least Baa by Moody's or BBB by Standard Poor's	Lehman Brothers' Corporate Bond Index
5	Mortgage-Related Securities	Mortgage-backed or related securities	Lehman Brothers' Mortgage-Backed Securities Index
6	Large-Capitalization Value Stocks	Stocks in Standard and Poor's 500 stock index with high book-to-price ratios	Sharpe/BARRA Value Stock Index
7	Large-Capitalization Growth Stocks	Stocks in Standard and Poor's 500 stock index with low book-to-price ratios	Sharpe/BARRA Growth Stock Index
8	Medium-Capitalization Stocks	Stocks in the top 80% of the capitalization in the U.S. equity universe after the exclusion of stocks in Standard and Poor's 500 stock index	Sharpe/BARRA Medium Capitalization Stock Index
9	Small-Capitalization Stocks	Stocks in the bottom 20% of the capitalization in the U.S. equity universe after the exclusion of stocks in Standard and Poor's 500 stock index	Sharpe/BARRA Small Capitalization Stock Index
10	Non-U.S. Bonds	Bonds outside the U.S. and Canada	Salomon Brothers' Non-U.S. Government Bond Index
11	European Stocks	European and non-Japanese Pacific-Basin stocks	FTA Euro-Pacific Ex Japan Index
12	Japanese Stocks	Japanese stocks	FTA Japan Index

Source: William Sharpe, "Asset Allocation: Management Style and Performance Measurement," *Financial Analysts Journal*, 18, no. 2 (1992): 7–19.

In this case, the regression coefficients are estimated by the ordinary least squares (OLS) method. The R-square is 95.20 percent, which indicates that a substantial portion (95.20%) of the total monthly variance of the fund is explained by the 12 selected asset classes. The R-square in factor models is regarded as an appropriate measure of the model's ability to explain the portfolio's returns. In this example, the 12 selected asset classes explain well the returns of the fund. The sum of the 12 coefficient estimates is 72.71 percent. Because the coefficient estimates do not sum to 100 percent, they do not indicate the actual investment weights.

TABLE 19.2 Regression and Quadratic Programming Results (in %) for Trustees' Commingled U.S. Portfolio, January 1985 through December 1989

	Name of asset class	Unconstrained regression	Constrained regression*	Quadratic programming**
1	Bills	14.69	42.65	0
2	Intermediate-term government bonds	−69.51	−68.64	0
3	Long-term government bonds	−2.54	−2.38	0
4	Corporate bonds	16.57	15.29	0
5	Mortgage-related securities	5.19	4.58	0
6	Large-capitalization value stocks	109.52	110.35	69.81
7	Large-capitalization growth stocks	−7.86	−8.02	0
8	Medium-capitalization stocks	−41.83	−43.62	0
9	Small-capitalization stocks	45.65	47.17	30.04
10	Non-U.S. bonds	−1.85	−1.38	0
11	European stocks	6.15	5.77	0.15
12	Japanese stocks	−1.46	−1.79	0
	Total	72.71	100.00	100.00
	R-squared***	95.20	95.16	92.22

*The constraint on the regression coefficients is $\sum_{k=1}^{12}\beta_{ik} = 1$.
**The constraints on the regression coefficients are $\sum_{k=1}^{12}\beta_{ik} = 1$ and $0 \leq \beta_{ik} \leq 0$ for $k = 1, \ldots, 12$.
***The R-square is calculated as $R^2 = 1 - \text{Var}(\varepsilon_{it})/\text{Var}(r_{it})$.

The constrained regression column in Table 19.2 shows the multiple regression estimation results of equation (19.5) with one constraint: The sum of the slope coefficients should be 100 percent (i.e., $\sum_{k=1}^{12}\beta_{ik} = 1$). The analytical solution for the estimation of the regression coefficient with this constraint is provided in the end-of-chapter appendix. Because the coefficient estimates sum to 100 percent, the current slope coefficient estimates could indicate the actual investment weights, unless short sales (represented by negative weights) are prohibited. The R-square is slightly reduced from 95.2 to 95.16 percent. The slope coefficient estimates are not consistent with the fund's actual investment policy, because the investment policy of the fund does not allow short sales. Thus, further constraints are necessary in estimating the regression coefficients of equation (19.5) to produce the estimates consistent with the fund's actual investment policy.

The quadratic programming column in Table 19.2 shows the estimation results of equation (19.5) with two constraints: the constraint of the slope coefficients sum to 100 percent and the constraint that each coefficient lies between 0 percent and 100 percent (i.e., $\sum_{k=1}^{12}\beta_{ik} = 1$ and $0 \leq \beta_{ik} \leq 1$ for $k = 1, \ldots, 12$). By using a quadratic programming algorithm, Sharpe (1992) obtained the coefficient estimates on large-capitalization value stocks and small-capitalization stocks, which are 69.81 percent and 30.04 percent, respectively. The sum of these two estimates almost equals 100 percent. These results indicate that the fund has invested so as to obtain returns similar to those from a portfolio with roughly 70 percent invested in a portfolio of value stocks and 30 percent in a portfolio of small-sized stocks. In other words, the fund's returns are almost *attributable* to value stocks and small-sized stocks. With the addition of the new constraint, the R-square also is decreased slightly from

95.2 to 92.22 percent. This indicates that 92.22 percent of the total variation of the fund's returns can be explained by the variation in the returns from this portfolio's mixture of value stocks and a portfolio of small stocks.

19.3 RETURN DECOMPOSITION-BASED ANALYSIS

Rather than focusing on risk-adjusted returns, performance attribution with return decomposition-based analysis focuses on decomposing the managed portfolio's return. The managed portfolio's return in excess of the benchmark portfolio's return is decomposed into the components attributable to the portfolio manager's allocation and selection decisions. The excess return may be expressed as the sum of the effects from the allocation and selection decisions.

The portfolio managers determine investment weights in each asset class, w_{p_i}, based on their expectation of the future performance of the asset class. Then, they select a portfolio of the securities (or sectors) within each asset class based on their security (or sector) analysis, and the portfolio earns r_{p_i}. Thus, the managed portfolio's return is calculated as $r_p = \sum_i w_{p_i} r_{p_i}$. Likewise, the benchmark portfolio's return is calculated as $r_B = \sum_i w_{B_i} r_{B_i}$. The difference (or the excess return) between the managed portfolio's return (r_p) and the benchmark portfolio's return (r_B) is calculated as

$$\text{Excess return} = r_p - r_B = \sum_i w_{p_i} r_{p_i} - \sum_i w_{B_i} r_{B_i} = \sum_i \left(w_{p_i} r_{p_i} - w_{B_i} r_{B_i} \right) \quad (19.6)$$

where w_{p_i} $\left(w_{B_i} \right)$ is the managed (benchmark) portfolio's weight invested in asset class i and $r_{p_i} (r_{B_i})$ is the return of asset class i in the managed (benchmark) portfolio.

To illustrate this analysis, consider a hypothetical managed portfolio p that invests in three asset classes: stocks, bonds, and cash (or money market securities). Returns and weights of the managed portfolio and the benchmark portfolio are shown in Table 19.3. Based on the data shown in Table 19.3, the managed portfolio's return is 7.58 percent and the benchmark portfolio's return is 5.25 percent. Thus, the excess return is 2.32 percent. Because the performance of the managed portfolio may result from active management and the benchmark portfolio is passively managed, this excess return can be regarded as the consequences of active management. The question to be raised is: Which decisions made by the portfolio manager resulted in this excess return? In other words, how do we decompose the excess return into the contributions made by the manager's decisions?

Figure 19.1 illustrates a framework to answer this question. This figure assumes that portfolio managers actually make two active decisions regarding asset allocation and security selection. Thus, Quadrant I indicates the benchmark return (earned from both *passive* asset allocation and security selection), and Quadrant IV indicates the return of a managed portfolio (earned from both *active* asset allocation and security selection). Difference III-I (Quadrant III–Quadrant I) indicates the excess return earned from the manager's decision that allocates the funds across assets differently from the benchmark weights given, while holding constant the security selection decision. This is the asset allocation effect. Meanwhile, Difference II-I (Quadrant II–Quadrant I) indicates the excess return earned from the manager's

TABLE 19.3 Performance of a Hypothetical Managed Portfolio

	Asset class (i)	Managed portfolio (p)		Benchmark portfolio (B)	
		Return (r_{p_i})	Weight (w_{p_i})	Return (r_{B_i})	Weight (w_{B_i})
1	Stocks	9.20%	0.75	7.30%	0.60
2	Bonds	3.10%	0.20	2.80%	0.25
3	Cash	1.20%	0.05	1.20%	0.15
	Total		1.00		1.00

Portfolio return: $r_p = 7.58\%$ $r_B = 5.26\%$
Excess return: $r_p - r_B = 7.58\% - 5.26\% = 2.32\%$

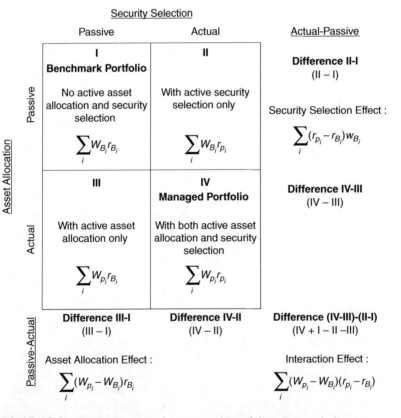

FIGURE 19.1 Decomposition of a Managed Portfolio's Return in Excess of the Benchmark's Return
Source: Adapted from Gary P. Brinson, L. Randolph Hood, and Gilbert L. Beebower, "Determinants of Portfolio Performance," *Financial Analysts Journal* 42, no. 2 (1986): 39–44.

decision that selects securities differently from securities of the benchmark, while holding constant the asset allocation decision. This is the security selection effect. Difference (IV-III)-(II-I) indicates the excess return earned from the manager's asset allocation decision when the performance of the selected securities in the managed portfolio differs from the benchmark. This results from the interaction effect of the asset allocation and the security selection. The sum of these three effects equals the total excess return of the managed portfolio.

Based on Figure 19.1, the excess return in equation (19.6) can be rewritten as the sum of the components attributable to the asset allocation effect, the security (or sector) selection effect, and the interaction effect. That is, the excess return can be decomposed into the following three attributes:

$$\text{Excess return} = r_p - r_B \qquad (19.7)$$

$$= \sum_i \left(w_{p_i} r_{p_i} - w_{B_i} r_{B_i} \right)$$

$$= \underbrace{\sum_i \left(w_{p_i} - w_{B_i} \right) r_{B_i}}_{\substack{\text{Asset allocation} \\ \text{effect}}} + \underbrace{\sum_i \left(r_{p_i} - r_{B_i} \right) w_{B_i}}_{\substack{\text{Security} \\ \text{selection effect}}} + \underbrace{\sum_i \left(w_{p_i} - w_{B_i} \right) \left(r_{p_i} - r_{B_i} \right)}_{\text{Interaction effect}}$$

This decomposition allows investors to view the sources of the overall performance and their manager's ability of asset allocation and security selection.[2] The *asset allocation effect* measures the value added by the manager's decision to allocate the funds across asset classes differently from the benchmark. Thus, the difference between the actual weight and the benchmark weight of each asset class, $w_{p_i} - w_{B_i}$, is the key element in measuring the asset allocation effect. The value added by this effect is calculated as the sum of the multiplications of this difference and the benchmark return of the asset class. The *security selection effect* measures the value added by the manager's decision to select securities that may or may not outperform those of the benchmark. Thus, the difference between the actual return and the benchmark return of each asset class, $r_{p_i} - r_{B_i}$, is the key element in measuring the security selection effect. The value added by this effect is calculated as the sum of the multiplications of this difference and the benchmark weight of the asset class. *The interaction effect* measures the value added by the manager's asset allocation decision when the performance of the selected securities in the managed portfolio is different from that of the benchmark. The value added by this effect is calculated as the sum of the multiplications of the difference in the weight, $w_{p_i} - w_{B_i}$, and the difference in the return, $r_{p_i} - r_{B_i}$. The value added by the interaction effect will be positive when the portfolio manager places more weights in the asset class where the manager exhibits good security selection ability.[3]

Table 19.4 shows the calculation of the value added by the asset allocation effect, by the security selection effect, and by the interaction effect. Panel A of Table 19.4 shows that the portfolio manager increased the allocation in stocks whose return is higher by decreasing the allocation in bonds and cash whose returns are lower. Due to this asset allocation decision across the asset classes, the excess return of 0.835

TABLE 19.4   Performance Attribution of the Managed Portfolio in Table 19.3

Panel A: Contribution of the asset allocation to the excess return

Asset class (i)	Actual weight (w_{p_i})	Benchmark weight (w_{B_i})	Difference in the weight $(w_{p_i} - w_{B_i})$	Benchmark return (r_{B_i})	$(w_{p_i} - w_{B_i})r_{B_i}$
1 Stocks	0.75	0.60	0.15	7.30%	1.095%
2 Bonds	0.20	0.25	−0.05	2.80%	−0.140%
3 Cash	0.05	0.15	−0.10	1.20%	−0.120%
Total	1.00	1.00	0.00		0.835%

Panel B: Contribution of the security selection to the excess return

Asset class (i)	Actual return (r_{p_i})	Benchmark return (r_{B_i})	Difference in the return $(r_{p_i} - r_{B_i})$	Benchmark weight (w_{B_i})	$(r_{p_i} - r_{B_i})w_{B_i}$
1 Stocks	9.20%	7.30%	1.90%	0.60	1.140%
2 Bonds	3.10%	2.80%	0.30%	0.25	0.075%
3 Cash	1.20%	1.20%	0%	0.15	0%
Total				1.00	1.215%

Panel C: Contribution of the interaction to the excess return

Asset class (i)	Difference in the weight $(w_{p_i} - w_{B_i})$	Difference in the return $(r_{p_i} - r_{B_i})$	$(w_{p_i} - w_{B_i}) \times (r_{p_i} - r_{B_i})$
1 Stocks	0.15	1.90%	0.285%
2 Bonds	−0.05	0.30%	−0.015%
3 Cash	−0.10	0.00%	0%
Total			0.270%

Panel D: Sum of all contributions to the excess return

$0.835\% + 1.215\% + 0.270\% = \mathbf{2.32\%}$

percent was earned. Panel B shows that the actual returns of stocks and bonds in the managed portfolio are greater than those of the benchmark. The actual returns of stocks and bonds in the managed portfolio are 1.90 percent and 0.30 percent greater than those of the benchmark, respectively. This indicates that the portfolio manager made a good selection of sectors and/or securities in stocks and bonds that outperform the securities in the benchmark. Thus, the excess return of 1.215 percent can be attributed to this security selection decision within each asset class. Panel C shows that the excess return of 0.270 percent can be attributed to the interaction effect. Panel D shows that the sum of these excess returns exactly equals the total excess return of 2.32 percent.

Panel B of Table 19.4 shows that the stock component of the managed portfolio has a return of 9.20 percent, whereas that of the benchmark has a return of 7.30 percent. The excess return of 1.90 percent in the stock component of the managed portfolio may be attributed to good allocation across sectors (or industries) and a good stock selection within each sector. In other words, the excess return attributable to the security selection within a particular asset class i can be decomposed into finer contributions than the decomposition in equation (19.7):

$$\text{Excess return within an asset class } i = r_{P_i} - r_{B_i} \tag{19.8}$$

$$= \sum_j \left(w_{P_{ij}} r_{P_{ij}} - w_{B_{ij}} r_{B_{ij}} \right)$$

$$= \underbrace{\sum_j \left(w_{P_{ij}} - w_{B_{ij}} \right) r_{B_{ij}}}_{\substack{\text{Sector allocation} \\ \text{effect within an} \\ \text{asset class } i}} + \underbrace{\sum_j \left(r_{P_{ij}} - r_{B_{ij}} \right) w_{B_{ij}}}_{\substack{\text{Stock (or Security)} \\ \text{selection effect} \\ \text{within an asset} \\ \text{class } i}} + \underbrace{\sum_j \left(w_{P_{ij}} - w_{B_{ij}} \right) \left(r_{P_{ij}} - r_{B_{ij}} \right)}_{\substack{\text{Interaction effect} \\ \text{within an asset class } i}}$$

The *sector allocation effect* measures the value added by the manager's decision to allocate the funds across sectors differently from the benchmark. Thus, the difference between the actual weight and the benchmark weight across sectors within a particular asset class i, $w_{P_{ij}} - w_{B_{ij}}$, is the key element in measuring the sector allocation effect. The *stock* (or *security*) *selection effect* measures the value added by the manager's decision to select stocks that may or may not outperform those of the benchmark. Thus, the difference between the actual return and the benchmark return of each sector within a particular asset class i, $r_{P_{ij}} - r_{B_{ij}}$, is the key element in measuring the stock selection effect. *The interaction effect* measures the value added by the manager's sector allocation decision when the performance of the selected stocks in the managed stock portfolio is different from that of the benchmark.

Suppose that the managed stock portfolio ($i = 1$) in Table 19.3 is invested in five sectors ($j = 1, 2, \ldots, 5$): technology, utilities, consumer goods, capital goods, and financials. Further suppose that five different portfolio managers each manage one of these five sector portfolios. Returns and weights of the managed stock portfolio and the benchmark stock portfolio (such as Standard & Poor's 500) are shown in Table 19.5. The excess return of the managed stock portfolio over the benchmark stock portfolio is 1.90 percent. Which portfolio manager's decisions account for this excess return?

Table 19.6 shows the decomposition of the excess return of the managed stock portfolio into the components contributed by the sector allocation effect, by the stock selection effect, and by the interaction effect. Panel A of Table 19.6 calculates the contribution of sector allocation to the excess return of the managed stock portfolio. The stock portfolio manager earned the excess return of 0.614 percent over the benchmark stock portfolio by increasing the allocation of funds to technology stocks and capital goods stocks whose returns are higher and decreasing the allocation to the other sectors whose returns are lower. In other words, this excess return results from the manager's good sector allocation decision. Moreover,

TABLE 19.5 Performance of the Managed Stock Portfolio in Table 19.3

Sector (j)	Managed stock portfolio (p_i)		Benchmark stock portfolio (B_i)	
	Return ($r_{p_{ij}}$)	Weight ($w_{p_{ij}}$)	Return ($r_{B_{ij}}$)	Weight ($w_{B_{ij}}$)
1 Technology	12.40%	0.35	9.10%	0.19
2 Utilities	5.50%	0.16	5.80%	0.28
3 Consumer goods	10.20%	0.10	9.80%	0.13
4 Capital goods	9.60%	0.20	8.26%	0.10
5 Financials	5.48%	0.19	6.16%	0.30
Total		1.00		1.00

Stock portfolio return: $r_{p_i} = 9.20\%$ $\qquad r_{B_i} = 7.30\%$

Excess return: $r_{p_i} - r_{B_i} = 9.20\% - 7.30\% = 1.90\%$

the stock portfolio manager selected stocks that outperformed overall those of the benchmark stock portfolio. Due to this good stock selection, Panel B shows that the excess return of 0.525 percent was earned. Panel C shows that the excess return of 0.762 percent can be attributed to the interaction of the sector allocation and stock selection decisions. The sum of these excess returns exactly equals the excess return of 1.90 percent by the security selection within the stock portfolio in Panel B of Table 19.4.

As done to the stock portion of the managed portfolio shown in Tables 19.5 and 19.6, a similar sector analysis for performance attribution can be done to the other asset classes.

Performance attribution analysis can be done from the broadest asset class level to progressively finer levels. Tables 19.3 and 19.4 illustrate performance attribution analysis at the asset class level. In other words, the overall excess return is decomposed into components contributed by the manager's asset allocation and security selection. Tables 19.5 and 19.6 illustrate performance attribution analysis at the sector level within an asset class. The excess return in a particular asset class is decomposed into components contributed by the manager's sector allocation and selection. The performance attribution analysis can be done at even finer levels (e.g., at the security level). For example, the excess return in a particular section can be decomposed into components contributed by the manager's security allocation and selection. Panel B of Table 19.6 shows that the excess return by stock selection in the utility sector is 3.3 percent. This excess return can be decomposed into the contributions of the individual securities.

The highest level at which performance attribution is analyzed in this chapter is the asset class, such as stocks, bonds, and cash (or money market securities) *within one country*. The performance attribution analysis at a higher level than this can also be performed *across countries*. The performance attribution analysis at the country level, which involves foreign currencies, is illustrated in Singer and Karnosky (1995).[4]

TABLE 19.6 Performance Attribution of the Managed Stock Portfolio in Table 19.5

Panel A: Contribution of the sector allocation to the excess return of the stock portfolio

Sector (j)	Actual weight $(w_{p_{ij}})$	Benchmark weight $(w_{B_{ij}})$	Difference in the weight $(w_{p_{ij}} - w_{B_{ij}})$	Benchmark return $(r_{B_{ij}})$	$(w_{p_{ij}} - w_{B_{ij}})r_{B_{ij}}$
1 Technology	0.35	0.19	0.16	9.10%	1.456%
2 Utilities	0.16	0.28	−0.12	5.80%	−0.696%
3 Consumer goods	0.10	0.13	−0.03	9.80%	−0.294%
4 Capital goods	0.20	0.10	0.10	8.26%	0.826%
5 Financials	0.19	0.30	−0.11	6.16%	−0.678%
Total	1.00	1.00	0.00		0.614%

Panel B: Contribution of the stock selection to the excess return of the stock portfolio

Sector (j)	Actual return $(r_{p_{ij}})$	Benchmark return $(r_{B_{ij}})$	Difference in the return $(r_{p_{ij}} - r_{B_{ij}})$	Benchmark weight $(w_{B_{ij}})$	$(r_{p_{ij}} - r_{B_{ij}})w_{B_{ij}}$
1 Technology	12.40%	9.10%	3.30%	0.19	0.627%
2 Utilities	5.50%	5.80%	−0.30%	0.28	−0.084%
3 Consumer goods	10.20%	9.80%	0.40%	0.13	0.052%
4 Capital goods	9.60%	8.26%	1.34%	0.10	0.134%
5 Financials	5.48%	6.16%	−0.68%	0.30	−0.204%
Total				1.00	0.525%

Panel C: Contribution of the interaction to the excess return of the stock portfolio

Sector (j)	Difference in the weight $(w_{p_{ij}} - w_{B_{ij}})$	Difference in the return $(r_{p_{ij}} - r_{B_{ij}})$	$(w_{p_{ij}} - w_{B_{ij}}) \times (r_{p_{ij}} - r_{B_{ij}})$
1 Technology	0.16	3.30%	0.528%
2 Utilities	−0.12	−0.30%	0.036%
3 Consumer goods	−0.03	0.40%	−0.012%
4 Capital goods	0.10	1.34%	0.134%
5 Financials	−0.11	−0.68%	0.076%
Total	0.00		0.762%

Panel D: Sum of all contributions to the excess return of the stock portfolio

$0.614\% + 0.525\% + 0.762\% = \mathbf{1.90\%}$

19.4 CONCLUSIONS

This chapter discusses three different forms of performance attribution. Sponsors or managers can choose the form of performance attribution analysis they desire. If they want to analyze the portfolio manager's selection ability and market timing ability, the factor model analysis can be used. If they want to analyze the style of a mutual fund, Sharpe's (1992) return-based style analysis would be useful. To analyze the portfolio manager's skill in allocating the funds across asset classes or sectors and in selecting outperforming securities, they can use return decomposition-based analysis.

19.4.1   Detrimental Uses of Portfolio Performance Attribution

The ways in which portfolio performance attribution might have a detrimental impact on Markowitz portfolio theory are difficult to imagine. For example, portfolio performance attribution may be viewed as being a fast, simple, easy-to-use investment selection device that competes with Markowitz portfolio analysis. But because it is not an optimum-seeking procedure, portfolio performance attribution can be expected to yield solutions that are usually dominated by the Markowitz efficient frontier. And, because performance attribution is not a form of comprehensive analysis, it yields only suggestions, not precise conclusions. Thus, as stated at the outset, Markowitz's theory seems to have little to fear from the simpler portfolio performance attribution tools.

19.4.2   Symbiotic Possibilities

Portfolio performance attribution is typically used to delineate a portfolio manager's strengths and weaknesses. Even a scientific portfolio manager who uses Markowitz portfolio analysis expertly can benefit from criticisms and suggestions obtained with the simple tools that comprise portfolio performance attribution. In fact, because the models shown in equation (19.1) and Figure 19.1 exist independently from Markowitz portfolio theory, they can provide useful and insightful findings about how a Markowitz-efficient portfolio is being managed. Thus, we conclude that modern portfolio performance attribution is a valuable tool that supplements the older Markowitz theory–based performance evaluation tools discussed in Chapter 18.[5]

APPENDIX: REGRESSION COEFFICIENTS ESTIMATION WITH CONSTRAINTS

This appendix provides the solutions to the estimation problem of the regression coefficients with no constraints and with the constraint that the slope coefficients sum to one, respectively.

The linear factor model for an asset i to be estimated is

$$r_{it} = a_i + \beta_{i1} r_{F_1,t} + \beta_{i2} r_{F_2,t} + \cdots + \beta_{iK} r_{F_K,t} + \varepsilon_{it} \qquad (19.5)$$

The preceding model can be rewritten in a vector form as

$$r_{it} = a_i + R_t' B_i + \varepsilon_{it} \qquad (A19.1)$$

where $B_i = (\beta_{i1}, \beta_{i2}, \ldots, \beta_{iK})'$ is the $(K \times 1)$ regression coefficient vector and $R_t = (r_{F_1,t}, r_{F_2,t}, \ldots, r_{F_K,t})'$ is the $(K \times 1)$ factor return vector.

A19.1 With No Constraints

The solution to the problem of minimizing the squared error variance (or the tracking error variance) is obtained from

$$\underset{a_i, B_i}{\text{Min}} E\left[\left(r_{it} - a_i - R_t' B_i\right)^2\right] \tag{A19.2}$$

When there are no constraints on the coefficient vector B_i, the regression coefficients are estimated by the ordinary least squares (OLS) method. In this case, the OLS coefficient estimate of B_i is

$$\hat{B}_i = \hat{\Sigma}_{RR}^{-1} \hat{\Sigma}_{rR} \tag{A19.3}$$

where $\hat{\Sigma}_{RR}^{-1}$ is the inverse of the $(K \times K)$ variance-covariance matrix estimate of R_t and $\hat{\Sigma}_{rR}$ is the $(K \times 1)$ covariance vector estimate between r_{it} and R_t. Because there are no constraints on the coefficients, the values of $\hat{B}_i$ do not necessarily constitute positively weighted portfolios. The values shown in the unconstrained regression column of Table 19.2 are obtained by using equation (A19.3). The estimate of the intercept a_i is

$$\hat{\alpha}_i = E\left(r_{it}\right) - E\left(R_t'\right) \hat{B}_i \tag{A19.4}$$

A19.2 With the Constraint of $\sum_{k=1}^{K} \beta_{ik} = 1$

When the constraint of the slope coefficients sum to 100 percent (i.e., $\sum_{k=1}^{K} \beta_{ik} = 1$) is imposed on the optimization problem of equation (A19.2), the formulation for optimization is

$$\underset{a_i, B_i}{\text{Min}} E\left[\left(r_{it} - a_i - R_t' B_i\right)^2\right] \tag{A19.5}$$

$$\text{subject to } B_i' l_K = 1$$

where l_K is a $(K \times 1)$ column vector of ones. Based on DeRoon, Nijman, and Werker (2001) and DeRoon and Nijman (2001), the solution to the optimization problem of equation (A19.5) provides the slope coefficient estimates as

$$\tilde{B}_i = \hat{B}_i + \left(1 - \hat{B}_i' l_K\right) \hat{\Sigma}_{RR}^{-1} l_K \left(l_K' \hat{\Sigma}_{RR}^{-1} l_K\right)^{-1} \tag{A19.6}$$

Note that $\tilde{B}_i$ is the restricted OLS estimate of B_i, whereas $\hat{B}_i$ is the unrestricted OLS estimate of B_i, which is equal to equation (A19.3). Equation (A19.6) shows that if the sum of the OLS coefficient estimates equals 1 (i.e., $\hat{B}_i' l_K = 1$), $\tilde{B}_i$ equals $\hat{B}_i$.

The expression in the last term of equation (A19.6), $\hat{\Sigma}_{RR}^{-1} l_K \left(l_K' \hat{\Sigma}_{RR}^{-1} l_K\right)^{-1}$, equals the weights for the global minimum variance portfolio (MVP), which consists of the K factor portfolios. That is,

$$w_{\text{MVP}} = \hat{\Sigma}_{RR}^{-1} l_K \left(l_K' \hat{\Sigma}_{RR}^{-1} l_K\right)^{-1} \tag{A19.7}$$

This is exactly the same as the expression in equation (A7.6) of Chapter 7. Let $v_i = \hat{B}_i' l_K$. Then, $\tilde{B}_i$ of equation (A19.6) can be rewritten as

$$\tilde{B}_i = \hat{B}_i + (1 - v_i)\, w_{\text{MVP}}$$

$$= v_i \left(\frac{\hat{B}_i}{\hat{B}_i' l_K} \right) + (1 - v_i)\, w_{\text{MVP}} \tag{A19.8}$$

Equation (A19.8) indicates that the fund i's restricted exposures to the styles, $\tilde{B}_i$, are equal to a weighted average of the global MVP and a hedge portfolio $\hat{B}_i/\hat{B}_i' l_K$. Note that $\hat{B}_i/\hat{B}_i' l_K$ is the normalized weight vector for the K factor portfolios. The estimate of the intercept a_i in the optimization problem of equation (A19.5) is

$$\tilde{\alpha}_i = E(r_{it}) - E(R_t')\, \tilde{B}_i$$

$$= \hat{\alpha}_i + (\hat{B}_i' l_K - 1)\, E(r_t^{\text{MVP}}) \tag{A19.9}$$

where $\hat{\alpha}_i$ is the OLS intercept estimate of equation (A19.4), $E(r_t^{\text{MVP}})$ is the expected return of the global MVP, and $r_t^{\text{MVP}} = R_t'\, w_{\text{MVP}}$.

The restricted coefficient estimate in equation (A19.6), $\tilde{B}_i$, yields the style portfolio that is closest to the fund i. In this sense, it is the best mimicking portfolio. The difference between the fund's return, r_{it}, and the return on the mimicking portfolio, $R_t'\tilde{B}_i$, indicates the tracking error, $r_{it} - R_t'\tilde{B}_i$. Thus, the mimicking portfolio is the portfolio that yields the smallest tracking error variance.

NOTES

1. Lehmann and Modest (1987) found that the Jensen measure for selection ability is quite sensitive to the method used to construct the APT benchmark and there are considerable differences between the performance measures yielded by the CAPM benchmarks and those produced with the APT benchmarks. Their findings suggest the importance of knowing the appropriate model for risk and expected return.
2. This decomposition approach was suggested by Brinson and Fachler (1985) and Brinson, Singer, and Beebower (1986, 1991).
3. Ankrim (1992) suggested a risk-adjusted performance attribution to avoid the distortion in the measurement of the determinants of portfolio performance in the case that portfolio managers systematically choose portfolios whose risk levels differ from their appropriate benchmarks. The returns in equation (19.7) are replaced with the returns predicted by the CAPM.
4. Allen (1991) analyzed the performance attribution of a global equity portfolio in six different types of the manager's decision: country selection (equity), security selection, country selection (currency), timing effect, policy hedge effect, and active hedging effect.
5. One of several easy-to-read books that focus on portfolio performance attribution is Bruce J. Feibel's *Investment Performance Measurement* (Hoboken, NJ: John Wiley and Sons, 2003).

CHAPTER 20

Stock Market Developments

Stock markets have changed more since the year 2000 than they did during the 50 years before 2000. Technological advancements have reshaped securities markets, new high-tech stock markets have been created, old stock exchanges have consolidated in new and unusual ways, the Securities and Exchange Commission (SEC) has written new laws to encourage and facilitate these changes, stock exchanges' trading orders have been implemented in new ways that increase market liquidity, and there have been other developments that may have implications for Markowitz portfolio theory. This chapter assesses the impact of these recent developments on Markowitz portfolio theory and analysis. Conclusions are reached about what stock market changes favor the use of Markowitz portfolio analysis, and what changes are not favorable.

A *market* is a public arena where buyers and sellers come together to trade. Traditional stock exchanges like the New York Stock Exchange (NYSE) and the London Stock Exchange (LSE) have impressive physical locations. In recent years, electronic technology has made the existence of a physical location less important. The National Association of Securities Dealers Automated Quotations, or Nasdaq, for example, is a successful market that is not associated with any physical location.[1] And the informal interbank foreign exchange market (forex), which is the largest financial market in the world, has no central headquarters. It seems that having an impressive edifice and/or a centralized trading floor has become an unimportant determinant of a stock market's success. But having a liquid market is still important.

Ideally, it should be possible to sell the assets traded in a market quickly without suffering significant price declines. This kind of stock market liquidity can only be achieved if competing buyers and sellers always stand ready and willing to trade. An electronic trading network can obtain the flow of buy and sell orders needed to create market liquidity by drawing in transactions from a large geographic area. And stock market consolidations increase the geographic area from which a market can draw liquidity-creating traders.

20.1 RECENT NYSE CONSOLIDATIONS

This section reviews important NYSE acquisitions and mergers that diversified the exchange geographically and also diversified its product line. The acquired markets are described before the consolidation is evaluated.

20.1.1   Archipelago

In 2000 Archipelago was an *electronic communications network (ECN)* for direct securities trading without the need for a trading floor or market makers (such as NYSE specialists). It operated the first all-electronic stock exchange in the United States. In 2004 Archipelago had an initial public offering (IPO) and became a privately owned, publicly traded, profit-seeking corporation. Other stock exchanges found Archipelago's characteristics attractive.

20.1.2   Pacific Stock Exchange (PSE)

The PSE is a venerable regional stock exchange that can be traced back to the founding of the San Francisco Stock and Bond Exchange in 1882. The PSE has been officially registered with the SEC for decades.

20.1.3   ArcaEx

Archipelago purchased the PSE in 2004 and a new corporation named ArcaEx was born. ArcaEx was an old stock exchange on the day it was born because the PSE had been an SEC-registered securities exchange for decades. But the PSE changed its name and adopted modern technology in 2004. The computer technicians from Archipelago immediately began implementing improvements that permitted ArcaEx to trade all Nasdaq-listed stocks, all NYSE-listed stocks, and all American Stock Exchange-listed stocks on one electronic trading platform. This was a leap forward from the technologically backward U.S. stock market that existed in 2004. Today ArcaEx can trade all these U.S. stock exchange-listed stocks and also options. ArcaEx is on the cutting edge of electronic stock exchange developments. ArcaEx made it possible for a small individual investor to determine the national best bid and offer (NBBO) prices for stocks and transact at those prices, as first suggested by the National Market System law of 1975.[2] In the years since the merger ArcaEx morphed (as will be explained shortly) into NYSE Arca.

20.1.4   New York Stock Exchange (NYSE)

From the Depression in the 1930s to 2006, the NYSE was a mutual company that was owned by its members. It was a not-for-profit *self-regulating organization (SRO)* that was supposed to be managed for the public welfare. In other words, the NYSE should have been operated somewhat like a library or a hospital. Between 1940 and 2006 the stock exchanges that compete with the NYSE (a) adopted more modern electronic technology, (b) diversified into things like bond trading, options trading, futures trading, and/or new products like exchange-traded funds (ETFs), and (c) merged to gain geographical diversification. But during those years the NYSE remained a labor-intensive stock market with an active trading floor primarily run by about 400 market makers called NYSE specialists.[3] Some of these specialists were grey-haired traders who resisted technology because it might automate them out of their high-paying positions. By 2000 each specialist had a PC and used it to keep track of his or her inventory and execute small routine trades. But the NYSE lagged behind other securities exchanges in technology and diversification. When Richard Grasso was CEO, the NYSE tended to maximize the specialists' wealth rather than improve the public welfare.[4] As a result of such policies, on December 1, 2005, one NYSE seat (one membership in the NYSE) sold for the all-time high price of $4 million.

20.1.5 NYSE Group

On December 30, 2005, with the highly qualified John Thain as its new CEO, the NYSE ceased selling seats and, instead, started selling annual trading licenses. In March 2006 the NYSE and ArcaEx (previously Archipelago and the PSE) announced the completion of a merger that created the NYSE Group. Concurrently, the NYSE demutualized by having an initial public offering (IPO) and became a publicly-traded, profit-seeking corporation. In the decades during which the NYSE was still a mutual company it could make important decisions based on the votes from its 1,366 member/owners. But the new profit-seeking NYSE had to earn competitive returns for its new external investor/owners instead of misusing its previous SRO status to maximize the profits of the previous NYSE members. Shares of stock in the NYSE Group stock began trading on the NYSE under the ticker symbol: NYX.

Following the 2006 NYSE-ArcaEx merger, ArcaEx's electronic technology replaced the NYSE's labor-intensive specialist system and diversified the NYSE's product line to include options trading. After the NYSE's floor trading became electronically capable in the spring of 2007, hundreds of NYSE floor traders were automated out of their jobs—they resigned or were laid off. Before the end of 2007 the NYSE closed three of its five trading rooms, which means it had shut down approximately half of its trading floor space. The NYSE joined the electronic age, belatedly, in 2007, after getting rid of top management (CEO Richard Grasso exited in 2005) that had resisted modern technology.

After reformulating the NYSE to become a modern securities exchange, John Thain resigned to become CEO of Merrill Lynch in November 2007.[5] Duncan Niederauer, whom Thain previously hired from Goldman Sachs, became the CEO of the NYSE Group in November 2007.

20.1.6 NYSE Diversifies Internationally

In 2005 Euronext was a technologically advanced stock exchange in Paris. Euronext's electronic trading platform included European securities exchanges in Paris, Amsterdam, Brussels, Portugal, and a London derivatives exchange named London International Financial Futures Exchange (LIFFE). On June 2, 2006 the NYSE Group, under the leadership of John Thain, merged with Euronext to create an international stock exchange with an aggregate total value of $21 billion. The SEC approved the NYSE-Euronext merger in 2007. Thus, the NYSE Group diversified its product line to include derivatives trading and, simultaneously, diversified its market geographically into Europe.

20.1.7 NYSE Alliances

Before resigning in November 2007 John Thain steered the NYSE Group into other consolidations. In January 2007 the NYSE Group and three other investors agreed to cooperate in buying small (five percent apiece) stakes in the National Stock Exchange (NSE) of India, located in Mumbai (formerly Bombay). The NYSE Group formed an alliance with the Tokyo Stock Exchange (TSE), the second-largest stock exchange in the world in 2007. A document describing this alliance states that the TSE and NYSE would cooperate in aligning their regulations, electronic trading platforms, and other factors that would facilitate an eventual merger of the two exchanges. In January 2008 NYSE/Euronext agreed to pay $260 million in stock to purchase the NYSE's Wall Street neighbor, the American Stock Exchange (AMEX). (It might be clarifying to note that Nasdaq merged with the AMEX in 1996 and later reversed that merger. AMEX became independent again circa 2005.) NYSE/Euronext and the Tel Aviv Stock Exchange (TASE) signed an agreement in June 2008 with the objective of increasing the cross-listing of securities on each other's stock exchanges.[6]

20.2   INTERNATIONAL SECURITIES EXCHANGE (ISE)

In February 2000 four New York City entrepreneurs registered the newly conceived International Securities Exchange (ISE) with the SEC. ISE was designed to be totally electronic because that technology offered faster transactions, low variable costs per transaction, fewer opportunities to introduce human errors, and the increased transparency that facilitates competition with other exchanges. Initially, the ISE concentrated on making an options market because options promised more growth in trading volume and wider profit margins than stock trading. By 2002 ISE grew to list options representing 90 percent of the average daily options-trading volume in the United States. Within a few years the ISE was competing directly with the older Chicago Board of Options Exchange (CBOE). In 2005 the ISE became the first securities exchange to sell its shares in an initial public offering (IPO). The *ISE Stock Exchange* was launched in 2006. A subsidiary of Deutsche Bourse Group named Eurex (ticker: DB1) acquired ISE and its new stock exchange on April 30, 2007 for $2.8 billion, creating the world's first trans-Atlantic derivatives exchange. Within seven years the four founders of ISE were rewarded for their ingenuity and risk taking by becoming multimillionaires.[7] Today the combined Eurex and ISE markets are the world market leaders in individual equity derivatives and in equity index derivatives. A large part of ISE's success can be attributed to its use of the electronic technology that the older U.S. stock and commodity exchanges had resisted. The newer, internally financed ISE did not have to fight this internal anticomputer bias.

20.3   NASDAQ

The National Association of Security Dealers Automated Quotations (Nasdaq) is the electronic portion of the over-the-counter (OTC) stock market in the United States. Nasdaq sold its stock and became a publicly-owned profit-seeking stock exchange in 2000, although Nasdaq's stock was not listed for public trading until 2005. Nasdaq was the second-largest stock exchange in the United States in 2007. Nasdaq had purchased an ECN named Instinet in 2005. Instinet is a well-known (third-market) firm operating an ECN that trades exchange-listed securities in the OTC market. The merger was not a marriage made in heaven and the combination was unwound a few years later. Then, when Nasdaq saw that its New York City neighbor and competitor, the NYSE, was carrying out exciting improvements under John Thain's leadership, Nasdaq started seeking new ways to grow. For starters, Nasdaq imagined that the London Stock Exchange would make an attractive partner.

20.3.1 London Stock Exchange (LSE)

The London Stock Exchange (LSE) is noteworthy in several respects. The two-century-old LSE was the world's third largest stock market in 2007. In 1997 (a decade before the NYSE) LSE made a switch to electronic technology that left its trading floor without any significant human activity. The LSE went on to spend four years and 40 billion euros developing a high-speed trading system named Infolect that went active in 2007. Infolect increased the Exchange's trading volume significantly. In the first half of 2007 LSE purchased its small Italian rival, Borsa Italiana, for 1.6 billion euros ($2.15 billion), after fending off several competing offers. Other than making a few small acquisitions, LSE's management chose to remain independent at a time when many other exchanges were consolidating. The LSE had a female CEO with a royal title—Dame Clara Furse.

In March 2006 Nasdaq offered $4.1 billion to acquire the LSE, but the offer was rejected. Later in 2006 Nasdaq purchased 30 percent of LSE's outstanding shares in hopes this would increase the likelihood of the merger. Recast as a 30 percent owner, in January 2007 Nasdaq raised its bid price for LSE to $5.7 billion. Dame Clara Furse wrote a letter to the LSE shareholders suggesting they reject Nasdaq's proposal, and the majority did. In August 2007 Nasdaq gave up and announced it would soon liquidate all its LSE shares. Nasdaq never liquidated those shares, and, as explained next, those shares later turned out to have an unanticipated impact on Dame Clara Furse and on the LSE.

20.3.2 OMX Group

The OMX Group is a Swedish-Finnish financial services company with two divisions. First, OMX Exchanges operates seven stock exchanges in Nordic and Baltic countries. Second, OMX Technology creates markets systems for financial transactions used by OMX Exchanges and other stock exchanges. OMX is a technology powerhouse that supplies technology to 60 stock exchanges in 50 countries. OMX also controls stock and derivatives exchanges in Copenhagen, Stockholm, Helsinki, Iceland, Riga, Tallinn, and Lithuania.

Very early in 2007, Nasdaq tentatively agreed to merge with OMX to form the Nasdaq-OMX Group. After a Nasdaq-OMX merger, the combined firm would trade 4,000 stocks (including European stocks like Volvo and Nokia) from 39 countries with an aggregate market capitalization of approximately $5.5 trillion. It seemed like Sweden's financial regulator, Finansinspektionen, and the SEC only had to approve the OMX-Nasdaq merger to complete a "marriage made in heaven". But the forthcoming marriage was brought to a sudden halt by Arabs from Dubai that had deep pockets.

20.3.3 Bourse Dubai

Dubai is the name of a city located on the Persian Gulf coast. In addition, Dubai is the name of an emirate that is part of (a state in) the United Arab Emirates (UAE), and that emirate contains the aforementioned city of Dubai. The emirate has the largest population in the UAE and, after Abu Dhabi, has the second-largest land area. Some people are surprised to learn that petroleum and natural gas generate only a small fraction (6% in 2006) of Dubai's national income. Historically, Dubai has been a trade center. More recently, Dubai has attracted worldwide attention for its real estate and financial developments.

The Bourse Dubai is a state-owned institution that owns both of Dubai's two stock exchanges. Bourse Dubai stopped the forthcoming Nasdaq-OMX merger by making an unsolicited $4 billion cash offer to buy the OMX Group, which exceeded Nasdaq's $3.6 billion bid for OMX. Nasdaq and Bourse Dubai immediately went into secret negotiations about the OMX deal. By May 30, 2007, Dubai, OMX, and Nasdaq came up with the following complex deal, which provided desired benefits for each party: (a) Bourse Dubai would buy OMX and then immediately sell OMX to Nasdaq for $3.7 billion. Thus, Nasdaq and OMX could merge, a marriage which both were eager to consummate. (b) Bourse Dubai would be permitted to buy a 20 percent stake in Nasdaq. This acquisition gave Dubai a respectable position in the U.S. financial market, which it was seeking. (c) Bourse Dubai would also buy the 30 percent share of the LSE that Nasdaq still owned. This acquisition would give Dubai a significant position in Britain's financial market. All the relevant nations' regulators approved the deal. As the dust from the Nasdaq-OMX deal settled, some observers hypothesized that the LSE's CEO, Dame Furse, might have been too independent when she rejected Nasdaq's earlier proposal. Dame Furse resigned her LSE post in May 2009.

20.3.4   Boston Stock Exchange (BSE)

While negotiating to buy OMX in Sweden (on October 2, 2007), Nasdaq purchased the Boston Stock Exchange (BSE). After being independent for 173 years, this purchase put the BSE under new managers. The deal included almost everything the BSE owned except the Boston Options Exchange. The BSE's options market was sold to the Montreal Exchange. In addition to another trading venue, Nasdaq also gained a clearing license that allowed it to clear and settle its trades through the BSE's back office. Clearing and settling is the process by which buyers and sellers actually exchange money and shares. Acquiring the BSE permitted Nasdaq to stop paying a third party approximately $14 million a year to clear and settle its transactions.

20.3.5   Philadelphia Stock Exchange (PHLX)

In 2007 the Philadelphia Stock Exchange (PHLX) was the oldest stock exchange in the United States, and the third-largest options exchange in the United States. Nasdaq was interested in the PHLX's options business because trading in financial futures, options, and derivatives was expanding more rapidly than stock exchange trading, and trading derivatives offers larger profit margins than stock trading. Thus, in November 2007, while negotiating to buy OMX in Sweden, Nasdaq also acquired a large (controlling) share of PHLX's stock for $652 million.

20.4   DOWNWARD PRESSURES ON TRANSACTIONS COSTS

The preceding rapid-fire consolidations between securities exchanges contributed to worldwide advances in electronic trading technology. While these advances proceeded, stock market regulations were being revised. These developments also put downward pressure on the transactions costs in U.S. stock markets. The legal changes are considered first.

20.4.1   A National Market System (NMS)

A loosely defined concept of a national market system (NMS) was introduced by Congress in the Securities Act Amendments of 1975. Regulation National Market System of 2005, nicknamed Reg NMS, formalized the previously vague NMS concept. The 2005 Reg NMS included an Access Rule, which granted the investing public access to all stock price quotations. This made it illegal for market professionals to reserve the best trading prices for only their largest clients. And the Order Protection Rule (or Trade Through Rule) was included to require that competing market-makers immediately and automatically share access to inter-market stock price quotations. The Trade Through Rule increased the likelihood that small investors find and trade at the national best bid and offer (NBBO) prices, rather than be shown stock price quotations that were less desirable. Reg NMS also suggested the desirability of creating a larger number of competing stock markets within the United States. Having the NYSE and Nasdaq control over 90 percent of the U.S. stock market transactions, as Table 20.1 shows they did in 1995, did not create enough competition to please the SEC lawyers. So, the SEC enacted Reg NMS and took the other steps listed next to achieve the fragmented stock market Table 20.1 shows existed in 2010.

We can conclude from Table 20.1 that the NYSE and Nasdaq market shares of total U.S. share-trading volume shrank substantially from 1995 to 2010. These

TABLE 20.1   Percentages of Share-Trading Volume in the U.S. Stock Market, 1995 and 2010

	1995	2010
S.E.C.-registered stock exchanges		
Nasdaq	52%	19%
Nasdaq OMX BX	0	3%
Nasdaq subtotal	52%	22%
NYSE	39%	14%
NYSE Arca	0	14%
NYSE subtotal	39%	28%
BATS in Kansas City	0	10%
Other exchanges	9%	4%
Subtotal for all exchanges	100%	64%
Dark pools (e.g., Liquidnet)		
Total for 32 pools	0	8%
Electronic communication networks (ECNs)		
Direct Edge	0	10%
Other ECNs	0	1%
Subtotal for ECNs	0	11%
Internalized trading within brokers and dealers	0	17%
Total Volume	100%	100%

Sources: "Origin of the Scare on Wall Street Eludes Federal Regulators," *New York Times*, May 8, 2010, pages A1 and B7. NYSE Factbook, 1996. Nasdaq Factbook 1997.

changes occurred for two resons. First, the U.S. stock market was fragmented by the arrival of new electronic markets. Second, Reg NMS encouraged the formation of competing markets.

20.4.2 The SEC's Reg ATS

Reg ATS is the nickname for an SEC regulation covering automatic trading systems (ATS). Reg ATS was enacted in 1999 and revised thereafter. Reg ATS encouraged every competing market maker to either (a) register as a broker with the National Association of Securities Dealers (NASD), (b) register with the SEC as an exchange, or (c) operate as an unregulated ATS that operates within small trading volume limitations. Any ATS with a trading volume of less than 5 percent of the total market volume in any stock or bond was not required to register as an exchange and was forbidden to use the word "exchange" in its name. But any ATS with over 20 percent of the trading volume in any stock or bond was required to register with the SEC and publish rules that helped merge that ATS into a competitive national market system (NMS). Reg ATS also permitted small electronic communications networks (ECNs) to develop and compete in the NMS without being encumbered to register with the SEC as an exchange. Thus, Reg ATS set the stage for dark pools (e.g., Liquidnet, Pipeline), high-frequency traders (BATS, Getco, etc.), and other ATSs to spring up and compete with the NYSE and Nasdaq, as illustrated in Table 20.1.

20.4.3 Reg FD

The SEC's Full Disclosure Regulation, called Reg FD, was adopted in 2000. It addresses the selective disclosure of information by publicly traded companies and other issuers of securities. Reg FD requires publicly traded corporations to immediately make full public disclosure of any material (i.e., significant) information that they disclose to securities markets professionals (such as stock analysts or holders of the issuer's securities). The purpose of this law was to make inside information public and help small investors share in the new information made available by the latest technological developments.

20.4.4 Decimalization of Stock Prices

The SEC ordered all U.S. stock markets to convert their prices to decimal prices[8] by April 9, 2001, to eliminate the inconvenient fractions of pennies. Decimalization reduced the smallest price change permitted, called a *tick*, to one penny instead of continuing to use price ticks of six and one-quarter cents. Decimalization squeezed much of the profit out of the bid-ask spread. In other words, in addition to writing new SEC regulations that encouraged the creation of a larger number of competing U.S. stock markets, the decimalization decree also enabled investors to enjoy the declining transactions costs illustrated in Figure 20.1.

20.4.5 Technological Advances

While cloud computing was beginning to take off in the United States, other technological developments were evolving. Scientists were using optical fibers to

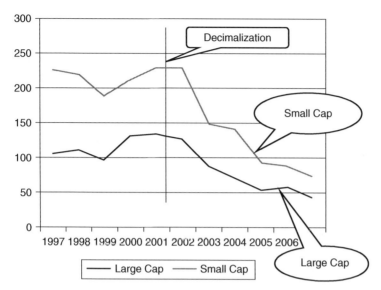

FIGURE 20.1   Declining Transactions Costs in the United States
Source: Wayne H. Wagner and Ralph A. Rieves, *Investment Management* (New York: John Wiley & Sons, 2009), 304, Exhibit 21.1. The figure was computed from transactions between institutional investors; no retail investors were involved. However, the transactions costs between institutional investors and retail investors declined similarly.

provide more bandwidth for transporting the continually growing Internet traffic. And the NYSE's 2006 merger with Archipelago created the first intercontinental stock market. All the while, technology continued to make electronic trading cheaper, faster, and less prone to clerical errors. Technology also fostered the use of a type of securities trading order called the limit order.

20.5   THE VENERABLE LIMIT ORDER

Trading with limit orders facilitates making automated trading decisions and provides additional market liquidity.

20.5.1   What Are Limit Orders?

A *limit order* is an order to buy or sell at an advantageous price. Limit orders require that the minimum selling price to be received or the maximum purchase price to be paid must be either equal to or more desirable than the limit price. These orders are sometimes called *limit or better orders*. If the limit order cannot be executed immediately, the order is recorded in the market maker's *limit order book (LOB)* and held for future execution if and when the market reaches the limit price or a better price. If the client attaches an expiration time to a limit order, that order may expire before it is executed. A problem with limit orders is that, very infrequently, in a fast-moving market a limit order might accidently be passed over without being executed as the security's market price moves quickly past the limit price without being noticed.

20.5.2 Creating Market Liquidity

If all other factors are equal, liquid securities (such as NYSE stocks) are more desirable than illiquid securities (such as unlisted stocks that are traded infrequently), because liquid securities can be quickly and easily converted into cash without causing significant price changes.

The limit orders listed in a market-maker's limit order book (LOB) are trading opportunities that offer valuable liquidity to other traders who may be considering whether to buy or sell. Traders who post limit orders for other traders to consider provide free options for others to trade known securities at posted prices. Some U.S. securities exchanges pay traders small fees of $0.002 per share to post limit orders to buy and/or sell at their exchange, because having a large menu of limit orders available increases the exchange's liquidity and draws investors away from trading at less-liquid exchanges. These securities exchanges also charge small fees of $0.003 per share to dealers who reduce the exchange's liquidity by placing stop orders. A stop order is an order to sell (buy) when the price of a security falls (rises) to a designated level. The cost of posting a (liquidity-producing) limit order is ($0.002 + $0.003 = $0.005 =) one-half cent per share below the cost of posting a (liquidity-consuming) stop order.

20.6 MARKET MICROSTRUCTURE

Securities markets are made by people, computers, or companies called *market makers*. Market makers are *dealers* who supply a market with liquidity. For example, if a dealer wants to make markets in a dozen stocks, the dealer should post 12 different *bid prices* for the dozen stocks in an active electronic market and buy whatever number of shares clients offer for sale at those 12 bid prices. In addition, that dealer should post *ask prices* for the same dozen stocks and sell whatever numbers of shares the clients want to buy at the posted ask prices. The new dealer should set competitive bid and ask prices and always be ready to transact quickly, because securities brokers prefer active dealers who make liquid markets over inactive dealers.

20.6.1 Inventory Management

Because dealers compete by standing continually ready to buy and sell securities at their posted bid and ask prices, they sometimes accumulate inventories. It is risky and expensive for market makers to carry inventories, so they continually try to minimize them. Market makers control the size of their inventories of securities by altering their bid and ask prices at frequent intervals. The asked (or offer) price for any given security is usually pennies (but, occasionally, dollars) above the bid price. Because a large part of a dealer's income is earned from the *bid-ask spread* on each trade, smaller bid-ask spreads require dealers to transact more volume to earn as much as they earned in the years past.[9]

When clients unexpectedly sell large quantities of a security, many dealers eagerly accumulate an inventory of long positions in that security rather than miss those opportunities to buy. As a result, dealers sometimes build up large inventories of long positions in one or more securities. A dealer with an uncomfortably large positive inventory can shrink that inventory (downward toward zero) by either lowering the dealer's bid price, lowering the dealer's ask price, or lowering both prices.

Dealers would like to carry no inventories, but this would hinder their ability to make markets. Profitable dealers see their inventories as necessary evils that cannot be eliminated.

When clients unexpectedly place large orders to buy a security in which a dealer has insufficient inventory, many dealers will sell that security short rather than miss an opportunity to sell. As a result of short selling, dealers sometimes accumulate large inventories of short positions in one or more securities. A dealer with an uncomfortably large negative inventory can shrink that negative inventory (upward toward zero) by either raising the bid price, raising the ask price, or raising both prices.

20.6.2 Brokers

Brokers are commissioned sales people who are typically employed by dealers. Some brokers claim they have salaried jobs; however, it has been noted that their salaries are frequently realigned with the sales revenues they generate. Brokers do not have their own money invested in the securities they buy and sell. Unlike brokers, dealers must continually maintain risky investments in inventories of the securities in which they choose to make markets. Merrill Lynch is one of the largest securities dealers in the world; Merrill employs about 16,000 brokers and carries inventories in a few thousand stocks. There are also thousands of owner-operated dealers operating out of their home offices who compete with Merrill by making markets in only one or a few securities. In between huge Merrill Lynch and the numerous tiny owner-operated dealers are hundreds of medium-sized securities dealers that make markets in 10 to 1,000 stocks.

20.7 HIGH-FREQUENCY TRADING

By 2008 alternative trading systems (ATSs) were stealing transactions from the organized exchanges by offering faster and cheaper places to trade. Their lightning-fast computers are valued by high-frequency traders who measured their trading times in microseconds, or millionths of a second.[10] These new electronic markets are inexpensive for brokers to use because they offer commission rebates to liquidity providers who post their bid and ask prices and, in so doing, increase the depth and breadth of securities available in the market.

High-frequency trading providers include a private company named Getco, headquartered in Chicago.[11] Getco was founded in 1999 and is a registered market maker with operations around the world in stocks, bonds, options, futures, and currencies. In 2009 Getco employed 250 people and sometimes generated 10 to 20 percent of NYSE's daily trading volume. Other high-frequency providers include the BATS Exchanges in Kansas City, Goldman Sachs Group in New York City, a Chicago hedge fund named Citadel Investment Group, a hedge fund named Renaissance Technologies, Jane Street Capital LLC, Hudson River Trading LLC, Wolverine Trading LLC, Jump Trading LLC, and Chi-X in Europe. If they desire, high-frequency traders can pay a fee to exchanges like Nasdaq for the privilege of seeing other clients' incoming buy and sell orders, called *flash orders*, 30 milliseconds (0.03 seconds) before the general public.

Flash orders were pioneered at the CBOE in the early 2000s to speed options trading. Market makers who pay to gain access to flash orders obtain split-second indications of interest from forthcoming buyers and sellers. The market makers respond to these indications of interest in milliseconds by posting limit orders to supply the liquidity the forthcoming buyers and sellers want and need. This allows the market to work more quickly by providing ample pools of securities whenever investors need them. In 2009 some stock exchange executives and politicians announced they disliked flash orders because flash orders seemed to give high-speed traders an unfair 30 millisecond head start on the public traders. These critics asked the SEC to outlaw high-frequency trading. These critics seem to attach no value to the valuable market liquidity that is supplied by the high-frequency traders. In 2009 high-frequency trading accounted for 73 percent of all U.S. equity trading volume.[12]

20.8　ALTERNATIVE TRADING SYSTEMS (ATSs)

After thinking about high-frequency trading, people often ask: How can so many shares be traded so rapidly? The answer: High-frequency traders get the shares they need to create liquidity by using alternative trading systems (ATSs) like crossing networks and dark pools.[13]

20.8.1　Crossing Networks

Crossing networks were initially developed early in the 2000s. A crossing network is an electronic network that matches identical but offsetting orders to buy and sell a given security without first routing the order to a stock exchange where the buy and sell orders would be displayed to the public. Most crossing networks use computers to aggregate nonpublic quotes and match buy and sell orders at a price that, typically, is halfway between the bid and asked prices posted on the competing organized exchanges. Two big advantages of the crossing network are that it has no impact on the publicly quoted price and the traders can remain anonymous. Active crossing networks are operated by large brokerage houses, Liquidnet, ITG's Posit, Nasdaq Crossing Network, Pipeline, and Goldman Sachs's Sigma X. Crossing networks are opaque because they never display to the public any bid or asked prices or information about the shares traded.

20.8.2　Dark Pools

Dark pools are institutional trading organizations that are available to institutions and a few very wealthy individual investors. The execution prices and volume of shares transacted within dark pools cannot be seen by the public. Dark pools obtain their liquidity from block trades (transactions of 10,000 shares or more) that are done away from the stock exchange in what is sometimes called the *upstairs market* (that is, on an upper floor in an office building that is located away frome the stock exchange floor). This type of market liquidity can remain hidden from public view by using reserve orders posted on electronic limit order books run by competing market makers. Crossing networks provide another source of dark pool liquidity that is unreported to the public. And wealthy speculators are always ready to provide liquidity to any market where they see an opportunity to profit. Most of these wealthy investors prefer to remain unnamed. The crossing networks, dark pools, and wealthy speculators are available to instantly supply liquidity to high-frequency traders.

20.9   ALGORITHMIC TRADING

Buy-and-hold investors hope to profit by collecting cash dividend income, coupon interest income, and price appreciation that accumulates gradually with the passage of time. They often study the risk and return characteristics of various asset classes, and then buy a mutual fund that is indexed to the asset class they find attractive. Buy-and-hold investors are usually *passive investors* that trade infrequently. In contrast, *active investors* who seek to buy low and sell high usually trade frequently as they endeavor to profit from short-term price movements. These active investors study current news about different corporations as they seek to buy before the price of a stock rises and sell before a stock's price declines.

Recently a combination of technologically advanced securities markets, decimalized stock prices, and limit orders have enabled a third new group of traders to generate substantial portions of each day's national trading volume by employing computer programs referred to as *trading algorithms*. Trading algorithms are computer codes that enable stock market traders to do algorithmic trading, or automated trading. In 2006 a Boston-based financial research and consulting firm named Aite Group estimated that one-third of all the stock trading in the European Union and in the United States was done by algorithmic trading. Algorithmic trading has also been popular in the world's largest financial market, the informal interbank foreign exchange (forex) market. It has been estimated that 25 percent of all forex trading in 2006 was automated trading.[14] The profitability of algorithmic trading is harder to estimate, but an August 2009 report issued by a financial services research firm named the TABB Group was informative. The TABB Group, which specializes in algorithmic trading, estimated that the 300 securities firms and hedge funds that used algorithmic trading had aggregate earnings of $21 billion in 2008.[15] Algorithmic trading has been shown to significantly improve the liquidity of a market.[16]

20.9.1   Some Algorithmic Trading Applications

One of the earliest applications of algorithmic trading was the development of electronic order working systems to reduce trading costs.

Electronic Order Working Systems   An electronic order working system is an electronic communications network (ECN) that handles a client's buy and/or sell orders electronically by performing one or more of the following eight tasks.

1. Initial data gathering: Gather input data about the client's trading goals. Gather price information from the relevant markets and array the best alternatives for further consideration.

2. Order crossing: Internalize the client's order flow and, in the process, offset identical but opposite buy and sell orders from the software provider's own accounts, where possible. Endeavor to cross these opposite but matching transactions.
3. Time slicing: Time-slice the client's order by breaking a large order into smaller pieces that are executed at intervals throughout the day rather than all at once, to disguise the true size of a large order and minimize its market impact.
4. Risk management: Monitor the trading portfolio's risk by continuously reevaluating its profit and loss, leverage, sector risk exposures, volatility, and by keeping the trading activities within the client's pre-specified limitations.
5. Basket trading: Execute basket trades by simultaneously buying and/or selling hundreds of individual stocks in one aggregate transaction in a fraction of a second.
6. Iceberging: Allocate small parts of an order to market segments that have the best prospects. Essentially, advantageously disaggregate an order to (a) maximize profits in a fragmented market, and, (b) conceal the size of a large order.
7. Shopping data collection: Collect data and evaluate different market makers' historical order-fill rates and other factors that might suggest profitable trading possibilities, and save this data to facilitate future trade searches.
8. Search extending: Broaden searches by using telecommunications and satellite connections to search opportunities in international markets.

To utilize an electronic order working system it must first be loaded with input data about the securities that are to be traded (customers' orders and the software operator's own orders), any relevant limit order prices, quantities available to be traded at different prices, time limitations, markets where the securities are traded, historical and current data about trading partners, and additional information the electronic order working system might request while it processes the order. The smart system uses this information to seek out markets where the whole transaction or parts of the transaction might be consummated. During its search process, the order working system continually gathers newer information that will affect the way the transactions progress. The order is typically passed to market makers, order crossing networks, and competing order working systems around the world that might be able to execute all or part of the trade. Feedback is gathered from these competing markets and computer software utilizes this real-time trading information to make decisions about whether or not to execute all or part of the order. Some systems analyze the stock market's short-term volatility in search of advantageous moments to trade. If the transactions, or at least a portion of them, are not executed within some prespecified time limit, the order working system will send the remaining part of the order to a dark pool, an external crossing network, a foreign system for immediate execution, or to some designated trading desk operated by human traders. Or, the order might be canceled.

The following software may be hired to work large trading orders: (a) Investment Technology Group (ITG)'s electronic order working system named QuantEX; (b) Instinet's Order Management System; (c) Credit Suisse First Boston's Lattice Trading System; (d) the partnership of several large brokerages and investment banks around REDIBook; and (e) Primex, an electronic auction system for stocks developed by several large investment banks.

Program Trading The NYSE defines *program trading* to be an order to simultaneously buy or sell 15 or more stocks with a total value of over $1 million. Such transactions require the submission of so much input data that virtually all program trades employ algorithmic trading. By 1980, program trading in the S&P 500 index's 500 stocks and the associated contracts in the financial futures market had become popular. Stock index arbitrageurs would buy (sell short) a stock index futures contract on the S&P 500 index and simultaneously sell short (buy) the 500 stocks that make up the S&P 500 index (or a representative sample of those 500 stocks). This transaction would be executed at an instant in time when the index price (representing the market values of the 500 stocks) and the futures price were far enough apart to yield a risk-free arbitrage profit. Decimalization facilitated stock index arbitrage trading by allowing arbitrage profits to be earned from small tracking errors in the S&P 500 index futures contract. Such trading enforces the economic law of one price and benefits the public by increasing the market's liquidity.

Statistical Arbitrage Statistical arbitrage is usually based on the mean-reversion tendencies of securities prices and returns. Dozens or hundreds of securities are analyzed simultaneously; the number of securities is limited only by the amount of capital available and the technological capabilities of the arbitrageur. Large amounts of market data, many computations, and a substantial amount of high-speed market trading are employed to capture short-term arbitrage profits. For instance, some poorly performing stocks might be purchased in long positions with the expectation that their prices will climb back to their mean values and, at the same time, some high-performing stocks are sold short with the expectation that their prices will fall back to their mean values. These offsetting long and short positions can be assembled to create a beta-neutral arbitrage portfolio that is unlikely to be hurt by market movements and, if the stocks' prices revert to their means, profits are earned from this statistical arbitrage. Statistical arbitrage is also employed in trading matched pairs of stocks, exploiting lead-lag relationships, trading on short-term momentum strategies, and other strategies.

High-Frequency Trading High-frequency trading was reviewed in Section 20.7. The algorithms that perform high-frequency trading are faster and more expensive than the electronic order working systems and the program trading algorithms mentioned earlier in this section. Furthermore, most high-frequency trading programs run for days without human intervention.[17] Fears that this kind of high-speed algorithmic trading can disrupt normal stock market trading have led to the establishment of various trading curbs.

20.9.2 Trading Curbs

Stock market authorities have established trading curbs that are designed to prevent the collapse of continuous stock market trading.

Black Monday Monday, October 19, 1987 is called Black Monday. Stocks around the world lost a huge amount of value in a very short time that day. Black Monday began in Hong Kong and then spread west through Europe. The *trading collapse* hit the United States after many other markets had already declined significantly earlier that day. The S&P 500 index dropped 23 percent on Black Monday. Some observers blamed program trading and an option strategy called portfolio insurance, although these claims have never been proven.

To prevent the recurrence of another Black Monday event, the NYSE created market curbs called circuit breakers. The NYSE *circuit breakers* give traders time to reconsider their trades in hopes that these trading pauses would result in reduced market volatility and reduced panic selling. Essentially, the NYSE automatically stopped all trading for one hour in response to declines of 10 percent in a stock market average, two hours in response to market declines of 20 percent, and halted all trading for the rest of the day if the market fell 30 percent. The Chicago Board of Trade adopted similar circuit breakers to halt the trading of financial futures on that exchange.

Because many of the trades on the NYSE are program trades based on momentum strategies, circuit breakers were implimented to limit volatility by moderating the ability of lightning-fast computer trading to drive stock prices down by following and accentuating stock price trends (called trading on momentum). In November 2007 the NYSE cancelled its circuit breakers because they were judged to be ineffective volatility curbs.

The Flash Crash of 2010   The aggregate speed and power of the high-speed trading programs manifested itself in a *flash crash* that occurred on the afternoon of May 6, 2010. The following details outline the stock market problems that prevailed for 20 minutes during the flash crash. On May 6, 2010, the Dow Jones Industrial Average (DJIA) started plunging at about 2:00 P.M. and fell nearly 1,000 points before recovering by the end of the trading day at 4:00 P.M. For example, the price of Proctor & Gamble's stock fluctuated between $63 and $40 in 20 minutes. Apple Computer's stock price rose from below $300 to almost $10,000 per share at one point. Stock in the large consulting firm Accenture PLC fell from $41 to one cent per share between 2:30 and 2:50. So many things went wrong in the stock markets that the SEC and the Commodities and Futures Trading Commission (CFTC) jointly prepared an in-depth report. Contrary to initial hypothesis, the high-frequency traders did not contribute to the flash crash.[18] But one widely held conclusion did emerge about the flash crash. Many Wall Street trading veterans believed that another flash crash would probably happen again because the high-speed computer-driven stock market had become more fragile than previously realized.

To reduce the danger of more flash crashes, in June 2010 the SEC implemented a simple new circuit breaker rule that applied to 1,300 popularly traded stocks. All stock market trading in any of these popular stocks is supposed to halt for five minutes if that stock experiences either a price gain or a price drop of more than 10 percent within the previous five minutes of trading.

20.9.3   Conclusions about Algorithmic Trading

New competing U.S. stock markets and decimalization reduced bid-ask spreads and made it profitable to use algorithmic electronic trading. Algorithmic trading reduced the size of economically feasible trading quantities and improved the liquidity of the U.S. stock market. These developments facilitated international trading, contributed to the international consolidation of stock exchanges, and opened new avenues for profit-seekers. Highly automated stock markets like Direct Edge and BATS in the United States, dark pools like Liquidnet and Pipeline in the United States, and the crossing of trades within dozens of brokerage houses around the world have fragmented the U.S. stock market. These developments have taken substantial pieces of market share away from the NYSE and Nasdaq within the past decade. Table 20.1 illustrates this fragmentation of the U.S. stock market.

20.10   SYMBIOTIC STOCK MARKET DEVELOPMENTS

A symbiotic relationship between two entities is an association that is mutually beneficial for both entities. Symbiotic relationships yield a positive net gain from cooperation that can benefit both counterparties. This section lists four stock market developments mentioned in this chapter that seem to bear a symbiotic relationship with portfolio theory.

1. Decimalization of the stock markets in 2001 increased the volume of trading and market liquidity by reducing bid-ask spreads. Minimizing these liquidity problems allows portfolio analysts to focus more directly on asset allocation.
2. The 2005–2007 consolidation of the Pacific Stock Exchange in San Francisco; Archipelago from Chicago; New York's NYSE; and Euronext, with trading floors in Paris, Amsterdam, Brussels, Portugal, and London, formed the NYSE Group. This and the other recent acquisitions and mergers created a better forum for international diversification than what existed previously.
3. Limit orders can be entered in an electronic market to await execution. The presence of limit orders attracts researchers and traders because publicly displaying these valuable options to trade at predetermined prices entices the relevant parties to consider these possibilities. Widespread use of limit orders creates a countably infinite number of investment alternatives.
4. Widespread use of computers and electronic communication tends to generate higher levels of expertise and reduced computation costs. These developments facilitate the use of Markowitz portfolio analysis and other computationally intensive techniques of investment analysis.

20.11   DETRIMENTAL STOCK MARKET DEVELOPMENTS

Some of the stock market developments touched on in this chapter could conceivably have a negative impact on portfolio theory and/or portfolio analysis. This section lists four developments that, within this context, could have some negative impact(s).

1. Electronic order working systems, program trading, statistical arbitrage, trading curbs, and other electronically generated transactions introduce statistical white noise into stock market prices that can confound the price-discovery processes based on fundamental economic information.
2. Algorithmic trading can disrupt stock market trading by creating counterproductive events like Black Monday and, more recently, a flash crash. Unfortunately, knowledgeable people are forecasting more flash crashes in the future.

3. Algorithmic trading may distract and discourage some individual investors from doing valuable financial analysis based on fundamental financial information and intuition, because they feel too small and insignificant to compete effectively against massive databanks and multimillion-dollar electronic technology.

4. Certain algorithmic trading techniques, for example, high-frequency trading, might drain resources away from portfolio analysis because automated trading is more attractive. For instance, a highly qualified analyst might choose to ignore portfolio analysis in order to work on high-frequency trading because working with high-frequency trading offers higher pay, more glamour, more excitement, or some other attraction. As algorithmic trading techniques draw hardware resources, software resources, research people, and other resources away from scientific portfolio analysis, the costs of performing the analysis will be driven up.

20.12   SUMMARY AND CONCLUSIONS

The tick size in U.S. stock markets remained one-eighth and then one-sixteenth of a dollar since the founding of the NYSE in 1792 until the SEC decreed decimalization in 2001.[19] The SEC's decree to decimalize reduced trading costs and increased the liquidity of the U.S. stock markets.

The NYSE, followed closely by Nasdaq, led the way in reorganizing the stock market industry by forging a number of mergers, carrying out some important acquisitions and fashioning key alliances. As a result, the world of equity trading grew smaller and international diversification was expedited.

Orders to trade at the limit or better, or, more simply, limit orders, fit nicely into computer programs that automatically accumulate or liquidate investment positions. High-frequency trading programs are one of the more lucrative trading algorithms that resulted. However, on the afternoon of May 6, 2010, a flash crash occurred because some high-speed computer trading programs became intertangled. More flash crashes are expected in the future.

Algorithmic trading techniques like high-frequency trading are probably draining valuable resources away from scientific portfolio analysis. This resource allocation could make portfolio research increasingly expensive.

Overall, the new developments reviewed in Chapters 19 and 20 do not seem to involve any serious detrimental consequences for Markowitz portfolio theory. To the contrary, these new developments appear to be making Markowitz portfolio theory more valuable than ever.

NOTES

1. Nasdaq's mainframe computer is located in Connecticut, but this location is not important. Nasdaq's mainframe computer could be relocated to many different locations.
2. This section draws on an article by Jack Clark Francis, Arie Harel, and Giora Harpaz, "Exchange Mergers and Electronic Trading," *The Journal of Trading*, Winter 2009, 36–42.
3. "What's Wrong with Wall Street?" *The Economist* 381, no. 8505 (November 25, 2006): 11. In the early 2000s the NYSE specialists constituted the highest paid and most powerful subset of the 1,366 NYSE members (seat owners).

4. "Down on the Street, No Longer Can America Take for Granted Its Global Superiority as a Market for Capital," *The Economist*, November 25–December 1, 2006: 69–71.

5. Unknown to many, Merrill Lynch was headed into bankruptcy when it hired John Thain. To avoid having the largest investment bank in the United States go bankrupt, the U.S. government pressured Bank of America into acquiring Merrill Lynch. John Thain had the misfortune to become a scapegoat that Bank of America discharged a few months after hiring him.

6. Reuters, June 30, 2008.

7. One of the four founders is a friend of Baruch College named Mr. David Krell.

8. February 15, 1971, was the day the United Kingdom and Ireland decimalized their currencies. Decimalization of the stock markets is, of course, an unrelated event with a similar name.

9. For more theory about inventory management see Thomas Ho and Hans Stoll, "Optimal Dealer Pricing under Transactions and Return Uncertainty," *Journal Financial Economics* 9, 1981: 47–73. Also see Marcia O'Hara, *Market Microstructure Theory* (Cambridge: Blackwell, 1997).

10. Scott Patterson and Serena Ng, "NYSE's Fast-Trade Hub Rises Up in New Jersey," *Wall Street Journal*, July 30, 2009, page C1; Scott Patterson, Kara Scannell, and Geoffrey Rogow, "Ban On Flash Orders Is Considered by SEC," *Wall Street Journal*, August 5, 2009, page C1.

11. Scott Patterson, "Meet Getco, High-Frequency Trade King," *Wall Street Journal*, August 27, 2009, page C1.

12. Rob Iati, "The Real Story of Trading Software Espionage," AdvancedTrading.com, July 10, 2009.

13. In 2005, 79 percent of the U.S. trading volume was conducted on the NYSE. By 2009 the trading volume on the NYSE fell to 25 percent. ECNs took about 11 percent of the volume, dark pools took 8 percent, and crossing networks took 17 percent. These ATSs barely existed in 2005.

14. Heather Timmons, "A London Hedge Fund That Opts for Engineers, Not MBAs," *New York Times*, August 18, 2006.

15. TABB Group, "*Opalesque* Exclusive: High Frequency Trading under the Microscope," *Opalesque*, August 4, 2009.

16. Terrence Hendershott, Charles M. Jones, and Albert J. Menkveld, "Does Algorithmic Trading Improve Liquidity?" *Journal of Finance* 66, 2010, 1–33.

17. For more information about high-frequency trading programs see Irene Aldridge, *High-Frequency Trading: A Practical Guide to Algorithmic Strategies and Trading Systems* (New York: John Wiley & Sons, 2009).

18. Jonathan A. Brogaard, "High Frequency Trading and Its Impact on Market Quality," Northwestern University, unpublished manuscript, August 25, 2010, 80 pages.

19. On March 13, 1997, the American Stock Exchange and Nasdaq reduced their minimum tick size from US$0.125 to US$0.0625, but the NYSE stuck with US$0.125.

Mathematical Appendixes

APPENDIX A. EXPECTATION PROOFS

This appendix furnishes proofs that may be studied to develop an understanding of the expected-value operator, and to explain certain statistical relationships that will aid in understanding the subject matter of this book.

Given two random variables X and Y having a joint probability distribution $p(x_i, y_j)$ for $i, j = 1, 2, \ldots$, the following theorems may be derived using the expectation operator.

Theorem A1: $Var(X) = E(X^2) - [E(X)]^2$

Proof:
$$Var(X) = E[X - E(X)]^2 \text{ by definition}$$
$$= E\left[X^2 - 2XE(X) + (E(X))^2\right]$$
$$= E(X^2) - 2E(X)E(X) + [E(X)]^2$$
$$= E(X^2) - [E(X)]^2 \qquad \text{Q.E.D.}$$

Theorem A2: $E(X^2) = Var(X) + [E(X)]^2$

Proof:
$$Var(X) = E(X^2) - [E(X)]^2 \text{ by Theorem E1}$$
$$Var(X) + [E(X)]^2 = E(X^2) \qquad \text{Q.E.D.}$$

Theorem A3: $Var(aX + b) = a^2 Var(X)$ for any constants a and b

Proof:
$$Var(aX + b) = E\left[(aX + b) - E(aX + b)\right]^2$$
$$= E[aX + b - aE(X) - b]^2$$
$$= E\left[a^2(X - E(X))^2\right]$$
$$= a^2 E[X - E(X)]^2 = a^2 Var(X) \qquad \text{Q.E.D.}$$

Theorem A3 implies that the standard deviation of $(aX + b)$ equals $a\sigma_X$ — the square root of $a^2 Var(X)$.

Theorem A4: $E(XY) = E(X)E(Y)$ if and only if X and Y are independent.

Proof:
$$E(XY) = \sum_i \sum_j x_i y_j \, p(x_i, y_j)$$

but $p\left(x_i, y_j\right) = p\left(x_i\right) p\left(y_j\right)$ if X and Y are independent, so

$$E\left(XY\right) = \sum_i \sum_j \left[x_i y_j p\left(x_i\right) p\left(y_j\right)\right]$$

$$= \sum_i \sum_j \left[x_i p\left(x_i\right) \; y_j p\left(y_j\right)\right]$$

$$= \sum_i \left[x_i p\left(x_i\right)\right] \cdot \sum_j \left[y_j p\left(y_j\right)\right]$$

$$= E\left(X\right) \cdot E\left(Y\right) \qquad \text{Q.E.D}$$

Theorem A5: $Cov\left(X, Y\right) = E\left(XY\right) - E\left(X\right) E\left(Y\right)$

Proof: $Cov\left(X, Y\right) = E\left[\left(X - E\left(X\right)\right)\left(Y - E\left(Y\right)\right)\right]$ by definition

$$= E\left[XY - X E\left(Y\right) - Y E\left(X\right) + E\left(X\right) E\left(Y\right)\right]$$

$$= E\left(XY\right) - E\left(X\right) E\left(Y\right) - E\left(Y\right) E\left(X\right) + E\left(X\right) E\left(Y\right)$$

$$= E\left(XY\right) - E\left(X\right) E\left(Y\right) \qquad \text{Q.E.D}$$

Theorem A6: $Cov\left(X, c\right) = 0$, where c is a constant.

Proof: $Cov\left(X, c\right) = E\left(X c\right) - E\left(X\right) E\left(c\right)$

$$= c E\left(X\right) - c E\left(X\right) = 0 \qquad \text{Q.E.D.}$$

Theorem A7: $\text{Cov}\left(aX + b, cY + d\right) = ac\, Cov\left(X, Y\right)$

Proof:

$$\text{Cov}\left(aX + b, cY + d\right) = \text{E}\left\{\left[aX + b - E\left(aX + b\right)\right]\left[cY + d - E\left(cY + d\right)\right]\right\}$$
$$\text{by definition}$$

$$= \text{E}\left\{\left[aX + b - aE\left(X\right) - b\right]\left[cY + d - cE\left(Y\right) - d\right]\right\}$$

$$= \text{E}\left\{a\left[X - E\left(X\right)\right] c\left[Y - E\left(Y\right)\right]\right\}$$

$$= ac\, \text{E}\left\{\left[X - E\left(X\right)\right]\left[Y - E\left(Y\right)\right]\right\}$$

$$= ac\, Cov\left(X, Y\right) \qquad \text{Q.E.D.}$$

Theorem A8: $Cov\left(X, \; Y + Z\right) = Cov\left(X, Y\right) + Cov\left(X, Z\right)$

Proof: $Cov\left(X, Y + Z\right) = E\left[X\left(Y + Z\right)\right] - E\left(X\right) E\left(Y + Z\right)$ by Theorem A5

$$= E\left(XY + XZ\right) - \left[E\left(X\right) E\left(Y\right) + E\left(X\right) E\left(Z\right)\right]$$

$$= E\left(XY\right) + E\left(XZ\right) - \left[E\left(X\right) E\left(Y\right) + E\left(X\right) E\left(Z\right)\right]$$

$$= \left[E\left(XY\right) - E\left(X\right) E\left(Y\right)\right] + \left[E\left(XZ\right) - E\left(X\right) E\left(Z\right)\right]$$

$$= Cov\left(X, Y\right) + Cov\left(X, Z\right) \qquad \text{Q.E.D.}$$

Theorem A9: If the random variables X and Y both undergo a linear transformation (for example, $aX + b$ and $cY + d$, where a, b, c, and d are constants), their correlation coefficient (ρ_{xy}) is invariant. Symbolically,

$$\rho_{xy} = \rho\left(aX + b, cY + d\right)$$

Proof:

$$\rho\left(aX + b,\ cY + d\right) = \frac{Cov\left(aX + b,\ cY + d\right)}{\sigma_{aX+b} \cdot \sigma_{cY+d}} \text{ by definition of } \rho_{xy}$$

$$= \frac{ac\, Cov\left(X, Y\right)}{a\sigma_X \cdot c\sigma_Y} \text{ by Theorems A3 and A7}$$

$$= \frac{Cov\left(X, Y\right)}{\sigma_X \cdot \sigma_Y}$$

$$= \rho_{xy} \text{ by definition} \qquad \text{Q.E.D}$$

Theorem A10: $Var\left(\sum_i X_i\right) = \sum_i \sigma_i^2 + \sum_i \sum_j \sigma_{ij}$ for $i \neq j$

Proof:

$$Var\left(\sum_i X_i\right) = E\left(\sum_i X_i - \sum_i \mu_i\right)^2, \text{where } \mu_i = E\left(X_i\right)$$

$$= E\left[\sum_i \left(X_i - \mu_i\right)^2\right]$$

$$= E\left[\sum_i \sum_j \left(X_i - \mu_i\right)\left(X_j - \mu_j\right)\right]$$

$$= \sum_i \sum_j \sigma_{ij}$$

$$= \sum_i \sigma_i^2 + \sum_i \sum_j \sigma_{ij} \qquad \text{Q.E.D.}$$
for $i \neq j$

Theorem A11: Consider the regression $y = \alpha + \beta x + \varepsilon$, estimated by ordinary least squares (OLS) with $E\left(\varepsilon\right) = 0$. The expected value of this regression is the conditional expectation $E\left(y|x\right)$. This conditional expectation implies that $E(y)$ and $E(x)$ move together in a linear fashion.

Proof:

$$E\left(y\right) = E(\alpha + \beta x + \varepsilon)$$

$$= E\left(\alpha\right) + E\left(\beta x\right) + E(\varepsilon)$$

$$= \alpha + \beta E(x)$$

Thus, $E\left(y|x\right) = \alpha + \beta E\left(x\right)$

Theorem A12: The difference between a random variable y and its expectation conditioning on x, $y - E(y|x)$, has zero covariance with the conditioning variable x. Symbolically, $\text{Cov}[y - E(y|x), x] = 0$.

Proof:
$$\text{Cov}[y - E(y|x), x] = E[yx - xE(y|x)]$$
$$= E[E(yx|x)] - E[xE(y|x)]$$
$$= E[xE(y|x)] - E[xE(y|x)]$$
$$= 0$$

APPENDIX B. SIMULTANEOUS SOLUTION OF LINEAR EQUATIONS

Consider the two linear equations:

$$x + y = 5 \tag{B.1}$$

$$2x - y = 4 \tag{B.2}$$

There are many pairs of values of x and y that will satisfy either equation (B.1) or equation (B.2). The problem is to find whether there are pairs that will simultaneously satisfy both equations and, if so, how they can be found. If such pairs exist, the equations (B.1) and (B.2) are called *simultaneous equations*. Four methods of finding the simultaneous solutions to the two equations will be demonstrated.

Elimination

This method consists of multiplying one or both of the equations by appropriate constants and then adding or subtracting the equations. When this has been done, one of the unknowns will have been eliminated. This process is called the *elimination* method. If, for example, equation (B.1) is multiplied by -2 and added to equation (B.2), the result is

$$-2 \text{ times (B.1)} = -2x - 2y = -10$$

$$\text{plus (B.2)} \qquad + (2x - y = 4)$$

$$\text{equals} \qquad -3y = -6$$

$$\text{so} \qquad y = 2$$

This value of y can be substituted into equation (B.1) or (B.2) to find x. Thus, from equation (B.1),

$x + 2 = 5$ or $x = 5 - 2 = 3$

Again, the simultaneous solution is $(x, y) = (3, 2)$.

Substitution

The second method is called the *substitution* method. Using one of the equations, one unknown is solved in terms of another. This solution is then substituted into the remaining equation, giving the value for the remaining unknowns.

$$x + y = 5 \tag{B.1}$$

$$y = 5 - x$$

$$2x - y = 4 \tag{B.2}$$

Substituting for y,

$$2x - (5 - x) = 4$$

$$3x = 9$$

$$x = 3$$

This value of x can be substituted into equation (B.1) or (B.2) to determine y. Using equation (B.2),

$$2x - y = 4$$

$$2(3) - y = 4$$

$$y = 2$$

Once again, the solution is $(x, y) = (3, \ 2)$.

Cramer's Rule

Cramer's rule is based on matrix algebra. The two equations in general form can be written:

$$a_1 x + b_1 y = c_1$$

$$a_2 x + b_2 y = c_2$$

where $a_1 = 1$, $b_1 = 1$, $c_1 = 5$, $a_2 = 2$, $b_2 = -1$, and $c_2 = 4$. The coefficients (that is, a_1, b_1, a_2, b_2) in matrix form and their determinant are

$$[A] = \begin{vmatrix} a_1 & b_1 \\ a_2 & b_2 \end{vmatrix} = \begin{vmatrix} 1 & 1 \\ 2 & -1 \end{vmatrix} = a_1 b_2 - a_2 b_1 = -1 - 2 = -3$$

The determinant obtained by replacing the coefficients of x by the constants on the right side of the equations (that is, c_1 and c_2) is

$$[B] = \begin{vmatrix} c_1 & b_1 \\ c_2 & b_2 \end{vmatrix} = \begin{vmatrix} 5 & 1 \\ 4 & -1 \end{vmatrix} = c_1 b_2 - c_2 b_1 = -5 - 4 = -9$$

The determinant obtained by replacing the coefficients of y by the numbers on the right side of the equations is

$$[C] = \begin{vmatrix} a_1 & c_1 \\ a_2 & c_2 \end{vmatrix} = \begin{vmatrix} 1 & 5 \\ 2 & 4 \end{vmatrix} = a_1 c_2 - a_2 c_1 = 4 - 10 = -6$$

Cramer's rule states that the value of the unknown is found by dividing the determinant of the matrix obtained by replacing the coefficients of that unknown by the constant values on the right of the equations, by the determinant of the original coefficients. Using Cramer's rule,

$$x = \frac{[B]}{[A]} = \frac{\begin{vmatrix} c_1 & b_1 \\ c_2 & b_2 \end{vmatrix}}{\begin{vmatrix} a_1 & b_1 \\ a_2 & b_2 \end{vmatrix}} = \frac{\begin{vmatrix} 5 & 1 \\ 4 & -1 \end{vmatrix}}{\begin{vmatrix} 1 & 1 \\ 2 & -1 \end{vmatrix}} = \frac{-9}{-3} = 3$$

$$y = \frac{[C]}{[A]} = \frac{\begin{vmatrix} a_1 & c_1 \\ a_2 & c_2 \end{vmatrix}}{\begin{vmatrix} a_1 & b_1 \\ a_2 & b_2 \end{vmatrix}} = \frac{\begin{vmatrix} 1 & 5 \\ 2 & 4 \end{vmatrix}}{\begin{vmatrix} 1 & 1 \\ 2 & -1 \end{vmatrix}} = \frac{-6}{-3} = 2$$

As usual, the solution is $(x, y) = (3, 2)$.

Matrix Inversion

The two equations written in matrix form are

$$\begin{bmatrix} a_1 & b_1 \\ a_2 & b_2 \end{bmatrix} \begin{bmatrix} x \\ y \end{bmatrix} = \begin{bmatrix} c_1 \\ c_2 \end{bmatrix}$$

Premultiplying both sides of the equation by the inverse of $\begin{bmatrix} a_1 & b_1 \\ a_2 & b_2 \end{bmatrix}$ yields

$$\begin{bmatrix} x \\ y \end{bmatrix} = \begin{bmatrix} a_1 & b_1 \\ a_2 & b_2 \end{bmatrix}^{-1} \begin{bmatrix} c_1 \\ c_2 \end{bmatrix}$$

$$= \begin{bmatrix} 1 & 1 \\ 2 & -1 \end{bmatrix}^{-1} \begin{bmatrix} 5 \\ 4 \end{bmatrix} = \begin{bmatrix} 1/3 & 1/3 \\ 2/3 & -1/3 \end{bmatrix} \begin{bmatrix} 5 \\ 4 \end{bmatrix} = \begin{bmatrix} 3 \\ 2 \end{bmatrix}$$

because $\begin{bmatrix} a_1 & b_1 \\ a_2 & b_2 \end{bmatrix}^{-1} = \dfrac{1}{det\,[A]} \begin{bmatrix} b_2 & -b_1 \\ -a_2 & a_1 \end{bmatrix} = \dfrac{1}{(a_1 b_2 - a_2 b_1)} \begin{bmatrix} b_2 & -b_1 \\ -a_2 & a_1 \end{bmatrix},$

and thus

$$\begin{bmatrix} 1 & 1 \\ 2 & -1 \end{bmatrix}^{-1} = \frac{1}{(-3)} \begin{bmatrix} -1 & -1 \\ -2 & 1 \end{bmatrix} = \begin{bmatrix} 1/3 & 1/3 \\ 2/3 & -1/3 \end{bmatrix},$$

where $det\,[A]$ is the determinant of matrix A.

Although two simultaneous equations with two unknown variables are given, the unique solution for the two unknowns cannot be sometimes obtained. For example, suppose that equation (B.3) instead of equation (B.2) is given together with equation (B.1) as follows

$$x + y = 5 \tag{B.1}$$

$$2x + 2y = 10 \tag{B.3}$$

In this case, the unique solution for (x, y) does not exist. The reason is as follows: Equation (B.3) does not provide any additional information about the unknowns (x, y), because equation (B.3) is simply equal to equation (B.1) times two. Equation (B.3) is redundant. We call these equations *linearly dependent equations*, which are explained in the next appendix.

APPENDIX C. LINEARLY DEPENDENT EQUATIONS

Consider the following two equations system.

$$x_1 + x_2 = 2 \tag{C.1}$$

$$x_1 - x_2 = -1. \tag{C.2}$$

From equation (C.2),

$$x_1 = x_2 - 1 \tag{C.2a}$$

Substituting equation (C.2a) in equation (C.1) yields

$$x_2 - 1 + x_2 = 2$$

Thus, $x_2 = 1\frac{1}{2}$ and $x_1 = x_2 - 1 = \frac{1}{2}$.

These solutions can be graphically obtained. The two equations can be graphed in Figure C.1.

The two equations cross, and the equations are said to be *independent*. The location at which the two equations intersect satisfies both equations.

The two simultaneous equations (C.1) and (C.2) can also be solved in a matrix form.

$$\begin{pmatrix} 1 & 1 \\ 1 & -1 \end{pmatrix} \begin{pmatrix} x_1 \\ x_2 \end{pmatrix} = \begin{pmatrix} 2 \\ -1 \end{pmatrix}$$

$$\Rightarrow \quad \begin{pmatrix} x_1 \\ x_2 \end{pmatrix} = \begin{pmatrix} 1 & 1 \\ 1 & -1 \end{pmatrix}^{-1} \begin{pmatrix} 2 \\ -1 \end{pmatrix} = \begin{pmatrix} 1/2 & 1/2 \\ 1/2 & -1/2 \end{pmatrix} \begin{pmatrix} 2 \\ -1 \end{pmatrix}$$

$$= \begin{pmatrix} 1/2 \\ 1\frac{1}{2} \end{pmatrix}$$

In this case, the inverse of the coefficient matrix exists, and so does the solution for x_1 and x_2.

The two equations are independent. The coefficient matrix is said to be non-singular. For the computation for an inverse matrix, refer to Section B in the appendix.

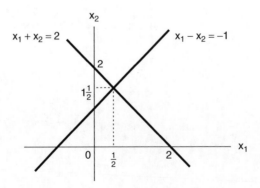

FIGURE C.1   Two Equations Cross

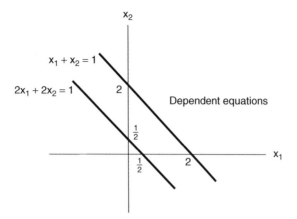

FIGURE C.2 Two Equations are Parallel

Now, we consider another equations system.

$$x_1 + x_2 = 2 \tag{C.1}$$

$$2x_1 + 2x_2 = 1 \tag{C.3}$$

The preceding equations are graphed in Figure C.2.

The two equations have the same slope and are parallel. There is no intersecting location, and no solution simultaneously satisfies both equations. Parallel equations are said to be *dependent*

If we rewrite equations (C.1) and (C.3) in a matrix form,

$$\begin{pmatrix} 1 & 1 \\ 2 & 2 \end{pmatrix} \begin{pmatrix} x_1 \\ x_2 \end{pmatrix} = \begin{pmatrix} 2 \\ 1 \end{pmatrix}$$

the solution can be represented as

$$\begin{pmatrix} x_1 \\ x_2 \end{pmatrix} = \begin{pmatrix} 1 & 1 \\ 2 & 2 \end{pmatrix}^{-1} \begin{pmatrix} 2 \\ 1 \end{pmatrix}$$

However, the inverse of the coefficient matrix does not exist, because its determinant is equal to zero. The solution for x_1 and x_2 also does not exist. A matrix whose inverse does not exist is said to be *singular* and its determinant equals zero. In singular matrices, one vector has a linear relation with the other vector(s). For example, the first row vector in the coefficient matrix $(1, 1)$ has a linear relation with the second row vector, $(2, 2)$, as $(1, 1) = \frac{1}{2} (2, 2)$, or vice versa. In $(n \times n)$ singular matrices, the vectors are said to be *linearly dependent*, and one vector can be represented as a linear combination of the other vectors.

APPENDIX D. MATRIX AND VECTOR DIFFERENTIATION

Let f be a differentiable function and

$$z = f(\mathbf{x}) \tag{D.1}$$

where z is a scalar and $\mathbf{x}$ is an $(n \times 1)$ column vector. Then, the first-order derivative of a scalar with respect to an $(n \times 1)$ vector $\mathbf{x}$ is denoted

$$\frac{\partial z}{\partial \mathbf{x}} = \left\{ \frac{\partial z}{\partial x_j} \right\}_{j=1,\dots,n} = \left(\frac{\partial z}{\partial \mathbf{x}}, \frac{\partial z}{\partial \mathbf{x}}, \dots, \frac{\partial z}{\partial \mathbf{x}} \right)' \tag{D.2}$$

This is an $(n \times 1)$ column vector.

The differentiation of a vector with respect to another vector is as follows. Let

$$\mathbf{y} = f(\mathbf{x}) \tag{D.3}$$

where $\mathbf{y}$ and $\mathbf{x}$ are $(m \times 1)$ and $(n \times 1)$ column vectors, respectively. Then, the first-order derivative of $\mathbf{y}$ with respect to $\mathbf{x}$ is denoted

$$\frac{\partial \mathbf{y}}{\partial \mathbf{x}} = \left\{ \frac{\partial y_i}{\partial x_j} \right\}_{\substack{i=1,\dots,m, \\ j=1,\dots,n}} = \left(\frac{\partial y_1}{\partial \mathbf{x}}, \frac{\partial y_2}{\partial \mathbf{x}}, \dots, \frac{\partial y_m}{\partial \mathbf{x}} \right)'$$

$$= \begin{bmatrix} \dfrac{\partial y_1}{\partial x_1} & \dfrac{\partial y_1}{\partial x_2} & \cdots & \dfrac{\partial y_1}{\partial x_n} \\ \dfrac{\partial y_2}{\partial x_1} & \dfrac{\partial y_2}{\partial x_2} & \cdots & \dfrac{\partial y_2}{\partial x_n} \\ \vdots & \vdots & \ddots & \vdots \\ \dfrac{\partial y_m}{\partial x_1} & \dfrac{\partial y_m}{\partial x_2} & \cdots & \dfrac{\partial y_m}{\partial x_n} \end{bmatrix} \tag{D.4}$$

This is an $(m \times n)$ matrix.

Based on equations (D.1) to (D.4), we obtain the following differentiation results.

i. If $z = \mathbf{a}'\mathbf{x}$, where $\mathbf{a}$ is an $(n \times 1)$ column vector, then

$$\frac{\partial \mathbf{z}}{\partial \mathbf{x}} = \mathbf{a}$$

ii. If $\mathbf{y} = \mathbf{A}\mathbf{x}$, where $\mathbf{A}$ is a $(m \times n)$ matrix and does not depend on $\mathbf{x}$, then

$$\frac{\partial \mathbf{y}}{\partial \mathbf{x}} = \mathbf{A}$$

iii. If $\mathbf{y} = \mathbf{x}'\mathbf{A}\mathbf{x}$, then

$$\frac{\partial \mathbf{y}}{\partial \mathbf{x}} = (\mathbf{A} + \mathbf{A}')\mathbf{x}$$

If $\mathbf{A}$ is symmetric, then

$$\frac{\partial \mathbf{y}}{\partial \mathbf{x}} = 2\mathbf{A}\mathbf{x}$$

Bibliography

Admati, Anat R. "A Noisy Rational Expectations Equilibrium for Multi–Asset Securities Markets." *Econometrica* 53, no. 3 (May 1985): 629–657.

Adesi, Giovanni B., Patrick Gagliardini, and Giovanni Urga. "Testing Asset Pricing Models with Coskewness." *Journal of Business and Economic Statistics* 22, no. 4 (October 2004): 474–485.

Agmon, Tamir, and Donal R. Lessard. "Investor Recognition of Corporate International Diversification." *Journal of Finance* 32, no. 4 (September 1977): 1049–1055.

Akgiray, Vedat. "Conditional Heteroscedasticity in Time Series of Stock Returns: Evidence and Forecasts." *Journal of Business* 62, no. 1 (January 1989): 55–80.

Akgiray, Vedat, and G. Geoffrey Booth. "Compound Distribution Models of Stock Returns." *Journal of Financial Research* 10, no. 3 (Fall 1987): 269–280.

_____. "The Stable-Law Model of Stock Returns." *Journal of Business and Economic Statistics* 6, no. 1 (January 1988): 51–57.

_____. "Stock Price Processes With Discontinuous Time Paths: An Empirical Examination." *Financial Review* 21, no. 2 (May 1986): 163–184.

Aldridge, Irene. *High-Frequency Trading: A Practical Guide to Algorithmic Strategies and Trading Systems*. Hoboken, NJ: John Wiley & Sons, 2009.

Alexander, Gordon J. "An Algorithm for Deriving the Capital Market Line." *Management Science* 23, no. 11 (July 1977): 1183–1186.

Alexander, Gordon J., and P. George Benson. "More on Beta as a Random Coefficient." *Journal of Financial and Quantitative Analysis* 17, no. 1 (March 1982): 27–36.

Alexander, Gordon J., P. George Benson, and Carol E. Eger. "Timing Decisions and the Behavior of Mutual Fund Systematic Risk." *Journal of Financial and Quantitative Analysis* 17, no. 4 (November 1982): 579–602.

Alexander, Gordon J., and Norman Chervany. "On Estimation and Stability of Beta." *Journal of Financial and Quantitative Analysis* 15, no. 1 (March 1980): 123–137.

Alexander, Gordon J. and Jack Clark Francis. *Portfolio Analysis*. 3rd ed. Upper Saddle River, NJ: Prentice-Hall, 1986.

Alexander, Gordon J., and Roger D. Stover. "Consistency of Mutual Fund Performance during Varying Market Conditions." *Journal of Economics and Business* 32, no. 3 (Spring–Summer 1980): 219–226.

Alizadeh, Sassan, Michael W. Brandt, and Francis X. Diebold. "Range-Based Estimation of Stochastic Volatility Models." *Journal of Finance* 57, no. 3 (June 2002): 1047–1091.

Allen, Gregory C. "Performance Attribution for Global Equity Portfolios." *Journal of Portfolio Management* 19, no. 1 (Fall 1991): 59–65.

Ambachtsheer, Keith P. "Portfolio Theory and the Security Analyst." *Financial Analysts Journal* 28, no. 6 (November–December 1972): 53–57.

_____. "Profit Potential in an 'Almost Efficient' Market." *Journal of Portfolio Management* 1, no. 1 (Fall 1974): 84–87.

_____. "Where Are the Customers' Alphas?" *Journal of Portfolio Management* 4, no. 1 (Fall 1977): 52–56.

Ambachtsheer, Keith P., and James L. Farrell, Jr. "Can Active Management Add Value?" *Financial Analyst Journal* 35, no. 6 (November–December 1979): 39–47.

Ankrim, Ernest M. "Risk-Adjusted Performance Attribution." *Financial Analysts Journal* 48, no. 2 (March/April 1992): 75–82.

Ang, James S. "A Note on the E, SL Portfolio Selection Model." *Journal of Financial and Quantitative Analysis* 10, no. 5 (December 1975): 849–857.

Angelidis, Timotheos, Alexandros Benos, and Stavros Degiannakis. "The Use of GARCH Models in VaR Estimation." *Statistical Methodology* 1, no. 1–2 (December 2004): 105–128.

Arditti, Fred D. "Another Look at Mutual Fund Performance." *Journal of Financial and Quantitative Analysis* 6, no. 3 (June 1971): 909–912.

_____. "Risk and the Required Return on Equity." *Journal of Finance* 22, no. 1 (March 1967): 19–36.

Arnott, Robert, Jason Hsu, and Philip Moore. "Fundamental Indexation." *Financial Analysts Journal* 61, no. 2 (March–April 2005): 83–99.

Arrow, Kenneth J. *Essays in the Theory of Risk-Bearing.* Chicago: Markham Publishing Company, 1971.

Ball, Clifford A., and Walter N. Torous. "On Jumps in Common Stock Prices and Their Impact on Call Option Pricing." *Journal of Finance* 40, no. 1 (March 1985): 155–173.

Banz, Rolf W. "The Relationship Between Return and Market Value of Common Stocks." *Journal of Financial Economics* 9, no. 1 (March 1981) 3–18.

Barberis, Nicholas, and Ming Huang, "Stocks as Lotteries: The Implications of Probability Weighting for Security Prices," *American Economic Review* 98, no. 5: 2066–2100.

Barry, Christopher B. "Effect of Uncertain and Nonstationary Parameters upon Capital Markets Equilibrium Conditions." *Journal of Financial and Quantitative Analysis* 13, no. 3 (September 1978): 419–433.

Barry, Christopher B., and Stephen J. Brown. "Differential Information and Security Market Equilibrium." *Journal of Financial and Quantitative Analysis* 20, no. 4 (December 1985): 407–422.

Basu, Sanjoy. "The Relationship Between Earnings Yield, Market Value, and Return for NYSE Common Stocks: Further Evidence." *Journal of Financial Economics* 12, no. 1 (June 1983): 129–156.

Bawa, Vijay S. "Admissible Portfolios for All Individuals." *Journal of Finance* 31, no. 4 (September 1976): 1169–1183.

_____. "Optimal Rules for Ordering Uncertain Prospects." *Journal of Financial Economics* 2, no. 1 (March 1975): 95–121.

Bawa, Vijay S., and Stephen J. Brown. "Capital Market Equilibrium: Does Estimation Risk Really Matter?" Chap. 6 in *Estimation Risk and Optimal Portfolio Choice*, ed. Vijay S. Bawa, Stephen J. Brown, and Roger W. Klein. Amsterdam: North-Holland Publishing Company, 1979.

Bawa, Vijay S., and Eric B. Lindenberg. "Capital Market Equilibrium in a Mean-Lower Partial Moment Framework." *Journal of Financial Economics* 5, no. 2 (November 1977): 189–200.

Beaver, William H. "The Information Content of Annual Earnings Announcements." *Journal of Accounting Research* 6 (Supplement), 1968: 67–92.

Beaver, William H., Paul Kettler, and Myron Scholes. "The Association between Market Determined and Accounting Determined Risk Measures". *Accounting Review* 45, no. 4 (October 1970): 654–682.

Berkowitz, Jeremy, and James O'Brien. "How Accurate Are Value-at-Risk Models at Commercial Banks?" *Journal of Finance* 57, no. 3 (June 2002): 1093–1111.

Bernstein, William J., and David Wilkinson. "Diversification, Rebalancing, and the Geometric Mean Frontier." Working Paper, 1997.

Bigman, David. "Safety-First Criteria and Their Measures of Risk." *American Journal of Agricultural Economics* 78, no. 1 (February 1996): 225–235.

Bildersee, John S., "Market-Determined and Alternative Measures of Risk," *The Accounting Review* 50, no. 1 (January 1975): 81–98.

Black, Fischer. "Capital Market Equilibrium with Restricted Borrowing." *Journal of Business* 45, no. 3 (July 1972):, 444–455.

Black, Fischer, Michael C. Jensen, and Myron Scholes. "The Capital Asset Pricing Model: Some Empirical Tests." in *Studies in the Theory of Capital Markets*, ed. Michael C. Jensen. New York: Praeger Publishers, Inc., 1972.

Black, Fischer, and Myron Scholes. "The Effects of Dividend Yield and Dividend Policy on Common Stock Prices and Returns." *Journal of Financial Economics* 1, no. 1 (May 1974): 1–22.

Blattberg, Robert C., and Nicholas J. Gonedes. "A Comparison of the Stable and Student Distributions as Statistical Models for Stock Prices." *Journal of Business* 47, no. 2 (April 1974): 244–280.

Blitz, David, and Laurens Swinkels. "Fundamental Indexation: An Active Value Strategy in Disguise." *Journal of Asset Management* 9, no. 4 (2008): 264–269.

Bloomfield, Ted, Richard Leftwich, and John B. Long, Jr. "Portfolio Strategies and Performance." *Journal of Financial Economics* 12, no. 2 (November 1977): 201–218.

Blume, Marshall E. "Betas and Their Regression Tendencies." *Journal of Finance* 30, no. 3 (June 1975): 785–795.

_____. "On the Assessment of Risk." *Journal of Finance* 26, no. 1 (March 1971): 1–10.

Blume, Marshall E., and Irwin Friend. "The Asset Structure of Individual Portfolios and Some Implications for Utility Functions." *Journal of Finance* 30, no. 2 (May 1975): 585–603.

Blume, Marshall E., and Frank Husic. "Price, Beta, and Exchange Listing." *Journal of Finance* 28, no. 2 (May 1973): 283–299.

Blume, Marshall E., and Robert F. Stambaugh. "Biases in Computed Returns: An Application to the Size Effect." *Journal of Financial Economics* 12, no. 3 (November 1983): 387–404.

Bollerslev, Tim. "Generalized Autoregressive Conditional Heteroscedasticity." *Journal of Econometrics* 31, no 3 (April 1986): 307–327.

Boness, James A., Andrew H. Chen, and Som Jatusipitak. "Investigations of Nonstationarity in Stock Prices." *Journal of Business* 47, no 4 (October 1974): 518– 537.

Bos, Theodore, and Paul Newbold. "An Empirical Investigation of the Possibility of Stochastic Systematic Risk in the Market Model." *Journal of Business* 57, no. 1 (January 1984): 35–41.

Brandt, Michael W., and Francis X. Diebold. "A No-Arbitrage Approach to Range-Based Estimation of Return Covariances and Correlations." *Journal of Business* 79, no. 1 (January 2006): 61–74.

Brealey, Richard A. *An Introduction to Risk and Return from Common Stocks*. Cambridge, MA: The MIT Press, 1969.

Breeden, Douglas. "An Intertemporal Asset Pricing Model with Stochastic Consumption and Investment Opportunities." *Journal of Financial Economics* 7, no. 3 (September 1979): 265–296.

Breeden, Douglas T., Michael R. Gibbons, and Robert H. Litzenberger. "Empirical Tests of the Consumption-Oriented CAPM." *Journal of Finance* 44, no.2 (June 1989): 231–262.

Brennan, Michael J. "Taxes, Market Valuation and Corporate Financial Policy." *National Tax Journal* 23, no. 4 (December 1970): 417–427.

Brennan, Michael J., and Alan Kraus. "Necessary Conditions for Aggregation in Securities Markets." *Journal of Financial and Quantitative Analysis* 13, no. 3 (September 1978): 407–418.

Brenner, Menachem, and Marti G. Subrahmanyam. "A Simple Formula to Compute the Implied Standard Deviation." *Financial Analysts Journal* (September–October 1988): 80–83.

Brinson, Gary P., and Nimrod Fachler. "Measuring Non-U.S. Equity Portfolio Performance." *Journal of Portfolio Management* 11, no. 3 (Spring 1985): 73–76.

Brinson, Gary P., L. Randolph Hood, and Gilbert L. Beebower. "Determinants of Portfolio Performance." *Financial Analysts Journal* 42, no. 2 (July/August 1986): 39–44.

_____. "Determinants of Portfolio Performance II." *Financial Analysts Journal* 47, no. 3 (May/June 1991): 40–48.

Britten-Jones, Mark, and Anthony Neuberger. "Option Prices, Implied Price Processes, and Stochastic Volatility." *Journal of Finance* 55, no. 2 (December 2002): 839–866.

Brogaard, Jonathan A., "High Frequency Trading and Its Impact on Market Quality," Northwestern University, unpublished manuscript, August 25, 2010.

Brown, Stephen J. "The Effect of Estimation Risk on Capital Market Equilibrium." *Journal of Financial and Quantitative Analysis* 14, no. 2 (June 1979): 215–220.

Brown, Stephen J., William N. Goetzmann, Roger G. Ibbotson, and Stephen A. Ross. "Survivorship Bias in Performance Studies." *Review of Financial Studies* 5, no. 4 (1992): 553–580.

Brown, Stephen J., William N. Goetzmann, and Stephen A. Ross. "Survival." *Journal of Finance* 50, no. 3 (July 1995): 853–873.

Brown, Stephen J., and Mark I. Weinstein. "A New Approach to Testing Asset Pricing Models: The Bilinear Paradigm." *Journal of Finance* 38, no. 3 (June 1983): 711–743.

Brownlees, Christian T., and Giampiero M. Gallo. "Comparison of Volatility Measures: A Risk Management Perspective." *Journal of Financial Econometrics* 8, no.1 (Winter 2010): 29–56.

Campbell, John Y., and John H. Cochrane. "Explaining the Poor Performance of Consumption-Based Asset Pricing Models." *Journal of Finance* 55, no. 6 (December 2000): 2863–2878.

Canina, Linda, and Stephen Figlewski. "The Informational Content of Implied Volatility." *Review of Financial Studies* 6, no. 3 (Fall 1993): 659–681.

Carhart, Mark M. "On Persistence in Mutual Fund Performance." *Journal of Finance* 52, no. 1 (March 1997): 57–82.

Carr, Peter, and Dilip B. Madan. "Towards a Theory of Volatility Trading." In *Volatility*, edited by R. Jarrow, 417–427. New York: Risk Publications, 1998.

Cass, David, and Joseph E. Stiglitz. "The Structure of Investor Preferences and Asset Returns, and Separability in Portfolio Allocation: A Contribution to the Pure Theory of Mutual Funds." *Journal of Economic Theory* 2, no. 2 (June 1970): 122–160.

Chamberlain, Gary, "Funds, Factors, and Diversification in Arbitrage Pricing Models," *Econometrica* 51, no. 5 (September 1983), 1305–1323.

Chamberlain, Gary, and Michael Rothschild. "Arbitrage, Factor Structure, and Mean-Variance Analysis on Large Asset Markets." *Econometrica* 51, no. 5 (September 1983): 1281–1304.

Chang, Eric C., and Wilbur G. Lewellen. "Market Timing and Mutual Fund Investment Performance." *Journal of Business* 57, no. 1 (January 1984): 57–72.

Chen, Nai-fu. "Some Empirical Tests of the Theory of Arbitrage Pricing." *Journal of Finance* 38, no. 5 (December 1983): 1393–1414.

Chen, Nai-fu, and Jonathan E. Ingersoll, Jr. "Exact Pricing in Linear Factor Models with Finitely Many Assets: A Note." *Journal of Finance* 38, no. 3 (June 1983): 985–988.

Chen, Nai-fu, Richard Roll, and Stephen A. Ross. "Economic Forces and the Stock Market." *Journal of Business* 59, no. 3 (July 1986): 383–403.

Cho, Chinhyung, Edwin J. Elton, and Martin J. Gruber. "On the Robustness of the Roll and Ross Arbitrage Pricing Theory." *Journal of Financial and Quantitative Analysis* 19, no. 1 (March 1984): 1–10.

Christensen, B. J. and N. R. Prabhala. "The Relation between Implied and Realized Volatility." *Journal of Financial Economics* 50, no. 2 (November 1998): 125–150.

Christoffersen, Peter F. *Elements of Financial Risk Management*. San Diego: Academic Press, 2003.

Christie, Andrew A. "The Stochastic Behavior of Common Stock Variances: Value, Leverage, and Interest Rate Effects." *Journal of Financial Economics* 10, no. 4 (December 1982): 407–432.

Christie-David, Rohan, and Mukesh Chaudhry. "Coskewness and Cokurtosis in Futures Markets." *Journal of Empirical Finance* 8, no. 1 (March 2001): 55–81.

Chunhachinda, Pornchai, Dandapani Krishnan, Shahid Hamid, and Arun J. Prakash. "Portfolio Selection and Skewness: Evidence from International Stock Markets." *Journal of Banking and Finance* 21, no. 2 (February 1997): 143–167.

Cochrane, John H. "Production-Based Asset Pricing and the Link between Stock Returns and Economic Fluctuations." *Journal of Finance* 46, no. 1(March 1991): 209–237.

Cohen, Kalman J., and Jerry A. Pogue. "An Empirical Evaluation of Alternative Portfolio-Selection Models." *Journal of Business* 40, no. 2 (April 1967): 166–193.

Copeland, Thomas E., and J. Fred Weston. *Financial Theory and Corporate Policy*. Reading, MA: Addison-Wesley, 1983.

Connor, Gregory. "A Factor Pricing Theory for Capital Assets." Unpublished paper. Northwestern University, 1981.

Cornell, Bradford. "Asymmetric Information and Portfolio Performance Measurement." *Journal of Financial Economics* 7, no. 4 (December 1979): 381–390.

Corrado, Charles J, and Thomas W. Miller Jr. "A Note on a Simple, Accurate Formula to Compute Implied Standard Deviations." *Journal of Banking & Finance* 20, no. 3 (April 1996): 595–603.

Davis, James L., Eugene F. Fama, and Kenneth R. French. "Characteristics, Covariances, and Average Returns: 1929 to 1997." *Journal of Finance* 55, no. 1 (February 2000): 389–406.

Day, Theodore E. and Craig M. Lewis. "Forecasting Futures Market Volatility." *Journal of Derivatives* 1, no. 2 (Winter 1993): 33–50.

_____. "Stock Market Volatility and the Information Content of Stock Index Options." *Journal of Econometrics* 52, no. 1–2 (April–May 1992): 267–287.

DeFusco, Richard A., Gordon V. Karels, and Krishnamurty Muralidhar. "Skewness Persistence in U.S. Common Stock Returns from Bootstrapping Tests." *Journal of Business Finance and Accounting* 23, no. 8 (October 1996): 1183–1195.

Demeterfi, Kresimir, Emanuel Derman, Michael Kamal, and Joseph Zou. "A Guide to Volatility and Variance Swaps." *Journal of Derivatives* 6, no. 4 (Summer 1999): 9–32.

_____. "More Than You Ever Wanted to Know about Volatility Swaps." *Quantitative Strategies Research Notes*, Goldman Sachs (1999a).

DeRoon, Frans A., and Theo E. Nijman. "Testing for Mean-Variance Spanning: A Survey." *Journal of Empirical Finance* 8, no. 2 (May 2001): 111–155.

DeRoon, Frans A., Theo E. Nijman, and Bas J. M. Werker. "Testing for Mean-Variance Spanning with Short Sales Constraints and Transaction Costs: The Case of Emerging Markets." *Journal of Finance* 56, no. 2 (2001): 723–744.

Dhrymes, Phoebus J., Irwin Friend, and N. Bulent Gultekin. "A Critical Reexamination of the Empirical Evidence on the Arbitrage Pricing Theory." *Journal of Finance* 39, no. 2 (June 1984): 323–346.

Dhrymes, Phoebus J., Irwin Friend, Mustafa N. Gultekin, and N. Bulent Gultekin. "New Tests of the APT and Their Implications." *Journal of Finance* 40, no. 3 (July 1985): 659–674.

Diamond, Douglas W., and Robert E. Verrecchia. "Information Aggregation in a Noisy Rational Expectations Economy." *Journal of Financial Economics* 9, no. 3 (September 1981): 221–235.

Dimson, Elroy. "Risk Measurement When Shares Are Subject to Infrequent Trading." *Journal of Financial Economics* 7, no. 2 (June 1979): 197–226.

Ding, Yuanyao, and Bo Zhang. "Risky Asset Pricing based on Safety First Fund Management." *Quantitative Finance* 9, no. 3 (April 2009): 353–361.

Dittmar, Robert F. "Nonlinear Pricing Kernels, Kurtosis Preference, and Evidence from the Cross–Section of Equity Returns." *Journal of Finance* 57, no. 1 (February 2002): 369–403.

Dupire, Bruno. "Pricing with a Smile." *Risk* 7, January 1994: 18–20.

Dybvig, Philip H. "An Explicit Bound on Individual Assets' Deviations from APT Pricing in a Finite Economy." *Journal of Financial Economics* 12, no. 4 (December 1983): 483–496.

Dybvig, Phillip H., and Stephen A. Ross. "The Analytics of Performance Measurement Using a Security Market Line." *Journal of Finance* 40, no. 2 (June 1985b): 401–416.

_____. "Differential Information and Performance Measurement Using a Security Market Line." *Journal of Finance* 40, no. 2 (June 1985a): 383–399.

_____. "Portfolio Efficient Sets." *Econometrica* 50, no. 6 (November 1982): 1525–1546.

_____. "Yes, the APT Is Testable." *Journal of Finance* 40, no. 4 (September 1985c): 1173–1188.

Elgers, Pieter T., and Dennis Murray. "The Impact of the Choice of Market Index on the Empirical Evaluation of Accounting Risk Measures." *Accounting Review* 57, no 2 (April 1982): 358–375.

Elton, Edwin J., and Martin J. Gruber. "On the Maximization of the Geometric Mean with Lognormal Return Distribution." *Management Science* 21, no. 4 (December 1974b): 483–488.

_____. "Portfolio Theory When Investment Relatives Are Lognormally Distributed." *Journal of Finance* 29, no. 4 (September 1974a): 1265–1273.

_____. "Risk Reduction and Portfolio Size: An Analytical Solution." *Journal of Business* 50, no. 4 (October 1977): 415–437.

Elton, Edwin J., Martin J. Gruber, and Joel Rentzler. "The Performance of Publicly Offered Commodity Funds." *Financial Analysts Journal* 46, no. 4 (July-August 1990): 23–30.

Engle, Robert F. "Autoregressive Conditional Heteroscedasticity with Estimates of the Variance of U.K. Inflation." *Econometrica* 50, no. 4 (July 1982): 987–1008.

Estrada, Javier. "Mean-Semivariance Behavior: Downside Risk and Capital Asset Pricing." *International Review of Economics and Finance* 16, no.2 (2007): 169–185.

_____. "Mean-Semivariance Optimization: A Heuristic Approach." *Journal of Applied Finance* 18, no. 1 (Spring–Summer 2008): 57–72.

_____. "Systematic Risk in Emerging Markets: The D-CAPM." *Emerging Markets Review* 3, no. 4 (December 2002): 365–379.

Eubank, Arthur A., Jr., and J. Kenton Zumwalt. "An Analysis of the Forecast Error Impact of Alternative Beta Adjustment Techniques and Risk Classes." *Journal of Finance* 34, no. 3 (June 1979): 761–776.

Evans, John L., and Stephen H. Archer. "Diversification and the Reduction of Dispersion: An Empirical Analysis." *Journal of Finance* 23, no. 5 (December 1968): 761–767.

Fabozzi, Frank J. "The Association Between Common Stock Systematic Risk and Common Stock Rankings." *Review of Business and Economic Research* 12, no. 3 (Spring 1977): 66–77.

Fabozzi, Frank J., and Jack Clark Francis. "Beta as a Random Coefficient." *Journal of Financial and Quantitative Analysis* 13, no. 1 (March 1978): 101–116.

_____. "Industry Effects and the Determinants of Beta." *Quarterly Review of Economics and Business* 19, no. 3 (Autumn 1979a): 61–74.

_____. "Mutual Fund Systematic Risk for Bull and Bear Markets: An Empirical Examination." *Journal of Finance* 34, no. 5 (December 1979b): 1243–1250.

_____. "Stability Tests for Alphas and Betas over Bull and Bear Market Conditions." *Journal of Finance* 32, no. 4 (September 1977): 1093–1099.

Fama, Eugene F. "The Behavior of Stock Market Price." *Journal of Business* 38, no. 1 (January 1965): 34–105.

_____. "Components of Investment Performance." *Journal of Finance* 27, no. 3 (June 1972): 551–567.

_____. "Efficient Capital Markets: A Review of Theory and Empirical Work." *Journal of Finance* 25, no. 2 (May 1970b) 383–417.

_____. *Foundations of Finance*. New York: Basic Books, 1976a.

_____. "Multiperiod Consumption-Investment Decisions." *American Economic Review* 60, no. 1 (March 1970): 163–174.

_____. "Reply." *Journal of Finance* 31, no. 1 (March 1976b): 143–145.

Fama, Eugene F. "Risk, Return, and Equilibrium." *Journal of Political Economy* 79, no. 1 (January–February 1971): 30–55.

_____. "Risk, Return, and Equilibrium: Some Clarifying Comments." *Journal of Finance* 23, no. 1 (March 1968): 29–39.

Fama, Eugene F., and Kenneth R. French. "Common Risk Factors in Returns on Stocks and Bonds." *Journal of Financial Economics* 33, no.1 (February 1993): 3–56.

_____. "The Cross-Section of Expected Stock Returns." *Journal of Finance* 47, no. 2 (June 1992): 129–176.

_____. "Multifactor Explanations of Asset Pricing Anomalies." *Journal of Finance* 51, no. 1 (February 1996): 55–84.

Fama, Eugene F., and James D. MacBeth. "Risk, Return, and Equilibrium: Empirical Tests." *Journal of Political Economy* 81, no. 3 (May 1973): 607–636.

Fama, Eugene F., and Merton H. Miller. *The Theory of Finance*. Hinsdale, IL: Holt, Rinehart and Winston, 1972.

Farnsworth, Heber, Wayne Ferson, David Jackson, and Steven Todd. "Performance Evaluation with Stochastic Discount Factor." *Journal of Business* 75, no. 3 (July 2002): 473–503.

Farquhar, Peter H. "Utility Assessment Methods." *Management Science* 30, no. 11 (November 1984): 1283–1300.

Farrar, Donald E. *The Investment Decision Under Uncertainty*. Englewood Cliffs, NJ: Prentice-Hall, 1962.

Farrell, James L., Jr. "Analyzing Covariation of Returns to Determine Homogeneous Stock Groupings." *Journal of Business* 47, no. 2 (April 1974): 186–207.

_____. "A Disciplined Stock Selection Strategy." *Interfaces* 12, no. 5 (October 1982): 19–30.

_____. "Homogeneous Stock Groupings: Implications for Portfolio Management." *Financial Analysts Journal* 31, no. 3 (May–June 1975): 50–62.

Feibel, Bruce J., *Investment Performance Measurement*, Hoboken, NJ: John Wiley and Sons, 2003.

Feller, William. *An Introduction to Probability Theory and Its Applications*, Vol. I. New York: John Wiley & Sons, 1968.

Ferguson, Robert. "How to Beat the Index Funds." *Financial Analysts Journal* 31, no. 3 (May–June 1975): 63–72.

Ferson, Wayne E., and Campbell R. Harvey. "Conditioning Variables and the Cross-Section of Stock Returns." *Journal of Finance* 54, no. 4 (August 1999:, 1325–1360.

Ferson, Wayne E., and Rudi W. Schadt. "Measuring Fund Strategy and Performance in Changing Economic Conditions." *Journal of Finance* 51, no. 2 (June 1996): 425–461.

Fertuck, Leonard. "A Test of Industry Indices Based on SIC Codes." *Journal of Financial and Quantitative Analysis* 10, no. 5 (December 1975): 837–848.

Fisher, Irving. *Appreciation and Interest*. New York: Macmillan, 1896.

_____. *The Theory of Interest*. New York: Macmillan, 1930.

Fisher, Lawrence. "Analysts' Input and Portfolio Changes." *Financial Analysts Journal* 31, no. 3 (May–June 1975): 73–85.

Foster, George. "Asset Pricing Models: Further Tests." *Journal of Financial and Quantitative Analysis* 13, no. 1 (March 1978a): 39–53.

_____. *Financial Statement Analysis*. Englewood Cliffs, NJ: Prentice-Hall, 1978b.

Fouse, William L. "Risk and Liquidity Revisited." *Financial Analysts Journal* 33, no. 1 (January–February 1977): 40–45.

————. "Risk, Liquidity, and Common Stock Prices." *Financial Analysts Journal* 32, no. 3 (May–June 1976): 35–45.

Fowler, David J., and C. Harvey Rorke. "Risk Measurement When Shares Are Subject to Infrequent Trading: Comment." *Journal of Financial Economics* 12, no. 2 (August 1983): 279–283.

Francis, Jack Clark. "Intertemporal Differences in Systematic Stock Price Movements." *Journal of Financial and Quantitative Analysis* 10, no. 2 (June 1975): 205–219.

————. "Skewness and Investor's Decision." *Journal of Financial and Quantitative Analysis* 10, no. 1 (March 1975): 163–172.

————. "Statistical Analysis of Risk Coefficients for NYSE Stocks." *Journal of Financial and Quantitative Analysis* 14, no. 5 (December 1979): 981–997.

Francis , Jack Clark, and Stephen H. Archer. *Portfolio Analysis*. Englewood Cliffs, NJ: Prentice-Hall, 1971. *Portfolio Analysis* (2nd ed.). Englewood Cliffs, NJ: Prentice-Hall, 1979.

Francis, Jack Clark, and Frank J. Fabozzi. "The Effects of Changing Macroeconomic Conditions on the Parameters of the Single Index Model." *Journal of Financial and Quantitative Analysis* 14, no. 2 (June 1979): 351–360.

Francis, Jack Clark, Arie Harel, and Giora Harpaz. "Exchange Mergers and Electronic Trading." *The Journal of Trading*, Winter 2009: 36–42.

Francis, Jack Clark, Christopher Hessel, Jun Wang, and Ge Zhang. "Portfolios Weighted by Repurchase and Total Payout." Forthcoming in *Journal of Portfolio Management*.

Frankfurter, George M., and Herbert E. Phillips. "Portfolio Selection: An Analytic Approach for Selecting Securities from a Large Universe." *Journal of Financial and Quantitative Analysis* 15, no. 2 (June 1980): 357–377.

Friedman, Milton. *Essays in Positive Economics*. Chicago: The University of Chicago Press, 1953.

Friend, Irwin, and Marshall E. Blume. "The Demand for Risky Assets." *American Economic Review* 65, no. 5 (December 1975): 900–922.

————. "Measurement of Portfolio Performance under Uncertainty." *American Economic Review* 60, no. 4 (September 1970): 561–575.

Garman, Mark B., and Michael J. Klass. "On the Estimation of Security Price Volatilities from Historical Data." *Journal of Business* 53, no. 1 (1980): 67–78.

Gibbons, Michael R. "Multivariate Tests of Financial Models: A New Approach." *Journal of Financial Economics* 10, no. 1 (1982): 3–27.

Gibbons, Michael R., Stephen A. Ross, and Jay Shanken. "A Test of the Efficiency of a Given Portfolio." *Econometrica* 57, no. 5 (September 1989): 1121–1152.

Gilster, John E., Jr. "Capital Market Equilibrium with Divergent Investment Horizon Length Assumptions." *Journal of Financial and Quantitative Analysis* 18, no. 2 (June 1983): 257–268.

Goetzmann, William N., and Roger G. Ibbotson. "Do Winners Repeat?" *Journal of Portfolio Management* 20 (Winter 1994): 9–18.

Gonedes, Nicholas J. "Evidence on the Information Content of Accounting Numbers: Accounting-Based and Market-Based Estimates of Systematic Risk." *Journal of Financial and Quantitative Analysis* 8, no. 3 (June 1973): 407–443.

Good, Walter R., Robert Ferguson, and Jack Treynor. "An Investor's Guide to the Index Fund Controversy." *Financial Analysts Journal* 32, no. 6 (November–December 1976): 27–36.

Gooding, Arthur E., and Terence P. O'Malley. "Market Phase and Stationarity of Beta." *Journal of Financial and Quantitative Analysis* 12, no. 5 (December 1977): 833–857.

Graham, John R., and Campbell R. Harvey. "Grading the Performance of Market Timing Newsletters." *Financial Analysts Journal* 53, no. 6 (November–December 1997): 54–66.

Grant, Dwight. "Market Timing and Portfolio Management." *Journal of Finance* 33, no. 4 (September 1978): 1119–1131.

_____. "Portfolio Performance and the Cost of Timing Decisions." *Journal of Finance* 32, no. 3 (June 1977): 837–846.

Grauer, Frederick L. A., Robert H. Litzenberger, and Richard E. Stehle. "Sharing Rules and Equilibrium in an International Capital Market under Uncertainty." *Journal of Financial Economics* 3, no. 3 (June 1976): 233–256.

Gressis, N., G. C. Philippatos, and J. Hayya. "Multiperiod Portfolio Analysis and the Inefficiency of the Market Portfolio." *Journal of Finance* 31, no. 4 (September 1976): 1115–1126.

Grinblatt, Mark, and Sheridan Titman. "Factors Pricing in a Finite Economy." *Journal of Financial Economics* 12, no. 4 (December 1983a): 497–507.

_____. "The Persistence of Mutual Fund Performance." *Journal of Finance* 47, no. 5 (December 1992): 1977–1984.

Grossman, Sanford J. "On the Efficiency of Competitive Stock Markets Where Traders Have Diverse Information." *Journal of Finance* 31, no. 2 (May 1976): 573–585.

Grossman, Sanford J., and Robert J. Shiller. "The Determinants of the Variability of Stock Market Prices." *American Economic Review* 71, no. 2 (May 1981): 222–227.

Grossman, Sanford J., and Joseph E. Stiglitz. "Information and Competitive Price Systems." *American Economic Review* 66, no. 2 (May 1976): 246–253.

_____. "On the Impossibility of Informationally Efficient Markets." *American Economic Review* 70, no. 3 (June 1980): 393–408.

Grubel, Herbert G. "The Peter Principle and the Efficient Market Hypothesis." *Financial Analysts Journal* 35, no. 6 (November–December 1979): 72–75.

Handa, Puneet, S. P. Kothari, and Charles E. Wasley. "The Relation between the Return Interval and Betas: Implications for the Size Effect." *Journal of Financial Economics* 23, no. 1 (June 1989): 79–100.

Hansen, Lars Peter., "Large Sample Properties of Generalized Method of Moments Estimators." *Econometrica* 50, no. 4 (July 1982): 1029–1054.

Hansen, Lars Peter, John Heaton, and Erzo G. J. Luttmer. "Econometric Evaluation of Asset Pricing Models." *Review of Financial Studies* 8, no. 2 (Summer 1995): 237–274.

Hansen, Lars Peter, and Ravi Jagannathan. "Assessing Specification Errors in Stochastic Discount Factor Models." *Journal of Finance* 52, no. 2 (June 1997): 557–590.

Hardouvelis, Gikas A., Dongcheol Kim, and Thierry A. Wizman. "Asset Pricing Models With and Without Consumption: An Empirical Evaluation." *Journal of Empirical Finance* 3, no. 3 (September 1996): 267–301.

Harrington, Diana R. "Whose Beta Is Best?" *Financial Analysts Journal* 39, no. 4 (July–August 1983): 67–73.

Harvey, Campbell R. "Time-Varying Conditional Covariances in Tests of Asset Pricing Models." *Journal of Financial Economics* 24, no. 2 (1989): 289–317.

Harvey, Campbell R., and Akhtar Siddique. "Conditional Skewness in Asset Pricing Models Tests." *Journal of Finance* 55, no.3 (June 2000): 1263–1295.

Hendershott, Terrence, Charles M. Jones, and Albert J. Menkveld. "Does Algorithmic Trading Improve Liquidity?" *Journal of Finance* (2010).

Henderson, James M., and Richard E. Quandt. *Microeconomic Theory.* New York: McGraw-Hill, 1980.

Hendricks, Darryll, Jayendu Patel, and Richard Zeckhauser. "Hot Hands In Mutual Funds: Short-Run Persistence Of Relative Performance, 1974–1988." *Journal of Finance* 48, no. 1(March 1993): 93–130.

Henriksson, Roy D. "Market Timing and Mutual Fund Performance: An Empirical Investigation." *Journal of Business* 57, no. 1, pt. 1 (January 1984): 73–96.

Henriksson, Roy D., and Robert C. Merton. "On Market Timing and Investment Performance. II. Statistical Procedures for Evaluating Forecasting Skills." *Journal of Business* 54, no. 4 (October 1981): 513–533.

Hentschel, Ludger. "All in the Family Nesting Symmetric and Asymmetric GARCH Models." *Journal of Financial Economics* 39, no. 1 (September 1995): 71–104.

Hirschleifer, Jack. "Efficient Allocation of Capital in an Uncertain World." *American Economic Review* 54, no. 3 (May 1964): 77–85.

Ho, Thomas, and Hans Stoll. "Optimal Dealer Pricing Under Transactions and Return Uncertainty." *Journal Financial Economics* 9, no 1 (1981): 47–73.

Hodges, Stewart D., and Richard A. Brealey. "Portfolio Selection in a Dynamic and Uncertain World." *Financial Analysts Journal* 29, no. 2 (March–April 1973): 50–65.

Hodrick, Robert J., and Xiaoyan Zhang. "Evaluating the Specification Errors of Asset Pricing Models." *Journal of Financial Economics* 62, no. 2 (November 2001): 327–376.

Hogan, William W., and James M. Warren. "Computation of the Efficient Boundary is the E-S Portfolio Selection Model." *Journal of Financial and Quantitative Analysis* 7, no. 4 (September 1972): 1881–1896.

Huang, Chi-hu, and Robert Litzenberger. *Foundations for Financial Economics*. Upper Saddle River, NJ: Prentice-Hall, 1988.

Huang, Dashan, Shu-Shang Zhu, Frank J. Fabozzi, and Masao Fukushima. "Relative Robust CVaR in Portfolio Management." *European Journal of Operational Research* 203, no.1 (2010): 185–194.

Huberman, Gur. "A Simple Approach to Arbitrage Pricing Theory." *Journal of Economic Theory* 28, no. 1 (October 1982): 183–191.

Hull, John. *Options, Futures, and Other Derivatives*. Prentice Hall, 2008.

Ibottson, Roger G., Laurence B. Siegel, and Kathryn Love. "World Wealth: Market Values and Returns." *Journal of Portfolio Management* 12, no. 1 (Fall 1985): 4–23.

Ingersoll, Jonathan E., Jr. "Multidimensional Security Pricing." *Journal of Financial and Quantitative Analysis* 10, no. 5 (December 1975): 785–798.

_____. "Some Results in the Theory of Arbitrage Pricing." *Journal of Finance* 39, no. 4 (September 1984): 1021–1039.

Jacob, Nancy L., and R. Richardson Pettit. *Investments*. Homewood, IL: Richard D. Irwin, 1984.

Jacquillat, Bertrand, and Bruno Solnik. "Multinationals Are Poor Tools for Diversification." *Journal of Portfolio Management* 4, no. 2 (Winter 1978): 8–12.

Jagannathan, Ravi, Keiichi Kubota, and Hitoshi Takehara. "Relationship Between Labor-Income Risk and Average Return: Empirical Evidence from the Japanese Stock market." *Journal of Business* 71, no. 2 (April 1998): 319–348.

Jagannathan, Ravi, and Yong Wang. "Lazy Investors, Discretionary Consumption, and the Cross-Section of Stock Returns." *Journal of Finance* 62, no.4 (August 2007): 1623–1661.

Jagannathan, Ravi, and Zhenyu Wang. "The Conditional CAPM and the Cross-Section of Expected Returns." *Journal of Finance* 51, no. 3 (March 1996): 3–53.

Jarrow, Robert A., and Eric R. Rosenfeld. "Jump Risk and the Intertemporal Capital Asset Pricing Model." *Journal of Business* 57, no.3 (July 1984): 337–351.

Jean, William H. "The Extension of Portfolio Analysis to Three or More Parameters." *Journal of Financial and Quantitative Analysis* 6, no. 1 (January 1971): 505–515.

_____. "More on Multidimensional Portfolio Analysis." *Journal of Financial and Quantitative Analysis* 8, no. 3 (June 1973): 475–490.

Jegadeesh, Narasimhan, and Sheridan Titman. "Returns to Buying Winners and Selling Losers: Implications for Stock Market Efficiency." *Journal of Finance* 48, no.1 (March 1993): 65–91.

Jensen, Michael C. "Optimal Utilization of Market Forecasts and the Evaluation of Investment Performance." in *Mathematical Methods in Investment and Finance*, eds. G. P. Szego and Karl Shell. Amsterdam: North-Holland Publishing Company, 1972.

_____. "The Performance of Mutual Funds in the Period 1945–1964." *Journal of Finance* 23, no. 2 (May 1968): 389–416.

_____. "Risk, the Pricing of Capital Assets, and the Evaluation of Investment Portfolios." *Journal of Business* 42, no. 2 (April 1969): 167–185.

Jiang, George J., and Yisong S. Tian. "Model-Free Implied Volatility and Its Information Content." *Review of Financial Studies* 18, no. 4 (Winter 2005): 1305–1342.

Jobson, J. D., and Bob Korkie. "Estimation for Markowitz Efficient Portfolios." *Journal of the American Statistical Association* 75, no. 371 (September 1980): 544–554.

_____. "Performance Hypothesis Testing with the Sharpe and Treynor Measures." *Journal of Finance* 36, no. 4 (September 1981a): 889–908.

Jobson, J. D., and Bob Korkie. "Potential Performance and Tests of Portfolio Efficiency." *Journal of Financial Economics* 10, no. 4 (December 1982): 433–466.

_____. "Putting Markowitz Theory to Work." *Journal of Portfolio Management* 7, no. 4 (Summer 1981b): 70–74.

Johnson, Keith H., and Donald S. Shannon. "A Note on Diversification and the Reduction of Dispersion." *Journal of Financial Economics* 1, no. 4 (December 1974): 365–372.

Jorion, Philippe. *Value at Risk*, 3rd ed. New York: MacGraw-Hill, 2007.

Jorion, Philippe, and William N. Goetzmann. "Global Stock Markets in the Twentieth Century." *Journal of Finance* 54, no. 3 (June 1999): 953–980.

Judge, George G., W. E. Griffiths, R.C. Hill, H. Lütkepohk, and T. C. Lee. *Introduction to the Theory and Practice of Econometrics*, 2nd ed. New York: John Wiley & Sons, 1988.

Kahneman, Daniel and Amos Tversky, "Prospect Theory: An Analysis of Decisions under Risk," *Econometrica* 47 (March 1979): 263–291.

Kan, Raymond, and Cesare Robotti. "Model Comparison Using Hansen-Jagannathan Distance." *Review of Financial Studies* 22, no. 9 (September 2009): 3449–3490.

Kandel, Shmuel. "On the Exclusion of Assets from Tests of the Mean Variance Efficiency of the Market Portfolio." *Journal of Finance* 39, no. 1 (March 1984): 63–75.

Kaplansky, Irving. "A Common Error Concerning Kurtosis." *Journal of the American Statistical Association* 40, no. 230 (June 1945): 259.

Kataoka, Shinji. "A Stochastic Programming Model." *Econometrica* 31 (January–April 1963): 181–196.

Keim, Donald B. "Size-Related Anomalies and Stock Return Seasonality" *Journal of Financial Economics* 12 (June 1983): 13–32.

Kendall, Maurice G. "The Analysis of Economic Time Series, I: Prices." *Journal of the Royal Statistical Society*, Ser. A, (December 1953): 11–25.

Kim, Dongcheol. "A Bayesian Significance Test on the Stationarity of Regression Parameters." *Biometrika* 78 (September 1991): 667–675.

_____. "The Errors-In-Variables Problem in the Cross-Section of Expected Stock Returns." *Journal of Finance* 50, (December 1995):1605–1634.

_____. "The Extent of Nonstationarity of Beta." *Review of Quantitative Finance and Accounting* 3 (June 1993): 241–254.

_____. "On the Information Uncertainty Risk and the January Effect." *Journal of Business* 79 (July 2006): 2127–2162.

_____. "A Reexamination of Firm Size, Book-to-Market, and Earnings-Price in the Cross-Section of Expected Stock Returns." *Journal of Financial and Quantitative Analysis* 32 (December 1997): 463–489.

Kim, Dongcheol, Tong-Suk Kim, and Byoung-Kyu Min. "Future Labor Income Growth and the Cross Section of Equity Returns." *Journal of Banking and Finance* 35, no. 1 (January 2011): 67–81.

Kim, Dongcheol, and Stanley J. Kon. "Alternative Models for Conditional Heteroscedasticity of Stock Returns." *Journal of Business* 67 (October 1994): 563–598.

_____. "Sequential Parameter Nonstationarity in Stock Market Returns." *Review of Quantitative Finance and Accounting* 6, (March 1996): 103–131.

_____. "Structural Change and Time Dependence in Models of Stock Returns." *Journal of Empirical Finance* 6 (September 1999): 283–308.

Kim, Dongcheol, and Yaxuan Qi. "Accruals Quality, Stock Returns, and Macroeconomic Conditions." *Accounting Review* 85 (May 2010): 937–978.

Kim, Moon M., and Kenton J. Zumwalt. "An Analysis of Risk in Bull and Bear Markets." *Journal of Financial and Quantitative Analysis* 14, no. 5 (December 1979): 1015–1025.

King, Benjamin F. "Market and Industry Factors in Stock Price Behavior." *Journal of Business* 39, no. 1 (January 1966): 139–170.

Klemkosky, Robert C. "The Bias in Composite Performance Measures." *Journal of Financial and Quantitative Analysis* 8, no.3 (June 1973): 505–514.

Klemkosky, Robert C., and John D. Martin. "The Adjustment of Beta Forecasts." *Journal of Finance* 30, no. 4 (September 1975): 1123–1128.

Kon, Stanley J. "Models of Stock Returns–A Comparison." *Journal of Finance* 39, no. 1 (March 1984): 147–165.

Kon, Stanley J., and Frank C. Jen. "Estimation of Time-Varying Systematic Risk and Performance for Mutual Fund Portfolios: An Application of Switching Regression." *Journal of Finance* 33, no.2 (May 1978): 457–475.

_____. "The Investment Performance of Mutual Funds: An Empirical Investigation of Timing, Selectivity, and Market Efficiency." *Journal of Business* 52, no. 2 (April 1979): 263–289.

Korkie, Bob M. "Comment: Systematic Interest-Rate Risk in a Two-Index Model of Returns." *Journal of Financial and Quantitative Analysis* 9, no. 5 (November 1974): 723–725.

Kothari, S. P., Jay Shanken, and Richard G. Sloan. "Another Look at the Cross-Section of Expected Stock Returns." *Journal of Finance* 50, no. 1 (March 1995): 185–224.

Kraus, Alan, and Robert H. Litzenberger. "Skewness Preference and Valuation of Risk Assets." *Journal of Finance* 31, no. 4 (September 1976): 1085–1100.

Kritzman, Mark. "Can Bond Managers Perform Consistently." *Journal of Portfolio Management* 9, no. 4 (Summer 1983): 54–56.

Kroll, Yoram, Haim Levy, and Harry M. Markowitz. "Mean Variance versus Direct Utility Maximization." *Journal of Finance* 39, no. 1 (March 1984).

Kryzanowski, Lawrence, and Minh Chau To. "General Factor Models and the Structure of Security Returns." *Journal of Financial and Quantitative Analysis* 18, no. 1 (March 1983): 31–52.

Kupiec, Paul H. "Stress Testing in a Value at Risk Framework." *Journal of Derivatives* 6, (Fall 1998): 7–24.

_____. "Techniques for Verifying the Accuracy of Risk Management Models." *Journal of Derivatives* 3 (Winter 1995): 73–84.

Lakonishok, Josef. "Stock Market Return Expectations: Some General Properties." *Journal of Finance* 35, no. 4 (September 1980): 921–931.

Lamoureux, Christopher G. and William D. Lastrapes. "Forecasting Stock-Return Variance: Toward an Understanding of Stochastic Implied Volatilities." *Review of Financial Studies* 6, no.2 (Summer 1993): 293–326.

Landskroner, Yoram. "Nonmarketable Assets and the Determinants of the Market Price of Risk." *Review of Economics and Statistics* 59, no. 4 (November 1977): 482–492.

Lanstein, Ronald J., and William W. Jahnke. "Applying Capital Market Theory to Investing." *Interfaces* 9, no. 2, pt. 2 (February 1979): 23–38.

Lau, Hon-Shiang, John R. Wingender, and Amy Hing-Ling Lau. "On Estimating Skewness in Stock Returns." *Management Science* 35, (September 1989): 1133–1142.

Lee, Cheng-few. "Investment Horizon and the Functional Form of the Capital Asset Pricing Model": *Review of Economics and Statistics* 58, no. 3 (August 1976): 356–363.

Lehmann, Bruce N., and David M. Modest. "Mutual Fund Performance Evaluation: A Comparison of Benchmarks and Benchmark Comparisons." *Journal of Finance* 42, no. 2 (June 1987): 233–265.

Leland, Hayne E. "Beyond Mean-Variance: Performance measurement in a Nonsymmetrical World." *Financial Analysts Journal* 55, (January–February 1999): 27–36.

LeRoy, Stephen F. "Efficient Capital Markets: Comment." *Journal of Finance* 31, no. 1 (March 1976): 139–141.

Lessard, Donald R. "International Diversification," *Financial Analysts Journal* 32, no. 1 (January–February 1976): 32–38.

––––––––. "World, National, and Industry Factors in Equity Returns." *Journal of Finance* 29, no. 2 (May 1974): 379–391.

Lettau, Martin, and Sydney Ludvigson. "Consumption, Aggregation Wealth and Expected Stock Returns." *Journal of Finance* 56, no. 3 (June 2001): 815–849.

Levhari, David, and Haim Levy. "The Capital Asset Pricing Model and the Investment Horizon." *Review of Economics and Statistics* 59, (February 1977) 92–104.

Levy, Haim. "Equilibrium in an Imperfect Market: A Constraint on the Number of Securities in the Portfolio." *American Economic Review* 68, no. 4 (September 1978): 643–658.

Levy, Haim. "Measuring Risk and Performance over Alternative Investment Horizons." *Financial Analysts Journal* 40, no. 2 (March-April 1984): 61–68.

Levy, Haim, and Yoram Kroll. "Ordering Uncertain Options with Borrowing and Lending." *Journal of Finance* 33 (May 1978): 553–573.

––––––––. "Stochastic Dominance with Riskless Assets." *Journal of Financial and Quantitative Analysis* 11 (December 1976): 743–778.

Levy, Haim, and Harry M. Markowitz "Approximating Expected Utility by a Function of Mean and Variance." *American Economic Review* 69, no. 3 (June 1979): 308–317.

Levy, Haim, and Marshall Sarnat. "International Diversification of Investment Portfolios." *American Economic Review* 60, no. 4 (September 1970): 668–675.

Levy, Robert A. "On the Short-Term Stationarity of Beta Coefficients." *Financial Analyst Journal* 27, no. 6 (November–December 1971): 55–62.

Lindenberg, Eric B. "Capital Market Equilibrium with Price Affecting Institutional Investors" in *Portfolio Theory, 25 Years After*, ed. E. J. Elton and M. J. Gruber. Amsterdam: North-Holland Publishing Company, 1979.

Lintner, John. "The Aggregation of Investor's Diverse Judgments and Preferences in Purely Competitive Security Markets." *Journal of Financial and Quantitative Analysis* 4, no. 4 (December 1969): 347–400.

––––––––. "Security Prices, Risk, and Maximal Gains from Diversification." *Journal of Finance* 20, no. 4 (December 1965b): 587–615.

––––––––. "The Valuation of Risk Assets and the Selection of Risky Investments in Stock Portfolios and Capital Budgets." *Review of Economics and Statistics* 47, no. 1 (February 1965a): 13–37.

Litzenberger, Robert H., and Krishna Ramaswamy. "The Effect of Personal Taxes and Dividends on Capital Asset Prices: Theory and Empirical Evidence." *Journal of Financial Economics* 7, no. 2 (June 1979): 163–195.

Livingston, Miles, and Edward S. O'Neal. "The Cost of Mutual Fund Distribution Fees." *The Journal of Financial Research* 11 (Summer 1998): 205–218.

Lloyd, William P., and Richard A. Shick. "A Test of Stone's Two-Index Model of Returns." *Journal of Financial and Quantitative Analysis* 12, no. 3 (September 1977): 363–376.

Lucas, Robert. "Asset Prices in an Exchange Economy." *Econometrica* 46 (November 1978): 1429–1445.

Lynge, Morgan J., Jr., and J. Kenton Zumwalt. "An Empirical Study of the Interest Rate Sensitivity of Commercial Bank Returns: A Multi-Index Approach." *Journal of Financial and Quantitative Analysis* 15, no. 3 (September 1980): 731–742.

Mains, Norman E. "Risk, the Pricing of Capital Assets, and the Evaluation of Investment Portfolios: Comment." *Journal of Business* 50, no. 3 (July 1977): 371–384.

Malkiel, Burton G. "Returns From Investing In Equity Mutual Funds, 1971–1991." *Journal of Finance* 50, no. 2, (June 1995): 553.

Mandelbrot, Benoit. "The Variation of Certain Speculative Prices." *Journal of Business* 36 (October 1963): 394–419.

Mao, James C.T. "Models of Capital Budgeting, E-V Versus E-S." *Journal of Financial and Quantitative Analysis* 4, (January 1970): 657–675.

Markowitz, Harry M., ed. *Harry Markowitz Selected Works*, Vol. 1. Singapore: World Scientific Publisher, 2010.

_____. "Investment for the Long Run: New Guidance for an Old Rule." *Journal of Finance* 31, no. 5 (December 1976): 1273–1286.

_____. *Mean-Variance Analysis*. New York: Basil Blackwood, 1987.

_____. "Nonnegative or Not Nonnegative: A Question about CAPMs." *Journal of Finance* 38, no. 2 (May 1983): 283–295.

_____. "Portfolio Selection." *Journal of Finance*, 7, no. 1 (March 1952): 89.

_____. *Portfolio Selection: Efficient Diversification of Investments*. New York: Wiley, 1959.

_____. "The 'Two Beta' Trap." *Journal of Portfolio Management* 11, no. 1 (Fall 1984): 12–20.

Markowitz, Harry M., Peter Todd, Ganlin Xu, and Yuji Yamane. "Computation of Mean-Semivariance Efficient Sets by the Critical Line Method." *Annals of Operations Research* 45, no. 1 (December 1993): 307–317.

Martin, C. G. "Ridge Regression Estimates of Ex Post Risk-Return Trade-off on Common Stock." *Review of Business and Economic Research* (Spring 1978): 1–15.

Martin, John D., and Arthur J. Keown. "Interest Rate Sensitivity and Portfolio Risk." *Journal of Financial and Quantitative Analysis* 12, no. 2 (June 1977): 181–195.

Mayers, David. "Nonmarketable Assets and Capital Market Equilibrium under Uncertainty" in *Studies in the Theory of Capital Markets*, ed. Michael C. Jensen. New York: Praeger Publishers, Inc., 1972.

_____. "Nonmarketable Assets and the Determination of Capital Asset Prices in the Absence of a Riskless Asset." *Journal of Business* 46, no. 2 (April 1973): 258–267.

_____. "Nonmarketable Assets, Market Segmentation, and the Level of Asset Prices." *Journal of Financial and Quantitative Analysis* 11, no. 1 (March 1976): 1–12.

Merton, Robert C. "An Analytic Derivation of the Efficient Portfolio Frontier." *Journal of Financial and Quantitative Analysis* 7, no. 4 (September 1972): 1851–1872.

_____. "An Intertemporal Capital Asset Pricing Model." *Econometrica* 41 (September 1973): 867–887.

_____. "On Estimating the Expected Return on the Market: An Exploratory Investigation." *Journal of Financial Economics* 8, no. 4 (December 1980): 323–361.

_____. "On Market Timing and Investment Performance: I. An Equilibrium Theory of Value for Market Forecasts." *Journal of Business* 54, no. 3 (July 1981): 363–406.

_____. "Optimum Consumption and Portfolio Rules in a Continuous-Time Model." *Journal of Economic Theory* 3, no. 4 (December 1971): 373–413.

_____. "A Reexamination of the Capital Asset Pricing Model," Sec. 7 in *Risk and Return in Finance*, Vol. I, ed. Irwin Friend and Hames L. Bicksler. Cambridge, MA: Ballinger Publishing Company, 1977.

Meyers, Stephen L. "A Re-Examination of Market and Industry Factors in Stock Price Behavior." *Journal of Finance* 28, no. 3 (June 1973): 695–705.

Miller, Merton H., and Myron S. Scholes. "Dividends and Taxes." *Journal of Financial Economics* 6, no. 4 (December 1978): 333–364.

_____. "Rates of Return in Relation to Risk: A Re-examination of Some Recent Findings," in *Studies in the Theory of Capital Markets*, ed. Michael C. Jensen. New York: Praeger Publishers, Inc., 1972.

Miller, Robert E., and Adam K. Gehr. "Sample Size Bias and Sharpe's Performance Measure: A Note." *Journal of Financial and Quantitative Analysis* 13, no. 5 (December 1978): 943–946.

Modigliani, Franco, and Leah Modigliani. "Risk-Adjusted Performance." *Journal of Portfolio Management* 23 (Winter 1997): 45–54.

Mood, Alexander M., Franklin A. Graybill, and Duane C. Boes. *Introduction to the Theory of Statistics*, 3rd ed. New York: McGraw Hill, 1974.

Morgan, I. G. "Market Proxies and the Conditional Prediction of Returns." *Journal of Financial Economics* 6, no. 4 (December 1978): 385–398.

Mossin, Jan. "Optimal Multiperiod Portfolio Policies." *Journal of Business* 41, no. 2 (April 1968): 215–229.

_____. "Security Pricing and Investment Criteria in Competitive Markets." *American Economic Review* 59, no. 5 (December 1969): 749–756.

Muralidhar, Krishnamurty. "The Boostrapping Approach for Testing Skewness Persistence." *Management Science* 39 (April 1993): 487–491.

Murphy, J. Michael. "Efficient Markets, Index Funds, Illusion, and Reality." *Journal of Portfolio Management* 4, no. 1 (Fall 1977): 5–20.

Neal, Robert. "Is Program Trading Destabilizing?" *Journal of Derivatives* 1 (Winter 1993): 64–77.

Niedermayer, Andras, and Daniel Niedermayer. "Applying Markowitz's Critical Line Algorithm," in *Handbook of Portfolio Construction: Contemporary Applications of Markowitz Techniques*, ed. John B. Guerard Jr. New York: Springer, 2010.

O'Hara, Maureen. *Market Microstructure Theory*. Cambridge: Blackwell, 1997.

Odier, Patrick, and Bruno Solnik. "Lessons for International Asset Allocation." *Financial Analysts Journal* 49 (Mar–Apr 1993): 63–77.

Ohlson, James, and Barr Rosenberg. "Systematic Risk of the CRSP Equally-Weighted Common Stock Index: A History Estimated by Stochastic-Parameter Regression." *Journal of Business* 55, no. 1 (January 1982): 121–145.

Ortobelli, Sergio, Svetlozar Rachev, and Frank J. Fabozzi., "Risk Management and Dynamic Portfolio Selection with Stable Paretian Distributions." *Journal of Empirical Finance* 17, no. 2 (March 2010): 195–211.

Osborne, M. F. M. "Brownian Motion in the Stock Market." *Operations Research* 7, (February 1959): 173–195.

Parkinson, Michael. "The Extreme Value Method for Estimating the Variance of the Rate of Return." *Journal of Business* 53 (January 1980): 61–65.

Pastor, Lubos, and Robert F. Stambaugh. "Liquidity Risk and Expected Stock Returns." *Journal of Political Economy* 111 (June 2003): 642–685.

Patell, James M., and Mark A. Wolfson. "The Ex Ante and Ex Post Price Effects of Quarterly Earnings Announcements Reflected in Option and Stock Prices." *Journal of Accounting Research* 19 (Autumn 1981): 434–458.

Pearson, Egon S and H.O. Hartley, eds. *Biometrika Tables for Statisticians*, Vol. 1, 3rd ed. Cambridge: Cambridge University Press, 1966.

Perignon, Christophe, and Daniel R. Smith. "The Level and Quality of Value-at-Risk Disclosure by Commercial Banks." *Journal of Banking and Finance* 34, no. 2 (February 2010): 362–377.

Perold, Andre F. "Fundamentally Flawed Indexing." *Financial Analysts Journal* 63, no. 6 (November–December 2007): 31–37.

Peterson, David, and Micheal L. Rice. "A Note on Ambiguity in Portfolio Performance Measures." *Journal of Finance* 35, no. 5 (December 1980): 1251–1256.

Pettit, R. Richardson, and Randolph Westerfield. "Using the Capital Asset Pricing Model and the Market Model to Predict Security Returns." *Journal of Financial and Quantitative Analysis* 9, no. 4 (September 1974): 579–605.

Pflug, Georg Ch. "Some Remarks on the Value-at-Risk and the Conditional Value-at-Risk." In *Probabilistic Constrained Optimization: Methodology and Applications*, edited by S. Uryasev. Dordrecht, Netherlands: Kluwer Academic Publishers, 2000.

Poon, Ser-Huang, and Clive W.J. Granger. "Forecasting Volatility in Financial Markets: A Review." *Journal of Economic Literature* 41, (June 2003): 478–539.

Prakash, Arun J., Chun-Hao Chang, and Therese E. Pactwa. "Selecting a Portfolio with Skewness: Recent Evidence from US, European, and Latin American Equity Markets." *Journal of Banking and Finance* 27, (July 2003): 1375–1390.

Press, S. James. "A Compound Events Model for Security Prices." *Journal of Business* 45 (July 1967): 317–335.

Price, Kelly, Barbara Price, and Timothy J. Nantell. "Variance and Lower Partial Moment Measures of Systematic Risk: Some Analytical and Empirical Results." *Journal of Finance* 37, no. 3 (June 1982): 843–855.

Quirk, James P., and Rubin Saposnik. "Admissibility and Measurable Utility Functions." *Review of Economic Studies* (February 1962): 140–146.

Rachev, Svetlozar T., Christian Menn, and Frank J. Fabozzi. *Fat-Tailed and Skewed Asset Return Distributions: Implications for Risk Management, Portfolio Selection, and Option Pricing.* New York: John Wiley & Sons, 2005.

Rachev, Svetlozar T., Sergio Ortobelli, Stoyan Stoyanov, Frank J. Fabozzi, and Almira Biglova. "Desirable Properties of an Ideal Risk Measure in Portfolio Theory." *International Journal of Theoretical and Applied Finance* 11, no. 1 (February 2008): 19–54.

Rachev, Svetlozar T., Stoyan Stoyanov, Almira Biglova, and Frank J. Fabozzi. "An Empirical Examination of Daily Stock Return Distributions for U.S. Stocks." In *Data Analysis and Decision Support*, edited by Daniel Baier, Reinhold Decker, and Lars Schmidt-Thieme. Berlin: Springer-Verlag, 2005.

Reinganum, Marc C. "The Anomalous Stock Market Behavior of Small Firm in January: Empirical Tests for Tax-Loss." *Journal of Financial Economics* 12 (June 1983): 89–104.

_____. "Misspecification of Capital Asset Pricing: Empirical Anomalies Based on Earnings Yield and Market Value." *Journal of Financial Economics* 9 (March 1981): 19–46.

Richard, Scott F. "A Generalized Capital Asset Pricing Model." In *Portfolio Theory, 25 Years After*, edited by E. J. Elton and M. J. Gruber. Amsterdam: North-Holland Publishing Company, 1979.

RiskMetrics Group. *RiskMetrics–Technical Documents.* New York: J.P. Morgan, 1996.

Roberts, Harry V. "Stock Market 'Patterns' and Financial Analysis: Methodological Suggestions." *Journal of Finance*, 14 (March 1959): 1–10.

Rockafellar, R. Tyrrell, and Stanislav Uryasev. "Optimization of Conditional Value-at-Risk." *Journal of Risk* 2, no. 3 (Spring 2000): 21–41.

Rogers, L. C. G., and Stephen E. Satchell. "Estimating Variance from High, Low, and Closing Prices." *Annals of Applied Probability* 1 (November 1991): 504–512.

Roll, Richard. "Ambiguity When Performance Is Measured by the Security Market Line." *Journal of Finance* 33, no. 4 (September 1978): 1051–1069.

_____. "Bias in Fitting the Sharpe Model to Time Series Data." *Journal of Financial and Quantitative Analysis* 4, no. 3 (September 1969): 271–289.

_____. "A Critique of the Asset Pricing Theory's Tests: Part I. On Past and Potential Testability of the Theory." *Journal of Financial Economics* 4, no. 2 (March 1977): 129–176.

_____. "Performance Evaluation and Benchmark Errors (I)." *Journal of Portfolio Management* 6, no. 4 (Summer 1980): 5–12.

_____. "Performance Evaluation and Benchmark Errors (II)." *Journal of Portfolio Management* 7, no. 2 (Winter 1981): 17–22.

Roll, Richard, and Stephen A. Ross. "The Arbitrage Pricing Theory Approach to Strategic Portfolio Planning." *Financial Analysts Journal* 40, no. 3 (May–June 1984a): 14–26.

_____. "An Empirical Investigation of the Arbitrage Pricing Theory." *Journal of Finance* 35, no. 5 (December 1980): 1073–1103.

_____. "On the Cross-Sectional Relation between Expected Returns and Betas." *Journal of Finance* 49, no. 1 (March 1994): 101–121.Rosenberg, Barr. "Extra-market Components of Covariance in Security Returns." *Journal of Financial and Quantitative Analysis* 9, no. 2 (March 1974): 263–274.

Rosenberg, Barr, and James Guy. "Beta and Investment Fundamentals." *Financial Analysts Journal* 322, no. 3 (May–June 1976a): 60–72.

_____. "Beta and Investment Fundamentals, II." *Financial Analysts Journal* 32, no. 4 (July–August 1976b): 62–70.

Rosenberg, Barr, and Vinay Marathe. "Common Factors in Security Returns: Microeconomic Determinants and Macroeconomic Correlates." In *Proceedings: Seminar on the Analysis of Security Prices*. Center for Research in Security Prices, Graduate School of Business, The University of Chicago, May 1976.

_____. "The Prediction of Investment Risk: Systematic and Residual Risk." In *Proceedings: Seminar on the Analysis of Security Prices*. Center for Research in Security Prices, Graduate School of Business, The University of Chicago, November 1975.

Ross, Stephen A. "The Arbitrage Theory of Capital Asset Pricing." *Journal of Economic Theory* 13, no. 3 (December 1976): 341–360.

_____. "The Capital Asset Pricing Model (CAPM), Short-Sale Restrictions and Related Issues." *Journal of Finance* 32, no. 1 (March 1977a): 177–183.

Ross, Stephen A. "The Current Status of the Capital Asset Pricing Model (CAPM)." *Journal of Finance* 33, no. 3 (June 1978a): 885–901.

_____. "Mutual Fund Separation in Financial Theory—The Separation Distributions." *Journal of Economic Theory* 17, no. 2 (December 1978b): 254–286.

_____. "Risk, Return, and Arbitrage." Sec. 9 in *Risk and Return in Finance*, Vol. I. Edited by Irwin Friend and James L. Bicksler. Cambridge, MA: Ballinger Publishing Company, 1977b.

Roy, A. D. "Safety First and the Holding of Assets." *Econometrica* 20, no.3 (July 1952): 431–449.

Rubinstein, Mark. "An Aggregation Theorem for Securities Market." *Journal of Financial Economics* 1, no. 3 (September 1974): 225–244.

_____. "The Valuation of Uncertain Income Streams and the Pricing of Options." *Bell Journal of Economics and Management Science* 7, (Autumn 1976): 407–425.

Samuelson, Paul A. "Proof That Properly Discounted Present Values of Assets Vibrate Randomly." *Bell Journal of Economics and Management Science* 4, no. 2 (Autumn 1973): 369–374.

Schaefer, Stephen M. "Taxes and Security Market Equilibrium." In *Financial Economics: Essays in Honor of Paul Cootner*, edited by William F. Sharpe and Cathryn M. Cootner. Englewood Cliffs, NJ: Prentice-Hall, 1982.

Schaefer, Stephen, Richard Brealey, Stewart Hodges, and Howard Thomas. "Alternative Models of Systematic Risk." In *International Capital Markets*, edited by Edwin J. Elton and Martin J. Gruber. Amsterdam: North-Holland Publishing Company, 1975.

Schneller, Meir I. "Are Better Betas Worth the Trouble?" *Financial Analysts Journal* 39, no. 4 (July–August 1983): 74–77.

Schoemaker, Paul J. H. "The Expected Utility Model: Its Variants, Purposes, Evidence and Limitations." *Journal of Economic Literature* 20, no. 2 (June 1982): 529–563.

Scholes, Myron, and Joseph Williams. "Estimating Betas from Nonsynchronous Data." *Journal of Financial Economics* 5, no. 3 (December 1977): 309–327.

Schreiner, John, "Portfolio Revision: A Turnover-Constrained Approach." *Financial Management* 9, no. 1 (Spring 1980): 67–75.

Schwert, G. William. "Size and Stock Returns, and Other Empirical Regularities." *Journal of Financial Economics* 12, no. 1 (June 1983): 3–12.

Shanken, Jay. "The Arbitrage Pricing Theory: Is It Testable?" *Journal of Finance* 37, no. 5 (December 1982) 1129–1140.

_____. "Multi-Beta CAPM or Equilibrium APT?: A Reply." *Journal of Finance* 40, no. 4 (September 1985): 1189–1196.

_____. "Multivariate Tests of the Zero-Beta CAPM." *Journal of Financial Economics* 14, no. 2 (September 1985): 327–348.

_____. "On the Estimation of Beta-Pricing Models." *Review of Financial Studies* 5 (Spring 1992): 1–33.

Sharpe, William F. "Asset Allocation: Management Style and Performance Measurement." *Financial Analysts Journal* 18, no. 2 (1992): 7–19.

_____. "Capital Asset Prices: A Theory of Market Equilibrium under Conditions of Risk." *Journal of Finance*, September 1964.

_____. "The Capital Asset Pricing Model: A 'Multi-beta' Interpretation." In *Financial Decision Making under Uncertainty*, edited by Haim Levy and Marshall Sarnat. New York: Academic Press, 1977.

_____. *Investments*. Englewood Cliffs, NJ: Prentice-Hall, 1985.

_____. "A Linear Programming Algorithm for Mutual Fund Portfolio Selection." *Management Science*, March 1967, 499–510.

_____. "Major Investment Styles." *Journal of Portfolio Management* 4, no. 2 (Winter 1978): 68–74.

_____. "Mutual Fund Performance." *Journal of Business* 39, no. 1 pt. 2 (January 1966): 119–138.

_____. *Portfolio Theory and Capital Markets*. New York: McGraw–Hill, 1970.

Sharpe, William F. "A Simplified Model for Portfolio Analysis." *Management Science* 9, no. 2 (January 1963): 277–293.

_____, ed. *William F. Sharpe: Selected Works*. Singapore: World Scientific Publishing Company Inc., 2011.

Sharpe, William F., and Guy M. Cooper. "Risk-Return Classes of New York Stock Exchange Common Stocks, 1931–67." *Financial Analysts Journal* 28, no. 2 (March–April 1972): 413–446.

Simkowitz, Michael A., and William L. Beedles. "Diversification in a Three-Moment World." *Journal of Financial and Quantitative Analysis* 13, (December 1978): 927–941.

Singer, Brian D., and Denis S. Karnosky. "The Global Framework for Global Investment Management and Performance Attribution." *Journal of Portfolio Management* 21, no. 2 (Winter 1995): 84–92.

Singer, Ronald F. "Endogenous Marginal Income Tax Rates, Investor Behavior and the Capital Asset Pricing Model." *Journal of Finance* 34, no. 3 (June 1979): 609–616.

Singleton, J. Clay, and John Wingender. "Skewness Persistence in Common Stock Returns." *Journal of Financial and Quantitative Analysis* 21, no. 3 (September 1986): 335–341.

Siriopoulos, Costas, and Athanasios Fassas. "Implied Volatility Indices–A Review." SSRN eLibrary.

Smith, Dariel R. "Conditional Coskewness and Asset Pricing." *Journal of Empirical Finance* 14 (January 2007): 91–119.

Smith, Gary. "A Simple Model for Estimating Intrinsic Value." *Journal of Portfolio Management* 8, no. 4 (Summer 1982): 46–49.

Solnik, Bruno H. "An Equilibrium Model of the International Capital Market." *Journal of Economic Theory* 8, no. 4 (August 1974b): 500–524.

_____. "Why Not Diversify Internationally Rather than Domestically?" *Financial Analysts Journal* 30, no. 4 (July–August 1974a): 48–54.

Stambaugh, Robert F. "On the Exclusion of Assets from Tests of the Two-Parameter Model: A Sensitivity Analysis." *Journal of Financial Economics* 10, no. 3 (November 1982): 237–268.

_____. "Testing the CAPM with Broader Market Indexes: A Problem of Mean-Deficiency." *Journal of Banking and Finance* 7, no. 1 (March 1983): 5–16.

Stapleton, R. C., and M. G. Subrahmanyam. "The Market Model and Capital Asset Pricing Theory: A Note." *Journal of Finance* 38, no. 5 (December 1983): 1637–1642.

Stehle, Richard. "An Empirical Test of the Alternative Hypotheses of National and International Pricing of Risky Assets." *Journal of Finance* 32, no.2 (May 1977): 493–502.

Stone, Bernell K. "A General Class of Three-Parameter Risk Measures." *Journal of Finance* (June 1973): 675–685.

_____. "Systematic Interest-Rate Risk in a Two-Index Model of Returns." *Journal of Financial and Quantitative Analysis* 9, no. 5 (November 1974): 709–721.

Stoyanov, Stoyan, Svetlozar T. Rachev, Boryana Racheva-Yotova, and Frank J. Fabozzi. "Fat-Tailed Models for Risk Estimation." *Journal of Portfolio Management* (Winter 2011): 107–117.

Stulz, Rene M. "A Model of International Asset Pricing." *Journal of Financial Economics* 9, no. 4 (December 1981): 383–406.

Sun, Qian, and Yuxing Yan. "Skewness Persistence with Optimal Portfolio Selection." *Journal of Banking and Finance* 27 (June 2003): 1111–1121.

Sunder, Shyam. "Stationarity of Market Risk: Random Coefficients Tests for Individual Stocks." *Journal of Finance* 35, no. 4 (September 1980): 883–896.

Swalm, Ro. "Utility Theory Insights into Risk Taking." *Harvard Business Review*, November–December 1966, 123–136.

Szakmary, Andrew, Evren Ors, Jin Kyoung Kim, and Wallace N. Davidson III. "The Predictive Power of Implied Volatility: Evidence from 35 Futures Markets." *Journal of Banking and Finance* 27 (November 2003): 2151–2175.

Tesler, Lester G. "Safety First and Hedging." *Review of Economic Studies* 23, January 1955–56:1–16.

Theil, Henri. *Principles of Econometrics*. New York: John Wiley & Sons, 1971.

Thomas, George B., and Ross L. Finney, *Calculus and Analytic Geometry*, 9th ed. (Reading, MA: Addison-Wesley, 1996).

Thompson, Donald J., II. "Sources of Systematic Risk in Common Stocks." *Journal of Business* 49, no. 2 (April 1976): 173–188.

Tobin, James. "Liquidity Preference as Behavior Towards Risk." *Review of Economic Studies* 26, no. 1 (February 1958): 65–86.

Treynor, Jack L. "How to Rate Management of Investment Funds." *Harvard Business Review* 43, no. 1 (January–February 1965),: 63–75.

Treynor, Jack L., and Fischer Black. "How to Use Security Analysis to Improve Portfolio Selection." *Journal of Business* 46, no. 1 (January 1973): 66–86.

Treynor, Jack L., and Kay K. Mazuy. "Can Mutual Funds Outguess the Market?" *Harvard Business Review* 44, no. 4 (July–August 1966): 131–136.

Upson, Roger B., Paul F. Jessup, and Keishiro Matsumoto. "Portfolio Diversification Strategies." *Financial Analysts Journal* 31, no. 3 (May–June 1975): 86–88.

Vasicek, Oldrich A. "A Note on Using Cross-Sectional Information in Bayesian Estimation of Security Betas" *Journal of Finance* 28, no. 5 (December 1973): 1233–1239.

Von Neumann, John, and Oskar Morgenstern. *Theory of Games and Economic Behavior.* New York: John Wiley & Sons, 1944.

Wagner, Wayne H., and S. C. Lau. "The Effect of Diversification on Risk." *Financial Analysts Journal* 27, no. 6 (November–December 1971): 48–53.

Wagner, Wayne H., and Ralph A. Rieves. *Investment Management*. New York: John Wiley & Sons, 2009.

West, Richard R. "Two Kinds of Market Efficiency." *Financial Analysts Journal* 31, no. 6 (November–December 1975): 30–34.

Whitmore, George A. "Third Degree Stochastic Dominance." *American Economic Review* 60, no. 3 (June 1970): 457–459.

Williams, Dave H. "Organizing for Superior Investment Returns." *Financial Analysts Journal* 36, no. 5 (September–October 1980): 21–23, 27.

Xiong, James X., and Thomas M. Idzorek. "The Impact of Skewness and Fat Tails on the Asset Allocation Decision." *Financial Analysts Journal* 67, no. 2 (March/April): 23–35.

Yang, Dennis, and Qiang Zhang. "Drift Independent Volatility Estimation Based on High, Low, Open and Close Prices." *Journal of Business* 73, (July 2000): 477–491.

Young, William E. and Robert H. Trent. "Geometric Mean Approximations of Individual Security and Portfolio Performance." *Journal of Financial and Quantitative Analysis* 4, no. 2 (June 1969): 179–199.

About the Authors

Jack Clark Francis was born in Indianapolis, Indiana and received his BA and MBA from Indiana University. He then enlisted in the U.S. Army, was commissioned as a lieutenant, graduated from paratrooper school, and was a company commander as he served two years of active duty. He then earned his PhD in finance from the University of Washington in Seattle. Francis was Assistant Professor of Finance at the University of Pennsylvania's Wharton School of Finance for five years. He was also a Federal Reserve economist for two years. He did monetary economics research, participated in monetary policy discussions, and spoke at numerous bankers' meetings while at the Fed. Currently, he is Professor of Economics and Finance at Bernard M. Baruch College in New York City. Dr. Francis authored and coauthored 22 books published by McGraw-Hill, Prentice-Hall, John Wiley & Sons, and Irwin publishing companies. Professor Francis's research focuses on investments, banking, and monetary economics. He has had dozens of research articles published in many refereed academic, business, and government journals. He periodically works as an expert witness and consultant. He resides in Stamford, Connecticut with his wife, Brenda.

Dongcheol Kim is Professor of Finance at Korea University Business School. He was formerly a tenured faculty member at Rutgers University Business School campuses in Newark, New Jersey and New Brunswick, New Jersey, for more than fifteen years. He holds a PhD degree in Finance and Business Statistics, and an MS in Statistics from University of Michigan in Ann Arbor, Michigan. And, he holds an MA in Management Science from Korea Advanced Institute of Science and Technology, and a BE in Industrial Engineering from Seoul National University. He served as President of the Korean Securities Association and as President of the Korean Finance Association in 2013. Professor Kim teaches investments, fixed-income securities, derivatives, and empirical finance. His research mainly focuses on investment and portfolio analysis, market efficiency, and empirical asset pricing models. He is the author of over thirty articles published in refereed finance, accounting, and statistics journals, including *Journal of Finance; Accounting Review; Biometrika; Journal of Business; Journal of Financial and Quantitative Analysis; Journal of Money, Credit, and Banking; Financial Management; Journal of Empirical Finance; Journal of Banking and Finance;* and *Journal of Futures Markets.* He has been honored with numerous research awards.

Subject Index

Printed and bound by CPI Group (UK) Ltd, Croydon, CR0 4YY

24/04/2025

14661405-0001